Cinematic Illuminations

Cinematic Illuminations

THE MIDDLE AGES ON FILM

Laurie A. Finke *and* Martin B. Shichtman

The Johns Hopkins University Press
Baltimore

© 2010 The Johns Hopkins University Press
All rights reserved. Published 2010
Printed in the United States of America on acid-free paper

9   8   7   6   5   4   3   2   1

The Johns Hopkins University Press
2715 North Charles Street
Baltimore, Maryland 21218-4363
www.press.jhu.edu

Library of Congress Cataloging-in-Publication Data
Finke, Laurie.
    Cinematic illuminations : the Middle Ages on film / Laurie A. Finke
and Martin B. Shichtman.
        p. cm.
    Includes bibliographical references and index.
    ISBN-13: 978-0-8018-9344-5 (hardcover : alk. paper)
    ISBN-10: 0-8018-9344-5 (hardcover : alk. paper)
    ISBN-13: 978-0-8018-9345-2 (pbk. : alk. paper)
    ISBN-10: 0-8018-9345-3 (pbk. : alk. paper)
    1. Middle Ages in motion pictures. I. Shichtman, Martin B. II. Title.
    PN1995.9.M52F56 2009
    791.43'635840902—dc22   2008052304

A catalog record for this book is available from the British Library.

Special discounts are available for bulk purchases of this book.
For more information, please contact Special Sales at 410-516-6936
or specialsales@press.jhu.edu.

The Johns Hopkins University Press uses environmentally friendly
book materials, including recycled text paper that is composed of at
least 30 percent post-consumer waste, whenever possible. All of our
book papers are acid-free, and our jackets and covers are printed on
paper with recycled content.

Contents

Figures

Acknowledgments

In our title, *Cinematic Illuminations: The Middle Ages on Film*, we have tried to imagine the connections between two distinctly different types of artistic production: the medieval illuminated book and cinematic representations of the Middle Ages as they have developed over the last century. Undoubtedly, the production of luxury manuscripts in the Middle Ages required the collaborative labor of many people, from the artisans who produced materials such as vellum and inks to the writers and artists responsible for the content. Similarly, the making of a major motion picture can involve hundreds, even thousands, of people. It requires actors and directors but also sound technicians, gaffers, and even caterers. Intellectual labor is always collective, even if the rewards accrue primarily to the *auteur*. This year, and with this book, the two of us celebrate our twenty-fifth year of collaboration. But we also recognize that many friends and colleagues make our work possible. This project, in particular, has been supported by "the magnificent seven," a network of wonderfully dynamic, funny, exciting medievalists; they have not only made us feel welcome, part of an intellectual community—as they have for so many others—but they have also inspired us with their brilliance, their conviviality, their liberality, and their fondness for good food, good drink, good lodging, and good times.

For their advice and criticism, encouragement and assistance, friendship and kindness, we thank Dorsey Armstrong, Sarah Blick, Larry Bogart, Margaret Bridges, Jennifer Cerny, Nina Clemens, Craig Dionne, Michelle Foster, Helen Fulton, John Ganim, Donald Hoffman, Amy Kaufman, Peter Larson, Russell Larson, David Lloyd, Alan and Barbara Lupak, Hannah Markley, Linda Mitchell, Joseph Murphy, Christine Neufeld, Jami Peelle, Arthur Pendragon, Edward Prichard, Tison Pugh, Lynn T. Ramey, Matthew Shichtman, Elizabeth Sklar, Ilan Troen, Elizabeth Uzelac, and Bonnie Wheeler. We deeply appreciate the feedback offered by the members of the Kenyon Seminar, the Ohio Medieval Symposium, the Michigan Medieval Seminar, and the Great Lakes College Association Women's Studies Committee Scholarship Roundtable, and we especially thank their organizers—Jim Carson and Reed Browning at Kenyon, Richard Firth Green at Ohio State, and Peggy McCracken and Catherine Sanok at the University of Michigan—for the opportunity to present our research. We owe special debts of gratitude to Kevin J. Harty for generously sharing his extensive knowledge of medieval film, as well as his extraordinary film collection, and to Mary K. Ramsey for generously agreeing to read the entire manuscript, for her proofreading help, and for her always insightful comments.

Portions of this book were presented as keynote lectures at the International Conference on Medievalism at Wesleyan College in 2008; the Women, Sexuality, and Early Modern Studies Conference at California State Long Beach in 2007; the annual conference of the Swiss Association of University Teachers of English at the University of Zurich in 2007; and the International Conference on Medievalism at Ohio State in 2006. We are grateful to those audiences for their helpful feedback. It goes without saying that all errors in the book are ours and ours alone.

Laurie A. Finke received a 2005 NEH Summer Stipend, which funded research on Joan of Arc, and a grant to participate in a 2005 Midwest Faculty Seminar on Edward Said. A Faculty Development Grant and a Summer Stipend from Kenyon funded research at the British Film Institute. Martin B. Shichtman was a participant in the 2006 Brandeis Summer Institute for Israel Studies, which contributed to our work on the Crusades. He also received from Eastern Michigan University a World College Travel Award and several Dean's Travel Awards. Sabbatical leaves in 2005 and 2006 from Kenyon College and Eastern Michigan University allowed us to complete the writing.

Portions of chapter 10 appeared in an earlier form in *Race, Class, and Gender in Medieval Cinema*, ed. Lynn T. Ramey and Tison Pugh, and are reprinted with permission of Palgrave Macmillan. We thank John Cramer of the Special Collections and the Collection Services Department of Leiden University; Suzanne Smailes, head of Technical Services of the Thomas Library at Wittenberg University; Catherine Paulus of Musées de Strasbourg; and Lita Garcia of the Manuscripts Department of the Huntington Library for their assistance with the images used in the book.

We thank our Johns Hopkins University Press readers, Susan Aronstein and Kathleen Coyne Kelly, for their careful, perceptive, and helpful commentary and our editor, Michael Lonegro, for his long-standing support of this project. Joe Abbott deserves high praise for his rigorous and sensitive copyediting; we owe him a great debt.

Of the many watering holes that have, over the years, facilitated our collaboration, Thai Bistro of Canton, Michigan, deserves special recognition. Without the lure of regular and generous portions of Pad Thai and Thai Spice this book probably would not have been finished. Finally, we thank our spouses, Robert Markley and Maryann Shichtman, and our children, Stephen and Hannah Markley and Matthew Shichtman, for their love, patience, encouragement, and good humor.

Part 1: Theory and Methods of Cinematic Medievalism

Chapter One

Traversing the Fantasy

Screening the Middle Ages

s early as 1936, in "The Work of Art in the Age of Mechanical Reproduction," Walter Benjamin recognized that film would become the quintessential art form of our time and that it would bring about profound changes in how we view the work of art and, by extension, our own past. Indeed, as Robert Rosenstone writes, most people "increasingly receive their ideas about the past from motion pictures and television, from feature films, docudramas, mini-series, and network documentaries. Today the chief source of historical knowledge for the majority of the population—outside of the much despised textbook—must surely be the visual media, a set of institutions that lie almost wholly outside the control of those of us who devote our lives to history" ("History in Images / History in Words," 1174). Most high school and college students come to their literature and history classes with vast experience viewing films but much less in reading literature and history. How much more will this state of affairs apply to the Middle Ages? We have found that most of what our students know about the history, literature, and art of the Middle Ages comes from their viewing of films (or playing Dungeons and Dragons or video games), and this volume is a response to that observation. In the classroom we use our students' experience of film to make them better readers of medieval literature—of its poetry, its history, and its art. In our scholarship we want to show that cinematic "repackaging" of the Middle Ages for popular consumption is important in its own right for what it can tell us about our own cultural fantasies.

Fantasy One: The Time Machine

Perhaps the ultimate fantasy for historians is the time machine. Imagine being able to travel back in time to observe historical events firsthand. Surely, such an invention would offer a privileged glimpse at the truth of history. Finally, we would be able to say with absolute certainty "what really happened" in the past. Several popular cultural texts have explored this fantasy, from the comic *Peabody's Improbable History,* part of the *Rocky and Bullwinkle Show* of the 1960s, to more serious science fiction, such as Orson Scott Card's 1996 novel *Pastwatch: The Redemption of Christopher Columbus* and Connie Willis's 1992 *Doomsday Book.*[1]

Doomsday Book offers a sustained speculation on what the time-traveling historian might learn about her subject. In the novel Oxford researchers in the year 2054 prepare to send their first historian back to the Middle Ages to document life in the early fourteenth century. The chosen scholar, a female undergraduate named Kivrin, comments on the paucity of documentation for the Middle Ages that makes travel to this period so attractive: "Nobody knows anything. There are scarcely any records, except for parish registers and tax rolls, and nobody knows what their lives were like at all. That's why I want to go." Time travel will take the historian out of the realm of speculation, out of the business of interpreting the holes in the historical record. It will offer plentitude; the Middle Ages will at last become fully and totally transparent. History will be able to say with absolute certainty not only what people in the Middle Ages did but how they lived as well.

It is worth pausing, however, to examine the technical details of this fantasy as Willis imagines it. In preparation for their travel, historians ironically need to learn the very details their time traveling is supposed to resolve: "I need to know the language and the customs," Kivrin says, "and the money and table manners and things. Did you know they didn't use plates? They used flat loaves of bread called *manchets,* and when they finished eating their meat, they broke them into pieces and ate them. I need someone to teach me things like that, so I won't make mistakes" (8–9). These are just the sorts of details one might need to know to make a movie about the Middle Ages, and, indeed, the laboratory that houses the time machine or "net" resembles nothing so much as a film set—"In the center of the laboratory was a smashed-up wagon surrounded by overturned trunks and wooden boxes. Above them hung the protective shields of the net, draped like a gauzy parachute" (4)—or the curtain at a theater, to call up a different metaphor. The historians resemble the actors and technicians; there are even "marks" they have to hit. As she prepares to step into the net, Kivrin "looked down at the marks on the floor, stepped forward a little, and arranged her dragging skirts around her" (11). The technician running the net picks up

> a carryboard that was lying on top of the console. He began checking items off with a brisk poke of the light pen.
>
> Kivrin said something to him and pointed at the brass-bound casket. Montoya straightened impatiently up from leaning over Badri's shoulder, and came over to where Kivrin was standing, shaking her head. Kivrin said something else, more firmly, and Montoya knelt down and moved the trunk over next to the wagon. . . .
>
> Gilchrist was messing with the flat metal box. He shook his head and then moved Kivrin's folded hands up a little higher. The too-long sleeve fell back. Her hand was cut. A thin brown line of blood ran down the cut . . .
>
> . . . Her temple was bloody, too. Her hair under the fillet was matted with it. (11–12)

These injuries, we are to understand, are part of the "costume." Stage blood is impossible; everything must be done to achieve total realism, total transparency:

> She knelt and then lay down on her side next to the wagon, turning so that she was on her back with one arm flung over her head and her skirt tangled about her legs. The tech arranged her skirts, pulled out the light measure, and paced around her, walked back to the console, and spoke into the ear. Kivrin lay quite still, the blood on her forehead almost black under the light. (16)

The historians' attempts at achieving absolute reality call attention to the very artifice of the undertaking: twenty-first-century technicians constructing fourteenth-century wagons, caskets, clothing. During the opening chapter the real and the artificial collapse in on one another as the mechanisms of the time machine simply introduce the artifice of the future into the imagined reality of the past. It stages, in other words, a movie about the Middle Ages, albeit a movie that no one will see. The only evidence of Kivrin's time traveling is her own account, audio recorded on a device implanted in her wrist to resemble a bone spur, again revealing artifice striving for maximal transparency, maximal "reality."

Perhaps the improbability of time travel is not the only reason Willis's novel is found on the fantasy shelf in bookstores. Even as Willis's novel holds out the possibility of recovering the truth about "what really happened" in the Middle Ages, the fantasy of full transparency deconstructs. The novel unfolds its dream of capturing the past from within the mechanisms (or at least the metaphors) of film, a medium that, according to Tony Barta, "was to bring truth and artifice, action and acting, documentary and drama, on to one and the same screen with not even a split second to tell them apart" (3). Like Willis's time machine, the cinema holds out the historian's dream of complete and unmediated access to the past at the same time that its efforts reveal the artifice required to hold such a dream in place. The cinema offers a quintessentially postmodern position, oscillating between the desire for plentitude, for total transparency and knowledge of the past, and the impossibility of ever achieving that goal.

Taking the metaphor of time travel as its starting point, *Cinematic Illuminations* examines popular films set in the Middle Ages as fantasies that hold out the promise of hyperreality, the fantasy of an utterly transparent past.[2] We examine the point at which the real and fantasy intertwine and interanimate one another as a means of understanding the ways in which our own historical period has imagined the Middle Ages and the uses to which that imagining has been put. We study medieval costume dramas—both popular and artistic—as a different way of thinking about the past as well as the present.[3] Taking seriously their contributions to our cultural past and their assessment of our present state, our analyses demonstrate that films present us, to paraphrase Hayden White, with a past from which we would like to be descended. Following Richard Burt, we call the process of imagining the Middle Ages on film "cinematic medievalism."[4]

Fantasy Two: Plato's Cave

Why should serious medieval scholars take the time to comment on movies about the Middle Ages? They are, all too often, neither great art nor important historical documents; few are topics for serious scholarship. The vast majority of movies about the Middle Ages may easily be dismissed as nothing more than mass-produced commercial fantasies. Do we not risk debasing our coinage, trivializing our scholarship by indulging such fantasies? A Platonic reading of cinematic medievalism might argue that in our fascination with the technological apparatus of the cinema and its capacity to produce hyperreality, we abandon truth and reality for hallucinations; we embrace the seductive images of Plato's cave.

The Platonic order of "*mimesis, aletheia,* and truth as self-presence" (Norris, 60), upon which judgments about history are usually based, is established in book 7 of the *Republic,* where Plato describes a group of prisoners chained in a cave "with their legs and necks tied up in a way which keeps them in one place and allows them to look only straight ahead, but not to turn their heads" (Plato 7.514a–b). These prisoners sit inside the cave, their backs "firmly turned to the world of daylight reality." All they perceive "are the shadows cast upon the wall of this prison by a moving puppet-show of figures projected by a flickering artificial fire" (Norris, 60). The prisoners in the cave see, Socrates concludes, only illusions, "the shadows cast by the fire on to the cave wall directly opposite them" (Plato 7.515a). Plato's "prisoners" resemble no one so much as Alex in *A Clockwork Orange,* Stanley Kubrick's modernist recreation of Plato's allegory. Alex is restrained and forced to watch violent cinematic images unfolding before him. Like the prisoner in the cave, a Platonic reader of the cinema might argue, film audiences are deceived, the prey to illusions that make the medium inappropriate as a carrier of our history.

What most accounts of the allegory of the cave leave out, however, is the pleasure that we derive from contemplating these images created by the play of light and shadow on the wall of a dark room. What is thoroughly occluded in Plato's account, as the French film theorist Jean-Louis Baudry recognizes, is the tension between our desire to perceive reality as it "really" is—to reconstitute reality through "a totalizing process that would finally subscribe to some ultimate truth behind or beyond the play of mimetic inscriptions" (Norris, 61)—and our pleasure in those flickering images, even when we know them to be an illusion. History does more than record "matters of fact."[5] It also records our fantasies, and our methods of deploying history both in and out of the academy often speak as much to those fantasies as to "what really happened." As medievalists we have a stake in understanding the nature of the collective fantasies we call the Middle Ages. *Cinematic Illuminations* is an attempt to unpack the social logic of the Middle Ages as it appears in contemporary film, the technology par excellence of modernity.[6]

A psychoanalytic reading of the allegory of the cave might well convince us of the need to consider the apparatus of film, to examine more closely the *form* of that which is coming into focus on the screen. "The allegory of the cave," Baudry quite rightly reminds us, "is the text of a signifier of desire which haunts the invention of cinema and the history of its invention" ("The Apparatus," 307). "Screening" in the subtitle to this chapter, then, refers not only to the process of projecting a film but also to film's peculiar ability to create fantasies that both reveal and obscure significant social content. It evokes the concept of the "screen memory," Freud's term for a memory whose apparently indifferent content conceals from consciousness some intense emotional event. Following Louise Fradenburg, we argue that fantasies do not necessarily separate us from reality; "they also have the power to remake the social realities in which we live and desire" (Fradenburg, 208).

Slavoj Žižek offers an even more radical reading of fantasy as ideology, arguing that "in the opposition between dream and reality, fantasy is on the side of reality: it is . . . the support that gives consistency to what we call 'reality' " (*The Sublime Object of Ideology*, 44). What does he mean by this? Žižek rejects the classical Marxist understanding of ideology as "a dreamlike illusion that we build to escape insupportable reality"; instead, "in its basic dimension it is a fantasy-construction which serves as a support for our 'reality' itself: an 'illusion' which structures our effective, real social relations and thereby masks some insupportable, real, impossible kernel," "a traumatic social division which cannot be symbolized" (45). Fantasies offer us not an escape from reality, as we usually understand them; rather they structure what we call reality, teaching us how and what to desire. Far from trivial, fantasies are central to Žižek's account of both art and political ideologies (Kay, 163) because they expose "social reality as an escape from some traumatic, real kernel" (*The Sublime Object of Ideology*, 45).

Fantasy works in tandem with the processes of subjectivization described by Lacan, in which the three psychic orders of the Imaginary, the Symbolic, and the Real situate the subject in dialogue with the external world. The Imaginary is the internalized image of the ideal self, or *imago*, organized around the idea of wholeness rather than fragmentation, the result of the Lacanian mirror stage. The mirror stage suggests that the subject must externalize itself (view itself in a mirror) to be a subject at all, opening up a gap between the fiction of totality provided by the image (the autonomous and coherent self) and the fragmentation that signals the impossibility of ever attaining that ideal image. The Symbolic constitutes most of what we call "reality," the realm of language, of symbol, and of law. The third order, and most important for Žižek, is the Real, which is not, as the word suggests, the way we encounter the world in everyday life (that would be the Symbolic); it is, in one sense, the world before it is carved up by language. Žižek would say that the Symbolic introduces a cut into the Real. But since we never encounter that prelinguistic world once we enter the Symbolic, except as a theoretical construct, it is perhaps more helpful to think of the Real as that which resists incorporation into the Symbolic. The Real is meaningless and senseless; it simply persists as a void in the Symbolic around which the Symbolic structures itself. Fantasy, then, is the name we give to those eruptions of the Real into the Symbolic; it is the way we make sense of them.

Two theoretical concepts Žižek employs to explain how fantasies work on both the individual and cultural level will figure heavily in our analyses of cinematic medievalism and of particular films: the anamorphotic blot and the process of interpellation. Fantasies, as we argue above, are structured around an element that "sticks out, which cannot be integrated into the given symbolic structure, yet which, precisely as such, constitutes its identity" (Myers, 99). Žižek uses several terms to describe this element; it is a stain, distortion, symptom *(sinthome)*, blot. But most frequently he relies on the concept of anamorphosis or "looking awry" to describe the element (the anamorphotic blot) in fantasy that sticks out. Anamorphosis describes a visual technique in which a distorted picture becomes legible when viewed from a particular perspective or with a device like a cylindrical mirror (see Kay, 50–51). Such pictures, as Bushy explains to the Queen in Shakespeare's *Richard II*, contain forms

. . . , which rightly gaz'd upon
Show nothing but confusion; ey'd awry
Distinguish form. (2.2)

The classic example of this kind of anamorphosis is Hans Holbein's *The Ambassadors* (1533). This fairly straightforward example of Renaissance portrait painting, which depicts two ambassadors to the court of Henry VIII, is disturbed by the presence of an elongated "stain" or blot that appears at the bottom of the painting. When viewed from "a precisely determined lateral perspective," the stain resolves into a skull (Žižek, *Looking Awry*, 91). This reminder of mortality, although not a "part" of the painting (the viewer cannot look at both perspectives simultaneously but must alternate between them by physically moving), becomes part of its meaning by challenging the complacency that underwrote the Renaissance myth of "progress" celebrated in the painting.[7] We will use the concept of the anamorphotic blot to understand the function of fantasy in cinematic medievalism. It allows us to access what may not be visible from "straight on," what may resist analysis: the inconsistent, troublesome, or even downright silly aspects of cinematic medievalism.

The second concept we will invoke to describe the working of fantasy in cinematic medievalism is Althusser's notion of interpellation, the process by which a subject comes to recognize herself as a subject when she is "hailed" by ideology (see Althusser, 127–88). Althusser likens this process to the state's hail in the form of a policeman's "Hey you!" to which we respond guiltily whether or not we are the ones being hailed (Kay, 105). To demonstrate this process, we might look briefly at a scene early in *Monty Python and the Holy Grail*, in which Arthur and Bedevere are called upon to determine the guilt or innocence of a witch. This scene perfectly encapsulates the sheer absurdity of the process of interpellation. The scene opens with a hail; a crowd chants, "A witch! A witch!" There is a contrast between the crowd's groundless claims and Bedevere's attempts to call on the law to "investigate" the charge and locate the truth of it: "How do you know she's a witch?" Because "she looks like one," they reply idiotically. Although the "witch" counters their assertion—"They dressed me up like this"—her protests and even the crowd's admission that they have indeed "constructed" her by dressing her up are ineffective in the face of the crowd's arbitrary and insistent hail: "She's a witch. Burn her." After a tortuous bit of logical reasoning, Bedevere "proves" her a witch to the law's satisfaction by weighing her against a duck, suggesting that the law's reasoning is perhaps no more rational than the mob's. The newly interpellated witch replies, "It's a fair cop," thus answering the hail and taking up her place within that ideology. But Žižek asks, why is it she who is hailed or addressed? Why does she answer? The inanity of this scene captures Žižek's response: it is not that she has some reason for answering the hail or that the cause (witchcraft) corresponds to something within the subject: "we don't believe in it because it makes sense to us; on the contrary, the reason we believe is that it is *senseless*" (Kay, 105). "The subject responds to a certain irrational injunction, that is, to the very fact of a groundless command" (Dean, 9–10). As this scene suggests, in this psychic structure the unconscious is to be found outside the subject, "not hidden in any unfathomable depths" of the psyche (Žižek, *The Plague of Fantasies*, 3).[8]

Fantasy Three: Enjoy Your Middle Ages!

If fantasy is, in Žižek's terms, "a point of excessive, irrational enjoyment" that accounts for the hold of an ideological edifice on the subject,[9] then we can only begin to unpack the pleasures of the cinema and its ideologies by "traversing the fantasy," by moving beyond our fascination with hidden meanings, with the "kernel of signification." We must look not at the "secret behind the form" but at the form itself (Žižek, *The Sublime Object of Ideology*, 14–16), recognizing that ideology is never carried solely by the content of utterances but by their form as well. We will explore the relationships between fantasy and form in cinematic medievalism more fully in chapter 2, but before we can turn to this relation, we must first describe those fantasies collectively known as medievalism.

In "Dreaming of the Middle Ages" (Eco, 61–72) Umberto Eco describes the ubiquity of the Middle Ages in the popular imagination: in books, music, films, television, medieval fairs, Societies for Creative Anachronism, even in the names of Las Vegas hotels, housing developments, shopping malls, and dry cleaners.[10] Within popular culture one can hardly call to mind a fantasy work in any genre or medium without calling up the medieval. Harry Potter, *The Lord of the Rings*, *Buffy the Vampire Slayer*, *Star Wars*, *Dr. Who*, *Dune*, *The Highlander*, *Sleeping Beauty*, *Snow White*, *Shrek*, Dungeons and Dragons, *The Chronicles of Narnia*, Wicca, and the sword-and-sorcery genre, particularly popular among adolescent males, all mobilize fantasies about the medieval, even when, as in *Buffy* or *Star Wars*, their settings are modern or futuristic. Scholars have given the name of "medievalism" to this fantasy, which may be as old as the medieval itself. *Beowulf*—with its proto–Middle Ages fantasy world populated by heroes and monsters—arguably belongs as much to the discourse of medievalism as the latest *Beowulf* movie (Robert Zemeckis, 2007). A central task for this book will be to theorize the fantasy of medievalism.[11]

Medievalism, as Leslie J. Workman, the founding editor of the scholarly journal *Studies in Medievalism*, described it, has two aspects: "One is the scholarship or historiography of the Middle Ages, the scholars and critics in several fields who are continually reinventing the Middle Ages. The other is the writers and artists who have employed the idea of the Middle Ages creatively."[12] However, as Kathleen Biddick notes in *The Shock of Medievalism*, the very notion of "medievalism" is dependent on a highly suspect differentiation created by academics of the late nineteenth century and early twentieth. These scholars insisted that their reconstructions of the Middle Ages were scientific and objective, that is, that they were part of the project of a learned, scientific history. They separated this "true" Middle Ages from the vulgar and sentimental fantasies about the Middle Ages found in popular culture, which they termed "medievalism" and excluded from the subject matter of "medieval studies." As a result of its exclusion, medievalism was free to develop over the last century into a scholarly field in its own right.

Contemporary medievalism repeats this initial gesture of exclusion, reinscribing the same rigid topography of interiority and exteriority that constituted the field of medieval studies one hundred years earlier.[13] Two things stand out in

Workman's editorial policy. The first is that although medievalism admits both "*serious* scholarship on the great scholars and critics of the field" (emphasis ours) and "writers and artists" who "creatively" deploy the ideal of the Middle Ages, his statement still requires a discursive boundary be drawn between "objective" scholarship of the Middle Ages and artistic recreations of it, between fact and fantasy. Recent critics of medievalism, however, including Biddick, argue that this objective scholarship, especially as medieval studies developed in the nineteenth century, was itself dependent on and generated fantasies of European nationalism, some of them even dangerous.[14] Second, Workman's statement excludes from the now respectable field of medievalism (respectable because it now has its own scholarly journal and conferences) the romantic Middle Ages, the sentimentalized Middle Ages of popular culture, the project, as Umberto Eco puts it, of "dreaming the Middle Ages." Howard Bloch and Stephen G. Nichols define medievalism as a field that "considers questions normally excluded from the canon of traditional or high medieval studies, topics such as connoisseurship, professionalization, and popularization." The "popularizations" they have in mind, however, are more like "the effects of Bédier's successful rewriting of *The Romance of Tristan and Isolde* upon contemporary medieval studies as well as upon modern poets such as Péguy and Cocteau" than, say, the effects of Brian Helgeland's *A Knight's Tale* on Chaucer scholarship or the discourse of race in Martin Lawrence's *Black Knight* on arguments about the "post-colonial Middle Ages" (Bloch and Nichols, 4). A cursory glance at the contents of *Studies in Medievalism* prior to, say, 1994 would confirm this exclusion of mass-produced popular medievalisms.

Of course, one might argue that such exclusions have been superseded by the spate of scholarly work that has appeared since the English translation of Eco's *Travels in Hyperreality* (1986) on forms of popular culture ranging from Disney (Aronstein and Coiner) to comic books (see Sklar and Hoffman) and, of course, popular film. Surely popular medievalisms are no longer excluded from the scope of medievalism, even if they once were. *Studies in Medievalism's* new editor, T. A. Shippey, enlarges on Workman's two categories of scholarship and artistic creation in his editorial policy:

> Medievalism is the study of responses to the Middle Ages at all periods since a sense of the mediaeval began to develop. Such responses include, but are not restricted to, the activities of scholars, historians and philologists in rediscovering medieval materials; the ways in which such materials were and are used

by political groups intent on self-definition or self-legitimation; and artistic creations, whether literary, visual or musical, based on whatever has been or is thought to have been recovered from the medieval centuries. The Middle Ages remain present, moreover, in the modern consciousness, both through scholarship and through popular media such as film, video games, poster art, TV series and comic strips, and these media are also a legitimate object of study, if often intertwined with more traditionally scholarly topics.[15]

Shippey adds to the journal's mission an attention to "the ways in which [medieval] materials were and are used by political groups intent on self-definition or self-legitimation" (for which Pamela Morgan's 1994 article on the Kennedy myth of Camelot might stand as an exemplar) and "popular media such as film, video games, poster art, TV series and comic strips," which are now a "legitimate object of study, if often intertwined with more traditionally scholarly topics." Yet even in this new policy, popular medievalism is segregated from its more "serious" counterparts by being confined in its own sentence, separated from the grammatical parallelism of the other three "proper objects" of medievalism by the conjunctive *moreover* as if it were an afterthought. Furthermore, one is hard pressed to know whether to take the concluding "if" clause of Shippey's statement as descriptive or imperative, but it does seem to suggest some anxiety about the inclusion of popular medievalisms; they must be disciplined by "more traditionally scholarly topics." Once again, "hard-edged" distinctions are rigorously policed, especially between "the activities of scholars, historians and philologists" who are "rediscovering medieval materials" and the work of artistic recreation, political legitimation, and popularization. This distinction is constitutive of the field. We do not intend to argue for a reconfiguration of medieval studies or a "new medievalism." That neologism has already been taken.[16] Instead, our study of cinematic medievalism explores those gestures of exclusion that mask the "illegitimate" leakages among medieval studies, medievalism, and popular culture. The subject of our book is the myriad ways in which contemporary popular culture uses the medieval past as a fantasy frame for making sense of our own world.

Neither the Middle Ages nor the texts and artifacts we designate as medieval exist simply as objects out there waiting to be discovered by scholars; rather, the scholarship of the Middle Ages creates its objects in response to very specific fantasies and desires, particularly, as Bernard Cerquiglini suggests, the desire for the authentic and original.[17] Medieval studies, in Cerquiglini's reading, shares with genealogy "a bourgeois, paternalist, and hygienist system of thought about the family" that "cherishes filiation, tracks down adulterers, and is afraid of contamination" (49): "Medieval philology is the mourning for a text, the patient labor of this mourning. It is the quest for an anterior perfection that is always bygone, that unique moment in which the presumed voice of the author was linked to the hand of the first scribe, dictating the authentic, first, and original version" (34). But as Žižek notes, when we perceive of a historical moment as a moment at which some quality is lost, that quality, in fact, is almost always a fantasy being created by the very act of mourning (*The Plague of Fantasies,* 12–13). The "authentic" Middle Ages produced by the academy through its practices (teaching and scholarship) is at best one among many fantasies that use the distant past to meet the particular needs and agendas of our own present (Cerquiglini's "patient labor of mourning"). We might well ask what "patient labor of mourning" the medieval philologist's fantasy of origins shares with an act of political legitimation, such as that of one Arthur Pendragon (né John Timothy Rothwell), a "British soldier, the son of a soldier, brought up in army camps and council estates, a truant, a persistent offender, a jack-of-all-trades, a traveler, a mad biker chieftain wielding an axe, who, in a moment of revelation, in a twentieth-century squat," claims to be a "post-Thatcher" King Arthur, who changes his name to reflect (create) that "reality" and who links his political struggles against the state to myths that mourn the always already lost original purity of ancient Britain, invoking "a time, long before history, when the people knew their place in the Universe, not as the centre, but as parts of a greater whole"?[18] Scholarship about the Middle Ages may or may not employ the same procedures as fictions about it, but we do not consider it purer for the differences—or any freer of fantasy.

Medievalism's desire to police the boundary between objective scholarship and artistic fantasy—in effect between fact and fiction, truth and artifice— springs from and feeds the need to secure yet another boundary, the boundary that differentiates modernity from that which came before: the medieval. Bruno Latour notes that modernity is the name for a fantasy that imagines "a new regime, an acceleration, a rupture, a revolution in time," which is always contrasted to "an archaic and stable past" (*We Have Never Been Modern,* 10). The archaic that precedes and opposes the modern exists both in the past—Arthur Lindley writes, "We tend to figure Western history in terms of a break between medieval and Renaissance in which the latter is the beginning of modernity and the former that which is discarded: . . . the despised and rejected Middle Ages" ("The Ahistoricism of Medieval Film")—as well as the present in those non-

Western cultures designated as "premodern." The Middle Ages as the "dark ages" is metonymically linked with those geographic areas that to Western and "modern" minds are the "dark continent" or the "inscrutable east." It is our name for what is yet to be modern, the antithesis of the modern. The Middle Ages functions as "an enabling premise in the construction of a distinctive character and destiny for Western Europe" (A. Middleton, 12–13), which is to say the Middle Ages is the excluded other of the narratives about progress and enlightenment that are major themes in Western history without which those narratives would lose their consistency.

Three Little Medievalisms

The master narrative of modernity has spawned three opposing yet complementary fantasies about the Middle Ages, three distinct, yet related, medievalisms. In the first the Middle Ages has become synonymous with a peculiarly modern form of nostalgia for a past organic society that mourns the sterility of modernity.[19] Many popular medievalisms are about the rejection of technology (*Star Wars, The Highlander, Buffy the Vampire Slayer*) in favor of a closer connection with nature (the force) and suggest considerable anxiety around the break effected between the Middle Ages and the Enlightenment, a belief that the progress promised by the Enlightenment comes at too high a cost and that the cure can only be regression to a simpler past. David Lloyd describes this nostalgia when he remarks that the Middle Ages is the "site of an elegiac labour of reinvention that laments the lost immediacy of personal relationships, the individuality of artisanal crafts in a pre-industrial mode of production, the clarity of authority and hierarchy, the surety of religious faith" (14). Paul Zumthor seems to echo Žižek's contention that acts of mourning create the qualities being mourned when he argues (while carefully distancing himself from contamination by the popular through his use of the impersonal *they*) that popular interest in the medieval "is based in part on a vague desire to escape the oppressiveness of the civilization they have created: in that case their 'Middle Ages' takes on more or less the same qualities as their ecological myths" (9). He attributes popular medievalism to the "decline in our belief in scientific progress," the promise of the Enlightenment (10).[20] Extreme versions of nostalgic medievalism inform the work of ecologists like Carolyn Merchant, who argues in *The Death of Nature* that modernity has led to a mechanistic and sterile view of the world, creating fragmentation, alienation, and objectification leading to the "death of nature"; the remedy seems to be a rejection of the modern and a return to a more natural past that leaves the break between the two untouched.

The nostalgia for a less technologically developed past, even as it runs counter to the rationalism on which the academy is based (it is modern), bleeds into the academic, fostering an implicit belief that because the medieval is so closely associated with fantasy, because it precedes the break that precipitated the modern, it lies somewhere outside of an institution whose reputation is based in rationality and critique.[21] John Ganim has argued that critical discourse "imagines the Middle Ages as a romance" ("The Myth of Medieval Romance," 149), while romance is relegated to "a form of history before historical consciousness takes place" (151). In this view the Middle Ages becomes "a lost Golden Age, perhaps even a childhood, to which we can never return" (149) or a "critique of modernity, . . . of industrialization, urbanization, and democratization" (152).[22] Angela Jane Weisl flirts with such nostalgia in her introduction to *The Persistence of Medievalism*. Describing the network of phenomena that accompany "fandom" as modern versions of "saints, relics, and pilgrimage," she misses what might be most radical about this insight that troubles the distinction between past and present by invoking the longing for the Middle Ages left behind by modernity, claiming that the "medievalization" of these phenomena witnesses the desire "for community and unification often lost within modern technological society" (18–19).

A film like Ben Stiller's *The Cable Guy* (1996) comments on the fantasies that fuel the return to the Middle Ages as nostalgia for an organic past. The anxieties of the title character about the very modernity he represents (as "cable guy")— the isolation and alienation produced by the technology of television (ironically despite the fact that cables literally "connect")—draw him to "the finest restaurant in town," a medieval-themed chain restaurant called "Medieval Times," where "serving wenches" dispense food and drink, and knights engage in tournaments for the amusement of twentieth-century American audiences. Jim Carrey's "Chip Douglas" (the alias the cable guy uses in the film) has been shaped as a creepy, antisocial loner, abandoned by his mother to the care of the "electronic babysitter," his worldview determined by a medium that, even by his mother's assessment, will "rot his brain." He imagines Medieval Times, which he visits "two times a week," as a cure for the trauma of modernity. If *Monty Python and the Holy Grail* offers, in Eco's terms, an "ironical revisitation" of the Middle Ages (69), *The Cable Guy* offers us a Middle Ages in which the pain of modernity can be held at bay by the nostalgic recreation of an earthy past. Retreat into a fantasy of the distant past—however cheesy—enables "Chip" to establish the community and bonds of friendship denied him by his world of alienated labor (even his assumed name, Chip Douglas, places him within the fictional family that he longs for, the Douglas family of television's *My Three Sons*, even as it links him to technology—to computer chips, microchips, V-chips). He brings with him to Medieval Times a befuddled Steven Kovacs (played by Matthew Broderick) to recuperate the kinds of homosocial bonds between men represented by the chivalric community of medieval knighthood. As the two men engage in combat, first on foot and then on horseback, "Chip" fashions an extremely bewildered Kovacs into his "sworn enemy." Not surprisingly, Kovaks, at first, does not get it. The camera indicates his perplexity through disorienting point-of-view shots, one shot through his helmet and another from a camera held upside down, representing Steven's view from the ground. As the battle ensues, however, Kovacs is gradually drawn into the fight, and after he defeats his opponent, the two embrace in fraternal companionship, as "Chip" holds his new friend's hand aloft in the conventional sign of victory, at least momentarily establishing the kind of homosocial connection his life lacks.

The irony is that *The Cable Guy*'s Medieval Times is a tawdry recreation of the past in which the Middle Ages becomes a commodity just like any other, so much junk, like the paper crowns audience members wear. At one point, after being offered a refill on his Pepsi by his ostentatiously bored waitress (played by Janeane Garofalo), Kovacs asks if he can have some utensils. She intones: "There were no utensils in medieval times, hence there are no utensils at Medieval Times." Kovacs remarks that there was no Pepsi in medieval times either. She responds: "Dude, I have a lot of tables." Her response, of course, is not really a response at all. It is a frustrated acceptance of the alienation of her own labor, whereby she requires her customers to consume the Middle Ages as though it were just another commodity, to accept that they participate in a fantasy because of their authenticity as consumers, to paraphrase Eco (41). Even for the filmmakers this is no doubt true. Pepsi's appearance in this scene is no accident, though it was not determined by the needs of the plot. It is the result of the film industry's economics of product placement, in which both Pepsi and the Middle Ages are to be consumed as so many commodities (that there is actually a restaurant chain called Medieval Times with franchises from New Jersey to California only reinforces this irony).

Such commodity fetishism reduces everything to equivalents. Douglas and Kovacs are permitted to become part of the show, allowed the privilege of homosocial contestation because, as the Cable Guy notes, he gives the knights "free cable." The battle itself offers the promise of hyperreality, the reproduction of the medieval tournament. But, Douglas, whose notion of reality has been overdetermined by the commodity fetishism of television, cannot distinguish between fantasies about medieval armed engagement and futuristic fantasies like *Star Trek*. At one point their battle morphs into a complete shot-by-shot parody of a *Star Trek* episode ("Amok Time")—complete with distinctive music identifiable by any casual Trekkie—in which Kirk and Spock, best friends, as Douglas points out, must fight one another to the death. Past and future fantasies of homosocial bonding become interchangeable, both answering to anxieties about modernity. Ultimately the combat, with all its attendant fantasies, provides Douglas and Kovacs with a brief respite from unrewarding employment, the isolation of contemporary urban life, and sexual frustration (after fixing Kovacs up with a prostitute, Douglas explains, "You think women like that would hang out with us if we weren't paying?").

But nostalgia for the organic wholeness that preceded modernity does not by any means exhaust modern fantasies about the Middle Ages, either popular or academic. The flip side of the nostalgia we have been examining is to associate the medieval with the barbarity, superstition, and violence from which civilization (modernity) is supposed to have rescued us. According to Carolyn Dinshaw, "it is ritualized sexual torture, it is dark and perverse, and it must be met by a personal vengeance that is itself ritualized, torturous, dark and perverse" (185). For modern film audiences, the Middle Ages are just as often savage and atavistic as organic. They represent superstition in opposition to reason, dogma opposed to inquiry and critique, magic opposed to science, myth and legend opposed to history. The medieval "comes to connote not only intellectual and religious obscurantism of various kinds, but a kind of sluggish fixity that inhibits progress and development in face of the mobile, abstracting tendencies of capital" (Lloyd, 10).[23] More important for our analysis of film, it has become the name, as David Lloyd argues, for "an archaic that may indeed be still lodged in the recesses of the modern psyche and to which the latter at times regresses" (8).

This version of the Middle Ages might best be represented by a recent series of advertisements created by Ogilvy and Mather for IBM Consulting, which juxtaposes iconographies of the modern business boardroom with those of a primitive Arthurian Round Table. In one version medieval trumpets introduce Arthur, a twenty-first-century corporate executive who, we are told, has just been knighted. The office space, complete with Bauhaus-style furnishings, is marked by large picture windows that look out on an urban environment. Arthur's corporate board is composed of executives right out of central casting: well-tailored, conservatively coifed, speaking in the dialects of England's upper crust—they are crisp, clean, and deferential. The camera then cuts to a scene out of the Middle Ages, where King Arthur reigns in a gloomy room, lit by torches. Furnishings are bulky, ponderous. The same actor who played Sir Arthur now plays the king, and the actors who played executives compose the medieval court. But the king and his knights have long beards and shaggy hair. Their couture is decidedly medieval: heavy robes, and some—including the king—wear armor breastplates. One of King Arthur's knights speaks in a thick cockney dialect.

There is a kind of Monty Pythonesque silliness in the association of contemporary business problems with those of a medieval court. The commercials exploit their audience's expectation of hyperefficient modernity in contrast to a sluggish Middle Ages that impedes the flow of capital. The advertisements invoke twenty-first-century fears of the medieval, of slipping into a culture of filth and superstition, and offer the solutions of IBM Consulting as an antidote. Ultimately, the commercials would have us believe, realizing the full potential of modernity is not possible without the intervention of Big Blue.

On one level the IBM advertisements suggest that things have not changed significantly during the last thousand years. There is still top-down governance, and, most important for the commercials' central conceit to function, powerful governing bodies continue to meet at round tables. However, the comparison serves to demonstrate the kind of "medieval" abyss a company can descend into if it allows its problems to go unchecked. In the commercial entitled "Sir Arthur's Business Round Table," corporate inefficiency is compared to the threat posed by "a giant sloth." In another, "Sir Arthur's Quest Remains Elusive," we are asked to consider how difficult it is to discern "the big picture." In the medieval portion of the ad the audience is informed that the "big picture" is hiding in a cave and cannot be extricated because "it is too big." A third sixty-second advertisement asks viewers to make the association between a company's services becoming commoditized and "an evil wizard [who] has cast a hex upon our empire." The Ogilvy and Mather spots play with Umberto Eco's notion that we continue to live in the Middle Ages, but they suggest that, as moderns, we have it in our power to choose a smarter, cleaner, more efficient way of going about business—the modern way.

A similar point is suggested by a series of Capital One commercials in which hordes of pillagers descend on a man and woman about to make an ill-advised credit card purchase. These are generic pillagers—it is impossible to determine if they are Vikings, Visigoths, or Huns, although in his blog, "In the Middle," Jeffrey J. Cohen identifies them as the "Norsemen" or Vikings from whom the Normans descended.[24] Whoever they are, there can be no question that the pillagers have somehow emerged from the Middle Ages. They are a mass of large, barbaric men, an angry mob, filthy, dressed in animal skins, carrying weapons such as swords, shields, and maces. They growl more than speak, even when asking the advertisement's signature question, "What's in your wallet?" Capital One's pillagers arrive from the Middle Ages to represent—in what has to be one of the strangest associations in Madison Avenue history—inflated credit card interest rates. They threaten the civilization of the twenty-first century, particularly the flow of twenty-first-century commerce. In these spots the medieval figures the instability created by middle-class spending habits (rampant consumerism).[25]

How is it possible that these commercials have been so successful that viewers tolerate—and even enjoy—this strained analogy? The simple answer is that they play on precisely the fantasies about the Middle Ages that Dinshaw outlines. In his blog Cohen surprisingly invokes what Richard Burt calls the "fidelity model" of medieval representation to make exactly this point (217), expressing impatience with Capital One's appropriation of "medieval Vikings, barbarians, and other louche fellows." He argues that the commercials do "a grave injustice to the early Middle Ages in offering such an unnuanced view of ancient proclivities towards raiding and pillage." He continues, tongue in cheek, scolding the credit card company: "your primitive and thuggish depictions of barbarians do a violence to history by flattening it beyond subtlety." His solution? "I ask you to grant these groups their full complexity, a first step towards which might be having the spokesbarbarian no longer declare the tagline 'What's in your wallet?' in a seriously poor Cockney accent." The commercials, however, depend on fantasies, not knowledge, of the Middle Ages to make their point. The antisocial behavior of competitor banks is equated with the violence of pillagers. For SUV-driving suburbanites, Capital One's target audience, medieval berserkers and usurious banks become one and the same. But what this audience really fears is its own prodigal spending, its own tendency to run berserk with credit cards, to pillage the local big box store for more and more useless junk. Capital One assists its customers in displacing this fear of their own consumption back onto fantasies about the Middle Ages. The comforts of modernity take the form of a Capital One credit card.

Cohen the consumer, however, gets what Cohen the medievalist resists when, at the end of his rant, he offers a more nuanced reading of the spots, coyly suggesting, "I am very sorry that I was tardy with my last payment. Could you please refund the $120 late fee and return my interest back to whatever it was before it shot to 23.7%?" Cohen the consumer seems to understand that, if the medieval in popular culture represents a break from a barbaric past, it also contains temporally the seeds of the modern, our third medievalism. The analogy created by Capital One's medievalism troubles the break between "medieval" and "modern" at the same time that it reinforces it. David Lloyd argues that we can understand the Middle Ages created by the modern mind as "the antithesis between a figuration of backwardness and a narrative of always incipient transition. . . . Even as the medieval becomes the very emblem of fixity, it is no less the type of fluidity, change and heterogeneity" (9). He continues, "This must be so if the middle ages are to contain the seeds of transition to capitalism. . . . The elements of individualism, rational inquiry and critique must be presumed already at work for the fullness of their later historical emergence to be at all possible" (13). Lloyd's argument that the Middle Ages already contain the seeds of capitalism suggests why viewers largely unfamiliar with the Middle Ages can make the strained analogy that the advertisements require.

With its series of barbarian commercials, Capital One equates contemporary notions about the lawlessness of the Middle Ages—the lack of restraint on human behavior, in general—with capitalism "gone wild." Capital One needs its consumers to be continually insecure, continually fearful of instability, which the advertisements link to the return of the repressed Middle Ages. These commercials have been successful enough that Capital One followed them with a number of sequels, the most delightful of which have the pillagers, defeated by Capital One's better business practices, seeking new kinds of work. In one advertisement a job counselor explains that men from the Middle Ages have few job skills and even fewer social graces—they are shown attending job preparation sessions in which they learn about the importance of soap. In other advertisements we find the pillagers at work in the kinds of service industry jobs available to men with few marketable skills. Still unkempt and incongruously garbed in clothing readily identifiable as "medieval," one serves as an airline attendant, accidentally hitting passengers' faces with his mace as he comes down the aisle; another as an ice cream server, scooping product literally by hand even as he wipes his nose; and the last as a ladies' shoe salesmen. We are told by the leader of the pillagers that one of his comrades, "Ivan the Terrible," has had a particularly hard time overseeing amusement-park rides. Thanks to Capital One, the Middle Ages have become domesticated, their barbarians broken and no longer able to run amok. This second series, however, seems to undercut the already stretched analogy between barbarianism and unrestrained capitalism by redirecting our attention, through cunning sleight of hand, replacing fears about big banking with anxieties about an underclass barely held in check by alienated labor. Can Capital One be suggesting that alienated labor is the mechanism by which the "barbaric" tendencies of capital can be harnessed? The instability created by alienated labor is confirmed by how badly the barbarians do their jobs. Rather than allowing viewers to remain focused on the depredations of big banks—on high interest rates and fees—(after all, as Cohen recognizes, Capital One is one of them), it shifts viewers' attention to "the masses" and the discontent created by capitalism's need for alienated labor.

Since we are interested not only in the social circumstances displayed openly in a given text but also in those that reside in its silences, gaps, and contradictions, we do not limit our analysis to the content of films but explore their forms as well. In our next chapter, we will consider how cinema functions as the locus of a multitude of intertextual and intermedial references, even as it transforms the ways we think about both textuality and the media. We will investigate the semiotic systems that signify the Middle Ages for contemporary filmmakers and film audiences—the genres, conventions, and iconographies that give structure to our imaginings of the antique past.

Chapter Two

Signs of the Medieval

A Sociological Stylistics of Film

In "Discourse in the Novel" M. M. Bakhtin criticized the divorce in literary studies between an abstract formal analysis of literary technique and an equally abstract sociological criticism. Unsurprisingly, this split has found its way into the academic study of film.[1] Although Bakhtin never wrote about film, he was a contemporary of the great Russian filmmaker Sergei Eisenstein, and there is ample warrant within Bakhtin's work and that of his circle for adapting his ideas to film theory.[2] Traditional film stylistics, contemporary Marxist analytics, and the structural semiotics of a Christian Metz, Bakhtin would argue, all fail to articulate an adequate film aesthetics because they have failed to understand that film requires a "sociological stylistics."

We take up this challenge of articulating a sociological stylistics of film by considering the mechanisms through which the cinematic apparatus mediates, and indeed remediates, our experience of medievalism.[3] This task requires that we understand film not simply as a neutral carrier of content but as a complex network of material, social, political, cultural, economic, and semiotic practices. We begin by examining film as a form of contemporary mass media, not distinct from all others but thoroughly integrated into a network of visual communication that makes claims both to immediacy and hypermediacy, transparency and opacity. From there we proceed to look at the cinematic codes that have developed over the last century for representing the Middle Ages.

Remediating the Middle Ages

Werner Wolf, in his study of intermediality, defines *media* as "a conventionally distinct means of communication, specified not only by particular channels (or one channel) of communication but also by the use of one or more semiotic systems serving for the transmission of cultural 'messages'" (35–36). This definition makes a good starting point for a consideration of film as a medium; it has the advantage of pointing out the ways in which all media bring together material, technological, and semiotic practices. While we might be tempted to think of media simply as the material or technological apparatuses through which we view our world (and note the metaphor of transparency)—i.e., books, newspapers, radios, televisions, film, computers—in fact, technology itself is thoroughly imbricated in cultural, social, political, economic, and semiotic networks, and we must examine them as such. By way of contrast, *The Oxford English Dictionary*'s definition of *media*—"the main means of mass communication, esp. newspapers, radio, and television, regarded collectively"—tends to focus attention only on the channel of communication, the technology. At the same time, the *OED* definition regards media (as in mass media) as a modern phenomenon, transpiring in Benjamin's "age of mechanical reproduction." As Fredric Jameson points out, however, the emergence of contemporary mass media (and particularly the multiplication of "new media" over the last few decades) has only made us more aware of the extent to which we have always been in its grip: "We have finally begun to get it through our heads that culture . . . was always that [media], and that the older forms or genres, . . . were also in their very different ways media products" (*Postmodernism, or, The Cultural Logic of Late Capitalism*, 68). Older media and their technologies, from the manuscript to the movie, he suggests, may be remediated, rethought through the lens (so to speak) of newer media.

We have chosen the phrase "cinematic illuminations" for this volume's title to suggest the tensions between immediacy and hypermediacy,[4] reality and fantasy, creation and recreation, tensions that are central to our readings of the cinema of the Middle Ages. To clarify these tensions, it will be helpful to investigate "the process whereby the traditional fine arts are mediatized: that is, how they come to consciousness of themselves as various media within a mediatic system in which their own internal production also constitutes a symbolic message and the taking of a position on the status of the medium in question" (Jameson, 162). As an example of latter-day media "remediating" earlier forms, we turn briefly to explore the visual (and narrative) pleasures of images in luxury manuscripts of the Middle Ages and in cinematic medievalism. Few media seem further removed in time and form from film than manuscript illumination. We tend to think of the former as part of mass media and the latter either as art or historical artifact. Yet the two are united as media by the kinds of pleasures and anxieties they mobilize around representation. Each "remediates"—improves upon and remedies—the other. The medieval illuminated manuscript both anticipates and provides inspiration for cinematic fantasy; the technology of film supplements the illuminated manuscript with sound and movement, all while enhancing the size and scope of display. Marilynn Desmond and Pamela Sheingorn have described fifteenth-century manuscript culture as "cinematic" in the ways in which it plays with the qualities of light, using it to interpellate—literally to call into being—a particular kind of spectator. The experience of viewing a manuscript illumination, according to Desmond and Sheingorn, "situates the reader as a spectator constructed by the luminous quality of the page. This aspect of the reading experience in late medieval manuscript culture is analogous to the modern cinematic experience" (2).

To demonstrate this remediation more specifically, let us turn to two images of the Round Table. The first is a manuscript illumination from a late-fourteenth-century copy of Wirnt von Gravenberg's Arthurian Romance *Wigalois*; the second is a still from John Boorman's 1981 film *Excalibur* (Figures 1 and 2). In the *Wigalois* manuscript the gold leaf adorning the crowns, the various dishes and cups arrayed on the table, and the decoration in the subjects' clothing reflect light and draw the viewer's eye in much the same way that light reflects off the brightly burnished silver metal of the knights' armor in Boorman's shot.[5] Both images depend, as Desmond and Sheingorn suggest, on light, on "illumination," not merely to represent—but literally to produce—the wealth, power, and authority of the Round Table. Their discussion of the "world system of production and trade" (19) that produced medieval manuscripts underscores this point. The raw materials required to produce the golds, as well as the intense blues and reds, characteristic of late medieval manuscript illumination, had to be imported to Europe, often from great distances. They describe luxury manuscripts as networks of material and technological practices—from lapis lazuli and gold mining in Asia and Africa to painting in the workshops of Paris (19)—that were largely mystified by the system of patronage that controlled production. Illuminated manuscripts like the

Figure 1. Manuscript illumination from *Wigalois,* Leiden, Universiteitsbiblio-
theek, ms. LTK 537, fol. 1v. Courtesy Leiden University Library.

Leiden copy of *Wigalois,* which was made for Duke Albrecht II von Braunschweig-
Grubenhagen (Meuwese, 30), were usually produced for a single owner, and the
work literally embodied the wealth, power, and authority of its owner and patron.
A film also represents a nexus of social relationships between producers and con-

sumers. It represents capital, technological and artistic labor, social organization and hierarchy, but those relationships are usually mystified by the operations of commodity fetishism, which, Žižek argues, occurs when the *value* of a certain commodity, which stands for a network of social relations, "assumes the form of a quasi-'natural' property of another thing" (*The Sublime Object of Ideology*, 23–24).

To illustrate the process Žižek describes, we might push this unlikely juxtaposition even further. Both images depict the Round Table, the object that most materially embodies the "medieval" ideals of Arthurian romance (whatever they happen to be at a particular historical moment) from an impossible point of view. Both show the Round Table from high above, from what in film is called a crane shot. In *Excalibur* the sequence that culminates in this image consists of a long tracking shot that follows the Fair Unknown, Perceval, through Camelot as he takes in the wonders of Arthur's court. The crane shot represents Perceval's first glimpse of the Table from a balcony high above it. The camera encourages us to share Perceval's point of view by positioning us behind his head, while he says in awe, "I must be dreaming." But as he leaves the shot, the camera lingers for a moment on the scene, and viewers enjoy a panoptical glimpse of the Round Table, which, as we argue in chapter 3, turns its human subjects into geometric patterns, creating a particular fantasy of political omnipotence. The manuscript illumination from *Wigalois* represents the opening scene of the romance, which emphasizes Arthur's custom never to sit down to eat before some kind of marvel or ad-

Figure 2. Crane shot of John Boorman's Round Table, *Excalibur* (1981).

venture has transpired, a mark of his considerable power. With its shifting perspective, this image seems to position viewers nowhere and everywhere at the same time. To understand how this image coherently interpellates its viewers, we must unpack the representational strategies of the medium. In this case we must understand that, in manuscript illuminations, temporality can be rendered spatially. If, rather than trying to take the entire image in all at once, we read it as a sequence, its method for situating the viewer becomes clearer. We can, in fact, follow this image as we might a tracking shot in film by simply turning the book around, as medieval readers most likely did.[6] The viewer is meant to focus first on the Round Table itself, shown from above as in the Boorman shot. The eye is drawn there because of its white space, punctuated by the geometric patterns created by the swords, and because of the light reflecting off of the illuminated cups. The eye then tracks down to the three maidens below. From there, rotating the image ninety degrees left will focus the viewer's attention on the three figures on the right. A rotation ninety degrees to the right will take us to the top, where the king and queen are represented; then another rotation to the right brings us to the three figures on the left. The figure on the far left bottom of the table points back to the starting point and closes the circle, ending the tracking shot. In the manuscript the reader must do the work of tracking (by rotating the image) that, in a film, the camera does through its movement (and through the illusion that the viewer moves with the camera). Of course, this means that readers have the power to move the book in other ways, backward or in any other way that might suit their fancies. Still, the medieval image manages something like the effect of Boorman's filmic one, turning the human figures into geometric patterns: note in particular the interlocking triangles created by the green and red dresses of three of the maidens (two at the top, one at the bottom) and the diaper-patterned clothing connecting Arthur at the top and two maidens below. Boorman's film image remediates the manuscript illumination; that is, it appears to offer us a better, more "realistic," more immediate experience of a particular way of looking (immediacy). Similarly, the highly formalistic patterns of the medieval image call attention to the hypermediacy of the filmic image, of Boorman's indulgence in the pleasures of artistic mediation.

Both images—the manuscript image and the film still—are emblematic of the power of the visual to record our histories, as well as our fantasies, and the pleasures and dangers aroused by this power. Both are also nodal points in a complex network of technological production and consumption that organizes social relationships, as well as inanimate objects (books, films, multiplexes, DVDs). Manuscript images continually haunt the cinema of the Middle Ages, most obviously because they are the best record we have of what the Middle Ages "really" looked like. For this reason they are often used in film to signify authenticity and immediacy. Documentary films routinely use manuscript images this way; in the next chapter, we discuss how Terry Jones's documentary on the Crusades plays with the authenticity of manuscript images, a strategy that at once authorizes his own historical views, even as his hypermediation of the illuminations parodies the process of authentication. Even fiction films call upon the authenticity conveyed by the manuscript. Carl Theodor Dreyer's 1928 *La Passion de Jeanne d'Arc* opens with a shot of the Bibliothèque Nationale manuscript of the saint's trial to signify the historical immediacy of his film. Some seventy years later, in a commentary accompanying the DVD of the 1999 Joan of Arc film, *The Messenger*, Milla Jovovich uses much the same strategy of authorization, describing the ways in which the production team scoured "the archives of France" for images that could be used to historicize Luc Besson's vision of the Maid of Orléans. Manuscript images, however, can also serve as a strategy for hypermediation, heightening the visual pleasures offered by both media (film and manuscript). The cinematography of Victor Fleming's 1948 *Joan of Arc* showcased the achievements of Technicolor in its lavish scenes of court spectacle whose brightness and saturated color "seemed lit from within as if they were indeed pages of illuminated manuscripts" (Andrew, 68). Terry Gilliam's playful animations for *Monty Python and the Holy Grail* (1975) remediate as cartoons the fantastic grotesques and caricatures found in manuscript marginalia (Burt, 227–28).

Is There a Text in This DVD?

Many of the new media's claims to immediacy and remediation, to improving on older media, rest on claims of their technological superiority. To unpack the social logics of film as a medium—especially the network of relationships in which it is embedded—we turn now to examine the social implications of recent developments in film technologies. Media technologies do not simply offer viewers transparent windows through which to view the past nor blank screens on which to project their fantasies. It is possible to explore the effect of technological change on both the production and consumption of film texts without falling into the trap of technological determinism or neglecting the nexus of social, political, cultural, and economic relationships in which technologies are embedded.[7] Because the end of the twentieth century brought about technologies that have revolutionized the ways in which we view films, we will limit our discussion to those technologies that have transformed film reception. In 1980, when Teresa de Lauretis and Stephen Heath examined the ideological effects of technological changes in the film industry in *The Cinematic Apparatus,* not one of the essays in the volume dealt with the cinematic apparatus of film reception. This is because, except for the introduction of television in the 1950s (which was considered inferior in quality to even the smallest theatrical screen), up until the mid-1980s, there had been no real qualitative changes in the technology of film reception since the invention of the film projector in the nineteenth century (we are counting sound and color as advances in the production process. Although they obviously had implications for viewing as well, they did not alter significantly the technologies of film consumption). The end of the twentieth century, however, saw new technologies that revolutionized the ways in which we view films.

Ever since film studies emerged as an academic discipline, *cineastes*—film purists—have insisted that the only true viewing of a film could occur through the experience of the film "text" on a large screen projected in a darkened theater. All other forms of viewing were at best secondary and at worst bastardized. In *The Dreamers,* Bernardo Bertolucci's 2003 paean to the French *cineaste* movement of the 1960s, one of the characters quips, "We don't watch television, we're purists." Home viewing technologies, whether in the form of television broadcasts (in which networks cropped the image using "pan and scan" technologies, inserted commercials, edited the film for content, and crammed it willy-nilly into preset scheduling blocks) or videotape, were especially looked down upon by film cognoscenti as not allowing for the appropriate kinds of concentration encouraged by the darkened theater. Television viewing, critics argued, was marked by interruption and a lessened concentration.

Even a glimpse at the film theory produced during the prevideo era (up through the 1980s), however, suggests the limitations for film analysis of theatrical viewing. As several film theorists have remarked, film theory in the prevideo age is characterized by its vagueness and, often enough, inaccuracy, the result of relying on memories of past viewings. In 1971 Stanley Cavell, while maintaining that even the most "ancient viewing" of a film takes precedence over a television viewing "in the hierarchy of film experience," remarked that "my way of studying films has been mostly through remembering them, like dreams." Cavell admits, "I am often referring to films I have seen only once, some as long as 30 year[s] ago. In a few instances I have seen a film three times, but in no case enough times to feel I possess it the way it deserves" (quoted in Barlow, 127). Raymond Bellour, writing a few years later, comments somewhat cryptically on "the vertigo of not being sure of my text, and with it, hidden by the relative impossibility of doing so, a different kind of profound vertigo determined by what the implications would be if I were someday able to be sure of it" (quoted in ibid.).

In fact, that day Bellour contemplated with a mixture of anticipation and dread arrived in 1997 with the introduction of the DVD. Since its introduction, DVD technology has been quietly transforming the viewing habits of movie audiences, for good or ill. Unlike earlier home video technologies, DVD offers a digital picture whose quality is equal to, and at times even superior to, theatrical viewing. While some cineastes are marginally less suspicious of the technology because it can preserve the widescreen aspect ratio of theatrical viewing so that films do not have to be recut and edited to fit the smaller screen, others are deeply suspicious of the technology because of the amount of control it gives to individual viewers. Quentin Tarentino, for instance, echoes earlier generations of purists in his distaste for the technology: "You don't want to have to think about the fact that people are having conversations and doing the crossword puzzle while your movie's playing. . . . The availability devalues films. . . . In an ironic way, by making art available we make it more disposable" (quoted in Barlow, 19). DVDs, in this view, exacerbate the privatization of movie watching. It used to be that we watched movies in large theaters with hundreds of others. The creation of the "multiplex" in the 1970s divided audiences into increasingly smaller segments. The transfer of movies to television and the arrival of videotape in the 1980s moved the whole enterprise into the privacy of the home, to the family living room. DVDs disperse it to the bedroom or to the personalized computer screen. Viewing has become individualized, even interiorized; with a portable DVD player and headphones, an individual can watch a movie on a crowded airplane or in other public spaces, effectively privatizing public spaces.[8]

DVDs "remediate" film by offering (literally) a whole menu of different ways in which an individual can watch a movie. If television viewers "lean back" as they watch (perhaps as good an image as any for the kind of passive, inattentive viewing Tarentino excoriates), computer users "lean forward," suggesting other, more active ways of watching a DVD (Barlow, 51). The interface between DVD and computers, in fact, allows for new ways to study movies. Until recently, precise and detailed analysis of film was nearly impossible except on a steenbeck, a flatbed editing machine (generally available only in specialist libraries) that allowed an individual to look at a film frame by frame.[9] The development of home video, whatever its flaws, created the potential for film scholars to view individual scenes from movies over and over again, subjecting them to the most minute scrutiny, a potential DVD technologies have exquisitely refined. It is now possible (as we have done in writing this book) to write on one half of a computer screen, while viewing the film one is studying on the other half, stopping as necessary and rewinding to check details (computer monitors with twenty-inch and larger screens have greatly aided this process). It is possible to turn on subtitles to pick up unintelligible lines of dialogue or to check quotations. Special features describe the making of the film, explain film technologies and processes, or offer historical documents related to the film. Commentaries offer the insights of directors, movie technicians, or film scholars. In his August 17, 2003, *New York Times* article, "Everyone's a Film Geek Now," Elvis Mitchell writes about how "the process of providing the best commentary was perfected by Criterion, a company that took as its mission eliciting lengthy interviews with directors and boiling them down into thoughtful, and often staggeringly intense, conversations about filmmaking." He notes that "Martin Scorsese's comments on the Criterion Collection's laser disc of *Taxi Driver* isn't just an interview; it's a master class, with an intoxicating wealth of raw data and insight into his perspective." In fact, DVDs offer the prospect that analysis by screenwriters, directors, and actors could render film studies superfluous. "For a time," Mitchell argues, "it seemed that Criterion's output might eliminate the need for film schools altogether, since their essential components, access to films and information about them, were packaged in two-disc sets." DVD enables even casual viewers to become fluent in film languages and techniques.

If, however, as Mitchell suggests, DVD audio commentary tantalizes with the potentiality of immediate access to a filmmaker's "original intention" (so much so that directors are willing to "sign off" on it),[10] it can also withhold or, at the very least, defer that authorization, calling attention to itself (hypermediation). A case in point might be Monty Python's Criterion commentary on their famous full-frontal-nudity scene in *Life of Brian*, when its eponymous hero, Brian Cohen (played by Graham Chapman), rises naked from bed, walks to a window, and opens it, exposing himself to the throng of disciples that has gathered outside of his home. While the Python group's audio commentary to the film hints at thoughtful, intense conversation, emphasizing a deep concern with historical and ethnic accuracy—this is, after all, a Criterion Collection film—during this scene it devolves into a hilarious discussion of efforts to insure the appropriate appearance of Brian Cohen's penis. We are told that in order for Graham Chapman, an uncircumcised gentile, to play the role of the Semitic Brian in this particular scene, he had to submit to having a foreskin-raising rubber band placed on his genitals. As with the frequently deconstructive content of their films, the Python group puts together an audio commentary that questions the process of audio commentary itself, calling attention to the mediating function of the commentary. Can it really be possible that the group cared so much about historical accuracy as to rubberband Graham Chapman's foreskin? We cannot remember how Chapman's apparatus looked on the big screen in 1979—its very presence would have been such a shock to original viewers that little time would have been spent pondering authenticity. Watching the DVD version of the film on television really does not allow the viewer to judge if Chapman's penis was altered to reflect the condition of Jewish genitalia in biblical Judea. It would seem, then, that the gloss provided by Monty Python's audio commentary may not be all that illuminating but just another equally inane text. It holds out the hope of immediacy, of authorized meaning—perhaps in the interest of truthfully reproducing the past, Chapman's penis really was bound for the scene—and simultaneously withdraws that meaning as a means of highlighting the hypermediated nature of commentary as a genre.

Robert W. Hanning, in his analysis of medieval textual glossing, suggests that "as an explanatory technique, glossing belonged primarily to the [medieval] schools and the pulpit, but as a concept it achieved a much broader cultural currency, functioning as a metaphor for all kinds of textual manipulation, even what might be called textual harassment, that is, the forcible imposition of special meanings on single words or entire verbal structures" (27). In so many ways, DVD audio commentary remediates this practice, functioning as a high-tech textual gloss. Like the medieval gloss, the audio commentary stands simultaneously in counterpoint to the text it analyzes and as its supplement. Proximity endows the gloss with an authority that overshadows all other possible commentaries, so much so that the gloss even threatens to overwhelm that which it analyzes. But ultimately the bonds that tie text and gloss together slip, as do the connections between a film and its DVD commentary. They become destabilized, susceptible to interpretations that require reassessments of their relationships.

These destabilizing elements extend to the filmic text itself. DVDs have had the effect of scattering the film "text" into variability, altering "the ontological status of the film itself" (Burt, 219). Today it is no longer possible, if it ever was, to speak of a single stable film "text." The DVD format enables directors to produce different versions of the same film and include them on a single disk or in packaged sets. They can recut films that have been altered by studio intervention. To appeal to his base of Tolkien fans, Peter Jackson issued extended-version DVDs, cuts of *The Lord of the Rings* trilogy significantly longer than the theatrical releases. In a move that has alienated many of his fans, George Lucas recut his 1977 classic *Star Wars* to include plot developments from the lesser "prequels" produced between 1999 and 2005. Scholarly restorations of films like Dreyer's *La Passion de Jeanne d'Arc* or Fleming's 1948 *Joan of Arc* offer versions of these films that had never been seen. When the original print release of Dreyer's film was destroyed in a fire, a newer cut based on outtakes was made, and it, too, was subsequently lost to fire. For a long time the film existed only in various forms cobbled together from inferior copies. In 1981 a nitrate print of the film was discovered in a Danish mental hospital; however, this print was not widely viewed until it was released on a DVD whose astonishing clarity showcases this cinematic masterpiece. The DVD restoration of Fleming's film includes nearly forty-five minutes that had not been seen in more than fifty years and that substantially alters the narrative. The ready availability of DVD technology has made it easier for scholars to study the variability of such film texts because it allows them to study different versions of the same film side by side.

We may need to speak today of many different ways to view a film, each of which has its advantages and disadvantages. We might watch a film on a large screen in a darkened theater, or we might watch it at home for a pleasant undemanding evening's entertainment. Our home viewing might be punctuated by bathroom breaks, snack forays, even casual conversation, something that would be heresy in a movie theater. Or we might view a DVD on our computer, stopping and rewinding, playing a single sequence over and over again to study it, to pick up the minutest technical details. We might view alternate versions of a single film, comparing them. In many ways a film text is becoming more like a medieval manuscript than like a printed book. Rather than being a text fixed through the processes of mechanical reproduction, the very technology that produces the film text has rendered it, as Cerquiglini notes of the medieval manuscript, variance itself. "The extension and dispersal" of the filmic text through the new digital and electronic media (Burt, 218), especially through DVD and other "new" media, have enabled the kinds of readings we undertake in this volume. The final part of this chapter turns to the interpretive practices that follow from these developments, especially the specific signs of medievalness that filmmakers draw on to make the Middle Ages legible to viewers.

Cinematic Mythologies

Roland Barthes was conscious of the mythologizing impulse in historical films, of what Burt calls "history effects" (217). One of the brief essays collected in *Mythologies*, "The Romans in Film," observes that in Joseph L. Mankiewicz's *Julius Caesar* (1953) all of the characters sport bangs. "What then is associated with these insistent fringes?" he asks:

> Quite simply the label of Roman-ness. We therefore see here the mainspring of the Spectacle—the *sign*—operating in the open. The frontal lock overwhelms one with evidence, no one can doubt that he is in Ancient Rome. And this certainty is permanent: the actors speak, act, torment themselves, debate "questions of universal import," without losing, thanks to this little flag displayed on their foreheads, any of their historical plausibility. Their general representativeness can even expand in complete safety, cross the ocean and the centuries, and merge into the Yankee mugs of Hollywood extras: no matter, everyone is reassured, installed in the quiet certainty of a universe without duplicity, where Romans are Romans thanks to the most legible of signs: hair on the forehead. (26)

Vivian Sobchack, in her essay "The Insistent Fringe," criticizes Barthes' analysis as "a view that far too quickly judges the iconic and synchronic signification of moving, yet 'fixed,' images in popular films (and popular consciousness) as 'mythological,' 'ahistorical' and 'bourgeois,' and the spectators who watch them as downright dumb, historically befuddled, and ideologically suspect" (5). Such an "elitist" view, she argues, must be complicated if we hope to understand "how historical consciousness emerges in a culture in which we are all completely immersed in images." Perhaps because of contemporary film viewers' almost continual immersion in mass media, Sobchack credits them with the knowledge "that histories are rhetorically constructed narratives, that 'events' and 'facts' are open to various uses and multiple interpretations" (5). But to what extent does Sobchack's criticism of Barthes "elitism" project onto an anonymous public a means of salving her own anxieties about the historical status of cinematic signs? It is not clear to us that, however sophisticated movie audiences have become about media, they understand how histories are "rhetorically constructed narratives" or that they understand what follows from such a premise. Rather, it seems to us that the social contract of cinema requires that all viewers—from the anonymous naive public to the sophisticated historian or cultural theorist—agree to enter into the world created by a film and learn its systems of signification. Viewers accept a Caesar haircut, for instance, as a sign of Romanness not because they are (or are not) unsophisticated or naive but because they have become competent readers of the cinematic shorthand that allows a two-hour visit to a remediated ancient Rome. The systems of signification that make up this shorthand resonate across any number of disparate films, triggering a willing suspension of disbelief that enables us to enter into the worlds these films create (at least momentarily), even when, as historians, we might be suspicious of the film's representation of the past.

In fact, the processes Barthes describes of learning and synthesizing cinematic signs require a different kind of sophistication on the part of the viewer than the kind of historical contingency Sobchack describes.[11] In our analysis of film medievalism we want to go beyond Barthes' "insistent fringe" to understand what such signs might mean for audiences "completely immersed in images." Most of the interpretive work done in watching a film consists of recognizing those features a particular film has in common with other films of its kind. Reading a film about the Middle Ages (or any historical film), because it draws on a discipline entirely outside of cinema—history—is complicated since the viewer must recognize not only those features the film has in common with other films but also those it has in common with the store of knowledge of dates, events, and characters that constitutes a culture's "historical capital" (Sorlin, 20). Because most twentieth-century Americans' historical capital for the Middle Ages is so impoverished, because the period has become so distant and alien to popular viewers, filmmakers have come to rely on a series of stock features—signs—whose function it is—like Mankiewicz's "insistent fringe"—to signify "medievalness" and so to locate the viewer within the medieval framework of the film. Oftentimes, like the "insistent fringe," these signs relate to nothing whatsoever except other films about the Middle Ages. They are not what scholars would consider historical references; rather they are cultural signs that signify popular ideas (even mythologies) about the period; these "history effects" remediate inaccessible or unfamiliar historical texts for cinema audiences. All films about the Middle Ages, from the most popular and formulaic to the most artistic and innovative, draw on these features as a sort of narrative shorthand. In this section we describe those practices of reception that viewers draw on—with astonishing facility—to make sense of cinematic medievalism.

In unpacking these "signs of medievalness," we find Bakhtin's notion of the chronotope useful. In his essay "Forms of Time and of the Chronotope in the Novel," Bakhtin coined the term to designate the "intrinsic connectedness of time and space," which, he argues, constitutes not only literary genre but social life itself. In a chronotope "spatial and temporal indicators are fused into one carefully thought-out, concrete whole. Time, as it were, thickens, takes on flesh . . . ; likewise, space becomes charged and responsive to the movements of time, plot and history" (*The Dialogic Imagination*, 84). For Bakhtin chronotopes are the basis of all representation; we literally cannot represent our world without them: "the chronotope makes narrative events concrete, makes them take on flesh, causes blood to flow in their veins." For Bakhtin this is what distinguishes a narrative from bare chronicle: "An event can be communicated, it becomes information, one can give precise data on the place and time of its occurrence" (250). For Bakhtin all genres—whether literary or social—are constituted by chronotopes. The peculiar chronotope of, say, the western—a long time ago in an unsettled American frontier—distinguishes it from the detective story—the here and now of urban space. The novel and its predecessors all have their characteristic chronotopes that Bakhtin's essay explores at great length.

If language, "as a treasure-house of images," is fundamentally chronotopic for Bakhtin (251), the languages of film must be even more so. If warrant were needed to extend the Bakhtinian chronotope to film, the art historian Erwin Panofsky's 1947 essay "Style and Medium in the Motion Pictures" suggests that film's "unique and specific possibilities" lay in its "dynamization of space and, accordingly, spatialization of time" (281). Christian Metz's "grande syntagmatique" was an attempt to articulate a set of syntagms by the ways in which they structure the spatiotemporal relations of a profilmic event (Miller and Stam, 93). Whatever the narrative time-space a film might represent, the cinematic chronotope is always limited by the fact that it is played out across a screen with specific spatial dimensions, and it always unfolds in literal time (usually twenty-four frames per second).

But this does not mean that either time or space is necessarily linear in film. Filmmakers are able to play, for instance, with viewers' sense of unfolding time in various ways. A film like John Boorman's *Excalibur* (1981) creates a romance chronotope, suggesting both a subjective and mythical view of time through the use of the seasons. The narrative plays out across the cyclic changes of the seasons, but seasonal time also appears to be sensitive to the health of the king and so of the land he rules, a technique noted by most commentaries on the film: "Winter signifies the barbarous world into which Arthur is born"; he "flourishes

Excalibur in a leafy forest hung with banners" and marries Guenevere amid "the flowers of May"; "Mordred's milieu is the dark world of autumn, where bare branches and brown bogs signify oppression and sterility" (Whitaker, 136). Monty Python, on the other hand, parodies the romance's subjective playing with time in the sequence in which Lancelot affects a wedding rescue "in his own idiom." Lancelot's approach to Swamp Castle parodies filmic conventions for dilating and contracting time. After a series of scenes showing the wedding preparations, an extreme wide-angle shot shows Lancelot running toward the castle, accompanied by a drum roll. Because of the wide-angle lens, he appears to be making no progress at all as he runs toward the camera. This shot loops five times, intercut with reaction shots of the guards (creating what Metz describes as an "alternate chronological syntagma" ["Problems of Denotation in the Fiction Film," 84]). Then, in the next cut, Lancelot is right on top of the guards. In the same scene, through cinematic tricks that would be familiar to even the most casual viewer, time has been dilated and then contracted, parodying the romance chronotope's manipulation of time.

Those syntagms most likely to signify "medievalness" include iconography, conventions, formulae, and genres. In our analysis, however, these syntagms do not function the way they might in a structural analysis based on Saussurean linguistics or a formalist analysis such as Metz's. Bakhtinian translinguistics,[12] in contradistinction to Saussurean linguistics, prefers the diachronic over the synchronic and *parole* over *langue;* or, more accurately, it deconstructs the oppositions set up between these Saussurean pairs. For this reason it is important to bear in mind that these four types of cinematic syntagms—iconography, conventions, formulae, and genres—never function abstractly as Saussureans imagine signs do. The interplay of these various signs with one another constitutes the whole sense of medievalness a film imparts. Indeed the extension of a Bakhtinian translinguistics to the "languages" of film might well help to bridge the gap in the study of film "between an abstract 'formal' approach and an equally abstract 'ideological' approach," a gap that Bakhtin clearly felt in the study of literature (*Dialogic Imagination,* 259) and that Robert Stam, in his insightful analysis of the work of Christian Metz (*Subversive Pleasures,* 37–56), demonstrates plagues the study of film today.[13] It may also provide us a language within which to theorize the relationship between the demands of historical accuracy and those of narrative structuration in historical film. The meaning of the cinematic sign is never determined in advance; it can only be realized through the utterance, which is always the minimal unit of analysis for Bakhtin. Meaning, for Bakhtin, is always particular, historical, contextualized. Embedded within a diachronic matrix (in the sense of an interconnecting network or system) of paradigmatic and syntagmatic relations, these signs combine to produce utterances, always in dialogue with other utterances. Because of the slipperiness of the concept of utterance, however (it can refer to everything from a single shot to an entire film), and because they function in different areas of the film, these four types of signs do make sense as discrete categories of analysis. Some of these tropes manage narrative structures, others shot sequences; still others organize the mise-en-scène.

Genre

We could hardly do better introducing the concept of genre in film than to look at the theory of genre developed by the Bakhtin Circle, especially in P. N. Medvedev's *The Formal Method in Literary Scholarship* and Bakhtin's late essay "Speech Genres." What these texts have to say about literary genres applies equally well to film genres. In his essay on speech genres Bakhtin argues that genres are not unique to literary aesthetics; they govern both thought and speech; genre is "a specific way of visualizing a given part of reality" (Morson and Emerson, 275). Medvedev defines genre as "the typical form of the whole work, the whole utterance" (Medvedev and Bakhtin, 129), where "utterance" might be an exclamation, a sentence, a scientific article, a novel, or even a film. As with all literary forms, analysis of film begins with its genre as the foundational block of its representational strategy: "genre appraises reality and reality clarifies genre" (Medvedev and Bakhtin, 136). One cannot understand a film without first understanding the genre on which it draws. Genre here is understood, however, not as a formal, ahistorical system of classification; rather particular genres are a "residue of past behavior." That is, they are created by repetition; they "crystallize" and "congeal" (Morson and Emerson, 290) diachronically around a set of formal features. As they do, they imply a set of values, a way of thinking about the world. They define the possible social relationships between characters, suggest possible or desirable action, convey information about time and space (chronotope), and suggest appropriate tone and languages. "Many people who have an excellent command of a language often feel quite helpless in certain spheres of communication precisely because they do not have a practical command of the generic forms used in the given spheres" (Bakhtin, *Speech Genres and Other Late Essays*, 80). Similarly, a film spectator with an incomplete understanding of a film's genre will be at a loss to follow its action.

We do not believe that medieval films constitute a genre in and of themselves;

they are too diverse a lot. Rather, different films draw on different generic frameworks to construct their chronotopes, especially their representations of time. Two possibilities occur to us. Some medieval films combine a contemporary genre with a medieval setting, playing with the genre's conventional chronotope. Jean-Jacques Annaud's 1986 adaptation of Umberto Eco's *The Name of the Rose* is a good example of a film that locates the modern genre of detection not in the chronotope of contemporary urban life but in the medieval monastery. In Eco's novel time and space are rationalized, precisely counted off by the days of the week, the liturgical hours, and the apportioning of space in the monastery. This rationalization is appropriate to the detective genre, which relies on the precise timing of events to work out its narrative; however, time in Eco's novel is not only rationalized; it is liturgical (counted through the canonical hours) and mythological as well (the novel spans seven days, the exact number of days attributed to the Creation). The film, which is billed as a "palimpsest" of Eco's novel, cannot manage Eco's temporal precision but conveys something of this dual sense of time in its contrast between daytime and nighttime. During the day, the public, cyclic, repetitive, and collective activities of the monks take place; these scenes are set in the church, the refectory, the chapter. Nighttime activities are personal, secretive, involving the individual; they take place in cells, hidden passages, and secret libraries. These two distinct chronotopes—that of the individual and the collective—come together in the climax, which involves a public fire at which heretics are to be burned before the entire community and a fire in the secret library, the result of a standoff between two individuals: the detective, William of Baskerville, and the murderer.

Monty Python and the Holy Grail, by way of contrast, offers up the television genre of sketch comedy in a medieval setting. Time and space are episodic, fragmented, undifferentiated. Based almost entirely on the form of the comedy troupe's successful television series, it mostly ignores traditional filmic plot construction in favor of a series of almost discrete sketches, loosely held together by a narrative that can be jettisoned at will. One adventure is not related by either time or space to another. Rather they build by random contingency; Arthur and the Black Knight just happen to be in the same place at the same time (chance simultaneity). There is no narrative logic building to a climax. As such, the film is free to focus the audience's attention on its parody of the formulae, conventions, and iconography of other medieval films. Even the actors are iconic, their presence signifying a particular type of comedy. Drawing on their previous familiarity with the comedy troupe's cult BBC television series, audiences who understand the film's humor will expect comedy that involves cross-dressing, comic violence, animation, and learned parody of literary, historical, and cultural events.

Still other films adapt medieval genres to the medium of film, our second possibility. Eric Rohmer's 1978 *Perceval le Gallois* is perhaps the most successful example of this type of film. Rohmer closely follows the text of Chrétien de Troyes, and all aspects of the film follow from the generic chronotope of medieval romance. This chronotope exhibits, according to Bakhtin, a "subjective playing with time, an emotional and lyrical stretching and compressing of it," along with an "emotional, subjective distortion of space," which is largely symbolic (*The Dialogic Imagination*, 155). The mise-en-scène of Rohmer's film attempts to recreate (often with stunning success) illuminations of medieval manuscripts; the music, sets, and style of acting contribute to the overall effect.

Formula

A formula is a "repeated series of actions that results in a predictable outcome" (Sobchack and Sobchack, 230). Generally, certain cinematic formulae structure particular genres. Analyses of such formulae illustrate the ways in which the development of the formal features of film depends not on the existence of abstract synchronic units (or syntagms, as Metz hypothesized) but on filmmakers' and viewers' diachronic experiences of film and other narrative texts. The dream vision, for example (usually the result of a knock on the head), is a common formula for medieval films, especially time-travel films that draw loosely on the plot of Mark Twain's *A Connecticut Yankee in King Arthur's Court*. The Bing Crosby star vehicle of that title, directed by Tay Garnett in 1949, offers an example even as it shapes viewers' responses to the same formula in later films, such as Gil Junger's 2001 *Black Knight*. This formula usually functions as the frame tale for the medieval part of the film and produces certain predictable plot and character developments. We know, even if we have never read Twain's novel, that the film's humor will derive from the exploitation of anachronism, as, for instance, when Crosby's character, Hank Martin,[14] mistakes the obtuse Sir Sagramore the Desirous for an escaped mental patient and parries the knight's challenge to a joust with a wisecrack, "Skip, run along, before they come and get you. . . . Your keepers should be here any minute." We know that Martin will succeed in this alien world by introducing technological marvels (a magnifying glass, an almanac, a safety pin, a revolver, western riding and rodeo skills, big band music) to the ignorant primitives. Our pleasure as viewers derives not from the plot's originality (it is utterly formulaic) but from the variations worked on the theme. Garnett's film, for instance, replaces Mark Twain's satire of late-nineteenth-century America—a critique that encompasses, among other things, America's struggles with slavery, civil war, rapid expansionism, and the genocide of Native Americans—with the exhilaration of a nation having just emerged from victory in World War II. Together, genre and formula manage the details of plot construction in narrative film.

For the Bakhtin Circle, however, any sign is a site of ideological contestation, and if our extension of Bakhtin's formulations to film holds, then this must be true for its formal features as well. In *Marxism and the Philosophy of Language* Vološinov writes: "The domain of ideology coincides with the domain of signs. They equate with one another. Wherever a sign is present, ideology is present too. Everything ideological possesses semiotic value" (10). What are the ideological consequences of a formula like the one described above? For one thing, it frames a contrast, as we suggested in chapter 1, between a superior "modern" technology and a benighted and atavistic past, and it links certain elements in contemporary culture to that primitive past. On the humorous side, Garnett's film links King Arthur, who is played by Sir Cedric Hardwicke as constantly plagued by a cold, to his twentieth-century descendant, Lord Pendragon, also played by Hardwicke, who seems to have inherited the infirmity. On a more serious side, much of the humor in Garnett's film is derived from the confident reserve Crosby's Hank Martin exhibits, no matter how ludicrous—or dangerous—his position. He cracks wise even as he is being led to execution. Hank Martin's bravado, however, is completely undone when he encounters poverty and injustice in medieval England, the same poverty and injustice that persist in his technologically advanced "modern" world. For the most part Garnett's film transports Hank Martin to a medieval past where, as representative of a superior, more advanced American culture, he is able to solve problems through the application of his wits and enhanced technology. But Martin's journey through time also helps him solve his own, modern-day difficulty. At the beginning of the film Martin is portrayed as the quintessential, twentieth-century bachelor, surrounded by and fond of children. He sings about American persistence overcoming obstacles to a group of neighborhood tots—but, finally, he is alone with his technology. For the post–World War II generation, whose notions of heteronormativity were stabilized in the institutions of marriage and family, Martin's situation would seem vexing, if not downright deviant. Martin is resituated through his encounter with the medieval past, where he encounters romance both of the generic and gendered varieties. Martin returns from the Middle Ages rehabilitated, grown-up, not entirely ready to put down his technological toys—if he did, how would capitalism advance?—but interested in dividing his time between those toys and a proper family life. The film provides for him an exact replica of his medieval love waiting in the present. He comes back from his time travel not miserable and disoriented, like the character in Twain's novel, but rather exactly as Hollywood imagined the GIs returning from World War II: ready to marry, raise a family, and promote the business of America.

Time travel to the Middle Ages provides a formulaic antidote to the adolescent aimlessness of Stephen Herek's suburban slackers in *Bill and Ted's Excellent Adventure* (1989). Bill and Ted are suburban primitives, innocent of the authority of the great Western tradition. They are postmodern blank slates on which oppressive and dominating educational institutions attempt to inscribe the teleological order of a Western civilization that culminates in the consumerist world of white, middle-class San Dimas, California. They are failing high school history. Threatened by the prospect of separation—Ted's father will send his son to military school if he doesn't straighten up—the boys are given an opportunity to expedite their history assignment, on which they must achieve an A+, by traveling to the past and literally kidnapping history, or at least historical figures. Their assignment reads: "express to the class how an important historical figure from each of your time periods would view the world of San Dimas, 1988." This assignment imagines history is progressive and teleological; it is also based on the individual, the "important historical figure." But the plot of *Bill and Ted's Excellent Adventure* circumvents the ideological meaning of the time-travel formula. Rather than rehabilitating its adolescent heroes, civilizing them and preparing them to take their place in the dominant order—the goal of the history project—their adventures reshape the world they occupy, bringing it more into line with their vision, an adolescent male fantasy of a future in which they are worshipped as rock stars. The history they have kidnapped becomes irrelevant, nothing more than a collection of free-floating signifiers they can assemble to accomplish their immediate ends. At the film's conclusion Ted notes that "we traveled through time. I mean, we met lots of great leaders, and we got an A+ on our history report and look at us—nothing is different." Rufus, their guide from the future (played by George Carlin), tells them, however, that their considerably less-than-competent garage band, Wyld Stallyns, will become "the foundation of our whole society. . . . Eventually your music will help put an end to war and poverty. It will align the planets and bring them into universal harmony, allowing meaningful contact with all forms of life, from extraterrestrial beings to common household pets—and it's excellent for dancing." Bill, Ted, and the futuristic world they have inspired have rejected the teleological march of Western history for a static cosmic order that resembles nothing so much as the medieval Great Chain of Being. Adolescents as postmodern consumers par excellence become so detached from any foundational historical narrative that they can move full circle to become futuristic medieval primitives.

Conventions

Conventions manage sequences of shots; they usually involve small, relatively self-contained, units of action. They translate formulae into visualized action, telling the director how to photograph or edit a particular sequence. Examples of medieval conventions include single combat and the joust. The conventions for editing fight sequences that involve violent confrontations between two individuals have been worked out over the last century in several film genres including westerns (the gunfight), martial arts films, action films, boxing films, as well as medieval films that include jousting and sword fighting. The scene in *Excalibur* in which Arthur and Lancelot first meet offers a fairly conventional example of how such sequences are visually managed. The scene of single combat is, of course, conventional in medieval Arthurian romance as a genre. Usually the opponents are unknown to the hero-knight, strangers, and so vaguely threatening (a good example is Gareth's encounter with a series of anonymous, color-coded knights in Malory's *Morte Darthur*).[15] But it is almost equally likely that the opponent will be a friend and fellow member of the Round Table (to achieve knighthood, the same Gareth must fight the knight he holds his dearest friend, Lancelot). *Excalibur* plays on this generic expectation in staging this fight scene. The sequence begins with an establishing shot of the two mounted knights at opposite ends of a bridge. Lancelot (who at this point in the film is the stranger and so threatening) is on the far left, riding a white horse and clad in the heroic shiny chrome armor that has already become part of the iconography of the film. He occupies the place of the hero. Arthur is on the far right, riding a brown horse and wearing black armor. Even though most of the previous scenes have worked to establish Arthur as the hero (in no other scene in the film does he wear black armor), in this scene he seems to occupy the conventional place of the villain (the black knight), perhaps to emphasize the threat his anger poses to his rule. *Excalibur* is a film that wants to suggest moral ambiguity, but it does so by mobilizing the oldest and most clichéd signs of good and evil (white and black hats).

The conventional fight scene also contains signs within its mise-en-scène for telling viewers who has the upper hand. At one point in this same sequence, when Lancelot has gained the advantage, we are shown Arthur in the bottom left of the shot, almost out of frame. He is literally cornered, with nowhere to go. Lancelot looms over him with a huge expanse of empty space in the frame to the right of him. The implication is that Lancelot has room to maneuver; Arthur does not. A few shots later the positions are reversed. Having called on the mystical powers of the sword Excalibur, Arthur now has the advantage (and indeed wins the encounter at the cost of the sword that legitimates his rule). Lancelot is cornered in the lower left portion of the screen, and Arthur looms above him with an expanse of space to his right. The allocation of space within the frame provides cues that enable viewers to follow the reversal of fortunes in the fight.

The Black Knight sequence in *Monty Python and the Holy Grail* mobilizes the same set of conventions, parodying the way in which such sequences are usually managed. To impart a sense of chaos to a fight scene, for instance, the editing will almost always be accelerated. In *Monty Python and the Holy Grail* the fight between the Black Knight and the Green Knight includes about twenty-five shots in a sequence that uses about eighty seconds of screen time. This averages out to a cut about every three seconds, much faster than the rate of cutting in earlier, more leisurely, scenes. The shots alternate among longer establishing shots, two-shots showing the combatants, shot–reverse shot sequences that alternate between the combatants (similar to the method for editing conversation), close-ups and extreme close-ups. The close-ups tend to contribute to the sense of chaos by denying us access to the whole scene and exaggerating particular small motions; the longer shots establish the spatial relations between the combatants. These shots alternately create suspense and relieve it. The Black Knight sequence, for instance, opens with an extreme close-up of crossing swords. The camera then pulls back to reveal a knight's helmet. It then cuts to a close-up of two sets of legs that frame the tiny figure of Arthur "galloping" into the shot.[16] Thus, the scene begins in confusion for viewers. We cannot easily tell what is happening; we do not know what kind of adventure Arthur will discover. Only in the fifth shot are we finally given an establishing shot that shows two knights engaged in single combat. The duel between Arthur and the Black Knight unfolds much like this earlier fight scene, using the same combinations of shots, although the camera is much more static, usually holding the two characters in a long two-shot once Arthur begins lopping off the Black Knight's limbs. The sequence ends with a visual joke—a point-of-view shot looking down on the now limbless Black Knight still itching for a fight.

"Because the eye tends to read a picture from left to right, physical movement in this direction seems psychologically natural, whereas movement from the right to left often seems inexplicably tense and uncomfortable" (Giannetti, 99), although this may be true only for those readers of languages that read from left to right. Conventionally, according to Giannetti, protagonists move from left to right and villains from right to left. The directors of *Monty Python and the Holy Grail*, however, exploit our expectations and increase the sense of chaos throughout the film by frequently having characters—both protagonist and antagonists—move from right to left in a scene. The ideological effect of this technique is ambiguity about the heroic, as part of Monty Python's send-up both of the Middle Ages and of the conventions of film. The film's originality lies in the variations that it creates on those conventions, for instance, in the way it turns customary screen violence into cartoon violence, parodying the anxieties of medieval (and modern) hyper-masculinity ("It's only a flesh wound," the Black Knight says of his severed arm).

At the level of ideology a Bakhtinian reading might notice that the same shot–reverse shot sequence that developed even before the introduction of sound film to represent dialogue is also used to make sense of these fight sequences.[17] This connection reminds us that such sequences represent not simply the enmity between two male antagonists. They are also implicated in an ideology of gender and violence in which honor becomes the only allowable form of homosocial bonding. Because, as the World War I poet Wilfred Owen so eloquently noted, the anonymous technologies of modern warfare—automatic weapons, tanks, bombs, and poison gas—hold little attraction for "children ardent for some desperate glory," cinematic representations of single combat, particularly those involving archaic weapons like swords, satisfy a nostalgic longing for a time when combat brought men together in close physical contact for the purpose of establishing honor. This ideology offers one explanation for the rather odd series of 1995 recruiting advertisements made by the J. Walter Thompson agency for the United States Marine Corps. These spots—which often appeared before the previews of Hollywood films—draw on the imagery of medieval swordplay to sell the marines to adolescent male audiences. They all prominently feature the sword—carried as part of the dress uniform of every marine—as a metonymy for a concept of honor that forges the "corps" into a new chivalric elite: "the few, the proud." One of these spots, which demonstrates the fluidity of cultural icons of archaic masculinity for twentieth-century adolescent males, begins with a muscular young man dressed in Banana Republic–like attire having an adventure in the idiom of Indiana Jones. After overcoming a number of trials that test his "body and mind" (but mostly his body), he finds himself in a chamber where he pulls a sword out of a globe, bringing to life a statue of an armed and armored knight. The two fight, and, in three quick strokes, he vanquishes the knight. Holding his sword aloft in victory, the young man morphs into a marine in full dress uniform. Indiana Jones and King Arthur merge in the figure of the marine (who will undoubtedly never use his sword except in parades). A second spot features a chess board in which a knight, armed in excessively metallic armor and riding a white horse, does battle with various opponents, including a sorcerer and a mounted black knight. The victorious white knight salutes the king and then morphs into an African American marine, again in full dress uniform, again prominently displaying the decorative sword. These spots suggest the extent to which the marines have a difficult time representing culturally the kind of honor that defines membership in a military elite except through archaic forms of single combat that bear no relationship to the realities of modern warfare.

If the U.S. Marines recruiting spots demonstrate the close connection between nontechnologized single combat and chivalric notions of honor, a film like *Bill and Ted's Excellent Adventure* humorously reveals the ways in which this ideology depends on a homosociality that demands affection between men be expressed only through physical violence. Single combat between close friends is not unusual, either in the medieval romance or in film medievalism; its purpose is almost always to forge closer, more physical, relationships among men. During their stint in "medieval times," Bill and Ted don full suits of armor and engage in brief swordplay, and, in many ways, they are just boys playing with swords. When Bill thinks Ted has been killed by another knight, however, he is distraught. When Ted is revealed to be uninjured, the two together overcome their medieval assailant. They embrace quickly in victory, celebrating their honor. But they part even more quickly, chanting in unison, "Fag," apparently to ward off any taint of contamination by the homoerotic. They displace their earlier physical conflict into friendly banter, both acknowledging and repudiating the relationship developed through violence. If further proof were needed of this connection between physical violence and homosocial bonding, we might point to *Shanghai Knights* (David Dobkin, 2003), which choreographs a martial arts sequence to the tune of "Singin' in the Rain," structuring the exchange of violence through the conventions of the musical, that most heterosexual and romantic of film genres.

Iconography

Iconography manages a film's mise-en-scène, aiding directors in setting up individual shots. These are the details caught within the frame (clothing, objects, landscapes, even performers) whose meanings come from their repeated use in similar films. Icons must be distinguished from symbols. Symbols usually appear in a single film and take their meaning from their repetition within the film. The sword Excalibur in Boorman's film of the same name is a symbol. While armor is iconic (and almost always anachronistic, serving the needs of the particular film rather than historical accuracy), the shiny chrome of the armor that runs as a motif throughout the film is symbolic. The game of chess between Antonius Block and Death in Ingmar Bergman's *The Seventh Seal* is symbolic; its parodic repetition in films like Woody Allen's *Love and Death* or Peter Hewitt's *Bill and Ted's Bogus Journey* (in which the heroes play Battleship, Clue, and Twister with Death) is iconic.

Perhaps the icon that functions most vividly to call up the Middle Ages for the popular viewer (the one that functions like Barthes' "insistent fringe") is filth, at least if Sobchack's examples from the email discussion list H-film are any indication. Films that realistically depict the Middle Ages, according to this scholarly forum, must represent "the muck and dirt and rushes on the floors," "graphic depictions of squalor," and "lots of mud, dirt, rain," in order to be "realistic," that is, in order to convey to the viewer the authenticity of medieval life ("The Insistent Fringe," 6). We would correlate the amount of filth present in a medieval film with the film's view of the Middle Ages. Those films subscribing to the fantasy of the Middle Ages as a lost organic society will tend to be cleaner than those that see it as barbaric and uncivilized. Compare the prettified Camelot of Joshua Logan's 1967 *Camelot* with Richard Lester's filthy Sherwood Forest in *Robin and Marian* (1976). The insistence on the filthiness of the Middle Ages seems to stem from a need to counter the romanticized, nostalgic view of the period, to proclaim its barbarity as a "dark age." The association of the medieval with "magic and mud, superstition and the thick sludge of wet soil, ignorance and the peasant," David Lloyd argues, suggests for modern audiences its status as a metaphoric representation of the material, "all that capitalism in its logic of ceaseless dissolution, melting all into air, fails to dissolve" (15). *Monty Python and the Holy Grail* parodies Pier Paolo Pasolini's and Ingmar Bergman's representations of the Middle Ages in its second scene, "Bring Out Your Dead." This scene uses a combination of close-ups and deep-focus photography to draw attention to the extreme filth of a medieval village. While we are watching an argument over a not-quite-dead man play out in the foreground, our eye also notices a woman beating a cat against a wall in the background. Here, however, the scene provides a buildup to a rather serious joke. As Arthur and his squire pass through the village, the characters speculate on his identity, "Who's that, then?" "I dunno. Must be a king." "Why?" "He hasn't got shit all over him." For the Monty Python troupe, the filth of the Middle Ages provides a commentary on class difference and privilege. The filth and squalor of the Middle Ages is an ideological sign of its backwardness and, by extension, of contemporary backwardness.

Winston Churchill, in his discussion of King Arthur in *The Birth of Britain*, noted that knights required not only "valour and physical strength" but "good horses and armour" as well (60). For most medieval movies the iconographic representation of valor and physical strength is metonymically linked to the visual representation of good horses and armor. In *Excalibur* the violence of the opening battle scene is marked by the insistent neighing of the horses and the steam issuing from their breath. The opening joke of *Monty Python and the Holy Grail* (banging coconuts to represent absent horses) is dependent on filmic conventions for representing horses (even sound can, as in this example, be iconic). Before we ever see horses, we hear the sound of "galloping," which, in a sound studio might well be made by banging two coconuts together. The joke brings the diegetic fiction and extradiegetic sound together on the same screen. In *Excalibur* Boorman heightens the connection between knightly valor and armor by exaggerating his armor's sheen. The flickering green lights glancing off the burnished chrome in scene after scene gives the film its characteristic look, which is supposed to suggest some kind of Celtic mysticism, a past with a more magical connection to nature.

But armor as an iconographic representation of the medieval provides filmmakers with a challenge because it tends to interfere with the typical Hollywood iconography of the hero. Because of the prominence of the "star system," in which the star becomes an icon, Hollywood narratives require that the audience have a hero with whom it can identify, and that hero (especially if he or she is a star) must be clearly marked by the processes of filming, by both mise-en-scène and editing, which distinguish the hero from all other characters in the film. A knight in full armor, however, will tend to be indistinguishable from other knights in armor. For this reason, in many medieval films, the hero will fight without armor or at least without a helmet. In *First Knight* (Jerry Zucker, 1995), for instance, Richard Gere's Lancelot sometimes wears armor but rarely a helmet. Zucker struggles against the logic of medieval warfare to showcase the well-known face of his leading man.

Boorman uses armor in *Excalibur* to mark the limits of heroism. Gabriel Byrne's Uther, who appears only in the film's first few scenes, wears full armor in almost all of his scenes, even when he is making love and holding his newborn child (Arthur). This makes him appear distant, unappealing. He cannot emerge, even temporarily, as a hero. Especially in the domestic scenes he appears mechanical, ruthless, and monstrous next to Katrine Boorman's warmly lit Igrayne; he is completely out of place. His rape of Igrayne seems all the more brutal because his armor makes him seem inhuman. By way of contrast, in Arthur's early scenes, Arthur draws the sword from the stone and unites the British under his leadership without ever donning armor. The reason? He has not been knighted. But his lack of armor, though motivated by the demands of the story, also means that in these early scenes we can identify with him as the hero because we can see his face. Later in the film, Arthur will recede into his armor, and we will lose all sense of him as a character; he becomes more symbol than hero. Perceval emerges in the second half of the film as a more compelling hero than Lancelot not only because he achieves the Grail and restores Arthur's kingdom but because we usually see him without his armor and so can identify with him more readily. It is Merlin, however, who appears as the film's real hero and most fully developed character. He never wears armor; his face is always visible. The chrome skullcap he wears connects him visually to the knights, while at the same time it emphasizes his difference—and distance—from them.

Credits are signs whose iconography may also contribute to the sense of "medievalness" a film imparts, not because of any intrinsic meaning that attaches to things medieval but because of viewers' diachronic experience of viewing films (Burt, 221–28). Both *Monty Python and the Holy Grail* and *Excalibur* establish their "seriousness" (or lack thereof) by drawing on conventions for managing opening credits derived from Bergman's *The Seventh Seal*. (Bergman's film has become so iconographic that virtually all medieval films reference it in some way.) For Bergman, credits were a necessary inconvenience, something to be gotten out of the way, yet his black screen with white letters in a simple font has accumulated significance, indeed portentousness, for films that followed. Both *Monty Python and the Holy Grail* and *Excalibur* deploy these meanings as signs of the Middle Ages. In *Excalibur* the titles begin with an exposition that locates the film in the mystical but indeterminate Middle Ages of Jessie Weston (see Shichtman, "Hollywood's New Weston"): "The Dark Ages," a vague, imprecise time in the far-distant past. "The Land Was Divided And Without A King. Out Of Those Lost Centuries Rose A Legend . . . Of The Sorcerer, Merlin, Of The Coming Of A King, Of The Sword Of Power . . ." Then the title, *Excalibur*, appears in shiny metallic capital letters, establishing the film's most dominant stylistic motif. As noted above, throughout the film, armor, swords, castles, and other accoutrements of aristocratic rule will be woven together through the image of bright, shiny metal.

The opening titles for *Monty Python and the Holy Grail* are remarkably similar. On a black screen white titles appear to the strains of very serious, highly percussive music reminiscent of Erik Nordgren's opening score for *The Seventh Seal*. Parody is immediately introduced, however, in the second screen through the use of subtitles in a kind of mock Swedish, a satiric homage to Bergman's film. After thirteen screens the serious music seems to wind down, as if someone has pulled the plug on a record player. There are then a number of comedic shifts in the style of credits that ultimately take the viewer to cartoon credits, in garish yellow and red with Mexican music in the background. After establishing the film's attitude toward the Middle Ages (parody), the screen returns to black, with the words "England 932" (or possibly "93²"). In contrast to *Excalibur*'s nebulous appellation of a "dark age," we are given a date that is gratuitously precise but meaningless in the context of Arthurian narrative.

In their opening shots, *Monty Python and the Holy Grail* and *Excalibur* transport viewers from the contemporary world to an ancient and distant medieval world by calling on the iconography of mist. Both films begin with a scene shrouded in mist, which may well serve two purposes. First, as the mist parts and the scene comes into focus, the film transports the viewer from the present into the past. Second, the use of mist softens the picture, keeps it out of focus, so that a very few strokes will serve to set the scene. A mise-en-scène more sharply in focus would require more verisimilitude—and hence more expense. As the mists part in *Excalibur,* we see scenes from an unspecified battle; we hear the horses hooves and the clanging of swords, and, through the mists, we make out the figures of armed knights. Then a large figure looms out of the mists, moving slowly from the back of the shot to the front. Shot from below, this figure appears imposing, powerful. On close-up we are first introduced to Merlin the magician. As the scene continues, the film cuts between the scenes of battle and close-ups of Merlin, almost creating the impression that he is managing this battle, as he will appear to stage manage much of the action of the film. Monty Python uses many of the same components to humorous effect. As the establishing shot dissolves in from the credits, we see nothing but mists. We hear the sound of birds and then what, because of our experiences with many films (both medieval and western), we interpret as horses' hooves. Gradually individuals can be discerned in the shot. We begin to make out the figure of a knight followed by his squire. But as they loom into focus (shot from above so that they appear rather small), we get the joke. The riders are without horses, and the squire is banging two coconuts together, creating, according to Michael Palin, the "authenticity of full equine motion" (DVD commentary).

Monty Python and the Holy Grail is a sophisticated parody of the claims of illusionistic film to immediacy, to the "real" Middle Ages; as such, it offers an illuminating study in hypermediacy, in how the various elements of a film work together to construct a chronotope of the Middle Ages. It is so in control of the signs of the medieval that it mercilessly parodies the straight-faced recreation of these filmic conventions in John Boorman's *Excalibur*, a film made nearly a decade later. At every turn *Monty Python and the Holy Grail* works to expose the artifice of filmmaking, to make viewers gaze on the technology itself. Despite its painstakingly accurate costuming and lush locations, it never allows viewers to settle into the illusion that they are seeing a seamless slice of the past, that they are witnessing the Middle Ages. As such it draws on all of the cinematic conventions and clichés about the Middle Ages developed over the last century.[18] Seven years later Boorman created the prototypical illusionistic medieval film. Whatever the film's anachronisms, silliness, or lapses in historical accuracy, *Excalibur* presents with sometimes excruciating earnestness and a stunning lack of self-consciousness a narrative about authority that *Monty Python and the Holy Grail* had so relentlessly mocked.

Chapter Three

Celluloid History

Cinematic Fidelity and Infidelity

I n this chapter we move from concerns about the forms of cinematic medievalism to explore its historical content as a means of articulating what
Richard Burt has called a "dialogical model of cinematic fidelity" (219). We
take up his challenge to move beyond a simplistic historicism to consider in a detailed way the mechanisms through which the cinematic apparatus mediates
(and indeed remediates) our experience of medievalism. We are not historians,
however, and we do not intend to read films about the Middle Ages in the same
way historians might. We approach film from the perspective of the cultural and
film theorist. But, because all of the films we examine—from *The Seventh Seal* to
Black Knight—mobilize history's claims to truth and authenticity to create their
fictions, history will figure into our analysis. If, as Pierre Sorlin argues, all historical films are fictional (21), then all such films are also, by their very nature, historical. We must examine the ways in which history functions as a trope in these
films with the same seriousness we apply to their fantasies.

The belief in unmediated access to the truth of the past dies hard in historians,
even in this skeptical postmodern age. History is a profession that places maximal value on authenticity, on the realness of the historical artifact: the authentic

and original manuscript, the painting, the tax rolls, the charter. History is characterized by its allegiance to truth and its insistence on verifiability (Rosenstone, "History in Images / History in Words," 1173). Film, on the other hand, is an art form based on the *reproduction* of reality. "The space of film," writes Stephen Heath, "is the space of reality, film's ambition and triumph is 'to reproduce life' (Louis Lumière)" (384). But however compelling this reproduction is, it partakes of the belatedness and absence of all reproduction. As we have already noted, the apparatus of film, with its flickering images of light passing across the walls of a darkened room, bears a remarkable resemblance to Plato's cave. As such, it dupes us into accepting as reality a fantasy—a simulacrum—of that reality.

This belatedness and, even more, the fear of succumbing to the temptations of fantasy breed skepticism among historians about film's utility to history. Caught between their desire to see the past laid out before them, their questions answered and debates resolved, and their suspicion of the apparatus through which that spectacle has been created, historians are understandably wary about film as a means of understanding the past: "no matter how serious or honest the filmmakers," Rosenstone argues, "and no matter how deeply committed they are to rendering the subject faithfully, the history that finally appears on the screen can never fully satisfy the historian as historian (although it may satisfy the historian as filmgoer). Inevitably, something happens on the way from the page to the screen that changes the meaning of the past as it is understood by those of us who work in words" ("History in Images / History in Words," 1173). Historians have on occasion even evinced an almost naive belief that their expertise could remedy the problem. Rosenstone, for instance, quotes the historian Louis Gottschalk of the University of Chicago, who in 1935 wrote to the president of Metro-Goldwyn-Mayer to decry the exclusion of historians from the sets of historical films: "If the cinema art is going to draw its subjects so generously from history, it owes to its patrons and its own higher ideals to achieve greater accuracy. No picture of a historical nature ought to be offered to the public until a reputable historian has had a chance to criticize and revise it" (Rosenstone, "The Historical Film," 141).

If the promise of complete transparency is the lure of the cinema, its artifice is the snake in the grass. Historians writing about film often reinscribe the same binaries between past and present and reality and fantasy that the medievalism we examined in chapter 1 does, separating academic history's proper objects from its bastardizations. In *A Knight at the Movies*, for instance, John Aberth argues that the best films about the Middle Ages revel "in the differences between those times and our own" by "drawing us into another world in order to better understand and appreciate those differences" (viii). Rosenstone, writing on "the new history film," argues that "the difference between such works and traditional historical films is a matter of intent, content, and form. Their aim is less to entertain an audience or make profits than to understand the legacy of the past" (*Revisioning History*, 4–5).[1]

Though Rosenstone doesn't admit it, the reason that film fails to satisfy the historian as historian is because it fails to deliver on the promise of transparency that is at the very heart of its fantasy. And, if historians are wary of films about the recent past, they are positively dismissive of those that document the distant past. Arthur Lindley, in an essay entitled "The Ahistoricism of Medieval Film," argues that "film narrative cannot do the work of analytic history" and that no film about the Middle Ages, however compelling, can reconstruct the past, primarily because such films are not "working from the assumption that the past [is] of inherent interest or historically connected to the present" (n.p.).

These beliefs about the inadequacy of film as a medium of historical analysis have found their way into studies of medieval films, which tend to focus, as the pun in the title of Kevin J. Harty's book, *The Reel Middle Ages*, suggests, on the accuracy of these films, how "real" they are in their portrayal of the past. Judged by such a yardstick, all medieval films come up lacking. Burt argues that this "fidelity model" of film criticism has largely been rejected by film scholars (217); however, it remains surprisingly salient in the criticism of medieval films. Lindley, for instance, criticizes *The Seventh Seal*'s setting as less 1340s than the subatomic 1950s, a "painfully familiar Nevernever-but-always-land of twentieth-century European high modernism," less *Everyman* than *Waiting for Godot* ("The Ahistoricism of Medieval Film"). Colin McArthur's account in "*Braveheart* and the Scottish Aesthetic Dementia" of the notorious historical inaccuracies in Mel Gibson's epic prefaces a fairly sophisticated examination of the appropriation of the film by Scottish nationalists. In a 1999 special issue of *Film and History* David John Williams writes that the medieval past in film "often appears not to be that historical in any direct sense. The cinema's Middle Ages specializes instead in myth, spectacle, and adventures in settings of psychological potency" (9). Most recently, Aberth's *A Knight at the Movies* insists that the only good medieval films are those that represent the Middle Ages with absolute fidelity. Harty's pun at least has the virtue of recognizing the deconstructive potential in cinematic medievalism's representations of the past, holding on to the tension between the artificiality of the "reel" and the authenticity of the "real."

Sorlin argues that "when professional historians wonder about the mistakes made in an historical film, they are worrying about a meaningless question" (21). As Angela Jane Weisl points out, even the most ridiculous anachronisms of cinematic medievalism have precedents in medieval texts, where Greeks and Romans routinely dress in medieval armor and a fifth-century Romano-Celtic chieftain named Arthur is transformed into a Norman king (4–5). Martha Driver, in an essay aptly titled "What's Accuracy Got to Do with It?" challenges as naive reflectionism complaints about inaccuracies in medieval films, citing a comment by the film critic Jonathan Rosenbaum: "It doesn't matter if the historical details of a film are authentic. They just have to look authentic to the audience" (20). Driver goes on to note astutely that "authenticity is a convention of costume drama, part of the visual language in the re-creation of history on screen" (20–21). However, her comment still misses what is most radical in her suggestion that authenticity is iconographic when she smuggles transparency back in the injunction that film is a "starting point for the recovery of the true historical elements underlying the fiction" (21).

Historians who defend the usefulness of historical films argue that the history they present is of a different kind and cannot be judged by the criteria used for scholarly, written history. If traditional history attempts to "sort out what is probable from what is false, to establish the chronology of events, [and] to show the relationships between them," there are other ways of thinking about history as "society's memory of itself" (Sorlin, 16). Historical films may do "mythographic work" (Lindley, "The Ahistoricism of Medieval Film") or they may fulfill "the need for that larger History, that web of connections to the past that holds a culture together, that tells us not only where we have been but also suggests where we are going" (Rosenstone, "History in Images / History in Words," 1175). For this reason, they argue, we cannot judge historical films using the criteria of contemporary written history; rather we must recognize films as a legitimate form of history, judging the medium on its own terms as "a way of recounting the past with its own rules of representation" (Rosenstone, *Revisioning History*, 3).

Can we begin to sketch out what the "rules of representation" for the cinematic historian might be? How, in practice, does the historical film manage the tension between the artifice required to create filmic images of the past and the criteria of truth and accuracy central to the claims of history? Earlier we invoked Umberto Eco's notion of hyperreality to describe the ways in which the historical film participates in "a philosophy of immortality as duplication" in which "the past must be preserved and celebrated in full-scale copy" (Eco, 6). Reproduction in the mode of hyperreality attempts to improve on the real, to make it better, all in the interest of selling something. Like the other forms of hyperreality Eco describes, film attempts "to establish itself as a substitute for reality, as something even more real" than reality (8). "For historical information to be absorbed," Eco argues, "it has to assume the aspect of a reincarnation. . . . The 'completely real' becomes identified with the 'completely fake.' Absolute unreality is offered as real presence. . . . The sign aims to be the thing, to abolish the distinction of the reference, the mechanism of replacement" (7), creating a hallucination that threatens to "level the various historical periods and erase the distinction between historical reality and fantasy" (42). Eco gathers together in the trope of hyperreality the oscillation Bolter and Grusin describe between media's claims to immediacy and contrary impulses toward hypermediation in which those media call attention to their own status as media.

Monty Python and the Holy Grail provides an illuminating instance of the intersection between the hyperreality of reproduction and the authenticity of experience in a brief reflection on the impossibility of history and its various media technologies. The film represents the deconstructive space of hyperreality in which reality and fantasy meet, self-consciously parodying the cinematic illusion in which "the 'completely real' becomes identified with the 'completely fake.' Absolute unreality is offered as real presence" (Eco, 7). Scene 9 of the screenplay shifts from King Arthur's failure to capture a French castle to the filming of a television documentary on that subject. An offscreen voice identifies the documentary as an educational one:

VOICE. Picture for Schools, take eight.
DIRECTOR. Action!

As the mise-en-scène of the fiction film merges with that of the documentary, the viewer sees a male figure, a "talking head" identified in subtitles not by name but only generically as "A Very Famous Historian." Framed in the center of a wooded medieval ruin, the historian, with wild white hair, dressed in a poorly fitted suit with bowtie and floppy mismatched pocket handkerchief, is a parody of the British academic. In a posh Oxbridge accent, he intones the dry facts of Arthur's search for the Holy Grail:

HISTORIAN. Defeat at the castle seems to have utterly disheartened King
    Arthur. The ferocity of the French taunting took him completely by surprise, and Arthur became convinced that a new strategy was required if
    the quest for the Holy Grail were to be brought to a successful conclusion.

> Arthur, having consulted his closest knights, decided that they should
> separate, and search for the Grail individually. . . . Now this is what
> they did.

As the historian speaks, the sound of a horse's hooves can be heard in the background. Suddenly, in swoops an unidentified knight from the film, who cuts the throat of the historian and rides off.

With unerring accuracy, this scene parodies the earnestness of documentary reproduction of the Middle Ages in the service of cultural nationalism. The Very Famous Historian is a reminder of the various historical industries capitalizing on the Arthurian phenomenon, including the apparatus of documentary filmmaking itself. Nostalgia for the Arthurian Middle Ages, desire for facts about the "real" historical Arthur, is indulged for "academic" audiences by "historians" such as Geoffrey Ashe—whose claims about Arthurian origin are based on a somewhat dubious archaeological discovery of "the Camelot" ruin—and reproduced, for popular audiences, by a documentary industry supported by the BBC, by U.S. cable networks like the History Channel, and by the educational apparatus of the schools.[2] The Historian is a kind of latter-day priest interpreting sacred texts of the nation and in doing so forcing on us a kind of hierarchy in which we must respect the subject position and not the man—he is an *anonymous* Famous Historian.[3] His anonymity guarantees his objectivity and omniscience. He has no individualized existence; rather his pomposity, his iconic accent, and even his sartorial failures are symbols of his cultural power.

The scene gives us the convergence of a past that never really happened (the search for the Holy Grail) being read as history by a "Historian" whose authenticity is authorized only by the conventions of the documentary film. But if the "Very Famous Historian" of the documentary film within the film is supposed to be reporting on the events of the Grail quest that unfold within the cinematic apparatus (which he seems to be), then his bias as a historian is revealing. He chooses to leave out of his dry "objective" account the utter imbecility of the English knights in the previous scene and overplays the "ferocity" of the French knights, who mostly launch livestock at the English and call them names in a bad stage-French accent. Official history, the history taught in the schools, to maintain its authoritative stance, must necessarily create a "serious" past without English knights who build Trojan rabbits and French knights who need English translations of their own language. The film reproduces in its ersatz documentary that genre's notions of authenticity and objectivity. The "talking head" is filmed against a certain kind of backdrop, a ruin, an *authentic* fragment of the past being recovered. But the ruin carries other, more deconstructive, possibilities that the scene also realizes. The ruin reminds us that it is the historian's task to fill in the holes, the gaps in an always fragmentary account of the past. Unlike Connie Willis's time traveler in *Doomsday Book,* the historian works never with plentitude, always with remnants, and these remnants are always interpreted through the lens of the historian's present.

The scene's eruption into violence—a break in the diegesis of the documentary film within the fiction film—offers a number of different readings, all of which, as it turns out, result in the death of history. The knight's attack on the historian might signal an eruption of the "real," the assault of the hyperviolent Middle Ages, on domesticated academic accounts of the past. History literally jumps off the screen and murders the historian. Plentitude, once achieved, results in the end of history. The dream of traveling in time to witness the real Middle Ages renders history superfluous. What need is there for the intercession of a dry academic when the audience has access to the "real thing"? The knight's actions create the illusion that the ancient texts rise up and consume their interpreter, offering themselves more immediately and democratically to the audience.

Such a reading, however, assumes cinema can recover a "real" Middle Ages, an assumption that the filmmakers never entirely indulge and go to some lengths to undermine. Hyperviolence has always been a cinematic convention of the medieval, a part of our fantasy of the Middle Ages as barbaric past. Ultimately this scene portrays not the real but the cinematic knight in shining armor, working in what John Cleese's Lancelot refers to as his "idiom," the reckless slaughter of bystanders, saving the audience from someone who is boring them to death.[4] The murder of the historian is carnivalesque in Bakhtin's use of that term. It is sudden, grotesque, and excessive (its bloodiness far in excess of what is needed to shut the historian up). The appropriate audience response is glee. The pleasures the scene affords us are the disruption of official discourses and the possibility of a primitive—a knight with a sword—overthrowing the technologies of power represented by the documentary. Baudry's notion of the narcissistic regression offered by the cinematic apparatus may well explain this violent fantasy—the pleasure principle winning out over the reality principle, the Lacanian Real erupting into the symbolic. But Cleese's use of the word *idiom* locates Arthur's knights' actions more precisely within specifically *narrative* conventions; they behave as such characters in movies are supposed to behave. This scene stages the eruption not of the real, or even of the imaginary, into the symbolic but of the swashbuckling cinematic Middle Ages into the "idiom" of academic historical discourse.

If the Historian is a product of academic and documentary discourse, the knight in this particular case is the product of cinematic discourse. Within the popular realm there is delight in the displacement of the academic and documentary real by the cinematic. But none of these discursive practices brings us back to origins, to the "real" knight of the Middle Ages, as the film reminds us in its closing sequence, which deconstructs the discourse of film and its efforts to create an illusionistic past by returning to the documentary claims to truth so thoroughly parodied in scene 9. At the end of scene 24 Arthur's army masses to attack the French castle in a formation (indeed, in an "idiom") whose roots lie as much in the American western as in cinematic medievalism. Before they can attack, however, the sound of police sirens disrupts the classic mise-en-scène of incipient battle, and the attack is broken up by the arrival of police vans come to arrest the knights (or rather the actors portraying knights) for the murder of the Historian. The scene is filmed using a handheld camera whose shakiness even in 1974 was an iconographic sign of documentary "realism." The film abruptly concludes when a policeman, in documentary newsreel fashion, places his hand over the camera lens, an eruption of the (supposed) real into the fictional space of the film. Monty Python simultaneously represents history and makes fun of historians' claims to truth, at the same time exposing the artifice of film's reproduction of reality.

Does this mean that those of us interested in the relationships between film and history are doomed to Monty Python's refusal of narrative closure? Are we forever condemned to an inconclusive oscillation between our desire for truth and its impossibility? If *Monty Python and the Holy Grail* deconstructs through parody the representational claims of documentary filmmaking, twenty years later Terry Jones, one of the film's directors, turned his hand to the making of an actual documentary about the Middle Ages. *The Crusades* (1995), a four-part documentary produced for the BBC and the History Channel, was written and narrated by Jones. Does this signal that an older and wiser Jones has abandoned the epistemological skepticism of documentary objectivity so evident in *Monty Python and the Holy Grail* in favor of the realism of the BBC documentary? Has he bought into the belief, expressed by Noël Carroll, that history is possible in the nonfiction film, a genre that can deliver objective information about the real world (283)?

Throughout the four-part series Jones uses all of the formal techniques developed for television documentaries, including an "objective" narrator (Jones himself), talking heads, authentic locations, and eyewitness accounts. He also uses a number of techniques designed especially for representing historical periods for which we have no photographic evidence and so must rely on "authentic" remnants. For the Middle Ages these remnants include ruins, manuscripts, and dramatic recreations; in fact, these three types of evidence make up the bulk of what is most visually interesting in the series. All of these documentary techniques are in fact iconographic; their ideological purpose is to persuade the audience of the authenticity, accuracy, and objectivity of the history the film is presenting. They claim an indexical relationship to the "real" world, a belief that history is readily accessible and that filmmaker and viewers alike can share untroubled access to knowledge about the past. But Jones is not ready to declare himself a true son of Grierson just yet.[5] Although Jones does develop, throughout the series, a consistent argument, which he substantiates with different kinds of evidence, he never allows the signifying mechanisms of the cinema to become too transparent, to recede into invisibility in the face of historical certitude. Through its Pythonesque humor the film constantly forces viewers to reflect not only on the view of the Middle Ages being presented but on the technologies through which they are being presented as well. *The Crusades* is an often quite funny and self-reflexive documentary that interrogates its own use of the generic conventions of documentary filmmaking. None of the genre's techniques are mobilized in *The Crusades* without comment.

The voice of the narrator in documentary film is usually an iconic representation of omniscience. "Studio protected," writes Robert Stam, "this voice speaks in regular and homogeneous rhythms. . . . [It] speaks of its subjects confidently in the third person. . . . The narrator becomes the voice of knowledge and mastery, while the narratees are the voice of undiscriminating experience. The voice translates their 'alien' words into the impersonal discourse of objective truth" (46). As narrator, Jones projects this "suave articulateness" beautifully. Viewers familiar with the Monty Python television series will remember the show's numerous parodies of BBC announcers and understand that Jones has the cultural authority, the accent (again Oxbridge), and the intonation to pull off this pose. But, as in the television series, Jones is constantly lampooning the authority of the announcer position. Throughout *The Crusades* Jones recreates the narrator as tourist. He eschews the traditional coat and tie for casual dress and the occasional silly hat as he visits the major sites of the Crusades: Constantinople, Jerusalem, Damascus, Acre. Crossing the Bosphorus to the Asian continent with a group of tourists, his voice-over carries on with the narration as he casually receives a cup of coffee from a waiter on the ferry. Throughout the series, point-of-view shots mock the current trend in television journalism for announcers to appear to speak to the audience more intimately and personally through asides. An example occurs in part three, "Jihad," in a scene in which Jones listens to a storyteller in a Damascus café retell the story of Al Findalawi's defense of Damascus. While appearing to participate as a member of the audience, Jones turns his back on the performance to address the film's viewers more intimately. The aside is shot through what appears to be an exterior window, looking through the window to Jones's face framed in the shot (shots of Jones framed by a window recur throughout the series, an ambiguous sign of the announcer's omniscience and voyeurism). Perhaps his most egregious violation of the decorum or "tact" of the documentary announcer, however, occurs in part four, "Destruction," when he appears wading in the surf at Acre nearly naked in a Speedo and straw hat as he discusses the importance of Richard the Lionheart's washerwomen to the Third Crusade.[6]

The Crusades is equally irreverent with its presentation of manuscripts and other medieval works of art. The function of a manuscript (or any visual artwork) in documentaries on the Middle Ages is twofold. The illuminations may illustrate a point with a visual reference. But more important, the manuscript functions iconographically as a sign of medievalness. Like ruins, manuscripts offer us only a fragment of a lost historical past, but their authenticity seduces us into believing we have captured the "real" Middle Ages. *The Crusades* frequently attempts to improve on this iconographic function, making manuscripts and other artworks literally come to life, offering viewers the plentitude of full vision, the promise of the "moving" picture. For instance, the viewer is presented with a shot of, say, a Byzantine mosaic. An actor, made up to resemble the mosaic, will step out of the picture and begin to recite an eyewitness account, as, for instance, Anna Comnena's account of the arrival of the crusaders in Constantinople in her *Alexiad*. Such scenes, however, expose the double logic of remediation we described in the previous chapter. Far from rendering the stylized medieval picture more immediate to the documentary's viewers, it calls attention to the status of the film as hypermediated artifact. In one scene Jones himself emerges as a spectator in a manuscript page depicting Pope Urban II at the Council of Clermont (1095). He is hidden in the bottom left corner, seated among a crowd of prelates in full ecclesiastical regalia, an "eyewitness" of sorts to the events he is recounting. The manuscript page becomes a *tableau vivant*. But the artifice, the computer generated "enhancement" of the manuscript, at the same time, undermines the value of the manuscript as an "authentic" remnant of the past. Digital technology, the film seems to suggest, enables the trick; we are meant to marvel at the sight. The shot is an example of what Tom Gunning has described as the "cinema of attractions"; it is pure visual spectacle, demonstrating the way in which the logic of hypermediacy can insinuate itself even (or perhaps especially) within the logic of immediacy (Gunning; Bolter and Grusin, 155).

All of these techniques that we have been discussing, while they impart authenticity to the documentary, are fairly static. The appearance of talking heads gives the documentary academic weight; however, a film that consisted of nothing but headshots of medieval historians, even of the stature of Sir Steven Runciman or Jonathan Riley-Smith, would be a dull film indeed. The medium of film is best suited to convey action and movement. For a topic like the Crusades, which, after all, happened about nine hundred years before the invention of the portable video camera, the only way to create action sequences within the film is through reenactment. The technique of restaging historical events, however, brings the documentary film dangerously close to the fiction film. Carroll argues that nonfiction film's sharing of such techniques does not threaten its objectivity or authenticity: "the distinction between nonfiction and fiction was never really based on differences in formal technique in the first place; so one cannot deconstruct the distinction [between fact and fiction] by citing shared techniques" (286). However, Bill Nichols notes, "Documentaries run some risk of credibility in reenacting an event: the special indexical bond between image and historical referent is ruptured. . . . It has the status of an imaginary event, however tightly based on historical fact" (*Representing Reality*, 21). Once a documentary film begins to recreate the events it is narrating, the only thing that separates it from the fiction film is its *claim* to authenticity.[7] Yet documentaries about the Middle Ages could hardly exist without such reenactments. In *The Crusades* Jones and his experts reconstruct catapults, demonstrate riding and fighting tactics, armor making, siege strategies, and undermining. In the final segment of part 1 and the first segment of "Jerusalem," part 2, to illustrate the hardships the crusaders experienced on their trek east to Jerusalem, Jones even dons eleventh-century armor, helmet, and shield and begins walking. But *The Crusades* takes pains to remind us of the status of these segments as "re-creations" of the past. At one point Jones is trudging and slipping through the rain; in a signature Monty Python move, the camera pulls back to reveal the rainmaking machines that produced the effect, exposing the mechanisms of reenactment. The scene could as easily have been filmed in California as the Middle East.

The Crusades plays with the contradiction between the claims of truth and the technologies of artifice in historical documentaries, pushing the limit of the nonfiction film, most insistently in the recreated scenes that bring the Crusades to life by providing some action for the exposition. Some of the recreations observe the conventions developed for such scenes in fiction film. In the first part, while Jones discusses the dilemma knights faced between Christian and warrior ethics, there is a scene showing two knights in chain mail fighting. In this scene the convention of transparency is observed; the actors in the scene, like actors in a fiction film, act as if they really are eleventh-century knights engaged in combat. But more frequently *The Crusades* violates the conventions established for such recreations in medieval documentary by refusing to allow them to be transparent. A few scenes later, as a way of illustrating the power of Pope Urban's call for the First Crusade, we are shown a recruiting film in the style of a 1950s movie trailer. It is in black and white, with titles in large bold Gothic letters: "A Pilgrim Adventure." The trailer's announcer (with the iconographic 1950s announcer voice) introduces us to the leaders of the First Crusade, "a cast of stars": "See Raymond, Count of Toulouse. He hammered the Moors in Spain; now watch him smash them in Jerusalem." Interspersed with the trailer are shots of Jones watching the trailer and making asides about these leaders to his viewers. Even fiction film is harnessed to create visual interest. The infighting among the crusaders on the First Crusade is illustrated by a game of chess that calls to mind iconographic scenes from Bergman's *The Seventh Seal*. The Battle of Hattin, in which Saladin defeated the crusaders, is illustrated by scenes from Youssef Chahine's 1963 film *Saladin*.[8] The practice of recreation in *The Crusades* places at odds the two most foundational promises of the nonfiction film: that it will entail action (otherwise, why use the medium?) and that it will present its subject "authentically."

It is not surprising that medieval historians have been less than enchanted by the documentary. Paul Crawford, reviewing the series for *The Orb: Online Reference Book for Medieval Studies*, dismisses the content of the documentary without interrogating what is at stake in its representations of the past: "As for the idea that crusaders were merely smelly, stupid barbarians: well, that would likely find acceptance with the same people who believe in the Dark Ages and *jus primae noctis*, and use 'medieval' as a pejorative adjective." But perhaps we should ask why Jones needs his crusaders to be "smelly, stupid barbarians"? In the final analysis, any debate over *The Crusades* is not about whether the "facts" presented are true or false but rather whether the argument the series makes about the Crusades is persuasive. What is at stake in the various historical controversies about the motives of the crusaders or the effects of the Crusades on the Christian or Islamic worlds? We might justifiably ask why contemporary historians like Crawford who criticize Jones's (and by extension Steven Runciman's) characterization of the crusaders as mercenary invaders of a superior culture are so anxious to reimagine them as pious pilgrims at a time when religious fundamentalism of both Eastern and Western varieties threatens the stability of the world (a question we will explore more fully in chapter 7).

We would argue that what is at stake in Jones's characterization of the crusaders is the very temporality of colonialism described by postcolonial theorists, the mapping of modernity's past (the medieval) onto present space, in this case, the space of the embattled Middle East. If Jones, following Runciman, represents the crusaders not romantically as a chivalrous host who captured the Holy Land, or even as religious fanatics, but as barbarian invaders who destroyed the last outpost of the Roman Empire (Byzantium), it is because, for him, nine hundred years after they began, the Crusades still resonate in Middle Eastern politics.[9] This point is underscored by editing practices that frequently crosscut medieval history with scenes from twentieth-century life and warfare in the Middle East. For example, in "Jihad," as Jones discusses the wedding of Reynald de Chatillon's stepson in al-Karak, there is a quick pan to a castle wall, followed by a shot of Jones walking down a castle corridor and turning into a passageway. The cut shows him entering into a contemporary Muslim wedding reception in an entirely different location. Perhaps the most inflammatory combination of medieval and modern occurs in a segment on the attack of Damascus during the Second Crusade. In this segment a shot of Jones is followed by a quick pan to a ruin of a castle wall. This shot dissolves into a shot of two jets overflying a desert. Footage from the First Gulf War follows, dissolving finally into a shot of a medieval manuscript. The connection between the European crusaders and contemporary American aggression in the Middle East, especially Iraq, is unmistakable.

Crawford describes Jones's series as "Monty Python Goes on Crusade," and this is an accurate description. The series displays the same skepticism toward historical referentiality at work in *Monty Python and the Holy Grail* and the same antipathy toward nostalgic and romanticized idealizations of the Middle Ages. Just because one is skeptical of film's ability to convey "reality" objectively, however, does not mean that one cannot have an argument to make, and *The Crusades* shares much of the political agenda of the 1974 film, including a healthy skepticism—Aronstein calls it antimedievalism ("The Violence Inherent in the System")—about the kinds of dangerous myths the Middle Ages engenders, especially in the medium of film. This argument is more sophisticated than Crawford gives it credit for.

Jones may not, however, be entirely immune to the fascination engendered by the medieval or for the clear hierarchies that attract filmmakers to the Middle Ages. Certainly his audience is not. The success of his documentary—like the success of *Monty Python and the Holy Grail*—resides in his manipulation of the uneasy space between the parodic and the reverential, and between the authentic and the artificial, that we are mapping. That Jones and his Monty Python cohorts continue to return to the Middle Ages (most recently in Eric Idle's Broadway musical *Spamalot*) suggests that their struggle (and ours) with this gap is ongoing. Their send-ups of all things medieval, including the cinematic apparatus that pretends to reproduce the Middle Ages, are always insufficient to overcome this longing.

Film can create the illusion that it provides access to a realistic past, and through its artifice it does. But because it can only present the hyperreality of reproduction rather than the authenticity of experience, historians will always find it wanting. No film about the Middle Ages will ever satisfy a medieval historian because no film can offer an unmediated access to the past, even though some may make such claims (Antoine Fuqua's 2004 *King Arthur*, for instance, claims to be the "untold truth that inspired the legend"). Rather historical films, including films about the Middle Ages, are hybrid networks of associations where such claims are simultaneously held together and deconstructed. We have begun by staging this encounter between history and film, between film's and history's claims to truth and their dependence on artifice and reproduction, as a means of examining some of the difficulties associated with representing the past through visual images and film. We believe the insistence on accuracy in medieval films imposes a historical standard on what is basically an aesthetic product, obscuring the very functions of fantasy in the process of "dreaming the Middle Ages."

We turn now to the specific social logics of those fantasies that structure films about the Middle Ages, turning to more detailed analyses of individual films and groups of films as a means of elaborating and extending these insights. In particular, we will be concerned with medievalism's representation of modernity's decisive break with its medieval past, and our readings of films will continually return to this moment. Since the late eighteenth century, the period credited with this decisive break, cultural institutions and media—including the cinema—have programmed their audiences to desire the signs of the medieval. Medievalism produces longing for the past by highlighting the inadequacies of modernity even as it promises a glimpse of an "authentic" Middle Ages. More specifically, in part 2 we turn to the political paradigm of absolutism and divine right, whose elimination was supposed to constitute modernity by enabling the creation of the modern political subject. As we read the social and political economies of the Middle Ages from the perspective of the liberal individualism that has dominated Western thought since the Enlightenment, we are at once drawn to and repulsed by a simpler time in which authoritative institutions dominated political activity. We can simultaneously desire (at least in fantasy) that which we abhor.

Part 2: The Politics of Cinematic Medievalism

Chapter Four

Mirror of Princes

Representations of Political Authority in Medieval Films

The most common expression of medieval political theory is the genre called the "Mirror of Princes." These texts—the most famous but perhaps least representative of which is Machiavelli's *The Prince* (1513)—instruct rulers on the appropriate ways to exercise political power. In the process they outline a medieval political hierarchy that is refracted in modern ideas about the Middle Ages. As early as the twelfth century, John of Salisbury, in his *Policraticus*, a book dedicated to his friend Thomas Becket, offers a more representative example of the genre:

> The position of the head in the republic is occupied . . . by a prince subject only to God and to those who act in His place on earth, inasmuch as in the human body the head is stimulated and ruled by the soul [in John's schema, the clergy]. The place of the heart is occupied by the senate, from which proceeds the beginning of good and bad works. The duties of eyes, ears and mouth are claimed by the judges and governors of provinces. The hands coincide with officials and soldiers. Those who assist the prince are comparable to the flanks. Treasurers and record keepers . . . resemble the shape of the stomach and intestines. . . .

Furthermore, the feet coincide with peasants perpetually bound to the soil, for whom it is all the more necessary that the head take precautions, in that they more often meet with accidents while they walk on the earth in bodily subservience; and those who erect, sustain and move forward the mass of the whole body are justly owed shelter and support.[1]

John of Salisbury's elaborate metaphor of the body stresses the organic status of this "natural" order whose central feature is hierarchy. The body politic is a single unified entity, analogous to the human body but without its mutability. Hierarchy and submission dominate the relations between the three estates. The authority of the prince over his people and of the aristocrat over the commoner assure the health of the body politic. The metaphor of the body is a secularized version of medieval representations of Christ and the church, reminding us of the extent to which medieval versions of order were authorized through religious dogma. The discarding of this political paradigm is supposed to represent modernity's decisive break with its medieval past; it is what constitutes modernity and enables the creation of the modern political subject. This break is clearly articulated by John Locke in *The Second Treatise of Civil Government:* "it is evident, that *absolute monarchy,* which by some men is counted the only government in the world, is indeed *inconsistent with civil society,* and so can be no form of civil-government at all" (7.90). "For he that thinks *absolute power purifies men's blood,* and corrects the baseness of human nature, need read but the history of this, or any other age, to be convinced of the contrary" (7.92; emphasis in original). The liberal discourse of individual freedom and rights, equality, and meritocracy was supposed to replace that of divine right, absolutism, and aristocracy.

From our post-Enlightenment perspective, in which we are likely to believe, with Locke, that "MEN being, as has been said, by nature, all free, equal, and independent, no one can be put out of this estate, and subjected to the political power of another, without his own consent" (8.95),[2] how do we judge the absolutist political philosophies of the Middle Ages? Films about the Middle Ages that explore issues of political economy provide some purchase on this question. They leave us with two contradictory views of political authority in the Middle Ages. On the one hand, these films depict the Middle Ages as a time of barbarity and violence, where the rule of law was all but nonexistent. On the other hand, the Middle Ages is represented as a time of absolute authority and hierarchy, when rulers ruled by a divine right at odds with post-Enlightenment political theories based on liberal individualism.

This chapter explores debates about authority, power, rule, law, state, government, and politics in several medieval films. What are the principles on which political life should be based, and what organization best realizes those principles? How do governments go about legitimating themselves? Who can participate in political life and how? What are the ends of politics? What kinds of obligations or obedience do individuals owe to the state? What are the origins of modern concepts like freedom and equality, rights, contracts, interests, and citizenship? The films we examine invariably set a prior and alien political worldview against the familiar pieties of post-Enlightenment political philosophy (freedom, rights, individualism, and consent of the governed), sometimes expressing nostalgia for a lost organic order and sometimes locating the origins of the modern squarely in the medieval, or in individuals' struggles against a benighted medieval.

"You Don't Vote for Kings": Medieval Political Theory

Winston Churchill called the legend of King Arthur "a theme as well founded, as inspired, and as inalienable from the inheritance of mankind as the *Odyssey* or the Old Testament" (60). What is it that makes it such an important and "universal" theme? Churchill goes on to explain: "Let us then declare that King Arthur and his noble knights, guarding the Sacred Flame of Christianity and the theme of a world order, sustained by the valour, physical strength, and good horses and armour, slaughtered innumerable hosts of foul barbarians and set decent folk an example for all time" (60). King Arthur deserves to be remembered for all time because he was able to impose, even if temporarily, a "world order," or at least a local order that excluded "foul barbarians" (60). Presumably for the same reason, the story of King Arthur has inspired filmmakers of all generations, from the 1917 *Knights of the Square Table* to *King Arthur* in 2004.[3] It is a narrative that explores the nature and exercise of political authority, providing ideological legitimacy for the political institution of the monarchy and defining the nature of the individual's political obligations within the institution. Two films by British directors that treat the legend of King Arthur reflect contemporary political discourses around issues of power and authority. Despite drawing on the same material, material that itself is concerned with the nature and exercise of power and proper kingship, their treatments could not be more different, reflecting and reproducing the dominant values of British (and American) society at the time of their production. *Monty Python and the Holy Grail*, as we have suggested, combines the television genre of sketch comedy with various formulae and conventions for representing the Middle Ages, parodying romanticized images of medieval chivalry and monarchy. John Boorman's *Excalibur,* steeped in Malory, Tennyson, Richard Wagner, and Jesse Weston, is a loving recreation of the Grail legend that announces its nostalgia for a lost immediacy with nature and clarity of order, hierarchy, and authority.

The opening scenes of both films examine myths of social order—particularly a social order based on aristocratic claims to power—*Excalibur* in a tragic vein, creating an idealized political order and then demonstrating its frailty in a world of greed and lust; Monty Python in a comic vein, exposing the delusions of the mystical political order *Excalibur* romanticizes. In both, repetition is a key structural feature. Each begins with three segments designed to explore the nature of aristocratic authority inscribed in the Arthurian legends. In *Excalibur* these scenes show order arising out of chaos, whereas in *Monty Python and the Holy Grail* the trajectory is reversed and the opening scenes devolve from an illusion of order to anarchy as attempts to impose order are rebuffed.

While the opening scene of *Excalibur* shows us a fairly gruesome battle, the opening of *Monty Python and the Holy Grail* stages a battle of wits in which the conflict between illusion and technique is played out in the dueling languages of the characters.[4] Graham Chapman's Arthur begins the film looking for ratification of his political authority by riding around the countryside seeking knights to join his Round Table. His first words simultaneously introduce his character and assert his claim to authority and power. Standing at the base of a castle and addressing a guard high above him, Arthur speaks a stilted, formalistic language in a posh accent that we are supposed to understand (anachronistically, since the received pronunciation is a modern linguistic concept) as a sign of his authority: "It is I, Arthur, son of Uther Pendragon, from the castle of Camelot. King of the Britons, defeater of the Saxons, Sovereign of all England! . . . We have ridden the length and breadth of the land in search of knights who will join me in my court at Camelot." His claims to authority are based on his place within an aristocratic order as the son of Uther and hence as king and sovereign. They are voiced within a linguistic register that asserts his pretensions to cultural and political power.

The battle is played out in the dialogical languages of the scene, with different social dialects working at cross-purposes. Arthur's formality serves as a sign of class privilege: "We have ridden since the snows of winter covered this land, through the kingdom of Mercia." Its periphrasis emphasizes his sense of cultural superiority. His interlocutor answers in a Cockney accent (a contemporary marker of lower-class status); his focus on the coconuts diverts Arthur's claims to power into an incongruous scientific discussion (the language par excellence of liberal theory) that ridicules the pretentious mystical quality of Arthur's language (see Osberg and Crow on the film's language): "It's not a question of where he grips it! It's a simple question of weight ratios! A five ounce bird could not carry a one pound coconut. . . . Listen. In order to maintain air-speed velocity, a swallow needs to beat its wings forty-three times every second, right?" Communication is impossible here because the two characters do not even speak the same language, perhaps do not even exist in the same space and time. A characteristic technique of the film's language is to contrast twentieth-century versions of English (Cockney, scientific) with a language of mystification that sounds vaguely "medieval," largely through its use of periphrasis. In this scene, once Arthur has been so completely cut off from any effective communication with the castle guards, he can do little more than slink away, defeated.

This scene establishes immediately the method by which the film comically undercuts Arthur's pretensions. Both mise-en-scène and editing suggest the social relations among the characters, highlighting Arthur's impotence in his exchange with the guard. The establishing shot of the scene is filmed in an extreme long shot from the side of the castle, showing a large expanse of wall, made larger still by the angle of the camera. There is a tiny figure—Arthur—at the bottom and another tiny figure—the guard—at the top, suggesting the distance between two characters dwarfed by their surroundings (Figure 3). During their conversation,

Figure 3. King Arthur and Patsy confront the castle guard in *Monty Python and the Holy Grail* (1975).

the shot–reverse shot editing always films Arthur from a high angle, emphasizing his insignificance, and the guard, who is at the top of the castle, from a low angle. Despite Arthur's claims to political power and his constant demands to be taken to the "master" of the castle, the mise-en-scène presents him ultimately as a tiny and impotent figure.

The second scene that attempts to establish Arthur's authority is the famous "Dennis scene." This scene perhaps most explicitly addresses the myth of political authority represented by the Arthurian legend. Once again, despite the "violence inherent in the system," the battle takes place solely in words. While Arthur's dialogue is primarily concerned to establish a hierarchy of social relations (what knight lives in that castle; who is your lord; I am king), his interlocutors, the scene's spatial relations, and the editing undermine him at every turn.[5] The establishing shot shows two peasants in the foreground digging.[6] Arthur and his squire "gallop" through the shot, but they are tiny figures in the background, just barely visible; the peasants (who are incidental to the scene) occupy the dominant ground in the shot. Many of the shots in this scene show the main interlocutors in three-shot (Arthur, Dennis, and the silent Patsy completing the set), insisting not on the hierarchical relations among them but rather on their basic equality. They occupy the same ground, the same space. If the spatial relations of the scene emphasize the characters' sameness, however, the dialogue contests the legitimacy of Arthur's claims to social rank:

> ARTHUR. I am Arthur, King of the Britons. . . .
> WOMAN. King of the who?
> ARTHUR. The Britons.
> WOMAN. Who are the Britons? . . .
>
> .   .   .   .
>
> ARTHUR. Be quiet! I order you to be quiet.
> WOMAN. Order, eh? Who does he think he is? Heh.
> ARTHUR. I am your king!
> WOMAN. Well, I didn't vote for you.
> ARTHUR. You don't vote for kings.

The language in this scene plays off the medieval belief in the divine election of kings against a liberal individualist notion of government by "a mandate from the masses," by consent of free individuals. It contrasts the vatic language of medieval mysticism with the hardheaded language of contemporary political science. Arthur intones: The Lady of the Lake . . . her arm clad in the purest shimmering samite, held aloft Excalibur from the bosom of the water signifying by Divine Providence that I, Arthur, was to carry Excalibur. That is why I am your king!" Arthur's claims are substantiated by "angelic" singing on the music track.

As Dennis understands all too clearly, Arthur's language is designed to put him in his place, to demonstrate his cultural inferiority, and he responds with a dual challenge: "Strange women lying in ponds distributing swords is no basis for a system of government. Supreme executive power derives from a mandate from the masses, not from some farcical aquatic ceremony. . . . You can't expect to wield supreme executive power just 'cause some watery tart threw a sword at you!" His language challenges Arthur's claims both in its coarse deflation of aristocratic pretension ("watery tart") and in its use of a sophisticated political discourse ("supreme executive power") at odds with the naive medieval mysticism Arthur endorses in place of political theory.

The editing reinforces Dennis's challenge to Arthur's aristocratic claims. As Arthur delivers his speech, the shot shows the two peasants (Palin and Jones) in the foreground, framing Arthur, who stands at a distance from the camera and appears smaller, thereby reducing his importance in the shot. Dennis's rebuttals are usually given in close-up, encouraging viewers to sympathize with his assessment of the political situation. Once again Arthur loses the battle of wits; the scene erupts into chaos as he can do little more than attack Dennis physically ("the violence inherent in the system"). Of Eco's ten little Middle Ages, this scene's antimedievalism represents number two, the ironic Middle Ages that "do not believe in the grotesque period they inhabit." It is a site of "*ironical revisitation*," where we "speculate about our infancy" but also about "the illusion of our senility" (Eco, 69).

The third scene, which establishes *Monty Python and the Holy Grail*'s antiauthoritarian (and hence antimedieval) stance, is the scene depicting Arthur's battle with the Black Knight (see chapter 2). Here again Arthur fails to interpellate the Black Knight, to constitute his identity as a knight of the Round Table by compelling him to join Arthur at his court in Camelot. In this scene the homosocial bonding that usually ends medieval single combat devolves into comic confusion. Interestingly, the next scene, which concludes the opening sequence, in which Arthur witnesses the trial of a witch, ends with as nearly perfect a shot of medieval authoritarianism as it is possible to construct. After presenting us with the chop logic of Bedevere, who argues that a witch is like both wood and a duck, the scene ends with a static shot proclaiming Arthur's authority. Arthur stands on the right side of the shot, receiving homage from Bedevere, who is kneeling on the left side. Nothing that has happened up to this point substantiates the power and hierarchy implicit in this shot, which looks like nothing so much as Victorian illustrations of Arthurian subjects that highlight themes of political authority and hierarchy (a good example is Edmund Blair Leighton's well-known *The Accolade*).[7] Yet once again, the hierarchy and order implied in this scene are immediately undercut by the "Camelot" musical number. The court at Camelot for which Arthur seeks knights is so chaotic and silly—

> Between our quests
> we sequin vests
> and impersonate Clark Gable.
> It's a busy life in Camelot.

—that Arthur can't even stay there. No icon of authority, however visually compelling, is allowed to stand without comment.

It is not at all surprising that *Monty Python and the Holy Grail* maintains such a consistently antiauthoritarian stance. *Monty Python's Flying Circus* was a product of the 1960s counterculture and as such expresses a social critique that was prominent in the late 1960s and early 1970s, a critique that was itself a product of Britain's postwar situation.[8] By 1960 Britain had lost its world power status and its colonies abroad; it faced economic crises and debilitating conflicts in Northern Ireland (for all intents and purposes its colony at home). Its queen was no longer fashioned "Empress of India" but more prosaically "Head of the Commonwealth" (Cannadine, 134). This sense of political impotence found an outlet in the emerging television industry. By the time *Monty Python's Flying Circus* premiered on the BBC in 1969, British television had become accustomed to the kinds of political satire featured in shows like *That Was the Week That Was, Beyond the Fringe, The Last Laugh,* and *The Goon Show.* With comedians like Peter Cook, Dudley Moore, Jonathan Miller, and Alan Bennett, Monty Python represented a new breed of political satirists, members of Britain's elite, largely coming out of Oxford and Cambridge and hired by the BBC to produce social and political satire. This satire was marked by reaction against conventional authorities of all sorts but especially against political authority. And yet, as Stephen Wagg argues, it would be premature to attribute to their comedy any particular political agenda. The antiauthoritarianism of the "Oxbridge satire movement" tended to evacuate the political entirely, elevating "the *private* sphere of individual activities and decision-making at the expense of the *public* realm of parliamentary and 'party political' deliberation" (Wagg, 255; emphasis in original). Its primary targets were politics and politicians, those who wielded power and authority, but it advocated unrestricted freedom and fun in the private realm rather than citizenship in the public. What sets Monty Python's satire apart from the many other satirical programs of the period is that its satire was directed more generally at the absurdities of politics (the "Ministry of Silly Walks" skit, for instance) rather than at specific targets. The comedy has aged well, which is why a film like *Monty Python and the Holy Grail* can seem relevant even to our current students, for many of whom the 1960s are ancient history. American audiences with little or no knowledge of British politics of that period could (and can) still "get" the film.

But the British satirists' antiauthoritarianism, their retreat from politics, was not without consequences. As Wagg argues, it "helped to redefine the boundaries of citizenship, moving them subtly away from public service toward the private domain of consumption" (280). In 1970 the Monty Python group turned political satire into a profitable enterprise by forming a production group, Python Productions, to produce *Monty Python and the Holy Grail*, their first feature-length film. The film was directed by Python members Terry Jones and Terry Gilliam and shot for a shoestring £250,000.[9] The film was financed by members of Pink Floyd and Led Zeppelin; members of the comedy group undoubtedly saw the film's financing by rock stars (their 1979 film *Life of Brian* was financed by George Harrison when other backers dropped out) as consistent with their counterculture antiauthoritarian image.

It may be a bit of an exaggeration to claim, as Wagg does, that "Python, and other 'satirists,' invented Thatcherism" (279). Surely, middle age and economic success have, with some exceptions, chastened rebellious youth. But the essence of Thatcherism was already present in the retreat from the political into the private sphere of consumption. Thatcherism, according to Zygmunt Bauman, "offers the public a massive programme of buying oneself out, singly or severally, from politics: of making politics irrelevant to the pursuit of individual or collective goals and ideas. This dismantling of effective citizenship is presented as the triumph of freedom: as liberation" (37). That program finds both its cinematic critique and its confirmation in a film like *Excalibur*, released less than a decade after *Monty Python and the Holy Grail*.

Despite its deep distrust of the individualist values of Thatcherism that grew out of the evacuation of the political—its promotion of the acquisition of wealth and consumption of goods at the expense of the public good (Quart, 20)—Boorman's film is still a product of the Thatcher-Reagan era, with its focus on conservative social values, including its myths of political authority and hierarchy. Like its American counterpart, Reaganism, with which it was closely aligned, Thatcherism was "a strongly authoritarian, antilibertarian strain that viewed freedom as primarily economic rather than political in nature" (Quart, 19). *Excalibur,* despite its vaguely ecological agenda, expresses the political side of Thatcherism, evincing at once distaste for the individualist consumerism promoted by Thatcherism and a nostalgia for a more organic society ordered through hierarchical social and political relations and traditional values.[10] Notes Boorman:

> For a century now, we've been rushing headlong into the future; we've made a cult out of progress and we've forgotten our former selves, our former patterns of behavior, whose origins can be traced to the Middle Ages. We no longer have any roots; and today, in particular, when we contemplate the possible destruction of our planet, there's a thirst, a nostalgia for the past, a desperate need to understand it. We are attracted to the legend of the Grail because it speaks to us of a period when nature was unsullied and man in harmony with it. (quoted in Ciment, 188)

Excalibur offers its audiences a glimpse of such harmony, a political society ordered by the rule of a single man whose regime is underwritten by no less an authority than nature itself, a medieval view of the Great Chain of Being.

Although we are indebted to Aronstein's brilliant discussion of the film's relationship to the mythopoetic men's movement (see *Hollywood Knights,* 148–50), our view of *Excalibur*'s political mythmaking differs somewhat from hers. Aronstein describes the "hijacking by the New Right" of a film she sees as liberal in its politics. While she concedes that the film "seemed to valorize the same conservative values—the celebration of militarism, the nostalgic longing for authority, the reinstatement of the white male hero and the return of the Father"—that marked both Reaganism and the mythopoetic men's movement (151), for her Boorman's "politics and history as a filmmaker" belie this reading of the film. We would argue to the contrary that, while a film like Boorman's 1974 *Zardoz,* with its witty play on *The Wizard of Oz,* clearly articulates the dangers of capitulating to the charisma of a mythical leader, *Excalibur* seems far too much in thrall to its myth of masculinity to achieve the distance required for an ironic critique of the very myths it adoringly invokes.

Excalibur opens with a series of three segments that together plot the rise of Arthur as the king who will unify all England under a single divinely inspired ruler; he is able to accomplish, however momentarily, what *Monty Python and the Holy Grail*'s Arthur consistently fails to do: interpellate his subjects as subjects. *Excalibur*'s opening scenes reverse the trajectory of those in *Monty Python and the Holy Grail*, beginning in chaos and moving toward order. The segments are explicitly connected by a series of motifs and symbols that legitimate Arthur's acquisition of absolute political power through his possession of the sword Excalibur. Ironically, these are the same symbols and political myths that *Monty Python and the Holy Grail* lampoons. In Boorman's Arthurian world, "strange women lying in ponds distributing swords" *is* a basis for a system of authoritarian government.

The first segment begins in the chaos of battle. The opening shot, filmed in the dark of night and lit ostensibly by firelight (Boorman frequently shoots his battle scenes at night, which, while arresting to look at, seems a highly inefficient military tactic), creates a mise-en-scène populated by fully armored, and so completely concealed, knights, making it difficult for viewers to discern who is fighting whom and why. The sides are not clearly delineated (perhaps because there are none). Gradually Merlin emerges as the one figure capable of forging order from this chaotic political scene. In the shot that introduces him, he emerges from the back of the shot moving toward the front. He is shot from a low angle, making him appear more imposing, gradually looming larger and larger until he fills the screen. The familiar Wagnerian musical phrase from the opening of "Siegfried's Funeral March" crescendos, reaching its peak as Merlin's figure fills the screen. After that he is shot in increasingly tighter close-ups, and, since he is the only one in the scene without armor, he is visible to us, identifiable as an individual. His commentary anchors the scene for the viewer so that his observations of the battle order it; through his eyes Uther emerges as victor. Whether Merlin merely observes Uther's victory or causes it is more ambiguous.

The opening battle ends with a close-up of Merlin that provides the transition to the next scene, which also opens on a close-up of Merlin. Instead of being surrounded by the smoke and flame of battle, he is now surrounded by lush green. Seasons in this film correspond iconographically to the emotional or mythic content of scenes rather than to chronology as we might expect. Although this scene appears to take place on the day after the battle we have just witnessed (or maybe it is three months later; the point is that the film doesn't offer a chronology), the bare wintry trees of the previous scene have been replaced by the lush greens of summer. The first appearance of the sword Excalibur takes place exactly as Graham Chapman's Arthur describes it in *Monty Python and the Holy Grail*: "The Lady of the Lake . . . her arm clad in the purest shimmering samite, held aloft Excalibur from the bosom of the water signifying by Divine Providence that I . . . was to carry

Excalibur." Again the evocative strains from "Siegfried's Funeral March" crescendo as the sword becomes fully visible, linking the sword of power to Merlin.

Although we do not witness Uther being given Excalibur, in the next scene he wields it and is able, with Merlin's help, to forge a grudging peace. This scene gives us some insight into the film's representation of political power, its promise of plentitude in exchange for submission to the sword of power. Uther and Merlin use the sword to forge a truce based on a connection between the sword and the land; but how do they coerce the rebellious knights into accepting that connection? The knights appear already to know what the sword means, already to have been interpellated by it. When Merlin and Uther introduce the sword, the others seem impressed by it; one even kneels to it. Nonetheless, Merlin explains it, and his speech is designed more to command assent than to explain what the men seem already to know: "Behold the sword of power, Excalibur. Forged when the world was young and bird and beast and flower were one with man and death was but a dream." The sword represents a mystical and ritualistic promise of plentitude, of an organic unity between men and nature, one that might even forestall death. "One land, one king" promises that submission to the authority of one man (the wielder of the sword) will ensure not only peace but prosperity as well because it will connect the social and political institutions of men with nature (women are viewed in the film as outside of these institutions, as objects of exchange between men—like Guenevere—or as incomprehensible threats—like Morgana).

Uther, however, is not the "one." The various medieval practices designed to cement political power—feasting and the exchange of women and land—prove his undoing. His political authority lasts only long enough for him to beget a son, and England devolves once again into chaos, represented by Uther's war with Cornwall and with the murder of Uther after Arthur's birth. The mud and barren trees in Uther's death scene represent not the passage of time but the reemergence of chaos that follows his death. Uther's dying act is to thrust Excalibur into a stone, a narrative development that at least has the virtue of explaining, as Malory never does, why the sword is in the stone in the first place and why pulling it out is a test of legitimacy for his heir. This motif belongs to the aristocratic Middle Ages, where birth equals worth and the exercise of absolute political power is shrouded in mystical rituals.

Several seconds of black screen represent the passage of time. The second segment begins many years later, introducing Arthur as the Fair Unknown. It begins in the same chaos as the opening scene, except it is daytime instead of night, and, instead of engaging in real warfare, the knights fight one another in a tournament, a ritualistic "staged" battle. The effect of the vacuum in political leadership on the people is demonstrated by scenes of knights running down peasants and spectators in their rush to get to the tournament. This is the first glimpse in the film of any orders of society outside of the warrior class. In Arthur's first appearance in the film, his dirty, rough clothing and Welsh accent mark him as a social inferior, the fatherless boy who comes to the court to seek his fortune. He is spurned by his social superiors because of his apparent backwardness only to find out that he is of high birth, singled out for a particular destiny. Out of the chaos of the many knights competing for their chance to attempt extracting the sword from the stone, Arthur emerges triumphant, with Excalibur in hand, to the sweeping strains of Wagner.

Even though the sword in the stone clearly marks Arthur out for a particular destiny, the other knights are unwilling to accept a fatherless boy, a bastard, as their king. Once again conflict results when other knights refuse to submit to Arthur as they did to Uther. Arthur must forcibly impose order and bring the other knights into submission to the sword of power. Again Arthur emerges triumphant out of the chaos of battle in the third sequence. The scene of his triumph eschews traditional religious rituals of kingship (coronation and homage, for instance) in favor of some bizarre variations on traditional rituals of political sovereignty. Arthur receives a "battlefield commission" when he is knighted by Uriens. Having defeated Uriens in battle, Arthur stands over him with Excalibur pointed at his enemy's throat. Suddenly Arthur hands the sword to Uriens and places himself in a posture of submission by kneeling to him. He thus imposes on Uriens a moral dilemma. Does he keep the sword even though he has been defeated, or does he comply with Arthur's demand that he knight him? The traditional ritual of knighting then takes place as Uriens knights Arthur "in the name of God, St. Michael, and St. George." Their positions then reverse, and Uriens kneels before Arthur and offers his homage. The twist is that this scene takes place entirely in the castle moat, both characters waist-deep in water. The muddy water deprives the scene of the pomp and circumstance normally required of these rituals (knighting, homage), yet it also gives the scene the religious overtones of a baptism. As in earlier scenes musical phrases from Wagner's "Siegfried" punctuate the action as Arthur's success is assured.

In fact, the repetition throughout these three segments of the musical theme from "Siegfried's Funeral March" is central to forging the connection between political authority and Excalibur, between possession of the sword and the power to rule. Phrases from the opening of this piece from Wagner's *Götterdämmerung* play on the music track at key moments—the opening credits, the opening sequence, the scene in which Uther puts the sword in the stone, the scene in which Arthur pulls it out, and the segment in which Uriens knights Arthur and pledges homage to him.[11] Because at other times during these segments there is only a sparse musical score, the repetition of the musical theme from Wagner highlights the mythic qualities of the sword as a symbol of political authority. No one can exercise power unless he possesses the sword, and he who possesses it wields a supreme authority whose source is nature itself. By the time Arthur pulls the sword from the stone, the music's symbolic meaning has become overdetermined. This may be one of the film's flaws. Cynthia Clegg has argued that the film attempts to represent four modes of existence—the heroic, naturalistic, magical, and mythical—but is unable to unify them at the level of content and expression (103). The musical motif from Wagner represents the mythic, but in doing so it undercuts the heroic narrative of the Fair Unknown. It dissipates the element of astonishment at Arthur's feat in drawing out the sword. He already knows what the sword is and what it represents. Nigel Terry's acting in this scene alternates unconvincingly between studied bewilderment and studied nonchalance born of the predestination of his position: "I was your son before I was your king," he tells Hector, in a tone of voice that suggests he had known it all along.

The choice of Wagner's music to provide a leitmotif for the sword of power provides a clue to the film's aesthetics and its political mythmaking. In contrast to *Monty Python and the Holy Grail*'s consistently antiauthoritative stance (or indeed that of Boorman's own 1970s satire of political mythmaking in *Zardoz*), *Excalibur* imagines political order and prosperity as the result of submission to an authority legitimized by nature or divine will. Indeed, the film displays almost all of the characteristics Susan Sontag associates with the "fascist aesthetic," which, she argues, flows from and justifies "situations of control, submissive behavior, extravagant effort, and the endurance of pain; [it] endorse[s] two seemingly opposite states, egomania and servitude" (91). This aesthetic appears not only in the music but in the visuals as well. Sontag could be describing the visual style of *Excalibur* when she writes:

> The relations of domination and enslavement take the form of characteristic pageantry: the massing of groups of people; the turning of people into things; the multiplication or replication of things; the grouping of people/things around an all-powerful, hypnotic leader-figure or force. The fascist dramaturgy centers

on the orgiastic transactions between mighty forces and their puppets, uniformly garbed and shown in ever swelling numbers. Its choreography alternates between ceaseless motion and a congealed, static, "virile" posing. Fascist art glorifies surrender, it exalts mindlessness, it glamorizes death. (91)[12]

While pageantry is a common enough ritual of leadership and group membership from inaugurals to Fourth of July parades, Boorman's visual treatment of Arthur's kingship comes troublingly close to Sontag's "fascist dramaturgy."

Three shots from the middle of the film illustrate the specifically visual power of fascist aesthetics to compel assent and mobilize individuals around a charismatic figure that Sontag describes. Boorman presents the idea for the Round Table as occurring after victory in a battle that at last unites all England under Arthur's leadership. The battle takes place at night (again). The knights encircle Arthur and Merlin. The fires—the ostensible lighting source for the darkly lit scene—reflect off the burnished metal of the knights' armor, making them seem even more inhuman than they do elsewhere in the film. The aggressively bright armor, which is worn at all times in the film (even apparently in bed) as a symbol of knighthood, dehumanizes the knights, while its uniformity contributes to the effects of reification and massification. A similar tableau is enacted in Arthur's and Guenevere's wedding scene. Again lines of knights armed in brilliant armor surround the couple. Guenevere's costume picks up the knight's armor in a more subdued fashion. Her dress and veil are metallic, picking up the visual motif of shininess, but they are more translucent, less solid than the knights' armor. Finally, in the scene in which the film's other Fair Unknown—Perceval—is introduced to the court, Boorman presents a view of the Knights of the Round Table from Perceval's perspective. He stands on a balcony looking down on the assembly. The audience sees a crane shot of a huge round table with knights in glistening metal armor surrounding it (see Figure 2). The effect dissolves the humanity of the knights into geometric effect in a shot reminiscent of a Busby Berkeley musical. In this shot the attraction of the "fascist aesthetic" resides in its idealism: "the ideal of life as art, the cult of beauty, the fetishism of courage, the dissolution of alienation in ecstatic feelings of community; the repudiation of the intellect; the family of man (under the parenthood of leaders)" (Sontag, 96); and the idealism is carried by the aestheticization of its subjects.

The search for the Holy Grail completes Arthur's apotheosis into messianic leader (although Nigel Terry's understated performance hardly convinces). Boorman's audacious revisions to Malory's virtually incomprehensible Grail story change the meaning of the political myth it represents. In *Morte Darthur* Arthur laments his knights' pursuit of the Holy Grail; it represents a threat to the political bonds he has forged during his reign:

> ye haue berafte me the fayrest felaushyp and the truest of knyghthode that euer were sene togyders in ony royalme of the world. For whan they departe frome hens I am sure they alle shal neuer mete more in thys worlde, for they shal dye many in the quest. And so it forthynketh me a lytel, for I haue loued them as wel as my lyf, wherfore hit shal greue me ryght sore, the departycyon of thys fe-laushyp, for I haue had an olde custome to haue hem in my felaushyp. (Spisak and Matthews, 1:433)

Boorman's knights, however, follow the Grail at Arthur's request; he believes that the Grail is the only thing that can "redeem" him and restore the land that has become wasteland.[13] Perceval's Grail vision proves Arthur correct. The Grail is presented to Perceval as a gigantic golden chalice, brilliantly lit. A booming voice-over asks, "What is the secret of the Grail? Who does it serve?" Perceval replies, "You my Lord." At this point there is no reason not to believe that Boorman is calling up the usual Christian associations of the Grail with the chalice that Christ drank from at the Last Supper, that "my Lord" is Christ. But Perceval's (correct) answer to the voice's query—"Who am I?"—is surprising: "You are my lord and king." The chalice transforms into a brilliantly armored Arthur. While *Zardoz* reveals the "old man behind the curtain" of the political myth, *Excalibur's* vision of the Holy Grail invests him with a divine status. The Grail represents not the perfected social order of Christianity but the political authority of the monarchy; religion is mobilized in this scene only to buttress what is essentially a secular political order. Once Perceval has brought the chalice to Arthur, the incapacitated king is able to ride out with his knights (the oddly martial strains of Carl Orff's *Carmina Burana*—the oft-repeated "O Fortuna"[14]—playing in the background) to defeat the rebel Mordred and restore the land. Boorman's vision in *Excalibur* is a profoundly nostalgic one, an elegy to a lost organic society that never actually existed—one that unites nature and culture, high and low, sacred and profane under a single charismatic leader invested with mystical authority.

"It's 1183 and We're All Barbarians": Medieval Political Practice

The Grail scene in *Excalibur* represents the most complete synthesis of the abstract concepts of medieval political theory and the static ritualistic hierarchies of medieval political philosophy represented in John of Salisbury's *Policraticus*. In doing so, it feeds nostalgic fantasies of an organic fusion with nature. In this scene religion is placed in the service of an absolute monarchy in which the health of the land and the health of the king are indissolubly linked. The film fuses a political order that includes warriors, clergy, and peasants in the subject position of the king, who merges with the Holy Grail; all other perspectives are eclipsed by it. A film like *Becket* (Peter Glenville, 1964), however, explores in more depth the complex political realities involved in the relationships among those who fought, those who prayed, and those who worked the land during the Middle Ages and, in doing so, illuminates more contemporary questions of political authority. In *Excalibur* order and legitimate succession are ensured by a mystical ritual that links the "king and the land" through the symbol of the sword in the stone. In *The Lion in Winter* (Anthony Harvey, 1968) primogeniture and succession become the ground over which political battles for power are fought, not on the battlefield (physical violence is relegated to the status of background threat) but in the political scheming of the participants. The film, however, privatizes its politics, placing them within the nuclear, post-Freudian family; in doing so, it risks trivializing its political stakes. The second half of this chapter, then, explores two films that depict a medieval realpolitik that belies the static hierarchies of medieval political theory described above. But these films are not primarily interested in providing historical insight into medieval politics. Rather, medieval political practice exists in a position that Jeffrey Jerome Cohen describes as "extimate" to twentieth-century politics; it is "an 'inexcluded' middle at the pulsing heart of modernity" (5), at once alien and familiar. The "otherness" of medieval political practice becomes a means of imagining the birth of the liberal individual and of the modern nation out of the tyranny, chaos, and corruption of medieval "barbarism."

Glenville's *Becket* is based on Jean Anouilh's 1959 play *Becket, or the Honor of God*, its screenplay only lightly adapted by Edward Anhalt. The film, like the play, shows through the conflict between Henry II and Thomas Becket that, in practice, the relations between the twelfth-century church and state were far more tangled and conflicted than either medieval political theory or a film like *Excalibur* can suggest. Anouilh's drama also implies that this struggle between church and state helped give rise to the modern liberal state by replacing the personal affective loyalties that characterized feudalism with identification with an abstract corporate body (in Becket's case the church), a necessary precondition of the modern liberal state.

This may seem an unusual claim given the reactionary role usually assigned to the church in the development of modern liberal political thought, which required that the tyranny of state religion that marked the "medieval" be thrown off, especially what Francis Bacon referred to as the "degenerate traditions of the [Catholic] Church" (28). Religion, in the liberal state, lies outside the jurisdiction of civil government.[15] Medieval political theory, however—a theory written almost exclusively by clergymen—attempted to fuse church and state under a theocracy that inevitably created nearly unbearable tensions between two institutions—church and monarchy—with very different priorities and interests. In *Policraticus*, Becket's friend John of Salisbury suggests that the king's earthly authority derives exclusively from God. For this reason the clergy must submit to his rule: "I am satisfied and persuaded that loyal shoulders should uphold the power of the ruler; and not only do I submit to his power patiently, but with pleasure, so long as it is exercised in subjection to God and follows his ordinances." He goes on, however, to place limits on the king's authority and hence to the clergy's submission: "if it resists and opposes the divine commandments, and wishes to make me share in its war against God, then with unrestrained voice I answer back that God must be preferred before any man on earth" (Winston, 103). In fact, far from demanding subservience from the clergy, from the church's position and Salisbury's, the secular ruler was really subordinate to them: "The ruler is therefore a sort of minister of the priests and one who exercises those features of the sacred duties that seem an indignity in the hands of priests" (Nederman and Forhan, 33). In *Policraticus*'s complex allegory of the body politic the clergy are the soul and the ruler the heart. At the center of this metaphor, as Becket reveals, is massive uncertainty about the limits of each institution's authority. Anouilh attempts to sort through the contradictions inherent in this political impasse by substituting the metaphor of the ship for *Policraticus*'s convoluted metaphor of the body. In the council scene Becket asserts that England is a ship: "there must be one—and only one Captain on board ship." The Archbishop of Canterbury replies that "the Captain is sole master after God. . . . After God!" Becket counters, "Certainly God protects the ship by inspiring the Captain. But I've never heard that he determines the wages of the crew nor instructs the paymaster in his duties. God has more important duties" (Anouilh, 9).

Even a cursory reading of *Policraticus* suggests the inevitability of the conflicts that would emerge between secular and divine rulers during this time. The church did not limit its authority on earth to ministering to the spiritual needs of the kingdom. It also controlled vast amounts of material wealth and real estate and enjoyed privileges that frequently put its interests (and therefore God's interests) at odds with those of the secular ruler. None of the issues that divided Henry and Becket were new to Henry's reign nor even unique to England in the Middle Ages. The tensions were inherent in a political theory that attempted to join church and state while putting their interests at odds.

Historically, the key issue in the dispute between king and archbishop concerned the independence of the English church from secular interference. What was at stake was the recognition by the king of the pope's authority over the English church and the freedom of the church from secular interference. The political theory offered by the New Testament would seem to settle many of these questions for modern readers: "Render unto Caesar the things that are Caesar's and to God the things that are God's." Yet in twelfth-century England, God's things and Caesar's became inextricably linked, resulting in disputes that included primarily religious issues like canonical elections to episcopal offices; the freedom of the clergy to leave the country at will, to consult with the pope, answer papal summons, or carry appeals to the pope; free entry into England by papal legates; and the bishops' freedom to fill vacant sees promptly. But they also included matters that would strike the modern reader as more appropriately secular than religious, issues like episcopal control of real estate and clerical immunities from criminal prosecution (Winston, 164). Henry's position in the debate, represented by the sixteen clauses of the Constitutions of Clarendon (1164), a document Archbishop Becket reluctantly signed, asserted the king's jurisdiction over the English church, limited the powers of the pope in England, and asserted secular control over church property and over civil crimes committed by the clergy (Winston, 373–76).

Rather than getting lost in the complexities of feudal and canonical law, however, Anouilh the playwright chose to focus his drama about this conflict on the issue of clerical immunity. While the church vigorously defended its right to try clergymen accused of civil crimes in ecclesiastical courts, clause 3 of the Constitutions of Clarendon proclaimed: "Clerks cited and accused of any matter shall, when summoned by the king's justice, come before the king's court to be answerable there. . . . And if the clerk be convicted, or shall confess, the Church ought no longer to protect him" (Winston, 373). What often gets lost in the sheer drama of Anouilh's play, and O'Toole's and Burton's performances in the film, is the utter tawdriness of the issue they are ostensibly fighting over. A clerk accused of "debauching a young girl" is taken into custody to be tried in civil courts. "Is the priest guilty?" Becket asks when Bishop Folliot brings him the news. "That is immaterial," Folliot replies, because the accused can only be tried in "our ecclesiastical courts." In the film the great English martyr is required to defend the "honor of God" by protecting from civil prosecution a priest who is at best a seducer and at worst a rapist.

But both play and film are ultimately less interested in the details of Becket's arguments with the king than in representing a shift in the means of wielding political power: a transfer from the medieval to the modern. During the first half of the film, Becket finds himself negotiating a relationship with Henry structured not by contract or exchange of capital but by the medieval rules of patronage and gift giving. Patronage in the Middle Ages ordered a political system in which power was wielded through personal relationships, through bonds of love, both hetero- and homosocial, and through the exchange of gifts and women.[16] Patronage relations "differ from other forms of exchange in that they are not one-time exchanges, but involve long-term obligation and credit. They are particularistic and diffuse rather than legal or contractual. Unlike other, impersonal forms of exchange that alienate individuals from one another, gift giving draws individuals together, establishing personal bonds between them, which is why terms such as love . . . are often used to describe the relationship" (Finke and Shichtman, "Magical Mistress Tour," 484). The currency of power of the patronage relationship described in the first half of the film is a hypermasculinized heteronormativity tinged with homosociality and homoeroticism. Becket's "love" for the king, and the king's for him, is cemented through an exchange of gifts, those gifts being women. This is made clear early in the film, through the explicit use of the language of the gift. The "traffic in women"[17] establishes the homosocial bonds between the two men, at the same time providing cover for its obvious homoeroticism. In one scene, taking shelter from a rainstorm in a "Saxon hut," Becket and the king encounter a young Saxon girl to whom the king is attracted. This complicated scene brings together the various threads that link gender and the exercise of political power in the film. Becket, "wounded in the service of the King" when the girl's brother tries to stab him, is offered a gift. To rescue her from the king's lust, Becket asks for the girl: "I fancy her." Despite his own attraction, the king relents but extracts from Thomas the promise of a future gift in exchange: "favor for favor." Later, the king calls in his marker, demanding that Thomas hand over his Welsh mistress Gwendolen in exchange for his gift. In the king's understanding of the patronage system, this circulation of women as gifts is designed to promote solidarity in men, to create bonds of affection that are the only means by which the ruler can exercise power effectively.

Yet the king's strategy to secure Becket's loyalty through the exchange of women fails because Becket is a fish out of water in a world in which politics are conducted through personal loyalties. What Becket seeks is an escape from personal affiliation into an impersonal, individualistic "code" of honor. What is the "honor of God" except the opportunity to frame one's allegiances not personally but contractually through the institution of the church to an abstract ideal and thus free oneself from affective ties of all kinds? Archbishop Becket defends an abstract idea, which is why the audience can overlook the fact that the actual case at stake in his dispute with the king involves a potential rapist. Anouilh makes Becket's defining characteristic his inability to sustain personal affective ties—to love anyone—and his desperate search for an abstract cause in which to lose himself. "Somehow," he tells Gwendolen (played by Sian Phillips), "I can never support the idea of being loved." Becket is a type of the liberal individual who throws off the tyranny represented by feudal ties of patronage and kingship for the impersonal, individualistic "honor of God." "So long as Becket is obliged to improvise his honor, he will serve you. And if one day, he meets it face to face. . . . But where is Becket's honor?" (Anouilh, 26).

In the second half of the film Becket finds his answer; he finds "the honor of God." A central question for the play—and for the film—is, What does Anouilh mean by "the honor of God"? Anouilh does not make Becket a saint in the traditional sense. We are not given a glimpse of a single-minded religious devotion. Rather in the second half of the film Becket becomes the liberal individual required of the modern state. He cuts himself off from all patronage networks, all obligations and ties to others, pledging his loyalty to an abstraction—"the honor of God"—and to a corporate body—the church. His "conversion" from Becket the chancellor to Becket the archbishop frees him from all those ties—heterosexual and homosocial—that previously bound him. He can no longer marry, and he owes his allegiance not to a flesh-and-blood king but to the ideals attributed to an invisible God who will never contradict Becket. Becket wields power as archbishop of Canterbury not through the force of his relationships with others but through his ability to manipulate the symbols that represent this invisible corporate power and to associate his power with the power conferred by those symbols. In short, he displays an uncanny knack for the staging of spectacles of power—of fascist dramaturgy.

This should not be too surprising given the history of Anouilh's play. Alongside its depiction of the birth of the liberal individual, *Becket* evinces the anxieties about collaboration that were rife in post-Vichy France when the play was written. Anouilh, influenced by Augustin Thierry's 1825 *History of the Conquest of England by the Normans,* makes Becket a Saxon, though he was a Norman who happened to be born in London.[18] Anouilh's decision to adopt Thierry's romantic nationalism has more to do with drama than with historical accuracy.

> I decided that if history in the next fifty years should go on making progress it
> will perhaps rediscover that Becket was indubitably of Saxon origin; in any
> case, for this drama of friendship between two men, between the king and his
> friend, his companion in pleasure and in work (and this is what had gripped me
> about the story), this friend whom he could not cease to love though he became
> his worst enemy the night he was named archbishop—for this drama it was a
> thousand times better that Becket remained a Saxon.[19]

In fact, making Becket a Saxon enables Anouilh to frame the friendship and later enmity between king and archbishop in stark nationalistic terms as an encounter between conquering and conquered races. The relationship between Norman king and Saxon chancellor eerily parallels in reverse the relationships under the Vichy government between German invaders and their conquered French "collaborators," an anachronistic term Anouilh doesn't hesitate to use in his play.

The film's focus on collaboration is introduced in one of the early scenes, a scene that takes place in the king's bath. As Becket (Richard Burton) towels Henry (Peter O'Toole) off and helps him dress, the two discuss Becket's Saxon heritage. Their conversation is punctuated by rough-looking Saxon servants who scurry through the scene, stoking fires and lifting heavy buckets to supply water, only to be addressed by the king as "pig" or "dog."[20] Burton delivers Becket's explanation for the Norman contempt of the Saxons in an ironic and detached tone, making his point through the anaphoric repetition of the word *Saxon:* "When the Normans invaded England, you seized our Saxon land, burned our Saxon homes, and raped our Saxon sisters. Naturally you hate the Saxons." Everything in the scene is designed to highlight the vast gulf between the conquering Normans and what the film's opening titles call "the oppressed Saxon peasants." The only thing that seems incongruous is Becket, his rich and colorful garments contrasting the king's drab dress as he provides the services (toweling and dressing) usually performed by lower (and poorer) servants.[21]

When Henry calls Becket "a man of honor and a collaborator," he voices what, for Anouilh, is the heart of the matter: can one collaborate with honor? Anouilh's answer is characteristically ambiguous.[22] The two men go on to discuss Becket's "collaboration":

HENRY. How do you combine the two—honor and collaboration?

BECKET. I don't try. I love good living and good living is Norman. I love life
and the Saxon's only birthright is to be slaughtered. One collaborates
to live.

HENRY. And honor?

BECKET. Honor is a concern of the living. One can't very well be concerned
about it once one is dead. . . . Honor is a private matter within. It's an
idea, and every man has his own version of it.

The repetition of the term *collaboration* throughout this conversation can only
point to Anouilh's own anxieties about his activities during the Nazi occupation
of France. Collaboration is a modern, not a medieval, concept. Becket's ability to
move between cultures—Norman, Saxon, Celtic—would not have been characterized as collaboration in the twelfth century; it would have been a necessity.[23]
Although it has been usual to read Anouilh's wartime plays, especially his *Antig-
one*, as plays of resistance to tyranny, Mary Ann Frese Witt documents thirteen
articles Anouilh wrote for the collaborationist press during the occupation as evidence of his fascist leanings during the war (211–12), which, in these journal articles, took the form of typical Vichy propaganda: "the theme of the corruption of
money, including attacks on capitalism, Americans, and Jews" (Witt, 213). Although throughout his career Anouilh characterized himself as uninterested in
politics, he did speak out against the brutality of the postwar purges in France, especially the execution of the playwright Robert Brasillach, a fellow Vichy collaborator. He even attempted to collect signatures on a petition to prevent the execution and, after the execution, refused to allow any of his plays to be performed
in state theaters (Witt, 229).

Certainly this knowledge of Anouilh's wartime activity must send us back to
this curious conversation between king and servant on the compatibility of honor
and collaboration. One might read Becket's response to his king as the wishful
thinking of an immature hedonist who has not yet discovered his "honor." Even
the king recognizes, "I know there's something not quite right about your reasoning." And yet in the film collaboration is the cornerstone of Becket the chancellor's foreign policy. During the French campaign that immediately precedes
Becket's elevation to archbishop, Becket explains his strategy of collaboration to
Henry's barons, who are eager to increase their own wealth through looting: "I
want these people to collaborate with good grace." He later explains the policy to
the king: "Gentleness is better politics; it saps virility. A good occupational force

must never crush; it must corrupt," that is, it must create collaborators. Once again Becket's language describes less the political situation of twelfth-century England than that of post-Vichy France.

Becket's secular politics of collaboration are never condemned outright; rather they are represented as ambiguous, always shadowed by acts of futile resistance (the two attempts on Becket's life are examples). Becket's collaboration often has positive effects. His manipulation of the French townspeople saves them from Henry's bloodthirsty barons, who would "rather sack the town and slaughter the lot." He saves the life of the Saxon monk who would assassinate him, as earlier he had tried to save the Saxon peasant girl from a life of prostitution. The confrontation between Becket and the monk, John, offers a stark contrast between collaboration and resistance:

> JOHN. You used to be a Saxon. Now you belong to the Normans.
> BECKET. A Saxon knife for a Saxon collaborator. Did you think that by killing me you could liberate your race?
> JOHN. No. Not my race, myself.
> BECKET. From what?
> JOHN. My shame . . . and yours.
> BECKET. The Normans have occupied England for one hundred years, since Hastings. Shame is an old vintage to the Saxon. Your father and grandfather drank it to the dregs. The cup is empty now.
> JOHN. No, never.

What this dialogue says about the relative values of collaboration and resistance as strategies for the conquered is finally undecidable; in fact, it says very little. Visually, however, the choice between collaboration and resistance is stark, highlighted by the scene's deviation from traditional practices of continuity editing. This conversation is not presented through the usual technique of shot–reverse shot editing; rather the entire dialogue is filmed as a continuous two-shot. Furthermore, the interlocutors are not framed facing one another; they are not filmed in profile, a technique that tends to distance the audience from the action on-screen. They do not even appear to be talking to one another. Rather Becket stands behind John, and both face forward toward the audience, a composition that implicates the audience in the dialogue. The scene does not choose between Becket's policy of collaboration and John's of outright—and futile—resistance. It presents them in tension with one another, postponing the resolution of the conflict until later in the film. Yet even though he manages eventually to "convert" the angry monk, *Archbishop* Becket seems less intent on relieving the tyranny suffered by the Saxon peasants than in protecting the privileges of a powerful and rapacious church, a point that gets lost in the film's canonization of Becket's principled position.

Witt characterizes Anouilh's flirtation with fascism as an "aesthetic fascism," a term she uses to define "the nature of the fascist presence in art and literature and of the involvement of those writers, artists, and intellectuals who came to the movement primarily through aesthetics" (ix). Her formulation suggests a less than wholehearted devotion to fascism's political program on the part of "aesthetes" like Anouilh. However, the term cannot help but bring to mind Sontag's "fascist aesthetic." Like *Excalibur, Becket's* visuals at times—most notably in the opening scene—suggest Sontag's "fascist dramaturgy," a monumental form of pageantry that groups people and things around a charismatic figure, "a dissolution of alienation in ecstatic feelings of community" (91). In a tableau that suggests that Henry has at least learned from Becket the power of spectacle, the film opens with a sequence that shows how much Glenville has learned from Leni Riefenstahl. The establishing shot focuses on the tympanum of a cathedral, displaying the symbols of Christianity triumphant—Christ in a mandala seated in judgment. The camera tilts downward to massive open church doors. Hooded monks begin to file out of the doors in two orderly and identical lines, finally forming a semicircle in front of the church. There is a cut to a tolling church bell. As the bell moves back and forth, a large massed crowd is revealed, organized into two orderly blocks with an aisle between them. The shot is monumental and ritualistic. It resembles nothing so much as the famous scenes from the Nazi Party Congress in Leni Riefenstahl's *Triumph of the Will*.[24] In fact, this scene is almost a shot-by-shot parallel of the famous scene in that film depicting a rally commemorating the death of Field Marshal Paul von Hindenburg. In Riefenstahl's scene the establishing shot shows a statue of an eagle; the camera tilts down to reveal a swastika. Both are symbols that authorize Nazi power. A dissolve to a massed crowd follows (see Figure 4). Three tiny figures (Hitler is the center figure) are shown walking up the aisle toward the Hindenburg monument.

In *Becket* the king and his retinue ride up on horseback through the center aisle as a martial theme sounds in the musical score. Though he is generally a small figure in the shot, the king wears a red cape that marks him as the central figure. Emphasis in this scene, however, is on the monumentality of the whole rather than any single component. Individuals—even charismatic kings—are tiny figures who make up part of a vast whole. As the king makes his way through

Figure 4. Crane shot from *Triumph of the Will* (Leni Riefenstahl, 1935).

what is presumably the interior of Canterbury Cathedral to Thomas's tomb in a long tracking shot that follows him, he is a small figure set against a massive shadowy cathedral interior; only the red cape stands out. In this scene the attempt to link kingship with religious symbolism through spectacle seems a much more ambiguous and even cynical exercise than in *Excalibur*. Henry needs to harness the ritualistic power conferred by the church, so he humiliates himself by submitting to a flogging. But O'Toole's performance makes it clear that Henry's submission is largely for show: "Oh Thomas, I'm ashamed of this whole silly masquerade. So I've come here to make my peace with their Saxon hero because I need them now, those Saxon peasants of yours." The power struggle between church and state that created the conflict between Henry and Becket is not resolved by his penance, only temporarily eased through Henry's manipulation of public rituals of subordination and humiliation performed before massed crowds, through his own act of collaboration.

The fascist concept of the masses, as Klaus Theweleit has shown us, is contradictory, yet its contradictions encompass Henry's cynicism about the spectacle of his penance. "Alongside his capacity to mobilize great masses of human beings," Theweleit writes, "there exists within the fascist a simultaneous contempt for the masses; while he addresses himself to them, he feels himself at the same time to be raised above them, one of an elite standing against the lowly 'man-of-the-masses'" (Theweleit, 2:3). Theweleit explains this difference by recourse to two distinct kinds of masses. The first—"The mass that is celebrated is strictly formed, poured into a system of dams. Above it there towers a leader *(Führer)*"—corresponds to the orderly masses represented in Glenville's opening shot. "To the despised mass, by contrast, is attributed all that is flowing, slimy, teeming" (2:4), Henry's despised Saxons, Hitler's Jews.

Becket's comment that collaborationist politics is good occupational politics because it "saps virility" is a key to understanding the film's representation of medieval political power as gender politics. That gender is part of a fascist aesthetic cannot be in doubt after Klaus Theweleit's two-volume study of the gender politics of fascist fantasy. Whatever its flaws, *Male Fantasies* points to the glorification of masculinity that undergirds this film's fantasies and its representations of medieval politics. In Becket collaboration is effeminate because women can be conceived only as objects in exchanges between men; this traffic in women solidifies the homosocial relationships between men. But those relationships always border on the homoerotic. Henry is never shown in bed with a woman without Becket present. In the film's opening scene Becket plays the voyeur to Henry's debauchery. After Becket's mistress, Gwendolen, kills herself, the king spends the night in Becket's bed. During the French campaign, Becket and the king talk politics together in bed with a French whore—designated as one of the king's "French possessions"—between them, the prostitute providing a heterosexual "cover" for the erotic charge between the two men.

Needless to say, this representation of the trafficking of women creates only very circumscribed space for women, explaining the film's domestication of two of the most remarkable and powerful women in the Middle Ages—Eleanor of Aquitaine, Henry's wife; and Matilda, his mother. These characters do not even appear in the film until after the break between king and archbishop, and their primary function is to provide commentary on the break. The three scenes in which the two women appear collectively demonstrate with admirable economy the film's preference for homosocial bonding between men over heteronormative family life. "The joys of family life," Henry tells Eleanor, "are limited. Frankly you bore me." Both women recognize that Henry's response to the loss of his friend is that of a jilted lover, which is precisely how O'Toole plays it.

There is no room at all in the film for the considerable accomplishments of these two remarkable women, who historically led armies, instigated civil wars, and patronized the greatest intellectuals and artists of their day. Henry jeers at their "carping mediocrity," and, whereas Sian Phillips's Gwendolen is a heroically tragic figure, Eleanor and Matilda are represented as ineffectual shrews. Their daily occupations appear to be limited to gossiping, backbiting, nagging, (mediocre) sewing, and raising children (poorly). Nothing could be further from the historical—or legendary—truth than Henry's description of Eleanor's youth: "that withered flower pressed between the pages of a hymn book since you were twelve years old with its watery blood and stale insipid scent, you can bid farewell to that without a tear." Of Matilda, who was in fact engaged in a civil war for the English throne during his childhood and more likely to be attending a battle than dancing, Henry says, "I never saw you except in a passage way on your way to a ball."

Glenville shoots the scenes with Eleanor and Matilda to reinforce their circumscribed roles. Their scenes tend to be highly static and filmed in a way that minimizes movement. The two women are swathed—literally hemmed in—by elaborate gowns and wimples that limit their motion. They are almost always photographed in static three shots with Henry. They never move; the camera rarely does. If there is any movement in the scene, it is usually the hyperactive Henry who is moving, with the camera following him. Glenville's mise-en-scène underscores the film's homosocial and even homoerotic edge by denying any agency—even the sexual and maternal power usually attributed to women—to Henry's wife and mother.

In 1968 *The Lion in Winter*, based on James Goldman's 1966 Tony Award–winning play, restored to the figure of Eleanor of Aquitaine her historical grandeur by embodying her in the magisterial figure of Katharine Hepburn.[25] Whereas none of the actresses in *Becket* was particularly well known at the time of the film (although Sian Phillips went on to fame portraying Livia in *I, Claudius*, *Becket* was only her second film), Hepburn was a towering presence in Hollywood. A star for more than thirty years at the time, she won her third Oscar for her performance in this role. Her star persona alone—Hepburn was a Hollywood icon of aristocratic elegance—makes Eleanor's conflict with Henry (played once again by Peter O'Toole) central to the film's plot. *The Lion in Winter* explores the politics of succession, the transition of power in a state ruled by an absolute monarch, condensing the decades-long struggle over which of Henry II's three surviving sons would succeed him into a single Christmas court imagined to have occurred in Chinon in 1183. The event brings together Henry; his estranged and imprisoned wife, Eleanor of Aquitaine; his sons, Richard (the Lionheart, played by Anthony Hopkins), Geoffrey (John Castle), and John (Nigel Terry); as well as Henry's mistress, Alais (Eleanor's foster-daughter and betrothed to Richard, played by Jane Merrow), and her brother, Philip of France (Timothy Dalton).[26] The film orients its audience to the political significance of this struggle in the very first scene with a wildly anachronistic reference to Shakespeare's *King Lear*. Henry tells his mistress Alais, "There's a legend of a king called Lear with whom I have a lot in common. Both of us have kingdoms and three children we adore, and both of us are old. But there it ends. He cuts his kingdom into bits. I can't do that. I built an empire. I must know it's going to last. I'm the greatest power in a thousand years. And after me comes John."[27]

Is the play's Christmas court a family reunion or, as Goldman suggests in the historical note to his play, "a meeting of the French and English Kings" (vii)? The latter would suggest a political event of public significance, the former a private moment. Although the film's condensation of action to a single event allows for much tighter dramatic action, it also shrinks a dynastic struggle for succession that took place over decades and involved half of Europe to the sphere of the nuclear, post-Freudian family. Although the play appears to examine the relationship between family and politics at a time when public and private spheres are not easily distinguished, what it, in fact, does is foreclose the public sphere—the political scheming of its principals—altogether in favor of a pop psychology reading of family dynamics, of familial "dysfunction."[28] In the claustrophobic setting of Chinon castle, what Henry defines as the dynastic struggle over an empire that stretched from Italy to England is reduced to a medieval *Who's Afraid of Virginia Woolf?*

If Becket is, for Anouilh and Glenville, the prototypical liberal individual who frees himself from all ties of dependency to serve an abstraction like the "honor of God," the succession struggle over Henry's crown becomes, for James Goldman and Anthony Harvey, a means of exploring the mechanisms through which that liberal subjectivity is produced out of the atavistic Middle Ages. Liberal individualism, if it was to provide a philosophical legitimation for economic capitalism, required individuals to be freed from feudal patronage dependencies, to compete to sell their labor as atomistic and independent individuals. But the liberal narrative of the modern individual's birth is always partial at best. The sustaining feature of liberal democracy, as Carole Pateman and Zillah R. Eisenstein have both argued, is a split between the public sphere of government and work and the private sphere of family, a process that, by the eighteenth century, had largely been completed in the separation of the workplace from the home (Pateman, 123; Eisenstein, 22–26). The ties of dependency that marked public life under feudalism are gathered up in the private sphere under the direction of women, enabling the individual (usually male) to function independently in the public sphere, free from all hierarchies. "The family is based on natural ties of sentiment and blood and on the sexually ascribed status of wife and husband (mother and father). Participation in the public sphere is governed by universal, impersonal, and conventional criteria of achievement, interests, rights, equality, and property—liberal criteria, applicable only to men" (Pateman, 121).

While public and private spheres are functionally interdependent, ideologically the separation into two spheres is accompanied by a thorough repression of the private sphere: Pateman notes that liberal political theorists "base their inquiries on the assumption that their subject lies in the public world of the economy and state and that the private realm of the domestic, familial and sexual relations lies outside their proper concerns" (3). The family must be seen as the natural foundation of liberal society, existing outside of political discourse. The private sphere must be repressed, as it surely is in *Becket*, for the individual to emerge victorious in the founding political narrative of liberal democracy.[29]

In this regard Freud's articulation of psychoanalytic theory at the end of the nineteenth century was less a means of describing some kind of universal psychological truth than of suggesting a mechanism for producing the public liberal individual. The typology of the psyche, its division into conscious and unconscious, maps easily onto the public-private dichotomy: the rational conscious mind is separated from the irrational, highly sexualized unconscious. Freud's work describes the creation of the unconscious as a family romance; he locates it exclusively in the private sphere of the family, in the Oedipal triangle of father, mother, and child. In this he is as guilty as political theorists of occluding the interdependence of the two spheres. The effect of the public world of the economy and politics on the private bourgeois family is largely absent from his account of the Oedipal conflict; the family seems to exist in a social vacuum. Still his account of the formation of the unconscious describes the process Louis Montrose calls "subjectivization": the mechanism by which individuals are "endowed with subjectivity by certain cultural practices [in this case child rearing] which create the capacity for agency, at the same time [that] they position those individuals within a social network and subject them to cultural codes that ultimately exceed their comprehension and control" (21); it describes, in other words, the formation of a liberal individual who can separate from the domestic sphere and become a political subject of the state, a citizen. *The Lion in Winter* examines the effect on political life of a politics that is exclusively a family affair; however, its relocation of twelfth-century politics to the domestic sphere has the effect of evacuating the political altogether in favor of a popular psychoanalytic understanding of twelfth-century English history.[30] It is as if liberal theory, having separated the private from the public, cannot represent the two at the same time, cannot imagine a politics in which public and private are inextricably imbricated. Like those graphic illusions that oscillate between a vase and two faces, a rabbit and a duck, we can see only one view at a time, either the public or the private, but not both at once.

The opening of *The Lion in Winter* enacts a shift from public politics to the private sphere as three parallel scenes literally interpellate each of the three sons as family members. In at least two cases, they are called by their father (and king) away from their public duties to the bosom of the family. These simple acts of hailing, "the rituals of ideological recognition" Althusser calls them (117), are thoroughly ideological. The fact that we do not usually think of the act of hailing, of calling a person by her or his name, as ideological speaks to its ideological power. As the film opens, the youngest, Johnny, who is still a boy and still living with his father, is hailed as a soldier as he learns the basics of swordplay from his father; the first words of the film are words of interpellation as Henry calls to John: "Come for me." Both Richard and Geoffrey, however, are hailed as dutiful sons by William Marshal, Henry's messenger,[31] as they engage in public acts of violence on successively increasing scales. In the act of answering Henry's "hail," they cease to be soldiers and potential rulers and become family members, "our boys," a phrase repeated by Henry and Eleanor several times in the film. Richard is engaged in single combat when he is hailed simply by his name, "Richard," repeated twice. Geoffrey is called as he directs a large battle. All of the principals, including Eleanor, called from Salisbury castle, where she has been imprisoned for her rebellions against her husband, understand without being told that they are being called back to court and what that means, although Geoffrey perhaps best articulates it: "Christmas. Warm and rosy time. The hot wine steams, the Yule log roars, and we're the fat that's in the fire."

The opening scenes reveal in a very few strokes the characters of the men who would be king. They contrast John's inept youth and callowness with Richard's neurotic and conflicted bloodthirstiness and Geoffrey's detached indifference.[32] The rest of the film seems designed to explain, in terms of pop psychology, how the family dynamic that Henry and Eleanor have created could have produced such repulsive sons. The scenes that interpellate Richard and Geoffrey are the most interesting because they reverse the usual process, whereby the (male) subject moves from the family to independence in the larger world. Richard and Geoffrey already appear to be fully public personae, so these scenes give us the only glimpse in the film of a public world beyond the claustrophobic atmosphere of Chinon. It is a world of senseless violence. In both cases the audience is offered no indication of the purposes the characters' violent actions serve, no justification for them; it is simply what Richard and Geoffrey do as public figures.

Richard engages in single combat and is about to finish off his opponent. The audience is given no clues about what event precipitated this battle, what offense his opponent has committed that provokes Richard—a legendary chivalric figure—to ignore the injunction to give quarter. Richard begins the scene as an anonymous knight, an inhuman figure in monstrous armor. After he removes his helmet, he is shot in close-up against a crescendo of Latin chanting in the music track. The look he conveys in the close-up is an intensely private one of psychic pain and neurotic angst that contradicts his reputation in the popular imagination as a romantic hero. The next scene provides no information about the battle Geoffrey is directing; we don't know what precipitated it or whether it is just or unjust. The public world of rulers and warfare, politics and diplomacy exists only as a vague backdrop to the film. The movement from the intimacy of the first two scenes—Henry with John and Alais, Richard in single combat—both filmed in tight close-ups with a static camera—to the extreme long shots and sweeping camera work of the battle scene subtly suggests that Geoffrey's calculating indifference may make him more capable of ruling an empire, more his parents' child, "owner of the best brain in a brainy family," than his two brothers, the one vapid and callow, the other too tied up in the relentless pursuit of an old-fashioned and personal kind of chivalry to be an effective ruler. While Geoffrey's cynicism and detachment may not make him a likeable character (is anyone in this film likeable?), his intelligence and understanding of politics enable him to maneuver more skillfully than his brothers in the climate of political intrigue that Henry has created (although to little avail). But such intimations exist only as hints in the film's opening sequence; Harvey's camera is stilled once the film turns to the more claustrophobic Chinon.

Both Henry and Eleanor are also vaguely situated in the public sphere before the film turns to its family drama. Prior to Eleanor's first appearance, her character is suggested by others' references to her, and these references are, by and large, not complimentary. Henry tells Alais, "She is not among the things I love," calling her "the new Medusa," "a gorgon," and "the great bitch." John refuses to "kiss her hairy cheek." Yet the other characters' assessments of her are belied by her arrival at Chinon, a regal performance and perhaps the most lyrical sequence in the film. Eleanor is photographed being rowed on a barge down the river. The queen sits enthroned and smiling as her oarsmen row. The scene is bathed in the golden glow of a wintry sunlight (Anthony Harvey's DVD commentary notes at several points the qualities of the winter light in the south of France where the film was shot). What lends the scene its particular air of lyricism is John Barry's score (for which he won an Oscar), an elegant choral number in a minor key that begins with women's voices in a call and response, modulating at the end into alternating lines of male and female voices. The choral music imitates, and prefigures, the back-and-forth bickering between Henry and Eleanor ("Tusk to tusk through all eternity," Henry says), except that the tone of the music in this scene is elegant and harmonic—regal—rather than petty and shrill.[33] This single sequence, with its visual and musical lyricism, captures Goldman's description of his Eleanor, who is "sixty-one and looks nothing like it. She is a truly handsome woman of great temperament, authority and presence. She has been a queen of international importance for forty-six years and you know it. Finally, she is that most unusual thing: a genuinely feminine woman thoroughly capable of holding her own in a man's world" (11).

Unlike Eleanor, Henry wears his royalty much less comfortably. While he is undoubtedly in his element plotting and scheming as a king, he seems less so putting on the public trappings of royalty. Throughout the film, Henry wears drab brown, rough-looking clothes that seem little more than rags.[34] Only one time in the film does he put on the regalia of a king, and he does so solely for the purposes of show. In the scene immediately following Eleanor's arrival, as the family gathers to meet Philip, the French king, Henry carelessly throws a gilded purple robe over his ragged everyday wear and plops a crown on his head as he goes to receive Philip. Fanfare announces his progress across the courtyard; a crane shot tracks them processing through mud. The ragged crowd that gathers hardly looks more ragged than their king. (Harvey comments that he was trying to create a primitive feel for the film, to suggest the "ghastly conditions" under which even twelfth-century royalty lived.) As soon as the family has reassembled inside the castle, out of the eyes of the public, Henry removes both cloak and crown as quickly as he put them on and unceremoniously lounges in a chair. The gesture highlights his complete cynicism about the mystical trappings of royalty; they are public performance and no part of his personality. Henry's incongruous mixture of sartorial styles and informality contrasts not only with Eleanor's regal bearing but also with Timothy Dalton's Philip, who is always elegantly dressed, with a carefully trimmed beard. "He is tall, well-proportioned and handsome without being at all pretty" (13). The ceremonies of royalty come much more easily to him than to Henry. The English, by contrast, seem like barbarians, as Eleanor notes later to her sons ("It's 1183 and we're all barbarians").[35]

After this brief introduction to the public personae of the main characters, the walls of Chinon castle close in and *The Lion in Winter* becomes exclusively—even relentlessly—a family drama, exposing the convoluted private lives of the Plantagenet family. Of all of the characters in the film, Eleanor and Richard are, in the popular imagination, the most legendary; both are figures of romance and chivalry, Eleanor for her cultivation of courtly love and her flaunting of the conventional roles assigned to women in her age, Richard as a troubadour and crusader.[36] *The Lion in Winter* reweaves legends about the two into its steamy Oedipal drama, deflating their reputations by shrinking them to the domestic sphere of the family. Because the domestic sphere, women's place in the liberal narrative of American culture, provides women more scope for action than the public, the film restores to Eleanor some of the brilliance, denied her in *Becket*, that made her a figure of legend, "a queen of international importance," but it does so at the cost of trivializing her achievements, subordinating them to the Oedipal drama. It is as if between 1964 and 1968 feminism had become enough a part of the American consciousness that it could find its way, at least on a superficial level, into a Hollywood film. However, the simultaneously admiring and patronizing tone of Goldman's stage direction—the rarity of "a genuinely feminine woman thoroughly capable of holding her own in a man's world"—coupled with the cynical use of Alais as a token of exchange among all the men, ensures that Eleanor remains firmly imprisoned within the domestic world of Chinon. The person who relates Eleanor's legendary feats—her adventures on crusade with her first husband Louis, for instance—is Eleanor herself, and, even she is as often ironic as nostalgic about them. "Be sure to squint as you approach," she tells Geoffrey. "You may be blinded by my beauty."

The scenes between Eleanor and Richard seem more Freud's than Shakespeare's *Hamlet*'s. In one of their first exchanges, which takes place in an enclosed garden outside the castle, mother and son lacerate each other like a pair of jilted lovers, ending the scene in a lovers' clinch. "I loved you more than Henry," Eleanor tells him. "Don't you remember how you loved me? We were always hand in hand." But even in these moments the Oedipal drama is never simple; glimpses emerge of other agendas. Even in private, Eleanor is always onstage, always performing her public persona. When she says, "I want us back the way we were," Richard challenges her sincerity, and she admits, "I want the Aquitaine." "That's the mother I remember," he rejoins. Eleanor's performance in this scene, as Tolhurst has shown, depends on the invocation of her literary reputation. "I had, at one time, many appetites. I wanted poetry and power and the young men who created them both. . . . I taught you dancing, too, and languages and all the music that I knew and how to love what's beautiful." In the domestic world of Chinon castle, however, the performances of legend ring hollow; the myths seem more like tawdry melodrama than romance or legend.

Aristotle gave the term *peripeteia* to the sudden reversal of fortune on which tragedy turns. *The Lion in Winter*, far from turning on a single peripeteia, is composed of a series of such reversals that function less to reveal some truth about the tangle of political and familial relationships than to confuse and obscure further the players' motives. This dynamic is clearly at work in the relationship between Henry and Eleanor, a volatile mixture of love and loathing. The two seem at times to relish their quarrels, and Hepburn and O'Toole deliver their lines with irony and zest. Their scenes together are mercurial. A single scene, such as their initial exchange by the Christmas tree, moves with lightning quickness from good-natured bickering to anger and recrimination, to bitter irony, to pain, to triumph. Its multiple peripeteias turn on a dime as the advantage moves from one to the other. Fortunately, Harvey had the good sense to allow the language of Goldman's script and his actors to carry sequences like this one, adopting an austere visual style that relies on the actors—especially O'Toole and Hepburn—rather than his camera to convey the energy and action.[37] Actors move in and out of shots while the camera remains stationary. More than seven minutes long, the entire sequence contains only fourteen shots. Long takes with very little camera movement give the actors time to deliver complete speeches. There is one shot of Hepburn, in which she reminisces about going on crusade, that is a minute and a half long, and although the shot registers several shifts in tone, she never moves. The effect is mesmerizing. Harvey tends more often to frame his stars in two-shots, an important tactic that allows the audience to track the rapid shifts in mood and tone because they have simultaneous access both to the speeches and to the other character's reactions. This is significant because the scene's action is structured around two sudden reversals. At one point Eleanor believes she has beaten Henry: "I'm like the earth, old man; there isn't any way around me." Henry replies that he has an offer: "Your freedom." The two words stop her cold, generating a moment of utter silence in a talky scene. Later, after Eleanor appears to have capitulated to Henry's demands in order to win her freedom from imprisonment, he enjoys his triumph. Eleanor tells him she'll sign away the Aquitaine on one condition. "Have the wedding now." Again the simple declarative sentence stops the action and signals the reversal. This time it is Henry who is brought up short. These kinds of sudden reversals of fortune occur with such frequency in the film that by the end the maneuvering seems to lose all sense of purpose. There is no endgame, no final winners or losers, only strategy for the sheer pleasure of it. The implication is that this one-upmanship will continue indefinitely, one party besting the other and then in turn being bested.

If lust for power seems the characters' primary motivation, lust, in good Freudian fashion, seems on the surface to be the explanation. Sex, in Freud's account, shapes the individual exclusively in the private sphere, and in this film all of the relationships are sexually charged: "Such, my angels, is the role of sex in history," Eleanor tells her sons. By his own admission, Henry's sexual appetites are voracious: "In my time, I've known contessas, milkmaids, courtesans and novices, whores, gypsies, jades, and little boys." When Eleanor accuses him of having had "countless" others, he accuses her of being equally catholic in her tastes: "What's your count? Let's have the tally of the bedspreads you've spread out on." Incest—or the threat of it—lurks always near the surface. An absent father—"You never called for me. You never said my name"—and a steamy relationship with his mother seems to explain Richard's neuroses: both his propensity for violence—"I follow all your slaughters from a distance," Eleanor tells him—and his homosexuality.[38] The incest seems to be multigenerational, extending to Eleanor's relationship with her father-in-law. "Did your father sleep with me or didn't he," Eleanor asks Henry as he threatens to have her sons locked up in Chinon while he seeks an annulment of his marriage to her. "Would it upset you?" And Henry seems genuinely devastated by the thought that forty years earlier Eleanor may have slept with his father.

Sex is the weapon the characters wield against one another in their political squabbling. However, it is at once result *and* cause of their grievances. It shapes their political strategies and yet appears to generate a surplus—what Žižek would call a symptom—beyond its effectiveness as a political strategy. While psychoanalysis is a "hermeneutic of suspicion," in which the analytic work is supposed to reveal truths hidden by the "symptom," in this film, revelation conceals and concealment reveals. Misrecognition structures every encounter.

In the climactic sequence of the film all four of the Plantagenet men are gathered together in Philip's bedroom. This remarkable and remarkably Shakespearean scene, by revealing that what all the men truly desire is not Alais, and not the Vexin, but Philip, exposes the homoerotic underpinnings of the sexual exchange of women that has seemed to drive the film up to this point. Concealment becomes the mechanism for revelation. As each of the men furtively enters Philip's room to meet with him in secret, someone else is revealed to be hiding. Geoffrey arrives first to plot, but John is revealed already to be hiding behind Philip's tapestry. Richard's entrance sends Geoffrey and John to hide behind the tapestry yet again ("That's what tapestries are for," Philip remarks). Just as Richard and Philip conclude what can only be described as their love scene and retire to the bed, Henry knocks, sending Richard to hide in the bed curtains. The austerity of Harvey's camera work conceals his skillful direction of this complex scene, which could easily appear stagey. Harvey is able to realize what is cinematographic about the mise-en-scène. His task is to keep all five men alive in the scene, reminding the audience that they are all voyeuristically spying on one another. In a film in which constant revelation seems to conceal all meaning, he creates a scene in which revelation results precisely from concealment.

In the final analysis, however, we never know whether someone is lying or telling the truth. There is no way of telling what anyone's "true" feelings are, so that the film's vague psychoanalytic framework, rather than revealing all, conceals all. There are no official markers of what constitutes truth; information is always held within private exchanges. If Eleanor is, as Tolhurst describes her, the "queen of losses," she is hardly alone in this regard. Despite all of the intrigue and plotting, no one in the film seems to win; everyone seems finally to lose, or rather nothing seems to be decided, not Henry's successor, Richard's marriage, Eleanor's imprisonment, not John's, Geoffrey's, or Alais's fates. The film ends in a draw, with all outcomes deferred until Easter.

The Lion in Winter's relocation of the public personae of its royals to the domestic sphere may well reflect Great Britain's attitudes toward its own monarchy during the political turbulence of the 1960s. In a decade marked by social, political, and economic upheavals, in which the established order was being challenged on all fronts, there was a marked move in the representations of government and politics away from the public and toward the private. Britain in many ways led the field in the journalistic trend toward the scrutiny of politicians' private lives. In 1963, at a time when the American president's sexual exploits were a carefully guarded secret, the scandal of John Profumo's affair with Christine Keeler nearly brought down Harold McMillan's government, forcing him to resign and setting up Harold Wilson's Labour victory in 1964. The shock waves of that scandal paved the way for increasing press scrutiny of public figures' private lives, setting the stage for the royal scandals of the 1980s and 1990s. By midcentury, the monarchy was losing popularity; its most significant role in the modern world seemed to be to promote national identity. The monarch, according to a 1961 speech by Charles de Gaulle, should be "the person by whose presence and dignity, national unity is sustained" (Aronstein, "The Violence Inherent in the System"). The monarchy's role in legitimating Britain's colonial interests abroad and class privilege at home, however, made it seem increasingly "irrelevant and expensive" in the antiestablishment 1960s. Many were calling for an end to an obsolescent institution. The royal family responded to the threat by launching a public relations campaign that veered between portraying the royals as the "quintessential middle-class family," as in the 1969 BBC documentary *Royal Family,* and making them the center of huge and hugely expensive displays of grandeur and fairy-tale splendor, as in the 1969 Investiture of Prince Charles at Caernarvon (Cannadine, 135). Little wonder that *The Lion in Winter*'s antimedievalism, its attempt to show the Middle Ages as barbaric and lacking in any rational political process, relegates its royal family to the private sphere of the home, the family, and the sex scandal. Goldman got his royals exactly right, at least as far as the modern-day monarchy is concerned. In a world where monarchs no longer rule, they have been reduced either to icons of domestic rectitude or fodder for the tabloids, which is simply the obverse of the same psychoanalytic coin.

None of the films we have discussed in this chapter entirely succeed in portraying governance during a time of nascent capitalism, when far-reaching policies might be affected by personal relationships between patrons and clients, one-on-one relationships—forged through the circulation of "gifts"—creating psychological, social, economic, and political attachments in the public sphere. It is, perhaps, inevitable that contemporary cinema would resist the sort of didacticism necessary to explain how closely interconnected familial and personal bonds—relationships fusing and confusing the private and public definitions of "love"—were to affairs of state during the Middle Ages. What makes *Becket* and *The Lion in Winter* important is not their historical accuracy. Neither is any more accurate than Boorman's film, nor than *Monty Python and the Holy Grail* for that matter. What makes these films interesting dramatically (both are based on successful plays) are the ways in which they complicate medieval political theory by showing us political practice at the level of the nuclear family. They reveal the complex intersections of the medieval with the modern, a practice that sometimes creates stunning anachronism but sometimes also stunning effects. Where these films show their limitations is their inability to extend the scope of their drama, to show the associations between the politics of friendship and family and the politics of governance—to show why Becket, Henry II, Eleanor, Richard, and John were of consequence both within their own time and historically. In our next chapter we will discuss Carl Dreyer's *La Passion de Jeanne d'Arc,* Victor Fleming's *Joan of Arc,* and Luc Besson's *The Messenger,* movies that struggle, in very conscious ways, to explore the tensions between public and private spheres. We will consider how these movies imagine the contestation between the various machines of medieval governance—the church and the state—and how one young girl from Domrémy, France, so exacerbated this contestation as to subvert the authority of both institutions.

Chapter Five

The Politics of Hagiography

Joan of Arc on the Screen

n season six of the cult series *Buffy the Vampire Slayer,* in the episode called "Tabula Rasa," the "tough girl" character, Buffy, waking up with amnesia, decides that her name must be "Joan." No comment is given. The name alone is enough to conjure up images of the chosen one, the "warrior of the people." There is no need for any narrative explanation because Joan of Arc is a part of the cultural literacy of most television viewers. This example suggests the extent to which the story of Joan of Arc permeates American popular culture.[1] She has been, in particular, a rich source of inspiration for filmmakers almost from the inception of the industry. Beginning with Georges Méliès's 1897 *Jeanne d'Arc,* there have been no fewer than fourteen screen adaptations of the saint's life in English, French, German, and Italian (Harty, "Jeanne au cinéma," 237). However, throughout the twentieth century and the twenty-first, if she has been a popular figure, Joan of Arc has also been an ambiguous one in the popular imagination, the meanings attached to her life shifting and unstable. George Bernard Shaw referred to her as "the queerest fish among the eccentric worthies of the Middle Ages" (*Saint Joan,* v). In the early part of the century in the years leading up to her canonization by the Catholic Church (1920), her story provided a conflicted *mythomoteur,* what Anthony Smith has called "the constitutive myth of the ethnic polity" (A. Smith, 15) for French nationalism. Even today in France it fuels racist and xenophobic fantasies of right-wing politicians like Jean-Marie Le Pen.

Joan has been used both to support traditional gender expectations for women and to defy them. At the 2004 March for Women's Lives in Washington, D.C., a prolife placard could proclaim Joan's conservative orthodoxy: "Joan of Arc led men through inspiration, not through feminization." Similarly a California woman, Frances Marie Klug, claims to receive revelations from Saint Joan and regularly publishes them on the Internet.[2] And yet, because she challenged the rigid gender roles of her time that excluded women from participation in the affairs of state, Joan has also become a latter-day feminist heroine.[3] Her defiant cross-dressing has also made her a symbol for lesbian and transgendered communities (see Feinberg, 3–37). The transcript of her trial describes this "feminist" presumptuousness: "wholly forgetful of womanly honesty, and having thrown off the bonds of shame, careless of all the modesty of womankind, she wore with an astonishing and monstrous brazenness, immodest garments belonging to the male sex" (Barrett, 3).

Joan of Arc: poster girl for women's liberation or avatar of racial purity and nationalist cant? The contradictions in her story—a radical fighter for a reactionary cause—make her a fascinating figure in the history of film. This chapter, drawing primarily on three Joan of Arc films—Carl Theodor Dreyer's *La Passion de Jeanne d'Arc,* Victor Fleming's *Joan of Arc,* and Luc Besson's *The Messenger*—examines what these films reveal about the politics of hagiography, by which phrase we mean not the self-evident nature of the saint's sanctification (the ostensible subject of most hagiography) but the messiness of the process of creating a saint—the patronage, conflict, opposition, persecution, trial, ridicule, behind-the-scenes maneuvering, and danger that follow in the wake of audacious claims to sanctity such as those made by Joan. The creation of a saint—whether Christian, nationalist, or feminist—is plagued by such conflicts. Hagiographies—the stories that we tell about our saints—are designed to cover over those conflicts. In traditional hagiographies, including those created by the film industry, saints seem always already holy. Whatever trials or tribulations they might suffer, their beatification seems a foregone conclusion that follows from their lives; we are never allowed to doubt their sanctity. But frequently, and especially in the Middle Ages, the difference between a canonized saint and a rabble-rousing heretic burnt at the stake is, as in Joan's case, more often than not a matter of politics and patronage. A mere two years after the French poet Christine de Pisan was comparing Joan to such Christian and classical worthies as Moses, Joshua, Gideon, Esther, Judith, Deborah, Hector, and Achilles (see *Ditié de Jehanne d'Arc*), this woman warrior was burned at the stake as a heretic. Less than a quarter century after that, she was being rehabilitated by the same church that had condemned her. In the nineteenth century Joan seemed as likely to be canonized as Christopher Columbus, whose canonization proceedings began at about the same time as hers (his began in 1873; see Henry Kelly, 208). The fifty years between 1869 and 1920, during which Joan's sanctity was debated, were marked by growing nationalism in France and animosity between its socialist government and the Vatican and interrupted by a world war fought in the name of those nationalisms.[4] Throughout the twentieth century, the appropriation of "Saint Joan" as a cultural icon was, as Robin Blaetz demonstrates in her book on Joan of Arc in American culture, accompanied by ideological contestation. The readings of cinematic hagiographies of St. Joan in this chapter attempt to restore to the idea of sainthood the politics that inform the process. We are interested in what these films reveal about the politics of church and state, particularly those of the Catholic Church at various historical moments: the canonization process and conflicts between the Vatican and the socialist governments of France in the early years of the twentieth century, the politics of censorship led in the United States by the Catholic Church's Legion of Decency in the immediate postwar era, and the cultural influence of fundamentalist splinter groups at the end of the twentieth century. We will examine the ways in which the films sometimes repress and sometimes highlight these politics.

Whatever the politics of the films about Joan we examine in this chapter, the Middle Ages functions in them as a backdrop of intolerance, religious bigotry, and barbarism against which Joan's liberal virtues stand out in sharp relief. These films give us the atavistic Middle Ages, not the nostalgic ones. Joan is the lone hero who stands against establishments (church and state) that have grown corrupt, complacent, and self-interested. The Middle Ages becomes the icon of that corruption. As such, all of these films represent Joan as pointing the way out of a dark age of intolerance toward a more enlightened future, the future of the here and now. Joan of Arc is the hero called forth by nationalism, which requires her sacrifice to lay the ground for the imagined community of the nation. Ironically, this places this most radical of figures—the woman warrior—into the most conservative of plots. Matt Groening's Lisa Simpson articulates this point when, as Joan of Arc in "Tales from the Public Domain," she expresses the fear that English "individual rights" could "undermine the rule of our beloved tyrant." The historical Joan of Arc fought on the side of absolutism and the divine right of kings, principles that were swept away by the French Revolution. But as the French historian Michel Winock writes, "Joan of Arc did not disappear from history when she was burned at the stake in Rouen. . . . She became symbolic as a historical subject, as one of the things at stake in the partisan war waged by French ideologues, especially since the end of the nineteenth century" (Winock, 103). In the nineteenth century the cause of Joan's canonization was resurrected, by ideologues of both right and left, in the service of French nationalism.[5]

The three decades of the new century leading up to the 1928 release of Carl Theodor Dreyer's *La Passion de Jeanne d'Arc* were marked in France by particularly acrimonious and often violent confrontations between various political factions over Joan's legacy. For protofascist and antirepublican groups like Action Française (an anti-Semitic group founded in 1899 in the wake of the Dreyfus affair and popular among French Catholics), "Joan was the symbol of the absolute authority of the state, as represented by the king whom she had so faithfully served, whatever his shortcomings" (Warner, 260). The Thalamas affair, coming so quickly on the heels of the infamous Dreyfus trials,[6] further polarized these nationalist conflicts, creating a set of equivalences that allied Joan uncomfortably with French anti-Semitism. François Thalamas was a twelfth-grade teacher at the Lycée Condorcet who expressed to his class doubts about Joan's sanctity (a topic that was, after all, being vigorously debated at the time by the Vatican). Specifically, he argued that Joan did not actually fight; she was a mascot, and because she was most likely raped in prison, she did not die a virgin (Margolis, 278).[7] Though dismissed from his teaching post, four years later when he was authorized to give a series of lectures at the Sorbonne, street thugs connected with Action Française (Weber describes these *camelots du Roi* as the "storm troops of the Action Française" [69]) began a systematic campaign of terror: "Thalamas was beaten up; Jewish lecturers were prevented from reaching their classrooms; riots broke out between police and students through the winter of 1908 – 9. . . . There were other disturbances, particularly around Joan's statue in the Place des Pyramides" (Warner, 262; see also Winock, 105; Margolis, 278).

At the same time, for French Catholics Joan's canonization represented a means of mending the rift between the French socialist government and the Vatican over the disestablishment of the church in 1905. In fact, in 1920, the same year as Joan's canonization, the papal nuncio returned to Paris after a sixteen-year absence. As late as 1929, a year after the release of Dreyer's film, elaborate preparations were required at the fifth centennial of the relief of Orléans to keep the papal legate and the president of the Republic physically separated during the ceremonies (Warner, 256, 264–65). The president, however, signaled a spirit of reconciliation between the Vatican and the French state when he sought out the legate and told him that France "rejoices . . . in Joan of Arc who is at once a national heroine and a saint of the Church, to find again its traditions, national and Christian" (Warner, 265).

Dreyer's Theater of Cruelty

It was into this troubled political climate that *La Passion de Jeanne d'Arc* was released. Although its director, Carl Theodor Dreyer, was Danish, the film was financed by the Parisian Société Générale de Films. Dreyer's film, now considered a classic of the silent cinema, was by no means intended as a political film. Yet, given the choice of subject and the political climate of the decade, Dreyer could hardly hope, even as late as 1928, to steer clear of the controversies that swirled around the saint's canonization and appropriation as a symbol of French nationalism. Dreyer's intense focus on Jeanne's trial and subsequent execution and his exclusion of her military exploits ensured that the film would be controversial. Some of that controversy is suggested by the fact that the film was banned in England supposedly for its anti-English sentiments (perhaps because the uniforms of the British soldiers, according to one review, "curiously and unnecessarily resemble those of British soldiers in the late European war" [W. L. Middleton, 7]). In France, after its release, the archbishop of Paris demanded Dreyer cut several scenes, and his distributors complied without consulting him (*New York Times* review, Jan. 20, 1929; Bordwell, *Filmguide to "La passion de Jeanne d'Arc,"* 19). Right-wing reviewers, believing that Dreyer, as a foreigner, could hardly hope to capture the spirit of France that Jeanne represented, panned the film. It was not a financial success. Ironically, the same year saw the release of another film about the saint, *La Merveilleuse vie de Jeanne d'Arc,* directed by Marco DeGastyne. This film includes spectacular battle scenes, employing French troops as extras, and a magnificent coronation procession shot inside the newly restored Reims Cathedral. This film, unlike Dreyer's, was a commercial success and must have been far more satisfying to those promoting Jeanne's role as "the heart of France" (Dreyer, *Four Screenplays,* 76) and its national hero (see Harty, "Jeanne au cinéma," 246–47).

Much of the critical response to *La Passion de Jeanne d'Arc* has focused either on the film's formal experimentation or on the problem of establishing a reliable text of the film from among the five surviving key prints rather than on its participation in the politics of creating Jeanne's hagiography.[8] But closer attention to the critical vocabulary used to describe the film's formal features may point us toward its place in the social and political upheavals of its time. David Bordwell's analysis in *The Films of Carl-Theodor Dreyer* is representative of formal accounts of this film, which tend to treat it reverently as an art or avant-garde film. For Bordwell the film challenges virtually all of the conventions of filmmaking. It "deforms" and "ruptures" classical norms. Its "compositions swing radically, almost madly, out of balance." It "fails to stick together the film's narrative space in a coherent manner." It represents a "challenge to continuity editing" by denying viewers establishing shots. Through its editing practices "uncertainty bleeds across the cuts." Bordwell speaks of the film's "gaps and dislocations," "estranging features," "distortions," inconsistency, ambiguity, and "absence of firm certainties." Its camera angles are "contorted and awry," "skewed," "tilted or canted," "impossible," "oblique." The space of the film is "gravityless," "emptied out," "warped," "distorted and derealized," "impossible," "discontinuous," "virtually illegible." Its framings are "eccentric," "unbalanced," "decentered." Finally, movement is "gratuitous," "eccentric," "disorienting," and "bizarre" (66–80).

There is a certain consistency to Bordwell's characterization of Dreyer's film; he stresses distortion in the film's chronotope: its representation of a warped time and space, achieved through the techniques of film production—editing, camera angles and movement, lighting, mise-en-scène. But what is all of this disorientation and discontinuity in the service of? The film is not simply an artistic experiment for its own sake, as Bordwell suggests;[9] in fact, Dreyer denied that his film was avant-garde in any way, insisting that it was intended to appeal to a wide audience. Popular audiences, at least in the United States, have by and large been unwilling to accept bizarre camera work in the form of avant-garde experimentation but will accept almost any strange trick of the camera if it serves a clear narrative or special-effects function.[10] Unless we are to believe that he was simply creating a film experiment for its own sake (again, a goal he denied), we must assume that Dreyer had some reason for presenting a world so seriously out of joint. An example from the film may demonstrate this point more clearly.

Toward the end of the film, just before Jeanne's execution, there are two famous shots. The first shows a group of soldiers filmed from overhead so that as they enter the frame from the bottom, they appear upside down. As they march toward the upper edge of the frame, they are slowly viewed from directly above; just as they are about to exit the frame, the camera, which until this point has been stationary, tilts to track their forward progress and comes to rest on the portcullis and the gathering crowd behind it. Later, a similar shot inverts the point of view. In this shot, as the crowd disperses through the gateway, the camera views them from directly below, literally under their feet. Bordwell argues, reasonably enough, that these are not point-of-view shots. Unlike the expressionist camera work of German filmmakers in the 1920s, these shots express no single character's subjectivity, which was the point of expressionist camera work. But what purpose, then, do these shots serve? Bordwell can only answer this question in terms of technical experimentation: "The unmotivated inversions of the camera mark the paroxysmic culmination of the film's search for camera movement which dissolves the classical scenographic space and the stability of the viewer's vantage point" (*The Films of Carl-Theodor Dreyer*, 77). These shots, he seems to argue, are the culmination of Dreyer's search for a means of disrupting filmic space, an interpretation that aligns Dreyer's camera work with avant-garde experimentation. But we might ask, again and more insistently, whether this camera work serves any narrative function? If the camera movement does not express a subjective point of view, neither does it show objective reality. Rather, we would argue, it shows the subjectivity of the social formation—a world (literally) turned upside down. The isolation, despair, and lack of moral certainties that mark Jeanne's experiences with her judges finds its objective correlative in Dreyer's camera work. But is this upside-down world the world of fifteenth-century or of interwar France?

Other framing techniques in the film may provide some purchase on this question. Although details of setting and costume were meticulously researched and reproduced in the film, the audience frequently does not see the results of that research because of the way Dreyer frames his subjects. Dreyer had a large and realistic set built for the film—the most expensive ever made for a French film at the time—but little of it is shown onscreen (a fact that annoyed his producers, given the cost of the film; Bordwell, *Filmguide to "La Passion de Jeanne d'Arc,"* 17, 20). Dreyer insisted that his fifteenth century is historically accurate, although the film presents few of the signs of medievalness that we examined in chapter 2; there is little filth, only stylized armor, the carefully maintained tonsures of the priests are often covered with skullcaps. The film opens with a shot of a manuscript, the transcript of Jeanne's trial, presumably to add a kind of documentary authenticity. Yet the very plainness of the particular manuscript, which lacks illumination and is in a relatively unadorned hand, fails to provide a visual sign of the medieval in the same way that the often luxurious manuscripts do in Terry Jones's documentary *The Crusades*. Dreyer's technique in the film works against establishing a clear historical chronotope of the Middle Ages; rather, it tends to encourage a blending together of different historical moments, suggesting a conflation of Jeanne's fifteenth- and early-twentieth-century trials. The soldiers' uniforms, for instance, are accurate representations of fifteenth-century armor, but the helmets also look like those worn by British soldiers during World War I.

In fact, Dreyer takes his subjects out of history altogether. In his own writing on film Dreyer called this technique "abstraction," arguing that the film director must replace "objective reality with his own subjective interpretation." Dreyer argues that the film artist must "abstract himself from reality in order to strengthen the spiritual content of his work. More concisely, the artist must describe inner, not outer, life. The capacity to abstract is essential to all artistic creation. Abstraction allows the director to get outside the fence with which naturalism has surrounded his medium. It allows his films to be not merely visual, but spiritual" ("Thoughts on My Craft," 314–15).

Dreyer achieves this "simplification" by stripping away "all the accretions of props, make-up, costumes, and all the other paraphernalia that traditionally go into an historical costume drama. In this way, the audience is forced to focus on the actors' facial expressions and gestures" (Aberth, 279–80).[11] Even in medium and long shots, characters are often filmed against the backdrop of a white wall or the sky so that they appear without a spatial context to anchor them. When visual cues are present, they are frequently distorted and misleading. Dreyer tends to isolate individuals within the frame, denying them any spatial, and thus any historical, context and reinforcing the spiritual isolation and alienation of individuals in the world of the film, which might be located historically anywhere.

The film's art of abstraction, however, is not simply an aesthetic choice. It also has the effect of collapsing the distinction between the fifteenth century and the early decades of the twentieth, both historical periods that experienced the social disruptions of war, disease, political instability, and economic crisis. *La Passion de Jeanne d'Arc* belongs as much to the interwar generation as to the Middle Ages. This generation, which came of age between the two world wars, was not unacquainted with social disorder. Buffeted by the horrors of war, mass death, and economic collapse on a worldwide scale, this generation experienced a world bereft of the moral certainties of the past, a world in which millions had died fighting a war in the name of the nationalism that Jeanne's cause came to represent and in which millions more would soon be eliminated in the name of racial purity that Jeanne's right-wing French apologists promoted. For this reason Dreyer's decision to film only the trial and execution and to eliminate the military exploits cannot be viewed apart from the nationalist politics of early-twentieth-century France. Dreyer makes a choice to represent in his film the existential drama of the individual cut loose from the traditional kinds of communities that would sustain her.

To be sure, Dreyer's vision is as much religious as political. The term *passion* in the title refers unequivocally to the suffering and death of Christ, and the film's iconography connects Jeanne's suffering to his.[12] Dreyer's Jeanne is a saint and martyr, not a military hero. Dreyer has excised everything from her story but the means of her death. There are no glorious battles, no coronations, no nullification trial; there is not even really an apotheosis in the end. There is finally only Jeanne alone, despised, spat upon, brutally tortured, suffering an unimaginably cruel death. And this is perhaps the genius of the film, this intense concentration on the hero's existential suffering. *La Passion de Jeanne d'Arc* is an extremely bleak religious vision, perhaps finally even bleaker than Bergman's. In *The Seventh Seal* at least we are afforded the "holy family" of Jos, Mia, and their baby at the end of the film, representing community, salvation, and resurrection as a counter to Antonius Block's dour existentialism. In *La Passion de Jeanne d'Arc*, Jeanne is not the apotheosis of the French nation, which perhaps explains why many right-wing critics disliked the film (Tybjerg, DVD commentary). She is a lone woman—the only character named in the film—facing her anonymous judges, powerless to do more than passively provoke her own execution.[13]

Dreyer suggests the intensity of Jeanne's suffering through his powerful use of the close-up, the technique most closely associated with this film:

> My idea of telling the passion of Jeanne in close-up did not fit into the framework of what was then understood as a "normal film." It was an unwritten law that the individual close-up had to be part of the harmonious unity of the long shot and at the same time a detail in the pattern of the plot. Then my aggressive close-ups appeared, jumping unannounced on the screen and demanding the right to an independent existence. Close-up after close-up demanded space with no concern for the "harmonious" unity of the long shot—all those close-ups, close-ups that behaved like a flock of noisy troublemakers—but which are very useful not only because they made it possible for me to bring the audience very near to the physical and mental torture that Jeanne suffered but also because they showed how her judges and tormenters reacted to her tears. (quoted in Bordwell, *The Films of Carl-Theodor Dreyer*, 235n4)

What makes Dreyer's use of the close-up different from that of, say, D. W. Griffith (P. Cohen, 115–21) is his break with traditional practices of continuity editing, particularly his severing of the close-up from the "harmonious unity" of the long shot that provided the spatial cues for reading the close-up. This technique serves several functions in the film. The constant barrage of close-ups detached from longer establishing shots isolates individuals, especially Jeanne, underscoring their alienation from one another. We are generally not allowed to see characters together in longer shots; we don't know their relations in space to one another, and this increases the sense of dislocation and fragmentation. At times, we cannot even tell if characters are in the same location or not. This is especially true of the scene, early in the film after the first interrogation, that crosscuts between the judges forging the letter from Charles and Jeanne in her cell. Although these two actions do not take place in the same room, the paucity of spatial cues creates some confusion. The close-ups are powerful tools in creating the sense of isolation and alienation that is central to the film's existential view of the atomized individual cut off from sources of community.

The close-ups also encourage us to explore the geography of the face. They powerfully disrupt the techniques for looking—or at least the theoretical paradigm that for the last three decades has interpreted those techniques—established by classical narrative cinema. Those techniques were described by Laura Mulvey in her influential *Screen* essay "Visual Pleasure and Narrative Cinema" and have been continuously debated by film theorists since its appearance in 1975.[14] Mulvey describes a semiotics of the gaze in which looking is active and male, while being looked at is passive and female. In visual representations ranging from classical painting to contemporary film, man is the bearer of the look and woman is the object of that look. Drawing on the visual apparatus produced by Renaissance perspective, this gendered theory of the gaze posits a psychic apparatus that "positions the spectator, on this side of the screen, as the mirror of the vanishing point on the other side" (Doane, "Remembering Women," 51). The mirroring between these two points stabilizes the representational logic, "producing its readability, which is coincident with the notions of unity, coherency, and mastery" (51). The gaze that emanates from this point is the possession of the camera and, through identification with that position, of the spectating subject. In the work of psychoanalytic film critics the gaze works in the service of voyeurism. This geometric perspective maps space in the service of control, possession, and mastery of the objects under scrutiny. Several techniques of narrative cinema are designed to position the female body as a spectacle. These include the fragmentation of the female body into parts, makeup, the glamour shot, soft focus, the practice of putting Vaseline or gauze over the camera lens, particular kinds of lighting—especially soft lighting—and the star system itself, which creates iconic female stars to be gazed at, as well as whole armies of anonymous starlets whose purpose is to present themselves as spectacles.[15]

This theoretical paradigm of the male gaze has come under criticism from several quarters;[16] however, it does offer a way of understanding Dreyer's challenges to conventional methods of representing femininity. Dreyer avoids all of the techniques designed to display the female body as a passive object to be consumed, stripping his female lead of all the trappings of glamour. The extremity of his method is perhaps best illustrated by the cutting of his actress's hair, a moment Bordwell describes, perhaps hyperbolically, as "one of the most memorable moments in film history." We quote at length to give a sense of how radical Dreyer's contemporaries found his methods:

> In the silence of an operating room, in the pale light of the morning of the execution, Dreyer had [Renée] Falconetti's hair shaved. Although we had lost old prejudices [against short hair on women], we were as moved as if the infamous mark were being made there, in reality. The electricians and technicians held their breaths and their eyes filled with tears. Falconetti wept real tears. Then the director slowly approached her, gathered up some of her tears in his fingers, and carried them to his lips.[17]

But his boldest move—the one most frequently commented upon at the time—was to film without using any makeup. The development and affordability of panchromatic film stock—film capable of picking up the entire color spectrum—made it possible for Dreyer to do this (Bordwell and Thompson, 152–53). Orthochromatic film, used mostly on films before the mid-1920s, required heavy makeup to register skin tones properly. The bare faces in *La Passion de Jeanne d'Arc* make it a study in pain and the inflicting of pain. Her judges confront us like so many medieval gargoyles. In tight close-ups we see every crevice, every wart, every sneer. Jeanne's mental anguish is etched on her face, however, not on her body, which is only rarely shown in the film and which carries little visual interest. A close-up of a single tear running down Falconetti's cheek brings the viewer intimately into Jeanne's suffering in ways that all the histrionics of silent film acting could never accomplish.[18]

A brief comparison might illuminate Dreyer's art in this film, especially his manipulation of the gaze. The only other Joan of Arc film that limits its narrative to the trial is *Procès de Jeanne d'Arc*, released in 1962 by the French New Wave filmmaker Robert Bresson. The biggest difference between the two films is not, as one might expect, the addition of sound and color. Rather, Bresson's film uses almost exclusively medium to long shots and a fairly stationary camera. His technique focuses viewers' attention on the verbal exchanges between Jeanne and her judges but in a way that distances them and us from Jeanne's suffering, creating a kind of visual objectivity that contrasts with Dreyer's technique. Yet, like Dreyer, he does not allow the audience to become complacent about the power afforded by such a gaze. At key moments in the film he calls the mechanics of the gaze into question, stripping at least temporarily the power of the gaze. In both films there are shots in which the audience is positioned with Jeanne's judges, who peep at her through a peephole or crack in her prison wall. These shots allude to the mastery and possession of the male gaze at the same time they undercut it. They suggest, as Slavoj Žižek has argued, that the "dialectic of gaze and power" posited by feminist film theory is more complex than is usually allowed: "the gaze does connote power, yet simultaneously, and at a more fundamental level, it connotes the very opposite of power—*impotence*—in so far as it involves the position of an immobilized witness who cannot but observe what goes on" (*The Metastases of Enjoyment*, 73). Although the judges have control over Jeanne's body to the extent that they can spy on her and even have her burnt at the stake, ultimately they are powerless before what Žižek would call her *jouissance*, her refusal to subordinate her desire to the law as represented by the church (*The Metastases of Enjoyment*, 65–70).

In stripping away all glamour from his actress's performance, Dreyer comes closest to realizing artistically what George Bernard Shaw in 1924 understood was fundamental to representations of the newly canonized woman warrior of France. Joan should not be beautiful in the way that screen actresses typically are. Shaw writes, "Any book about Joan which begins by describing her as a beauty may be at once classed as a romance. Not one of Joan's comrades, in village, court, or camp, even when they were straining themselves to please the king by praising her, ever claimed that she was pretty. All the men who alluded to the matter declared most emphatically that she was unattractive sexually to a degree that seemed to them miraculous, considering that she was in the bloom of youth, and neither ugly, awkward, deformed, nor unpleasant in her person" (*Saint Joan*, xiii). A *New York Times* review describes Falconetti's success in achieving this vision: "Not a pretty heroine, but a rather stupid, short haired peasant maid, with a face supernaturally illuminated by faith, with lips parched through excitement and with a pair of eyes that see Heaven opening before them. An uncannily realistic spirit of the Middle Ages shines in these miens" (Jan. 20, 1929).

Dreyer's use of the close-up to represent Jeanne blends the medieval "eye of piety" (*oculis pietatis*; Stanbury, "Regimes of the Visual in Premodern England," 267) with what Paula Cohen has called, in reference to D. W. Griffith's close-ups of Lillian Gish, "existential exposure" (124).[19] One problem with psychoanalytic theories of the gaze, as Sarah Stanbury has noted, is that this visual regime, because it is based exclusively on the visual experiences of the modern, may be "unable or unwilling to address the medieval origins of later structures of visuality" ("Regimes of the Visual," 263). Medieval religious painting developed its own hermeneutics for structuring the gaze and these structures have found their way into the iconography of much conventional postmedieval religious art. Medieval religious art developed a "fluid set of gazes" that fracture distance, "fusing self with the object of devotional desire in a hybridized mix of maternal, infantile, and erotic impulses." These gazes are not unidirectional but "intersubjective, specular, and emotional" (267–68). If modern theories of the gaze work toward objectification and distance (sadism), the medieval religious gaze functioned to create empathy.[20] Furthermore, in medieval religious art, as Sarah Stanbury, Sarah Beckwith, and others have noted, "the body that consistently focuses a collective gaze through its display before a crowd" is not the female body but the body of the crucified Christ (265), so this gaze tends to disrupt conventional signs of gender, as well as those of objectivity and distance.

This "visual hermeneutic" is present not only in medieval religious art, as Stanbury demonstrates, but in its modern equivalents as well, and Dreyer exploits this hermeneutic in filming his Jeanne by inviting viewers to gaze on Jeanne as they would on the crucified Christ. At times Dreyer's images call to mind the kinds of popular religious ephemera still very much in circulation today—but with an existential twist. Often close-ups of Falconetti resemble nothing so much as Catholic holy cards (Figure 5).[21] The image of Christ crowned with thorns suggests at least the kind of iconography to which Dreyer is obliquely referring. This image is remarkable only for its conventionality, suggesting the kind of gaze mobilized by the "eye of piety." In this representation Christ's gaze does not meet the viewer's. Instead he gazes upward, his head tilted to the left, suggesting an intimate connection with the object of his gaze, presumably the unrepresentable divine. The internal averted gaze suggests visual disengagement, placing the central figure in a "separate plane of time and narrative" (Stanbury, "Regimes of the Visual," 271), one into which the viewer is invited but never fully present. Christ's suffering is present only in the prickly crown of thorns and the sad expression on his face. Other expressions of suffering are softened out in the image. The crown of thorns is doubled in the nimbus surrounding Christ's

Figure 5. "Crown of Thorns" holy card.

head, suggesting his sanctity. The soft lighting and warm colors reassure the viewer and mitigate the representations of suffering.

Figure 6 suggests the ways in which Dreyer has transformed the sentimental image of the holy card, exposing the existential anxieties of his subject. The pose duplicates the holy card almost exactly, the central figure of the suffering martyr, the tilted head, the averted gaze, sad face, and crown of thorns. However, the harsh lighting and stark black-and-white image remove any sentimentality from the moment, which holds in tension contradictory knowledges: it allows for a response based on emotion, on an identification with Jeanne's suffering, as well as one based on skepticism. Falconetti's Jeanne gazes not upward toward a transcendent reward but downward, almost in despair. The fake crown of straw and the "scepter" she is made to hold locate her "torture" entirely in the realm of parody. Dreyer's "eye of piety" is everywhere tinged with such anxiety.

The holy card is designed to offer a private intimate experience of viewing, as James Petruzzelli suggests in his study of holy cards. The owner is encouraged to carry the card around, use it in missals, Bibles, shrines, as an object to gaze on. "What I came to realize from my discussion with Maria [a thirty-three-year-old Catholic woman interviewed for the study]," he writes, "was that her holy cards were a part of the personal liturgy of her daily life. They not only 'help her get to heaven,' but they also provide her with an expression of Catholic identity and with personal history" (280). Maria notes, "They are remembrances of a saint, or

Figure 6. Renée Falconetti as Jeanne d'Arc in *La Passion de Jeanne d'Arc* (Carl Theodor Dreyer, 1928).

a church, or some place we have been to. They remind us of our religion. We believe in God, Mary, and the saints. I believe in the way my mom brought us up, with saying novenas and the rosary; it is our tradition" (280). Dreyer's gaze on the tortured Jeanne, however, is a very public gaze based on technologies of display. He reminds us that in film, "the private look is repeatedly generalized and constructed through a commercial enterprise that depends on multiple viewers that number in the thousands or even millions, such that an image, always perceived by a single eye, is arrested before a collective identity" (Stanbury, "Regimes of the Visual," 277). He reminds us that even the private look (such as that mobilized by the holy card) is always implicated in a social collectivity.

What social collectivity is the object of this very public display of the suffering body? Dreyer is clearly less interested in the political issues at stake in Jeanne's trial, either for the fifteenth century or the twentieth; he downplays these, focusing instead on Jeanne's suffering. To be sure, we must consider the extent to which the medium of the silent film dictates the filmmaker's interests. Dreyer stages a film about a trial—a dramatic situation in which speaking is the central action—yet speech is exactly what he cannot represent.[22] Instead, he had to develop the resources of a silent cinema, in particular those of the close-up, to convey his story without language and to show through his character's facial expression its "intimate expressiveness." Paula Cohen writes that "the silence of early film was crucial in establishing this effect, for the medium was forced to take advantage of the close-up in its effort to render cinematically what novels and plays had been able to do through language" (115).

The final intertitle suggests that the social collectivity for which Jeanne suffers is, finally, France. "The flames sheltered Jeanne's soul as it rose to heaven. Jeanne whose heart has become the heart of France. Jeanne whose memory will be cherished for all time by the people of France."[23] This is the only nondialogue intertitle of the film. According to David Bordwell, "The sentence collapses the historical/spiritual dialectic of the discourses of the film: both nation and martyr achieve immortality" (*The Films of Carl-Theodor Dreyer*, 92). Jeanne's martyrdom adds a spiritual dimension to French nationalism. Dreyer's representation of it abstracts the historical Jeanne, making her the *mythomoteur* of French nationalism. Jeanne's scapegoating allows the formation of an imagined community of the nation by providing a locus for a collective national mourning (Redfield, 61).

Postwar Joan

During the years following World War II, Hollywood studios made several attempts to bring the story of Joan of Arc to the screen again, but it wasn't until 1948 that *Joan of Arc*, produced independently by Walter Wanger, directed by Victor Fleming, and conceived as a star vehicle for Ingrid Bergman, became the first American version of the story since DeMille's 1917 *Joan the Woman*. Fleming had directed two of the most successful films of 1939, *The Wizard of Oz* and *Gone with the Wind*, while Bergman had appeared in four films that in 1947 had collectively grossed $21.7 million, making her the top-ranked star in Hollywood's best grossing year in history (Bernstein, "Hollywood Martyrdoms," 91). The reviews in the Catholic press of *Joan of Arc* reveal much about the social and political climate in which the film was made and perhaps suggest why the film was ultimately doomed to failure, despite the magnitude of the talent thrown at it. An anonymous *Commonweal* reviewer praised the film for its refusal to recruit Joan's image for any political cause: "In the face of present day skepticism and the tendency of writers to visualize the saint as the patron of everything from Protestantism to equal rights for women, her portrayal as an instrument of the Divine Will does credit to the comprehension of those who made the film" (Nov. 20, 1948, 189–90). Jerry Cotter, in the Catholic periodical *Sign*, notes that the film is (improbably) "historically accurate and sympathetic to the church's position. The distinction between politically minded bishops involved and that of the church itself is carefully and forthrightly presented. There is no whitewash of a tragic mistake" (53).

Convinced that they had produced a film that contained nothing subversive, promoted no causes (such as equal rights for women), and criticized no religious or political authority, the filmmakers could revel in the Catholic Church's imprimatur. In his *Sign* review Cotter gushes: "The lexicon of criticism is sorely tried in any endeavor to give full credit to all concerned in the production of *Joan of Arc*. It is the finest motion picture ever made" (53). Catholics were urged to patronize the film by Father Paul Doncoeur, S.J., the film's historical adviser, who wrote, "Catholics owe it to themselves to insure this film the success it merits" (28). Yet the film was a notorious flop, nearly bankrupting Wanger, who had invested much of his own money in its production.[24]

If reviews in the mainstream press were not as congratulatory,[25] the reception by Catholic authorities of this Joan of Arc film provides a means of exploring the unprecedented control the Catholic Church exerted on the American film industry between 1934 and 1960. None of the moral uncertainties of Dreyer's 1928 film taint this overblown Hollywood biopic; such existential angst would not have been tolerated by Catholic censors either in or out of Hollywood. Instead, the film, even in the face of Joan's historical defiance, promotes proper respect for authority—especially religious authority—and a view of female heroism that conforms to traditional gender norms; female heroism is redefined "to encompass the faithful service to and inspiration of the returning soldier" (Blaetz, 119). The film's gendered meanings were created primarily through the manipulation of Ingrid Bergman's star persona, although this careful public relations exercise was all but short-circuited when Bergman disclosed her extramarital affair with the Italian director Roberto Rossellini (Blaetz, 128; Damico, 242), revealing the extent to which the "Catholic crusade against the movies," despite its notable successes, was, by the late 1940s, beginning to unravel.

By the time *Joan of Arc* went into production, the Catholic Church, according to Frank Walsh, "played a major role in determining what Americans saw and what they didn't see on the silver screen" (2). The 1930 Production Code—a system of bylaws designed to head off government censorship of the motion picture industry—was written by a Jesuit priest and a Catholic layman, Daniel Lord, S.J., and Martin Quigley, publisher of the *Exhibitor's Herald*. The Production Code Administration (PCA), which was set up to administer the code, ostensibly under the directorship of former postmaster general William Hays, was actually being run on a day-to-day basis by another Catholic layman, Joseph Breen. By 1934, any film that lacked the PCA seal of approval could not be shown in any MPPDA (Motion Picture Producers and Distributors of America) theater; a violation could result in a $25,000 fine (F. Walsh, 104). The PCA's ability to censor films was limited, however. It exercised power most effectively in the planning stages of production. Once a film was completed, while it retained the ability to preview, the PCA had less control: "censors participated in the decision-making process by which the studio hierarchy orchestrated and controlled production" (Jacobs, 91). As Geoffrey Shurlock, Breen's assistant and successor at the PCA, noted, "The whole purpose of our existence was to arrange pictures so that we could give seals. You had to give a seal" (Jacobs, 90). This the administration did through negotiation during the production process.

The Catholic Church, however, not satisfied that the PCA was sufficiently independent of studio control, created an independent reviewing agency, the Legion of Decency, whose New York Office was established in 1934 to preview and classify films according to Catholic sensibilities. Its classifications used the following categories:

A-I   Morally Unobjectionable for General Patronage
A-II   Morally Unobjectionable for Adults and Adolescents
A-III Morally Unobjectionable for Adults
B   Morally Objectionable in Part for All
C   Condemned

The Legion of Decency, staffed by volunteer reviewers (most of them women), ultimately had the power to alter scripts, force edits, and even shelve projects it deemed unsuitable for Catholic viewers. *Joan of Arc* received the Legion of Decency's highest rating, A-I. By way of contrast, a decade later Otto Preminger's *St. Joan* would receive an A-II, and Bergman's *The Seventh Seal* would receive an A-III in 1957.[26]

To be sure, nationally the Legion of Decency was never anything more than a loose confederation of local Catholic organizations. Each diocese appointed its own director, usually a parish priest, to coordinate local activities. Given a tradition of episcopal autonomy, the activism of any local chapter was entirely dependent on the commitment of the local bishop. Most, however, did publicize the Legion's classifications and administered the following pledge annually, around the feast of the Immaculate Conception (December 8):

> In the name of the Father and of the Son and of the Holy Ghost. Amen. I condemn all indecent and immoral motion pictures, and those which glorify crime or criminals. I promise to do all that I can to strengthen public opinion against

the production of indecent and immoral films, and to unite with all who protest against them. I acknowledge my obligation to form a right conscience about pictures that are dangerous to my moral life. I pledge myself to remain away from them. I promise, further, to stay away altogether from places of amusement which show them as a matter of policy. (Black, 27–28; F. Walsh, 145)

While the church gave the impression that violation of this pledge was a grave sin, it never issued any definitive statements about penalties associated with breaking it (F. Walsh, 93). Despite the amorphousness of the national organization, however, the New York office responsible for rating films was sufficiently powerful that "from the mid-1930s until Otto Preminger's release of *The Moon Is Blue* in 1953, no Hollywood studio seriously challenged the right of the priests to censor their films" (Black, 5).[27]

As early as 1936 George Bernard Shaw commented on Catholic censorship in a letter of complaint to the *New York Times:*

I am of course aware that there has been in the United States a genuine revolt against pornography and profanity in the picture theatres by good Catholics who want to enjoy a beautiful art without being disgusted and insulted by exhibitions of silly blackguardism financed by film speculators foolish enough to think that such trash pays. A body called the Hays Organization [PCA] has taken the matter in hand so vigorously that it now has Hollywood completely terrorized. Without its sanction nothing can be done there in the film business. (Sept. 14, 1936)

Shaw can perhaps be forgiven for misunderstanding the relationship between the PCA (the Hays Organization) and the Legion of Decency when he registered his amazement at learning "that the Hays Organization includes . . . a body called Catholic Action, professing, on what authority I know not, to be a Roman Catholic doctrinal censorship" (ibid.). While they did not always agree, the Production Code Administration and the Legion of Decency worked hand-in-glove for nearly three decades; the same individuals—including Lord, Quigley, Father John Devlin, and Breen—were prominent in both organizations. According to Gregory Black, "for more than three decades the Hollywood film industry allowed religious groups to determine what was moral and immoral, what was socially acceptable political comment and what was not" (244).

We might well wonder why studio executives caved in to the demands of Catholic pressure groups at this particular historical moment. Frank Walsh suggests that in the 1930s the cost of converting studios for sound film production and the economic effects of the Depression left the studios vulnerable to outside pressure, especially from bankers to whom they were increasingly indebted. Catholic groups were organized enough to appeal to those bankers to put pressure on the studios to comply with the crusade.[28] While World War II alleviated some of these economic pressures—by 1945 motion picture revenues reached an all-time high—studios also suffered from a loss of profits from the overseas market during the war (F. Walsh, 60, 188). After the war economic pressures resulted from the movies' shrinking portion of entertainment dollars, the impact of television, and an antitrust ruling in 1948 that ended such economic practices as vertical integration (ownership of the means of production, distribution, and screening of motion pictures) and block booking (agreements extracted from theater owners to purchase all of a studio's product as a package [F. Walsh 189; Turner 15]). By the late 1940s, these economic factors had contradictory effects on studio owners, whose first goal was to turn a profit, not to create great art or to shape the morals of Americans. On the one hand, studios feared the loss of revenues that might result from a Catholic boycott of their films, especially in urban areas with large Catholic populations; on the other hand, it was often the very material that the Catholic censors wanted to eliminate that sold the most tickets—adult subjects like sex and crime.

Danae Clark has suggested that this moral crusade also played into the studios' strategies for containing labor unrest, especially among its stars. The control of the MPPDA over "independent producers, exhibitors, and labor groups" could be justified as concern for the nation's morality (66). Specifically, it could redirect actors' demands for control over their own labor into a narrative about the extravagance and immorality of Hollywood life, blaming the industry's problems on the "spiraling costs of stardom": its "debauchery, riotous living, drunkenness, ribaldry, dissipation, [and] free love." Actors "do not know what to do with their wealth, extracted from poor people in large part by 25 cents or 50 cents admissions fees, except to spend it on riotous living, dissipation, and 'high rolling'" (71). By keeping public attention focused on morality, the MPPDA could contain labor unrest by playing off the poverty of the Depression era moviegoer against the high salaries commanded by Hollywood stars.

Hollywood frustration over the chilling effects of combined PCA and Legion censorship is suggested by an "ad" appearing in *Screen Writer:* "Wanted, an idea: Established writer would like a good updated idea for a motion picture which avoids politics, sex, religion, divorce, double beds, drugs, disease, poverty, liquor, senators, bankers, wealth, cigarettes, congress, race, economics, art, death, crime, childbirth, and accidents (whether by airplane or public carrier)" (quoted in F. Walsh, 190). Given the long list of subjects rendered taboo by the Production Code, it seems reasonable to assume that religious films—especially the genre of hagiography—would provide sufficient material for the kind of morally uplifting entertainment the Legion's founders envisioned. Certainly they ought to be able to avoid subjects like profanity, sex, politics, drugs, alcohol, and violence. And indeed, the 1940s and 1950s established the saints' biopic as a relatively "safe" film genre: *Song of Bernadette* (1943, A-I), *Joan of Arc* (1948, A-I), *Miracle of Our Lady of Fatima* (1952, A-I), *The Robe* (1953, A-I),[29] *Saint Joan* (1957, A-II), *Francis of Assisi* (1961, A-I), and *Becket* (1964, A-II)[30] joined biblical films like *Samson and Delilah* (1949, A-II), *David and Bathsheba* (1951, B for "suggestive sequences"), and *The Ten Commandments* (1957, A-I), which had existed since the beginning of the industry. In 1954 *Newsweek* commented that "obviously Hollywood has once more become aware of the box office magic of the Christian tradition and is exploiting it to an unprecedented degree" ("Biblical Boom," 79; see also Bernstein, "Hollywood Martyrdoms," 92).

Yet religious films could prove to be every bit as troublesome as the steamiest potboiler. The case of *Joan of Arc* is instructive. The Production Code specified that religious material must be handled carefully. Films could not ridicule any religion; they could not use clergymen as comic characters or villains. "The reason why ministers of religion may not be comic characters or villains is simply because the attitude taken toward them may easily become the attitude taken toward religion in general. Religion is lowered in the minds of the audience because of the lowering of the audience's respect for a minister" (Black, 251). Joan of Arc's biography provided some real challenges to this standard. After all, Joan was not martyred by some sybaritic Roman emperor; the same institution that canonized her in the twentieth century had cruelly martyred her in the fifteenth. The Catholic Church was clearly the villain in this case, and as Martin Quigley noted to David Selznick, "the fact remains that Catholic people are not going to be pleased by a presentation of a Catholic bishop [Cauchon, the bishop of Beauvais who presided over her trial] in a despicable light" (F. Walsh, 224). Furthermore, the central issue in Joan's trial, as Shaw recognized, was Joan's defiance of the church's authority: "would she adopt the church as the inspired interpreter of the will of God instead of setting up her own private judgment against it and claiming that her conduct was a matter between God and herself?" (Shaw, *New York Times*, Sept. 14, 1936).

Shaw had already had his own run-in with the Hollywood censors in 1936 over a project based on his *Saint Joan*. Fox sought advice about a Saint Joan film from Joseph Breen. Breen in turn consulted Quigley and Father Devlin, as well as Father William L. Lallou, a Joan of Arc scholar who taught at St. Charles Seminary in Philadelphia. Arguing that the play was "a satire against Church and State which are made to appear stupid and inept" (*New York Times*, Sept. 14, 1936), these three convinced Breen that the film would incite controversy unless Shaw agreed to major changes in the story (F. Walsh, 224). Fox dropped the project.[31] Since neither a script nor a film had ever been formally submitted to the PCA, Hays could deny Shaw's charges that his work had been censored. Hays told the *Times*, "We have no knowledge whatsoever concerning the advice given to Mr. Shaw relative to the changes and deletions in his play which he says were suggested" ("Shaw 'Muddled,' Catholics Hold"). This is a good example of how PCA censorship exercised power most effectively over the production process rather than over the finished product; its agents could claim not to be censoring at all.

Joan of Arc next surfaced a decade later when Wanger, along with Bergman and her husband, Peter Lindstrom, and Victor Fleming, created the independent film company Sierra Pictures to capitalize on Bergman's popularity (Bernstein, "Hollywood Martyrdoms," 90). They chose for their first project a film based on Maxwell Anderson's play *Joan of Lorraine*, in which Bergman had already successfully played Joan. Wanger envisioned the film as a prestige film, along the lines of Olivier's *Henry V* (1944), with the highest production values. His goal, according to Bernstein, was to demonstrate that Hollywood could make sophisticated movies for mature audiences ("Hollywood Martyrdoms," 95). Unfortunately, that agenda could not survive the moral climate of postwar Hollywood, at least not in a film with $4 million in negative costs.

To ensure that the film received the church's imprimatur, the film employed no less than four Catholic advisers: Devlin and Lallou, who had both consulted on the Shaw project; Father Andrew Snoeck, a Belgian theologian; and Father Paul Doncoeur, a French priest who was an expert on Joan of Arc (F. Walsh, 225). The collaboration was anything but smooth, with a rift developing between Devlin, who wanted to ensure that the film conveyed the proper Catholic viewpoint, and the French historian, Doncoeur, who was more concerned about the film's historical accuracy. For Doncoeur the culpability of Joan's judges was not an impediment to the film: "historically there is no doubt about the bishops and other clerics who condemned St. Joan. They were deeply in error, and Cauchon . . . was an ambitious and venal tool of the English" (F. Walsh, 225).

Since the film received the Legion of Decency's highest rating (A-I), we might well ask how Joan's story was shaped to bring it in line with the industry's requirements for the respectful representation of religious authority. Although Maxwell Anderson is credited, along with Andrew Solt, for the screenplay, the film radically alters Anderson's much more skeptical stage version of Joan's life. In *Joan of Lorraine,* Joan's story unfolds as part of a play within a play as actors rehearse a play about her life. This conceit allows Anderson to introduce some critical distance between the simple faith of the Middle Ages and a more modern agnosticism; as the director of the play within the play states, "We live by illusions and assumptions and concepts, everyone of them as questionable as the voices Joan heard in the garden" (Blaetz, 124). The film's screenplay drops the contemporary parallel story in favor of a straightforward historical account of Joan's rise to prominence, her military exploits, her trial, and her death. This change has the effect of increasing the modality—the truth claim—of Joan's story. As a play within a play, the contemporary plotline emphasizes the fictional status of Joan's story; the audience encounters it at a remove as a story. The screen version—at least the shortened version that has circulated for the last fifty years—mobilizes the signs of historicity—maps, an "objective" narrator's voice-over, and period costumes and sets—to assert the story's authenticity, its *claim* to historical accuracy.[32]

From its first frame *Joan of Arc* works to align the Catholic Church securely with Joan's heroism. In the opening series of shots all of the tracks of the film are channeled to create a tone of pious reverence by mobilizing iconic signs of holiness—pealing bells, candles, a cathedral, sun streaming down from a church rotunda, a choir singing sacred music—in a series of six dissolves that move from pealing bells to the interior of a cathedral (presumably St. Peter's) to a book, a life of St. Joan. Together these shots suggest that the experience of viewing the film resembles the experience of going to church. The event represented is Joan's 1920 canonization; however, the shots seem necessary more to rehabilitate the church—which after all was responsible for Joan's martyrdom—than Joan. In the short version an authoritative voice-over—an iconic representation of omniscience—sets the tone for what follows: "In the year of our Lord 1920 the Church makes its uttermost reparation to one who five hundred years before stood a heretic accused before her enemies." While the term *reparation* acknowledges wrongdoing on the part of the church, the segment emphasizes the perfect alignment between Joan's heroism and the church's symbols of sanctification. The opening sequence's final shot shows a book, a life of "St. Joanna de Arc." A voice-over (the only voice-over in the restored long version) intones, "Joan of Arc, whose history is recorded here, lived only nineteen years on this earth." The deictic "here" is purposefully vague. Is it referring to the book or the film? The ambiguity aligns the film with the official hagiography or *vita* required of all Catholic saints, the written proof of the saint's exceptional holiness. Ironically, unlike the opening shot of Dreyer's *La Passion de Jeanne d'Arc*, this shot does not represent a real medieval manuscript. Instead it represents the ultimate contradiction of hyperreality—a faked manuscript designed to command assent to the historicity of the film that follows.

Having secured the connection between the church and Joan's sanctity in the opening segment, the film still has the problem of apportioning responsibility for Joan's execution. If she was so saintly, why did the church excommunicate her and turn her over to the British for execution? To distance the official church from Joan's execution, the film creates a villain in Cauchon, the bishop of Beauvais who presided over Joan's trial at Rouen. Bosley Crowther, the *New York Times* film reviewer, praises Francis L. Sullivan's "elephantine volume and his cruel cunning arrogance" in his performance of Cauchon. Cauchon's first appearance in the film literally insinuates him into the plot in a scene after the battle of Orléans that brings together "the defeated leaders of Burgundy and England" (according to the voice-over). The scene opens with a three-shot of the secular lords routed by Joan—the earl of Warwick, the duke of Burgundy, and the count of Luxembourg; there is no hint that anyone else is present. As the camera tracks right, however, a figure is revealed standing at a window, back to the camera. The figure turns and walks into the shot while the camera moves in to a close-up revealing Cauchon, who is made to seem more sinister by this indirect introduction. Luxembourg articulates the bishop's motive for casting his lot with the English; Joan had chased the rapacious bishop from his palace at Beauvais. Later, after Joan's capture, he is shown negotiating the price of turning Joan over to the English with J. Carrol Naish's villainous-looking Luxembourg.[33]

This device of scapegoating a single individual would still seem to put the film at odds with the Production Code, which forbade representing the clergy as villains at all. A *Variety* review of *Joan of Arc* noted that "there will be those who will look askance at the clergymen-peers whose political skullduggery and avarice transcend their ecclesiastic obligations, for their machinations in the prolonged trial at Rouen are completely lacking in piety" (Oct. 20, 1948). To offset the negative image of Cauchon, the second half of the film incorporates several "good" clergymen who comment on the bishop's mismanagement of the trial, leaving no

doubt as to its dubious legal status. Early in the proceedings, Nicholas de Houppe-
ville objects to the trial out of conscience and, as in Dreyer's film, is imprisoned.
Father Massieu is traditionally represented as sympathetic to Joan; in the long
version he and two other clergymen visit Joan in jail to advise her to end the trial
by demanding a papal hearing. Finally, when Joan has made her request to move
the trial to Rome, the bishop of Avranches appears and condemns the trial as unlawful; his remark that "Rome will declare the truth about this girl" suggests the
extent to which, in the genre of hagiography, the saint is always already canonized. Joan's appeal to Rome, as several judges comment, renders the trial unlawful and Cauchon's dismissal of the objections absolves the pope—and hence the
official church—of any complicity in her execution. This strategy of containment
was recognized by the Production Code by 1938: "Where a given member of any
profession is to be a heavy or unsympathetic character, this should be off-set by
showing upright members of the same profession condemning the unethical acts
or conduct of the heavy or unsympathetic character" (Vasey, 106).

While these strategies effectively isolate the clergymen responsible for Joan's
execution and absolve the official church of any blame, Joan's defiance of church
authority also had to be handled in a way that did not threaten the church. Ultimately, Joan, who claimed that her "voices" told her to lead an army against the
English, had to be seen as a faithful and obedient daughter of the church and, in
the conservative postwar period, that undoubtedly meant that she needed to conform to traditional notions of femininity. The "traditional standards of morality"
being upheld by the Production Code and the Legion of Decency included ideologies of gender—a set of beliefs, practices, values, and institutions—that determined appropriate roles, behaviors, modes of dress, and occupations for men and
women. *Joan of Arc* began production shortly after World War II, a time when
gender ideologies were shifting and unstable. During the war, women had flocked
in unprecedented numbers to factories to fill the jobs previously held by men
who had been called off to war. These women wore trousers, paid the bills, and
presided over their families as breadwinners. After the war, as servicemen demo-
bilized and the wartime economy began to gear down, attempts were made to
lure women back into the home by creating a cult of domesticity and hyperfemi-
nity that positioned women out of the workforce and in the home as consumers
of the products that would be produced by returning servicemen. This ideology
of domesticity required women to be "docile wives and ever-present mothers"
(Blaetz, 119), not to mention dutiful consumers.[34] According to Brett Harvey's

oral history of women in the 1950s, "marriage and family were expected to be a woman's whole world. Her intelligence, energy, creativity, and sexuality all were funneled into the constricted sphere of family life" (xv–xvi).

Despite the fact that she wears armor and male clothing, rides a horse, and carries a sword into battle, Bergman's performance as Joan is nearly a caricature of 1950s femininity. Harvey could be describing Bergman's costumes in the film when she notes that female clothing in the 1950s was "like armor": "Our cinched waists and aggressively pointed breasts advertised our availability at the same time they warned of our impregnability" (xi). Bergman's elegant "male dress," designed by Dorothy Jeakins and Barbara Karinska, emphasized her femininity, highlighting her long legs, waist, and breasts. Unlike Falconetti's Jeanne, Bergman is made to appear beautiful using all of the conventions of Hollywood stardom. Arguably, her appearance in the film suggests the ethereal by mobilizing a more conventional male gaze rather than, as in Dreyer's film, the medieval eye of piety.

Although much of Bergman's star persona was based on her "unmade-up look" and her so-called "naturalness," instructions were issued to photograph her "avoiding the bad side of her face; keeping her head down as much as possible; giving her the proper hairdress, giving her the proper mouth make-up, avoiding long shots so as not to make her look too big, and, even more importantly, but for the same reason, avoiding low cameras on her . . . but most important of all, on shading her face and invariably going for effect lighting on her" (Damico, 245). Bergman's "natural femininity" in this and other films was the result of much artifice. In *Joan of Arc*, Bergman is frequently photographed in medium shot to close-up, from a slightly low angle, lit from the front. Her head is canted to the right, her gaze upward, suggesting her saintliness (even though this contradicts some of Selznick's suggestions; see Figure 7). Although many reviewers described Bergman as possessing a "spiritual spark," James Damico argues for the "almost totally sexual nature of her screen persona" (245, 249). In this perhaps her performance best captures the contradictions of 1950s femininity that Harvey describes.

Both cut and uncut versions of the film go to great lengths to neutralize the threat Joan's military exploits pose to traditional femininity, which is metonymically represented by references to female occupations like spinning and sewing and by the female garments she repeatedly refuses to wear.[35] Changes in the narrative structure of the film when the film was abbreviated further emphasize Joan's femininity. For instance, a brief excerpt from the trial scene was moved forward out of chronological order to the opening of the film, making it the first live-action scene in the film.[36] In the first scene of the abbreviated version, a high-

Figure 7. Ingrid Bergman as Joan in
Joan of Arc (Victor Fleming, 1948).

angle shot shows Joan kneeling humbly before her judges and swearing an oath
"to speak the truth on matters concerning the faith." What this version sup-
presses (and what the 146-minute version restores) is Joan's defiance toward her
judges, her refusal to swear to answer all questions truthfully. In the trial transcript, when Joan is asked to swear an oath "on the holy gospels," she replies, "I
do not know what you wish to examine me on. Perhaps you might ask such things
that I would not tell." She goes on to say that "concerning her father and her
mother and what she had done since she had taken the road to France, she would
gladly swear; but concerning the revelations from God, these she had never told
or revealed to any one, save only to Charles whom she called King; nor would she
reveal them to save her head" (Barrett, 37–38). Since it is the status of the revelations from God that were at issue in the trial, the alterations present Joan as
submissive and obedient from the opening scene, eliminating references to the
acts of defiance that led to her execution.[37]

Although the restored version of the film includes much more of Joan's defiance of the church's authority (together with what survives of her own words in
her letters and in the trial transcript), it too attempts to bring her accomplishments, and even her rebellion, into line with traditional femininity by underplay-
ing her military career elsewhere in the film. This tactic is especially evident in
the scene in which Joan is introduced to the captains of the French army. Of
course, any film about Joan of Arc must come to terms with the question of what
Joan actually did at Orléans. Warfare is an occupation inappropriate not only for
women but for saints as well. A filmmaker can hardly show a saint, let alone a female saint, hacking off limbs and skewering enemy soldiers. Dreyer had side-
stepped the issue altogether by eliminating Joan's military exploits from his film.
He focuses on what seems to him the core of her story—her martyrdom, which

provides a focus for national mourning and the creation of an imagined community of the nation. Fleming makes Joan a figurehead, a cheerleader for the French army. The scene in which she is first introduced to the French captains sets careful limits on Joan's military leadership. When Poton de Xaintrailles tells her "so long as you promise not to give any commands we shall get along well," Joan replies, "I wouldn't know what commands to give"; yet the next words out of her mouth are precisely that, in response to La Hire's swearing: "There must be no swearing in this army among high or low." When Xaintrailles reminds her that she had agreed not to give any orders, she replies, "This is not a military order, sir. Surely you must see that." Xaintrailles's conclusion sets the terms of Joan's participation in the battle: Joan "is not to lead us. She's to ride before us a sort of symbol, a figurehead for the soldiers to rally around. I don't expect she'll be of much use in battle." In fact, Joan is imagined as a kind of maternal superego (Žižek, *Looking Awry*, 99), a mother figure who sets the moral tone for the crusade by banishing swearing, gambling, drinking, and whoring from the army, which she does in a rousing battlefield speech that begins as a conversation and modulates into an oration. Yet the morality Joan preaches is also shown as threatening the very masculinity that is established through warfare. Even as it accepts Joan's presence on the battlefield, the film expresses the quite common fear that allowing women into traditionally male spaces will contaminate the masculinity of the men engaged in that enterprise.[38]

The traditional femininity of Bergman's Joan was also established by a public relations campaign that consciously connected Bergman, Joan, and the emerging 1950s cult of domesticity, nearly canonizing the actress as the patron saint of postwar family bliss. As Graeme Turner reminds us, the meanings we attach to stars depend not only on the film roles they inhabit but on a range of other media as well, including fan magazines, the mainstream press, talk shows, and, these days, the Internet (Turner, 120). Stars carry with them across these media a set of identifications and meanings that can work either for or against any particular characterization. In this case Bergman's star persona aligned her performance as Joan with traditional femininity. Both James Damico and Robin Blaetz describe how David Selznick's publicity campaign for Bergman focused as much on the actress's domesticity as on her beauty or acting talent. A 1948 *Look* article, for instance, describes how the actress "takes great pride in her husband's career" and "looks forward to Sundays—cook's day off—when she can sort laundry, fix Pia's [her daughter] clothes, and try her hand at cooking" (quoted in Blaetz, 128–29). This domesticity is linked pictorially in the same article with her portrayal of

Joan. The cover of the magazine features her on horseback in full armor. She is quoted as saying, "I always felt I looked like Joan of Arc, who was a big peasant girl. And all my life I dreamed of playing her" (Blaetz, 128). In the Catholic periodical *Sign*, Father Doncoeur, the film's historical adviser, notes, "As a little girl, Miss Bergman was enthralled when she heard the story of Joan of Arc. She dreamed of wonderful adventures in the service of her people." He quotes Bergman as saying, "If . . . on the screen I could bring back to life in my person that marvelous Joan, it seemed to me that I could also accomplish something to stimulate faith and love in my people" (Doncoeur, 27–28). As late as 1972, in her memoir, Bergman reiterates her desire to portray the saint: "I've always wanted to play Joan of Arc, I don't know where the desire came from, but ever since I can remember I have wanted to play Joan" (Bergman and Burgess, 83). This metonymic link between star and role created nearly perfectly the image of Hollywood the Catholic crusade against the movies was designed to promote. It was an image that would founder on the rocks of reality, as Bergman's affair with Rossellini became public at almost the same moment the film was released.

That *Joan of Arc*, despite its sumptuous production values, was a notorious flop that nearly bankrupted its producer is something of a critical commonplace. Its failure has been attributed to Bergman's private life, to economic changes in the industry, to the producers' inability to market a "prestige" film to a mass audience (Bernstein, "Hollywood Martyrdoms," 92–95). However, in creating a film that fit the idea of wholesome entertainment promoted by groups like the Legion of Decency, in excising from Joan's story any subversive or disturbing elements, the filmmakers produced a film as flat as its Technicolor, a film lacking all substance, depth, or shading. For an industry notoriously averse to risk, the financial and aesthetic failings of Fleming's *Joan of Arc* would serve as a caution to future filmmakers. It would be another decade before Otto Preminger would succeed in bringing George Bernard Shaw's shelved *Saint Joan* to the screen. But Graham Greene's conservative rewrite of Shaw's script removed much of its bite, particularly its displeasure with the Catholic Church. Indeed, it would take until almost the end of the twentieth century for the story of Joan of Arc to be reimagined in the light of cinema's involvement with modernist and even postmodernist thought.

Millennial Joan

One of the novel inventions Luc Besson adds to *The Messenger*, his 1999 screen version of Joan of Arc, is an allegory that dramatizes the doubts—both Joan's and our own—about her mission. In her prison cell in Rouen Joan is visited by a hallucination in the form of Dustin Hoffman, who is billed in the credits as "The Conscience." Her interrogation by this enigmatic figure interrupts and dramatically overshadows scenes of the historical trial, despite the fact that they consist almost entirely of dialogue taken from the trial transcripts. Critics have largely derided Besson's conceit.[39] The *Washington Times* called Hoffman "oddly rabbinical for a figment of a fifteenth-century girl's fantasies," while the *Village Voice* labeled him "a sort of Old Testament shrink" in a burnoose. Andy Klein in the *Dallas Observer* summed up critical disdain for Besson's representation of the heroine's inner struggle:

> Poor Joan is in the throes of a crisis of faith, and who does God send? A sixty-ish, five-foot-four Jew with an American accent, all done up as if it's Halloween and he's trick-or-treating as Obi-Wan Kenobi. It's Ratso Rizzo in Rouen . . . Rain Man in robes.
>
> It's ludicrous. It's not so much the Jewishness, though Hoffman's voice and intonations evoke memories of Mel Brooks's take on Joan of Arc. But Hoffman is so recognizably, distractingly himself and so irrevocably modern.

Besson, however, saw these scenes as central to his vision of the film. He writes of them, "c'était pour moi le cœur du film" (For me, it was the heart of the film) (Besson and English, 13). They were the very first dialogue he wrote for the screenplay. Although Nickolas Haydock suggests that credit for this invention (at least as "Man") should go to screenwriter Andrew Birkin ("Shooting the Messenger," 257), an interview with the French newspaper *Le Monde* suggests that Besson had this idea in mind before filming began: "In the first history book I read, I got the idea (for the film) . . . a debate between Joan and her conscience" (Oct. 27, 1999).[40] Given the importance Besson ascribes to these scenes, it may be useful to explore briefly how The Conscience functions within the film and how this role affects Besson's characterization of the saint. In doing so, we are less interested in commenting on the aesthetic quality of the film or its historical accuracy than in understanding the obsessions and anxieties that may have motivated it.

The critics' reactions offer some clues. They see the casting of Hoffman in this role as the problem; he is both too Jewish and too modern for a fifteenth-century costume drama. The meanings his star persona carries and the insinuation of contemporary psychiatric practice disturb the film's sense of historical verisimilitude. Whether or not this disturbance works aesthetically, it may offer some insight into anxieties about hagiographic claims that hover not far beneath the film's epic surface. Hoffman's presence may function precisely as a kind of ana-morphotic blot, a distortion on the film's surface that "persists as a surplus and returns through all attempts to domesticate it" (Žižek, *Looking Awry*, 91). It rep-resents, finally, not fifteenth-century doubts about the saint's sanctity—which were expressed in the trial, in the charges of witchcraft and heresy that con-demned her—but a peculiarly twentieth-century skepticism that would have re-course to psychiatric explanations for Joan's voices (only schizophrenics hear voices). Besson is well aware that twentieth-century viewers have no real emo-tional stake in the fears of witchcraft or heresy that fueled the fifteenth-century trial, but they understand all too well the terrors of insanity. In this regard Hoffman's Jewishness, his modernity, and his invocation of the analyst's couch may be precisely the point (Haydock, "Shooting the Messenger," 261–62). To a twentieth-century audience steeped in scientific rationalism, Joan's visionary fer-vor can only seem finally mad. Besson's strategy in these scenes is to break the il-lusion of the costume drama.

There are many signs in the film's paratext that Besson intended to trouble the genre of hagiography by making Joan's sanctity more ambiguous than any of the previous Joan biopics.[41] The filmmaker Ron Maxwell recognizes this in his scath-ing but often incisive review when he comments that "Luc Besson attempts to prove what even the best prosecuting clerics of her day could not: that Joan was a demented, misled, hysterical, confused and guilt-ridden phony" (Maxwell). Even the film's advertising bears out this intention. In one of the film's trailers Joan moves in dreamy slow motion, shot through a romantically lit field of sunflowers. Although dressed as a woman, with long hair streaming, she wields a sword. As mysterious music plays in the background, a series of words are super-imposed on the image: "witch," "leader," "lunatic," "warrior," "saint," "after 500 years the questions live on." The trailer, then, advertises the film as one that raises doubts about miraculous visions and voices but that balances hagiography (leader, warrior, saint) with rational skepticism (lunatic). Narratively, the film carefully maintains that balance up until Joan's capture. Of course, her allies raise ques-tions about her "voices." During the siege of Orléans, Gilles de Rais asks, "Is she really sent by God?"[42] And even her closest adviser, Aulon, has doubts. "How do you know these voices aren't really just you?" he asks her, a peculiarly twentieth-century question. But such doubts still fit within the framework of the hagio-graphic genre; they are never given authority since overcoming such doubts is precisely what is expected of a saint, however differently they might be expressed in different times and places. The inclusion of a fictional rape scene at the beginning of the film more thoroughly muddies the hagiographic picture. The English attack Joan's village and rape her sister, a sister unattested in the historical record, providing Joan with a psychological trauma—she witnesses the rape in a grotesque parody of the primal scene (she is gazing through a hole in a door)[43]—and a revenge motive for her crusade against the English.

The Conscience scenes, however, overturn whatever balance the film achieves between belief and doubt. In both composition and placement, they tend to settle the issue of Joan's visions rather than trouble it as the other scenes have done. The compositional simplicity of the scenes presents a stark contrast to the rest of the film, and in particular to the busy trial scenes with which they are intercut (the transitions between the two are virtually seamless). According to Besson, in filming the scenes with Jovovich and Hoffman, "Il y'a Jeanne et sa conscience, moi et la camera sur l'epaule (ou le steadicam), et c'est tout" (It was Joan and her conscience, me and the camera on my shoulder [or the steadicam], that's all) (Besson and English, 52). With a few exceptions the five scenes in Jeanne's cell are filmed in very tight close-up, a nod, no doubt to Dreyer's film (rather than Bresson's, as Dufreigne suggests). These close-ups are shot against a dark background so that the faces fill most of the screen. Besson chooses to shoot all his films in CinemaScope, which has the effect of creating a sweeping but largely flat horizontal space that works against the art of the close-up. Conventional wisdom suggests that, in a scope format, head-and-shoulder shots are preferable to extreme close-ups because the camera's distortion renders the latter grotesque. Besson and his cinematographer, Thierry Arbogast, however, use the distortion produced by the anamorphic lens to create the grotesque effect of Dreyer's close-ups. There is virtually no movement in these scenes, and the music track is minimal. A notable exception is the third scene in which The Conscience questions Joan about her use of violence. In this scene Joan circles restlessly around her cell, the steadicam relentlessly pursuing her. After the noise and commotion of the preceding battle scenes, the stillness of these scenes is eerie, but the minimalism of Hoffman's performance grants it certain weight, particularly in comparison to Timothy West's hearty, but mostly ineffectual, Cauchon.

Like the judges in the trial, The Conscience interrogates Joan's visions. He does so, however, not from the position of fifteenth-century theology (are these visions the work of God or the Devil?) but from that of scientific logic. Of Joan's "signs" he notes, "Every event has an infinite number of causes, so why pick one rather than another? There are many ways a sword might find itself in a field." To drive home his point, he offers a number of practical explanations for how a sword might end up in a field. Each is enacted in a "flashback" vignette. Finally, he offers a Monty Pythonesque parody of a filmic vision (a shiny sword floats down from the sky in a beam of light while triumphant choral music is heard in the background). He concludes, "You didn't see what was, Joan; you saw what you wanted to see." In each of these scenes The Conscience always has the last word. On her role as God's messenger: "How can you possibly imagine that God, the creator of heaven and earth, the source of all life, could possibly need you? You don't think he's big enough to deliver his own messages?" About her use of violence: "When did your pleasure begin with that . . . sword in your hand." And about her recantation, his most damning words: "You just signed away his existence. For you, he's a lie, an illusion." The cumulative effect of these scenes is an emptying out of any religious significance we might attach to Joan's life. By the time The Conscience finally hears her confession and absolves her, just before she is burned, her exploits have been evacuated of anything spiritual; they are reinterpreted through the lens of twentieth-century psychiatric rationalism (admittedly of a decidedly popular bent). These five scenes underscore the similarities (however strained) that Foucault articulated between the medieval confessional and modern techniques of psychiatric investigation ("Sexuality and Solitude," 367). In the end, like a good schizophrenic, Joan admits her visions were a lie, finds peace, and dies at the stake.

The skepticism, and even cynicism,[44] that marks Besson's characterization of Joan's sanctity makes all the more puzzling John Aberth's declaration that Besson is a member of the "notoriously secret" conservative Catholic organization Opus Dei and that the film is marked by the organization's "horribly flawed agenda" (297), an assertion echoed by Haydock in a long footnote ("Shooting the Messenger," 266). Both critics make this assertion without any corroborating evidence or anything to suggest where this information came from. Our research has failed to turn up any substantiation for this statement. Aberth claims that Opus Dei's focus on lay vocations, on the work *(opus)* of the laity, lies behind those scenes in *The Messenger* in which Joan claims a more direct relationship to God, bypassing the clergy. He mentions two examples that suggest that "if the clergy cannot satisfy lay people's spiritual yearnings, they must help themselves" (297). Early in the film, the child Joan, anxious to experience communion, simply takes the wine from the altar and drinks it.[45] At the film's end, before her execution, Joan is refused confession by Cauchon and so must be given absolution by The Conscience, presumably a figment of her imagination. These scenes, which suggest an unmediated relationship between the saint and God, in which the intercession of the clergy is unnecessary, seem to us more in line with the kinds of access to God claimed by charismatic medieval mystics, who frequently claimed to have received absolution or communion from the hands of God, than with the disciplines of conservative—and usually authoritarian—Catholicism, of which Opus Dei represents only one strain. Opus Dei, though founded to promote lay piety, is traditional in the authority it grants to the clergy and the submission it demands from its adherents. It does not encourage the audacity of a medieval visionary like, say, Angela of Foligno, who wrote, "the Word was made flesh to make me God."[46] Indeed, the scene in which Joan raids the tabernacle would seem blasphemous to someone raised within the pre–Vatican II Catholic Church, when laypeople never dared to cross the altar railing into the sanctuary or even so much as touch the Eucharistic wafer, let alone drink the wine.

It seems unlikely that someone who would evoke the weird apocalyptic vision Besson creates in his earlier *The Fifth Element* (1997) would win the imprimatur of a group as traditionally Catholic—and authoritarian—as Opus Dei. Yet Aberth's error does suggest a direction for further exploration, one that might help to unpack the kinds of skepticism about the hagiographic genre Besson's device of The Conscience reveals. There is no question that Besson's films evince an interest in religion and even, as in *The Fifth Element*, a fascination with millenarianism, although his vision in that film of Earth's savior as a scantily clad fashion model wearing a Gaultier Ace bandage is hardly a traditional Catholic one. His 1997 film presented pop religion and pop millennialism designed to appeal to the youth audience that supported his films. *The Messenger* was released in November of 1999, just a little more than a month before we would cross the threshold of the year 2000, a crossing that many awaited with fear and trepidation, having heard that a computer-date glitch known as Y2K may well cause the end of the world by crashing the world's computers. Planes would fall out of the sky; banks and utilities would fail; the food supply would be cut off; the catastrophe might even result in the accidental launch of nuclear weapons. Mild panic ensued as people began to stockpile food, water, and supplies in anticipation of disaster. While fears about a millennial bug were never realized, Y2K was certainly not the only example of millennial thinking that emerged in the closing decades of the twentieth century. As the millennium drew to a close there were plenty of signs that the Enlightenment consensus that yoked reason, truth, the individual, liberty, equality, and fraternity was beginning to crack (if it ever held together) under economic, political, and cultural pressures. Millenarian consciousness certainly made itself felt in religious fundamentalism worldwide in the decades leading up to 2000.[47] *The Messenger* might be read as a reproach to this fundamentalism, one designed to speak to a generation of European and American youth dispossessed by the economic contractions of the last decades of the twentieth century but not yet prepared to abandon secularization. If right-wing and fundamentalist Catholics have hijacked the cult of Joan of Arc in support of conservative, even reactionary, and authoritarian religious and political policies at odds with the postmodern sensibilities of the youth culture to which Besson's aesthetic owes its success, *The Messenger* attempts to invent a postmodern Joan for the millennium designed to appeal to participants of that youth culture.

Some background may help create a cultural context for Besson's peculiar brand of medievalism. Because *The Messenger* is in every sense a joint French-U.S. production (a French film in English), the fundamentalism that has emerged within the Catholic Church in both countries in the wake of the reforms of Vatican II will concern us. That fundamentalism became more vocal and more organized in the politically conservative environment at century's end, so the connections of this fundamentalism to right-wing politics will also concern us. The Second Vatican Council (1962–65), called by Pope John XXIII in 1959, initiated a thorough reform of the Catholic Church, moving it toward a more progressive and pluralistic stance of religious tolerance, at a time when movements devoted to social protest and political reform—even talk of revolution—were sweeping across both the United States and Europe. In response to a belief that the church was becoming increasingly "irrelevant" to people's lives, John XXIII proclaimed, "I want to throw open the windows of the church so that we can see out and people can see in" (E. Brown). The centerpiece of the church's liberalization was liturgical reform, which replaced the Tridentine (Latin) mass with the Novus Ordo mass in the vernacular. In subsequent decades the Latin mass would emerge as the central symbol for those Catholics who rejected the reformism of Vatican II. Organized resistance to these changes began to emerge in the 1970s and 1980s at a time when the political environment in both the United States and Europe was becoming increasingly conservative as well. All of the so-called Catholic traditionalists reserve their most virulent criticism for what they consider to be the heresy of modernism perpetrated by Vatican II; Michael Cuneo quotes one traditionalist Catholic: "As I saw it, the council had brought a completely new religion into being. The new post-Vatican church—with its liberal theologies, its ecumenism, its secular liturgies, and its ethical pluralism—wasn't the Catholic Church any longer. It was a new and heretical creation."[48]

Although clearly conservative, Opus Dei is perhaps the most mainstream of the "traditionalist" movements that dot the landscape of late-twentieth-century Catholicism; it is not even unambiguously traditionalist in that a return to pre–Vatican II Catholicism is not its primary mission. Founded in 1928 by the Spanish priest Josemaría Escrivá (who was canonized in 2002), in 1982 it was officially incorporated into the church as a "personal prelature" whose mission is to encourage "ordinary people of all backgrounds to seek holiness 'in the middle of the world'" (O'Connor, 21), in secular pursuits. To this day, despite controversies about its wealth, elitism, secrecy, and influence over its members, it remains firmly within the church hierarchy; it has benefited from the Vatican's patronage and supports its popes.[49]

In France the most vocal and controversial opponent of Vatican II was Marcel Lefebvre, who founded the Society of Saint Pius X (SSPX) in 1970 to oppose modernism and secularism in the church. By 1974 SSPX had established traditionalist chapels in several U.S. cities. From the 1970s until his death in 1991 Lefebvre was in almost constant conflict with the Vatican. In 1974 he publicly proclaimed Vatican II and the Novus Ordo mass heretical; in response the Vatican suspended him from his priestly duties in 1976. The Vatican attempted to reconcile with Lefebvre in 1984, issuing an indult that allowed priests to say the Tridentine mass under special circumstances and again in 1988 by trading recognition of SSPX for a profession of papal loyalty (Cuneo, 91–92). In 1988, however, "SSPX passed into a state of formal schism" (Cuneo, 92) when Lefebvre was excommunicated for ordaining four bishops without papal approval. Yet SSPX is considered to occupy the moderate ground among traditionalists; despite its criticism of Vatican II, it still officially professes its loyalty to the pope in Rome.[50]

To the right of SSPX are schismatic, sedevacantist, and millenarian groups that are so authoritarian and traditionalist that, paradoxically, they openly defy the oldest tradition of the Catholic Church—the supreme authority of the pontiff. In 1983, after being expelled from SSPX for refusing to pray for John Paul II, and highly critical of what they saw as Lefebvre's concessions to the Vatican, a group of nine American priests founded a splinter organization, the Society of Saint Pius V (SSPV), going back more than three centuries to find a pope even more traditionalist and authoritarian than Pius X—a counterreformation pope (elected in 1566). Sedevacantists deny the legitimacy of every pope since Pius XII, spinning conspiracy theories of Byzantine complexity to explain why the seat of St. Peter is vacant. Millennial sects such as the Fatima Crusade or the Bayside movement of Veronica Lueken believe, based on prophecies like those revealed to three Portuguese peasant children in Fatima—or on more recent revelations such as those claimed by

Lueken—that the end of days is at hand. Some, like the Apostles of Infinite Love, are so far outside the Catholic mainstream they even ordain women (Cuneo, 125). Michael Cuneo aptly describes the world of Catholic dissidents as "a complex shadowlands of steamy prophecy, exotic conspiracy, and sectarian intrigue" (87), but what is perhaps most striking about these groups is their medievalism. All look backward to the medieval church as the model of Catholicism and evince a form of spirituality that can only be described as medieval, wedding an idealized past to "carefully selected features of modernity" (Aho, 69).[51]

The religious politics of the Catholic Church do not take place in isolation from the world around it. Religious movements can and do channel the political frustrations and aspirations of both the left and right. Most of the traditionalist, sedevacantist, and millenarian groups described above tend toward extreme right-wing politics. Lefebvre's links with fascism have been documented not only by conspiracy theorists such as the authors of *Holy Blood, Holy Grail*, who link him with the prewar anti-Semitic right-wing Action Française (Baigent, Leigh, and Lincoln, 212), but also by the *New York Times*, which in 1989 reported Lefebvre's involvement in attempts to shelter the French war criminal Paul Touvier, who had been sentenced to death for Nazi war crimes (Oct. 1, 1989). The Francoist sympathies of Escrivá have been well documented (Estruch, 90–94). Father Clarence Kelly, an American SSPV priest interviewed by Michael Cuneo, claimed ties to the John Birch Society (Cuneo, 96), while the Fatima Crusade seems largely stuck spinning outdated cold war conspiracy theories. In France, many of the Catholics who worship at SSPX churches like St. Nicholas de Chardonnet in Paris are also supporters of groups like Jean Marie Le Pen's National Front.

Founded in 1972 "as a big-tent movement, uniting the long-divided factions of the extreme right," by 1984 the National Front had risen from obscurity to win 11 percent of the vote in the presidential election; in 1995 it won 15 percent. In 2002 its charismatic leader, Jean Marie Le Pen, came in second in the first round of the presidential elections, forcing a runoff with incumbent Jacques Chirac. In some parts of the country the National Front can count on as much as 30 percent of the vote (Gourevitch). The National Front's successes depend on its ability to mobilize not only fears of economic insecurity and political abandonment but also, in the words of a 1997 *New Yorker* profile of Le Pen, to speak to "a deeper psychic uncertainty about the future—of fears that the new liberal world order, heralded by economic globalization and European union, somehow saps the national essence" (Gourevitch, 111). Le Pen is notorious for his appropriation of Joan of Arc as both mascot and patron saint in the name of his platform of racism, anti-

Semitism, xenophobia, and nationalist isolationism; virtually every news story about him mentions the French saint (Margolis, 281). The nationalist Greek Hellenic Front, reporting on a Le Pen visit to Athens in 2005, reported the following anecdote from Le Pen's speech: "Allow me to tell you one parable from the Dark Ages. When Joan D'Arc was asked by her judges why as a Christian she did not love the British, she answered that she did love them, but she loved British in their country. In the same way, we do not hate the Turks, we love them, but in their country."[52] The National Front's is only the most recent in a long history of right-wing appropriations of Joan of Arc—from Action Française to the Vichy government—that have shaped the development of the saint's iconography in this century and the last (Margolis, 265, 280–81).

James Aho has argued that religious fundamentalism (and the right-wing politics that accompany it) offers one response to the dislocations, uncertainties, moral relativism, and breakdown of social cohesion that marked the second half of the twentieth century under advanced capitalism. Another possible response, he claims, is postmodernism. For Aho, however, the latter is almost exclusively an intellectual project that embraces the loss of moral and conceptual certainty and of the master narratives of modernity, replacing them with free play and language games, which he sees as a postmodern version of "let them eat cake." Aho does not consider that postmodern intellectuals, however securely placed, might be engaged in a painstaking attempt to understand the painful political ramifications that follow from this "intellectual" position. In Aho's binary formulation, those less privileged than the academic philosophers of postmodernism find its acceptance of a moral vacuum less playful than threatening and even terrifying. They attempt to fill the gap with the kinds of authoritarianism and religious fundamentalism described above (Aho, 66–67).

Aho's argument that religious fundamentalism and millennialism appeal to groups and individuals dispossessed by the economic crises of advanced capitalism, while compelling in some respects, oversimplifies responses to what Fredric Jameson calls the "postmodern condition" that might connect corporations like Sony and Gaumont to the "t-shirt deconstructionists of Paris" (Maxwell). It is, first and foremost, empirically false, as Aho himself admits later in the essay: "One of the paradoxes of political sociology is that radical reform and reactionary movements alike originate not among the most downtrodden, but in the discontents of those who have recently experienced improvements in their condition." Religious fundamentalists are not children of despair but "offspring of hope"

(68). Equally shaky, however, is his belief that the postmodern alternative to religious fundamentalism appeals only to those whose position under late capitalism as intellectuals is reasonably secure and comfortable. Those "already residing in chaos," he believes, can only find postmodernism terrifying (67). We would argue, however, that the group that offers the most explicit challenge to this either/or model is youth, especially those left out of the master narrative that linked education to economic prosperity, those most affected by high unemployment and contracted opportunities in both France and the United States (Hayward, 23–27; Gourevitch). In both countries the youth culture that expresses the discontent of this group, what Susan Hayward calls their "no-hopism," seems to embody most of the characteristics Jameson associates with postmodernism. Youth culture rejects older forms of culture as stultifying and dead, "reified monuments that one has to destroy to do anything new" (Jameson, "Postmodernism and Consumer Society," 1961) at the same time it evinces a paradoxical attraction to forms of nostalgia (1965–66). It is at once cynical and sentimental. It is marked stylistically by pastiche and schizophrenia, fragmentation and a breaking down of the boundaries between high art and mass culture. Postmodernists, in Jameson's formulation, "have been fascinated precisely by that whole landscape of advertising and motels, of the Las Vegas strip, of the late show and Grade-B Hollywood films, of so-called paraliterature with its airport paperback categories of the gothic and the romance, the popular biography, the murder mystery and the science fiction or fantasy novel" (1961). This style and this attitude characterize not only academics but also a youth generation that is as likely to embrace Elvis sightings, aliens, and ghosts as evolution or the atom.

This is the culture and audience toward which all of Besson's films are directed (Hayward, 27), and *The Messenger,* despite its superficial resemblance to an older genre of costume drama, is no exception. J. Hoberman's description in his *Village Voice* review of the film as a "comic book of revelations" and its fashion model star as the "Babe of Orléans" captures both its postmodern style and its attempt to reach youth audiences. Maxwell complains that "Ms. Jovovich's Joan is a thoroughly modern Milla who struts and poses across the battlefield as if she's having a temper tantrum in the middle of a photo layout for Vogue." That, as Maxwell complains, "nothing in the character and belief system of this portrayal takes the slightest step out of the pop culture of the late twentieth century" is precisely our point. However misguided one might feel Besson's treatment of the historical Joan of Arc, rather than pass it off with a one-liner or excoriate the film for it, it is worth asking if there is any serious purpose behind the choices Besson makes. Might the director have been attempting to reclaim Joan's iconography from right-wing fanaticism in the name of his postmodern youth audience?

We intend to explore this question by looking more closely at Besson's manipulation of Joan's iconography. There are at least three shots in the film in which Besson depicts Joan with her arms outstretched in the position of a crucified Christ (it is a shot he uses in *The Fifth Element* as well, with similar religious connotations). The first occurs in the opening scene, when Joan is a child, experiencing her first vision. She is lying in a field on her back. The second occurs when she is wounded in battle as she attempts to scale the walls. She falls backward off the ladder with her arms outstretched (Figure 8). The final shot (two distinct shots actually) occurs during her capture. As she falls off her horse with arms outstretched, there is a jump cut to a repetition of the first scene, this time with an adult Joan lying in a field in full armor. These shots bear an eerie resemblance to one of the illustrations Margolis includes in her article on Joan and the French right, Octave Guillonnet's cover illustration for *Jeanne d'Arc*, Funck-Brentano's 1912 biography (Figure 9). Here the newly beatified Joan is depicted as a Christ figure, passively suffering her martyrdom. Although her arms imitate a crucifixion scene, she is not nailed to a cross, not suspended from it; her feet stand squarely on some kind of pedestal (perhaps an oblique reference to the stake). The cross against which she stands is not a wood cross but a pattern of repeated fleurs-de-lis, the royal dynastic symbol of France, linking Joan's martyrdom to French royalism and nationalism (Margolis, 275).

Despite the fact that his actor is lying down or falling in all three shots, oriented horizontally rather than vertically, Besson achieves the vertical effect of crucifixion through his exploitation of CinemaScope photography. CinemaScope

Figure 8. Milla Jovovich as Joan of Arc in *The Messenger* (Luc Besson, 1999).

Figure 9. Octave Guillonnet's cover illustration for Funck-Brentano's 1912 edition of *Jeanne d'Arc*. Courtesy Wittenberg University Archives.

generally creates a widescreen shot that offers horizontal sweep but little vertical effect. To create any sense of vertical line requires artful composition. In all three of these shots Besson has filmed Joan (Jovovich) from above, giving the impression that a horizontal body is arranged vertically, as in a crucifixion (in the first shot the child Joan even appears to have been crucified upside down). In the shot from the battle scene (Figure 8) the mass of soldiers is reduced by CinemaScope's flattening effect to mere patterning, the background against which Joan's wounded body is displayed, as in Guillonet's drawing of her triumphant body displayed against a pattern of fleurs-de-lis. Besson's iconography and these shots have all the flatness of an icon, tropes on both religious and nationalistic imagery associated with Joan's martyrdom not to reinforce it but to probe it in a cinematic language accessible to a youth audience grown cynical of the genre of hagiography. Joan's martyrdom is presented with a sly nod toward an iconography overdetermined by French nationalism.

We do not finally believe, however, as Maxwell does, that Besson intended wholly to deny either Joan's sanctity or her heroism. Rather he seems to envision a tortured saint and a flawed hero, more in line with his earlier *Nikita* (1990) than with the dictates of Catholic hagiography, even if the result is a "boorish, screaming, hysterical, frenzied, petulant, angry and weepy" Joan (Maxwell). As in his earlier films, from *Le Dernier Combat* to *The Fifth Element*, Besson explores the complex relays that link the star's body both to violence and to the gaze, the gaze to violence on the body, and violence to the pleasures of looking.[53] *The Messenger*, like most of Besson's films, is an extraordinarily violent film: it opens with a gruesome necrophilic rape and wolves chewing on entrails and climaxes in a bloodsplattered Battle of Orléans that features decapitations, hacked-off limbs, impaled bodies, slit throats, and literally buckets of blood. Joan's actual execution is probably the tamest rendering of violence in the film; it seems almost a symbolic gesture in comparison to the explicit violence that has come before. We might dismiss all this violence as simply gratuitous, as several critics have done, but we might also consider the sorts of questions it raises about Joan's sanctity, as well as about the genre of hagiography.

Hayward argues that Besson's films all have violence written on the body at their core. The star's body in particular becomes a site for the inscription of violence, but she is as often the perpetrator as its victim. Jovovich's Joan is not simply the victim of violence; she is surrounded by violence committed in her cause and at her behest. She is implicated by it even if she never strikes a blow. By the time the Battle of Orléans is over, Joan appears literally bathed in blood from head to foot. *The Messenger* takes on, in a way that previous films we examine have not, the unasked question that continually haunts the story of Joan of Arc: what did she actually do? Joan's sainthood rests exclusively on the unusual claim of her military exploits, unusual not only because she is a woman. Catholic saints—either male or female—are generally not revered for their brutality. The genre of hagiography requires that they be the targets of violence—martyrs—rather than its perpetrators.[54] This makes Joan an uncommon sort of saint. If she participated in the violence of the battles in which she fought, then her position as a saint seems compromised. But if she did not, if she is just some kind of mascot, as Thalamas suggested, then her life does not seem all that heroic and her claims to sainthood suspect. For a filmmaker this presents a tricky balancing act. Dreyer avoided the problem altogether by beginning with the trial scenes; his Joan's heroism lies exclusively in her passive acceptance of martyrdom, a perfectly acceptable role for both women and saints. Fleming turned his Joan into a mascot, a domestic angel on the battlefield, offering inspiration to the troops, the den mother of Orléans. Besson shows Joan actively engaged in military feats (storming a drawbridge, for instance, or jumping her horse over a barrier), but he refrains from having her engage in any acts of explicit violence. At the same time, he makes clear that the brutality and gore of the Battle of Orléans must be laid at the feet of the Maid of Orléans; the battle-hardened French soldiers are bemused by Joan's hysterical reaction to the violence of the battle.

Hayward goes on to link the violence in Besson's early films to the sadistic properties of looking. In particular, she notes the connection forged between acts of violence and the technologies of surveillance (rifles with telescopic lenses, etc. [90]). *The Messenger* differs from Besson's previous films because its medieval setting militates against the use of technologies that, of course, would not have existed in fifteenth-century France. Given what Hayward describes as Besson's fetishization of technology, this is surprising. While *The Messenger*'s technology does facilitate military violence in the form of the various siege machines, like the captured trebuchet that seems to fascinate the French soldiers during the battle for Orléans,[55] the film primarily investigates the violence of the gaze in the absence of technologies of surveillance. Besson's medievalism locates the origins of modern surveillance in the investigative procedures of the medieval church, in the Inquisition, much as Foucault does. As such, the gaze frequently organizes power relationships among the characters, especially during scenes depicting investigations (trials). However, analyses of the filmic gaze, such as Hayward's, based on Mulvey's 1975 essay run the danger of seriously oversimplifying the complex dynamics at work in film's representations of looking.

Analyses that draw on Mulvey's essay tend to describe the gaze as a weapon. In this regard Hayward's study of Besson's early films is exemplary (89–93). Drawing on Mulvey and other theorists of the gaze, she locates the power of the gaze on the side of the one who looks. The gaze sadistically investigates—probes—its victims, who are rendered powerless by this scrutiny. For Mulvey, as we argued above, this difference is gendered; men look, women are looked at: "pleasure in looking has been split between active/male and passive/female. The determining male gaze projects its fantasy onto the female figure" (Mulvey, 39). Mulvey's argument, which has set the terms of feminist film theory since the 1980s, maps a formal feature (the gaze) onto gender and, in doing so, fixes the meaning of the gaze too rigidly. If the act of looking—whether it is the gaze of a character in the film, the camera, or the audience (Mulvey, 46–47)—is a signifier, its signification cannot be fixed once and for all. Meaning does not reside in the formal device; it is bound to a context. *The Messenger* offers scenes that contest the meaning attributed to the cinematic gaze; two scenes in particular stand out: the rape scene that opens the film and the examination of Joan's virginity. Both scenes explore the centrality of sexuality—and of the voyeuristic gaze—to the hagiographic conventions of the virgin martyr.

While one might criticize the film's rape scene for its historical inaccuracy or its gratuitous violence, it does challenge conventional theoretical accounts of the cinematic gaze. Besson replaces the "voices"—the three saints, Catherine, Margaret, and Michael—the historical Joan claimed spoke to her (they are never mentioned in the film), giving her, instead, a sister named Catherine after one of them. In this scene Catherine hides Joan in a cupboard as English soldiers enter the house. Joan watches as one of the soldiers impales her sister on the door of the very cupboard in which she is hiding and rapes the dead body (see Haydock, "Shooting the Messenger," 249). The composition of shots clearly aligns the gazes of the camera and the audience with Joan's as she voyeuristically watches the rape unfold. Several close-ups of Joan's eyes as she looks out of a hole in the door establish her point of view. One shot even frames the soldiers in a blurry partially blocked out shot, as if we were watching them through a peephole. Yet this grotesque parody of a primal scene does not confer power on the one who looks. It does not confirm the pleasures that Mulvey associates with scopophilia and voyeurism. Joan is clearly powerless in the scene, horrified and traumatized, and the audience is made to share her terror. The look of disgust and shock on the faces of the other soldiers who witness the rape provides a kind of choral support for this reading. But the gaze in the scene belongs to Joan, and it forces the audience to share in Joan's powerlessness and paralysis. The audience occupies, in Žižek's terms, "the position of an immobilized witness who cannot but observe what goes on" (*The Metastases of Enjoyment,* 73). As if to underscore his point, Besson repeats this scene later in the film. In her delirium after she is wounded in battle Joan relives the experience. She dreams as an adult, dressed in full armor, she is watching the rape again through the same peephole. This shot of a character peering through a hole is hardly unique or novel to this film. Many films depict characters "peeping through keyholes," and those characters usually appear powerless or pathetic.[56] Both Dreyer and Bresson include in their Joan of Arc films scenes that depict Joan's judges spying on her through holes in her cell wall. These scenes indicate the extent to which the judges have failed to break her. Despite their juridical power, they are reduced to impotence, required to steal glances at her while they hide. These filmmakers' voyeurism is supported by the historical record. At Joan's nullification trial one scribe testified that, after she had been captured, Joan was examined to ascertain her virginity either by the duchess of Bedford or her women, while "the Duke of Bedford concealed himself in a place from which he could watch Joan's examination" (Kathleen Coyne Kelly, 18, 146).

Even in scenes where Joan is clearly the object of a potent male gaze, the power dynamics of this gaze are more complex than Mulvey's model allows. For instance, testimony at her nullification trial confirmed that Joan's virginity was examined by Queen Yolanda (the dauphin's mother-in-law) before she was given command of an army. Her squire, d'Aulon, testified that "the said Maid was seen, visited, and privately looked at and examined in the secret parts of her body" (Kathleen Coyne Kelly, 17). Besson is the only filmmaker who depicts the examination of Joan's virginity. Other filmmakers most likely avoided it precisely because the scene is difficult to pull off without succumbing to a kind of leering prurience that would attest to male power to master women through the gaze and would largely dilute the force of the saint's holiness. As Howard Bloch has pointed out, virginity exposed is virginity lost (109). Besson seems aware of the delicate balancing act required to pull off this scene, which he structures through an interplay between concealment and scrutiny that manages to convey simultaneously both the sanctity and the prurience with which the Middle Ages invested virginity.

In this scene the audience is invited to look at Joan and forbidden at the same time. She is at once the object of a sexualized gaze and the sacred and sacrificial body that draws the "eye of piety." Besson achieves this effect by constructing the scene as a ritual. Rather than making it private, it is public and ceremonial. It becomes a sacred spectacle in which the audience's gaze is paradoxically drawn to witness that which it cannot see, which turns out to be a fairly good description of medieval virginity's evanescence.[57] The scene begins with a solemn procession that creates a sacred space. Each of a series of groups enters in a procession and takes up its assigned position in a hall that has been divided by white screens that face a raised platform at one end. Entering first are a group of similarly black-clad men, presumably clerics, who file by a scribe who is recording the proceedings.

The scribe functions as a kind of precursor to more modern forms of surveillance like the tape recorder or video camera and the close-up ensures that we register his continual presence. The clergy's entrance is also juxtaposed to a close-up of various instruments. Are these instruments for torture or gynecological examination? Curiously, although the camera lingers on them and we are invited to gaze on them, they are never used in the scene. They are an implied threat only. Both scribe and instruments are associated metonymically with the first group in the processional, the clergy, signifying their control over the proceedings. Next a group of nuns files in, followed by members of the court. The nuns and clerics take up their places in front of the screens facing the place where Joan will stand. Members of the court, however, both male and female, take their places behind the screens where they cannot see anything. The one exception is the dauphin's mother-in-law, Queen Yolanda (Faye Dunaway), who is ostensibly carrying out the examination.[58] She enters last and takes her position in a chair placed squarely in the center of the room where she can see everything.

The setup of the space calls to mind the spatial arrangement of a medieval mass in which, in some areas of Europe at least, clergy and laypeople were separated by an altar screen that prevented the congregation from seeing the central mysteries of the mass. By calling up this spatial configuration, Besson constructs Joan simultaneously as a passive victim of ecclesiastical investigation *and* a sacred figure. She enters last, dressed in white, with a white diaphanous veil. She is placed as if on an altar. A makeshift tent is lifted up around her to conceal her from everyone in the room except the four nuns holding up the tent and the elderly nun who actually examines her. At the moment of examination, the film becomes silent. Despite the detail he lavishes on setting the scene, Besson leaves vague the specifics of Joan's examination; we have to imagine how her virginity was confirmed. In this way Besson simultaneously creates Joan both as the object of an eroticized gaze and of the "eye of piety," a Christ-like figure displayed before an assembled congregation. Simultaneously seen and unseen, she attests both to the spiritual power medieval Christianity associated with virginity and the impossibility of ever establishing it once and for all. This scene is one of a series of scenes in which Joan is subject to an investigative gaze. These culminate, of course, in her trial and the Conscience scenes with which we began our analysis of this film, with a gaze that constructs Joan not as a medieval saint but as a modern subject, disciplined by both juridical and medical gazes.

It is perhaps fitting that the end of the twentieth century and the millennium should be marked by the release of a new cinematic hagiography of Joan of Arc, however problematic. Throughout the twentieth century, the history of the saint's canonization and the history of film intersected regularly to structure narratives of nationalism, morality, and millenarianism through a cinematic brand of Christian heroism. Something of the sweep of those histories can be seen in the three Joan of Arc films that have been the subject of this chapter. All three films remediate the struggle to define the proper place of religion within an ostensibly secular state; Joan's narrative suggests the ways in which religion can overtly and covertly structure national identity in a secular state. In the next chapter we will further consider the imbrications of politics, particularly U.S. politics, with religious iconography, moving from the politics of hagiography to the hagiography of politics.

Chapter Six

The Hagiography of Politics

Mourning in America

*I*f, as we have seen, cinema can serve as a potent medium for examining the secular politics that participate in the creation of a saint, it has even more often contributed to the nationalist politics underlying the creation of secular saints. In the process of what we are calling political hagiography, cinema provides spiritual endorsements for what are fundamentally political gestures. In this chapter we explore two movies about the Middle Ages—Joshua Logan's *Camelot* (1967) and Mel Gibson's *Braveheart* (1995)—movies with very different ideological investments—that cover over twentieth-century American realpolitik with the veneer of moral idealism, drawing on the narrative structures of religious hagiography to link an iconographic figure with particular political ideals.

Alan Jay Lerner's and Frederick Loewe's *Camelot* came to Broadway in December of 1960, drawing sellout audiences (after a shaky opening) and generally favorable reviews, thanks in large part to Ed Sullivan's decision to include four of the play's songs on his program in an hour devoted to the songwriting team (Mordden, 27–28).[1] The musical won a Tony Award for Richard Burton and a nomination for Julie Andrews, as well as awards for scene and costume design. By the time it closed in January of 1963, it had run 873 performances, not as long as

Lerner and Loewe's earlier collaboration, *My Fair Lady*, which ran 2,717 performances, but longer than Peter Glenville's *Becket* (193), *The Unsinkable Molly Brown* (532), and *West Side Story* (249), all of which opened or closed in 1960.[2] Since 1963, the connection between the Lerner and Loewe musical and the career of John Fitzgerald Kennedy, who assumed the presidency barely a month after *Camelot* opened and was assassinated less than a year after it closed, has permeated the American political landscape. As several commentators have noted, the play's themes of idealism were self-consciously echoed in Kennedy's political rhetoric, and the link was vigorously promoted after his death by his widow, *Life* magazine, and Theodore H. White in an audacious act of political hagiography.[3] The Kennedy association with Camelot was a public relations exercise marking the first but hardly the last presidency to owe its success to the marketing of a specific image. Kennedy was a star in the Hollywood sense of the term. He represented wealth, glamour, youth, charisma, idealism, and energy, qualities that were an easy fit both with Hollywood and with the optimism that marked the postwar American imperium. His early death fixed those qualities in the public consciousness, creating a narrative of national loss that was given coherence by the Camelot myth.

What might it mean, in the context of American presidential politics, to sing:

Don't let it be forgot
That once there was a spot
For one brief shining moment
That was known as Camelot.

The association between Kennedy and Camelot would seem to suggest that good kings and good presidents are more or less equivalent. Yet the United States was established on a political philosophy that resolutely rejected the authority of kings. The modern political subject, as we have argued, was founded on the break with monarchy and all its trappings. In *The Federalist Papers* James Madison dismisses as "impious doctrine" the belief "that the people were made for kings, not kings for the people" (no. 45). Yet the first song in *Camelot*, "I Know What My People Are Thinking Tonight," expresses just that belief, that these are *Arthur's* people, starstruck watchers of royalty in awe of the trappings of the monarchy. A similar contrast between "the simple folk" and the "throne folk" is created in act 2 in "What Do the Simple Folk Do?" which offers the age-old justification for aristocracy, that commoners are really happier because their simpler life insulates them from the painful complexities aristocrats must endure as governors. In an article entitled "Arthur and President Kennedy: The Myth of Kingship," Ronald Garet notes, "It offends rudimentary political theory to call upon the values of kingship to judge presidential administrations; after all, by design presidents are not kings" (5). Yet the connection between the Kennedy administration and Camelot has remained powerful in contemporary politics even as it has been debunked by a slew of books with titles like *From Camelot to Kent State*, *The Dark Side of Camelot*, and *Rethinking Camelot* (this last by Noam Chomsky, as antiroyalist a political commentator as one might find). If, however, presidents are not like kings—are, in a sense, antikings—then what is the basis of the analogy between Kennedy and King Arthur? Garet's reading of Malory may well suggest why Arthur is a good king, but it does not help us understand how the analogy of kingship with presidential leadership might help forge the imagined community of the American nation.

A turn to romantic theories of the state might better explain why this analogy worked so well in the context of 1960s politics. The state, according to this philosophy articulated by, among others, Schiller, Hegel, and Matthew Arnold, "represents the community to itself, thereby giving the community form and in a certain sense giving it an ethical imperative and a future" (Redfield, 59). According to Arnold the state represents "our best self," and for Schiller it is "the archetype of a human being." This view of the aesthetic and pedagogical functions of the state is very much alive even today, as suggested by the historian F. R. Ankersmit, who writes that "[aesthetic] political representation is required since each [civil] society needs an image of itself in order to function properly; without such an image of itself it will stumble around erratically and aimlessly like a blind man."[4] The Broadway musical (whether staged or filmed) has always been a peculiarly American phenomenon, despite its roots in other musical cultures. It has always functioned pedagogically, as Raymond Knapp argues, to construct the imagined community of the American nation, which has always been "the central theme in American musicals" (8).[5] Arthur's own sense of loss before his final battle echoes Ankersmit's metaphor of the blind man: "When did I stumble? Where did I go wrong? . . . If I am to die in battle, please, please, do not let me die bewildered." We might postulate that the connection between King Arthur and the Kennedy presidency caught on (the cleverest public relations ploy to work must strike some kind of chord in its target audience) because of the Camelot myth's ability to fuse in the figure of a single man the self-image from which American civil society and politics at midcentury desired (and in many ways still desires) to be descended. The public relations machine, which was just beginning to discover the power of the new medium of television, exploited those characteristics. Kennedy shared with the Arthurian myth youth and charisma, both of which struck a chord in baby-boom youth stultified by the blandness of the Eisenhower 1950s and newly aroused by the Vietnam War, civil rights, women's rights, and by the glamour of revolutionary politics.

Singing and Dancing on the Edge of a Volcano

Camelot (both the musical and Joshua Logan's 1967 film) presents us with an eclectic mix, equal parts musical, political philosophy, love story, and political hagiography. Insofar as this mélange works, it does so because it stages the originary moment of civil society—the establishment of democratic principles of government—in the life's work of a single individual and then creates a "fiction of an impossible, ineradicable mourning" that encourages identification with that ideal at the moment of its irretrievable loss (Redfield, 61). It reenacts not only the loss by assassination of John F. Kennedy, a beloved leader, but silently makes that loss into a metonymy for all the other losses of the decade, for the loss of the American imperium—for Vietnam, the chaos of civil unrest, and the rebelliousness of youth culture and its rejection of the Pax Americana of postwar American society—in short, the collective loss of confidence in the ability of the state to mirror our "best selves." Marc Redfield has argued that it is through the work of mourning that the nation most effectively imagines itself. Alan Jay Lerner's account in his memoir of a performance of *Camelot* in Chicago on November 22, 1963, the day Kennedy was shot, condenses this process of mourning into a single dramatic—if apocryphal—moment: "Louis Hayward was playing King Arthur. When he came to those lines ['one brief shining moment'], there was a sudden wail from the audience. It was not a muffled sob; it was a loud, almost primitive cry of pain. The play stopped and for almost five minutes everyone in the theater—on stage, in the wings, in the pit, and in the audience—wept without restraint. Then the play continued" (quoted in Everett, 155; see also Davidson, 65).

Although Gene Lees maintains in his biography of Lerner and Loewe that if this incident ever happened, it did not take place in Chicago (205), this is precisely the sort of narrative that focuses national mourning. The interpellation that results from this collective and public wail "calls forth" the citizen subject and "permits the mourning subject to transform a particular loss—real or imagined— into the general loss suffered by the nation" (Redfield, 69). In *Camelot* perhaps the most significant instance of this interpellation occurs in the final reprise of the theme song, "Camelot," at the film's end enjoining the viewer to "think back on all the tales that *you* remember / Of Camelot," encouraging the viewer in his or her mourning to identify with the child, young Tom of Warwick (who, we are to understand, is Thomas Malory), and so with a particular image of the nation.

Joshua Logan's 1967 film version of *Camelot* stages this process of mourning. It opens on a dark, foggy predawn outside a castle. To the melancholy choral strains of the song "Guenevere," a single dark figure is revealed to be King Arthur in the film's present, awaiting the dawn and his final battle with Lancelot, the battle that will destroy Camelot, the fantasy world of the film, forever. The film opens, then, with loss—and the mourning of loss—already firmly established. In this it differs from the opening of the stage play, which lacks this framing device. Like Merlin, we will live the film backward in time from the end, from irrecuperable loss. What loss is being mourned in this version of *Camelot*, and who is being called upon to mourn? Lerner and Loewe could not have imagined in 1960 that their musical would spawn a national myth of mourning and lost innocence. Logan's film, however, opened in a very different America. It appeared four years after the Kennedy assassination, long after the myth of the Camelot presidency had gelled. The placid 1950s had morphed into the turbulent 1960s. The administration of Lyndon Johnson continued to press a losing war effort in Vietnam, while facing mounting opposition at home; American cities were burning as African Americans campaigned and even rioted for civil rights long overdue; disaffected suburban youth had created a counterculture—increasingly driven by radio, television, and record sales—more interested in sex, drugs, and rock and roll than Broadway show tunes and chorus lines. The Rolling Stones, the Doors, and Bob Dylan had replaced George Gershwin, Cole Porter, and Rogers and Hammerstein on the charts. *Wild in the Streets,* which would be released a year later, captured more fully than a once and future Broadway musical could the political imagination of this generation of young Americans.[6]

It has become something of a critical commonplace to associate the film version of *Camelot* with an escape from the turbulence of the 1960s. Alice Grellner, for instance, maintains that "by the time the film came out, four years after John F. Kennedy's death, its mystique and lyrics had come to be associated with that 'one brief shining moment,' and the public was ready to accept the ideology and the romance, the humor, the satire, and the fantasy of the movie as an escape from the disillusionment of Vietnam, the bitterness and disenchantment of antiwar demonstrations, and the grim reality of the war on the evening television news" (74–75). Aberth similarly argues, in *A Knight at the Movies,* that "by 1967, when the movie version of *Camelot* came out, America was beginning to question its involvement in Vietnam and experience an imperial hesitancy that is perhaps echoed in Arthur's song of self-doubt, 'What Went Wrong?' sung at the opening of the film. The country was ready for the return of the 'once and future king,' for another Kennedy presidency" (19–20). According to his memoir, however, Logan was far more interested in the politics of the Broadway stage and the Hollywood studio system than with Vietnam, the civil rights movements, or the counterculture (although these upheavals could not help but find their way into the film, if only indirectly). Except perhaps for opera and the symphony, it is difficult to imagine an American entertainment genre that by 1967 was more conservative and less responsive to the social movements of the 1960s than the Broadway stage. With its extravagant ticket prices, Broadway theater—and the Broadway musical, in particular—targeted during the post–World War II period a coterie audience of older, affluent patrons, "blue-haired ladies" from the suburbs, "theater party ladies," as Logan calls them, who, he insists, exerted a dominating influence over the prospects of Broadway productions (192). Although Logan's film version of *Camelot* takes a number of liberties with the original, it advances the play's fundamental 1950s conservatism, creating its own nostalgia for past greatness, for a simpler time when everyone knew his or her place (especially the younger generation, women, and other disenfranchised members of society), when the holy triumvirate of patriarchal religion, patriarchal family, and patriarchal government made the world safe for American capitalism.

This is not to suggest that the film's producers did not attempt to tap into the lucrative youth market—a market that was just beginning to emerge during this period—especially in casting.[7] Both Vanessa Redgrave (who replaced Julie Andrews as Guenevere) and David Hemmings (Mordred) had appeared the year before in *Blowup*, Michelangelo Antonioni's paean to 1960s mod London, and Redgrave was a notorious antiwar protester; in 1967 she took out a full-page advertisement in the *London Times* denouncing the U.S. bombing of North Vietnam. *Life* magazine reported in its September 22, 1967, issue that Richard Harris (who replaced Richard Burton as Arthur) was also associated with the leftist American Theater of Being. Logan cast Harris, despite the actor's reputation for being unreliable, because he played several scenes "with verve, excitement, and truth" (197); that is, he resonated with Logan's ideas about youth. The costuming was also designed with a youth audience in mind, especially in the production number "Simple Month of May," which Aronstein describes as a "hippie picnic" (*Hollywood Knights*, 93). The DVD of the film includes a feature on the film's premiere, complete with commercials for the "Camelot-inspired collection from

Stevens" showcasing nightgowns, slips, "opulent robes," and "graceful sleepsets" that look part-medieval, part–flower child: "You don't have to be Guenevere to have the romance of Camelot," the ads proclaim.

But in a year that produced such politically challenging films as *Bonnie and Clyde, Guess Who's Coming to Dinner, The Graduate,* and *In the Heat of the Night, Camelot*'s target demographic was not America's rebellious youth culture. Rather, the film was always more likely to appeal to older moviegoers, suburbanites who had lived through World War II and Korea. As Aronstein has noted, *Camelot* is about the power of story and myth to shape lived reality, to focus ideals and unite a political community. At a time when films like *Bonnie and Clyde* and *The Graduate*—products of an independent "cinema of dissent"—were questioning "the viability of the 'tales' that adults tell their children" (Aronstein, *Hollywood Knights,* 90) for a generation in the throes of rejecting their parents' values, "*Camelot* attempts to wrest control of 'the stories people tell' by revalorizing the myths at the heart of the 1950s' consensus of the center" (98). Logan's *Camelot* creates a ritualized mourning for the loss of youth and gentility, vigor and elegance, oxymoronic pairings that, not coincidentally, come to be associated with the Kennedy administration. But the film finally offers the mourning of "theater party" ladies and their spouses, the mourning of America's postwar suburbs.

How does *Camelot*, a film that mourns for and hyperbolically heaps adoration on a mythical English king, attempt to align itself against the tyranny of aristocracies and with the American values of individualism, equality, and democracy? We might consider its use of the generic conventions of the film musical as a means of exploring this issue. Three of the six musical numbers in act 1 occur in the opening moments of the film. These musical numbers recapitulate the form of that most American of film genres, the musical, and at the same time they introduce the main characters and chronotope of the film. The film opens by establishing a contrast between two opposing chronotopes—the space-time of the film's opening "real" world (Camelot just before the final battle that will destroy it), where political ideals prove impossible to live by and loss has already happened; and the space-time of Camelot, an idealized world where those political philosophies can be realized, a place "for happ'ly ever aftering." The movement from the chronotope of realism to that of fantasy is established through what Rick Altman calls an "audio dissolve" in which the characteristic subordination of the film's sound track to diegetic action is reversed and the extradiegetic music motivates the action (*The American Film Musical,* 62–73). There is a brief flashback to Arthur's childhood—a false start, so to speak—since Merlin locates the proper beginning of the story as the day Arthur met Guenevere, his bride. The underscoring at this point modulates from Merlin's theme, "Follow Me," to "How to Handle a Woman" (though the audience has not yet heard either of these numbers sung). Then Arthur, in the present, utters, "I know what my people are thinking tonight." A cut reveals a bright winter setting in which the youthful Arthur "talksings" the same line, "I know what my people are thinking tonight," as a segue into the opening song and into the idealized space-time of political myth.

The film's opening numbers, "I Wonder What the King Is Doing Tonight" and "Where Are the Simple Joys of Maidenhood," figure an opposition between new world populism and an old world aristocracy that will be reconciled through heterosexual romance leading to marriage. Romantic relationships, according to Raymond Knapp, provide "a readily adaptable dramatic 'surface' for the musical, with the shining possibility of marriage standing allegorically for the resolution of seemingly incompatible peoples—or families, classes, races, ideas, ideologies, or whatever—into a stabilized partnership" (9).[8] Romance and marriage are central to the plot of musicals not only because they can figure a symbolic reconciliation of ideological opposites but also because they can signify the proper relationship between a public sphere, which is male and embodies and reproduces the spirit of "Americanness," and a private sphere, a female space to nurture and support this idea of the nation. The musical, then, becomes a method for naturalizing proper gender relationships within an ideology of a specifically American nationalism. If *Camelot* returns obsessively to the originary moment of civil society, it stages that moment first within the institution of marriage, contrasting an old-world aristocracy represented by Guenevere with Arthur's brash new-world populism.

"I Wonder What the King Is Doing Tonight" establishes Arthur's character as childlike, even naive, a young king "uneasy in my own crown." Harris's Arthur is introduced climbing trees and singing about his fear of his approaching nuptials: "What occupies his time while waiting for his bride / He's searching high and low for someplace to hide." Though a formidable warrior ("You mean that a king who fought a dragon, / Whacked him in two and fixed his wagon"), he "goes to wed in terror and distress." Arthur's discomfort with his regal status, his youth, and his mastery of American colloquialisms like "whacked him in two" or "fixed his wagon" mark him as an oxymoron, an American king (despite Harris's Irish roots). So, too, does his first encounter with Guenevere. Dropping out of a tree, he lacks the confidence to introduce himself as Arthur, King of England. Instead he uses his childhood nickname: "They call me Wart." The film highlights Arthur's constant desire to retreat into an idealized "natural" childhood in a forest where he learned with Merlin and the animals. Throughout the film Harris emphasizes Arthur's childlike characteristics. Whereas Lancelot is frequently shot from below, making him appear larger than life, Arthur is either shot in close-up or in long shot. The long shots, particularly those filmed indoors, diminish Arthur in comparison to the majestic sets surrounding him. Props also function to infantilize the king; frequently they are produced on a scale that dwarfs him. In one scene, late in the film, when Arthur is introduced to his bastard son, Mordred (*Camelot* conveniently leaves out the incest of the source texts), the king literally curls up on his throne in a fetal position while Mordred stretches and boasts. During the "Follow Me" segment near the film's conclusion, Arthur is paired with a child double and the gestures of the two are matched, as Arthur retreats, at least momentarily, into his childhood.

In the opening segment Arthur relates to Guenevere the story of the sword in the stone.[9] Arthur describes how he pulled a sword out of a stone that was left there "by the old king Pendragon." However, he never mentions a filial connection between himself and the old king. By sidestepping the issue of lineage, *Camelot* creates the impression that Arthur becomes king of England not through an archaic ritual that identifies him as a true blood prince and heir to the throne but through a magical event that prophesies his own undiscovered wit and initiative. Doubtless the characterization of Arthur as childish owes much to Disney's Americanization of T. H. White's novel *The Once and Future King* (see Aronstein and Coiner, 214–20). The important difference is that in the Disney cartoon Arthur *is* a child. In this film he is supposed to be an adult and a political leader. The film emphasizes Arthur's childlike qualities precisely because those qualities contravene ideas about aristocracy and lineage. Like America, Arthur is youthful, brash, rebellious of protocol, informal (like the Kennedy White House with its Jack, Jackie, and Bobby, everyone in Camelot has a nickname: Wart, Jenny, Lance), and impetuous. Although he is surrounded by the trappings of intellectualism (he talks a lot about thinking, casting his ideas in pseudophilosophic "propositions"), he thinks like a child, slowly, ponderously, and painfully; it is always an effort. Especially in the opening sequence, Arthur seems like nothing so much as a royal Huck Finn, at any moment ready to "light out for the territory."

Guenevere's song "Where Are the Simple Joys of Maidenhood," which immediately follows Arthur's opening song, establishes her as Arthur's opposite. Guenevere may be a maiden, but she is no innocent. She is aristocratic and haughty, first glimpsed being conveyed by servants in a litter and attended by her nurse and anonymous "hairdressers." She is elegantly dressed. Her song characterizes her as a young girl in love with the aristocratic ideology of romance and chafing at the aristocratic practice of arranged marriage ("was there ever such an inconvenient marriage of convenience?"). Her song laments those "harmless, convivial joys" of maidenhood, like knights who "leap to death in woe for me," or who "let their blood be spilt for me." Throughout the film Guenevere will demonstrate that she is most adept at deploying the institutions of the old aristocracy, particularly the institution of royal patronage in the "Take Me to the Fair" segment, which nearly results in the death of Sir Dinadan, to reinforce her privilege. Guenevere's characterization of chivalry in "Where Are the Simple Joys of Maidenhood" is cheerfully marked by a violence that in act 2 will turn much darker; the alliteration in "shall kith not kill their kin for me" pretty much predicts the story's outcome.

Alice Grellner argues that Guenevere is the serpent in Arthur's garden, "a wanton, who will ultimately succumb to her penchant for illicit adventure" (75–76), but such a reading misses Guenevere's function in the garden's creation. If Joshua Logan's *Camelot* teaches America to mourn for Arthur, an American king, Arthur mourns at least partly for what Guenevere represents, the old aristocratic structures that provide the foundation for his vision and against which his ideas will be measured. Like old money, he takes his privilege from looking obsessively back to a mythologized past largely, but never totally, sanitized. Such nostalgia must be cleansed of the history of unsavory practices by which wealth and power were produced—a selective amnesia that allows possessors of old money the freedom to replicate the abuses of their ancestors while still believing themselves innocent. The myth of empire *Camelot* espouses demands that Arthur's new world order be built on the remains of the old, or, at least, on fantasies concerning those remains. Whether the medieval in popular culture represents a break from a barbaric past or the loss of an organic one, it also contains temporally the seeds of the modern. Guenevere—like King Pellinore, who will be introduced later in the musical—represents a fantasy of aristocracy, of monarchy, charming but wrongheaded, that must, for a period, be subordinated to Arthur's dream. Joshua Logan wanted a Guenevere who was "a true femme fatale: shadowed, threatening, romantic" (194). Julie Andrews had played Guenevere on Broadway, but Logan rejected her for his film because, after starring in *Mary Poppins* (1964) and *The Sound of Music* (1965), she was simply too "cozy and little girlish and adorable . . . just not that kind of world-shaking figure" (194). In Vanessa Redgrave he found an actress descended from British stage royalty; her father, Michael Redgrave, had been knighted in 1959 for service to the English stage.[10] Logan believed that he had found an actress whose patrician elegance, demeanor, and beauty could carry the aristocratic insouciance suggested by "Where Are the Simple Joys of Maidenhood." When Guenevere falls in love with Arthur and his ideals, she puts aside—though by no means completely—the values of Britain's antique past, or at least some benignly domesticated version of those values, to accept the inherent superiority of Arthur's American principles of individualism, equality, and democracy.[11]

Together, the two opening numbers, "I Wonder What the King Is Doing Tonight" and "Where Are the Simple Joys of Maidenhood," establish the staple of musical comedy—two apparently incompatible lovers who will be brought together by the power of their musical interaction. Rather than occupying the rest of the film, however, their reconciliation occurs immediately in the third number, the title song "Camelot," in which the magic of the place—the time-space of musical fantasy—brings about the union of the lovers. Perhaps the quickness of this resolution suggests its impermanence. The musical world—Camelot—is a world in which political ideals have been so perfectly realized that even the weather cooperates. Even the instability of the climate, nature itself, is controlled by "legal laws," though oddly enough the political revolution the film envisions has not yet happened. Camelot simply creates an environment in which Arthur's incipient political transformation might come to fruition. In *Camelot* Arthur and Guenevere together embody the aspirations and anxieties of America's affluent middle class. Lerner's lyrics imagine Camelot as a 1950s American suburb—safe, placid, conformist, and not a little dull, a place where autumn leaves do not "fall into neat little piles"; rather they "blow away completely. At night of course."

In musicals the incompatibility of the heterosexual couple becomes the carrier of other dualities and other ideologies; the success or failure of these personal relationships becomes, Raymond Knapp argues, "an emblem for larger possibilities, . . . a marker for the resolution or continuation of conflicts between larger antagonistic forces" (9; see also Altman, *The American Film Musical*, 46–50). The reconciliation of social opposites within heterosexual romance in the American musical exemplifies what Lauren Berlant and Michael Warner call "national heterosexuality": "a mechanism by which a core national culture can be imagined as a sanitized space of sentimental feeling and immaculate behavior, a space of pure citizenship." National heterosexuality creates "a familial model of society [that] displaces the recognition of structural racism and other systemic inequalities" (313). The opening segment of *Camelot* concludes with a wedding that unites

Arthur and Guenevere—metonymies for their respective political systems—in a "triumphant moment of union and reconciliation" (Aronstein, *Hollywood Knights*, 93), creating a foundational political moment that resolves the tension between political and companionate marriage, as well as the conflict between old world and new, via the power of the chronotope called "Camelot." Of course, this "happily ever after" is transient; it will soon be disrupted by the adulterous union of Guenevere and Lancelot that creates the necessary "fiction of an impossible ineradicable mourning" (Redfield, 61).

The marriage between Arthur and Guenevere naturalizes the origins of the state in marriage and the family (despite the fact that their union produces no offspring): "Government is simply a question of proper marriage, and, conversely, marriage is but a question of proper government" (Altman, *The American Film Musical*, 149). For Lerner and Loewe civilization emerges out of middle-class heteronormativity, literally out of the marriage bed itself. As if to demonstrate this, shortly after their marriage, *Camelot* offers a glimpse of the Pendragons at home. This cozy segment stages the founding of the social contract known as the Round Table as domestic comedy, placing Arthur's new social order "firmly within the framework of America's vision of itself as the 'City on the Hill,' entrusted with a divine mission to educate and protect (police) those less fortunate" (Aronstein, *Hollywood Knights*, 92). The segment proceeds initially without song or underscoring. It is morning as the scene opens. Arthur, who has dressed, points to a map of England. He is disturbed and perplexed: "The map of England. Map, indeed. A fishnet of ill-begotten kingdoms ruled by immoral lords battling with their own unlawful armies over illegal borderlines. And who is king of this jungle, hmmm? A man who four years ago promised he would become the greatest king who ever sat on any throne. I, Arthur of England." Arthur's term of power replicates that of the American president, and, now that he has served for four years—apparently doing little more than setting laws to adjust the weather in Camelot—it is time to offer a more ambitious political agenda, one that will put an end to the chaos in the land. Guenevere, naked in bed—looking luminous, clearly no longer a maiden and enthroned in her proper sphere—listens to the husband she adores. The conversation is childish, but the couple, in their political naiveté, believes it profound:

ARTHUR. Proposition. It is far better to be alive than dead.

GUENEVERE. Far better. Ummmmm.

ARTHUR. If that is so, then why do we have wars in which people can get killed?

GUENEVERE. I don't know. Do you?

ARTHUR. Yes. Because somebody attacks.

GUENEVERE. Why do they attack?

If, as Terry Eagleton argues, the child is a natural theorist, this scene depicts Arthur as a childish political theorist, asking impossible questions about the nature of civil society and the place of warfare in such a society (171). Arthur's questions lead him back to his education by Merlin in the forest, where, as a child, he had been taught to understand that "boundaries are what somebody always attacks about." And because boundaries are not real but socially created, "we have battles for no reason at all." Arthur's answer to his own question, of course, still leaves open the original childish question: why risk one's life to fight a war? The impossibility of answering this question may reside in the fact that *Camelot* is set in the Middle Ages, a time when a militarized aristocracy enriched and empowered itself strictly through the acquisition of property, through the violent expansion of borders. While individuals in the late 1960s might dream of a medieval king as a peacemaker, consolidating power through conversation rather than violence, the reality of the Middle Ages would have been more like *Beowulf*'s Scyld Sceffing, who is praised as a "good king" for his ability to take control of and dominate the territory of others, than John F. Kennedy, who sought to fight the cold war at the level of metaphor, the winner determined by which side got to the moon first. Arthur's question may have been one that the post–World War II generation wanted asked, but it is one that a medieval king could not contemplate for too long.

In this scene, however, we are constantly reminded that this political theorizing is taking place within a cozy domesticity. The king ducks behind a curtain from which he soon emerges, in a bathtub, on wheels, no less, perhaps a suggestion that Arthur's Camelot is a technologically inventive place where "progress is our most important product" (as General Electric's popular 1960s slogan would have it). As Guenevere washes his back, Arthur exclaims, "That's it, Jenny. That's it. It's the armor. It's the armor, Jenny, the armor. Only the knights are rich enough to have armor. The foot soldiers, they have nothing. So all that can happen to a knight is an occasional dent." Knights—members of the aristocracy—keep perpetuating wars over nonexistent boundaries because they never really place themselves in harm's way. To them battle is an interesting game—the equivalent of Monday Night Football—where reputations can be made and wealth amassed with little risk. The inequalities within the system, between those who possess armor (superior technology) and those who do not, perpetuate the violence in society.

Arthur's reality, therefore, must necessarily deconstruct his rhetoric. He is not innocent of battle; Guenevere admiringly refers to him as "the greatest warrior in the land." But neither he nor the film can acknowledge the means through which his own reputation and political power have been consolidated; he is unwilling to consider what kinds of violence and bloodshed or how many knights in armor it might take to centralize authority sufficiently for him to be recognized as "the greatest king who ever sat on any throne." *Camelot* passes over the series of bloody civil wars, described both by Malory in the *Morte Darthur* and by T. H. White in *The Once and Future King*, necessary to secure Arthur's throne. The film passes over the brutality of aristocratic succession and dominance and Arthur's necessary complicity in this brutality. *Camelot* figures a naive childlike past, suggesting, at the same time, that this past contains the seeds of a future liberal democracy that emerges out of the comforts of domesticity and the family. *Camelot*'s fantasy teaches us to mourn this man-child and the loss of his dream. It is, of course, impossible to mourn a butcher.[12]

Most of Arthur's bathtub speech is offered as the extradiegetic overlay to the beginning of the next scene, which takes place in Camelot's town square. Arthur, struck with inspiration, runs about announcing his new social contract: "a new order of chivalry, a new order where might is only used for right, to improve instead of destroy; look, we'll invite all the knights, all the kings of all the kingdoms to lay down their arms to come and join us. Oh yes, Jenny, and we'll take one of those large rooms in the castle, put a table in it, and all the knights will gather at it." Initially, Arthur's notion of a table where knights will "debate, make laws, [and] plan improvements" rather than engage in acts of violence doesn't sit well with Guenevere, who pronounces the idea "ridiculous." But she is persuaded by Arthur's vision of a knightly order that would be "very fashionable; everyone will want to join," and she offers her father's round table: "It seats 150. He had it as a wedding present and he never used it." The entire sequence screams of the affluence of suburban domesticity. It is market day, and the Pendragons are out shopping. Although the square is filled with people of all classes, little deference is shown to either king or queen. The Pendragons behave like newlyweds in the neighborhood, envisioning the perfect country club and wondering what unused furniture might be liberated from their parents' basements. Word announcing the creation of the Round Table is circulated as though Arthur and Guenevere are preparing for a yard sale. The founding of a just society is imagined as a pleasant domestic interlude. Leaflets are thrown from the castle tower, falling into the hands of peasants and the nobility alike. In 1967, a time of extraordinary social unrest, *Camelot* offered white, conservative, middle-aged, middle America a Middle Ages from which it would like to be descended, a Middle Ages in which visionary kings and their patrician wives longed for a life similar to those developed just a short expressway trip away from great cities.

Arthur envisions a social order in which the Round Table serves as an icon for an imagined political equality. This social order, this image of a shining "City on the Hill" that can become "a force for good in the world, making 'just' laws and enforcing them for the people's benefit," as Susan Aronstein has argued, "coincides with America's post–World War II self-definition" (*Hollywood Knights*, 92), which also turned dark in the 1960s. As the scene closes, the score reprises the theme song, "Camelot," and Arthur and Guenevere make their real ambition known. It is an ambition that cannot be publicized by arbitrarily circulated leaflets and cannot be supported by men sitting around a table engaging in discourse. The dark underside of aristocratic ambition is voiced by both Arthur and his queen when they sing:

> We'll send heralds riding through the country
> Tell every living person far and near
> That there is simply not
> In all the world a spot
> Where rules a more resplendent king
> Than here in Camelot.

In juxtaposition to their democratic, populist rhetoric, Guenevere insists that Arthur's rule must be the most "resplendent." Her fixation with aristocratic dominance passes over in complete silence the gestures that will be necessary to achieve this state of resplendency. What political or military mechanisms must be deployed to make other potentially jealous knights and kings acknowledge Arthur's superiority? How many un-armored foot soldiers must die before such acknowledgment is achieved?

The fantasy of *Camelot*, of course, also contains the seeds of the ideal order's undoing. After a brief montage sequence showing various of Arthur's male subjects answering his call, one of the invitations finds its way to Lancelot's castle in France, where he is shown, in the next musical sequence, holding a leaflet and singing his appropriateness for Round Table membership. The musical number "C'est moi" serves two purposes. From a practical point of view the song overlays and organizes a montage sequence condensing Lancelot's journey from his castle in France to Camelot.[13] But it also accomplishes Lancelot's inscription as a political subject, as a knight and, more specifically, as a knight of the Round Table. By answering Arthur's "hail," he enacts the complex processes of recognition and misrecognition that Althusser argues inscribe us into ideology. Lancelot musically interweaves into his song the Camelot theme that has played throughout the transitional montage sequence. We hear its first musical phrase, ascending thirds, as a fanfare that Lancelot picks up, singing "Camelot. From far off France I hear your call."[14] In his answer to this hail Lancelot literally internalizes the chronotope of Camelot, inscribing it as his own subjectivity in the song's title and refrain, "C'est Moi, c'est moi, 'tis I." The song's first verse describes the physical prowess the Round Table knight should possess; he should be able to

> Climb a wall no one else can climb
> Cleave a dragon in record time,
> Swim a moat in a coat of heavy iron mail.

The second verse outlines his spiritual perfection. When he sings "He could easily work a miracle or two," the camera, which usually films Lancelot from below or at eye level, suddenly looks down on him from above as he devoutly looks up, suggesting divine approval for a heart and mind "pure as morning dew." Like Gawain in *Sir Gawain and the Green Knight*, Lancelot interpellates himself as the exemplar of knightly perfection both physical and spiritual. And like Gawain in the Middle English poem, Lancelot's virtue is here set up only as a prelude to his fall into sin, in Lancelot's case the sin of adultery.

Lancelot's opening number also serves a musical purpose; it differentiates him from Arthur and from the other men in the film. When he sings, Lancelot sings all of his pitches.[15] By contrast, Arthur frequently "talk-sings" at least the opening lines of his songs: in "I Wonder What the King Is Doing Tonight," in the reprise of "Camelot" after the founding of the Round Table, in "How to Handle a Woman," and in the final reprise of "Camelot" at the end. This is a technique Lerner and Loewe first developed for the character of Henry Higgins in *My Fair Lady* to suggest that Higgins lacks some essential humanity (and perhaps because Rex Harrison did not have a particularly musical voice; see Everett, 153). In *Camelot* Lerner and Loewe use the binary opposition between singing and talking to introduce variations on the theme of masculinity. The men are distinguished by the fact that Lancelot sings all the time, Arthur sometimes sings and sometimes talks his songs, and the villain Mordred never sings (the two songs given to him in the musical have been cut). William Everett argues that this distinction suggests that Arthur lacks something, "that very thing which Guenevere desires and cannot find—the thing which Guenevere finds in Lancelot and sacrifices everything to obtain. . . . Whatever the answer to this mystery may be, Lerner and Loewe offer a musical explanation." Everett argues that Guenevere is captivated by Lancelot's "soaring baritone" (153)—perhaps a metaphoric explanation of what T. H. White calls the "passion of romance" (*The Once and Future King*, 363) or of the danger, novelty, and excitement—the sexuality—that Lancelot represents.[16] Mordred does not sing because he lacks all humanity; Lancelot sings perhaps because he is a creature of pure passion. Arthur falls in the middle because of his ability to sacrifice his passions for a political ideal of the public good. This distinction may be suggested by Arthur's agonized speech after Lancelot's knighting, when he suspects Lancelot and Guenevere of betraying him: "I demand a man's vengeance. Proposition. I'm a king. Not a man. And a very civilized king. Could it possibly be civilized to destroy the thing I love? Could it possibly be civilized to love myself above all? By God I shall be a king. . . . This is the time of King Arthur when violence is not strength and compassion is not weakness." Apparently having read Freud's *Civilization and Its Discontents* centuries before it was written, Arthur, unlike either Lancelot or Mordred, understands that, as king, he must sublimate his human instincts—for love, for revenge, for violence—in the service of "civilization," and that repression is suggested by his hybrid singing style.

Camelot returns obsessively to the originary moment of civil society, to the beginning of the social contract, mythologizing it, erasing the very violence Freud argued was necessary to hold it in place. "The Lusty Month of May," Lancelot's introduction to the court of Camelot, enacts a subtle shift in the political structure of Arthur's court, a move away from the private sphere of the family, represented by the Pendragons at home, to the public sphere of politics, of civil society. This song, adapted from a passage that opens the final book of Malory's *Morte Darthur*, celebrates the pleasures of peace.[17] It is springtime for Arthur in Camelot. May is "that darling month when everyone throws self-control away," a "time for ev'ry frivolous whim, proper or im." Aronstein remarks that the scene is "more like a hippie picnic than a political utopia" (*Hollywood Knights*, 93); however, it is worth remembering that hippie fashion arose first as a politics of utopia. In this scene Logan appropriates youth counterculture to enact the originary split of liberal society, the split between the public sphere of politics and work and the private sphere of love and family.[18] Up until this point Arthur and Guenevere have worked together to establish the Round Table. They are shown discussing its shape in their bedroom, in the marketplace, and, in the montage sequence, surveying their kingdom on a map. "The Lusty Month of May" sequence subtly edges Guenevere out of the political sphere and into the private sphere of love. If the family is the natural basis of civic life, the foundation of the state, it is also antagonistic to it and so must be isolated from the public sphere of politics, which must be freed from the obligations of family ties: "the demands of love and of family bonds are particularistic and so in direct conflict with justice which demands that private interest is subordinated to the public (universal) good" (Pateman, 21).[19] At the end of the number Lancelot is introduced into the company. The comedy in the scene emerges from the contrast between his deadpan seriousness in discussing his physical and moral standards for knighthood and the frivolity of the event. When Arthur invites Guenevere to hear of the plans the two men had been discussing, Lancelot is puzzled: "Would not Madame find it tedious?" Guenevere responds, "I have never found chivalry tedious—[beat]so far." And from this moment Guenevere will be systematically excluded from the public affairs of the Round Table. The initial antagonism between the lovers is no doubt a feature of the genre (Altman, *The American Film Musical,* 168), but here it is given motivation. Lancelot displaces Guenevere. No longer Arthur's business partner, no longer a consort, she is reduced to mere decoration, exiled to the world of love and leisure. As he departs, Arthur dismisses her political advice: "You look far too beautiful, my dearest, to have anything on your mind other than frolic and love."

Guenevere's exclusion is formally marked in the final scene of act 1, when Arthur and his knights enter the Round Table hall and move to take their seats. Logan employs a crane shot, as well as all of the possibilities of CinemaScope, to emphasize the scale of Arthur's enterprise, the grandeur of his ambition (see Figure 10). As lavish as the Broadway production of *Camelot* might have been, it was limited in scale by the size of the theater, the size and shape of the stage, and the difficulty a crew would encounter in having to move an enormous prop onto the stage and off, night after night. Logan, on the other hand, could construct his Round Table in a massive Hollywood soundstage where it could serve to create a single breathtaking shot. Logan's Round Table fills the CinemaScope screen, which, with its flattened horizontal space, provides the perfect medium for recreating the inflated romantic aspirations of the Arthurian legend. The shot fulfills the fantasy of a king so open, so noble, so popular that nobles would flock from throughout Christendom to serve him, a king so wealthy and powerful that he could provide appropriate accommodation for this onslaught of knights and control their violent tendencies. The shot, with its emphasis on size, strength, and

Figure 10. Crane shot of Joshua Logan's Round Table in *Camelot* (1967).

dominance, offers a hyperbolic display of masculinity. As Arthur's knights gather around the Round Table, it is clear that women have no place in his imperial ambitions.

Yet Lerner and Loewe appear to have understood, at least at an intuitive level, the complex imbrication of public and private spheres both in medieval monarchies and in modern liberal democracies. The public sphere depends on the private sphere of the family for its very existence, yet modern Western democracies attempt to enforce a strict division between the two: love in the private sphere, justice in the public. Elements from the private sphere, however, frequently advance essentially public and political ends, as contemporary controversies around the issue of gay marriage, to cite only one example, suggest. In the Middle Ages the separation between public and private spheres was less clear-cut. The final songs of act 1, "Take Me to the Fair" and "How to Handle a Woman," set up the tournament scene that is the climax of act 1 by staging the struggle between Arthur and Guenevere to control private patronage networks to achieve public political ends. Lancelot and Guenevere initially respond to one another out of jealousy over access to Arthur, as they do in White's *The Once and Future King.*[20] Guenevere resists Lancelot's attempts to exclude her from the public affairs of the realm in "Take Me to the Fair," which reads Guenevere's involvement in the affairs of court (in the tournament) as a kind of meddling. This number, which in the stage musical is listed as an optional "additional number,"[21] depicts Guenevere and various knights engaged either in domestic duties (winding wool) or in leisure activities (horseback riding, lying in a hammock, drinking) as Guenevere manipulates them into challenging Lancelot in exchange for her favors (taking her to the fair, sitting beside her at the ball, escorting her to London). These "scenes" are integrated by the music, though separated temporally and spatially, as indicated by changes in location and costume (it is another musical montage). Interestingly, the insouciant violence of Guenevere's and the knights' language—

GUENEVERE. You'll bash and thrash him?
SIR LIONEL. I'll smash and mash him.

· · · · · · · · · · ·

GUENEVERE. A mighty whack?
SIR LIONEL. His skull will crack.

—in the midst of the smug domesticity surrounding them locates the bargaining entirely in the private sphere. The knights' talk-singing, in contrast to Guenevere's legato, however, aligns them with the public and civilized Arthur, troubling the neat distinction between public and private.

The film might interpret this song as Guenevere's meddling in public affairs, except that Arthur explicitly asks for her cooperation in the dialogue that precedes "How to Handle a Woman." He asks her to withdraw her favors (her kerchief) from at least one of the knights and offer them to Lancelot, whom, Pellinore remarks, the court finds unbearable precisely because "he has no lady"; that is no proper private life. When she refuses, Arthur says, "Why this is appalling. . . . It will seem to the court that you are championing his defeat." Guenevere responds to Arthur's anger by accusing him of jealousy. "Absolute rubbish," he replies; "I'm delighted the court adores you so." Within the medieval institution of courtly love, the private ties of affection were necessary to bind the knights publicly to the king within a homosocial community based on personal intimacy rather than social contract.[22] This scene shows the delicate balancing act required for Arthur to rule successfully. He must dangle the possibility of "love" between the queen and his knights—or at least her favors as rewards for their loyalty—at the same time that he must maintain her fidelity exclusively to himself, through violence if necessary. While Arthur keeps trying to make their dispute a private, familial one ("If I ask as your husband, will you, as a favor?"), Guenevere wants to cast it as a public-sphere issue, one of government, as she sides with the other knights against Lancelot's "improvements" to chivalry and in favor of the status quo: "If the King wishes me to withdraw what I have given, let him command me! And Yours Humbly [that is, your royal subject] will graciously obey."

Act 2 of *Camelot* attempts to place the blame for the destruction of Arthur's ideal polity on Lancelot's and Guenevere's adultery and on the villainy of his bastard son, Mordred (himself the offspring of Arthur's unchecked desires), as the violence that surrounds Camelot turns darker. Yet we might well ask how, at the end of the twentieth century, an essentially private transgression such as adultery might be imagined to have such far-reaching public political consequences? We might get some purchase on the blame assigned to adultery for the destruction of Camelot in the film if we return to the images promoted by the theme song, "Camelot." The attractions that Camelot offers, as we have already noted, are the attractions of the suburbs, a place where not a blade of grass is allowed to be out of place. Camelot offers the attraction of orderliness achieved through regulation and a social control that extends its influence even over the natural world. Camelot is a place in which everything—including nature—is subject to the capitalist regimentation of calendar and clock: "The winter is *forbidden* till December / and exits March the second on the dot." "The rain *may never* fall till after sundown. / By eight the morning fog *must* disappear" (the emphases are ours). Nothing disruptive can mar its placid and orderly surface. While the song praises this "congenial spot," this utopian community, it phrases Camelot's attractions in the negative and legalistic language of interdiction and prescription. Camelot as a chronotope reflects postwar optimism, the belief that American ingenuity and enterprise could conquer any problem, even the disruptions and unpredictability of nature itself. In such a place the chaos of desire must be managed in the same way. In such a world "the languages of rectitude and renunciation" must extend to and "successfully bind errant desire to socially sanctioned structures" (Kipnis, "Response," 434). Just as the postwar suburbs were conceived of as an orderly space structured around the monogamous nuclear family, so, too, the social order of Camelot is based on what Laura Kipnis, in her essay on adultery, has called "surplus monogamy," the binding of one woman and one man to create the nuclear family as the foundation of civil society. Surplus monogamy becomes the emotional prop for the surplus labor that makes the suburban "good life" economically feasible (Kipnis, "Adultery," 18).

In such a social structure adultery becomes more than simply private betrayal. *Camelot* projects the public face of adultery—its larger social and political meanings—back onto a precapitalist, and so originary, moment when such transgressions were treasonable—at least for queens a capital offense—because they threatened legitimate orderly succession, in this case of the crown. Although in 1967 legitimate inheritance was less of an issue than it was in the Middle Ages, monogamous marriage, founded on "the private property relation," still bound couples together juridically, as well as emotionally (Kipnis, "Adultery," 19). The orderliness of postwar suburban life depended on stable monogamous families. Despite such widely perceived threats to this stability as the women's movement, the sexual revolution, and the development of an effective birth control pill, in 1967 the legal bonds of marriage were much more difficult to break than they are today. No-fault divorce laws were still three years in the future, and one of the most common means of ending an unhappy marriage was for the couple to collude in staging an adultery for the sole purpose of obtaining a divorce.[23] Beyond the legal effects of marriage laws, however, adultery then, as now, functioned as "the favored metonym for all broken promises, intimate and national, a transparent sign for tawdriness and bad behavior" (Kipnis, "Adultery," 14). Adultery in this view functions as a "cover story," as it would two years later, in 1969, when the Chappaquiddick scandal put an end to Edward Kennedy's presidential aspirations and the last hopes for a revival of a Kennedy Camelot. Public outrage over adultery, particularly as it applies to our national leaders (as it increasingly has over the last two decades), as Kipnis argues, is "about the fear that adultery *puts things at risk:* from the organization of daily life to the very moral fabric of the nation" (14): "Infidelity makes you an infidel to the law, for which your spouse becomes an emblem, the hinge between the privacy of your desires and the power of the state installed right there in your master bedroom" (20). *Camelot* literalizes this metaphoric connection between injury to the spouse and injury to the state by fusing spouse and state into a single figure—Arthur.

Camelot simultaneously glamorizes and condemns adulterous love. In glamorizing the affair between Lancelot and Guenevere, the film implicitly recognizes the sort of liberatory potential in this transgressive behavior that Kipnis describes: "Under conditions of surplus monogamy, adultery—a sphere of purposelessness, outside contracts, not colonized by the logic of productivity and the performance principle—becomes something beyond a structural possibility. It's a counterlogic to the prevailing system" ("Adultery," 18). This possibility is recognized in Guenevere's song, "I Loved You Once in Silence," in the contrast between its language of restriction, imprisonment, and desolation—"I loved you once in silence / And misery was all I knew," "Your heart filled with dark despair"—and images suggesting release and loss of control—"Thinking love would flame in you forever," "The raging tide we held inside would hold no more," "We flung wide our prison door." But even the song's liberatory language is phrased negatively to emphasize loss of control rather than freedom, a freedom the film ultimately condemns as license. Guenevere's sentence—to be burnt at the stake—literalizes the song's metaphors of fire in her punishment, even if the film finally displaces that punishment onto the war between Arthur and Lancelot.

If the first act uses the founding of the Round Table to idealize the origins of government based on equality, the second act's concern with replacing trial by combat with a jury system idealizes the origins of an independent judicial system for which Lancelot's and Guenevere's adultery becomes the test case. The second-act song "If Ever I Should Leave You" accompanies a montage showing Lancelot and Guenevere conducting their affair in a series of private, even secret, spaces (bedrooms, private gardens, hidden houses). After Guenevere's arrest a trial specifically for the crime of adultery provides the film's climax, perhaps hinting at other judicial injuries to the family unit during the postwar period. The shifting of this crime from private injury to public trial might register dismay over the erosion of the domestic ideal of the 1950s nuclear family. Logan's film opened in the shadow of one of the most notorious murder trials in U.S. history, one that suggested that the white middle-class American dream of suburban affluence might hide darker currents. The previous year (1966) saw the retrial of Dr. Sam Sheppard, the suburban Cleveland man convicted in 1954 of having murdered his pregnant wife, Marilyn. Sheppard's motive for the crime was supposed to have been his wife's adultery. During the 1960s this case was rarely out of the public eye since it was the inspiration for the popular television series, *The Fugitive*, which ran from 1963 until 1967.

Guenevere's trial is shown only in a montage covered by the choral song "Guenevere." Before that, however, two scenes in the second half enact the origins of the system that will condemn her. Both are decidedly unmusical scenes; neither includes musical numbers, and both proceed with little or no musical underscoring of any kind. The first, added for the film, in which Arthur and Pellinore discuss the details of a jury system, provides some comic relief for the darker second act, but it also illustrates the evolution of jury trials out of the medieval blood feud. As Pellinore recognizes, the jury trial that, Arthur explains, pits prosecutor against defender is merely combat by other means, merely shifting the "trial" of the two parties from arms to words. For him the result is the same: "If that jury finds me guilty, there'll be plenty of bloodshed. I'll have a whack at every last one of them." When Arthur patiently explains that he would then be charged with murder, Pellinore replies, "The ruddy thing's endless. Another jury finds me guilty, and I'll have to have a whack at them and so on and so on and whacking and . . ." As a representative of the old aristocratic order, Pellinore can only understand the workings of this new system in terms of the blood feud rather than as the suppression of violence that will inaugurate civilization.

It is easy enough to point to Arthur's betrayal by Lancelot and Guenevere as the tipping point in the destruction of Camelot, the moment when public and private spheres collide, undermining Round Table governance and the new justice system. It is easy enough to blame Mordred for exposing Lancelot's and Guenevere's adultery. But Lancelot isn't really to blame for the destruction of Arthur's vision, nor is Guenevere; it is even difficult to hold Mordred entirely responsible since he does little more than capitalize on the transgressions already committed by others. In the scene that follows the haunting and nostalgic "Follow Me" into the woods and Arthur's childhood "schoolhouse," Mordred's challenge to Arthur's new judicial system sets in motion the events that will result in the arrest and trial of Guenevere. Mordred prompts Arthur to test Lancelot and Guenevere by arguing that virtue untried is not virtue at all—"Isn't your civil law marvelous? No proof, no crime; ergo virtue, happiness." Both at the beginning and at the end of the film Arthur asks "what went wrong," a question the film is finally unable to answer because to do so would require an examination of the violence on which the dream of Camelot is founded. Arthur's new world order disintegrates before it can reach fruition. An equally interesting question might have been "What went right?" It is not the loss of the perfect society that we mourn; it is the loss of the dream of a perfect society.

During the 1960s many members of America's left grew disillusioned with Kennedy-style liberalism. Impatient with their perception of John Kennedy's cold war posturing, his commitment to "domino theory" international policy, and his timidity about passing legislation addressing racial inequality, they became increasingly radical. For old-time Kennedy liberals—and their more conservative brethren as well—the film version of *Camelot* offered a counterpoint to the discourses that fueled the antiwar, civil rights, and women's movements of the late 1960s. Just as throughout the film King Arthur constantly speaks of the necessity to exert "might for right" to impose civilization in his realm and beyond, *Camelot* allowed Americans the fantasy that, even in its failures, well-intentioned Kennedy-style progressivism could inspire positive change. During the two months leading up to the premiere of *Camelot*, *Life* magazine ran articles and pictorials about U.S. citizens and soldiers working in Vietnam to improve the lives of the Vietnamese people and in America's inner cities to restore peace after the chaos of the 1967 riots. *Life* magazine, self-consciously fashioned to speak to "middle America" and self-consciously edited to fashion "middle America," stood as a pillar of stability, addressing the anxieties of white, middle-class members of the postwar generation, anxieties fanned by prospects of all-out war in Southeast Asia and escalating violence on the streets of the United States. Like Arthur of *Camelot* and John Kennedy—both charismatic, perhaps even messianic, figures whose personalities overshadowed their achievements—readers of *Life* could imagine themselves reaching out beyond their comfortable suburban domiciles (even as they remained in those comfortable suburban domiciles, just imagining) to help the disadvantaged, the disenfranchised. On September 22, 1967, however, *Life* magazine covered neither Vietnam nor urban racial unrest. Instead ten pages were dedicated to Logan's film, "The Shining Pageant of Camelot," and its star, Richard Harris. How could *Life* possibly resist the story of the movie's premiere? *Camelot*, mourning simultaneously the losses of King Arthur and John Kennedy, offered a nostalgia that suggested innocence could coexist with empire, that complacency could coexist with good samaritanism. Sweeping aside the complex and deeply divisive politics of the late 1960s, Joshua Logan wrapped members of America's bourgeois class in myths of privilege. Instead of turbulence *Camelot* gave them singing and dancing on the edge of a volcano.[24]

The Passion of the Scot

In the shadow of a revolution on the streets of America, Joshua Logan's *Camelot* offered nostalgic consolation to an anxious, middle-aged, suburban middle class through its reverence for King Arthur and, by extension, John F. Kennedy. But the film offered much too little, much too late for its message to make a political difference, and America greeted *Camelot* with indifference.[25] Mel Gibson's 1995 film, *Braveheart*, elevates the Scotsman William Wallace to the status of secular saint to precipitate a revolution of an entirely different character from the one that rocked American streets in the 1960s, a conservative revolution that celebrates "traditional" Christian values and virtues. Many commentators, including John Aberth and Colin McArthur, fault *Braveheart* for its "many, many historical mistakes" (Aberth, 304; McArthur, 167–69) in its depiction of Wallace's late-thirteenth-century rebellion against Edward I's England. But *Braveheart's* "historical mistakes" seem calculated revisions of history designed to articulate an agenda for a latter-day revolution. Gibson uses the revolt of what he characterizes as traditional, religious, family-oriented Scots against a permissive, decadent English aristocracy almost as an allegory of the sort of rebellion, even revolution, he believes necessary to reinvigorate religion in a secular and permissive modern world. *Braveheart* prefigures Gibson's controversial 2004 film, *The Passion of the Christ*, by promoting ideologies consistent with the U.S. religious right's peculiar mélange of nationalism, populism, patriarchy, and religion.[26] Ironically, while the cultural politics of Gibson's *Braveheart* may have eluded most literary and cultural critics of filmic medievalism, they were immediately understood by the makers of Comedy Central's *South Park*.[27]

In an episode entitled "The Passion of the Jew," *South Park*'s resident racist and anti-Semite, Eric Cartman, recognizes that he has come close to realizing his dream when his "friend" Kyle, a Jew, admits to feeling guilt after seeing Mel Gibson's *The Passion of the Christ* (2004). Cartman adjourns to his room and falls to his knees in prayer: "I want to thank you for the blessings you have brought me. You have shown me the way so many times in the past, and now you are making all my dreams come true. You give me strength where there is doubt, and I praise you for all you have done."

The expectation of the cartoon's audience is that Cartman is praying to God, but that is not the case. The cartoon cuts from the kneeling Cartman to the object of his adoration, a movie poster from Mel Gibson's *Braveheart*. The image of kilted, claymore-wielding Gibson remains as Cartman's voice-over continues: "Only you, Mel Gibson, have had the wisdom and the courage to show the world the truth." The scene finally moves back to the kneeling Cartman, who proclaims: "From this day forward, I will dedicate my life to making sure that your film is seen by everyone. I will organize the masses so that we may do thy bidding. Hail Mel Gibson. Amen."

This *South Park* moment is of interest because it reminds us that Mel Gibson had already accrued considerable political and religious capital prior to the release of his controversial religious biopic *The Passion of the Christ*. With *Braveheart*, which won Oscars both for direction and best picture, Gibson emerged not only as a powerful force in the filmmaking industry but also as a dominating influence on the cultural landscape of late-twentieth-century America. Eric Cartman participates in a hagiographic moment as he looks on and prays to the hypermasculine figure of Gibson's William Wallace—who, for Cartman, is never really separable from the star persona of Mel Gibson. For Cartman, Mel Gibson is canonized in and by *Braveheart* as the avatar of nothing less than a cultural revolution. Cartman accepts Mel Gibson as a saint, as the intercessor between a supplicant and God. But this canonization also has an unsettling political edge—Cartman later calls Gibson *mein Führer*. A Catholic priest has already informed Kyle—and, by extension, the *South Park* audience—that "the *Passion* was actually done as a performance piece, back in the Middle Ages, to incite people against the Jews." Staring at the publicity poster from *Braveheart*, Cartman is called to action, inspired to perform what he sees as an *imitatio Gibsoni*, fusing medieval religious hatred with the spirit of the modern pogrom. Cartman believes that doing Mel

Gibson's "bidding" involves putting on a brown jacket and leading crowds of South Park "Christians" as they mindlessly reply "wir müssen die Juden ausrotten" (we must exterminate the Jews) to his admonition, "es ist Zeit für Rache" (it is time for revenge).[28]

The *South Park* cartoonists use Eric Cartman's adoration of Mel Gibson's William Wallace to satirize America's turn to the political right, a move marked by an obsessive desire to return to patriarchal values signaled by the hard-bodied masculinity of Hollywood heroes like Gibson. *Braveheart*, in fact, gives a new twist for the 1990s to what Susan Jeffords has called the "remasculinization" of U.S. politics and culture in the 1980s.[29] In *Hard Bodies: Hollywood Masculinity in the Reagan Era* she suggests that the "hard-bodied" films of the 1980s, successful franchises like *Rambo* and *Die Hard*, capitalized on the sense of impotency emerging from America's political and military failures by attempting to recuperate for American nationalism traditional forms of masculinity as a response to America's loss of "face" in the Vietnam War, the gains of feminism in the 1970s, and feelings of national vulnerability arising from the Iranian hostage crisis of 1979. By promoting hard-bodied, hypermasculine heroes who were not restricted by diplomacy, military protocol, or police procedure, these films both anticipated and supported ideals of the Reagan presidency, ideals that included "militarism, patriotism, individualism, family values, and religious beliefs" (Jeffords, *Hard Bodies*, 13). In these films the camera's obsession with the toned male body, its rippling muscles and stoic endurance of suffering, made the male body into a cultural icon of the nation, a carrier of specific ideological markers of masculinity. The hard body is competitive, athletic, decisive, unemotional, strong, aggressive, powerful, and, above all, never feminine (Jeffords, *Hard Bodies*, 35). The hard-bodied males described by Jeffords, however, were not simply promoting a return to chest-thumping machismo. What the architects of the new politics of masculinity had in mind was at once more far-reaching and subtle. The political climate of the Reagan presidency enabled both political strategists and cultural mythmakers (like Sylvester Stallone or Bruce Willis) to create heroes who could simultaneously stand in opposition to certain authoritative institutions (primarily so-called big government) and advance politically conservative and socially authoritarian agendas: "In each case these heroes are shown to be representing the will and desires of 'average' citizens against the self-serving empowerment of government bureaucracies who are standing in the way of social improvement. . . . The hard-body films of the 1980s pose as heroes men who are pitted against bureaucracies that have lost touch with the people they are to serve, largely through the failure of bureaucrats themselves to attend to individual needs" (19). During the presidency of George W. Bush this political mythmaking would reach its apogee, enabling right-wing Republicans to blame feminized Democrats for all the mistakes of a government controlled in all three branches by conservative Republicans.

In the midst of the Clinton presidency, *Braveheart* offered a new kind of hard-bodied hypermasculinity, as well as a new paradigm for America's political right. By the time *Braveheart* reached U.S. audiences in the mid-1990s, American conservatives had already begun to grow somewhat restive with the political direction the country had taken. For the so-called religious right, primarily Christian fundamentalists and evangelicals concerned with "family values" issues such as abortion, prayer in school, and homosexuality, Ronald Reagan's actions had insufficiently supported his rhetoric and George H. W. Bush's brand of patrician Republicanism had been only slightly more satisfying than the swill of cultural decadence that accompanied the Clintons.[30] For "social conservatives," Sylvester Stallone's Rambo and Bruce Willis's *Die Hard* hero, John McClane—the hard-bodied heroes of the 1980s—may have possessed an ethical compass, but they lacked a religious one. When these heroes suffered, their sufferings, designed more often than not to show off their musculature, were done in the interest of correcting the mistakes of political liberalism. Rambo refought the Vietnam War; McClane battled criminals and terrorists.

In its call for "freedom" *Braveheart* echoes the militant nationalism, ushered in by the Reagan presidency, that ties the greatness of the nation to the exercise of military power, to the strength and courage of the soldier (Ryan and Kellner, 194). It is never entirely clear what Wallace's call for freedom means, though it is frequently repeated, as in one of the film's taglines, "They may take our lives, but they'll never take our freedom." Thomas Byers argues persuasively that the film taps into American nationalist ideas about freedom through its appropriation of the foundational narrative of the American Revolution in which a ragtag band of colonial upstarts throw out the British.[31] The ideas of freedom embodied in the American Revolution, however, derive from the liberal individualist belief that freedom consists of inalienable rights that are the same for all, regardless of social, economic, or racial distinctions. In the context of late-thirteenth-century Scotland, however, the film must elide the specificity of medieval ideas about freedom, which would include the ability to inherit land, to leave the village one was born in, or to choose a different lord; such freedoms would be neither inalienable nor universal. They would differ greatly by social rank; a knight like

Wallace, even of the minor nobility, would have many more freedoms than, say, a serf or a free man of the laboring classes. For medieval Scotland's underclasses, "freedom" from English rule could only mean exploitation by a Scottish aristocracy instead of by a British one.[32]

Yet with his portrayal of Scotland's William Wallace, Mel Gibson ties conservative religion to conservative politics. At the same time, he brings religious faith to the hypermasculine hard-bodied hero of American cinema. The film leaves no doubt that Gibson believes that the fight for freedom (whatever it means) can be accomplished only by a man of faith. Mel Gibson is a Traditionalist Catholic, a Catholic who would like to restore the faith to what it was before the liberalizing reforms of Vatican II. In *Braveheart* he appears to be more concerned with engaging in the cultural wars of the late twentieth century than with reproducing the complex, and perhaps not very cinematically interesting, politics of the late thirteenth. When Wallace suffers, he suffers as a Catholic martyr, complete with all the iconographic images of hagiography. Gibson's *Braveheart* offers the kind of muscular Christianity that would anticipate and ultimately support the arrival of George W. Bush to the White House. And yet there is a certain inconsistency in Gibson's peculiar blend of Traditionalist Catholicism and patriotism and the kind of "born again" conservative Protestantism embraced by Bush. Conservative Protestants have historically distrusted Catholicism, while Traditionalist Catholics reject the ecumenical acceptance of other religions promoted by Vatican II. Gibson shares with other Traditionalist Catholics the belief that the "the right to the freedom of conscience and of religion" is an "erroneous opinion which cannot be more fatal to the Catholic Church and the salvation of souls; it is a 'freedom to be damned'" (Stoekl, 96). And yet he marketed *The Passion of the Christ* heavily to conservative Protestants, and they in turn enthusiastically patronized the film.[33] Indeed, the paradox of the religious right, and its most significant political liability, is that it is a coalition among Christian activists, all of whom believe that their faith is the only true one and that all those who reject it will be damned.

From the very beginning of *Braveheart* Gibson signals his intent to use the film to engage in historical revisionism, often suggesting an ironically postmodern sense of history as the imbrication of power and knowledge, ironic because of the tendency for cultural conservatives to engage in what Byers calls "pomophobia." In his DVD commentary Gibson claims that "the history [of this period] is pretty sketchy, so I had a lot of wide parameters to go in and make stuff up. . . . There's a lot of legend and history. We adhered to the history where we could but hyped it up where the legend let us." In point of fact the history of this period is well documented, especially the border skirmishes between the kings of England, both Edward I and Edward II, and Scotland and the civil war between Edward II and his queen and her lover, Roger Mortimer, a conflict that ultimately led to Edward's deposing and execution.[34]

Braveheart's revisionism begins with the opening helicopter shot. Titles place the scene in the misty Scottish countryside and the date at 1280. A voice-over articulates the film's cultural and political agenda, establishing for the audience who the players are and where sympathies must be placed: "I shall tell you of William Wallace. Historians from England shall say I am a liar. But history is written by those who have hanged heroes." Gibson begins by debunking English historians and their hero-hangers: "the King of Scotland had died without a son, and the King of England, a cruel pagan called Edward the Longshanks, claimed the throne of Scotland for himself." Gibson's insistence that Edward I was a "pagan" is gratuitous and entirely without historical merit. While in his DVD commentary Gibson is often candid about rewriting history for the sake of a more compelling film narrative, he is mysteriously silent about what amounts to his excommunication of an English monarch. In fact, Gibson visually acknowledges, albeit begrudgingly, that Edward was a Catholic—crucifixes hang on walls throughout Edward's castle. What seems to disappoint Gibson is that Edward's government was not guided by his faith. He may have been a Catholic and a king, but he was not, so far as Gibson is concerned, a Catholic king.

Gibson uses the court of the "pagan" King Edward I as foil to the Traditional Catholicism of William Wallace; it is, of course, easy for Wallace to be a Traditionalist since he lived nearly seven hundred years before Vatican II. In *Braveheart* faith is part of the everyday life of medieval Scots. On seeing the hanged bodies of the Scottish nobility executed by Edward I, Malcolm Wallace, "a commoner," exclaims "Holy Jesus" in stunned disbelief; he and his two sons quickly make the sign of the cross. But the simple faith of common folk like Malcolm Wallace is insufficient for the kind of Christian leadership that his youngest son, William, will exemplify. Following the deaths of Malcolm and his eldest son in battle against Edward I, William is adopted by his uncle Argyle. Argyle quizzes the young William about his father's funeral:

ARGYLE. Did the priest give a poetic benediction?
WILLIAM. It was in Latin.
ARGYLE. You don't speak Latin? Well that's something we shall have to remedy, isn't it?

In his DVD commentary Gibson insists on the necessity for Wallace's linguistic enlightenment, noting that "if you were educated back then, Latin was your main language." But there is nothing in the film to suggest that any other powerful political figures have received such schooling; certainly none of Wallace's retinue have. Gibson's greater concern appears to be that Wallace knows and understands the official language of the Catholic Church. Regarding Malcolm Wallace's funeral ceremony, Gibson insists that he "had to get a Latin expert . . . because they were all Catholic back then, of course . . . had to get the appropriate Latin rite funeral." When William's wife, Murron, is killed, her funeral is performed in Latin, as are the battlefield absolutions offered to Wallace's men. Gibson understands that most of his audience will no more understand the language of these ceremonies than did the young William Wallace. He remarks: "My father informed me that we made a couple of grammatical errors in Latin there. But only a couple of minor ones. But since it's a dead language, it's only guys like him that are going to pick up on it." Gibson's desire for precision is not solely for the sake of historical verisimilitude. The Scots do not speak Gaelic; there is very little French spoken in the court of Edward I, even though that likely would have been the dominant language among thirteenth-century English aristocrats. Gibson's obsession with Latin—following his father's obsession with the language—is much more likely the result of his Traditionalist Catholic beliefs, the result of a conviction that God's agents—Wallace, for example—and perhaps even God, must communicate in this official language of Catholicism, a language abandoned by Vatican II.

Gibson's participation in the culture wars of the late twentieth century extends beyond his desire for the Catholic Church to reinstate the Latin liturgy. Just as he turns to the Middle Ages to demonstrate how twentieth-century reform has debased Catholicism, he uses the antique past to show how liberal secularism has produced a culture of decadence. Like Jesus in *The Passion of the Christ*, Gibson's William Wallace confronts a degraded and degrading society. As Gibson would have it, the England of Edward I, for all of its colonial power, is headed toward collapse. Nowhere is this more evident than in the court's "deviant," self-destructive sexuality. England under Edward I seems virtually devoid of women. The only women in Edward's court have been imported from France, and the reasons for their immigration are unsettling. The film's voice-over tells us: "Edward the Longshanks, King of England, supervised the wedding of his son, who would succeed him to the throne. As bride for his son, Longshanks had chosen the daughter of his rival, the King of France. It was widely whispered that for the princess to conceive, Longshanks would have to do the honors himself. That may be what he had in mind all along." The voice-over alludes to the homosexuality of Edward II, a matter that has been addressed by a number of the film's critics.[35]

Gibson holds up Edward II's homosexuality as the preeminent sign of English cultural, political, and spiritual decadence. Sid Ray and others have noted that while the real Edward II had five children—four by Isabelle, the Princess of Wales, and one out of wedlock—Gibson turns him into a silly, sterile, and anachronistic stereotype of homosexual effeminacy. At about the halfway point of *Braveheart*, Edward I, frustrated with William Wallace's victories, proceeds to pitch his son's homosexual lover, Phillip, out of a window.[36] In his DVD commentary Gibson acknowledges the criticism that he received for the scene: "I got into a lot of trouble for that, presumably because it would seem to be some kind of antigay thing. But, um, everybody gets it in this film, gay and straight alike, so I didn't see it as discriminating. I mean, Wallace gets tortured for ten minutes." Despite his insistence to the contrary, Gibson does seem to have a very different attitude toward Phillip's homosexuality than he has about Wallace's hard-bodied heterosexuality. Prince Edward's sexuality comes under intense criticism through much of the film, not only in Edward I's expressions of hypermasculine contempt for the preening homosexual lovers—a contempt often demonstrated in physical violence against Edward II (Ray, 27)—but also in the ongoing whispered mockery of Isabelle and her chambermaid. The murder scene takes on a perversely comic tone; Longshanks enjoys both the humiliation of Phillip and the brutality of the moment, and the audience is manipulated into sharing his pleasure. The audience sees the death scene from above—Gibson uses a crane shot—watching as the king's guards scatter, cartoonlike, in all directions, to avoid Phillip's crashing body. Even in his protests of innocence, Gibson can't contain a certain amount of levity as he insists: "I learned a new term, *defenestration*, which is what that's called, death by pushing someone out of a window, defenestration."[37]

Every bit as interesting as Gibson's use of homosexuality to defame the English court is his hint that Edward I had—or, at the very least, desired—incestuous relationships with his daughter-in-law, Isabelle. Even though the king seems to have little interest in Isabelle, his court is tainted by the rumor of incest—a rumor that, to some degree, is borne out when an English soldier attempting to rape Wallace's wife, Murron, whispers to her, "you remind me of my daughter back home." In what Gibson recognizes is a pretty distant flight from the truth, however, the princess in *Braveheart* is impregnated by Wallace, not one of the Edwards. In the film's legend (if not in the actual history) the inability of both son and father to sire a royal child on Isabelle stands as an indictment of the court's behavior. For all its colonialist and militarist bluster, Longshanks's court is sexually inadequate. As Isabelle's chambermaid insists, Englishmen are miserable lovers who "don't know what a tongue is for."

Braveheart in fact suggests that English sexual ineptitude, the utter procreative failure of the English male, sparks the sequence of events leading to Scottish revolution in the late thirteenth century. At a war council early in the film, Edward I explains his strategy for controlling Scotland: "The key to the door of Scotland. Grant our nobles land in the north, give their nobles estates here in England and make them too greedy to oppose us." Historically, Edward's strategy of maintaining control of Scotland by blurring the boundaries between Scotland and England, giving English land to Scottish lords and Scottish land to English lords, happened to be largely successful. However, Longshanks's policy is questioned by one of his generals: "But sire, our nobles will be reluctant to uproot. New lands mean new taxes, and they are already taxed for the war in France." In Gibson's own historical flight of fancy Edward I proposes a solution to the problem: "The trouble with Scotland is that it is full of Scots. . . . Perhaps the time has come to reinstitute an old custom. Grant them *prima nocte*. First night. When any common girl inhabiting their lands is married, our nobles shall have sexual rights to her on the night of her wedding. If we can't get them out, we'll breed them out." As Richard Utz has argued, this solution was extremely unlikely. Even Gibson appreciates how fast and loose he has played with history: "Yes, I don't believe that they practiced this custom at that time. This was done for the purposes of cinematic . . . um . . . to be cinematically compelling. Make it a more villainous thing to do." Perhaps Gibson uses *prima nocte* as a metonymy for the economic rape of Scotland. It becomes a more titillating means of describing English appropriation of Scottish wealth and land, with women standing in for the possessions of men.

For Gibson colonial conquest and the cruelty of Scotland's English overlords is played out in the sexual domination of Scottish brides. It is almost as if Gibson cannot help himself, calling Edward I a "cross between Machiavelli and Hitler," and the right of the first night "their version of ethnic cleansing." Gibson's facile recasting of Edward I's crimes against Scotland as twentieth-century "racial" genocide should give us some pause. His invocation of Hitler—and even of ethnic cleansing—gets Nazi understandings of racial science exactly backward. Informed by the "racial" paranoia of Joseph Arthur Comte de Gobineau's *Essay on the Inequality of the Human Races* and Houston Stewart Chamberlain's *The Foundations of the Nineteenth Century*, Hitler so feared miscegenation that he mobilized the technologies of the modern Western state to engage in a program of genocide that murdered 10 million. Furthermore, the Nazis' Nuremburg Laws prohibited marriage—or even extramarital intercourse—between Jews and Aryans. *Braveheart*'s Edward I is not so much interested in mass murder or racial purity as in promising English aristocrats the colonialist's dream: a land filled with passive men and beautiful, sexually available women. He offers virgin land and virgins, all for the taking, the fantasy of rape to a depraved and sexually frustrated nobility.

In juxtaposition to the sexual deviance of England's aristocracy, Scotland stands as a shining example of healthy, monogamous heteronormativity. Gibson takes his audience to a Scottish wedding, a family affair, where men, women, and children celebrate a sacrament. Even when the wedding is disrupted by English soldiers, who arrive to enforce their lord's right to *prima nocte*, a sense of equilibrium is maintained. Gibson notes: "I like this scene a lot, because [the bride] is just able to calmly walk through it and put things right in a very quiet, graceful way and sort of, umm, sacrifice herself. It is important to me to put something quite lyrical into a scene that is essentially quite violent and nasty." In *Braveheart* Wallace courts Murron from the time they are children. She is his one and only love, and their love extends beyond the boundaries of life itself. Wallace and Murron elope, their wedding performed in secret to resist an overlord's insistence on *prima nocte*, to ensure Wallace's absolute claim to possession of his wife's body. Even so, their marriage must be properly consecrated by a priest, the scene framed with a Celtic cross in the background, centered between the cleric and the kneeling couple. Their marriage is consummated in a gloriously green Scottish forest, amid images of fecundity: a lake and a waterfall.[38]

Their relationship, however, is less romance narrative than hagiographic pretext. Wallace's and Murron's relationship begins when as children Murron gives William a thistle flower. In the course of the film, as they exchange this same flower, it is gradually transformed from an actual flower into a symbol that transcends their love to figure the imagined community of Scotland. Wallace gives back the flower to Murron on his return. At their wedding she gives him a handkerchief with the flower embroidered on it, no longer a piece of nature but a symbolic representation of it, of their love, and of the imagined community of Scotland. On the battlefield the handkerchief falls into the hands of the Scottish lord, Robert the Bruce, serving as a reminder of his duty to his "country." Wallace will eventually die with that handkerchief still in his hand. The violation of Murron's body, then, becomes nothing less than the violation of Scotland itself. Gibson emplots Murron's life as hagiography in preparation for his hagiographic treatment of Wallace. Following the paradigm of the female martyr, Murron resists the depraved infidels who want to rape her. She keeps her body intact—at least from her attackers—preferring death to corruption. Prior to Murron's murder, Wallace is a reluctant warrior, claiming: "I came back home to raise crops and, God willing, a family. If I can live in peace, I will." But after fighting off an attempted rape—with overtones of incest that even Gibson finds "pretty skanky"— Murron is publicly murdered by the English, her death used as an example to teach the Scots the futility of resistance. Wallace's heterosexual bona fides firmly established by his marriage, Murron's death frees him to become the warrior he needs to be to save Scotland from English depredations.

The sequence that follows Murron's death, in which an outnumbered and apparently defenseless Wallace avenges her murder, brings together the various strands of our argument, illustrating the means by which Gibson constructs Wallace as a mythic hard-bodied martyr saint. The sequence begins with the overlord intoning, "Now, let the scrapper come to me." This sequence, which is fairly simple on paper—Wallace rides up to the English fortress presenting himself in a posture of surrender, only to pull a mace out of nowhere and begin to bash heads left, right, and center—makes Wallace's apotheosis into warrior saint cinematic. In this highly stylized sequence time is dilated; Gibson draws out the action, increasing its suspense and lyricism, by drastically varying film speed, combining slow motion photography with fast cutting. The scene takes more than three minutes of screen time and consists of nearly sixty shots. Throughout the sequence, shots of the English fortress and its watchful soldiers are intercut with the briefest glimpses of Wallace, as he rides slowly past the stationed guards and up to the fort, apparently ready to submit to its overlord. All of the cinematic devices used in the scene are designed to mark Wallace as a legendary, even mythic, hero. The underscoring uses eerie pipe music syncopated by percussion to heighten the mystery and suspense; diegetic noise—horse's hooves, whinnying, the clank of chain mail—are all intensified for atmospheric effect. Gibson's Wallace is shot in a way that distinguishes him from the English soldiers in the scene. He is frequently shot from a low angle because he is on horseback, positioned above the other characters in the sequence. The soldiers are photographed from odd angles in asymmetrical shots that make them seem off-balance, while Wallace is framed in the center of shots as the "pure" heroic character. The composition of shots offers up the star's body as an object to be gazed at. Throughout the film Gibson's body is the focus of the camera's relentless gaze. Wallace is the only character who

Figure 11. Mel Gibson as William Wallace in *Braveheart*
(Mel Gibson, 1995).

routinely goes either sleeveless or shirtless and his hard body is visible in nearly every shot. The cinematography highlights his body's mass, its strength, its rippling muscles (Figure 11).

In this sequence the camera, as it does throughout the film, lavishes visual attention on Gibson's muscular body, objectifying his hard body. However, the shots are crafted to achieve a paradoxical effect of both display and concealment, increasing the sense that Wallace is a nearly supernatural figure who can appear and disappear at will. Although Gibson as Wallace appears in about 50 percent of the shots, in the early shots in the sequence he is visible only in the briefest of glimpses; his face and body are usually obscured by something in the landscape: bare branches, a tree trunk, a hovel. Occasionally he moves in front of one of the soldiers, an out-of-focus blur, barely recognizable. He seems almost a ghost. In several shots only his horse or a part of his horse (flanks, hooves, nose, head) is visible, a metonymy for Gibson's own hard body. As he nears the fort, the viewer's gaze is allowed to linger on the hard body for longer and longer periods. At one point, he rides into a shot framed by flames, in a symbolic pairing that later in the film will come to signify his legendary status. At the same time, the sequence carries more than a suggestion of the sacred. As he approaches the English fort, he places his muscular arms out, crucifixion style, as a gesture of surrender that anticipates his "martyrdom" at the end of the film. When a soldier reaches for his horse's reins, Wallace pulls a mace, and the screen erupts into a violent action sequence that climaxes when Wallace cuts the throat of the English lord, avenging his wife's death.

Murron returns from the grave both to haunt and inspire Wallace, and by extension her countrymen, to rebellion and sacrifice. As his betrayal and death near, Wallace's friend Hamish questions his motives: "Your dream isn't about freedom. It's about Murron. Your dream is to be a hero 'cause you think she sees you." Wallace replies, "I don't think she sees me. I know she does. And your father sees you, too." In *Braveheart* revolution is a marker of Christian faith, of spirituality, and revolutionaries are somehow connected to the spirit world. A later montage demonstrates the growth of William Wallace's reputation throughout Scotland. As word of Wallace's victories spreads across the countryside, from storyteller to storyteller, he becomes the stuff of legend: "William Wallace killed fifty men. Fifty if it was one. One hundred with his own sword. Cut through them like . . . Moses through the Red Sea." The action film, Rikke Schubart writes, takes on "biblical dimensions"; as "the hero is beyond secular law, he cannot be judged, but has himself become a figure rarely mentioned, an avenging and judging Christ" (196).

The film makes literal Gibson's hyperbolic observation that in Scotland "people just kneel and pray when Wallace's name is mentioned. The guy was the Second Coming of Christ" (quoted in Luhr, 240). In any number of ways Gibson's *The Passion of the Christ* is little more than a very elongated version of *Braveheart*'s final ten minutes.[39] Moved by his faith, moved by his love, William Wallace, like Christ, receives his apotheosis through suffering. There is even a Garden of Gethsemane scene in which Wallace looks toward heaven, admits "I am so afraid," and asks God: "Give me the strength to die well." And like *The Passion of the Christ*, *Braveheart* revels in its portrayal of the beautiful, half-naked male body in pain. But Gibson understands that heroism demands more than just taking a beating. It is not only the brutality of the punishment that makes its recipient holy. He notes, with some peculiar amusement, that Edward II, "a bad king," was tortured: "They took him in the town square and ran a hot poker up his posterior until it came out of his mouth. Apparently you could hear the screams across the English Channel." Gibson's anxieties about Edward II's homosexuality are reflected in his suggestion that the king's punishment was appropriate and deserved: "His French wife was the one who planned all this and carried it out because, apparently, she didn't like him much either, and she had French mercenaries come over and really take over. So really he let the kingdom slip through his fingers." Wallace's execution, on the other hand, visually resembles the crucifixion. Humiliated, dragged through the streets to the jeers of the rabble, Wallace submits to his "purification" willingly, refusing even to take a potion that will dull his senses: "If I am senseless or if I wail, then Longshanks will have broken me." Gibson refers to the scene of Wallace's death as "the big crane shot. It parallels Christ's death." Liberties, however, had to be taken with the way Wallace was actually killed. Gibson admits, "In fact, Wallace had it worse than this. He was, in fact, castrated before they even brought him here, and he wasn't brought on a wagon. They cut off his equipment and they dragged him over cobblestones for about three miles. . . . It was a pretty bad, bad way to go." It is not just good taste that prevents Gibson from exposing the audience to the sight of this punishment—consider, for instance, the pummeling Gibson's audience receives during *The Passion of the Christ*, which the *South Park* boys call a "snuff film." Rather, Gibson needs to deemphasize Wallace's lost masculinity because, in the final analysis, Christian masculinity is what Gibson's Wallace is all about. As Gilles Deleuze notes, "A close examination of masochistic fantasies or rites reveals that while they bring into play the very strictest of the law, the result in every case is the opposite of what might be expected (thus whipping, far from punishing or preventing an erection, provokes and ensures it)" (88).[40] The film ends with Wallace's seeds taking root and growing, both literally—he has impregnated Isabelle—and metaphorically: "In the year of our Lord 1314, patriots of Scotland, starving and outnumbered, charged the fields of Bannockburn. They fought like warrior poets; they fought like Scotsmen and won their freedom."[41] In 1995 Americans could no longer be satisfied with Rambo or John McClane. The American moviegoing public seemed to desire spiritual hypermasculinity, Christian machismo embodied in a hero-saint, and Mel Gibson gave us precisely that in William Wallace. In 2000 the Republican Party, responding to this need in the American psyche, proposed, without a hint of irony, that George W. Bush would fit the bill.

If Joshua Logan's *Camelot* revised medieval legend as a means of reviving the idealism of the Kennedy administration, an idealism lost to the war in Vietnam, racial unrest, rebellious youth, providing comfort to a generation of American white, middle-class suburbanites, Mel Gibson's *Braveheart* erases the failures of Vietnam and the 1960s by looking to the distant past to unearth a new paradigm of leadership for America. By telling the story of William Wallace, Gibson provides an example of Christian heroism for a nation that has lost its way, a "Christian nation" that has forgotten its fundamental values. Gibson could not have imagined George W. Bush emerging from the fantasy offered in *Braveheart*, but there can be no doubt that the image machines Karl Rove brought to the 2000 election were able to tap into the very desires that Gibson's film mobilized.

That movies have an enormous impact on how Americans think about themselves, on how we fashion our identities, and on how we evaluate political leadership is lost on neither screenwriters nor directors. John Ford lays bare the impulse toward hagiography at the conclusion of his classic western *The Man Who Shot Liberty Valance* when a reporter finds out the truth about the film's hero, Ransom Stoddard (James Stewart). Stoddard has built an impressive political career—he has become a U.S. senator—on his reputation for having killed a brutal criminal, Liberty Valance (Lee Marvin). As it turns out, Stoddard's friend, the laconic, unambitious marksman Tom Doniphon (John Wayne), was responsible for shooting Valance. When asked if he is going to expose Stoddard's fraud, the reporter replies pragmatically: "When the legend becomes fact, print the legend." What the reporter leaves unspoken is his understanding that the retelling of the legend transforms it into fact and cements its status as truth. He appreciates the importance of the media in political hagiography, appreciates that print capitalism has helped forge national identity by creating imagined communities drawn to myths of particular charismatic individuals. Both Joshua Logan and Mel Gibson embrace political hagiography with a passion. Of course, John F. Kennedy was no King Arthur—was there even a King Arthur to serve as his political paradigm?—and George W. Bush will never be William Wallace. These films, however, are not particularly interested in such facts; they prefer the legends.

The directors of the movies we turn to now—Youssef Chahine, Dominique Othenin-Girard, and Ridley Scott—attempt to reconfigure twentieth-century Middle East politics, a politics informed by national identity; regional, racial, and religious disputes; and the economics of oil, by coming to terms with the "legends" of the Crusades, the charismatic individuals who dominated these wars. Their films—*Saladin*, *Crociati (The Crusaders)*, and *Kingdom of Heaven*—suggest that current political and cultural rhetoric about the clash of civilizations, political and cultural rhetoric inspiring, it seems, war without end, can be unwound by "traversing the fantasy," by struggling with and rethinking the political hagiographies that have emerged from the medieval events that incited these hostilities and the motives behind the individuals involved. These filmmakers seek, in very interesting ways, to derive a politics of peace for the present by reimagining the violence of the past.

The Crusades

War of the Cross or God's Own Bloodbath?

One would be hard pressed to imagine a medievalism more prominent in contemporary political discourse than the Crusades. As the Muslim world replaced the Soviet Empire in American minds as the major source of global instability, as Ronald Reagan's "evil empire" gave way to George W. Bush's "axis of evil," the military-religious movements that swept across Europe nine hundred years ago suddenly became newsworthy. Of the president's response to the September 11, 2001, attacks on the World Trade Center and Pentagon, the *Boston Globe* columnist James Carroll writes, "George W. Bush plumbed the deepest place in himself, looking for a simple expression of what the assaults of September 11 required. . . . Speaking spontaneously, without the aid of advisors or speechwriters, he put a word on the new American purpose that both shaped it and gave it meaning. 'This crusade,' he said, 'this war on terror' " (J. Carroll, 2). Three years before, in 1998, when most Americans had never even heard of him, Osama bin Laden pronounced a *fatwa* against "Jews and Crusaders."[1] In November 2001, in response to the Bush remark, the historian Thomas F. Madden, writing in William Buckley's *National Review,* characterized the Crusades as a defensive war, "the West's belated response to the Muslim conquest of fully two-thirds of the Christian world" ("Crusade Propaganda"), but irrelevant to current politics in the Middle East. Yet if he was not suggesting a connection between the Crusades and the modern relations between Islam and the West, one wonders about the anxious need to cast the Crusades as a Christian response to Muslim aggression. A month later, the same magazine fanned the flames by publishing a cover caricaturing a vacant-looking George Bush in crusader garb, carrying a shield and banner emblazoned with red crosses. The picture carries the caption "Here We Go Again: Islam and the West," suggesting that the Crusades adequately sum up what Samuel P. Huntington calls the "clash of civilizations."[2] Jonathan Riley-Smith agreed with Madden in blaming Muslim aggression for the Crusades but saw more relevance to the post-9/11 situation when he wrote in the same magazine that "when Osama bin Laden and his followers refer, as they often do, to crusades and crusaders, they are not using language loosely. They are expressing a historical vision, an article of faith that has helped to provide moral justification for the actions of both Arab nationalists and radical Islamists" ("Jihad Crusaders"). Given the prominence of the Crusades in *National Review,* one might argue that they provided a moral justification for the Bush administration's response to those attacks as well. In fact, James Carroll reports that Colin Powell invoked the Crusades yet again in testimony before Congress as recently as March 23, 2005 (8).[3]

Despite claims about the word's semantic innocuousness, any analogy between the current war in Iraq and a holy war that played itself out nine hundred years ago raises important questions about how we justify the decision to go to war but answers them, disturbingly, almost exclusively through Huntington's "clash of civilizations" thesis. The Crusades analogy suggests "nothing less than apocalyptic conflict between irreconcilable cultures" (J. Carroll, 4). Such rhetoric reduces a complex historical interaction to a simplified fundamentalism—both Christian and Muslim—God is on our side, or, in crusader rhetoric, "God wills it."[4] James Carroll reports that when Bush's remark was translated into Arabic, the word *Crusade* was rendered "war of the cross" (5), suggesting that a word that in the English language has become a generalization so bland it could be invoked haphazardly by a president not known for his oratorical skills resonates in Arabic with the religious fervor (perhaps even fanaticism) that was supposed to have motivated the first crusaders. Imagine how Americans might have responded in the days after September 11, 2001, or before the invasion of Iraq in 2003, to a call to "take up the cross."

If we judge the Crusades by the ways in which Hollywood has popularly represented them, Americans apparently do not much like holy wars and do not look on the Crusades as one of the high points of Western civilization. Historians complained when Ridley Scott's *Kingdom of Heaven* offered a hero who articulates his crisis of faith, claiming to have "lost my religion." Certainly, by the standards of twelfth-century Christianity, the response to this statement by the Hospitaler who serves as his adviser seems even more blasphemous: "I put no stock in religion. I've seen the lunacy of fanatics of every denomination be called the will of God. Holiness is in right action and courage on behalf of those who cannot defend themselves. . . . By what you decide to do every day you will be a good man . . . or not." But this is a twenty-first-century movie, and such sentiments, notwithstanding the disturbing growth in religious fundamentalism in this country, do reflect the values of the majority of Americans who understand the separation between church and state and religious tolerance (including tolerance of those who choose not to be religious) as foundational American beliefs. Scott seems to understand that he needs to detach at least his heroes from both the religious zealotry and materialistic motives that drive his crusaders. His heroes, Balian and his father Geoffrey, must be seen as secular crusaders struggling for freedom and religious tolerance against the forces of fundamentalism on both sides.

The clash of civilizations has played itself out in films about the Crusades since the earliest days of Hollywood, in the silent period, during the studio period with Cecil B. DeMille's treatment of the Third Crusade in 1935 ("a flaming love story set in titanic world conflict!" the film's advertising proclaimed), and, in the postwar period, with such melodramas as *King Richard and the Crusaders* in 1954 (David Butler) and *El Cid* in 1961 (Anthony Mann). But it has not always played in predictable ways. Crusades films do not by and large pit Christian heroes against Islamic villains, even if they do predictably include a Christian hero. While medieval scholars scramble to revise Sir Stephen Runciman's thesis that the crusaders were greedy barbarians looting a vastly superior culture, recasting the Christians as pious pilgrims seeking redemption, popular movies continue to represent the crusaders as vicious, murderous, treacherous, greedy, and fanatic, often more villainous than their opponents.[5] Despite its rampant Orientalism, Ridley Scott's 2005 *Kingdom of Heaven* offers a pair of notable Christian villains in the mad and bloodthirsty Raynald of Chatillon and his greedy and treacherous patron, Guy de Lusignan (on the historical Guy see Lindley, "Once, Present, and Future Kings," 19). These sinister representations of crusaders may have something to do with Americans' ideological investment in post-Enlightenment philosophies that relegate religion to the sphere of private expression rather than public policy. Americans tend to think of their public selves, represented by their government, as secular. Religious fanaticism—and this includes holy war—belongs to a savage—and dare we say, medieval—past.[6] As we have tried to show throughout this book, the Middle Ages often function both within academic and popular discourses as the barbaric atavistic past against which modernity shaped itself. As a secular culture, we find it easier to imagine capitalist motives—greed—as the motor of crusading than religious fervor. Crusades movies, then, tend to present a benighted and savage Middle Ages out of which emerges a hero—usually a Christian one—who succeeds not because of his or her religious fervor but because of devotion to such American ideals as equality, rugged individualism, self-determination, action, progress, efficiency, honesty, informality, and public service: Balian can trace his lineage not from documentary histories of the Crusades but from such cinematic crusaders as Sir Kenneth in *King Richard and the Crusaders* and Rodrigo Díaz de Bivar in *El Cid*.

Despite its long cinematic history, during the last forty years of the twentieth century, filmmakers largely ignored the Crusades, relegating them to minor episodes in Robin Hood movies *(Robin and Marian; Robin Hood: Prince of Thieves)*. This seems curious at first glance given the significance of the Middle East in global politics during that period: a period marked by the Six Day War, the Yom Kippur War, the rise of OPEC and the energy crises of the 1970s, the Iranian Revolution, the Iran-Contra affair, and the First Gulf War, as well as the sheer number of violent acts claimed by Islamic groups that included hostage crises in Munich and Iran, the hijacking of the *Achille Lauro* in 1985, the crash of Pan Am flight 103 in Lockerbie in 1988, and the first World Trade Center bombing in 1993. Reasons for this neglect are doubtless many: the complexity of Crusades histories and Americans' unfamiliarity with them (compared, say, to Arthurian legends or even Joan of Arc), and their foregrounding of religion as politics. Most significant, the politics of the second half of the twentieth century was so overdetermined by cold war rhetoric that all other international politics could only be interpreted in terms of their relation to this other "clash of civilizations" that pitted a free West against a totalitarian Soviet Union. The cold war mentality dominated American culture industries, and, in film, anxieties about that conflict tended to be displaced onto a technological future as science fiction (*Invasion of the Body Snatchers*, 1956 and 1978), highlighting fears of Soviet superiority, rather than onto an atavistic Middle Ages. After the fall of the Soviet Empire global politics was reconfigured in terms of the "war on terror," in which Muslim fundamentalists became the central enemy of a Western ideology, which is paradoxically—

even inexplicably—both secular and Christian.[7] On the level of culture, then, the Crusades seem relevant again as an explanation or an analogy for the hostilities that destabilize world politics.

The years that separated the First Gulf War and the current war in Iraq ushered in a revival of interest in the Crusades. The period produced highly touted television documentaries on the subject, by Terry Jones for the BBC in 1995 and Stuart Elliot for the History Channel in 2005. Drawing on those discourses loosely described as "postcolonial," this chapter explores three fiction films about the Crusades that illuminate shifts in the ideology of warfare in a post-Vietnam, post-Soviet era in which both the means and ends of geopolitical conflict have shifted. Two of these—*Kingdom of Heaven* and the Italian miniseries *Crociati (The Crusaders)*—were released after 2001 and seem firmly rooted in post-9/11 political and cultural rhetoric about the clash of civilizations. However, as a reminder that religious fundamentalism has not always dominated the relations—even the hostile ones—between the Muslim and Western worlds, we begin with an examination of Youssef Chahine's 1963 film *Saladin,* a film that advocates a secular resistance to European hegemony in the form of pan-Arabic nationalism. In all of these films the Middle Ages becomes a necessary backdrop against which latter-day anxieties about the postcolonial Middle East play out.

European colonization and its aftereffects—economic, political, social, and cultural—have shaped Arab and Muslim identity over the last century, just as surely as they have overdetermined responses by Western governments to the political expressions of those identities by Arab leaders (most recently, for instance, Saddam Hussein, Osama bin Laden, al-Qaeda, and the Taliban) and popular responses to those expressions on both sides (Abu-Rabi, 128–29). For this reason our analyses of these films draw on the set of discourses loosely designated by the term *postcolonialism,* a theoretical orientation that might best be described as the "discourse of oppositionality which colonialism brings into being" (Jeffrey Cohen, 3), the social, economic, political, and cultural practices created in resistance to colonialism. Postcolonial theorists begin with the recognition that independence from European colonial rule has not necessarily meant independence from Western control. While acknowledging the West's continued hegemony in those regions it once ruled as colonies, it argues that the structures and techniques of dominance have shifted since independence.[8]

Four concepts central to most postcolonial analyses will guide our investigation of these films:

1. Colonialism deprives its subjects of history; to be a colonial subject is to be denied history, to be located in an atavistic and primitive past in need of modernizing. The Tunesian Jewish writer Albert Memmi writes that "the most serious blow suffered by the colonized is being removed from history," and this sentiment is repeated with astonishing frequency in postcolonial writing.[9] Crusades films displace the contemporary Middle East back into a legendary past that exists outside of time, eliding the tragedy and complexity of more recent histories.

2. A second critical concept follows from this denial of history; the African revolutionary Amilcar Cabral put it most succinctly: "The colonists usually say that it was they who brought us into history: today we show that this is not so" (quoted in Young, *Postcolonialism: A Very Short Introduction*, 18). Postcolonialism attempts to bring to light subaltern knowledges, to recover history and culture from below.[10] The historian Carole Hillenbrand, for instance, offers a historical interpretation of the Crusades drawn exclusively from Arab sources. Chahine's *Saladin*, although it draws on the idiom of the Hollywood epic, retells the story of the Third Crusade from an Arab perspective.

3. Postcolonialism engages with temporality, with history, but also with geographical space. Territorialization and deterritorialization have figured centrally in former colonial states, as well as in what Gilles Deleuze and Felix Guattari describe as "nomadism" (which might alternatively be described through concepts like migration or diaspora).[11] The Crusades names an ancient struggle over a strip of land in the desert—the "holy land" and especially the city of Jerusalem—that is no less acrimonious and tragic today than it was nine hundred years ago. The establishment of the state of Israel in 1948 on more or less the same ground as the medieval Crusader Kingdom has fueled instabilities in the region for the past sixty years. What most often gets repressed in Crusades films that pit Arabs against Europeans, Muslims against Christians, is the presence of Jews in the medieval Crusader Kingdom and their imposing presence there today. It is as if Christians come to stand in for, become metonymic of, present-day conflicts between Palestinians and the state of Israel over this same land.

4. Postcolonial culture resists attempts "to give a hegemonic 'normality' to the uneven development and the differential, often disadvantaged, histories of nations, races, communities, peoples," by focusing attention on hybridity and acts

of cultural translation (Bhabha, "Postcolonial Criticism," 437). It is crucial not to turn Bhabha's concept of hybridity into a vague synonym for *multiculturalism,* a kind of bland pluralism that "tolerates" difference while enforcing the cultural hegemony of the West. Against a reading of the Crusades that highlights holy war and the clash of two irreconcilable civilizations we must set an exploration of borders, the spaces where the two (or more) cultures interact and mingle, as well as collide. Although it lies outside the scope of this chapter, such an exploration might well include the Arabic origins of much of what we consider Western culture and epistemology.

To these we would add a fifth element that will loom large in our postcolonial analyses of Crusades filmmaking: Gender is frequently the contested site of cultural differentiation (as in the practice of veiling, for instance, or the creation of what Susan Jeffords calls "hard-bodied" masculinity through warfare), as well as of translation and hybridity, of intercultural mingling, or what Sharon Kinoshita has called "miscegeNation" (113, 126).

Medievalists' engagement with postcolonial theory over the last decade has produced almost ritualistic declarations that mingle anxieties about anachronism, frustration over the marginalization of the Middle Ages within a theory that seems to stake its claims on the ground of modernity, and the conviction that what we call modernity emerged out of the rupture with the medieval past that underwrites the colonial *mentalité*.[12] They fret over statements, like that of Arif Dirlik, who argues that extending postcolonial studies to the "pre-modern" will result in "a confounding of present and past," flattening out historical specificity and promoting false or misleading analogies (Ingham and Warren, 9). Others fear that "reading the colonial histories of premodern Europe" might collude with the very colonialist fantasies postcolonialism was designed to critique (Ingham, "Contrapuntal Histories," 48). However, if, as medievalists, we believe that claims about Western cultural superiority rest on claims of Western modernity, on a break with a primitive and barbaric—and hence medieval—past, then not only do medievalists have the obligation to traverse those fantasies by engaging with medieval histories of colonization, but so must postcolonial theorists. This is not to reduce all colonialisms to the same thing, but rather it is an argument for careful and specific histories, for what Patricia Ingham calls "contrapuntal histories," comparative studies of different temporalities and geographies, the "intertwined histories and overlapping territories of colonial rule" (48).

Hollywood Orientalism

Despite the more than forty-year gap between *Saladin* and *Kingdom of Heaven*, movies about the Crusades have a long history in Hollywood. For this reason it is worth considering how Hollywood imagined the Crusades before *Saladin*. Hollywood films about the Crusades connect medievalism to the discourse Edward Said identified more than thirty years ago as Orientalism, by which he means not only the academic discipline created to study Oriental cultures but also the four-thousand-year-long historical and cultural relationship between Europe and Asia and the "ideological suppositions, images and fantasies about a currently important and politically urgent region of the world" ("Orientalism Reconsidered," 14). Crusades films orientalize not primarily, as we might expect, by demonizing the Arab and Muslim world as irredeemably violent and barbaric, a world of hyper-masculine aggression, as so much of the political rhetoric does (although they sometimes do that as well). Rather filmmakers locate Muslim antipathy toward America and the West in this earlier, almost legendary, time, bypassing altogether a complicated history of political and economic colonization by the West, the creation of the state of Israel in 1948, the rise of a pan-Arabic nationalism in the 1950s and 1960s, the politics of oil, and the growing power of religious fundamentalism—both Christian and Islamic—in the twenty-first century. It is far easier to see Muslim hostilities toward the West as the "clash of civilizations," pitting such romantic and legendary figures as Richard the Lionheart and Saladin against one another, than as a nearly insoluble and tragic political, economic, social, and religious tangle involving oil production and the Western dependency on fossil fuels, the state of Israel (the latter-day Crusader Kingdom) and territorial dispossession, the aftermath of the Holocaust and national and local rivalries, the World Bank and poverty, modernization and the place of religion in the modern world. Hollywood films frequently figure the Orient geographically as the historical medieval. Both the medieval and the Orient in these films are marked by barbarism and violence and, with the exception of the hero, as lacking in such liberal virtues as freedom, tolerance, and self-determination; at the same time, they are cultures of exotic romance, display, spectacle, and excess.[13] More than any other event associated with the Crusades, the Third Crusade, launched in 1187 in response to news of Saladin's reconquest of Jerusalem, has seized the Hollywood imagination because it features two imposing figures of medieval chivalry, Richard the Lionheart, the king of England, and Saladin, the sultan who united Syria and Egypt (Aberth, 70).

King Richard and the Crusaders, a film adaptation of *The Talisman*, Sir Walter Scott's novel about the Third Crusade, provides an illustration of Hollywood Orientalism that might have been culled from the pages of Said's book. Rex Harrison, who receives star billing, plays the legendary Arab leader Saladin literally in blackface. Described grandly in a vaguely Orientalist (that is, "unremittingly bombastic")[14] style by the opening voice-over narrative as the "Sultan of the one thousand tribes of Araby, master of the arts of desert warfare, genius of the methods of swift entrapment," Saladin is portrayed as an honorable man whose virtues are seen only as a function of his contact with a superior Western culture whose reputation for chivalry seems little in evidence in the film. While the film is largely taken up with internecine treachery among the crusaders, in the scenes in which he appears, Saladin's association with the Orientalist stereotypes Said enumerates is noteworthy: "In the films and television the Arab is associated either with lechery or bloodthirsty dishonesty. He appears as an oversexed degenerate, capable, it is true, of cleverly devious intrigues, but essentially sadistic, treacherous, low" (286–87). In *King Richard and the Crusaders*, Saladin, despite or perhaps because of his many virtues, functions simultaneously as a confirmation of these stereotypes and an exception.

Saladin is an exception because he is associated in the filmmakers' and the crusaders' minds with chivalry. Early in the film, the hero, Sir Kenneth, a Scottish knight,[15] is sent as a vanguard for Richard's wife, Berengaria, and cousin Edith, who have determined to go on pilgrimage. In the desert Kenneth encounters a Saracen who, he later discovers, is none other than Saladin himself. This scene presents an opportunity to introduce the "good Arab" through the lens of Orientalist fantasies. Kenneth returns Saladin's friendly greeting with aggressive hostility and the two engage in single combat, Kenneth furiously, Saladin with ironic detachment. Saladin defeats Kenneth, calls for peace between them, and the two engage in friendly conversation. At this point Kenneth is still unaware of his interlocutor's identity, believing him a physician sent by Saladin to cure Richard of the poisoned arrow that has struck him down. Kenneth remarks on his opponent's "civilized" behavior: "By Our Lady, this is chivalry from one enemy who has never seen the other. The warriors of Saladin and the Knights of Richard have a goodly creed in common: Chivalry." Saladin explains how he learned from the crusaders to become "at heart a knight." Yet like all "Saracens," Saladin is treacherous—"We Saracens have ears in the boughs of trees"—and violent—the crusaders fight, according to Kenneth, "against you who live by the sword." The scene calls attention to cultural differences between the crusaders and their opponents. Muslims are feminized by their curious customs. Muslim's don't drink: "Allah forbids it." "You delicate creatures," the hearty Scotsman exclaims. Everything, even their postures, calls attention to the gulf that separates these two. Kenneth lounges against a palm tree, while Saladin sits cross-legged in a modified lotus.

Gender seems to be the ground on which European and Arab are distinguished. Nothing in the film separates Christian from Muslim more definitively than their treatment of women. Saladin tells Kenneth, "You could never teach me to be so mindless as to make goddesses of women." The Scotsman replies, "You make slaves of women." The reference to goddesses no doubt invokes the tradition of courtly love, which elevated the beloved in poetry but bore very little relationship to the actual treatment of Christian women during the Middle Ages. Whatever the historical situation,[16] however, the film is at pains to contrast Muslim treatment of women to a more "enlightened" Christian approach. It does so by having Richard bring along with him on crusade a whole courtful of women, including his wife and his cousin Edith, who falls in love with the humble Kenneth.[17] Muslim contempt for women is amply demonstrated later in the film when Kenneth is expelled from Richard's court and finds himself a guest in "the camps of Islam." In the previous scene, having been defeated by a dishonorable Richard in single combat, Kenneth lies nearly unconscious on the ground, attended by Edith, with whom he is in love. A dissolve indicating a change of scene reveals Kenneth returning to consciousness, with an Arab woman in a diaphanous veil and an exotic headdress occupying the same spot Edith had in the previous scene. The two shots are identical in composition, drawing attention to the comparison between Christian and Muslim treatment of women. The camera pulls back to reveal Saladin sitting cross-legged on a throne of pillows. Pulling back further into a long shot, the camera reveals that except for the two men, all the occupants of the room are women; this is Saladin's harem, suggestive both of opulence and a thinly veiled eroticism (which appears to be what the diaphanous veil connotes for Hollywood filmmakers). The sequence ends with a belly dancer performing in a sexualized costume for the pleasure of Saladin and Kenneth. As the scene ends, the belly dancer, contorted into a nearly impossible backbend, appears to be offering her genitals to Saladin, suggesting his court is a site of sexual excess. The purpose of this scene appears to be to cement a homosocial relationship between the two men through an exchange of women.

The scene also serves to show Saladin's despotism, another trait associated with Orientalism. As Saladin and Kenneth emerge from the sultan's tent, a voice cries, "Fall ye down before the light of the world, the hand of the holy prophet on earth." The crowd in the courtyard falls to its collective knees; even Kenneth is forced to his knees by two nearby guards. The Arab ruler, even one "enlightened" by contact with Westerners, exercises an arbitrary power, untempered by laws and political institutions or by the rugged individualism that bows to no man: Kenneth, though forced to kneel, refuses the obsequious kowtowing that marks the Orientalist performance of submission. Most of the film is designed to contrast the complexities of the Christian political system in relation to this simple but tyrannical form of government. Indeed, much of the infighting among the Christians in the film is taken up with political debates about who should lead the Crusade. The crusaders are seen as politically fractious but more liberated than their Muslim counterparts, represented almost exclusively through Harrison's Saladin. Although the infighting is seen as detrimental to the crusaders' cause, it is also a sign of their greater freedom and social mobility. The plot, which revolves more around romance than warfare, requires that Kenneth surmount his humble origins and marry the cousin of the king, who, in contrast to Saladin's bombastic self-reference, refers to himself quite informally as "Dick" Plantagenet.

Anthony Mann's epic film *El Cid* reproduces its share of Orientalist tropes (see Aberth, 125–47; Ganim, "Reversing the Crusades"), and, although not technically a Crusades film, it reminds us that media images of black-robed Muslims rioting against the Christian West have a surprisingly long cinematic history. Set against the eleventh-century reconquest of Spain, *El Cid* presents three types of Muslims—the good, the bad, and the effeminate—but the Muslim enemies of Spain are dominated by an image of religious fanaticism. The film opens with a voice-over describing the "savage" forces of the African Ben Yusuf, leader of the fundamentalist Almoravids who are attacking Spain from across the sea. Against a heavy drumbeat, Yusuf is introduced as a wild-eyed religious fanatic, swathed in black robes and headscarves, bent on world domination: "The Prophet has commanded us to rule the world! . . . And when they are weak and torn, I will sweep up from Africa." His costume (and those of his followers) reminds us that women are not the only ones veiled in Muslim cultures. The meanings of the veil, however, are quite different for men than those associated with women's veiling. On men turbans and headscarves hide identity; they carry associations of wearing a mask, "of romantic banditry, of being outlawed, adopting a disguise as a means of self-protection against the odds of the authority in power" (Young, *Postcolonialism: A Very Short Introduction*, 88). In addition, the uniformity of the veil, Young argues, "increases the masculine subversive resonance. The male veil is as-

sertive" (88); the female veil, at least for Europeans, signifies submission and frequently eroticism.[18]

Yusuf rejects the wealth and civilization of Islamic Spain (Al-Andalus) as
effeminate. In the film's opening sequence he inveighs against Spain's Muslim
leaders: "When men speak of you they speak of poets, music-makers, doctors, scientists. Where are your warriors! . . . You have become women. Burn your books.
Make warriors of your poets. Let your doctors invent new poisons for our arrows.
Let your scientists invent new war machines. And then kill! Burn!" The scene
ends with a close-up of a veiled Yusuf in which all we can see are his mad eyes and
outstretched arm, dissolving to scenes showing the destructive effects of his war
on Spanish Christians. The film later bears out Yusuf's assessment of Muslim
Spain as weak and womanish, portraying the king of Valencia, in contrast both to
Yusuf's and El Cid's hard-bodied masculinities, in makeup and jewelry, as an orientalized and effeminate stereotype of opulence. In contrast to both these images
is the good Arab, the Westernized Moutamin, who gives Rodrigo his name, El
Cid, and swears allegiance to him. *El Cid* embraces the masculinist warrior ethos
of the epic film, luxuriating throughout in large sweeping crane shots of massed
armies. But Mann reserves his most disturbing imagery for Yusuf's armies, at
times presenting "Islamic mobs" whipped into an anti-Christian frenzy all too familiar to viewers of American newscasts.[19] At others, drawing on a "fascist dramaturgy" that might have been culled from Leni Riefenstahl, the film depicts masses
of identically black-robed and veiled Muslim soldiers moving silently against a
midnight-blue sky accompanied by a muffled drumbeat in preparation for a siege
of Valencia. As day breaks over this army, the music swells and Mann's choreography, the "the orgiastic transactions between mighty forces and their puppets,
uniformly garbed and shown in ever swelling numbers . . . alternates between
ceaseless motion and a congealed, static, 'virile' posing" (Sontag, 91). Nothing,
however, captures this "static virile posing" as spectacularly as the film's final shot
of El Cid, a dead inert body strapped to a horse, riding into his final battle.

Contrapuntal Histories

Chahine's *Saladin* is as much about the Arab nationalism that remapped the
post–World War II Middle East as it is about the medieval Crusades. Most commentators on the film point out Chahine's deliberate reference in his Arabic title,
Al-Nasir Salah al-Din, to the charismatic Egyptian president Gamal Abdel Nasser,
who, like the medieval Kurdish liberator of Jerusalem, in 1958 succeeded in unit-

ing Syria and Egypt (in a union that would last only until 1961).[20] The epithet Al-Nasir, "the victorious" (Kiernan, 135), cements the connection between Chahine's film and the flowering of pan-Arab nationalism in the 1950s and 1960s that began when Nasser became Egyptian president in 1956. Nasser became the symbol of Arab nationalism, a movement that attempted to unite Arabs on the basis of a common history, culture, and language, calling at its most extreme for the creation of an independent Arab state. Nasser's formulation of Arab nationalism, though no less hostile to the state of Israel or to U.S. interests in the region than today's religious fundamentalism, was primarily a political and secular movement, relying on socialism and modernization to achieve its aims. Chahine, a Christian, shared Nasser's political commitments, and these are reflected in *Saladin*, which appeared midway between the Suez Crisis of 1956 (when Nasser successfully nationalized the Suez Canal) and the disastrous Six Day War (1967) with Israel that marks the end of pan-Arab nationalism. As Joseph Massad notes, "Historical epics are not simply used by Chahine to illustrate historical events, but as a lens on the present. In this sense, his epics emerge more as national allegories" (Chahine and Massad, 81). The film illustrates—even enacts—the creation of a symbol around which the "imagined community" of an Arab nation might cohere.

Carole Hillenbrand suggests that the Arab and wider Muslim worlds remained largely indifferent to the legacy of medieval crusading—and Saladin's role in those conflicts—until relatively recently, perhaps because other colonial incursions—the Ottomans, for instance—were more pressing. The Arabic term, *harb al-salib* (war of the Cross), a European borrowing, was only introduced in the middle of the nineteenth century in response to the European colonization that followed the collapse of the Ottoman Empire. Saladin, who, for the West, became one of the great romantic heroes of history and "a knight without fear or blame who often had to teach his opponents the right way to practise chivalry" (Hillenbrand, 593), was ignored in the Middle East. Both Nur al-Din, Saladin's predecessor, and Baybars, the thirteenth-century Turkish ruler of Egypt, achieved wider recognition for their defeat of crusading armies. But European colonization undoubtedly shaped Arabic understanding of what was for centuries seen as simply a series of invasions from the West by "an aggressive, backward and religiously fanatic Europe." This historical memory would shift again in the nineteenth and twentieth centuries "as Europeans arrived once again to subjugate and colonize territories in the Middle East" (Hillenbrand, 590). In the fight for independence from European colonial rule Saladin's reputation grew. Even before the First World War an anonymous Arab author took the pseudonym *Salah al-din* to protest the growing Zionist threat in Palestine, and a university named after the twelfth-century sultan opened in Jerusalem in 1915. Bitterly ironic is the appropriation of Saladin, a Kurd, to promote the career of the Iraqi dictator Saddam Hussein. Hillenbrand reproduces a propaganda picture from the 1980s that juxtaposes Saladin and Hussein (Hillenbrand, 594–95).

Chahine's film draws on Saladin's legendary status to enable Arabs to experience a shared sense of connection and community, to "imagine" something like an Arab nation in the form described by Etienne Balibar: "a narrative which attributes to these entities [nations] the continuity of a subject," that enables its citizens to believe "that the generations which succeed one another over centuries . . . have handed down to each other an invariant substance," and "that the process of development from which we select aspects retrospectively, so as to see ourselves as the culmination of that process, was the only one possible, that is, it represented a destiny" (Balibar, 86). If, as John Ganim has argued, films about the Crusades, about medieval East-West conflict, orientalize the Middle Ages as excessive, autocratic, and barbaric ("Reversing the Crusades," 48–50), then Chahine, in creating a contrapuntal history of the Crusades, inverts the ideological perspective of Orientalism by returning to an older nineteenth-century model of medievalism in which the Middle Ages represents a utopian ideal, a "fierce reproach" to the present framed in political and explicitly secular terms (Ganim, *Medievalism and Orientalism*, 4; on the reversal of Orientalism see Matar).

Chahine's political and artistic goal in the film seems to be to create subjects capable of recognizing (or misrecognizing) themselves as subjects of an Arab nation whose experience of nationality extends back nine hundred years to the medieval Crusades. Like the title, the opening credit sequence works to link past and present, with Chahine literally issuing a "call" to his fellow countrymen to throw off their colonial subjectivity and to reimagine themselves as members of an Arab nation, united behind a charismatic leader (hence the desire to link the legendary Saladin to the contemporary leader, Nasser). While several critics have pointed to Chahine's use of Eisensteinian montage later in the film in the famous shots of Christians attacking a Muslim pilgrim caravan (Aberth, 92–94; Ganim, "Reversing the Crusades"; Fawal, 160–61), we would argue that, from the opening shot, Chahine deploys montage as a mechanism of interpellation to create and resolve perceptual puzzles. The credit sequence, in an astonishingly economical three-part progression that lasts a little more than seven minutes, takes us through a process of perception, of "recognizing," that interpellates the subjects of an Arab nation.

In the first part the leader is called to his task. Before any credits appear, before we are even given the title of the film, there is a brief "teaser" scene that begins with a simple shot of an unknown man entering a room. What is most significant about this shot is all that we, as viewers, don't know. It becomes a perceptual puzzle because we lack the information that would enable us fully to understand what is going on and how it relates to the film we are about to see. Disregarding the filmic convention of providing narrative exposition at the beginning, this scene plunges us into the action. The viewer must put the situation together piece by piece and, in so doing, answer its "hail." A second, establishing shot reveals the entire space to be a large hall, a court; nothing, however, explains where it is or whose it is except that it seems vaguely Middle Eastern.[21] Conventional editing techniques would require the establishing shot to come first. Montage sequences work best (that is, they are most easily "recognized" by a viewer) when the whole gives way to an examination of parts rather than the reverse.

The dialogue establishes that the entering man is Hossam Edin, a commander, but all we know about his interlocutor is that he is a sultan who is "our last hope."[22] The interlocutors discuss the "lamentable state" of Jerusalem. A montage follows, illustrating that state, with a voice-over by Hossam Edin, who represents the *cri de cœur* of that city. An attack by a crusading army is followed by scenes illustrating the people's suffering: "young and old have lost their smiles." For Arab audiences in 1963, such scenes would resonate with loss, both past and present. They seem almost documentary in style, reminding an Arab audience of recent humiliations, of the creation of Israel, of the heartbreak of Palestinian refugees, and of internecine Arab conflicts. If the first sequence creates a puzzle by giving us fragments without a whole, the montage sequence reverses that strategy. The establishing shot depicts a long line of refugees stretching horizontally across the screen, the line framed by the expanses of barren desert that surrounds it. This is juxtaposed with a series of shots that put a face on this anonymous suffering by showing its parts: a starving "refugee" family being fed by too few loaves of bread; a heartrending violin playing behind the expository voice-over, suggesting desolation; the patriarch of this family inquiring of a small veiled girl whether the water in the well is drinkable; the mute girl indicating that it is not. Such scenes could not fail to call to mind the dispossession of Palestinians from their homes when the state of Israel was created, the issue that precipitated the 1956 Suez crisis and would provoke the Six Day War four years after the appearance of *Saladin*. These scenes are a reminder not only of Arab dispossession, hunger, and thirst in the medieval past but of contemporary problems a disunited Arab world is unable to address.

At the very moment the audience is struggling to resolve this opening sequence into a coherent narrative, Chahine encourages the audience to desire a solution to these problems. He places his audience in the scene through a point-of-view shot that begins inside a hut looking out through a door. The shot represents no identifiable intradiegetic perspective and so compels the audience to take up that position. The shot slowly tracks toward the door and outside, as a voice-over promises that "Allah would not forget us." At this moment the audience is included in that "us." The music, which has modulated to a Middle Eastern air, crescendos and, as an elder promises a "liberator," suddenly stops. A silence, interrupted only by the sound of the wind, ensues as a series of brief shots shows the faces of the refugees awaiting their salvation. As the audience, we are interpellated as we wait with them. From the crowd, the small veiled girl emerges, and the camera tracks her to a pond. She points to vibrations on the surface of the water. The refugees and the audience together, united in a single point of view, see these vibrations and then hear the sound of drums signaling the coming of this unnamed liberator. Suddenly the music swells, and, as if in answer to the call, the name *Saladin* covers the screen in Arabic, both resolving the perceptual puzzle and interpellating the viewer. It is both answer to a prayer and the title of the movie that will follow. The scene has built to this moment, the moment that calls Saladin to his destiny as liberator of Jerusalem. And, while it does build suspense using conventions wholly familiar to Hollywood audiences, that is not the scene's primary purpose; rather it allows the audience to participate in the call to arms, to be interpellated along with the film's title character.

The credit sequence that follows plays over a loud martial sounding musical theme, with lots of percussion and a minor key that we have come to associate with the East.[23] Although viewers may pay little attention to credits, Chahine uses this time to create a second level of interpellation on the scale of the body. While the credits roll and the chorus swells, the camera tracks slowly over what appears to be a nonrepresentational textured background, an abstract play of light and shadow. Curiously, our inability to resolve the image into something coherent does not create perceptual uncertainty, does not create suspense. The camera lulls us into complacency; we think we know what we are seeing (background décor we can safely ignore) until the camera zooms out and suddenly reveals first an eye, then the outline of a nose, and finally, the complete image of a face, a portrait of Saladin. This strategy shows how interpellation happens on the scale of the body; it requires that the performer's body be recognizably human to the viewer's perception. At what point in this shot does Saladin emerge as recognizably human? At what point does his humanity cohere from a series of tiny dots, an abstract play of light and shadow? This involves the perceptual apparatus of the body in the process of interpellation.[24] Once recognized, the portrait could not fail to call to mind the propagandistic uses of large-scale photographs of national leaders—such as Nasser—as symbols to provide an imaginative focus for the community of the nation. Such images of charismatic leadership echo in popular culture, in cinema, and in song, as for instance, in the 1954 celebration of Nasser by the famous Egyptian chanteuse Umm Kulthum:

> Gamal, emblem of patriotism
>
> .   .   .   .
>
> You have freed the Nile from its usurpers
>
> .   .   .   .
>
> . . . you have lit a guiding light
> In its shine all countries converge
> You have united the Arab world (Valassopoulos, 102)

Chahine simultaneously calls on this practice to create his pan-Arab hero and dissolves it into nonrepresentational abstraction. The something that emerges from the pictorial disorder teaches us to desire the coherent, the recognizable, and to translate that desire into political action. Unfortunately, rather than desiring the institutions and structures that could cope with the suffering created by dispossessions both medieval and modern, we are taught to desire the charismatic leader, a desire that arguably led to the failure of Arab nationalism in the 1960s.[25]

But despite Chahine's play with Eisensteinian montage in the credits (and elsewhere in the film, as we will show), *Saladin* remains an epic film in the tradition of Hollywood realism (see Ganim, "Reversing the Crusades," 46). By the time the opening credits have finished, the whole has come into focus. Saladin has accepted his mission; he has been interpellated. "The Arabs await you," his commanders tell him. "I can't ignore their call." Note the emphasis on Arabs rather than, say, Muslims, which identifies the film's nationalist rather than religious allegiances. "My dream is to see the Arab nation united under one flag." The film's interests are finally political, not religious, which is not surprising since Chahine himself, though Egyptian, is Christian, not Muslim. Saladin, in turn, "hails" the subjects of his new polity, the Arabs. Note the circularity of this process: "the Arabs" call for a liberator, which endows Saladin with subjectivity, and the call of the masses is followed by Saladin's call to "the Arabs" to rally around him and constitute themselves as a nation. The success of this call is illustrated by a second montage showing the Arabs answering Saladin's hail: a crowd scene of turbaned and veiled men running up over a hill, a city in the background, a series of dissolves showing troops superimposed over an image of Saladin. This montage effectively exploits the potential of CinemaScope, whose anamorphic lens, as we noted earlier, tends to orient the mise-en-scène horizontally at the expense of flattening out the picture: "one gets the sense of viewing figures on a frieze with all that this connotes in terms of the heroic, the grandiose, the 'Homeric' in scope" (Halim, 82). This montage uses CinemaScope effectively to convey the size of the response to Saladin's call. On the horizontal level one sees the multitudes rushing off to war; on the vertical plane Saladin's superimposed face (a reference back to the credit photograph) establishes his larger-than-life heroism (Halim, 82).

Having forged a connection between Arab unity in the heroic past and the current situation, *Saladin* plays out the events of the Third Crusade, a crusade precipitated by the reconquest of Jerusalem. Saladin emerged as an Arab leader—a successor to the celebrated Nur al-Din, the sultan of Syria from 1154 to 1174—after taking Egypt in 1169 and Damascus in 1174. He was able to unite enough Arabs to defeat a factionalized crusader army at the Horns of Hattin in July of 1187, capturing and ultimately executing Raynald of Chatillon, a man known for his extraordinary cruelty toward Muslims, including raids on pilgrim caravans (one of which is depicted in a famous scene from *Saladin*) and the capture of Saladin's sister.[26] Afterward he moved on to Jerusalem itself, easily dispatching the exhausted remnants of the crusaders. The Third Crusade was launched by Gregory VIII when news reached Europe that Jerusalem had been retaken by the "infidel." It attracted such European luminaries as Richard I, king of England; Philip II of France; and the Holy Roman emperor Frederick Barbarossa, who died en route. Although his feats in the Holy Land made Richard legendary—he was able to recapture Acre and Jaffa—he failed to retake Jerusalem and left the Holy Land in 1192, having settled a truce with Saladin that left Jerusalem under Muslim control but allowed Christians access to the city.[27]

By all accounts, Saladin was a brilliant politician and military strategist. Chahine expands this characterization, portraying him not only as a warrior but as urbane and multifaceted, a physician and a scientist. Saladin is shown not only planning and directing battles but performing scientific experiments and, after Richard is wounded by a poisoned arrow, healing him. Saladin does not merely tolerate Jerusalem's Christian population; he seems an enthusiastic advocate of multicultural exchange. He maintains Christians—or at least one, Issa—in his retinue. Saladin is a Renaissance man before the Renaissance, an enlightened man before the Enlightenment; the East, in fact, becomes the source of Enlightenment ideology as he is able to impose his beliefs on an intellectually backward European Middle Ages. Chahine inverts Hollywood's Orientalism, representing the Christians generally as bloodthirsty, avaricious, treasonous, and intolerant. They kill pilgrims and steal their money, slaughter prisoners, plot against each other, and bribe officials. This opposition between enlightened East and barbaric West is initially set up early in the film in the events leading up to the Battle of Hattin, which represents Raynald of Chatillon as wild-eyed, maniacal, and yet effeminate, with long blond locks cut Prince Valiant style, ordering a bloody attack on a pilgrim caravan to finance his war. His wife, Virginia, is scheming, her sexual promiscuity evidenced by a willingness to offer her sexual favors to all who can aid in her political ambitions.

Chahine's version of the Battle of Hattin conforms to the requirements of Hollywood hagiography in portraying Saladin leading a wildly outnumbered army against Raynald (in fact Saladin had slightly more troops than the crusaders). Saladin wins by his wits, destroying the Europeans' water supply and forcing them off of the high ground they occupy and into the desert. But Raynald is a singularly bad commander. His characterization embraces the stereotype of the third world despot as he steals water from his parched men and blithely sacrifices the lives of the underclasses. However, to maintain his hagiographic portrait of Saladin and the mythologies of pan-Arabism, Chahine must gloss quickly over Saladin's conquest of Jerusalem. He does not even include Saladin's triumphant entrance into the city, although historically Saladin chose October 2 to mark the occasion because that day commemorated the prophet's Night Journey to Heaven from that city (Aberth, 71). Instead, Chahine compresses a four-month campaign into the single Battle of Hattin. Soon after the battle has commenced, Virginia indicates to the king of Jerusalem, watching the battle from atop the hill, that "Saladin is at the gates of Jerusalem," although the battle has just begun. Chahine most likely does this to avoid having to portray Saladin as a siege general who brings suffering on the Muslims of Jerusalem, his own people. The battle for Jerusalem that is played out in the film occurs much later, after Saladin has occupied the city, when he can defend the inhabitants of Jerusalem against besieging crusaders. We see Saladin killing only crusaders—other soldiers—never civilians. This enables Chahine to portray Arabs as "a peace-loving people who fight only when attacked by the aggressively warlike Christians of the West" (Aberth, 102).

The crusaders, on the other hand, in an inversion of conventional Orientalism, are consistently depicted, if not as barbarians, as irredeemably savage. While the Christians live as opulently as Saladin's retinue, they seem to depend on the spoils of war for their wealth. They produce no culture of their own, except the culture of warfare; they conquer and appropriate. The one exception is King Richard, whom Chahine sets up as a foil for Saladin, a Christian king capable of becoming a worthy foe. Most of the other Europeans in the movie desire the Crusades only as a mechanism to accumulate wealth. The distinction is made clear in a pair of scenes as Raynald's widow, Virginia, embarks on a kind of "shuttle diplomacy," going first to Richard's court in England, then to Philip's in France, to raise a crusading army to retake Jerusalem after it is lost. The parallels between the scenes reveal the different tactics she uses. In England Virginia appeals to Richard's idealism, in France to Philip's greed. The scene at Richard's court begins with Virginia, in a mirror image of the opening credits, enumerating the atrocities allegedly suffered by Christians at the hands of the Arabs. In fact, she is projecting onto Arabs the crimes her own dead husband has committed, as the transition from the previous scene makes clear. In the previous scene Saladin kills Raynald and laments, "If I could punish him for all his crimes, I'd kill him a thousand times over." Immediately there is a cut to Richard's court and Virginia's accusations: "Christian children are dying of thirst, pilgrims to Jerusalem taken prisoner, places of worship are being destroyed, the priests are fleeing to the desert." Richard's reply indicates the extent to which he fashions himself through the romantic conventions of hagiography and chivalry: "The Age of Martyrs is back!" he exclaims hyperbolically, vowing that "the Arabs will never occupy Jerusalem as long as there lives a Christian knight called Richard the Lionheart." The film validates this self-assessment when it closes with a crane shot depicting Richard and his knights in a "war council" at a round table, explicitly linking Richard with the paradigmatic British narrative of Christian chivalry—King Arthur and his Round Table (Figure 12).

Richard's idealism is necessary as a counterpoint to Saladin's. He is not, however, a hero yet; he will become one through his multiple encounters with Sala-

Figure 12. Crane shot of Youssef Chahine's Round Table in *Saladin* (1963).

din in the Holy Land (encounters that never took place historically; see Aberth, 73). At this point in the film Chahine must establish credibly Richard's idealism but undermine it by filtering it through the treachery of his court. For this reason the scene in which he first appears is shot largely from the perspective of Richard's brother John and a courtier, ironically named Arthur, who are plotting in the foreground of the shot while Virginia continues her mendacious pleas in the background. Richard's ability to act heroically is undercut throughout the film by the scheming of everyone around him.

Two scenes later, in a parallel scene, Virginia makes a very different appeal to the French king, Philip. The scene opens on a close-up of female hands scooping up jewels, a direct reference to the earlier raid on the pilgrim caravan, which features shots of crusaders luxuriating in the treasures they have stolen. The camera tilts upward to reveal that the hands belong to Virginia. In contrast to the sober black mourning she wears at Richard's court, here she wears an elegant blue gown and heavy jewelry. While the English court is dark and somber, the French court is colorful, bright (it is outdoors), and apparently wealthy. Philip is elaborately dressed in sky blue and furred robes decorated with the fleur-de-lis. Yet the scene carries orientalizing overtones. In the background we see figures cavorting. They are all women; no other men appear in the scene. Chahine insinuates the kinds of stereotypes about the Oriental harem found in films like DeMille's *The Crusades* and David Butler's *King Richard and the Crusaders*. Philip fondles the jewels Virginia has offered him. She tells him that "all the treasures of the East . . . can be yours if you liberate Jerusalem." Visually Chahine creates a metonymic link between Virginia's eroticized and commodified body and the "treasures of the East," making it clear that Philip's motivations are entirely materialistic. He will crusade to increase his possessions. This connects him with virtually every other crusader; Raynald's sacking of the pilgrim caravan, Virginia's machinations, John's and Arthur's plots against Richard, and Conrad of Montferrat's scheming have only one aim: to satisfy their greed and ambition.

Up to this point it is possible to read the film as an instance of the "clash of civilizations," even as a postcolonial celebration of the conquered and colonized rising up against their European and Christian conquerors. Saladin and Richard present us with two larger-than-life figures, symbols of their respective nations (forgetting for the moment that Saladin was, in fact, a Kurd), who square off against each other, as Nasser stood up against the British in the conflict over the Suez Canal. In this formulation the nation is understood as a coherent intersection of linguistic, historical, geographic, religious, ethnic, racial, and cultural commonalities. However, just as the credit sequence introduced a kind of contrapuntal "free play" that disassembles the apparently seamless perceptual processes of recognition by which the subjects of the nation are interpellated, the text of the film unpacks the nationalist narrative of pure origins that buttresses the clash of civilizations thesis. Against both the self-serving treachery of the factionalized crusaders and the harmony and idealism of the Arabs, Chahine sets three ancillary characters who complicate the film's representation of pan-Arabic unity and cultural purity: the governor of Acre, Issa, and Louise de Lusignan. Not every Arab is virtuous, and not every Christian is evil—a banal statement to be sure but an observation that enables us to begin to explore Homi Bhabha's concept of "hybridity": "the creation of new transcultural forms within the contact zone produced by colonisation" (Ashcroft, Griffiths, and Tiffin, 118). In *The Location of Culture* Bhabha locates this hybridity in what he calls "the third space of enunciation," a third space that "quite properly challenges our sense of historical identity of culture as a homogenizing, unifying force, authenticated by the originary Past, kept alive in the national tradition of the People." This third space, "though unrepresentable in itself, . . . constitutes the discursive conditions of enunciation that ensure that the meaning and symbols of culture have no primordial unity or fixity; that even the same signs can be appropriated, translated, rehistoricized and read anew" (37). *Saladin* explores this postcolonial hybridity by interweaving plot sequences involving these characters in espionage and heterosexual romance, both narrative devices that threaten the purity of racial, national, and religious origin in the film and so gesture toward the third space of enunciation; these devices confound the integrity of borders, mingling differences (between races, nations, religions) in ways that both threaten and encourage.

The film's opening portrays economically the governor of Acre as a mercenary courtier proffering his services to the side that will offer him most. His treachery is announced from the beginning; the credit sequence that calls for all Arabs to unite and liberate Jerusalem ends with a shot of the governor of Acre offering his homage to Saladin. A woman's voice in the last seconds of the shot anticipates and covers a cut that takes us to Virginia and Raynald's court, to a parallel scene in which the same governor is scheming with the crusaders to betray Saladin in exchange for Virginia's sexual "favors." The governor of Acre dramatizes the orientalized stereotype, the obsequious, greedy, hypersexual Arab who has become a player, a linchpin in the machinations of both sides. As the politician who controls the seaport that provides access to Jerusalem, he is courted by Arab and crusader alike. But his position disempowers him as well, forcing him to play one side against the other to gain advantage. Ultimately his dealings require the betrayal of one side—the one he judges least likely to advance his own ambitions. At the battle of Acre he disarms his people and opens the gate to the crusaders, who easily overwhelm the city. The film casts his alliance with the crusaders as a kind of race treason, far worse than an imprudent political judgment. Having relinquished his hybrid position, his "middle" position between the two sides, he becomes for the crusaders little more than a servant and for the Arabs a traitor who must be tried and executed.

Set against the governor's treachery is the romance between the "star-cross'd lovers" Louise de Lusignan,[28] a knight Hospitaler, and Saladin's most trusted adviser and companion, his "dearest commander," a Christian Arab named Issa (Arabic for Jesus). Louise is a hybrid figure marked by her transgression of conventional gender ascriptions; she is a woman warrior, an anachronism that leverages the presence of women on the Crusades perhaps to gesture toward the presence of women in the Israeli military. Issa represents the hybrid cultural space of the conflict between Christians and Muslims, Arabs and Europeans and as such functions as a stand-in for Chahine himself, who is also a Christian Arab. While identifying ethnically with Saladin's Arab nation, Issa also shares with the invading crusaders a religious commitment to Christianity. Chahine's Saladin allows more space for hybridity than his Christian opponents do, perhaps a reflection of his desire for a secular rather than religious pan-Arab state. Saladin's tolerance allows Issa to take his social status in Saladin's court for granted—until he falls in love with Louise. His desire for Louise forces both of them to articulate and defend their own cultural hybridity. The Crusades have allowed Louise the fantasy that she can, at least temporarily, erase the difference that gender makes—that she can ignore her hybridity as a woman warrior. After she has been captured at the Battle of Hattin and given to Issa as a prize, she bristles at being treated not as a prisoner of war but as a slave girl, that is, as a woman rather than as a soldier. As Issa presses his love for her, the cracks in her fantasy emerge, forcing her hybridity to the surface. Though at first she demands to be treated as a man, when he tells her he desires her not as a slave but as a wife, her response reveals a fear of miscegenation, a fear that her purity as a white Christian and European *woman* will be violated: "I the wife of an Arab. Were it not a mortal sin I'd kill myself first."[29]

Louise's insistence on her own and her cause's purity forces Issa to articulate his allegiance to Saladin in terms of his hybridity. He responds to Louise's Christian intolerance—"Jerusalem must remain in our hands. We are the custodians of Christianity"—with a secular argument that "Jerusalem has always been an Arab land. We shall prove that we can rule it in peace and with respect." He goes on to offer his existence as a reproach to the colonizing mentality of the crusaders: "You'd rather follow those to whom religion is a trade, who turn the holy places into markets in which to swindle the poor. Pay for your blessings. The money goes into Europe's coffers. Anyone who poses a threat to these profits faces fire, war, and death. Blackmail in the name of the Holy Scriptures. I am a better Christian than you. I believe that taking what is not mine is an unforgivable sin. My belief in justice is the basis of my faith."

This speech accomplishes several political ends, and it is interesting that Chahine puts it into the mouth of his most hybrid character. It justifies Jerusalem as an Arab space; it explains why Issa takes Saladin's side in a holy war despite their religious differences; it marks European Christianity as corrupt, proposing a pan-Arabic nation as an alternative; and finally its echo of Christ's expelling the money changers from the Temple suggests that crusading is not something Jesus ("Isa" [sic], a proper Christian; Shafik, 34) would do, not an appropriate occupation for a Christian. And indeed, when Louise next appears in the film, she is no longer a knight; she has given it up for nursing; tending the sick was the original occupation of the Hospitalers, as she notes, but also a more properly feminine occupation.

Issa's hybridity allows him not only to fall in love with Louise but also to become, like the governor of Acre, a spy. It is "Issa the swimmer" who is chosen to slip behind enemy lines to bring back the Damascene with his "Greek fire," the technological expertise that enables Saladin to repel the crusaders' siege engines.[30] He inadvertently recruits Louise to his cause when, injured, he is brought to the crusaders' camp and nursed back to health by her. Love makes her a traitor to the crusaders' cause when she helps Issa escape once his identity, which had been disguised by the cross that he wears, has been discovered.

All of these narrative strands converge when Louise is put on trial by the crusaders for her treachery in helping Issa escape at the same time Saladin tries the governor of Acre for his betrayal. Chahine begins the scene by using a conventional crosscutting technique to indicate that the trials are happening simultaneously but in different locations: Louise's in Richard's court, the governor's in Saladin's. He presents us with two apparently separate scenes but encourages us to compare Saladin's evenhandedness in meting out justice with the crusaders' authoritarian bigotry. Conrad of Montferrat, who is prosecuting Louise, condemns her for refusing to accept the rhetoric of the Crusades, that Saladin and the Arabs are savages. Against Conrad's accusations of Arabic barbarity, Chahine offers a

second tableau in which Saladin oversees the processes of enlightened government, trying the traitor before a jury of his peers and, in a reversal of the kinds of
Orientalist tropes that turn up in Hollywood films like *King Richard and the Crusaders*, refuses to allow the traitor to kowtow to him, ordering him to "Bow down
to none other than your God."

While *Saladin* generally operates within the filmic conventions of Hollywood
realism, there are moments when Chahine abandons realism for a kind of abstract expressionism. Such devices are never simply experimentation for its own
sake; rather they are put to ideological and symbolic use. As the two trials play
themselves out, Chahine gradually abandons the conventions of realism in favor
of a stylized presentation more reminiscent of the stage than the cinema, eventually merging the two tableaux until crusaders and Arabs appear, at least for the
benefit of the film audience, to be talking back and forth to one another across
the distance that separates them. As Fawal points out, Chahine could have created the same effect in a laboratory. Instead, he built two contiguous sets and al-
ternated between them by turning the lights on and off (Fawal, 160). As the climactic trial scene progresses, Chahine uses three stage techniques to create the
illusion that the two sides are talking to each other. He begins by using expressive
lighting to isolate the four major players—Conrad of Montferrat, Richard, Saladin, and Louise. Gradually the lights in each tableau disappear, leaving a spot on
whichever character the filmmaker wishes to highlight. He turns the monologues
recited by Conrad, Richard, and Saladin into dialogue through crosscutting and
eyeline matches. Having done that, he then sets the two tableaux side by side
using a split screen. The Arab tent on the left is distinguished by the design of
crescents on the arch above, the crusaders' tent on the right by its crosses. Finally,
the speeches themselves employ rhetorical devices like chiasmus and anaphora
so that one speaker picks up the language of the previous one:

CONRAD. She no longer has the sacred hate in her *heart*.

SALADIN. Your *heart* is like a city without walls.

CONRAD. The enemy found a way to your *heart*. She gave her Christian body
to an Arab, threw herself into his arms forgetting the war and that we will
not win if we don't hate them.

SALADIN. His envy led him to seek refuge with the invaders, forgetting Arab
chivalry and traditions.

CONRAD. *Love* has replaced the sacred *hatred* in your heart.

SALADIN. Hatred replaced love in your heart; thus you are cursed.

And:

> CONRAD. There's no victory without hate.
> SALADIN. And there's no liberation without love.
> CONRAD. Bring back the sacred hatred.
> SALADIN. Down with hatred.

The sum of these devices is that even though the words uttered by the orators are not directed to the other side, it appears as if they are. Chahine uses the power of montage to create meaning by connecting shots to transform what are essentially two monologues into a dialogue. While this scene depicts simultaneous events happening in different locations, the montage creates the illusion that the characters occupy the same space, while the sight lines create the illusion that they are talking to one another. The result is that the text can be read on at least three levels. Most literally, each prosecutor (Conrad, Saladin) is presenting, in a separate location, the case against the two spies. The verbal intersections between their speeches, however, suggest that what the prosecutors are talking about transcends the specifics of the governor's and Louise's transgressions to encompass the justification for the holy war itself. Finally, the scene also becomes the occasion for Richard's discovery of Conrad's and Virginia's treachery. The scene's climax occurs as Conrad condemns Louise to "burn as witches do." In a long shot of the crusaders' tableau Richard rises from his throne and steps forward. He appears ready to condemn Louise when he says, "This must be the ultimate punishment for all those who betrayed Jerusalem." Then a peripeteia occurs; rather than condemning Louise, he accuses Conrad: "Damnation to you, Conrad. Take off your mask. All the masks fall off before the Lord's will. You betrayed Jerusalem, you betrayed us, you betrayed the blood of our martyrs who came to place the cross on the tomb of Christ. The curse of God will follow you to the grave. The Arabs have refused your filthy conspiracy; Saladin refused to put his hand in your dirty hand! . . . May God smite those who conspire against Jerusalem."

The devices of split screen and montage suggest that Richard somehow has been listening to Saladin, and not Conrad, all along. Although there is no historical evidence of a meeting between the two, Chahine makes it clear that the Christian king learns from his Arab counterpart. Saladin ratifies Richard's pronouncement at the same moment that he condemns the governor of Acre to death: "We shall give you the traitor's punishment as those who conspire against their brothers." The film's theatrical device becomes the apparatus by which Saladin educates Richard in the application of the kind of evenhanded justice for which the European Enlightenment has always taken credit.

The trial scene is the climactic moment of the film. Up to this point Richard's idealism has been consistently manipulated by his fellow crusaders for their own ends. Through Saladin's intervention, however we imagine it, the trial teaches Richard to be a just king. Subsequent events—Richard's wounding, Saladin's clandestine visit to the enemy camp to heal him, and Richard's attack on Jerusalem—all follow from this moment, providing opportunities to demonstrate the superiority and benevolence of Arab civilization. The film's conclusion sets up between the two kings an interesting patron-client relationship in which Arab culture, scientifically and morally advanced, instructs a backward crusader Christianity in a politics of peace. Chahine's inversion of the standard tropes of Orientalism is completed through diplomacy, not warfare. The film marks the settlement between Saladin and Richard through the exchange of a woman, what Gayle Rubin would call the "traffic in women." Richard goes home, and Louise stays to become Issa's wife. She, in effect, becomes the prize when she decides to remain in Jerusalem with Issa. Aberth has criticized what he sees as the antifeminism of Chahine's film, especially his diminution of Louise from crusading knight to nurse to wife (98–101).[31] We would argue, however, that the film complicates what is usually a homosocial gesture between men, by allowing Louise at least some degree of agency in choosing to become Issa's wife and, in doing so, becoming the mechanism by which hybridity is literally created (their offspring would be both European and Arab). In a different context Kinoshita applies the hybrid term *MiscegeNation* to encapsulate the ways in which marriage—at least in the Middle Ages—functioned as that third space of enunciation that could move beyond simple agonism, beyond the conflict between oppressor and oppressed, dominator and dominated, master and slave, providing a mechanism for imagining a different kind of nation. In the film's final scene Saladin wishes Issa a Merry Christmas. As the *muezzin* calls Muslims to prayer, the strains of a choir singing (anachronistically) *Adeste Fidelis* intertwine, the two musical styles, the two religions, coming together, signaling the hybridity (perhaps only imaginary) of Chahine's vision for a pan-Arabic nation.

The Remasculinization of the Middle Ages

In his advocacy of Gamal Abdel Nasser's pan-Arabism, with its explicit ambitions to wipe out the state of Israel, Chahine must limit Saladin's celebrated religious tolerance. The Jerusalem of Chahine's fantasy is a holy place only for Muslims and Christians. Although Jews lived in the Holy Land during the time of the Crusades, make an important claim to the Holy Land as a religious site, and are in possession of Jerusalem at the time of *Saladin's* production, they are conspicuously absent from Chahine's film. *The Crusaders (Crociati)*, a virtually unknown Italian miniseries directed by Dominique Othenin-Girard that appeared in 2001, makes an effort to identify Jerusalem as an ecumenical space, even as it addresses the nearly constant violence among all three of the "religions of the book" that locate their most sacred relics in the holy city. The film argues against the clash of civilizations thesis, offering the medieval city of Jerusalem as a site of extraordinary ethnic, cultural, religious, and economic hybridity that was destroyed by the crusaders, barbarian invaders from the West. In the film's ending, this dream of a space for intercultural exchange—a third space—more fluid than the rhetoric of crusading allows concludes with a fairy tale of assimilation that smooths over a great deal of violence and intolerance—both past and present—and, more problematically, eradicates difference to make its fantasy work. Even casual viewers will recognize the hopelessness of the film's concluding vision—however uplifting—of social and cultural synergy.

The film is set during the First Crusade (1095–99), moving from the southern coast of Italy to Jerusalem and back again. Although the most spectacularly successful of all the waves of crusading, the First Crusade has never before been the subject of a feature film. For this reason its history may be somewhat obscure, and some background is in order. The First Crusade was initiated by Pope Urban II in 1095 in response to a letter from the Byzantine emperor requesting aid in defending Constantinople against incursions by the Seljuq Turks. Alexis I had hoped that the pope would send a small force of maybe three hundred knights that the emperor could then deploy as he saw fit. What he got was an invading army of some thirty thousand. The main force of crusaders consisted of four armies that set out in 1096 from different parts of Europe to meet up in Constantinople, the capital of the Byzantine Empire: the Normans and Flemish under Hugh of Vermandois, brother of Philip I of France; the nobility of northern France and western Germany under Godfrey of Bouillon; the Provençals under Raymond of Toulouse; and the Italian Normans under Bohemond and Tancred (Prawer, 12). Three years and three thousand miles later, on July 15, 1099, following a five-week siege, the crusaders captured Jerusalem, slaughtering between twenty and thirty thousand Muslim and Jewish defenders: "Thanksgiving prayers were celebrated in a silent Jerusalem, reeking with the stench of decaying corpses and amidst burned mosques, synagogues and houses" (15). The first crusaders had less incentive, by and large, than their later counterparts to return home. They had won the war, after all, and their numbers included no reigning monarchs. The hosts of the First Crusade became "the foundations upon which all the social classes in the [crusaders'] kingdom developed" (61). Godfrey of Bouillon would become the first ruler of the Crusader Kingdom, and his descendants would be kings of Jerusalem until its reconquest by Saladin a century later (63).

The Crusaders follows the exploits of three crusaders from the Italian coastal town of Aurocastro, in the duchy of Taranto, the tiny principality ruled by Bohemond, the leader of the Norman Italian force, although he does not figure in the film.[32] At the heart of *The Crusaders* are three impossible love stories, each of which will be uneasily worked out against the background of the conquest of Jerusalem. The first of these love stories deals with Peter and Maria. Peter, the son of a Muslim father and Christian mother, raised by a bell founder who has taught him to read and write in multiple languages, is dark-skinned, poor, and an outsider; he is taunted as "a bastard" and accused of witchcraft within his own community. Maria, the daughter of a farmer, has been promised in marriage to Bastiano, a wealthy and politically well-connected soldier. Peter goes off on the First Crusade to make some sense of his hybrid identity and to forget about Maria. The second of the love stories involves Richard, the son of a baron, William of Aurocastro. Richard joins the crusading armies of Christendom to escape from his uncle, Corrado, who has murdered his father and stolen his lands. Although Richard is religious at the beginning of his journey, he discovers his love of God as he finds himself in the presence of holy men and holy relics in Jerusalem. Finally, Andrew, Maria's brother, disdains the life of a miller destined for him, seeks upward mobility on the battlefield of the East—he insists, early in the film, "I want to grind heads, not grains of wheat"—and meets his beloved, Rachel, a Jew, on his way to Jerusalem.

At the ideological heart of this film is a sequence of iconographic shots that occurs about midway through. Peter and Richard, having deserted the crusaders—Richard to find his faith and Peter his Muslim roots—travel to Jerusalem with Rachel, whom they have met (disguised as a boy) in a Yeshiva. The film makes clear that the three have embraced peace, that they have become pilgrims rather than crusaders. The film cuts from the tumult and noise of the crusaders saddling up for the battle to take Jerusalem to a vision of the three rising up over a hill and getting their first glimpse of the holy city.[33] Their arrival is conveyed as a romantic long shot encompassing all three characters arrayed in a V with Rachel in the middle at the lowest point. Expressive warm lighting plays off softly rolling hills that frame the three. A melancholy Middle Eastern air plays on the sound track. They display the symbols that identify them with their particular religion and culture: a pilgrim staff, a yarmulke, and a turban. A reverse shot shows the city of Jerusalem in all its glory from behind the pilgrims. The city takes up nearly the entire screen, its luminous white buildings rising out of the drab desert. Rachel says, "There it is, the city of God." Richard responds reverently, breathlessly, "Jerusalem," and kneels. His kneeling creates a perfect diagonal running from the upper right hand of the shot to the lower left. Finally, the camera pans across the city; the panning and the crowd of tiny figures in the middle ground between the pilgrims and the city give a sense of the huge scale of the city. The shot generates nostalgia for an ecumenical Jerusalem that will be destroyed by the invading crusaders. It is virtually impossible to convey the nostalgic force of this ecumenical moment without turning it into an ethnic joke in the retelling: "An Arab, a Christian, and a Jew arrive together before the Holy City of Jerusalem. . . ." This vision of religious syncretism devolves into a joke in the retelling precisely because as listeners we desire the fantasy, but we don't believe it. Only the romanticized filming of the sequence manipulates us into accepting it.

There is much in the three hours and twenty minutes of the film to convince us of this fantasy's impossibility. Sandwiched between the love stories of Maria and Peter, Andrew and Rachel, the dream of ecumenical coexistence encapsulated in our heroes' entry into Jerusalem and the fairy-tale ending are scenes of ignorance, violence, shortsightedness, greed, and hatred, even hostility between brothers. The film is haunted by the geopolitical shifts made visible by the First Gulf War, a war precipitated by Iraq's invasion of Kuwait, an ally of the West. The film's opening sequence echoes the Gulf War's political situation, focusing briefly on the devastation caused by a band of Arab invaders. The film suggests that the Crusades may have been as much a response to Arab incursions into Europe as they were about the reclaiming of Jerusalem for Christianity (an argument repeated vociferously by conservative medieval historians like Thomas F. Madden in the months after 9/11).[34] In both the Crusades and the Gulf War the Western response to Arab expansionism is both overwhelming and overwhelmingly brutal. Operation Desert Storm, the name given to the effort to expel Iraq from Kuwait, required a UN-mandated force of thirty, mostly Western, nations— 660,000 troops. In the two months of combat, as many as 100,000 Iraqis may have been killed, as many as 300,000 wounded. (Coalition losses were miniscule by comparison—345 fatalities and 1,000 injuries.) But no matter how many arguments are made that the First Gulf War was about the liberation of a sovereign nation, the West has had to deal with lingering suspicions that it was also about greed, about access to Middle Eastern petroleum. It seems no coincidence that the United States, the world's leading petroleum consumer, deployed more than 80 percent of the coalition forces. The war put a decisive end to the pan-Arab ambitions of Iraq's president, Saddam Hussein; as a result, the West enjoyed inexpensive fuel for more than ten years.

The Crusaders portrays an overwhelming coalition of Westerners descending on the Middle East to fulfill a host of assorted desires, not the least of which is satiating themselves on the riches of the Holy Land. However much this description echoes the political situation in the Middle East over the last decade, there is one significant difference that the film highlights. Western imperialism, including U.S. imperialism in the Persian Gulf, has, since the nineteenth century, been predicated on a belief in the superiority of Western civilization to the civilizations it invades. In *The Crusaders* Europeans, whatever their rank or status, are depicted almost exclusively as primitive and ignorant, especially in comparison to the elegance, luxury, and learning of the Easterners—both Muslims and Jews—they defeat. They are barbarians overrunning an advanced and learned civilization. In Aurocastro, although there is a suggestion of something like a castle, most of the scenes are set outside. Its inhabitants live in hovels and dress in rags. They appear to live only slightly better than the animals they raise. Except for Peter, who has been taught by his learned foster father, Alessio, even the aristocracy is shown as illiterate, largely ignorant, and often vicious in its dealings with the underclasses.

Much like contemporary politics, the film is marked by what Stephen Ducat calls "anxious masculinity." The last decade of the twentieth century and the early years of the twenty-first have been marked by ideological shifts resulting not only from geopolitical changes in the wake of American defeat in Vietnam and the collapse of the Soviet Empire but also from women's liberation and the feminist challenges to patriarchal domination. Anxieties about masculinity are represented in popular media through representations that simultaneously critique and reinscribe a hard-bodied masculinity within narratives about war. Perhaps in reaction to the Gulf War as primarily a U.S. initiative, *The Crusaders*, an Italian film, captures much of the spirit—and the themes—of the American antiwar movie. The film's invocation of the horrors of war cannot fail to call to mind the conventions of the Vietnam War film, a genre that emerged in response to an American loss that has haunted the nation's foreign policy—and its war movies—

ever since.[35] The film recreates, almost to the point of parody, the stock formulae through which post–Vietnam War films reimagined masculinity in the face of humiliating loss at the hands of an enemy perceived as weaker.[36]

The film includes a medieval version of a boot camp sequence modeled on formulae derivative of Hollywood war films from *Stripes* (1981) to *Full Metal Jacket*: ritualized humiliation interspersed with combat drills. When Peter, Andrew, and Richard reach a crusader training installation on the Italian coast, its inhabitants can hardly believe that the "drill sergeant" of this "boot camp," the Norseman Olaf Gunnarson, is a lord. He is enormous, and his size only serves to accentuate his vulgarity. Utterly lacking in chivalry—willing to break rules of engagement to ensure victory—the "Jarl," as Gunnarson fashions himself, is brutal, greedy, and none too smart. His training methods resemble those of Gunnery Sergeant Hartman in Stanley Kubrick's *Full Metal Jacket*. That Gunnarson is a sadist who takes pleasure in humiliating his troops, peasants who have come to him with little taste and even less preparation for violence, seems almost beside the point. His task of turning the peasant recruits into hard-bodied killers requires that he strip away anything that might soften them. He will turn "little boys," "dwarfs," and peasants into "real men." The feminine especially must be neutralized: "Don't call me 'my lord.' I'm not your betrothed." His success is determined by turning these men into versions—albeit much smaller versions—of himself, hard-bodied killers who will follow orders without question and without thought. Peter, Richard, and especially Andrew fall under Gunnarson's sway for a time. Andrew is singled out when he nearly defeats Gunnarson in hand-to-hand combat, losing only after the Jarl beans him with a rock. When Andrew complains that he has broken the rules, Gunnarson tells him, echoing Kubrick's Gunnery Sergeant Hartman (can the echo of *Gunnery* in *Gunnarson* be entirely coincidental?), "You think your enemies on the battlefield will respect rules. They're infidels. There is only one rule. Kill them before they kill you."

While Gunnarson's tactics tell us more about post-Vietnam attempts to recuperate a military masculinity than about the military training of eleventh-century crusaders, his motives seem to underlie what for many represents the project of the First Crusade, motives that predictably lead in the film to atrocity; the film's middle section reproduces the trajectory of Kubrick's film, a trajectory that links atrocities in the field to the soldiers' reeducation into hard-bodied masculinity. Following the Jarl's training program, the crusaders wait for the invasion of Jerusalem, their hypermasculine aggressiveness, their desire for blood, just barely kept in check. One of their Armenian guides offers a diversion, a "Saracen lair" ripe for the plundering. He invokes the time-honored propaganda device of creating a defensive posture, imputing prior atrocities to those who will be attacked: "These people are animals," he tells them. "They have attacked a Christian monastery, massacred all the monks, and stolen some very precious relics." The Saracen lair that is the object of their first engagement turns out to be a peaceful Yeshiva. The slaughter captured on film goes on for more than ten minutes, and it includes the sacking of the temple and the cold-blooded murder of the Yeshiva's rabbi, identified throughout as both a theologian and a scientist. Rachel, a rabbinical student, a lover of learning so committed that she is willing to hide her identity as a woman to be in this institution of knowledge, is bewildered by the attack: "Why have you done this? This was a Yeshiva, a place of study. People come here from all over the world to learn." In a scene that is gratuitous, at best, she is assaulted by Gunnarson, stripped of her garments, grabbed by her genitals, and threatened with slavery. The crusaders are easily deceived into attacking the defenseless Yeshiva because they are too ignorant to decipher the simplest "signs" that would identify the people they are attacking, signs that are clearly legible to the audience: the Star of David, prayer shawls, a Torah scroll.

That the Christian spirit of the Crusades has been exploited for mercenary gain is of little consequence to Gunnarson, who is seen luxuriating in a bath while examining some of the spoils of his conquest (perhaps a visual reference to similar scenes in Chahine's *Saladin*). At this point the film must distance our three heroes from the Jarl's hard-bodied masculinity, from his greed and brutality. Richard is appalled by what has transpired: "This is not the lair of plunderers. It is we who are plunderers." So, too, is Andrew, who impugns the Jarl's integrity and eventually kills him: "You made a deal with the Armenians. You know that these people weren't hostile Saracens but peaceful Jews. These men, we, didn't come here to steal, murder, and plunder. We didn't come here as thieves." Gunnarson's reply indicates, perhaps, that the Crusades were never about faith—and, by extension, the Gulf War never about liberation: "Moors, Jews, what does it matter? They're all the same. What does matter is that we have won our first battle. Who knows what wealth is hidden within these walls?" The *real* interest of the Christian West in the film is to enrich itself.

A parallel sequence takes place toward the conclusion of the film when, after the walls of Jerusalem are breached by the crusader army, both Muslims and Jews—who have, ironically enough, put themselves under Muslim protection—

gather together in the city's central mosque. There are women, children, and the elderly in this group—including Rachel's Muslim mentor, the astronomer Ibnazul (played by *Camelot*'s Franco Nero). The crusaders demand a ransom from these huddled masses, and a very handsome one is paid. But the crusaders set fire to the mosque anyway, locking its inhabitants inside. Andrew tries to prevent the atrocity, screaming, "We're crusaders. We're not here to massacre innocent people." He is corrected by Robert of Flanders, a crusader commander, and one of Andrew's patrons: "You fool. Those are just empty words. They don't mean a thing."

In case viewers are inclined to miss *The Crusaders*' heavy-handed point about the un-Christian nature of the Crusades, the film brings it home when Richard, holding a piece of the "true cross," pleads with his fellow crusaders to stop the carnage. He has learned that Christians have always lived in Jerusalem—coexisting peacefully with Muslims and Jews—and it is only the Crusades that have threatened their existence there. His devotion to God brings him to believe: "This is a holy city. There must be no more blood." Unfortunately, neither Richard's pleas nor his display of the relic can stop the crusaders, who, in the name of Christ, have embarked on a program of murder, rape, and looting. Richard is stabbed and the piece of the "true cross" falls into the flames emanating from the mosque.[37] In a moment of despair and recognition he reminds the audience of this Italian miniseries, "We have burned the cross." The first-person plural relates to more than just Richard's contemporaries, eleventh-century crusaders. It implicates Christendom from the Crusades onward. Hence Peter's reply: "Perhaps that is why God sent you here. So you could go back and tell everyone the horror," a horror compounded by images of the mosque's collapse.

But if *The Crusaders* intends to critique the West's plundering of the Middle East, its message is washed away by the film's conclusion, which gestures toward the virtues of imperialistic assimilation, a peace marked by exactly the opposite of the hybridity Bhabha urges. On his return to Aurocastro Peter discovers that all pasts have been obliterated: Aurocastro's usurping ruler has died, and Maria has not married the repulsive Bastiano. The film offers no explanations for the lack of political succession nor any mention as to how Maria could have avoided fulfilling her contract with such a powerful patron. Peter laments at Richard's tomb: "We were wrong, Richard. I believed in peace. You believed in the power of your faith to change things. Why did we go there?" What is left is a bright future in which Peter can marry Maria, have a child, and become, like his foster father, an exceedingly well-read bell founder. Andrew, too, returns home, having received a number of battlefield commissions, the last of which made him lord of Aurocastro. Andrew has married Rachel. The happiness of the film's conclusion is cemented as Peter, Maria, Andrew, and Rachel surround the grave of an unknown pilgrim (only Peter knows that it is, in fact, Richard's grave), nearly canonizing him for his faith. Peter says, "This is why this pilgrim came here to Aurocastro. To bring peace to others and light to us all." Richard's anonymity is what allows him to become a focus of communal mourning and a symbol affirming the imagined political community of Aurocastro that can finally assimilate both Peter's and Rachel's ethnic differences. Richard's tomb presents us with an early version of the Tomb of the Unknown Soldier. According to Benedict Anderson, "void as these tombs are of identifiable mortal remains, they are nonetheless saturated with ghostly national imaginings."[38] But there are far too many disconcerting elements about the film's conclusion to go unnoticed. Is it really possible that, as a Muslim, Peter can be assimilated into medieval Italian society? He was, after all, the crusader who was told by an African child: "You are not like the others. Your face . . . You are like me." Rachel, too, must make enormous concessions, which seem, to say the least, out of character. She appears in Aurocastro dressed in women's clothes. Does this mean that she is also willing to convert to Christianity to be Andrew's wife? Is she willing to put aside her love of learning to become the lady of Aurocastro? Given the history of European anti-Semitism beginning with the Crusades, how likely is she to be assimilated? The harmony of the film's conclusion cannot tolerate such questions because it denies Bhabha's "third space of enunciation," returning us, inevitably, to the causes of war—the need to eradicate difference.

The fantasy of the multicultural Aurocastro at the conclusion of *The Crusaders* is, at best, a vision of European hegemony, requiring the sacrifice of Jerusalem's Muslims and Jews to create a tolerant society at home. At worst, the fantasy is simply preposterous, its impossibility attested to by the history of Middle East discord, from the Middle Ages—there will be many more Crusades—to the present. But the notion of a multiracial, multiethnic, multireligious harmony built on the ashes of the Crusades persists. Ridley Scott's *Kingdom of Heaven* resists some of *The Crusaders* feel-good idealism, offering a much more nervous assessment of Middle East conflict grown out of the First Gulf War, the 9/11 attacks on the World Trade Center and the Pentagon, and George W. Bush's war in Iraq. Focusing on the events leading to the Third Crusade, Scott's film longs for harmony in the Middle East, even as it understands that impediments to peace are formidable.

Kingdom of Heaven: Orientalism Redux

As a culture, we have had thirty years to absorb the feminist critique of a John Wayne masculinity that must violently abject anything feminine, yet we are still reluctant to rethink this masculinity in spite of its manifest failures both thirty years ago in Vietnam and again in the context of the current Iraqi war. This ideology has become a form of cynicism in that we understand (at least at some level) that its ideal is ideologically produced and doomed to repeated failure, and yet we continue to reproduce it (on cynicism see Žižek, *The Sublime Object of Ideology*, 28–29). Like *Crociati, Kingdom of Heaven,* by viewing structural shifts in the relations between warfare and gender in the current Middle Eastern conflict through the lens of the Crusades, attempts to refashion and reclaim a hard-bodied masculinity for a post-9/11 world defined largely in both U.S. foreign policy and the popular media by the "clash of civilizations." Susan Jeffords argues that films like *First Blood*, the first film in the Rambo series, attempted to wash away American failures in the Middle East—in particular, the Iranian hostage fiasco of the Carter administration—by reimagining the conclusion of the Vietnam War. "*First Blood*," she maintains, "clarifies the consequences of the 'weakened' years of the Carter presidency, when strength and preparedness were, according to the Reagan historians, abandoned in favor of negotiation and capitulation. . . . [It] shows audiences that inadequate, unprepared, and weakened masculine bodies simply cannot compete with the forces of a strengthened and prepared body" (32). Warfare and, especially in the post-9/11 world, the war on terror provide a ground on which to prove masculinity and the occasion for reasserting its necessity (as the 2004 election demonstrated; see Ducat). The close relationship between warfare and a certain form of hegemonic masculinity, Jeffords argues, underwrites patriarchy, as the structure of gender supports not only the dominance of men over women but also of some groups of men over other "feminized" groups. We see this process at work in Orientalism, which alternates between representations of an orientalized version of hard-bodied masculinity (the subjection of women, cruelty, violence) and its effeminizing mirror image.

Ridley Scott, however, offers a new paradigm in explaining the successes of postcolonial upstarts to an American audience overwhelmed by the politics of loss. Beginning with his 2001 film *Black Hawk Down*, Scott manages to celebrate retreat. *Black Hawk Down* tells the story of U.S. Delta Force commandoes and Army Rangers, elite corps of particularly well-trained and hard-bodied men, assigned on October 3, 1993, to capture or kill a number of Somali war lords—who, we have since learned, may have been al-Qaeda operatives—in the war-torn city of Mogadishu. Either betrayed by their informants, or just unlucky, the soldiers become trapped when Somali militia down two Black Hawk helicopters, and they must fight their way out of the city. The battle, on some level, demonstrated the clear superiority of American military muscle over poorly trained—though heavily armed—Somali gangs. Eighteen Americans were killed compared to more than one thousand Somalis. But the incident, which reaches its climax in the film with American soldiers literally running the distance from Mogadishu to the U.N. military enclave outside the city, brought about a major change in U.S. foreign policy and a withdrawal of U.S. troops from Somalia. *Black Hawk Down* recognizes the failure of hard-bodied masculinity to transform the politics of Africa—or of the Middle East. The film recognizes the futility of American exceptionalism—U.S. forces were inserted into Somalia to stop internecine conflict and genocide, but, at best, this "can-do" spirit only gets soldiers out of harm's way.

Kingdom of Heaven functions as a companion piece to *Black Hawk Down* in glorifying hard-bodied masculinity and American exceptionalism even as it simultaneously shows the futility of such fantasies to secure a lasting peace either in the twelfth century or in the twenty-first. As a figure of American exceptionalism, the hero, Balian of Ibelin, encounters a European Middle Ages that is, in the eyes of the film's audience, decidedly atavistic. *Kingdom of Heaven*'s plot is set into motion because Balian—no matter how resourceful he may be—is unable to offer his wife consolation after the death of her child, unable to prevent her suicide, and unable to prevent representatives of the Catholic Church from desecrating her body prior to its internment; she is decapitated by a priest and his henchmen who, to add insult to injury, also steal the crucifix from around her neck. But Balian's journey to Jerusalem does not provide him with the expected opportunities to overcome the widespread ignorance, brutality, and greed he encounters. Instead, he finds only escalating frustrations. The model of masculinity that requires the protection of women linked to the protection of the city/state/nation is undermined by the events it represents. Set just before the beginning of the Third Crusade, the film chronicles the events leading up to the crusaders' loss of the city of Jerusalem to Saladin.[39]

For this reason narrative interest in *Kingdom of Heaven* focuses not on the outcome of the conflict between the Crusader Kingdom and Saladin but on the way it was fought, on means rather than ends, performance rather than goals. In the end, how the hero performs is more important than the fact that he lost the battle and surrendered the city. All of Balian's military training—abbreviated, to be sure, but sufficient to allow him, on his arrival in the Holy Land, to defeat what he takes to be a Saracen champion—all of his American ingenuity, are little more than preparation for him to strike a truce with Saladin and lead Christians in a retreat from Jerusalem after its fall. Drawing on the work of Jean-François Lyotard to describe the ideologies that drive Vietnam War narratives, Jeffords argues that "the goal of such an ideology is 'no longer truth, but performativity—that is, the best possible input/output equation.'" We evaluate the hero not on the "quality or character of results" but on the "efficacy of performance" (5). One explanation for this shift might be because the goal is not worthy of the hero's efforts. Surveying the carnage of the lost Battle of Hattin with Balian, Tiberius (played by Jeremy Irons) articulates just this sentiment before riding off into the sunset, leaving Balian to defend Jerusalem alone: "I've given Jerusalem my whole life. First I thought we were fighting for God, then I realized we were fighting for wealth and land. I was ashamed."

Scott perhaps best encapsulates the anxieties that surround hard-bodied masculinity and the mourning for its loss in his uncanny image of Baldwin, the leper king of Jerusalem, whose death precipitates the destruction of the Crusader Kingdom.[40] Rather than focusing the audience's attention on the ravages of the disease of leprosy (at least until after his death), Scott depicts him in a funereal image of a male body swathed in white robes and veils, his face hidden by a beautiful but lifeless silver mask (Figure 13). Baldwin is beautiful but inanimate on the outside—a hard-bodied shell—living but hideous on the inside. His voice detached from his body, Baldwin becomes a ghostly acousmatic,[41] despite his physical presence onscreen. His voice seems to issue from an inanimate shell, cut off from its origin in a human body. He is his own—and his kingdom's—funeral effigy. In this figure the hard-bodied masculinity of the crusaders in *Kingdom of Heaven* is exposed as a performance, a disguise that hides the rottenness within the kingdom beneath its beautiful but dead veneer. The image allows not only the crusaders but Scott's audience to mourn lost glories.

Figure 13. Baldwin, the Leper King of Jerusalem, in *Kingdom of Heaven* (Ridley Scott, 2005).

Kingdom of Heaven, however, gives us not the clash of civilizations—East against West—but the clash between medievalism (in particular the belief that the Middle Ages represents intolerance, religious bigotry, and rigid class hierarchies) and American exceptionalism (the belief that not only is the American character free from all of these social ills, but it also embodies certain positive qualities like enterprise, rugged individualism, and self-reliance). Against the orientalized natives and the snobbish European invaders (when he first meets Balian, Sibylla's husband, Guy, sniffs, "In France 'this' would not inherit. Here there are no civilized rules"), Scott sets the Americanness of his hero, Balian.[42] That is why his screenwriter must transform the Balian of Ibelin of historical record from an aristocratic insider, a member of the ruling caste of the Crusader Kingdom, to a man with no history, a man cut off from his past and free to refashion himself in a "new world." The film places at its core cherished American values like the attraction to new frontiers, the triumph of the individual against social restrictions, and the melting pot—creating confusing and contradictory ideological messages that it holds together only with great difficulty. Early in the film, for instance, Balian's father, Geoffrey, describes Jerusalem as "the very center of the world for asking forgiveness," invoking the medieval trope of Jerusalem as "the naval of the region and of the whole world."[43] But it is not only for him the center of the known world; it is also a "new world," brimming with possibilities, where a man can determine his own fate. This new world erases ascribed status, allowing Balian, a bastard son, to be recognized by his aristocratic father: "A man who on Friday had not a house is in the Holy Land the master of a city. He who was the master of a city begs in the gutter. There at the end of the world you are not what you are born but what you have it in yourself to be." Geoffrey's geographical metaphors are revealing; a place cannot be simultaneously the center of the world—the cradle of civilization—and its outermost periphery, a no-man's land freed from the regulations that govern civilization. References to a "new world" at "the end of the world" deliberately call to mind rhetoric about the discovery of the Americas. But in the mouth of a crusader they suggest an uncomfortable intimacy between the rhetoric of American exceptionalism, especially the belief that America is a land of opportunity for the taking by those willing and able to exploit it, and the "benevolent" imperialism that created that opportunity. The justification for Balian's occupation of his lands comes straight out of nineteenth-century justifications of imperialism: the duty to bring enlightenment to backward primitives. If *Kingdom of Heaven* depicts the Holy Land as a land of wealth and riches to be exploited by the clever, it also marks it as technologically backward, in need of "modernization." Where both Chahine and Othenin-Girard insist on the superior science and technology of the Arab world, Scott sees backwardness. In one scene Balian, the blacksmith who had never before left his tiny village in France, must teach the desert inhabitants how to irrigate their own land. Indeed Balian's success in the Holy Land—his success in defending Jerusalem against Saladin and protecting its citizens from slaughter—clearly stems not from his superior fighting skills but from his technological inventiveness.

When Balian knights the men of Jerusalem during the final battle, using the same words his father had used to knight him, he enacts a shift from what is essentially an aristocratic ritual designed to inculcate status hierarchies among men to an egalitarian homosociality in which men bond together in the face of certain defeat. Scott calls on every cinematic trick at his disposal to punctuate this point. After Balian has ordered his men to "rise a knight," the bishop of Jerusalem (played by Jon Finch) scoffs, "Who do you think you are? Will you alter the world? Does making a man a knight make him a better fighter?" As the music in the underscoring crescendos, the camera cuts from a close-up of Jerusalem to a series of reaction shots of the crowd. The score climaxes and fades into silence. Balian turns and into the silence says simply, "Yes," the point being carried largely by the contrast between the swelling music and its abrupt silencing. Even though we know that Balian and his new knights will be defeated, we are to marvel at their performance of "true grit."

We might shed more light on Scott's project of rehabilitating masculinity in the face of defeat by contrasting the film's homosocial relations between men with its heteronormative romance plot. In the climactic battle sequence, as Orlando Bloom's Balian of Ibelin struggles to defend Jerusalem against Saladin's besieging armies,[44] conventional shot-countershot close-ups of Balian and Saladin, complete with eyeline matches, imply an impossible relationship between the two men in the midst of the chaos of battle. Shots like these serve a psychological rather than mimetic purpose. A wider perspective shows the same individuals as anonymous members of opposing mobs who could not possibly distinguish one enemy from another. The close-up offers an economical device that a filmmaker can exploit to create visual connections between characters in chaotic epic sequences—battle scenes, for instance. What, then, are we to make of another series of close-ups Scott offers us during the same sequence? During this scene the camera cuts away from the action at several points to offer a brief close-up of Sibylla (played by Eva Green), the sister of the recently deceased king of Jerusalem and the only female character of any significance in the film. He does this roughly twelve times in this thirty-minute sequence alone (the same technique appears at other points in the film as well). What is the significance of this set of rather static—and apparently unnecessary—shots? A simple answer might be that they keep alive the character, and the heteronormative coupling she offers the hero, in an otherwise homosocial film that chronicles the affairs of male warriors. Yet Balian never returns her gaze as he does Saladin's; there is no reverse shot. The settings establish that these two characters are in different locations. A more complicated answer might begin by noting that Scott uses these close-ups to establish Sibylla, the last surviving member of the ruling family, as an important observer of the destruction going on all around her. By establishing Sibylla as a witness to the fall of the Crusader Kingdom, he parallels her destruction with the city's. One of the last close-ups shows Sibylla sitting at a table gazing at her distorted image in a primitive mirror as she cuts off her hair. As she stares at her image, it morphs into the grotesque leprous image of her deceased brother, Baldwin. The destruction of Sibylla's considerable beauty, the shot implies, parallels the destruction of the city.

The connection in the film between Sibylla and Jerusalem, between woman and land, is always implied, never explicit. But it drives the plot. Twice in the film each of the two kings of Jerusalem, first Baldwin (the leper king played by Edward Norton) and then Guy de Lusignan (played by Marton Csokas), utters the phrase, "I am Jerusalem," claiming the customary link between king and land to bolster his authority: Baldwin as he chastises Reynald for his disobedience, Guy as he prepares his army for the upcoming battle with Saladin at the Horns of Hattin. The film's visuals, however, imply that it is Sibylla who really *is* Jerusalem; the manipulation of the simple close-up creates a metonymic link between women and land on which the homosocial order of Scott's medieval world is built. Sibylla becomes the site of the contests between men (Balian, Saladin, Guy) over the land—the holy city of Jerusalem. The two—queen and city—occupy equivalent positions in the film, at once economically and strategically insignificant but symbolically vital. At the end of the four-day siege Balian asks his victorious opponent, Saladin, "What is Jerusalem worth?" "Nothing," he responds. After a beat, he clenches his fists in victory and says, "Everything." Historically Sibylla's husband, Guy, never became king of Jerusalem. Instead, Sibylla ruled in her own right as queen, the last Frankish queen of Jerusalem in a line of remarkable women who, in a warrior society where husbands might be dead or continually at war, were often required to shoulder the responsibilities of government.[45] Scott (or his screenwriter, William Monahan) needed to alter the historical record because the film requires Sibylla to be a metonymic equivalent of Jerusalem, a passive object of exchange, not a ruler. She must not wield power in her own right; instead, she must remain, like the city itself, adaptable to the needs of the men who use her to achieve their own political ends.

Despite its liberal agenda of multiculturalism, an agenda reviled by most of the historians who reviewed it,[46] *Kingdom of Heaven* is, as we have been suggesting, a deeply reactionary film in almost every way. In particular, we would single out the connections between the film's masculinist and imperialist ideologies. Scott's reduction of women to passive objects of exchange in a male-dominated world creates Orientalist fantasies that the film recycles in twenty-first-century garb. Though Americans like to believe they live in a "postfeminist" world in which the aims of feminism have largely been achieved, Scott presents perhaps the most hypermasculine of any of the crusader films we have examined in this chapter. The film's homosocial politics begins with its manipulation of the star system, in a Hollywood film perhaps the most ideologically revealing of sign systems. In a cast of male stars that includes not only Bloom (capitalizing on the success of Peter Jackson's *Lord of the Rings* trilogy) but also such established male stars as Liam Neeson, Jeremy Irons, Edward Norton, and Jon Finch, Eva Green was a virtually unknown French actress at the time, blank but comely (to paraphrase Don Hoffman paraphrasing the *Song of Solomon*), whose only previous film credit was Bernardo Bertolucci's 2003 *The Dreamers*. Even during the 1950s period of high domesticity, the director of *King Richard and the Crusaders* found room in his film for Virginia Mayo and Paula Raymond, both seasoned actresses with more than thirty films each to their names. That film's casting allowed for at least a nod to the fact that women did participate in the Crusades, even if the film limits their participation to romance rather than, say, fighting or politics. The Arab filmmaker, Chahine, supposedly a member of a hypermasculine culture famous for its suppression of women, could even imagine a woman warrior.[47] But in the twenty-first century, Scott can only give us something beautiful to look at. He films the virtually unknown starlet Green in ways that conform to Laura Mulvey's notions of the male gaze. She is spectacle in the film, something to be looked at, while the men drive the narrative. She is a prize to be won, along with the city of Jerusalem. Even the romance between Sibylla and Balian begins as a political maneuver to prevent Guy from becoming king; she offers herself to Balian in the hopes that he will assassinate her husband and become king of Jerusalem himself.[48] In playing to a straight homosocial white European masculinity, the film brings back Orientalism with a vengeance through its representation of the prizes—women, land, and wealth—crusading offered. Scott's objectification of the film's women fuels and is fueled by his Orientalism.

To cement visually this connection between Sibylla and the land for which she serves as conduit, Scott orientalizes both her and the city, using imagery that would be visually familiar to the most casual viewer. Sibylla is as exotic to Balian as the new land in which he finds himself. By contrast to the grim and impoverished France depicted in the film's opening scenes, Balian finds himself in a Holy Land that is civilized, wealthy, and exotically beautiful. He first rides into Jerusalem in a shot reminiscent of Richard's, Peter's, and Rachel's entrance into the city in *The Crusaders*; the enormous gleaming city rises up out of the barren desert. Though in Frankish hands at the time, Jerusalem is represented as an Oriental city, indicated by the Middle Eastern sounding music (composed by Harry Gregson-Williams) that is its leitmotif. Hamilton describes the kind of wealth that Balian encounters in Jerusalem, which Scott showcases through a series of tracking shots that display its prosperity as Balian enters the city: "Many of the Franks lived in stone-built houses and could afford to dress in fabrics such as silk and cotton, which were prohibitively expensive in the West. They made regular use of public baths which existed in all the main cities and they ate the more varied and exotic foods which the land supplied" (Hamilton, *The Leper King and His Heirs*, 57). In fact, the Franks of the Crusader Kingdom exported luxury to the "impoverished" West: "Damascus steel, Arab goldsmith's work and jewelry, incense, Persian carpets and ceramics, Chinese silks, and spices and medicinal drugs from the East Indies" (Hamilton, *The Leper King and His Heirs*, 53). In his new home, in what are practically the first interior shots of the film, Balian surveys incense, soft beds, beautiful windows, luxury clothing, carpets, statuary, urns. It is almost as if he has been transported from Kansas to Oz, from the frozen blue hues of his home in France to the vibrant and colorful East.

Shortly after encountering the exoticism and luxury of Jerusalem, Balian meets Sibylla for the first time, riding into his courtyard on a white horse. Everything about her costume and makeup in this scene suggest not Western royalty but an exoticized Orient. She is completely swathed in cloth made of rich and colorful fabrics. She sports a jeweled turban and an embroidered veil that hides all of her face except for darkly made-up eyes. The veiling may represent her modesty, or it may simply be a convenient mode of dress for riding through the desert; however, it cannot fail to evoke contemporary controversies in the Arab world around veiling.[49] It even offers a bit of a tease, calling up for Western eyes the image of the harem and its fulfillment of the European male's wish to uncover its hidden sexual secrets. Her eyes are heavily made up to invoke the association between kohl and Middle Eastern women. Henna tattoos cover her hands. She wears jewelry everywhere. Her turban, veil, and forehead are set off by coins, chains, and jewels. She wears rings on every finger and ropes of pearls around her neck. Her dress reflects her social status as a member of the royal family, but it is also heavily orientalized. She is decorative, like the wealthy city of Jerusalem, an exotic prize to be won and so a spectacle offered up for the gaze of the males, but only the Frankish males, who surround her. When Balian next meets her at the king's table, she is similarly arrayed. As the film progresses, however, her dress becomes more Westernized as she is domesticated into the fold of Western Christianity. After her brother's death, as queen she abandons her Oriental dress altogether; her mourning and her coronation gown look much more Western, preparing us visually for her final decision to abdicate her claim to the throne of Jerusalem and follow Balian back to France.

Visually Sibylla, sister to the reigning Frankish king of Jerusalem, is linked through her costume to the only other woman in the film of any significance (Balian's first wife having committed suicide before the film even begins). This is Saladin's sister, who appears only once in the scene in which Reynald attacks the pilgrim caravan. This scene is striking precisely because of the way it deploys Orientalist fantasies about Arab women to create shock and horror around Reynald's attack on the defenseless caravan. From scenes showing the violence and gore of the attack, including a blood-spattered Reynald, there is a cut to a lone black figure kneeling in a sea of tall blowing grasses (meant undoubtedly to signify the oasis in the desert). The figure is veiled in black from head to toe. The camera tracks into focus on the figure as the sound of blowing grasses and a melancholic Eastern tune, sung by a lone female voice, make up the sound track. The figure rises and turns around (and this is the first indication that we have been looking at the figure's back; her heavy black veil obscures even the difference between her front and back). Saladin's sister is revealed, like Sibylla, completely veiled, her face framed by gold coins and chains; only her darkly made-up eyes are visible. As the sound track climaxes in a highly percussive tune, Reynald rips the veil off her face in what amounts to a cinematic signifier of rape. In the next scene we hear obliquely of her death, as Saladin's emissaries petition for the return of her body, along with the surrender of Jerusalem, the two clearly linked as demands. Not even Saladin, who in the film becomes a figure of imposing masculine power, can protect his women from the violence of warfare. Nor, despite his victory, can he ensure that Jerusalem will forever remain in Arab hands. In one of the last glimpses we get of Ghassan Massoud's Saladin, he strides through a destroyed courtyard in an elaborate black robe and turban, the embodiment of orientalized virility, master of a ruined city.

The film suggests that men can only suffer humiliation and defeat and then take revenge, a cycle that has fruitlessly continued to reproduce itself from the time of the Crusades. In the final battle for Jerusalem, Scott attempts to distance Balian from this cycle of loss, destruction, and violence, from the ethos of hard-bodied masculinity that fuels warfare. His speech to his troops exonerates him from any wrongdoing in what amounts to a breathtakingly specious defense of imperialism: "None of us took this city from Muslims. No Muslim of the great army now coming against us was born when this city was lost. We fight over an offense we did not give against those who were not alive to be offended." When the battle finally begins, it presents us with an aestheticization of violence that detaches the viewer from what is being represented, using techniques that have become all too familiar from Vietnam War movies. In the midst of the chaos of battle, suddenly the images move into slow motion, while the sound track shifts from the noise of battle to a sad and poignant musical theme (think Barber's "Adagio for Strings" in *Platoon*); in *Kingdom of Heaven* it is a variation on the Middle Eastern–sounding Jerusalem theme that encourages us to mourn the city's destruction. The camera pulls back into a crane shot, giving us the battle from a "God's-eye view," distancing us from the brutality and discouraging reflection on the political implications of the violence we are witnessing, focusing our attention on the beauty of the imagery. In the end we are left simply to be impressed by the soldiers' performance, their staunch defense against insurmountable odds. As Balian's Arab friend Nasir (played by Alexander Siddig) later tells him, "If God does not love you, how could you have done all the things you have done?"

For Ridley Scott, however, the weight of history is too unbearable to allow for the sort of hard-bodied masculinity that might reside in the realm of nostalgia. Scott's Middle Ages echoes in our present, as America's way of fashioning a new kind of masculinity, more appropriately responsive to such catastrophes as Vietnam, Somalia, and September 11, 2001: a masculinity ennobled in defeat and in retreat. In the aftermath of 9/11, when the world's only remaining superpower fell victim to eleven hijackers armed with box cutters, it becomes impossible to imagine even the most hard-bodied—or the most ingenious—men protecting their women or their cities. The film's message seems to be that the politics affecting the Holy Land for the last thousand years haven't changed, and the people behind those politics are also much the same. The film's message seems to be that we are still living in the Middle Ages, at least so far as we continue to be motivated by the same sorts of ignorance, brutality, and greed. The only choice, at least for "civilized" and "modern" people—and these, in Scott's film, are, of course, people of European descent—is to hide, to go underground. Scott offers his audience a fantasy that requires an aristocrat to give up his title and his holdings and a queen to abdicate her throne so that they may retreat from the terror of history.

If, at its end, *Crociati* offers the Middle Ages as a kind of "It's a Small World" fantasy in which the orientalized Middle East comes under the sway of the imperialistic West, *Kingdom of Heaven* suggests an escape no less fantastic, as Balian and Sibylla flee from Jerusalem into the disaffection of modernity. After the battle for Jerusalem, Balian tells Sibylla, "Your brother's kingdom was here [pointing to his head] . . . and here [pointing to his heart]." Sibylla replies that she is still a queen, queen of Acre, Ashkelon, and Tripoli, cities much richer and militarily more important than Jerusalem. "Decide not to be a queen and I will come with you," Balian replies. This fantasy draws on America's fundamental belief in second acts, on the fluidity of identity in American culture, where it is less desirable to be a king or a queen than to be able to light out for the territory and reinvent oneself (a theme we will explore more fully in our final chapter). But it is still difficult to imagine that an aristocrat and a queen would somehow choose lives as peasants as their platonic conceptions of themselves (and only because it is Orlando Bloom asking do we buy it even for a second). In the film, Balian and Sibylla recede into anonymity (no longer a priest killer turned aristocrat; no longer a queen), to partake of a kind of self-imposed witness-protection program, and indeed they have witnessed too much of the unrelenting struggle between two cultures over the bodies of women and the structures of cities in which, inevitably, both the bodies and cities are desecrated if not destroyed. The fantasy of fluid identity saves *Kingdom of Heaven*'s love story, providing the audience with a generically satisfying sense of closure—lovers galloping off toward the horizon. But it does so at the expense of history; the fantasy is finally impossible. The ongoing story of Jerusalem leaves no real happy endings, only the potential for more conflict.

The films of Chahine, Othenin-Girard, and Scott return to the Middle Ages as the moment of origin for today's violence in the Middle East, "apocalyptic conflict[s] between irreconcilable cultures" (J. Carroll, 4). By looking backward these directors seek to exorcize history of its demons, to resolve cultural and religious differences between Christians, Jews, and Muslims. But *Saladin*, *Crociati*, and *Kingdom of Heaven* all ultimately fall into an uneasy space, recognizing on the one hand politics of intolerance that over time have tended more toward escalation than understanding and on the other hand indulging fantasies wherein some hope may yet reside. All three films attempt to stare down the apocalypse with wishful thinking. Such is not the case with the films we examine in part 3, where we deal with films that see in the Middle Ages the seeds of modernity's isolation and alienation. This cinema finds no redemption in the past, only the failure of signification, hopelessness, and a profound despair insufficiently relieved by the commodification of nearly everything. We begin with a discussion of three European films—Robert Bresson's *Lancelot du lac,* Eric Rohmer's *Percival,* and Hans-Jürgen Syberberg's *Parsifal*—that explore the consequences of modernity's confrontation with irrecoverable loss, when mourning itself loses meaning.

Part 3: Cinematic Medievalism and the Anxieties of Modernity

Looking Awry at the Grail

Mourning Becomes Modernity

R obert Bresson's 1974 *Lancelot du lac* opens with a crawl that functions not only as a necessary exposition but also as a means of disengaging his redaction of the Arthurian material from its romance associations, establishing from the beginning what Julien Gracq describes as the film's "Arthurian realism," even if—or perhaps because—"the words protest at being placed side by side" (Cunneen, 153). The crawl explains that the "marvelous adventures" of the Arthurian world have passed into history. Merlin is dead; Perceval "the Pure" has disappeared; and Arthur's knights have failed to achieve the Grail, the cup of Joseph of Arimathea that promises "supernatural power." By stripping away all romance elements from the start, Bresson invests his absent Grail with significance without the aid of the marvelous, supernatural, or mystical, without the Middle Ages of fantasy. The blood-red letters of the crawl are superimposed over a simple picture of a chalice. The sounds of a drum and bagpipes accompany the exposition, one of only two instances of music in the film. The setup seems a simple if conventional way of managing a complicated exposition, and yet, in Bresson, simplicity is never simple. Closer scrutiny of the Grail image reveals that jutting out of the bowl of the chalice on the right side is an unidentifiable object, a stain. It is impossible to make out the image, but it looks a bit like the kind of distortion one gets in an anamorphic picture.[1] Žižek uses the phrase "looking awry" to describe a theoretical method that explores fantasy as "an element that 'sticks out,' which cannot be integrated into the given symbolic structure, yet which, precisely as such, constitutes its identity" (Myers, 99). The stain, distortion, or symptom that calls for this kind of reading strategy Žižek calls the anamorphotic blot. The anamorphotic blot, he argues, resists symbolization, resists explanation, but "persists as a surplus and returns through all attempts to domesticate it" (*Looking Awry*, 91).

As Bresson's opening image suggests, the Grail might easily be read as just such an anamorphotic blot. For what else is the Grail except a fantasy of freedom from the limitations of physical embodiment and so an object of mourning that holds out the promise of mastering the loss entailed by the incomprehensible knowledge of mortality? In the various Perceval stories from Chrétien to Wagner, the king who is served by the Grail is fed from it, not by earthly food but by a single consecrated host, while in Malory, the vision of the Grail feeds Arthur's knights: "euery knight had suche metes an drynkes as he beste loued in this world" (1.432). The association between the Grail and the fantasy of plenitude likely dates back to its Celtic roots in the story of Bran, who possessed a platter on which appeared whatever food one wished, a cauldron of rebirth, and a horn of plenty. After his death, his head ensured the fertility of the land and protected it from invasion. This is also the source of the Grail's associations with death and mourning. The head of Bran appears in the Welsh tale *Branwen*, where it serves as an object of mourning, enabling the inhabitants of the Isle of the Mighty to come to terms with their losses in the war against the Irish. By the thirteenth century, the Grail had morphed into the chalice of the Last Supper, into which Joseph of Arimathea collected Christ's blood and which he had with him when he arrived in Britain in AD 63. This extension of Eucharistic doctrine and symbolism into romance co-opts the theology of the Eucharist—theology that both memorializes Christ's death and offers the promise of eternal life—to serve an aristocratic ideology. While the sacrament of the Eucharist is theoretically available to all communicants, rich or poor (the Fourth Lateran Council of 1215 required annual communion), only knights could quest for the Grail (and only a select few among them can achieve it). This vessel containing a part of Christ that remained after his death, this "blood which continues to shine and give life," Žižek reads as a "little piece of the 'real' which immediately legitimizes power" ("The Wound Is Healed," 207). Why would a church that so assiduously rooted out heresy elsewhere tolerate this secular appropriation of its most central dogma, of an object "which 'naturally' belongs to and defines the locus of power" (207)? While the church certainly did not embrace the legend, it did not particularly attempt to suppress it as heresy either.[2] The rise of the military orders of knighthood in the early twelfth century may offer one explanation for the popularity of Grail legends in medieval romance—that is, romances that explicitly link chivalry to Eucharistic imagery—beginning in the late twelfth century. The Knights Hospitaler were founded in the wake of the First Crusade, while the Knights of the Temple (Templars) were given official church recognition by the Council of Troyes in 1128 (Shichtman, "Politicizing the Ineffable," 164). Troyes of course was the home of the first Grail poet—Chrétien de Troyes, whose *Conte du Graal* was composed c. 1175.

In the Middle Ages, then, the Grail, whether pagan or Christian, is an object of mourning, a piece of a "primitive elegiac labor" (Santner, *Stranded Objects*, 20). Ordinarily we understand mourning as negative; like pain it is something to be avoided. But, like pain, mourning may well have an orientation toward creativity as well, encompassing activity that enables both artist and audience to "transform . . . lost omnipotence into a form of empowerment" or power (20). Julia Kristeva calls this empowerment whose source is loss "that adventure of body and signs that bears witness to affect," in particular to "sadness as the mark of separation and the beginnings of the dimensions of the symbol" ("On the Melancholic Imaginary," 108). In psychoanalysis the paradigmatic procedure by which the individual masters and incorporates loss is described in Freud's account of the fort-da game he had observed in his grandson. "By staging his own performance of disappearance and return with props," the child masters the grief caused by separation from the mother (Santner, *Stranded Objects*, 20). D. W. Winnicott called these props "transitional objects" (20); they are part of the process by which the child comes to take up a subject position separate from the mother. But this process of coming to terms with loss through the creation of transitional objects is not just an individual psychic event. Santner points to several examples in ancient mythology of this same mechanism for mourning loss on a cultural scale (22). Following his lead, we are arguing that, in medieval romances, the Grail serves as a kind of cultural transitional object, a means by which an entire culture—in this case the culture of the medieval aristocracy—comes to terms with death and loss, with its own impotence, and in doing so legitimizes its own claims to power as the only class capable of acquiring the Grail.

This kind of elegiac labor, however, whether individual or cultural, never takes place in a social vacuum. While the interaction seems to involve only the mourner and the object, in fact, mourning is an intersubjective process, the object mediating the exchange between subjects. Social context, then, may either support or block the labor of mourning, whether a successful outcome is defined as the consolidation of a "cohesive and vital self" or the ability "to survive loss and to discover new possibilities and satisfactions of a life in the symbolic order" (Santner, *Stranded Objects*, 24). In a context of social alienation, in the absence of an empathetic environment, projects of mourning (on both the individual and cultural scales) fail to produce either outcome. Mourning becomes a mechanical procedure, an "elegiac loop that must repeat itself endlessly" (25). Eventually the object loses its efficacy, becoming a "stranded object," compulsively returned to but without effect or affect.

Under the conditions of modernity, in which "there are virtually no direct relationships between men, and in which each person has been reduced to a social atom" (Adorno, 152), the Grail becomes a stranded object. At least, that is the claim we explore in this chapter, which uses the Arthurian Grail as a kind of *point de capiton*, or quilting point, that organizes the ideological field of modernity in three European films about the Grail—Robert Bresson's *Lancelot du lac*, Eric Rohmer's *Perceval le Gallois* (1979), and Hans-Jürgen Syberberg's *Parsifal* (1982). These are not lovable films—at least not at first viewing. They are difficult and require patience to watch. They are the product of cultures perhaps more used to grappling with intellectual issues and less afraid of challenging viewers than the culture that produces Hollywood films. At the same time, they are the work of directors known for their conservatism: Bresson and Rohmer for their Catholicism, Syberberg for his reactionary politics and anti-Semitism, as well as his distaste for consumer culture. We hope to illuminate some small corners of these films through the method of "looking awry." To grasp the challenge of these films, we must focus our attention not only on their content but on their form as well. This is not to argue for an apolitical formalism. These three films by conservative, even reactionary, directors, all released within a decade of each other, were sandwiched between the utopian dreams of revolution that were crushed with the failure of France's student uprising in May of 1968, the end of the Vietnam conflict, and the emergence of global Reaganism in the 1980s, and they must be understood within those contexts. All three films locate the alienation that characterizes modernity in the kind of reified consumer society represented by the Hollywood film (Syberberg perhaps most explicitly) and attempt to discover a distinctive cinematic idiom to challenge the hegemony of Hollywood illusion-ism. More specifically, all three films subvert the photographic illusion of depth of field by which Hollywood films achieve their appearance of reality, with the effect that David John Williams describes for Rohmer's *Perceval* as an "odd conjunction between vigorously expressive, strongly characterized—even caricatured—actors and the purely theoretical space they occupy, which puts unusual emphasis on those characters and their destinies" (16). These directors create flat, featureless dreamscapes of modernity. Against this perspectiveless background the Grail works in all three films not by creating new meanings but by reorganizing meanings that were already present, "binding them to the same signifier" (Žižek, "Grimaces of the Real, or When the Phallus Appears," 64). This chapter explores the anamorphotic blot represented in Bresson's opening shot of the Grail, literally "looking awry" at the Grail as a stranded object of modernity.[3]

Bresson's First Knight

For Bresson the absence of the Grail becomes the hole—the stain—around which *Lancelot du lac* is structured. As the film opens, the Grail quest has ended in failure "as bloody as it is pointless" (aussi sanglants qu'inutiles).[4] Of the hundred knights who set out on the Grail quest, only thirty remain; the rest have been horribly slaughtered. Except for the brief image of it, described above, in the film's opening crawl, however, the Grail is not seen or mentioned. Instead, the film chronicles the decline of the Round Table and the senseless slaughter of Arthur's remaining knights in a moral wasteland from which God and Grail have retreated. The audience is made to feel this social anomie—the alienation resulting from the absence of any supporting social or moral framework—in the film's disorienting opening sequence, which takes place even before the crawl explains what is going on. This sequence relies on metonymy and parataxis, rather than causal connections, to create uncertainty and anxiety, as well as meaning.

The very first shot shows a knight's hand holding a sword. Metonymically, we know we are seeing a knight, but we have no idea who the knight is. The camera pulls back to reveal two knights in full armor fighting—or at least their hands and swords; there is no establishing shot that reveals the whole scenario. The knights' identities are effectively disguised by the armor they wear, which makes them appear anonymous and threatening. The sound track, in the absence of any music, loudly conveys the clanking of the swords coming together and the knights' grunts. These parts—the noises—stand for the whole, which remains inaccessible. A second shot shows us one knight's sword fallen on the ground. The opposing knight's sword crosses it. We feel the exertion required to lift the sword with enough force to decapitate the other knight. The third shot shows the decapitation in fairly gruesome (almost Monty Pythonesque) detail.[5] This sword fight can be conveyed in only three shots because it is represented entirely through metonymy, with the part always standing for the whole. Everything else, including any information about who is fighting, what they are fighting about, and who is right or wrong, good or bad, has been stripped away, a typical Bressonian technique. As Bresson explains it, "If you take a steam iron to your image, flattening it out, suppressing all expression by mimeticism and gestures, and you put that image next to an image of the same kind, all of a sudden that image may have a violent effect on another one and both take on another appearance" (Schrader, 68). What Bresson denies his audiences in his paratactic editing is the system described by film theorists as "suture." As Žižek explains it, suture describes the ways in which a film effaces "the traces of its own production": "Traces of the production process, its gaps, its mechanisms, are obliterated, so that the product can appear as a naturalized, organic whole" (*The Fright of Real Tears*, 55). In continuity editing the relationship of the long shot to the close-up is one such suturing technique. The long shot advances narrative by orienting the viewer spatially, the close-up creates intimacy. Knit together, they present the illusion of wholeness. Bresson's editing technique immerses viewers in the disorienting world of the film by refusing to suture the cinematic field to create a sense of a self-contained whole.[6]

The opening sequence that precedes the expository crawl is a study in parataxis, in the refusal of suture. It is composed of thirteen shots that alternate between acts of violence—a decapitation, a disembowelment, a burning building with charred corpses, a knight pillaging a church—and shots of knights riding through the forest. Who are these knights? They are never identified. Before a single title or credit appears, these thirteen shots disorient viewers by refusing to anchor the narrative in either time or space beyond the blank forest through which the knights ride. Opening titles and the presence of well-known stars are common procedures in Hollywood films for orienting viewers to the narrative they are watching, and Bresson rejects both. The long shots show only the heavy armor that obscures identity. The close-ups reveal only fragments, usually hands or feet. Who is fighting? Why are they fighting? Where are they fighting? Who are the good guys and who the bad? The film critic Jonathan Rosenbaum notes that "the appalling violence that opens and closes *Lancelot* presents us with war as anonymous and indifferent slaughter, with faceless phantoms in the darkness battling and perishing beneath heavy armor that instantly turns into scrap metal as soon as the bodies become mute" (205). It is hard not to see Bresson's film, re-leased only a year after the last American troops had left Vietnam, ending nearly thirty years of bloodshed, as haunted by the bloody postwar conflicts over French colonial losses in Vietnam (1956), as well as Algeria (1962).

To elucidate Bresson's refusal of suture, we might compare this sequence to the opening of Jerry Zucker's *First Knight* (1995). Although this Hollywood block-buster was made some twenty years after Bresson's film, it shares with it a focus on Lancelot as the Arthurian hero par excellence, while its opening sequence dis-plays at least some superficial similarities to Bresson's opening. As in *Lancelot du lac, First Knight* delays its credits in favor of an establishing sequence (a teaser). But while Bresson proceeds paratactically, Zucker's style, like most Hollywood films, relies on hypotaxis. While one reading of the theory of montage contends that all films make meaning paratactically by juxtaposing shots, the system of continuity editing that developed in Hollywood during the classical period cre-ated a system of suture capable of conveying hypotaxis.[7] Whereas Bresson rejects that system, Zucker relies on its editing procedures to orient his viewers in the narrative. *First Knight* opens with an extreme long shot of an army marching across the screen—an establishing shot. The tiny figures are all but swallowed up by the mountains, hills, and lakes through which they march. For a split second, but only a second, the audience knows nothing about where this army comes from or where it is going. Almost immediately, however, a crawl relieves our cu-riosity, explaining that this is Arthur's army returned from the wars to discover the treachery of Malagant, the film's villain. While Bresson delays his exposition until after the opening sequence, in *First Knight* exposition precedes action. The crawl explains the army, then introduces Lancelot as "a wanderer who never dreamed of peace or justice or knighthood" before we ever see him. By the time we have finished reading, we have every piece of information we need to make sense of the narrative that follows. The crawl supplies the necessary hypotactic connections that link cause and effect, something Bresson denies his viewers.

First Knight, like *Lancelot du lac,* stages a sword fight before title or credits roll. That fight also begins with a close-up shot of crossed swords (a metonymy), but the camera quickly moves back to reveal the whole—the hero, Lancelot, imme-diately identified as Richard Gere, the film's star. Unlike the knights in *Lancelot du lac,* the combatants wear no armor, so Gere is easily identified. While Bresson relies on unknown "models" rather than actors, much of the meaning in this scene is carried by Richard Gere's star persona, and the camera is careful to dis-play his face frequently, focusing on his good looks and banter as he dispatches his two opponents. Together these strategies suggest cause and effect within the single opening shot. This sword fight is not, as in Bresson, mortal combat. Rather it is a performance. If the crawl didn't already make it clear, the scene reiterates the setup. Lancelot is an itinerant showman who makes his living displaying his prowess with a sword; he is not, as the film opens, a knight. The editing of the sword fight follows the classic Hollywood formula for cutting fight sequences. Long shots establish the spatial relations of the combatants. These shots are interspersed primarily with close-ups of Gere and a few reaction shots from Gere's opponents, whom he easily defeats (but does not kill), and from the crowd.

In contrast to Zucker's rationalized images, Bresson's opening sequence gives us the violence of the medieval world in the alternating rhythms of bodies (both human and animal), color, sound, motion, light, and shadow. In an interview Bresson states, "I believe that the form leads to rhythms. Now the rhythms are all-powerful. . . . Even when one makes the commentary of a film, this commentary is seen, felt, at first as a rhythm. Then it is a colour (it can be cold or warm); then it has a meaning. But the meaning arrives last" (Thompson, 314). Viewing the opening sequence, we come to understand the anomie of this violent world and the devastation caused by its violence. However, we are almost completely in the dark about the causes until we arrive at the film's expository crawl. Only the rhythm of the editing paratactically connects the knights riding through the forest with the knights fighting. As the French press book puts it, "We are in an obscure world. It is certain that Arthur and his knights are battling against the Invisible which manipulates them" (Nous sommes dans un monde obscur. Il est certain qu'Artus et ses chevaliers sont aux prises avec l'Invisible qui les manœuvre).

This opening sequence is characteristic of Bresson's minimalist style. As Bresson describes it, "As far as I can I eliminate anything which may distract from the interior drama. For me, the cinema is an exploration within. Within the mind, the camera can do anything" (Schrader, 65). Bresson takes the thirteenth-century romance *La Mort le roi Artu* and pares away the plot. While this final romance of the Vulgate cycle is positively terse as medieval romances go, lacking the fantasy and chivalric elements of the first two romances of the cycle, Bresson strips the narrative down even further, replacing the magic and fantasy of romance with the mortality of the knights, the vulnerability of the body, death, tawdriness, limitation, and lack, creating the Arthurian realism Julien Gracq praises (Cunneen, 153). To represent this interiority, as well as the emotional poverty of the Arthurian community, Bresson gives us affectless characters projected against blank, contextless backgrounds. Despite the realistic look of his locations, Bresson films his actors (his "models") against blank illuminated tent walls, white stone castle walls, and featureless forests that make his geography seem more psychological than physical. Furthermore, he does not use actors, preferring to use individuals without acting experience, whom he calls "*modèles*." None of the *modèles* Bresson used in *Lancelot du lac* had appeared in a film before, and neither Luc Simon, who plays Lancelot, nor Vladimir Antolek-Oresek, who plays Arthur, ever appeared in another. Of the principal parts only Humbert Balsan, who plays Gauvain, went on to a career in film, acting in more than fifty films and serving as Bresson's assistant in *Le Diable probablement* (Reader, 117). In *Notes on Cinematography* Bresson describes how he works with his models to achieve the effects he desires: "Your models, pitched into the action of your film, will get used to the gestures they have repeated twenty times. The words they have learned with their lips will find, *without their minds' taking part in this,* the inflections and the lilt proper to their true natures. A way of recovering the automatism of real life" (32).

These techniques for establishing the automatism Bresson associates with modernity create in *Lancelot du lac* the effect of a pervasive melancholia, a sense that the mourning for lost comrades and lost possibilities has been blocked. The malaise that paralyzes King Arthur's court is explored through the other great stranded object in the film, the Round Table. In a scene that follows Lancelot's first meeting with Guinevere, Arthur, Lancelot, and Gauvain enter the room that holds the Round Table, where they contemplate the future of Arthur's fellowship. Arthur wants to close the room off, effectively repudiating this symbol of Arthurian fraternity. Gauvain clings to the stranded object, to the Round Table, as that which holds the knights together: "Shall we never assemble again?" Arthur replies, "Here sat Ydien, Clamadeau, Urien, here Galeschin and all the others we shall see no more. Here Perceval, there Claudas, and there, there, there. . . . No, too many dead and too many memories. I lack the heart when we have lost so many noble companions to replace them so quickly."[8] The Round Table, as stranded object, lurks in this sequence, never fully visible, represented only metonymically by bits and pieces: a few chairs and the curve of the table (see Figure 14). There is no establishing shot to give us the whole table, no crane shot investing it with the power to unify the Arthurian community. The camera follows the three knights as they gaze at the table, but the object of their gaze—the reverse shot—is denied to the viewer. Bresson refuses to suture cinematographic space. The scene focuses instead on Arthur's inability to mourn effectively his lost knights. It depicts the anomie of a culture cut off by its inability to come to terms with loss, creating a melancholia that results in isolation and alienation. The iso-

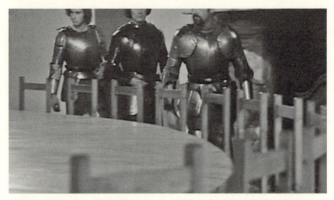

Figure 14. Robert Bresson's Round Table from *Lancelot du lac* (1974).

lation of the three men from one another is evident in the composition of the scene's last shot, which shows Lancelot, Arthur, and Gauvain all facing in the same direction. The white background of the walls flattens out perspective, so they look as if they are standing in a line, even if they, in fact, occupy different planes. They do not connect; they do not address one another.

If the Grail "quilts" the symbolic field of Bresson's film through its absence, the anamorphotic blot that persists throughout the film is acoustic rather than visual. Jeff Rider and his colleagues describe ways in which sound effects in *Lancelot du lac* pretend to invoke a "naturalistic ambience" at the same time that they are invested with an ominous, if unspecified, significance: "the audience hears horses whinny and gallop, hears the knights' armor clanking as they walk, hears an earthenware vessel being emptied. . . . However, they take on a life and significance of their own. . . . They are hyper-real intrusions that create a sense of anxiety and hidden meaning, both because one cannot attach them to anything in the film and because their peculiar quality undermines their credibility" (153). Bresson calls attention to that aspect of film that frequently goes unnoticed: sound. Historically, the achievement of the sound film was twofold. First, it wedded sound to the image so thoroughly that we rarely notice synchronous sound because it seems so much of a piece with the image; sound is "perceived *through* or *in terms of* the image" (Belton, 377; emphasis in original). If we see a door close, we expect to hear a slam, and when we do, the sound is "swallowed up" by the fiction; we attribute its meanings and effects to the image, even when it is created by Foley techniques (Chion, 3). In this sense sound becomes another mechanism for suturing the cinematic field. While most savvy filmgoers know that sound effects are artificially produced, their seamless inclusion in the film becomes part of the illusion of self-enclosure the film creates.[9] Sound only becomes significant if we fail to hear it when we expect it, if the door slams and there is no sound (even our writing here indicates the extent to which image and sound coalesce; we have used a term for sound, *slam,* to indicate something seen).

The second accomplishment of the sound film was to establish a hierarchy of sound that privileged human speech over other sounds. "In every audio mix, the presence of a human voice instantly sets up a hierarchy of perception. . . . The presence of a human voice structures the sonic space that contains it" (Chion, 5). As Rider and his colleagues suggest, Bresson exploits and frustrates these expectations in his films, linking them to his desire to represent the interiority of his characters: "When a sound can replace an image, cut the image or neutralize it. The ear goes more toward the within, the eye toward the outer" (28). Throughout *Lancelot du lac,* sounds—whinnying horses, clanking armor, horns—whether tied to something in the visual field (visualized sound) or cut free of the frame— are "fetishized and employed to 'thingify difference'" (Chion, 1). Bresson's manipulation of sound creates mystery, but, more important, it creates anxiety. Particularly important are those sounds the French theorist Michel Chion calls "acousmatic," sounds that wander in and out of the diegesis and that may not be anchored to an image (18). Although Chion is primarily interested in the acousmatic human voice, much of what he says about the power of the *acousmêtre* applies equally well to the kind of acousmatic sound heard throughout *Lancelot du lac.* The powers Chion attributes to the *acousmêtre* are "the ability to be everywhere, to see all, to know all, and to have complete power . . . : ubiquity, panopticism, omniscience, and omnipotence" (24). Such power cannot fail to signify and, because we generally don't know what the sounds signify, generate anxiety. To cite one example: throughout the scene in which Lancelot returns to Arthur's castle, sounds compete with—and at times drown out—the terse dialogue. We hear horses' hooves, whinnying, bells clanging, footsteps. One sound in particular is disturbing because it is, like the distortion projecting out of the chalice at the film's beginning, completely unidentifiable. A sound like a car horn is repeated throughout the scene, but nothing either in or out of frame explains it.[10] It remains a baffling distortion in the sonic field. Its repetition arouses anxiety, making it seem in some inexplicable way portentous. The *acousmêtre* becomes another anamorphotic blot, a distortion in the cinematic field that structures it, a trauma that returns through all attempts to rationalize it.

Bresson's manipulation of editing and sound create throughout the film a sense of anxiety and melancholy, of a world lost. But, as David Eng and David Kazanjian note, to ask the question "what is lost?" prompts the question "what remains?" Indeed, what is lost can only be known by what remains (2), and this is the focus of *Lancelot du lac*. At the film's opening, Lancelot, failing to acquire the Grail, has returned from his quest to find Arthur's court decimated by the Grail quest and torn apart by rival factions, the Round Table in tatters. What has been lost is social cohesion, fellowship. What remains, it seems, is Guinevere. Bresson puts the affair between Lancelot and Guinevere at the center of the film, yet as an explanation for the destruction of the fellowship of the Round Table, it remains inadequate, especially in the face of the devastation already wrought by the Grail quest. While Lancelot's failure to achieve the Grail is attributed to his adulterous love for Guinevere, one might argue that, in the absence of the affair, he would have arrived at the same results. Had he succeeded in his quest for the Grail, most likely, he would have disappeared as Perceval did, and the Round Table would still have been destroyed. "The external hindrances [in this case Lancelot's illicit love for Guinevere]," as Žižek argues, "that thwart our access to the object [the plenitude promised by the Grail] are there precisely to create the illusion that without them, the object would be directly accessible—what such hindrances thereby conceal is the inherent impossibility of attaining the object" (*The Metastases of Enjoyment*, 94). Guinevere is the only woman in the film (at least the only one with a speaking part), so it seems necessary to interrogate her presence in a film that defines masculinity through acts of violence rather than sexual difference. Žižek's logic suggests that she is there to create the illusion that, if she were not there, the Grail would have been achievable. The unattainable object Žižek is speaking of in this passage is the "Lady-Thing" of courtly love, but he might just as easily be describing the Grail, suggesting that the Grail and Guinevere serve similar structural functions in the film; they are black holes around which the male subject's desire is structured. Bresson's Guinevere illustrates the Lacanian formulation, "Woman is the symptom of man," as read through Žižek.[11] Žižek understands the symptom or *sinthome* to be a "signifying formation in which an individual subject organizes its relationship to enjoyment or jouissance" (Myers, 86).

Let us examine how Guinevere occupies this position in the film by looking at a scene that encodes Guinevere's place as a symptom not only for Lancelot but for all of Arthur's knights and for the viewer. After his return Lancelot attempts to renounce his adulterous relationship with Guinevere. Finally, he surrenders to his enjoyment, an enjoyment that in courtly fashion involves both pleasure and pain since it requires the renunciation of masculine reputation. He agrees to remain behind, arranging a rendezvous, as the other knights attend a tournament in Escalot. Mordred, identified as the cause of much of the unrest in Arthur's court (indeed the destruction of the Round Table seems overdetermined by far too many causes), sets the knights in his faction to spy on Guinevere. The scene we have in mind begins with an establishing shot of two knights hiding in a doorway, spying on Guinevere's room. As is typical of this film, it is not entirely clear who these knights are, since the previous scene has shown us Arthur's knights saddling up for the tournament. Only Lancelot is supposed to have remained behind. The knives they wield connect them with the two knights who, with Mordred, had spied on Guinevere's room in an earlier scene. Ladies-in-waiting enter and leave the room with buckets of water, suggesting that Guinevere is taking a bath, most likely in preparation for receiving Lancelot. Suddenly, a cut takes the viewer inside of the room, where we see Guinevere (played by Laura Duke Condominas) nude in a large tub. As the shot begins to track, we can see only the back of her left hip and buttock. Is this a point-of-view shot from the perspective of the spies, or is the viewer being granted a privileged peek inside Guinevere's boudoir? If so, why? From the point of view of the spies, this is an impossible shot. Earlier shots clearly establish that they cannot get more than a brief glimpse of the inside of the room where Guinevere is bathing. The viewer's privileged view, however, is from inside the room immediately behind the tub. The shot tracks rightward and up. We follow the gaze of the camera as it slowly moves from her legs and feet up to her buttocks. The camera lingers on her backside. Finally, it continues its upward movement to reveal the back of her head and then Guinevere in three-quarters profile. She is holding a small mirror and gazing at herself in it.[12] The shot is a cinematic recreation of the medieval iconography of Vanity, as, for instance, in Hans Memling's 1485 representation (Figure 15).

What John Berger says of the Memling painting in *Ways of Seeing* applies equally to Bresson's shot: "The mirror was often used as a symbol of the vanity of women. The moralizing, however, was hypocritical. You painted a naked woman because you enjoyed looking at her, you put a mirror in her hand and you called the painting *Vanity*, thus morally condemning the woman whose nakedness you had depicted for your own pleasure. The real function of the mirror was otherwise. It was to make the woman connive in treating herself as, first and foremost, a sight" (51). It seems likely that Bresson has this iconography of vanity in mind in framing this shot, which has all the flatness of an icon. He eroticizes a gaze that at once fetishizes and sadistically investigates Guinevere, as the knights in the

Figure 15. Vanity, by Hans Memling. Reproduced by permission of the Musée des Beaux-Arts de Strasbourg. Photo: Musées de la Ville de Strasbourg, A. Plisson.

film do. The viewer is invited to gaze on and judge Guinevere as a sexualized object. While, as we have suggested, Bresson is famous for his rejection of traditional Hollywood film idioms, in this scene he indulges in what Laura Mulvey identifies as the paradigmatic classical Hollywood shot: woman as object of the controlling male gaze, woman as a spectacle, a fetish. This shot stops the narrative in its tracks (Mulvey, 39–43). Guinevere is offered up in this shot purely as a symptom that organizes the enjoyment of the (presumably) male viewer.

We might notice further the ways in which this iconography splits the gaze. Like Memling, Bresson is careful to show us Guinevere's face reflected in the mirror. We can see that Guinevere sees only her own face, while as viewers we survey her naked body (although only from behind). While the viewer is treated to a highly sexualized display of nudity, Guinevere's gaze (as well as our access to her face) is severely restricted by the small mirror she holds. What is revealed in the gap between these two gazes? What Guinevere is thinking or feeling, perhaps represented by the image of her face in the mirror, is represented as an enigma. Women don't think; they are body. Or are they? The reflection of Guinevere's face in the mirror allows for just enough ambiguity. Bresson's Guinevere is a cipher, however, not because she doesn't express her feelings; she does so forcefully in her meetings with both Lancelot and Gauvain. Rather the film makes clear that she is not allowed her own desires. "It's not what you want that matters," Lancelot tells her in one of their meetings after she has refused to deny her love for him. That Guinevere functions as a symptom in the film for all of Arthur's knights is suggested by Gauvain's words to Lancelot: "She is our one woman, our sun." Throughout the film Guinevere is frequently reduced to metonymy by a shot of her lit window. Two symmetrical cutouts in an otherwise massive and blank wall constantly attract the gazes of the knights, to whom she is otherwise inaccessible. What, then, do we make of this moment of complete accessibility in a film that otherwise denies the human body, either refusing to show it altogether, representing it by its parts, or showing it almost invariably clad in inhuman metallic armor? The shot suggests that Guinevere—the woman as symptom—organizes enjoyment for the viewer just as surely as she does for Lancelot, Arthur, and all of his knights.

Like the Grail, Guinevere is more a pretext for the violence that ensues than its cause. And, like the Grail, she becomes a stranded object, unable to provide the social cohesion the knights seem to need from her. Finally, she is trapped—overdetermined—by the knights' desire to project onto her their failures, anxieties, and grief. In an earlier scene Guinevere is shown in church, wearing her crown, which resembles the iron bars of a prison. Later Lancelot will rescue her from a literal prison. Finally, he will return her to Arthur to prevent war, and the last view we have of her in the film is a long shot of her back as she walks away with Arthur, a man whom she "despises and loathes." We do not see her again; we do not know what becomes of her. Her restoration as queen fails to prevent the violence that is made to seem all but inevitable in the montage of rhythmic images showing Lancelot's knights saddling up for battle. In her absence the Arthurian world falls apart; the images of dissolution coalesce around the figure of a riderless horse galloping through the forest. The last word of the film is a knight—presumably Lancelot—crying Guinevere's name as he dies, falling among a pile of iron-clad corpses.

Système de la Mode

A 1959 discussion of Alain Resnais' *Hiroshima mon amour* produced Jean-Luc Godard's famous—if enigmatic—dictum, "Tracking shots are a question of morality" (Hillier, 68). André Bazin had elucidated this theoretical axiom of New Wave auteurs a few years earlier when he wrote that "if they prize mise-en-scène it is because they discern within it to a great extent the very material of film, an organization of beings and things that make up its meanings, moral as well as aesthetic. . . . Every technique refers to metaphysics" (Marie, 43). Bresson's shot of Guinevere bathing reveals the role "the woman" plays in the constitution of masculine subjectivity in *Lancelot du lac*. We turn now to what might be revealed— metaphysically speaking—about the morality of the gaze in a tracking shot that occurs near the end of Eric Rohmer's Arthurian film, *Perceval le Gallois*. It is a shot that reveals the place of material culture in the film's nostalgic fantasy of chivalry and spiritual transcendence. Unbeknownst to him but not to the audience, Gauvain arrives at the town of Escavalon, where he is supposed to be headed to prove that he has not committed an act of treason against its lord (that is, to prove his reputation as the exemplar of Arthurian chivalry). His arrival is accomplished in a long, slow tracking shot that translates the following narrative from Chrétien de Troyes' *Conte du Graal* into a cinematic grammar:

> He gazes at the whole town and its very good-looking inhabitants, and at the money-changers' tables entirely covered with gold, silver and coinage; and he sees the squares and streets thronging with good workmen occupied in various trades. With their different crafts one makes helmets, another hauberks, this

one saddles and that one escutcheons, this man bridles and that one spurs, whilst others burnish swords; these people pull cloth and those weave it, some card it, others shear it. Some for their part smelt silver and gold, others make beautiful, costly objects: cups, goblets and bowls, enameled jewelry, rings, belts and buckles. One might well have gained the firm impression that there was a continual fair in the town for it to be so full of goods: wax, pepper, scarlet material, vair and grey furs and all manner of merchandise. (Chrétien de Troyes, 450)

The camera tracks past a series of arches within which we see various artisans plying their trades; the exposition is carried by the artisans as each names his or her trade. This shot encapsulates economically the production of the material culture of medieval chivalry, fragmenting the chivalric subjectivity established by Perceval and Gauvain into a series of objects, commodities that are the result of social relations of labor and production that up to that point have been resolutely banned from the narrative. (In the previous episode Gauvain's unwillingness to fight was held up as proof that he was a merchant disguising himself to avoid paying taxes on his wares, a transgression so dire it is punishable by death.) Chrétien's passage contains two sentences, more or less (depending on which edition you read). Rohmer chooses stylistically to represent each sentence through a tracking shot, the cuts coinciding with the end of sentences, a method that creates a visual counterpart to the fluidity of Chrétien's verse.

Rohmer's tracking shot, furthermore, evokes metaphysically the "thingness" of things, which is what Chrétien's prose aims for—chain mail, helmets, saddles, shields, bridles, spurs, swords, cloth, as well as cups, goblets, rings, belts, clasps, enameled jewels, skins, furs, foods, and spices—which, far from merely reflecting court culture, can be seen as agents in social relations that, in the words of Roberta Gilchrist, "construct, maintain, control, and transform" the chivalric identities Perceval and Gauvain represent (Gilchrist, 15; see also Burns, *Courtly Love Undressed,* 15–16). The shot renders Gauvain's point of view as he rides into the town toward the castle where he will be lodged. If he is riding from right to left across the shot, then for him to see the various workers as the audience does (if his gaze is to merge with that of the audience), he must literally "look awry." In his sidelong glance at the labor required to sustain his chivalric identity, we might tease out the thread that unravels conventional readings—including Rohmer's own—of this film as Christian allegory. Gauvain's gaze reveals the important role of material culture in the process that Louis Montrose calls "subjectivization," the mechanism by which individuals are endowed with subjectivity by certain cultural practices (chivalry) that create the capacity for agency at the same time that they position those individuals within a social network and subject them to cultural codes that ultimately exceed their comprehension and control (21). Although this focus on the superficialities of material culture may seem diametrically opposed to what appears to be a universalizing psychoanalytic narrative of subject formation, our analysis is designed to deconstruct the illusion of psychic depth created by narratives about the formation of the subject. In this section, through an analysis of the material culture of chivalry, we describe the ways in which subjectivization, which we have outlined in our reading of Bresson's *Lancelot du lac,* inscribes its effects on the surface of the body.

Critics conventionally interpret the Gauvain digressions, both in Chrétien and in Rohmer, as a secular counterpoint to Perceval's spiritual adventures. Gauvain is a well-established knight of Arthur's court with a reputation for perfection, the exemplar of the chivalric subject, so the concentration on the place of the material in his subjectivity is unsurprising. We are meant to see Perceval as a more unformed knight, one who lacks Gauvain's savoir faire but who is destined, precisely because of his lack of earthly knowledge, to acquire the Grail. The two sets of adventures contrast different orders of chivalry, spiritual and worldly. The film, according to Linda Williams, replaces "a confused, secular ideal of the court with the Christian ideal of divine love" ("Eric Rohmer and the Holy Grail," 584). Indeed, Rohmer seems to hint at this contrast by having his knights travel in opposite directions. Perceval moves from right to left as he travels through the "forests," while Gauvain sets off from Arthur's court moving from left to right. Presumably, the "proper" Grail quester is the knight who abandons the things of the flesh to pursue the spiritual quest.

To be sure, the spiritual interpretation of Perceval's education accords well with Rohmer's own conservative Catholicism and his reading of Chrétien. He wants to stage Chrétien's text as "a return to the basics of Catholic morality," in the words of one reviewer (Wise, 49): in an interview Rohmer notes that "it very much seems that the text is centered on the Christian, Christly, idea that God is Christ" (quoted in Rider et al., 157). This religious reading of the film as an attempt, in Donald Hoffman's words, "to *remystify* Christian doctrine and the practice of penitence" ("Re-Framing Perceval," 47) depends heavily on the Passion play that concludes the film, in which Perceval takes on the role of the crucified Christ. This scene seems doubly authoritative because of its length and placement in the film. It takes up more than eighteen minutes of screen time, 13 percent of the film's running time, according to Bruce Beatie (258), and its placement makes it appear to be the end toward which the romance has been moving; we are invited to read the film retroactively through it. Medievalists who have written on the film, even as they affirm the role of the Passion play as a kind of transcendental signified that ensures the religious significations of both Chrétien's and Rohmer's texts, describe the episode as "jarring" (Grimbert, 39) or, at best, "affectively different from the rest of the film" (Hoffman, "Re-Framing Perceval," 46).[13] It is not an apt conclusion to the film because there is nothing in the preceding two hours of film that hints of such an ending. It comes literally, like the Loathly Lady, out of nowhere. To be sure, it does have some basis in Chrétien's text, but even there Perceval's visit to the hermit seems far from conclusive, nothing more than yet another episode in a relentlessly episodic—and ultimately unfinished—text. Rohmer clearly wants to create a spiritual film that reflects his Catholic morality and his scholarly sense of the Middle Ages, but he is, in the end, thwarted by his adherence to the letter of Chrétien's resolutely courtly text. The Passion play is not the logical conclusion of the film but a "tearing rupture" (Rider et al., 157) in its fabric that imposes a false sense of closure on the narrative, whose primary interests lie elsewhere.[14]

We would like to resist conventional readings of the film, to "look awry" at it. If the two knights are meant to contrast earthly and spiritual chivalry, it is instructive to note how much Perceval's and Gauvain's adventures actually have in common, especially in their foregrounding of what is repressed by the Grail's fantasy of plenitude: the material culture of chivalry. The plenitude promised by the Grail mythology must float free from the labor required to sustain it and the aristocratic ideology of superiority that encodes it. Yet that material culture continually returns through articles of dress and adornment whose production is glimpsed in the long tracking shot as Gauvain enters Escavalon.

Medieval Grail narratives tend toward the rambling, inconsistent, and inconclusive. They probe a wide range of themes that include not only this contrast between secular and spiritual orders of knighthood, the spirit and the flesh, but also the nature of political authority, the inscription of subjectivity within a particular social order, and the instability of signification as well. Most filmmakers attempt to iron out this narrative confusion (Boorman provides a good example in *Excalibur*), to reduce it to a coherent exposition that ironically robs the Grail of its very mystery, its sense of the uncanny. Since the Grail's mystery derives, as we suggest above, from its narrative function as a stranded object, as anamorphic blot, any attempt to look at it head-on, to explain it logically, will destroy its capacity to serve as a quilting point that holds together the symbolic field. It becomes just another material object. This is what happens in Rohmer's film, which chooses to stage Chrétien's twelfth-century romance (perhaps the most incoherent and inconclusive of all the Grail stories) and follows closely the source narrative, at least until the end. To explore the contradictions in Rohmer's text as a means to unravel its metaphysics, we need to linger over the incoherence of Rohmer's Grail story, turning to some of the narrative impasses Rohmer's recreation of Chrétien's romance creates. In doing so, we emulate John Sutherland's series of investigations into such literary mysteries as "Is Heathcliff a murderer?" "How long is Alice in Wonderland?" "Why is Moll Flanders' younger brother older than she is?" (Sutherland). Chrétien's texts, and *Conte du Graal* more than any of the others, offer us more than enough material for puzzlement. Here is just a small sample. Why is Perceval so relentlessly dimwitted? What happens to the romance between Perceval and Blanchefleur? Does Perceval return, as he promises, to rule Blanchefleur's lands (and presumably to marry her)? Is Gauvain really a traitor, or does he clear his name? Is the Maimed King ever healed? Does Perceval ever return to ask the appropriate questions? What did Perceval do that was so horrific that it brings down on his head the dire predictions of the Loathly Lady ("Cursed be whoever wishes you well")? And perhaps most important for any inquiry into material culture, what in the fashion system of twelfth-century France do small sleeves signify?

Perhaps this last question is of a different order than the others. Even so, this method of reading, by focusing our attention on apparently trivial details of a text, by asking what seem like impossibly childish questions of it, enables us to "reframe" it (to use Hoffman's term) in new ways (or to look awry at it). The last question, for instance, shifts our attention away from the privileged Passion play and its religious implications that have dominated critical discussions of Rohmer's film and toward the two hours that precede it, with its exploration of the intricacies of chivalric subjectivity. In particular our question about fashion prompts us to note the ways in which the sumptuous garments so conspicuously displayed in medieval romances participate in the processes of subjectivization, as Jane Burns argues in *Courtly Love Undressed* (25). In its faithfulness to its source romance, Rohmer's film reproduces a late-twentieth-century version of the medieval fashion system, which features heavily in the constitution of knightly masculinity in the film.

Style and technique have figured centrally in religious readings of Rohmer's film. Commentators have examined the abstract stylization of the film's mise-en-scène and acting. Its "planar geometry" (Crisp, 82) constructing a decorative space reminiscent of medieval manuscript painting, its flat lighting, lack of architectural scale, use of the third person and indirect discourse, lack of camera movement, long takes, and primary colors establish visually a chronotope in which time is seasonal and cyclical rather than linear and space symbolic rather than historical or geographical. Rohmer's style translates the "symbolic space of medieval iconography . . . into the three dimensional space of film," according to Linda Williams.[15] The interpenetration of space and time that realizes the film's "idealized, hierarchical world of symbolic meanings" (Williams, "Eric Rohmer and the Holy Grail," 585) is indicated by Perceval's stylized and repetitive movement through a landscape of abstract metallic trees and cardboard castles. Rohmer's realism, Beatie argues, is realized not in the desire "to show the Middle Ages as we would see it if we could go back in time and photograph it" but in his attempt "to rediscover the vision of the medieval period as it saw itself" (264).

Yet most critics have little to say about the film's costumes, designed by Jacques Schmidt, the one aspect of the film that runs counter to this abstractly formalist aesthetic.[16] The characters' relatively realistic clothing provides most of the visual interest in the film. The costumes are the primary source of color, texture, light, and shadow; they present a palate of brilliant blues and reds, purple, burgundy, and rose. Though perhaps simpler than the elaborate descriptions provided by medieval courtly romances, they nonetheless point us away from the abstract symbolization of the sets, immersing us in the material culture represented in Chrétien's poem and pointing toward its opulence and wealth. In the courtly culture of twelfth-century French romance, as Jane Burns argues, the ostentatious display of luxury dress provided a means of self-definition for the elite, marking out the symbolic space of court life. In medieval romance, clothing is never simply functional, nor does it simply overlay the supposedly raw material of the body. Rather, clothing in the courtly world must be understood as "a kind of 'social skin' that combines corporeal features of the physical body with adornment that significantly transforms and alters that body" (Burns, 25). Burns uses the term "sartorial bodies" to describe social bodies "forged from fabric and flesh" (12).

Chivalry is a gender system that defines norms for aristocratic behavior (see Armstrong, 1–8). Why, one might ask, in an "age of permissiveness" (Žižek, *The Metastases of Enjoyment*, 89) should Rohmer be interested in this code, in what his leading man called "a scholarly project, touched with insanity" (Crisp, 86)? We might point to the psychoanalytic significance attached to the "libidinal economy of courtly love" by Lacan, Kristeva, and Žižek (among others); notes Žižek, "The logic of courtly love still defines the parameters within which the two sexes relate to each other" (*The Metastases of Enjoyment,* 89).[17] Žižek's comment reminds us of the binary logic that organizes gender: "gender is not a free-standing identity; it is constructed in relationship and we come to our understandings of masculinity and femininity through a process of differentiation. One is masculine precisely by not being feminine, and vice versa; thus masculinity must simultaneously repudiate and rely on a notion of femininity as its defining and constitutive difference" (Tripp, 6). Gender, then, as Žižek would hold, is founded not on substance but on "difference from"; it forms around a hole, a void. But the situation is even more complicated. Chivalry is not simply a series of binary oppositions; it is also a narrative, "a structure of desire . . . that both invents and distances its object and thereby inscribes again and again the gap between signifier and signified that is the place of generation for the symbolic" (Susan Stewart, quoted in Weisl, 15). To cite just one example, the contrast between female weakness and male strength must be translated into a very specific narrative in which knightly prowess is demonstrated by the rescue of damsels in distress.[18]

The functions we have assigned to the Grail are in fact functions that Žižek, in his essay "Courtly Love, or Woman as Thing," attributes to the inaccessible woman in courtly love. However, in *Perceval le Gallois* women simply are not unattainable; au contraire, they are all too available. Perceval easily steals both a kiss and a ring from the unprotected Tent Maiden. Blanchefleur sleeps with him on their first date. The Maiden with Small Sleeves maneuvers Gauvain into carrying her favors in the tournament, and the lady at Escavalon entertains him willingly, defending him when the townspeople attack. Yet, while women seem merely ornamental in Rohmer's film—it is, after all, a film about Perceval's subjectivization—they are not simply passive conduits for male power. Attention to the details of the medieval fashion system will illuminate the place of women in Rohmer's medievalism.

In *Perceval le Gallois* fashion becomes a primary vehicle for carrying such narratives. In *The Fashion System* Barthes asks, "Is there any system of objects, a system of some magnitude, which can dispense with articulated language? Is not speech the inevitable relay of any signifying order?" His answer is that clothing can "signify without recourse to the speech that describes it." The fashion system "provides it [clothing] with signifiers and signifieds abundant enough to constitute a system of meaning" (xi). The fashion system is a "vestimentary code" based, like gender itself, on binary logic (narrow versus wide ties, short versus long skirts) and so might be mapped onto gender. The code works by building chains of equivalences (paradigmatic relations like narrow and wide lapels) and combinations (syntagmatic relations like skirt and blouse) creating a large set of terms or "functions" that can be used to build messages visually. Hence the usefulness of fashion—or costume design—for filmmakers.

Women's fashions not only serve to define female identity but, by putting certain narratives into play, can function as a marker of masculine identity as well, returning us to the question we posed about Rohmer's film: the meaning of small sleeves within the courtly fashion system. As the film turns to Gauvain's adventures, we are introduced to Tybald of Tintaguel's two daughters, who are watching a tournament. The elder daughter is being courted by Meliant of Lis, to whom she gives one of her sleeves to display during the tournament. When she brags about the prowess of her lover, her younger sister claims that Gauvain, who is observing the tournament, is clearly the better knight. This younger daughter is introduced as "the Maiden with Small Sleeves" (La Pucelle aux Petites Manches). Her identity—and the conflict between the two sisters—is marked only by the difference of her sleeves from those of her elder sister and the other ladies ("she alone wore cuffs so tight"). What does this difference signify? The courtly lady's sleeve, as Burns has noted, belongs to "a well-known constellation of courtly traditions involving the exchange of love tokens and the concomitant exchange of women as valuable beauties to be won in combat" (4). It does not take a psychoanalyst to see a potential connection between sleeves and female genitalia. In this instance the sleeves signify availability; the knight who carries the sleeve is advertising his possession of the lady whose sleeve he carries, inspiring him to "accomplish feats of extraordinary prowess that bring honor and credit to his name" and so win him the lady's love and favor. The film describes the arms of the younger sister as "modestly clad." Her small sleeves are a sign of her sexual inaccessibility. She is, perhaps, still too young to be trafficked. This reading is borne out when the maiden asks Gauvain to fight for her in the tournament to right the wrong her sister has done to her by proving he is the better knight. Her father tells Gauvain to "pay no attention to her foolishness. She's but a child." Tybald gives the younger daughter a bolt of silk and orders made "a sleeve, ample in width and length," which she can give to Gauvain to carry in the tournament. What is most remarkable about this episode is that the sleeve, in this instance, becomes completely detached from its function as clothing (to cover the arms as a part of a dress) and becomes pure signifier. This is the younger daughter's coming out. In the fashion system of courtly love large and small sleeves form a paradigmatic binary code signaling sexual availability.

This reading takes us back to earlier episodes to look for similar codes. After his experience in the Grail Castle, Perceval has two encounters that further refine the vestimentary code of courtly romance. Immediately after his adventures in the Grail Castle, he happens on the Loathly Lady (La Demoiselle Hideuse), whose loathsomeness is signaled in the film by her brown featureless dress, wild hair, weird eye makeup, and electronically distorted voice, which is harsh and guttural. Perceval's second encounter with the Tent Maiden (La Pucelle de la Tente) stresses her nakedness. Her dress is "so ragged . . . not a palm of it was whole." When she encounters Perceval, she "tries to cover herself only to reveal more, covering up one place, closing one hole, she opened a dozen more." Both women, who are described not by name but by plot function, are given no separate subjectivity. They are distinguished by a lack or deficiency in their clothing; both enter the narrative to chastise deficiencies in Perceval's chivalric behavior. The Tent Maiden's nakedness and the Loathly Lady's ugliness seem to be literally called forth by Perceval's inadequacies as a knight.

Although it might be tempting to think of fashion as a domain pertaining only to women, clothing literally makes the man from the opening scene of *Perceval le Gallois*. Masculinity is expressed primarily in clothing, not bodies. In the opening scene Perceval is hunting in the forest when he comes across five knights in full armor. Following Chrétien, the chorus identifies them first by the noise their armor makes—"chain mail quivering, thud of wood, ring of iron, clatter of shield and armor"—then by the visual effects of lighting they produce: "helmets glistening," "all red and white in the sun." Rohmer's armor is more or less realistic looking, adding depth to his otherwise flat mise-en-scène. Perceval mistakes the knights for devils and then for angels because they are literally nonhuman, encased in a second skin from head to foot. Once disabused of his error, he questions them about the function of each article—lance, shield, armor—a narrative device used to instruct the audience in the material culture of knighthood—"What is that you hold? How is it used? What's it for?" His response—"If God had given deer such armor, I couldn't kill another one"—suggests that Perceval does not at this point understand that the elaborate armor he marvels at is not the knights' own skin. Yet his error elucidates the concept of "social skin." "Were you born like that?" he asks. "No youth," the knight responds. "One can't be born like this." In this exchange the text has arrived at the central contradiction of knighthood, a contradiction that Žižek describes in *Looking Awry* (32–34). An identity—in this case, masculinity—that was always already there must be continually created and recreated through social (that is symbolic) interaction and conferred by the Law (King Arthur). One is born noble; it is an inherited position that carries with it the ideology that birth equals worth. Yet knighthood—chivalry—is a social status one must attain through training, initiation rites, and, most important, through investiture (which literally means the putting on of clothes, of a social skin).[19] Thus when Perceval asks "Who put it on you?" he understands his question practically. The knight, however, answers ideologically. The armor was given to him (put on him) by King Arthur as a symbol of his achievement of his inherent status as a knight. Social skin, indeed.

Perceval arrives at Arthur's court with one purpose. Having learned the lesson that a knight *is* his armor—is what he is wearing—he tells Arthur, "I want to *be* the Red Knight," which means, "I want the clothing that the Red Knight is wearing." Yet after killing the Red Knight, he has no idea how to separate the armor from the dead knight's body, short of skinning him like a deer: "I'll have to cut up this body to remove the armor, so well is it attached, as if the inside and the outside were all of a piece and refused to be parted." Yvonet must school him on how to put on and remove his "social skin" before he can set out on adventures. He does so in a montage sequence that displays the material culture of medieval chivalry, as each piece of the knight's social skin is displayed in a series of close-ups as it is named by the accompanying choral song: "Yvonet helps him, strips the body down to its toes, removing chain-mail and breeches, the helmet from the head and all else, laced his breeches, and to his boots attached the spurs. And over him put the tunic. Then he fitted on the armor so fine. And on his head placed the helmet which suited him well. The sword he taught him to wear loosely. Then placed his foot in the stirrups and helped him to mount the steed." By the end of the sequence, Perceval has been transformed into the Red Knight. His actual training in arms, which occurs in the next scene at the castle of Gornemant, is handled in a far more perfunctory manner, with only a few shots of Perceval riding his horse in circles in front of Gornemant's "castle." He masters the skills effortlessly, "as if he'd spent his life in tournaments and wars, traveling far and wide to do battle. It came to him from nature. With nature as your guide and a willing heart besides, all is learned with ease." In a series of shots much more abstract than the literal clothing sequence, Perceval learns to become what he always already must have been, illustrating again the central contradiction of subjectivity as Žižek formulates it.

How, we might well ask, does the actual body figure in the sartorial body of chivalric masculinity? In a film, characters cannot easily be dissociated from the actors cast to play them, who literally embody them. Rohmer treats his actors' bodies as just so much costume. He devised a system of stylized gesticulation

based on the relation of the elbow to the body and spent a year in rehearsals before a single frame of film was shot, teaching his actors how to "pivot their fore-
arms with outstretched palms around the elbow" (Williams, "Eric Rohmer and
the Holy Grail," 585). With the exception of Perceval, all of the characters, but especially the women, move in this fashion. Rohmer wrote *Perceval le Gallois* with
Fabrice Luchini in mind for his hero, and much of American critics' dissatisfac-
tion with the film derives not so much from Luchini's performance, which is ad-
mirably befuddled, as from his physique. Accustomed to more "hard-bodied" Arthurian knights (Franco Nero in *Camelot*, Richard Gere in *First Knight*, or, more
recently, Clive Owen in *King Arthur*), American critics found Luchini physically
unimposing. In a *Time* review Gerald Clark wrote: "Luchini is more a suggestion
of a knight than a knight himself. With a receding chin, concave chest, and dangling half-opened mouth, he looks as if he would be afraid to kill a mouse with a
trap, much less joust with a man in armor" (quoted in Rider et al., 151). Stripped
of his knightly accoutrements, and Luchini appears naked or near naked both in
Blanchefleur's castle and in the Grail Castle, it is evident that his body requires
the supplement of his armor, even as his naked body is incorporated as decoration into the ornamentation of the courtly mise-en-scène.

   The sartorial body in *Perceval le Gallois* reveals the mechanisms of subjectivization that are the focus of this chapter. Perceval's journey enacts Freud's description of the analytic process—"where there is id, let there be ego." He begins as
pure id, thoroughly dimwitted. Perceval does not know how to "get on" in social
life; in particular, he is unable to sublimate his desires (for a kiss from a comely
maid or a gift). Through the injunctions of the superego, represented by Perceval's several "guides," the unconscious is socialized, brought under the rule of the
symbolic. Freud thought that this process of sublimation would emancipate the
subject from "the heteronomous rule of his unconscious" (Žižek, *The Metastases
of Enjoyment*, 18). Later theorists, including those of the Frankfurt School and
Žižek, are more skeptical about Freud's liberal individualist project, coining the
term "repressive desublimation" to describe the "short circuit" between the id
and superego that bypasses the ego (18). This short circuit, they argue, characterizes modernity. Herbert Marcuse argues that repressive desublimation is a by-
product of "the social controls of technological reality" that extends certain forms
of liberty while intensifying domination (*One-Dimensional Man*, 72). According
to Adorno, "The contemporary types are those in whom any Ego is absent. . . . Together, they participate in this senseless ritual, following the compulsive rhythm

of repetition, and grow poor affectively: the demolition of the Ego strengthens narcissism and its collective derivations" (quoted in Žižek, *The Metastases of Enjoyment*, 19).

It is as if Rohmer's "scholarly project touched with insanity" attempts to conflate the prebourgeois (medieval) subject who did not know the conflict between drives and their prohibition with the contemporary "socialized, administered world," which does not know it any longer (Žižek, *The Metastases of Enjoyment*, 18–19). Ego does not replace id in Perceval. Perceval does not become the liberal bourgeois individual, autonomous and independent, that Freud predicted. At the end of the film he is as much a naif as he was at the beginning. While he has perhaps learned from his encounter with the Tent Maiden not always to take what he desires, he has simply acceded to the superego's injunction to enjoy. He inhabits a world in which desires are answered instantaneously. He never seems to lack what he needs; food, drink, women, lodging, training all seem to appear magically when desired. He doesn't labor for it; he doesn't pay for it. But the authority to which he accedes is capricious and, ultimately, unknowable. At the end, after having wandered lost for five years, Perceval happens on a hermit, who just happens to be his uncle (and who can occupy the place of the father). In a spectacular show of circular logic, the hermit's explanation of Perceval's sin fails to explain anything at all except the complete absurdity of the world he inhabits: "This sin was what silenced you. . . . When you saw the Bleeding Lance, you did not inquire of it. When you saw the Grail and asked not who was served from it, you erred." For Perceval the Grail must be understood as the hole, the blot or symptom, around which, Žižek argues, the symbolic, in this case the symbolic of chivalry, is structured. The external obstacles that thwart Perceval's access to the Grail (for instance, his not having asked the correct questions) cannot be explained. They are senseless, outrageous, capricious, and arbitrary precisely "to create the illusion that without them, the object (the plenitude promised by the Grail) would be accessible" (Žižek, *The Metastases of Enjoyment*, 94). Might we read into Perceval's silence before the Grail procession the operations of repressive desublimation, as Perceval's inquisitiveness is silenced by Gornemant's (the superego's) injunctions to hold his tongue, for which he suffers a kind of Kafkaesque punishment for doing exactly as he is told? Perceval's quest—the endless repetition of an interrupted gesture—quilted together by the search for the always already unattainable Grail, enacts a socialization process; it becomes the means by which Perceval begins to inhabit the "social skin" of chivalry, begins to become part of an aristocracy that takes its identity from materials, objects, fashions, and performances that have transcended their original functions and become symptomatic of a meaningless injunction to enjoy consumption for its own sake.

Goose-Stepping toward Avalon

The Frankfurt School formulated the paradoxical notion of repressive desublimation (paradoxical because repression was supposed to result in sublimation, in a rechanneling of libido rather than indulgence in it) as a means to explain the central trauma of twentieth-century European history: Nazism and the Final Solution. The success of totalitarian regimes in the late twentieth century, for which the totalitarian fantasies of Nazi Germany seem emblematic, depended, in Adorno's words, on "the expropriation of the unconscious by social control." But because he believed fascism was the result of conscious manipulation, external coercion, and conformist adaptation (see Žižek, *The Metastases of Enjoyment,* 19–21), for Adorno this mob psychology is mostly performative: "If they would stop to reason for a second, the whole performance would go to pieces, and they would be left to panic" (quoted in Žižek, 17–18). Žižek, however, argues that Adorno's model did not go far enough toward explaining the power of fascist fantasies, which represent a massive failure of rationality and so cannot be entirely explained or dispelled by conventional rational explanations of evil (selfish calculation or greed). The first half of *The Metastases of Enjoyment* attempts to find a way out of the "deadlock" of repressive desublimation as a means of coming to terms with the violence of late capitalism, for which the racial and sexual violence in Žižek's own homeland in the wake of the collapse of communism might stand as yet another exemplar.

The enjoyment that binds the masses under totalitarian regimes like Nazism is not, for Žižek, the product of rational calculation (though it might be manipulated by individuals acting out of rational calculation); it gains its strength through the force of a fantasy, and the only way to counter it is to go through that fantasy. Unfortunately, going through the fantasy, as Žižek recognizes, can look an awful lot like indulging the fantasy; indeed, it requires overidentification with it to rob it of its power (*The Metastases of Enjoyment,* 71–72). Hans-Jürgen Syberberg's 1982 film of Richard Wagner's *Parsifal* must surely be read as an attempt to come to terms with the trauma of Nazism and the failure of Germany to work through its fantasies of National Socialism. In his film of Wagner's final opera (released in its centennial year), the particular fantasy being explored is Wagner's medievalism. In *Religion and Art* Wagner turns to the Middle Ages as that prelapsarian moment that has been lost in the postindustrial world, which, for Wagner, is represented by the Jews: "This peculiar pride of race that still gave us in the Middle Ages such towering characters as Princes, Kings and Kaisers, may be met even to-day in the old nobility of German origin, although in unmistakable degeneration; and that degeneration we should have to take seriously into account if we wished to explain the fall of the German Folk, now exposed defenceless to the inroads of the Jews" (Wagner, *Religion and Art*, 269–70). Syberberg's *Parsifal*, in its overidentification with Wagner's fantasy of the Middle Ages, a medievalism that was also embraced by the Nazis, often looks chillingly like it, despite the film's carefully cultivated ironic distance.[20] It suggests the extent to which Wagner, Hitler, and some modern German conservatives—Syberberg among them—have all at times invested in the same fantasy, the fantasy of the return to origins, the Germanic spirit and state as they believe once existed in some time of purity, before the depredations—cultural, aesthetic, and environmental—of modernity.

Fredric Jameson has suggested that Syberberg's filmmaking amounts to something like a cultural psychoanalysis, an investigation of the German cultural unconscious ("In the Destructive Element Immerse," 109). Syberberg himself has characterized his filmmaking as a project of mourning that laments the sterility of German culture since it was tainted by Nazi atrocities.[21] Wagner figures centrally for him in this struggle over postwar German culture. Susan Sontag writes, "It is true that Hitler has contaminated Romanticism and Wagner, that much of nineteenth-century German culture is, retroactively, haunted by Hitler" (151). One chapter of Syberberg's *Filmbuch* (published in 1979, before the release of *Parsifal*) carries the title, *Meine Trauerarbeit für Bayreuth* ("My Mourning Work for Bayreuth," a reference to the site of the opera house constructed specifically for the performance of Wagner's operas). As Syberberg is painfully aware, Hitler believed Wagner a kindred spirit. In the most famous scene of *Hitler: A Film from Germany*, Syberberg portrays Hitler in a toga, emerging from the opened grave of Wagner "like a vision at a black mass in back of Wahnfried" (the home in Bayreuth that Ludwig II built for Wagner): "he is the color of a corpse as he comes out of hell, as in Doré's Dante illustration. Two figures, a life-size puppet in a Wagner cloak and the child, her face shrouded. Music from *Rienzi* [an 1842 opera by Wagner]" (Syberberg, *Hitler: A Film from Germany*, 127). This scene suggests much more than the recognition of Hitler's fondness for and appropriations of the composer's music and ideas. It implies that Hitler and Wagner are inextricably linked—buried together, in hell together. Perhaps it even hints at a kind of interchangeability, suggesting that one can replace the other, speak in the other's stead so that the composer's music is reduced to "theme music for fascism" (Abbate, 118). If, as Jameson contends, after World War II "people stopped blaming Wagner for Nazism," it was only because Wagner was thought to be irrelevant to the realities of postwar reconstruction ("In the Destructive Element Immerse," 99). More recently, however, a space has opened up among German conservatives for a reconsideration of both Wagner's and Germany's cultural legacy; it represents a repudiation of the "Frankfurt School–inspired, left-liberal consensus regarding standards of political correctness in artistic production in the postwar period" (Santner, "The Trouble with Hitler," 718; see also Jameson, "In the Destructive Element Immerse," 99). *Parsifal,* like *Hitler: A Film from Germany,* attempts from a conservative perspective to decathect images of Nazism, to settle the symbolic debts of National Socialism, while recuperating Wagner for German national identity. It is a project flawed by Syberberg's own brand of anti-Semitism and redeemed by the fact that frequently the film's meanings, like those of Wagner's opera, exceed their creator's occasionally offensive politics precisely because they plunge us into our most obscene fantasies.[22] His project seems doomed from the beginning by his attempt to create a very uneasy and unstable space between Wagner and Brecht. Syberberg is at once enthralled by Germanic romanticism and suspicious of it, appreciating how the politics of that romanticism turned, almost inevitably, to Nazism in Germany. He imposes on it an ironic, often surreal, vision that seeks its destruction. Yet, for all his desire to move into the genre of irony in this film, to deconstruct simultaneously medieval romance, nineteenth-century romanticism, and the fascinations of Nazism, Syberberg is drawn to them. His *Parsifal* is mesmerizing and erotic but also dark and uncomfortable.

Syberberg's film presents a daunting challenge to its viewers. Where does one even begin to engage this four-and-one-half-hour staging of Wagner's final opera? Played out on a series of complex sets—dominated by an enormous death mask of Richard Wagner—the film attempts both to celebrate the composer's art and to deploy that art in recovering a mythology of Teutonic origin transcendent of both fascism and the sterility of commodity culture that Syberberg believes the failure of Nazism ushered into late-twentieth-century Germany. What Eric Santner says of Syberberg's 1978 *Hitler* pinpoints the impossible demands of Syberberg's art: "this work crowds the imagination, forcing the viewer into an exegetical frame of mind. What one sees must be read and deciphered if one is not to feel hopelessly overwhelmed. It is a film that demands not so much criticism as commentary. Every object in the film functions as an ornament in the ancient sense of cosmos, that is, as a marker of a position in a social or cosmological hierarchy or genealogical construction" (*Stranded Objects*, 133). If every object in Syberberg's overcrowded mise-en-scène is steeped in meaning, then the only sensible approach requires that we abandon analysis for exegesis—finally, work for a medievalist. Such a process of commentary, however, quickly implodes (as Barthes' *S/Z* was designed to illustrate). A frame-by-frame commentary could not possibly account for the sheer number of "stranded objects" with which Syberberg litters his mise-en-scène.[23] Here the method of "looking awry," of focusing on the ideological investments revealed by the film's anamorphotic blots, may offer some purchase on this otherwise nearly unapproachable film. It enables us to discern the heart of darkness in Syberberg's work, his "programmatic insistence on the perverse perspective—the perspective stained by desire and fantasy—as a necessary condition of all aesthetic creation and reception" (Santner, "The Trouble with Hitler," 724).[24]

Syberberg's ambivalence toward Germany's past, its cultural heritage that includes Wagner but also National Socialism and the Holocaust, infects every aspect of his production. A deep melancholia pervades the film. Parsifal crosses a barren set representing the wasteland. But this wasteland is never empty. Rather, from the opening credits on, it is littered with the remnants of Western civilization, "monumental and tiered traces of the past" (Jameson, "In the Destructive Element Immerse," 102), but always in ruin, always wreckage and rubble: ruins, photographs of ruins, dead leaves, abandoned puppets, skulls. The hero arrives at a giant death mask of Richard Wagner (in its own way another ruin).[25] The mask opens onto the Grail kingdom. Before Parsifal enters the chamber holding the Holy Grail, he passes through an anteroom draped in flags and banners, the first and most prominent being the swastika flag of the Third Reich. John Christopher Kleis dismisses the shock we experience at this moment, arguing that the banners, "baroque, medieval, Nazi, abstract, kitschy . . . remind us of the many twists that have been given to Wagner, and at the same time stress that Syberberg is going in a different, less programmatic direction" (114). Perhaps, but Syberberg's mise-en-scène gives the Nazi banner pride of place so that, to our eyes at least, it embraces all of the emblems in the Grail antechamber. Whereas the other flags and banners are largely faded and innocuous, the flag of the Reich is bright red, vivid—even menacing. The camera lingers just long enough so that the viewer cannot fail to register its presence and be appalled by it. Inside the Grail chamber, other icons of National Socialism jostle the Eucharistic symbolism of the Grail and the cruciform insignia of medieval military orders like the Knights

Templar. The Grail maidens are marked with the sign of the Iron Cross. Although this military insignia existed in Germany at least from the time of Frederick the Great, king of Prussia during the eighteenth century, it was appropriated by Hitler and has become part of the eroticized Nazi paraphernalia Susan Sontag discusses in "Fascinating Fascism." The Grail knights are marked with either a dove or an eagle, the "Hitler eagle," as Syberberg continually refers to it in *Hitler: A Film from Germany*. In this example of the politics of appropriation, the symbol, resembling the Hohenzollern Eagle, is transformed into yet another piece of Nazi iconography.

Despite Wagner's well-documented anti-Semitism,[26] however, *Parsifal* does not offer the most promising material for fascist opera. Although there were attempts to recuperate the story for Nazi ideology, the opera was not a favorite of the Nazis; it was banned from 1939 until the end of the war (Hutcheon and Hutcheon, 270; Abbate, 114). On the surface the "brotherhood of the Grail" might seem to be just the sort of aggressive hypermasculine and homosocial "brotherhood of the initiated" about which Nazis fantasized—a brotherhood that could trace its lineage back to fantasies of medieval Teutonic military orders. This is precisely how the Hitler biographer Hermann Rauschning claims the Führer understood it: "Behind the absurd externals of the story, with its Christian embroidery and its Good Friday mystification, something altogether different is revealed as the true content of the most profound drama. It is not the Christian-Schopenhauerist religion of compassion that is acclaimed, but pure, noble blood, in the protection and glorification of whose beauty the brotherhood of the initiated have come together" (229–30). In the opera itself, however, the purity of that fantasy is undercut at every turn, not just by the external threat from the vaguely Semitic Klingsor, a device that, at any rate, would reinforce the fantasy, but by corruption at the community's very origins, corruption created not by Amfortas's sexual sins but by the very foundations of that order.

An anamorphotic look at this film, then, must begin with Titurel, the founder and first Grail king. Žižek calls him "the truly obscene presence in *Parsifal*" and "the ultimate cause of the decay of the Grail community" ("There Is No Sexual Relationship: Wagner as a Lacanian," 35), a utopia Syberberg himself described as a "society of the dead [*Totengesellschaft*]" (quoted in Santner, *Stranded Objects*, 192). Next to Titurel, Žižek claims, Klingsor, the ostensible villain, is nothing but a "small time crook" ("There Is No Sexual Relationship: Wagner as a Lacanian," 35). The father of Amfortas and the original guardian of the Grail, Titurel first appears in act 1 (although he has already appeared earlier in puppet form in the prelude), as the mysteries of the Grail are unfolding; he interrupts those proceedings, literally from his grave, with his insistent demand that the Grail be disclosed. He appears to be neither alive nor dead. Žižek calls him "an obscene undead apparition, a dirty old man who is so immersed in the enjoyment of the Grail that he perturbs the regular rhythm of its disclosure" ("There Is No Sexual Relationship: Wagner as a Lacanian," 35). Syberberg makes a significant alteration to Wagner's stage direction, which represents Titurel as an *acousmêtre*, a voice without a body. The stage direction reads, "Once all have arrived at their appointed places and after a complete silence has settled on the scene, the voice of Titurel is heard from a vaulted niche behind Amfortas' couch, as if from a tomb." Syberberg denies Amfortas's father the omnipotence accorded the disembodied—ghostly—voice by giving him body, by choosing to show him in his "tomb." In doing so, Syberberg emphasizes the liminal space Titurel occupies between life and death, making him more monstrous, the "undead" at the heart of the Grail community.

Syberberg places Titurel in a decaying subterranean vault, dripping with water. As with most of the sets, the ground is strewn with leftover objects we can hardly identify. Carolyn Abbate suggests Syberberg represents Titurel as Ludwig II, "fat and sick, sitting under the stage he has paid for" (153; see also Olsen, 200). Dressed in the regalia of a king, holding a wooden stick, Titurel is revealed in a long shot in a religious position of genuflection. His only exposed hand seems to be covered with some kind of wrapping—whether a shroud or bandage is unclear. Titurel sings only in the imperative;[27] even his questions carry the force of a demand: "Amfortas, my son, will you serve? Shall I once more look on the Grail and live? Must I die for want of my Deliverer?" The imperious nature of his demands is underscored by the musical composition. This "half dead basso" (the phrase is Abbate's [132]) sings without orchestral accompaniment in short phrases punctuated with strong caesurae indicated in the music by extended rests (the silence of the grave). His "immobile oppressive presence" contrasts with Amfortas's lengthy and agitated aria as he voices his suffering (Žižek, "There Is No Sexual Relationship: Wagner as a Lacanian," 35): "Alas! Woe is me for my pain! My father, oh once more serve the office! Live, live—and let me die!" When Titurel sings, "Uncover the Grail!" he turns his head upward and to his right as if that is the way out of his tomb to the place where the Grail mysteries take place. Syberberg's close-up places Titurel's head on the diagonal, a technique that increases his menacing presence. And, although Syberberg frequently expresses contempt for the conventional suturing technique of shot and countershot,[28] this is precisely how he indicates the spatial relationship between Titurel and Amfortas. He cuts between the one in his tomb and the other in the midst of the Grail ceremony, creating the impression that, even though they occupy different physical spaces, they are conversing. At the climactic moment of the Grail ceremony, as the Grail is being revealed, we hear Titurel's voice sing, "Oh holy joy." The next shot shows a funereal image of Titurel, this time lying on a bier, completely white, as if he were in an advanced state of decay. The Grail ceremony seems to make him more, not less, monstrous, an animated singing corpse produced by the Grail.

What do we make of this obscenity at the heart of the Grail mystery? The Grail ritual, as Syberberg stages it, resembles nothing so much as a mass, its monumental choral themes invoking the specific language of the Eucharist: "Take this my blood, take this my body, in remembrance of me!" How do we incorporate Titurel's disgusting enjoyment around which the "sacred" Grail community has formed itself? *Parsifal* can never be read simply as a Christian allegory, the film suggests. In the aptly titled "Grimaces of the Real" Žižek argues that the monster figures "the social impact of capital" and that each epoch of capitalism has had its own specific type of monstrosity. For the "postindustrial" age of late capitalism it is the living dead (67–68). *Parsifal* gives us Titurel, got up as King Ludwig, Wagner's moneyman, suspended between life and death, as well as Amfortas's wound, which will neither heal nor kill him, and Kundry's vamp who cannot die. These monstrosities are not incidental to the Grail's Eucharistic meanings; they are the anamorphotic blots around which those mysteries form. The film highlights the ways in which Wagner's music holds in tension both sacred and obscene: what has in Western civilization been most sublime and what has been monstrous. Often they end up being the same thing.[29]

Parsifal, we suggest, is a work at war with itself, and Syberberg does everything in his power to foreground the conflicts. To be sure, Wagner's music and libretto impose their own restrictions on the filmmaker. One suspects that the death mask set is meant to remind the viewer of the dead weight cultural tradition imposes on the material.[30] Yet Syberberg is still able to shape the opera visually on his own terms. Syberberg's film plays Wagnerian *Gesamtkunstwerk* (total work of art) off against the Brechtian *Verfremdungseffekt* (alienation effect). It attempts simultaneously to seduce us into the illusion of Wagner's opera and to distance us from it. Although Syberberg films on a set that is meant to call to mind the performance of opera in the theater, his *Parsifal* is not simply a film version of staged opera, as Edwin S. Porter's 1904 version was (Harty, "Parsifal and Perceval on Film," 301–3). Rather than using the technology of film to encourage audience identification with the film's illusion, as we might expect, Syberberg uses it to distance and alienate us, constantly reminding us that we are watching a movie, using the technologies designed to create the illusion of verisimilitude to dismantle it. He accomplishes this through several techniques. At the beginning of the film, while the prelude plays, he presents the story of Parsifal's youth in dumb show without comment, so that someone unfamiliar with the medieval tale of Parsifal (from Chrétien or from Wagner's source, Wolfram von Eschenbach's *Parzival*) would almost certainly be unable to follow it. Then, as the prelude continues, Syberberg gives us a synopsis of the libretto acted out in puppet show, while the child Parsifal watches his own life unfold. By the time we reach the end of the film and its final tableau—Amfortas and Kundry on their biers with the Grail Maiden behind them, surrounded by the film's various stranded objects—the actors themselves have begun to look much like puppets.

Syberberg's use of marionettes calls to mind the kind of ventriloquism performed by a film's sound editor long after the movie has been shot. Most filmgoers would not be shocked to learn that the singing in an opera film is added in the studio. They would not even think it a novelty to learn that an actor has been dubbed by another singer, splitting the specialized talents (acting and singing) required for performing opera for the sake of verisimilitude.[31] That device was old in 1952, when it was the basis of a plot twist in *Singin' in the Rain*. But Syberberg jolts us out of our cynical acceptance of film technologies designed to promote verisimilitude by splitting the operatic voice from the body that produces it, then resuturing it to a body it doesn't fit. In act 1 the two squires guarding the forest are sung by a single soprano whose voice clearly does not belong to the bodies of the two young boys playing the roles. The most famous instance of this splitting occurs in the title character, Parsifal (played by Michael Kutter), who, in the middle of act 2, is replaced with a girl Parsifal, played by Karin Krick. Reiner Goldberg, who has sung the role from the film's beginning, continues as though nothing has happened, though neither the slight, androgynous Kutter nor Krick could plausibly produce such a voice.[32] At the film's climactic moment in act 3, both Parsifals mouth the words sung by a single tenor who is not even present, except as voice. Žižek writes:

> The scene is thus composed of three elements: the (diegetic) subject (or, rather *two* of them); the spectral Thing in the background [Wagner's gigantic death mask] and the voice, *objet petit a*, the remainder of the mute Thing. . . . So what *is* this thing, if not the embodiment of that which remains the same in the

"passing of the torch (voice)" from one (masculine) to another (feminine) subject—namely *this voice itself?* This accounts for the spectral/ethereal character of the Thing: it is not an object which emits a voice, but an object which gives body to the impossible object-voice. (Žižek, *The Fright of Real Tears*, 41)

If Žižek explains the acousmatic voice of Parsifal as an anamorphotic blot, a stain, on the representational surface of the film, how are we to understand the splitting of Parsifal into male and female? Perhaps, as John Christopher Kleis suggests, Syberberg is indulging in some kind of misguided "feminism," perhaps to imply that "the fusion of masculine action and feminine intuition [is] essential to *Mitleid* [compassion]," the virtue Parsifal must acquire so that he can become the pure fool "by compassion made wise" and redeem the Grail community (117). Žižek, however, warns against reading into the split a too-easy Jungian androgyny (which, we would argue, is very far from feminist);[33] the split Parsifal does not stand for the reconciliation or unification of the sexes; they are, after all, split, perhaps to suggest some kind of originary incoherence in the subject. Krick appears and replaces Kutter at the moment in act 2 that the male Parsifal rejects Kundry's advances, when he tears himself away from the mother's sexual advances. It is as if Syberberg's conflation of Kundry with Parsifal's mother (they are played by the same actress) precipitates some kind of incest panic. Žižek reads the split as an embodiment of the Lacanian dicta that "Woman is a symptom of man." "Woman is the symptom of man, caught in the hysterical game of demanding that he refuse her demand, precisely to the extent to which she is submitted to the phallic enjoyment" ("The Wound Is Healed," 204). Syberberg recognizes that Parsifal's identification with Amfortas at the moment of Kundry's kiss is "feminine." The alternation between male and female Parsifals, then, "functions as a critical sting aimed at Wagner, a reminder that *Parsifal is not feasible as a unique psychologically 'coherent' personality*; he is split into himself and 'what is in him more than himself,' his sublime shadowy double (Parsifal-woman) first appears in the background as the ethereal double of Parsifal-man and then gradually takes his place" ("The Wound Is Healed," 205; emphasis in original). Because the splitting of Parsifal into two reveals the fundamental incoherence at the heart of "personality," and especially because it reveals masculinity as masquerade, "so that when we throw off its mask, a woman appears," Žižek reads the final scene of reconciliation between the two Parsifals, the final moment when they embrace before the Grail chamber, as an act of bad faith on Syberberg's part. He has given in to an ideology of false androgyny, losing his best insight into the incoherence of the subject: the subject can never confront its own "objective surplus correlative," the symptom around which the subject is constituted (260).

This splitting of the title character is just one of the mechanisms by which Syberberg explores the incoherence of the subject under modernity, the illusion of coherent subjectivity being the hallmark of the commercial filmmaking Syberberg denounces in his published manifestoes. His most spectacular conceit, spectacular precisely because it engages with the drama's spectacle, for undermining the coherence of his film's illusion is the way in which he dismantles embodiment, dissolving bodies into the landscape and resolving landscapes back into bodies. The death mask set is only the grandest and most persistent example of this device. In tighter shots we see a rugged terrain of hills and caves. The tracking camera reveals that what we thought was landscape is a large set constructed out of Wagner's face—death mask. The final shot of act 1, for instance, shows us Parsifal expelled from Monsalvat. The camera pulls back to reveal him standing alone in front of what once looked like a rocky landscape and now is revealed to be the death mask. Much of act 3 takes place in what looks like a grotto that turns out to be Wagner's nostrils. But the leitmotif is carried throughout the film in other ways as well. Act 2 opens with a medium shot of Parsifal standing in front of a projected set that looks like a series of stone hills and arches. On the far left is a set of stairs (presumably the entrance to Klingsor's castle) that seems to run underneath the arch. Again the camera pulls back into a wider shot, revealing that the backdrop is in fact a gigantic projection of a reclining naked woman with the entrance running right between her legs.[34] Inside, Klingsor's castle is simultaneously emasculating and erotic. The magician is surrounded by images that mirror his self-inflicted castration, sculptures of broken and damaged phallic objects. The castle is populated by scantily clad flower maidens—metamorphosing from flowers to human beings and back to flowers that wither, unredeemed (Abbate, 114)—who offer Parsifal the opportunity to "play" with them. Our first glimpse of Klingsor comes in long shot with what looks like a mound of rock (but which is, in fact, the death mask set) interposed between the viewer and Klingsor. On the top of it there looks to be a woman reclining, whom we might take to be Kundry since Klingsor is singing about her, "locked in deathlike sleep by the curse that my power alone can lift." As the mound moves apart, however, the image resolves; it is not Kundry but the entrance to the place where she sleeps, which the next cut reveals to be a prison. The final shot of act 2 is framed by what looks like an extreme close-up of two armor-clad feet and legs. Parsifal-girl enters from the right carrying Kundry, followed by Parsifal-boy. The actors provide a human scale that reveals these are not actual body parts but gigantic pillars through which the heroes pass as they leave Klingsor's destroyed kingdom. Finally, for the Good Friday Spell in act 3, the set is dominated by a large object that looks like a cross between a naked woman and a teapot (Olsen notes that it is described as a "female violin" [278]). Despite its enormous size (it dwarfs everything else in the scene), it is never noticed by the actors, and it serves no conceivable function except perhaps to mirror the silent Kundry's form.

Syberberg's visual play leaves no body intact. Truly the most bizarre stranded object of the film must be the wound Amfortas has received from the spear. Syberberg detaches it entirely from Amfortas's body. Carried on a pillow by a male and female attendant, the wound, representative of Amfortas's castration and the disease that infects the Grail Kingdom,[35] looks like a detached menstruating vagina. Having been castrated, Amfortas is feminized so that the appearance of Parsifal-woman weirdly doubles his feminizing wound. This disassembling and reassembling of bodies as a means of highlighting the incoherence of the psyche in its relation to the body is perhaps the reason why it seems almost necessary to bring a psychoanalytic perspective to bear on this film, to understand the ways in which the entity we call "psyche" is not buried in some deep recess within us but inscribed on the very surfaces of our bodies. The psychoanalytic framework does not need to be imposed on the film because it is called up by the film's own terms. In *Parsifal* the everyday world of historical event is never admitted. The opera unfolds in the spaces marked by bodies and by a "hysterically overexcited chromaticism," represented in the singing of Kundry, Amfortas, and Klingsor, and an "asexual purity," represented by Parsifal and by the "static diatonics" that are the leitmotif of the Grail community (Žižek, "There Is No Sexual Relationship," 212).[36]

Despite the abstraction of this pseudomedieval "dreamscape," however, the context of German culture and history returns through what David Levin has called the "heaps of ambivalent ur-German bric-a-brac" (quoted in Abbate, 111) scattered throughout the film. We have already mentioned the Nazi paraphernalia visible during the Grail ceremony in act 1. What, then, are we to make of the appearance of a concentration camp tower projected behind Klingsor in act 2 as he prepares for Parsifal's arrival? The question returns us to the anti-Semitism expressed by both Wagner and Syberberg. Is Klingsor the Jewish inmate or the administrator of this ghostly apparition? Whatever its orientation to Germany's past, Klingsor's castle stands in opposition to Amfortas's fallen but redeemable Grail kingdom. It is an enchanted den of perverse temptation; it stands for the "asocial excess of incestuous enjoyment"—where, at Klingsor's behest, Kundry attempts to seduce Parsifal, conjuring his mother and presenting him her naked breast as incestuous enticement—just as the Grail Castle figures the "incestuous rejection of any mingling with the Otherness" (Žižek, "There Is No Sexual Relationship," 226). Dressed in black leather, Syberberg's Klingsor is a pornographer/pimp, a man of the masses who has deployed the various sex industries at his disposal—Žižek has compared the dance of the Flower Maidens to "a cabaret performance from a high class nineteenth-century brothel" ("There Is No Sexual Relationship: Wagner as a Lacanian," 10)—to subvert and ultimately dominate a large portion of Amfortas's aristocratic military, to injure Amfortas, and bring about the onset of the wasteland.[37] One cannot help but make the connection between Klingsor's castle and Syberberg's critique of Hollywood—and mainstream German cinema—which he calls "cinema as brothel" (Syberberg, *Filmbuch*, 80). In his 1969 documentary *Sex-Business—Made in Pasing* Syberberg decries the popularity of German pornographic cinema and describes his own films as "a declaration of war against the present forms of cinema dialogue and of boulevard-type cinema in the tradition of Hollywood and its satellites, . . . a declaration of war against psychological chitchat, against the action film, against a particular philosophy endlessly linking shots and reverse shots, against the metaphysics of the automobile and the gun, against the excitement of opened and closed doors, against the melodrama of crime and sex" (Syberberg, *Filmbuch*, 11). Is Syberberg's imagery suggesting that the Jew who was tortured and exterminated at Auschwitz is reincarnated in the pornographer/pimp poisoning twentieth-century German culture, a sign for all that has failed in postwar Germany? The association is a reminder of Syberberg's insistence that Jews capitalized on German guilt following World War II and transformed that guilt into a soulless and vapid entertainment business: "And who is free of this plague of crimes against art? When McCarthy bribed and blackmailed, how many Jews in Hollywood were ready and willing to play along? And in Hollywood, jobs, not lives, were on the line—without Hitler, from whom they had fled to save their lives. The same Hollywood that made so many anti-Nazi movies" (Syberberg, *Hitler: A Film from Germany*, 82). We would note that what Žižek argues of Wagner's anti-Semitism applies equally to Syberberg's: between the pure German spirit and Jewish contamination there is always a third term—modernity, "the reign of exchange, of the dissolution of organic links, of modern industry and individuality" ("There Is No Sexual Relationship," 217). The desire to enjoy the fruits of modernity while avoiding its poisonous and disintegrative effects necessitates the figure of the Jew: "by rejecting the Jew who gives body to all that is disintegrated in modernity, we can retain its fruits" (218).[38]

Syberberg's Brechtian techniques for alienating his viewers, his invention of psychic dreamscapes crowded with fragmented bodies and the odds and ends of Germany's past, have their counterpart on the narrative level in his tendency to minimize action. While Wagner's drama of passive renunciation involves little enough action as written, Syberberg revises the endings of each of the three acts to rob them of their climactic moments. The "elevation" of the Grail at the end of act 1 involves a young girl (Syberberg's daughter) standing in front of the death mask, holding the Grail almost out of sight at her hip, as if it were a fashion accessory matching her faux-chain-mail vest. Act 2 is supposed to end with Parsifal catching in midair the spear Klingsor has thrown at him, at least a small demonstration of the prowess attributed to Parsifal in medieval narratives. In Syberberg, Klingsor lifts the spear over his head and then inexplicably falls down dead before he can even throw it. Finally, in act 3 we do not see Parsifal cure Amfortas's wound with the spear he has taken from Klingsor. Rather he narrates the event while Amfortas lies on a bed before him, apparently dead.

These changes rob the two central symbols of the opera—the Grail and the spear—of any efficacy; they become simply two more stranded objects. The association of the spear that pierced Christ's side with the Grail (which captured his blood) is traditional. A bleeding spear appears as part of the Grail procession in both Chrétien de Troyes's *Conte du Graal* and in von Eschenbach's *Parzival*. In Wagner their pairing allows for a symbolism that plays off female cup against phallic lance. But the spear also has connections with the occult, where it becomes more than the spear of Longinus, more than a Grail object associated with the Eucharist. It becomes a symbol of power and world domination. Elsewhere Syberberg indicates his familiarity with the writings of conspiracy theorists like Jean-Michel Angebert and Trevor Ravenscroft, who see the Grail and its accompanying objects as central to Hitler's plans for world domination.[39] Yet for all the hysterical agonizing over the display of these supposedly powerful magical objects, they seem curiously impotent (a theme that pretty much defines all of the male characters in the film as well). The Grail offers no more relief to Amfortas than Kundry's or Gawan's balsams; on the contrary, it seems to cause him great pain. And despite the talk about the spear's great power, we never actually see it do anything. In the film's final tableau the restored spear and Grail lie on the margins of the frame, one on the left and the other on the right, discarded, mingling with all the other abandoned objects in the frame: a cross, a musical score, a stuffed swan, a book, a crown, a statue, a skull, a model of the Festspielhaus at Bayreuth. In a frame literally crammed with portentous objects these two can have little significance since what gives a symbol its potency is precisely its singularity. By turning these portentous objects into so much rubbish, Syberberg attempts to decathect the central emblems of Grail mythology.

In the midst of "the icy loneliness of this utopia of our last stage of knowledge" (Syberberg, quoted in Santner, *Stranded Objects*, 192), this death cult of the Grail, what gives Syberberg's *Parsifal* life is Edith Clever's performance as Kundry (sung by Yvonne Minton). She dominates the film from beginning to end, appearing in nearly every scene, resisting easy interpretations. Thomas Mann called her "a desperate double personality, composed of a Circe and a repentant Magdalen, with cataleptic transition stages" (336–37). Kundry is unimaginably ancient, condemned to eternal life for having laughed at Christ when he was on the cross, but she does not seem, like Titurel, an undead vampire or zombie; she is more reminiscent of Shakespeare's Ariel. Against Parsifal's nearly catatonic and ritualized performance and Gurnemanz's static expositions, Kundry is all agitation and movement, at least for the first two acts. Representing difference and alterity, she is the force of resistance to the Grail community, and her ultimate subsumption into that community can only result in her death. Kundry seems a wonderful example of the ways in which the film's (as well as the opera's) meanings tend to exceed the intentions of both author and director. On the one hand, Kundry seems marked by both Wagner's and Syberberg's misogyny and anti-Semitism. A liminal character, forever wandering, associated with hypersexuality and perhaps sexually transmitted disease, Kundry is at once the "evil of woman," the Wandering Jew, and the exotic Oriental. On the other hand, the film seems to chart the course of Kundry's tragic descent into conventional femininity, where she can exist only insofar as she can attract the male gaze (Žižek, " 'The Wound Is Healed Only by the Spear That Smote You,' " 203). In act 1 she is the wild woman who has taken on the tasks of the knight errant that the Grail knights seem unable to perform; she seems to be the only one who can quest. She has just returned from Araby, bringing back balsams to ease Amfortas's wound. The only other character capable of such wide-ranging action is Gawan, who never appears in the opera because he has left Monsalvat to seek further medicines for Amfortas. By act 2 Kundry has been demoted to the conventional seductress, the femme fatale. In act 3 she is completely silenced, the model of ideal femininity. Though present throughout the act, she has barely a line to sing. Having finally been baptized into

the stasis of the Grail community, she can only die. Difference, alterity, and resistance are purged from the Grail community and purity restored, but the cost
seems to be life, energy, and pleasure. In Wagner's vision—and in the imagina-
tions of the medieval authors who inspired Wagner—acquisition of the Grail
promised the eternal return to a paradigmatic point of origin where celebrants
experienced fulfillment and redemption. Syberberg subverts this vision, offering
only emptiness; there is neither satisfaction nor solace. For the society of the
Grail, into which Kundry has become integrated—co-opted—there is only stasis
and, finally, death.

As we began this chapter with a mysterious shot from Bresson, we close with
two from Syberberg. These are inexplicable shots. During the prelude to Wagner's
music drama, Syberberg offers a long shot of Edith Clever, who plays both Parsifal's mother and Kundry—but has not yet been identified as either—lying on a
couch looking at a book. As the camera zooms in, we can see that she is staring
at a picture of the Round Table. At the film's conclusion Syberberg offers a long
shot of Clever lying crowned on a bier. These are shots that refuse to be subsumed
into the film's iconography. They are stains, blots that recall the Round Table, recall tombs for royalty. They would require, it would seem, a kind of mourning, for
a lost past, for the dead. But like Bresson and Rohmer, Syberberg suggests that
our returns to these objects of mourning are incomplete, insufficient, meaningless. In his famous opening to *Shakespearean Negotiations*, Stephen Greenblatt
tells us, "I began with the desire to speak with the dead" (1). The ghosts that
haunt Robert Bresson's *Lancelot du lac*, Eric Rohmer's *Percival le Gallois*, and Hans-
Jürgen Syberberg's *Parsifal* are unable to rest, yet they are also incapable of satis-
factorily telling their stories—or, perhaps, we are incapable of fully understanding these stories. Even as we seek their community—and the communities they
seem to promise—they leave us isolated, alienated, and alone.

Bresson, Rohmer, and Syberberg locate modernity's despair in the failure of
signification. These directors mock our desire for origin, for truth, for stability,
for history; even mourning has no meaning. They leave us with stranded objects,
blots that resist symbolization, refuse explanation. Continuing our analysis of the
ways in which films appropriate medievalism to indulge and perhaps assuage our
anxieties about modernity, our next chapter puts Ingmar Bergman's two medieval films, *The Seventh Seal* and *The Virgin Spring*, into dialogue with Vincent
Ward's *The Navigator: A Medieval Odyssey*. Like Umberto Eco, for whom the "chil-
iastic anxieties" of the modern world are "neomedieval," Bergman and Ward look
to the Middle Ages to understand the breakdown of modernity, to describe a frail

world on the brink of destruction. Like Eco, they see "the recurrent themes of atomic and ecological catastrophe" as a sign of "vigorous apocalyptic currents" (Eco, 73, 79). For Bergman and Ward images of rape and disease spring from the Middle Ages into our present, signaling the relentless dissolution of social institutions and an accompanying collapse of the human spirit.

Chapter Nine

Apocalyptic Medievalism

Rape and Disease as Figures of Social Anomie

E ven after the defeat in the 1940s of the modern fascist state, with its overt ultranationalistic, hypermasculine, and racist rhetorics—rhetorics that relied heavily on an idealized medieval past refracted through the lens of Nazi ideology (see Finke and Shichtman, *King Arthur and the Myth of History*, 186–97)—the Middle Ages reemerges as a locus for postwar anxieties concerning the corruption of the body politic in two films by Ingmar Bergman. Bergman's medieval films of the 1950s represent the great anxieties of that decade: fear of total annihilation in the face of a nuclear arms race; fear of a racialized underclass in a postfascist and postcolonial world; anxieties about rampant capitalism, materialism, and consumerism; and the fear of social and familial breakdown resulting from postwar changes in child-rearing practices. *The Seventh Seal* (1957), arguably the most famous film about the Middle Ages, and *The Virgin Spring* (1960) organize these fears on the scale of the body, expressing them in terms of rape and disease, and then offer by way of amelioration mythologies of genealogy (the intact nuclear family) and hypermasculinity (the hard-bodied aristocratic male). These films replace a defeated fascist neomedievalism with modernist fantasies that evince a conservative desire for authoritarian structures that can ensure the impermeability of both the physical body and the body politic from threats by rape, bomb, and disease. But why evoke the medieval to link fears about nuclear bombs, refugees, immigrants, and indulgent parents that seem so very modern? In these films the medieval does contradictory work. It expresses the desire to escape from the technological morass of the mid-twentieth century, where humans have it in their own power to destroy themselves, to a simpler time and place when that destruction was God's work. At the same time the medieval represents everything irrational that must be held in check by that very scientific rationality from which we desire retreat.

Influenced heavily by Bergman, Vincent Ward's 1988 film *The Navigator: A Medieval Odyssey* updates these anxieties about bodily invasion for a post-AIDS and postcolonial world. Ward stretches Bergman's analogies, invoking disease in the Middle Ages as the mechanism for unlocking the door to modernity, a paradigm-shattering experience requiring a revision and reconstitution of the structures of the body politic in the face of global capitalization. His vision of the apocalypse is more global, and less overtly reactionary, than Bergman's; his medieval characters can literally dig through time and space, burrowing through the world from fourteenth-century Cumbria to late-twentieth-century New Zealand—an almost perfect image for a transnational world, one that reflects the ways in which modernity is structured around the creation of an archaic postcolonial other, a medievalized "native." Ward's vision of a community of workers banding together to stave off apocalypse and preserve (though not intact) the body and the body politic offers both a critique of and an alternative to the social breakdown occasioned by globalization and by Bergman's vacillation between a bleak and alienated existentialism and retreat into the isolated nuclear family.

Our analyses of all three films, therefore, relocate discussions of the themes of world annihilation, social collapse, and family breakdown—the related crises of both the outer world and intimate sphere—to their historical context in postwar Europe. We rethink the filmmakers less in terms of modernism, auteurism, and existentialism than in terms of the anomie of postwar European society, of the disparity between individual aspiration and social constraint. The theory of social "anomie," articulated by the French sociologist Emile Durkheim and elaborated in the 1930s, with significant differences, by the American sociologist Robert King Merton, provides a means of relocating existential individualism within a specific social context from which it has been abstracted. Anomie theory flourished in the 1950s and 1960s, alongside existentialism, as a sociological (rather than philosophical) explanation for postwar angst; it then fell out of fashion, only to reemerge in the last couple of decades (Passas and Agnew, 1). The term describes the fragility of social integration under the conditions of modern capitalism, the alienation and anxiety that results from the discrepancy between cultural goals—the standards and values of modern liberal society—and the institutional mechanisms that prevent individuals from achieving those goals.[1] Anomie, according to its theorists, is the logical consequence of the "structural sources of modern individualism" in Protestantism, capitalism, and democracy: "Anomie is a substantive component of modernity, not an abnormal phenomenon, but a distinguishing trait of Western historical development" (Orru, *Anomie*, 142). Anomie results from liberal capitalism's gendered split between a public sphere that defines normative masculinity, consisting of individuals who pursue their self-interests in isolation from one another, and a private sphere that circumscribes normative femininity and that becomes claustrophobic precisely to the extent that it must supply all the individual's emotional needs for connection with others, becoming the sole locus of communitarian values.[2] Maria Bergom-Larsson argues that a theme that permeates Bergman's films is "the depiction of society as the menacing outer world, in sharp contrast to the intimate sphere, which in its isolation is also full of private demons threatening to destroy man. This balancing between outer and inner is a tightrope-walk over an abyss—with a sheer drop on either side" (7). While Bergman's two medieval films leave the individual stranded in this anomic state, immured within a family that has become less a refuge than an imprisoning fortress, Ward argues for the power of imagination in rethinking the individual's relation to a community on a larger scale than the family.

All three films work out their visions of social anomie on the scale of the body, which becomes a trope that connects several other intersecting (or nested) geographic sites or scales—in this instance, the scale of the family and the scale of the nation (or perhaps, in Bergman's case, European Christendom). We borrow the term *scale* from social geographers like Neil Smith and Linda McDowell to distinguish "not so much between places as between different *kinds* of places" (N. Smith, 64). Geographic scale (differences between places like the body, the family, the city, and the nation) "defines the boundaries and bounds the identities around which control is exerted and contested" (66). That these different scales intersect and interanimate one another allows for elaborate analogies among them, for the process Smith describes as "jumping scales," the "active social and political connectedness of apparently different scales, their deliberate confusion and abrogation" (66). Bergman's films conceive of and desire the healthy body as an impregnable fortress, one that figures the idealized hermetic space of the male body, of the family home, and, ultimately, of the nation. *The Navigator* rewrites Bergman's alienated individual, seeking more communitarian solutions to the condition of social anomie.

From Rape to Reverence: *The Virgin Spring*

It has become a commonplace to dismiss the first Bergman film to win an Oscar (Best Foreign Film of 1960) as his "least interesting work" (Ford). Bergman himself claimed it was "an aberration. It's touristic, a lousy imitation of Kurosawa" (Cowie, 182).[3] But for all the critical disparagement it received, *The Virgin Spring* touched on cultural anxieties that would reverberate through the remainder of the twentieth century, haunting its audience and heavily influencing the work of future filmmakers. *The Virgin Spring* updates a medieval ballad about a young virgin, Karin, who is raped and killed by three brigands while she is riding to church. A spring wells up beneath the dead girl that "still exists in the churchyard of Kärna parish and is thought to have healing powers" (Cowie, 182). According to Peter Cowie, Bergman thought that "by permeating the tale with the notion of therapy and the remission of sin through sacrifice, . . . he blurred and corrupted the original ballad and its stark outline" (182). The film does not proffer as its moral the wonder of a God who could work such a miracle and the exemplary life of the saint who provoked it, as a medieval tale might. Instead, it creates a virgin whose innocence results directly from her ignorance and willfulness, who is the spoiled child of indulgent parents. The film focuses our attention less on the miracle than on the father's bloody revenge and the violent reconstitution of the hermetic, intact nuclear family capable of standing as a bulwark against the deviance produced by modern anomie.

Perhaps the film is so disliked by the critics who lavish extravagant praise on *The Seventh Seal* because of its narrative roots not in Kurosawa's evocative psychological study of rape but in various lowbrow forms of popular entertainment. The film seems more like a 1950s American television situation comedy gone horribly wrong than an art house film. *The Virgin Spring* reminds us of the 1950s sitcom in that it plays on the arrogance of suburban life; it deviates from that genre by pointing to the anxieties masked by that arrogance. In sitcoms like *Leave It to Beaver* the coddled children of the privileged classes and their clueless, permissive parents occupy secure and innocent suburban spaces. The narratives are comedies precisely because the space in which the children's willfulness unfolds is safe; their disobedience has no serious consequences that extend beyond an episode's conclusion. In *The Virgin Spring*, however, the dangerous "other," the racialized and Godless underclass, intrudes itself into the secure space of the white and Christian nuclear family. For this reason the film would ultimately provide fodder for Wes Craven's first slasher film, *The Last House on the Left* (1972), a film about the intrusion of violent urban crime into the idyll of the American suburb.

The film's plot is simple and lurid enough to serve as the outline for a Wes Craven property. Töre's daughter, Karin, sets off from her home in the company of her foster sister and servant, Ingeri, to take candles to the church. Along the way she meets three goatherds who rape and murder her. When the murderers turn up at Töre's farmhouse, his wife recognizes her daughter's bloody clothes and sets into motion Töre's revenge. The film ends with his repentance for his acts of violence, the welling up of the eponymous spring, and Töre's vow to build an impregnable fortress of a church ("of stone and mortar") on the spot of his daughter's violation and the subsequent "miracle." *The Virgin Spring* figures violence to the larger imagined political community (which does not even appear in the film) through violation of both the intact female body and the intact nuclear family. The source of that violence is a racialized underclass that has not yet been regulated by Christianity.

Our title for this section echoes the title of one of the earliest book-length studies on women and film, Molly Haskell's *From Reverence to Rape*, to foreground two general points that we would like to make about cinematic rape in *The Virgin Spring*. The first may seem obvious from the title, that the crime of rape, sexual violence directed toward women, must be understood as intricately connected with—even the flip side of—idealizations of women that single out privileged women (those designated as wives and daughters, firmly under the regime of the private sphere and properly domesticated) for "reverence," while subjecting others to dehumanizing violence, a cultural habit Bergman and his screenwriter, Ulla Isaksson, highlight with a searing irony in their portrait of the "spoiled" virgin and her "pious" family. The second—and perhaps more important—point is that in narrative, as in law, rarely are we, as spectators, allowed to look directly at rape, to experience and empathize with the injury to the female victim. Rather, rape is almost always deflected onto something else. Rape becomes the object of a series of transformations and these displacements always serve other—often troubling—ideological ends. Rape functions in narrative as a blot or symptom, "a particular, 'pathological' feature, signifying formation, a binding of enjoyment, an inert stain resisting communication and interpretation." It is "a stain which cannot be included in the circuit of discourse, of social bond network, but is at the same time a positive condition of it, . . . a terrifying bodily mark which is merely a mute attestation bearing witness to a disgusting enjoyment" (Žižek, *The Sublime Object of Ideology*, 75–76). In *The Virgin Spring* the violation of the intact female body figures other boundary violations both geographical and temporal and so may be invoked ultimately to shore up a protectionist model of state and civil society in which the politics between men turn out to be, in the words of Wendy Brown, "always already the politics of exchanging, violating, protecting, and regulating women" (188). This seems to be Bergman's solution to the condition of postwar anomie.

Before we speculate further on the temporal and ideological boundaries Bergman's rape is meant to shore up, let us look directly at that rape itself, allowing the analysis to radiate from there. This rape scene was controversial both in Sweden and the United States when it was first screened in 1960. The State of New York Division of Motion Pictures, for instance, ordered twenty-four seconds of the scene removed, including "all views of one herdsman pushing up her dress, exposing her thighs, and holding her legs in a raised position while another herdsman moves his body into position over her body and between her legs" and of "all subsequent views of second herdsman in which his body is seen in position between Karin's legs." Other jurisdictions demanded similar cuts. In fact, in the United States, bowdlerized versions were the rule rather than the exception both for screenings and video release. Bergman, in justifying his scene against such censorship, wrote:

> For me, the rape scene has an ethical significance. It shows the crime in its naked atrocity, forcing us, in shocked desperation, to leave aesthetic enjoyment of a work of art for passionate involvement in a human drama of crime that breeds new crime, of guilt and grace.
>
> I should like to point out that the rape sequence, in its mercilessness and detailed objectivity, corresponds to Master Töre's administering of justice to the two malefactors, as well as—and this is of primary importance—to his bestial murder of the little boy. We must, in our very bowels and apart from all aesthetic judgment, take part in the two herdsmen's crime, but we must also, in despair witness the father's evil deed. We must not hesitate in our portrayal of human degradation, even if, in our demand for truth, we must violate certain taboos. (Criterion DVD)

Most striking in this defense is Bergman's insistence that his representation of rape involves not merely aesthetic enjoyment or ethical judgment but also passionate involvement felt "in our very bowels." The first two of these require objective distance and the last emotional cathexis. The scene suspends its viewers between two opposing kinds of gazes, two ways of looking at the violated female body—a sadistic objectifying gaze and a masochistic and subjective gaze—between an intimacy that fosters shock and a voyeurism that encourages detachment. Formal analysis of the sequence helps us to understand how Bergman achieves this oscillation. The beauty of his compositions aestheticize the rape. We notice the patterns created by the bare branches that obscure our view of the action, the play of light and shadow cast by the sunlight. The figures are artistically arrayed in carefully composed two- and three-shots or impossibly tight close-ups. The entire sequence alternates between long shots that encourage distance and objectivity and close-ups (especially of Karin) that invite emotional participation. The lack of camera movement and the extremely long takes in the sequence create stark objectivity and distance at the same time that they also perturb the placid beauty of the compositions. The actual rape and its aftermath are presented in two shots of unusually long duration (26 and 22 seconds) so that we are literally prevented from looking away; we are forced to watch with no respite offered by cutting or camera movement. There are long silences punctuated only by amplified ambient noise (birds, grunts, Karin's crying) with no musical underscoring to tell us what emotions we should feel. Our emotional responses are, to some extent, manipulated by point-of-view shots from the perspectives of two onlookers, the young brother of the two rapists and Karin's foster sister, Ingeri, both of whom we watch watching, powerless to intervene.[4]

Bergman's use of expressive lighting in the scene offers the most effective cues directing viewers' emotional responses. At the same time, however, it raises questions about the ideological meaning of the rape. In contrast to her rapists, who are frequently filmed in shadow and made to seem swarthier than they are, Karin is most frequently shot with her face bathed in light and her blond hair gleaming. From the first moments of the film, Karin's vulnerability to rape has been connected with her whiteness, which has been represented as a sign of her family's status and wealth. She is constantly compared to her darker, swarthier foster sister or to her rapists. In several close-ups the contrast between Karin's whiteness and her rapists' darkness literally composes the shots. The sole exception is during the long tracking shot immediately following the rape, when she walks toward the camera and suddenly the shadow of a pair of branches crosses her face, literally crossing her out and marking her with the blot, the stain, of the crime, marking her loss of innocence and purity (Figure 16). At that moment she becomes reverence destroyed by rape. The dialogue that precedes the rape reinforces the status difference between Karin and her rapists. This Little Red Riding Hood dialogue seems all the more ominous because throughout, the lighter of the two rapists has to translate the animalistic noises of his inarticulate much darker brother:

THIN HERDSMAN. My brother says the proud maiden has such white hands.

KARIN. Because princesses needn't do the washing or make fires.

THIN HERDSMAN. My brother says the proud maiden has such a pretty neck.

KARIN. To make a princess's gold necklace shine all the brighter.

Karin is a desirable object of rape because of her whiteness, her wealth, and her status.

To the extent that Karin invokes the fantasy of white femininity raped by a dark, animalistic, and racialized "other," the audience sympathizes with her ordeal, but it is, we would suggest, an uneasy sympathy for a twenty-first-century feminist viewer. In the events leading up to the rape, Karin's vulnerability is

Figure 16. Karin crossed out in *The Virgin Spring* (Ingmar Bergman, 1960).

everywhere visually tied to her whiteness and her status. As the two women stop to rest on their journey, Ingeri warns Karin that neither her pride nor her wealth will shield her from Ingeri's fate (becoming pregnant out of wedlock): "We'll see about your honor when a man takes your waist or strokes your neck." When Karin counters that she would only exchange her body properly within the economy of legitimate marriage (she wouldn't "give it away"), Ingeri counters: "And if he meets you in the pasture and pulls you down behind a bush?" At this point we have to wonder whether Ingeri's pregnancy could be the result of rape. Can she even be raped within the economy Bergman has set up? Ingeri's swarthier beauty makes her more sexually available than Karin, suggesting that women of the underclass have no real ability to refuse men's advances. If we indulge the belief that Töre (or someone like him) is the father of Ingeri's child (not an unlikely scenario), the film then structures its narrative around fantasies about the rape of white women by nonwhite lower-class "alien" men as a means of "disappearing," rendering invisible, the rape of lower-class women (while this account describes the sexual economy of American race relations, it might do service to describe the appropriation of lower-class or colonial sexualities by privileged men in Europe as well).

To read the rape not only in terms of its gendered meanings but its racial overtones as well, we must turn to the mechanisms by which Bergman displaces the rape onto other meanings. *The Virgin Spring* works out Bergman's vision of social anomie on the scale of the violated female body, which becomes a trope that connects several nested geographic sites—in particular the scale of the nuclear family and the scale of the nation. William Blake's poem "The Sick Rose" captures perhaps most succinctly the set of correspondences between the rape of the female body and racial "violation" that we are trying to analyze through the geographical concept of "scale":

O Rose, thou art sick!
The invisible worm
That flies in the night,
In the howling storm,

Has found out thy bed
Of crimson joy:
And his dark secret love
Does thy life destroy.

In this poem the worm's "defiling" of the rose's beauty figures defilement on a larger scale, on the scale of the human body through disease or sexuality and even on the scale of the political community, through fear of a racialized "other," a "dark secret love." Because, after fascism, it is no longer possible to declare openly in liberal societies the fear that the body politic (the nation) can be violated by an alien "other," those fears get displaced onto the scales of the body and the family, perennial loci for such anxieties.

The anomic and deviant individuals who threaten the idyll of Töre's nuclear family—the pregnant foster daughter, Ingeri, who accompanies Karin to church and the goatherds who rape Karin—are never specifically designated as non-white. However, the film's representation of earlier more "primitive" pagan religions and cinematographer Sven Nyqvist's manipulation of expressive lighting allude to a threat from "darker" races who have not yet been enlightened by Christianity and brought fully under the regime of the nuclear family. In postwar Europe, where the memory of the racial cleansing of the Jews under Nazism was still quite fresh, those darker races might be Jews or they might be the inhabitants of Europe's colonies in Africa, Asia, the Middle East, and the antipodes, many of whom were being begrudgingly welcomed as immigrants into Europe to facilitate postwar rebuilding. Though it maintained no colonies of its own in the twentieth century, Sweden would have felt the effects of the postwar dismantling of Europe's colonial empires and fears about threats to European racial purity, even as the guilt over Nazi atrocities would have inhibited direct expression of such fears. Bergman was not immune to Nazi propaganda about racial purity. Peter Cowie describes Bergman's youthful brush with fascism in the 1930s:

> After the war, when the newsreels of the concentration camps began to be shown in Sweden, Bergman realized the horror he had brushed shoulders with. "My feelings were overwhelming . . . and I felt great bitterness toward my father and my brother and the schoolteachers and everybody else who'd let me into it. But it was impossible to get rid of the guilt and self-contempt." In the 1970s, after almost thirty-five years of reticence, Bergman was able to admit to having been affected by the Nazi propaganda. "When I came home [from a trip to Germany in 1934 when he was sixteen] I was a pro-German fanatic," he has said, although none of his contemporaries recall any pronounced political leanings in him at that period. One of the most meaningful consequences of this episode was that Bergman turned his back on politics in every form. (Cowie, 16)[5]

However, if Bergman turned his back on direct political action (while remaining as he told one interviewer, "a good social democrat" [Bergom-Larsson, 8]) as a result of his early flirtation with fascism, anxieties about racial mixing do insinuate themselves into *The Virgin Spring.*

The film's opening scenes structure a series of ideologically charged binary oppositions around the expressive play of light and dark. These initial binaries—Christian/pagan, good/evil, innocent/guilty, virgin/whore, legitimate/illegitimate, leisure/labor—generate most of the film's subsequent narrative. The film opens without preamble on a medium shot of a young woman, a shot that follows her for more than a minute and a half as she goes about her morning labor—lighting a fire, putting the breakfast on the fire, opening a skylight. We later learn that the woman is Ingeri, an abandoned child taken in by Töre. Both servant and wayward daughter, she is beautiful but filthy, hypersexualized—so pregnant that she seems on the verge of bursting, wearing a dress whose buttons cannot contain her belly. She is the bastard who will produce yet another bastard. We never learn who the child's father is; could Töre possibly be both her foster father and her lover? Her rapist? The film is silent on these questions. She is characterized by the others in the household not as pregnant, overworked, and exhausted but as lazy and devious. She is most significantly marked by her darkness, not only by her dirty skin and dark hair color but also by the low-key lighting, which always places her in shadow, making her appear even darker than she actually is (Figure 17). Ingeri worships an older, discredited faith; she calls on Odin to deliver her from her servitude, the god of the parents she doesn't know, rather than the Christ figure worshipped by her foster family. She is the colonized other, forced into submissive labor yet subversive, readying her weapons of the weak to strike back at the institutions that have grudgingly provided space for her. She is welcomed into the home but continuously humiliated and, on occasion, beaten. She is a racialized Cinderella, the servant foster sister who seeks revenge on the privileged family that she serves. But Bergman's tale is told not from Ingeri's perspective, robbing it of the delight of the revenge of the underclasses. Instead, its conservatism requires that the underclasses finally confess, apologize, repent their rebellion, as Ingeri will do in the end, returning to her preordained place in the family economy.

An abrupt cut to a new location reveals a close-up of a cross, a stylized gesture toward a Gothic crucifix (an Ikea Jesus). The sculptor has captured the weight of Christ's suffering body hanging from the cross, and the low-key lighting creates a shadow across its surface not unlike the effects created in the previous scene. Yet if Christ's suffering in this shot is at least momentarily and subliminally linked to

Figure 17. Ingeri in *The Virgin Spring* (Ingmar Bergman, 1960).

Ingeri's, that moment passes quickly as the camera pans right to reveal Töre and his wife, Märeta, saying their morning prayers. Their faces are bathed in light, emphasizing their fairness in comparison to Ingeri. Märeta's face especially remains consistently well-lit and visible. The family's enlightened Christianity contrasts to Ingeri's dark paganism.[6]

Bergman's stark binaries between dark and fair, shadow and light, good and bad are undermined by the time in which *The Virgin Spring* is released—the late 1950s. Critics have been willing to give Bergman a pass, to aestheticize his simple, perhaps even clichéd, symbolism of light and dark. But in the aftermath of the Holocaust, when millions of "Untermenschen"—persons of dark complexion—were exterminated in the name of "racial science," it is impossible to overlook a disturbing political agenda informing Bergman's work. Bergman's conservative "family values" include a much more disturbing conservatism concerning race and class. He consistently depicts the underclasses of medieval Sweden as dark, disruptive, hypersexual, and subversive. They threaten both the individual bodies of the fair-haired, fair-skinned dominant culture and the body politic as well.

The household's morning breakfast is presented in a tableau arranged like da

Vinci's *The Last Supper* (a composition repeated in a later scene with the three goatherds), with Töre presiding in a large thronelike chair decorated with saints' heads. Even there, Ingeri occupies the dark outer edges. The economy of Töre's intact nuclear family, the film suggests, cannot exist without the labor provided by Ingeri's kind, by the same racialized underclass that threatens both virgin and family from the outside, but it must be disciplined; both the pure and the impure are contained within Töre's household.

The meal is marked by the absence of the daughter of the house, who has overslept. Our first view of Karin places her in sharp contrast to her foster sister. Whereas Ingeri occupies the darkness, Karin is always photographed bathed in light, her blond hair reflecting the light. Whereas Ingeri is a household drudge, Karin is the pampered child. The cinematography presents Karin as the treasure of this bare, sparse, and austere household—a pearl of great price. Her clothes are made of the finest materials and covered with precious objects—gold thread, pearls. Yet she is petulant and spoiled, manipulating her parents by cajoling, pouting, and even flirting with her father to deflect his anger. When we first saw the film we couldn't help wondering whether Bergman wasn't making some kind of statement about the postwar shift in child-rearing practices, locating in the spoiled offspring of indulgent parents (the scale of the family) the source of the anomie of modernity (Wes Craven clearly saw this when he adapted it as *The Last House on the Left*). Such a reading would certainly fit Durkheim's belief that anomie results from too little social constraint rather than too much: "If anomie is an evil, it is above all because society suffers from it, being unable to live without cohesion and regularity" (Orru, "The Ethics of Anomie," 509). The postwar publication of Dr. Spock's 1947 bestselling book *Baby and Child Care* became a contested focal point for a decided shift in Euro-American child-rearing practices away from authoritarian parent-centered customs of the past toward child-centered practices marked by flexibility, affection, and attention to the child as an individual. Many social commentators have been all too willing to link what they perceive as the pathological absence of moral norms back to the changes in the nuclear family, fearing that the "permissive" child-rearing practices promoted by Spock's book would result in spoiled children who would threaten the security afforded by the nuclear family under the protection of its patriarch. The link between the failure of patriarchal discipline in the private sphere and lawlessness in the public was made explicit in the late 1960s by Norman Vincent Peale, who claimed that "the U.S. was paying the price of two generations that followed the Dr. Spock baby plan of instant gratification of needs," and later in the 1970s by

Spiro Agnew, who, as vice president, denounced Spock as the "father of permissiveness," claiming that his child-rearing principles encouraged lawlessness.[7] A Swedish translation of Spock's book had appeared by 1956, suggesting that at least by the end of the 1950s the debate would have reached Sweden (in fact, in 1979 Sweden became the bellwether for controversies surrounding liberalized child-rearing practices by passing a law banning spanking). Bergman's biographers all note the authoritarian nature of the filmmaker's own upbringing, which stressed obedience and subordination to the parents', and especially the father's, authority and advocated the belief that the punishment of children be carried out objectively and without feeling (Cowie, 8).[8] By all accounts, Bergman, whose father was a Lutheran minister, was raised in just such an authoritarian environment: "It was a life-and-death struggle: either it was the parents who were broken or it was the children. The idea was not to shape you but to break you, never mind the methods used," he told Jörn Donner in 1975 (quoted in Bergom-Larsson, 14). As Maria Bergom-Larsson describes it, "Children were beaten, caned savagely and methodically, locked in a dark wardrobe, punished with icy silence or subjected to other forms of humiliation. The punishments were staged according to a strict procedure, with a trial in his father's study. It was an upbringing which aimed at humiliating the child into taking the strait and narrow. The whole atmosphere . . . was one of humiliation and guilt" (Bergom-Larsson, 14). Bergman himself noted the relationship between family dynamics in the private sphere and the state; for him the cold discipline of the family "led with inevitable logic to Nazism, even in such a little cell as our family, to trust in authority and the oppression of women and the most horrific cruelty in the name of family solidarity" (Bergom-Larsson, 14; see also Cowie, 5–19, on Bergman's childhood). But even if this childhood was as horrific as Bergman indicates, he also suggests that he did value that upbringing: "At the same time they taught me a number of values—efficiency, punctuality, a sense of financial responsibility—values which may be 'bourgeois' but are nevertheless important to the artist." In short, values which express everything his virgin Karin is not (Cowie, 19). In *The Virgin Spring* Bergman presents the same kind of stern and austere household but peoples it with parents who, while severe and frugal in their own conduct (Märeta is positively ascetic) and in disciplining other household members (the servants), are indulgent with their only child. Their indulgence leads not only to the horrific rape and murder of this child but the invasion of the household by the atavistic others the household was designed to (but can never successfully) expel.

By overdetermining Karin's fate within the racialized sexual economy we have described, Bergman ensures that the film will "jump scales"; that is, it will extend through allegory the violation of the white female body into fantasies about the violation of the nuclear family and ultimately of the modern "civilized" state—the successor state to the enlightened Christian Middle Ages that in an earlier "postcolonial" age vanquished the pagan Dark Ages. Predictably the goatherds' violation of Karin is followed by their invasion of Töre's household and his violent revenge for both crimes. But the film does not end, as Bergman and his critics have suggested, with Töre's repentance for his violent crimes. It ends with the welling up of the miraculous spring, a symbolic ejaculation that restores Töre's potency, asserts his legitimate sexual ownership of his women over the illicit encroachment of others. Töre promises to build an inviolable fortress of a church, "of stone and mortar," on that very spot. Karin's raped body becomes a scar, the symbolic wound on which the patriarchal order of the family is strengthened in order to sustain the emergent political state, the mark of modernity. Bergman's film repeats Max Weber's tale in *Economy and Society* about the origins of the modern state in which, to quote Wendy Brown, the "authority of the adult male derives not from his place in the division of labor but from his physical capacity to dominate and defend his household, a capacity significant only because of the omnipresent threat to household security" from "men's leagues," marauding bands of uncivilized men (W. Brown, 188). Sexuality, the scale of the body, in *The Virgin Spring*, becomes the prefigurative moment of the early modern, the temporal and geographical scale of civilization itself.[9] *The Virgin Spring* concludes with the promise of a modernity forged out of the assertion of a dominant male and aristocratic class. This dominant class destroys the racialized, hypersexualized "other" that, with its potential for sexual violence, continuously threatens progress, continuously evokes an atavistic Middle Ages; at the same time this dominant class creates an impregnable fortress—in this case a church—to house its ideologies. For Bergman this dominant class is best represented in the figure of the hard-bodied, hypermasculine knight, a character he had first experimented with three years earlier in *The Seventh Seal*.

Apocalypse Now and Then: *The Seventh Seal*

In 1957 Bergman had cast Max von Sydow in *The Seventh Seal* as Antonius Block, a knight returning from the Crusades after ten years to a home decimated by the plague.[10] This film, which propelled Bergman to international fame, probes the knight's inability to derive the promised meaning from his crusading in the face of the social dislocation caused by war and disease. Scholarship on the film has tended to read Bergman's preoccupations as intellectual, philosophical, and abstract. Reading *The Seventh Seal* through the philosophy of existentialism as an expression of nihilistic angst and doubt, critics have tended to focus on Block as the existential hero divorced from any social context; indeed Block's alienation from his social environment—evoked by the haunting beauty of the stunning opening shots of the knight washed up on a vast, empty, and desolate shore— seems for many precisely the point.[11] Andrew Sarris's and Birgitta Steene's readings in 1959 and 1968 respectively of *The Seventh Seal* as an allegory of the individual's struggle with death are typical. Sarris attempts to identify the sins that explain Death's choice of victims, and Steene argues the film's existentialist view that "a human life is decided not in intellectual questioning but in the choice of action."[12] These readings of the film through the lens of existentialism are only partial, however. The film does not merely dramatize the death of an individual, as, for instance, the medieval morality play *Everyman* does.[13] More recently, Hamish Ford shifts the discussion of this film slightly when he writes that "to late-'50s audiences [*The Seventh Seal*] asked what metaphysical schemas and values humanity can possibly live by in a time when apocalyptic death is a daily threat, and when structures of belief seem to bring only regression, blindness and servitude." As in *The Virgin Spring*, characters in *The Seventh Seal* oscillate between the poles of realism and allegory: death on the scale of the body figures apocalyptic breakdown on the scale of the community, even of the world. Block is both a medieval knight and an allegorical figure for the body politic; the health of his body represents the health of society itself. Block's chess match with Death becomes not only the individual's search to give meaning to his existence but a civilization's anguished death throes.

In his program notes for the film Bergman writes, "In the Middle Ages men lived in terror of the plague. Today they live in fear of the atomic bomb" (Aberth, 227). However, while *The Seventh Seal* unleashes all Four Horsemen of the Apocalypse—pestilence, war, famine, and death—its medieval framework serves only "as a mirror and an alienating device for viewing the mid-century present" (Lindley, "The Ahistoricism of Medieval Film"). In the Middle Ages only God would have the means to end the world; "none of the authors writing in the midst of the Black Death doubted for a moment that their terrible ordeal served a higher purpose" (Aberth, 210). Even as he reported the collapse of social order in the face of the plague, the fourteenth-century Italian poet Boccaccio understood the devastation of the plague as "God's just wrath as a punishment to mortals for our wicked deeds" (3). By the 1950s, however, technology had usurped God's prerogative; annihilation was in human hands. As if to reflect that reality, the film's opening "is a beach located midway between T. S. Eliot and Neville Shute. . . . If we are in any historical period, it is less the 1340s of the plot premise than the sub-atomic early 1950s, with universal death looming out of the northern sky. As Peter Cowie has written, the film 'reflect[s] the trepidation of the Cold War era' (2). A child of the fifties, I react to that [opening image of a] hawk by wanting to crawl under my school desk."[14] In the film's mélange of medieval and high modern, plague as death on a global scale becomes the mechanism for exploring postwar fantasies of apocalypse.

Bergman's own assessment of his concerns strikes us as less existential than anomic. Of the postnuclear world Bergman writes, "Our political systems are gravely compromised and unusable. Our social behavior pattern . . . has proved a fiasco. The tragic thing is that we have neither the ability nor the will nor the energy to change direction. . . . Around the corner there is an insect world waiting, and one day it will wash in over our highly individualised existence" (quoted in Bergom-Larsson, 8). Anomie, as we suggest above, describes a malaise peculiar to modern liberal societies that have freed individuals from authoritarian laws, ascriptive hierarchies, and moribund institutions (like religion). The autonomy of the modern individual fuels anomie (etymologically, self-law leads logically to no law). Yet it is unclear to us whether anomie should more accurately be described as the lack of structuring social constraints (normlessness) or as the discrepancy between the promise of individual autonomy and freedom and the tacit social constraints or norms that contradict that promise; undoubtedly it is some of both.[15] Autonomy and individual freedom are the hallmarks of liberal democracy—its greatest triumph—yet autonomous individuals may be alienated both by the loss of certainty that accompanies apparent unconditional freedom (the condition described by the existentialists) and by the continued presence of social constraint and obligation that impinge on that unconditional freedom, as well as by the social sanctions that police infractions of those constraints. If *The Seventh Seal* depicts a world in which "God is silent, lost, and/or absent and the religious and social institutions based on his authority void of any real value" (Blackwell, 76), then approaching the film through the concept of anomie improves on existential readings by placing the hero's isolation and alienation within a wider social context.

To illustrate the usefulness of the concept, let us reexamine *The Seventh Seal*'s opening sequence. The film begins with a series of tableaulike images that suggest the complete autonomy, the isolation of the individual in an indifferent and uncaring universe. The camera finds Block and his squire, Jöns, after they have washed up on a desolate beach. The landscape itself is an image of their alienation. The two are frequently shown in extreme long shot to suggest their insignificance and loneliness against a vast, empty natural space devoid of social context. Yet the two returning crusaders are not utterly detached from social life. Even against the backdrop of an indifferent silent universe, social constraint is present everywhere. The very first shot of Block includes his chess set, laid out next to him in perfect order, as if it washed up on the beach already set up for a game. The game of chess that sets the plot in motion tropes the social order that everywhere organizes and constrains individual action within the film. The defining feature of any game (chess included) is its rules. For instance, in what is perhaps the most frequently reproduced shot from the film, Block and Death enact the rule for choosing sides. Such rules are what Anthony Giddens calls "constitutive." That is, rules that seem to regulate the game end up being, in fact, that which constitutes the game. Every player agrees tacitly to abide by the rules of the game. Giddens extends this argument about rules to larger social systems (he jumps scales) whose structures he sees as consisting of "rules and resources." When Block proposes a game of chess with Death, they both agree to the rules that structure their social interaction. Even though the natural "rule" of Death is, "I grant no reprieve" (14), Block negotiates new rules: "The condition is that I may live as long as I hold out against you. If I win, you will release me" (14).[16]

Once we see the game of chess as an image of a rule-bound social order (whether those rules take the form of discursive laws or tacit understandings), we begin to see social constraint everywhere: "awareness of social rules, expressed first and foremost in practical consciousness, is the very core of the 'knowledge-ability' which especially characterizes human agents" (Giddens, 21–22), however free or unconstrained they might seem. The knight is always in the company of his squire, Jöns, and their hierarchical and ascribed relationship (master to servant) is governed by rules that they understand and reproduce without effort, though those rules are not of their own making. The song Jöns sings as they ride along reveals the social rules that govern their relationship:

Between a strumpet's legs I lie
That's the place for such as I
The Lord is aloft, you know
But Satan finds us here below.[17]

The two are aligned along a vertical social axis defined by higher and lower. The knight, by analogy with "The Lord . . . aloft," is "above" his servant, who represents the lower social strata. The knight is superior: ethereal, intellectual, and spiritual, unconcerned with the material needs of his body precisely because these needs are taken care of by his squire, who, as the song indicates, is immersed in the "lower bodily strata" that Bakhtin called the "grotesque body."[18] The relationship of these two individuals encapsulates the hierarchy of the medieval social order as Bergman represents it.

For both Bergman and his main character, Antonius Block, anomie takes the form of a mourning for the certainties of social orders that have been irretrievably lost, an inability to let go of a moribund past. In the preface to Malmström's and Kushner's translation of the script for *The Seventh Seal*, Bergman laments the descent of art into the cult of the individual: "Today the individual has become the highest form and the greatest bane of artistic creation. The smallest wound or pain of the ego is examined under a microscope as if it were of eternal importance. The artist considers his isolation, his subjectivity, his individualism almost holy" (8). As he mourns the loss of moral certitude (our inability to "distinguish between true and false, between the gangster's whim and the purest ideal"), Bergman also laments the loss of the art of the medieval cathedral, where "the artist remained unknown and his work was to the glory of God. He lived and died without being more or less important than other artists; . . . I want to be one of the artists in the cathedral on the great plain. . . . Regardless of whether I believe or not, whether I am a Christian or not" (8–9). Describing a kind of artistic anomie, Bergman nostalgically evokes a social order that has not existed for ages, desiring it despite, or perhaps even because, he cannot believe in it.

Block's anomie takes the same form of nostalgia for long-gone certainties, for a time when his aristocratic rank, his masculine privilege, and his religious devotion provided a framework for, and fantasies of, freedom, control, order. As much as he wants to believe that God is dead, he can't quite rid himself of the last vestiges of religious indoctrination. Echoing Bergman's nostalgia, he cries out, "Why can't I kill God within me? Why does He live on in this painful and humiliating way even though I curse Him and want to tear Him out of my heart?"[19] The knight has returned from his crusade empty, haunted by his participation. He went on crusade looking for God and found not God, not even the devil, but nothing. The most he can admit, even as he unburdens himself in the confessional, is a belief that "life is an outrageous horror. No one can live in the face of death, knowing that all is nothingness" (28). It is left to the materialist Jöns to evoke the physical sufferings of the crusaders: "For ten years we sat in the Holy Land and let snakes bite us, flies sting us, wild animals eat us, heathens butcher us, the wine poison us, the women give us lice, the lice devour us, the fevers rot us, all for the Glory of God. Our crusade was such madness that only a real idealist could have thought it up" (29–30).[20] But his account of these horrors represses the crusaders' own violence. Block is not empty because he has suffered physical discomfort in the Holy Land; he is empty because he committed atrocities that he cannot live with, that destroy whatever idealism sent him on crusade.

In the confessional the knight attempts to give voice to his anguish. The result is a confession that is not a confession at all; instead, it is a series of rhetorical questions, questions to which the knight can hardly expect an answer—even from a priest who turns out to be Death. The knight's anomie is carried less by von Sydow's stoic performance than by a series of crosscuts that return obsessively to a grotesque crucifix of a suffering Christ, emaciated, blood-spattered, face contorted in pain, fear, and despair (the same cross turns up again in the flagellants' procession later in the film). The crosscutting implies that the knight is experiencing what the Middle Ages might have called despair. But Block's anomie is really of a different time. In this as in so many ways, the film calls on the generic expectations of the medieval morality play, but its morality is not really medieval.[21] The image of a despairing Christ underlines what Susan Snyder calls the paradoxical nature of the medieval sin of despair (*tristitia*): "awareness of and sorrow for past sin, always the first step of fallen man on his way to salvation, may lead him into such self-loathing that he feels—and therefore is—beyond the reach of God's mercy" (20). Despair, unlike its modern counterpart, never denies God; rather, what the despairing sinner denies is that he or she can be touched by God's mercy. The Lutheranism in which Bergman was raised maintains this duality but takes it a step further; for Martin Luther despair is the very foundation of faith: "Luther found the experience of despair so necessary a part of holiness that he extended it to Christ himself. . . . Just like us, Jesus on his cross touched the depths of despair, believed himself forsaken by God" (Snyder, 27).

Against this theological background, invoked by the icon of the crucifix, Block expresses spiritual emptiness. The sentiments he expresses, however, are uniquely modern: "How can we have faith in those who believe when we can't have faith in ourselves?" he asks.[22] Block rejects the trappings of religion, the belief in the face of the uncertainty required by faith: "Why should he hide himself in a mist of half-spoken promises and unseen miracles? . . . I want knowledge, not faith, not suppositions, but knowledge. I want God to stretch out His hand towards me, reveal Himself and speak to me." These are not the outpourings of an existential atheist who confidently believes that God is dead. Block cannot imagine meaning in the absence of God: "Then life is an outrageous horror. No one can live in the face of death, knowing that all is nothingness." Block is caught between the security promised by religious faith and the absolute freedom of existential atheism. He inhabits the space between the medieval idea of despair and modern existential angst, a space we might call anomie.

Bergman's art, however, lies not in its philosophical speculation, which, to twenty-first-century ears seems stilted, even, at times, clichéd and pretentious, but in his visual realization of the anomie of midcentury life in a film of which one critic has said "stop it at almost every frame and you will find yourself looking at a striking, distinguished and often very beautiful composition" (Wood, 85). If Bergman's desire to return to the practices of medieval art articulates the anomie of aesthetics, his film accomplishes the aestheticization of anomie. As in the opening sequence, during the confessional scene Block is isolated from others; Bergman suggests this by filming him once again against barren stone, this time of an austere church.[23] This is one of the few scenes in which Block has been separated from his traveling companion. Block's "confession" is framed on either side by comic scenes between Jöns and the painter whose sociability (they are filmed almost entirely in two-shot) contrasts with Block's isolation (Blackwell, 79). The only other figure in the confessional sequence is Death, who is disguised as a priest. The interchange between the two is among the few in the film that show Block in a two-shot with another character. Yet the connection that might have been established by filming them together in the same shot is negated by placing them on opposite sides of a confessional grille that functions as a barrier between them, isolating the knight, who says, "Through my indifference to my fellow men, I have isolated myself from their company. . . . I am imprisoned in my dreams and fantasies" (27). As Marilyn Johns Blackwell has argued, *The Seventh Seal* visually portrays the knight's anomie through binaries of high and low, light and dark, closed and open (79). One panning shot illustrates the technique. It begins with Block in close-up, his face brightly lit. Block occupies the left side of the shot, the right taken up by the shadow cast by the confessional grille, a chessboard made of light and dark created by the harsh high-contrast lighting (Figure 18). The camera moves left and then upward until it reveals Death, obscured behind the grille, towering over a kneeling Block, who now occupies the lower right-hand side of the shot. Block appears trapped between the bars of the confessional grille and their shadows on the wall, nearly immured by the reli-

Figure 18. Antonius Block's prison in *The Seventh Seal* (Ingmar Bergman, 1957).

gious institutions that should give him comfort: "The confessional should be a place of liberation; instead, Bergman describes it in terms of incarceration—a cramped stall, the heavy iron bars like those of a prison, with Death as a jailer" (Cowie, 144).

Against Block's modernist anomie, Bergman sets the "holy family" of Jof, Mia, and the baby, Mikael, to suggest what we generally imagine the medieval religious mind-set to be: the simple, innocent, peasantlike experience of faith unmediated by the philosophy, logic, or scientific rationality that marks Block's tortured confession. Early in the film, after Block and Jöns move inland from the beach where they have landed, they are shown in long shot riding by a wagon in which a troupe of actors sleeps. At this point Bergman connects the two groups only by this momentary contiguity. The two crusaders pass by in silence, riding out of the shot, while the camera shifts its attention from them to the troupe. The contrast between this scene and earlier scenes is stark. If Block is shot against barren rocky wastes, the troupe of actors is first glimpsed in a setting of "lush grass, peace, fertility," bathed in a dappled soft and even light (Wood, 84; Blackwell, 84), birds chirping on the sound track. Bergman idealizes his "holy" family through simple techniques. If the first sequence alternates between close-ups and extreme long shots, the second follows the characters in long and medium shots with no camera movement and little enough movement on the actors' part. Jof recounts a vision to Mia in a medium shot that is held for over two minutes.

Jof and Mia are almost always filmed in two-shot, a style that, because it allows us to see the characters interacting with one another, "emphasizes fellowship and community, a sense of the integration of the individual into nature" (Blackwell, 85). Against Block's crisis of faith Bergman sets Jof's visions and his innocent belief precisely in the "half spoken promises and unseen miracles" Block rejects. After the riders pass by, Jof emerges from the wagon and, in a few deft strokes, Bergman creates the character of his "holy fool." Bergman chose the Swedish comic Nils Poppe to portray Jof as a buffoon whose performance is marked by slapstick comedy: dressed in multicolored tights, he slaps at fleas (carriers of plague), yawns, stretches in an exaggerated manner, does somersaults, dances, loudly gargles a drink of water, juggles badly, and talks to his horse.

In the midst of this performance, suddenly he stops and turns. As the camera tracks in toward his face, choral singing can be heard, the only music in the sequence, suggesting that Jof is experiencing some kind of extraordinary event. Jof, the performer—acrobat, juggler, clown—is the audience for what he believes is a divine performance, one in which the Virgin, "golden crown on her head," steps into the middle of a perfectly composed long shot—as if on a mark—and, as he recounts it, smiles at him. He rubs his eyes in a comic manner. Because he is a clown, his wife, Mia, does not entirely trust his reporting. She responds to his description of the vision with what the script describes as "gentle irony": "You have to keep your visions under control. Otherwise people will think you are a halfwit, which you are not." But she does not seem entirely convinced. Is Jof a halfwit or a saint? How can the buffoon become the vessel for the very revelation the introspective Block complains he is denied? What authority could the vision of a clown have? Bergman deploys his own, and the audience's, expectations of a romanticized innocent Middle Ages to frame Jof's vision; in a world gone so horribly wrong he, and we, await a child, or at least someone who thinks and behaves like a child, to provide leadership out of the wilderness of anomie. "I can't help it," he tells Mia, "if voices speak to me, if the Holy Virgin appears before me and angels and devils like my company" (19). But in a world gone so horribly wrong, why would anyone believe in the truth of such visions? The authenticity of the vision is undercut by the revelation that Jof had earlier made up fictitious visions: "I did it just so that you would believe in my other visions. The real ones. The ones that I didn't make up" (18). Although the audience is given a privileged glimpse of Jof's visions (we see what he sees of the Virgin, of Death, and of the final Dance of Death), we are here reminded that visions are, in the final analysis, performative.[24] The visions must be represented, literally translated into narrative for an audience. They depend finally on that audience's belief in the visionary's performance and, as Jof notes, the more vivid the performance, the more efficacious the vision.

Performance is everywhere in *The Seventh Seal*. Its plot is, in fact, structured by a series of performances to which Block and Jöns bear witness on their journey home: an acting troupe performs; a procession of flagellants passes by; a witch is executed. As Bergman interleaves these scenes with scenes from private life—an attempted rape, a seduction—even such private, secretive actions begin to seem like performances. The pair moves through a linear sequence of painterly montages vivified. Sequences replicate the narratives depicted by the painter Albertus Pictor in the church through which they pass, paintings that take their inspiration from frescoes Bergman had seen as a child. As Bergman recounts it, "In a wood sat Death, playing chess with the Crusader. Clutching the branch of a tree was a naked man with staring eyes, while down below stood Death, sawing away to his heart's content. Across gentle hills Death led the final dance towards the dark lands. But in the other arch the holy Virgin was walking in a rose-garden, supporting the Child's faltering steps" (Aberth, 221). In the film the pictorial is subsumed into the performative; frescoes are public art, narrative paintings that represent a shared cultural past. Bergman uses performances throughout *The Seventh Seal* to locate Block's alienation within a devastated and anomic public space. This social space contrasts the isolation of the confessional scene. Block and Jöns function, along with the film's viewers, as the audience for these performances, and through them the audience shares Block's perspective. The role of the spectator is to attend and judge. This is not simply a passive role, since out of the act of spectatorship the individual fashions him- or herself in accordance with the codes of conduct these spectacles encourage. In these public spheres the judgments of spectators are as much aesthetic as ethical, as a pair of scenes early in the film suggest.

The first occurs after Jof has recounted his vision to Mia. The director of the troupe, Skat, emerges from the wagon, complaining about the Death mask he must wear as part of his performance: "Is this supposed to be a mask for an actor? If the priests didn't pay us so well, I'd say no thank you" (20). The actors are being paid by priests to perform "right on the church steps" morality plays designed to "scare decent folk out of their wits," designed, that is, to create a docile public obedient to the priests. The actors are enlisted to perform something sober and moral to create sober and moral subjects. Jof argues for playing something "bawdy": "People like it better, and, besides, it's more fun" (20). This approach creates a public sphere of distraction and pleasure. Although medieval morality plays certainly knew how to mix laughter with doctrine, bawdiness with the fire and brimstone of hell, Bergman here envisions the two as mutually exclusive choices, resulting in the creation of different kinds of subjects, those who are scared "out of their wits" and those who have immersed themselves in the pleasures of the world. In a later scene Jöns and the painter enumerate the same alternatives when they debate the relative merits of Pictor's *Dance of Death*.[25] When Jöns asks him why he paints such "nonsense," Pictor replies, "to remind people that they must die." Jöns, who invariably represents the materialist approach to life, argues that "it's not going to make them feel any happier." Images such as those made by Pictor create particular kinds of subjects; as Jöns remarks, "They'll run right into the arms of the priests." Pictor counters, "Why should one always make people feel happy? It might not be a bad idea to scare them a little once in a while." Pictor expresses a realist's approach to art: "I'm only painting things as they are." Besides, he argues, the terrors he depicts do carry with them their own frisson that makes them entertaining in their own right: "A skull is almost more interesting than a naked lady." Together the two rehearse the terms of an aesthetic debate that has raged at least since Horace over the ends of art: should it instruct or delight? Pictor pragmatically opts for both because it's the best way to make a living at what he does: after presenting his horrific images, "I'll paint something amusing for them to look at" (26). And his patrons (as with the acting troupe, largely the clergy) will pay him for both.

Together these scenes articulate an aesthetic and ethical theory of performance as one mechanism for creating subjects in a public sphere, as if Bergman were using the film, in part, as a metacommentary on the participation of cinema in the creation of modern publicities.[26] We are adapting somewhat freely here Habermas's notion of the bourgeois public sphere. Habermas, writing on the historical emergence of the bourgeois public sphere in eighteenth-century Europe, argued that a public sphere of political debate could exist only once publicity could be thought of as distinct from the state. By contrast, the "medieval representative public sphere" was "directly linked to the concrete existence of a ruler": "as long as the prince and the estates of the realm still 'are' the land, . . . they represent their power 'before' the people, instead of for the people" ("The Public Sphere," 51). What differentiates the institution of the bourgeois public sphere from earlier collectives is "freedom of assembly and association and the freedom to express and publish their opinions" (49). *The Seventh Seal* fudges the differences between these medieval and modern forms of publicity.[27] The film does not represent the public sphere through the usual authoritarian mechanisms of church and state; there are no priests or bishops, no rulers or soldiers: the confessional lacks a priest; the corrupt cleric, Raval, is a seminarian (a student), not a priest; the knight remains a passive observer, never exercising his military authority; it is not soldiers or judges who carry out the execution of the witch but eight well-paid "volunteers." These absences give the film its eerie sense of temporal dislocation and isolation, its sense of being located nowhere and anywhere. Instead, the public sphere is consistently represented through performances, places where audiences gather together to watch and comment on some spectacle. These performances help to articulate a public sphere by making visible particular "modes of conduct" and cultivating in their audiences certain "practices of judgment." In this way the activity of spectating creates both particular subjectivities and a particular sense of communal identity appropriate to the spectacle (Donald and Donald, 114).

Habermas's notion of the public sphere, however, implies a good deal of social cohesion, cohesion that is not usually the mark of anomic societies.[28] What happens to the public sphere under the conditions of social anomie? The causes of social anomie in late-1950s Europe were not just fear of an arms race leading to nuclear annihilation. Just as the social dislocations Block and Jöns observe in *The Seventh Seal* seem to travel ahead of the plague, so the causes of fragmentation and anomie at midcentury included not only the kind of mass death produced by the Holocaust and the atom bomb but also the effects of rampant capitalism, materialism, and consumerism. They include the deleterious effects of the mass media that would be described by Guy Debord only a few years later in *Society of the Spectacle* (1967). Habermas and Debord, both writing in the turbulent 1960s, represent opposite poles in an argument about the nature of public spheres in late-twentieth-century democracies. Habermas insists that a healthy public sphere that fosters rational debate and critical engagement among social equals might counter the destructive effects of commercial mass media and so promote human emancipation through mutual understanding. At the other extreme Debord pessimistically contends that "in societies where modern conditions of production prevail, all of life presents itself as an immense accumulation of spectacles" (par. 1), which he defines not as "a collection of images, but a social relation among people, mediated by images" (par. 4). In such a society effective debate in a public sphere is all but impossible because "communication is always unilateral," one-sided; it is a monologue, never dialogue. Taken together these two theories of public discourse might serve as correctives for one another, such that we might imagine the public sphere as neither completely open and free communication between equal and active participants nor entirely passive brainwashing in which the tangible world is replaced by images (see Debord, par. 36). In an anomic society the public sphere is a site of struggle among individuals and groups with vastly unequal power and unequal access to mass media to articulate their needs, desires, and ambitions.

But the modern liberal individual, the subject of the anomie Bergman examines in the film, becomes a subject not only in the public but also in the private sphere of love, sexuality, and domesticity. The two are interdependent, mutually intertwined; both are necessary to the formation of the modern bourgeois subject. As Habermas notes, public and private spheres are not separate isolated social spaces; they can only be kept analytically distinct. Privacy was historically the "engine" of modern publicities: "The public's understanding of the public use of reason was guided specifically by such private experiences as grew out of the audience-oriented *(publikumsbezogen)* subjectivity of the conjugal family's intimate domain *(Intimsphäre)*" (Habermas, *The Structural Transformation of the Public Sphere*, 28). For Debord private life cannot be separated from public because "the commodity itself made the laws whose 'honest' application leads to the distinct reality of private life and to its subsequent reconquest by the social consumption of images" (par. 198).

In the central section of the film, the main characters have been reduced to audience surrogates; their primary function is to witness performances of social deviance. Bergman alternates scenes of performance in the public sphere with scenes from private life, using them to comment on the sources and manifestations of social dislocation and anomie. Leaving the church, knight and squire encounter the public display in stocks of a "witch," believed "to have caused the pestilence with which we are afflicted" (31). The witch is accused of "carnal intercourse with the Evil One" (30). This spectacle of public humiliation, coupled with the witch's later execution, is designed to purge improper private sexualities and to promote proper conduct among women. Private life is regulated by marriage, which is normative, idealized in the film both by Mia and by Block's wife, the image of Penelope patiently—and chastely—awaiting the return of her husband from the wars; its anomie is carried, as in *The Virgin Spring*, by scenes of rape and illicit sexual liaisons.[29]

The public torture of the witch for her private sexual crimes begins a series of scenes that depict anomie in the private sphere of intimacy, which, except for the relationship between Jof and Mia, is marked by alienation, conflict, exploitation, and extreme misogyny. In an apparently deserted village devastated by the plague, Jöns becomes the audience for an attempted rape. He voyeuristically watches the cleric Raval rob a corpse and then discover a mute girl. As the seminarian pushes her toward a more private place, they pass just beneath the squire's gaze, and the camera captures simultaneously both the act and the act of watching.[30] Jöns interrupts the rape, threatening the rapist with a knife, but suddenly decides he is not "bloodthirsty" and lets him go. Remarkably, Jöns turns around and tries the same thing. He introduces himself to the mute girl as "a pleasant and talkative young man who has never had anything but kind thoughts and only done beautiful and noble deeds" (33); he then grabs her just as Raval had. Once again, he loses interest almost immediately in the violence he has initiated: "I could have raped you. . . . I'm tired of that kind of love. It runs a little dry in the end" (34). However, he does take as his prize her labor, deciding that even though he has a wife, he could use a housekeeper. Jöns does not need to rape the girl to establish his stake in her sexuality and her labor. The threat is enough, sketching with remarkable economy the protectionist model by which men obtain rights in women's labor and sexuality in the private sphere by defending them from other men who threaten women who venture into public unsecured by their relationship to a man. The plague disrupts the social mechanisms that disguise the brutal logic driving the socialization of women like Mia or Karin (the knight's wife): the mute woman must attach herself to Jöns because he has proven himself the stronger protector.

The performances in the central portion of the film take place in an inn (the script calls it "The Embarrassment Inn") in an unnamed village not yet touched by plague, suggesting that the social anomie evident in both public and private spheres is not the result of the plague but, instead, precedes it. The next scene opens on the acting troupe, which has set up a makeshift stage next to the inn. Jof, Mia, and Skat are performing a pantomime set to lively music produced diegetically by a flute and drum. They wear clownish costumes; Jof has cuckold's horns. They are not performing on the church steps that Skat had earlier described, and they have opted to perform something bawdy rather than edifying. In the script Skat describes the performance, though his exposition has been cut from the film; it is a "tragedia about an unfaithful wife, her jealous husband, and the handsome lover—that's me" (35). The camera cuts between the performance and reaction shots of the crowd. In scenes of public performance this alternation of shot and reverse shot sutures audience and performance, shaping the audience into a particular kind of public sphere, an example of social relations mediated by images. The actors perform in front of an unruly, restive mob that heckles the performers and pelts them with rotten fruit. This lively amusing scene contains only a hint of darker elements that have, for the moment, been subdued. During one of the cutaway shots to the crowd, showing the smith Plog looking for his wife, we can make out just dangling from the top of the right hand of the screen a pair of legs. They are completely still. This glimpse of bare legs never resolves into anything coherent; the body is never shown in its entirety. The legs function as an anamorphotic blot, something to be glanced at but not fully comprehended. The implication is that this is a corpse, whether from a private lynching or a public execution is not clear because no officials are present. The public created by the troupe's performance is an undisciplined mob, amused and amusing, but hinting at something darker and more dangerous lurking just beneath the surface.

The actors' performance is intercut with a performance of a more private type, as the smith's wife performs an elaborate seduction with Skat. In their juxtaposition to public performances these scenes of private life come increasingly to seem every bit as theatrical as their public counterparts. The camera cuts from Skat playing his flute, and staring out at someone in the audience, to a reverse shot showing the object of his gaze, a buxom blond who stares back boldly. In the background we see her hulking husband, Plog, carrying a very large hammer, which he wields as a weapon. The woman turns, looks at the husband, turns back and winks suggestively at Skat. Later in the dance there is a shot of the wife furtively running behind the actors' wagon. As the dance ends, Skat exits the stage, free to pursue his seduction while Jof and Mia perform their next number. As the pair perform a nonsense song, Skat and the wife perform an elaborate and stylized pantomime of a seduction as stylized and theatrical as what has happened onstage.[31] The song, with its refrain referencing the activities of "The Black One," provides an ironic commentary on the lovers' actions, a reminder of death's constant presence, even during moments of triumph and celebration. Bawdy performance in the public sphere and illicit sexuality in the private create unruly publicities, publicities that will continue to dominate the film's narrative even after they have been chastened by the flagellants' performance of repentance.

The flagellants' procession proves the painter's argument that horror (a corpse) is more fascinating to an audience than a bawdy performance; at the same time, it achieves (at least temporarily) its religious aim to shape this unruly public into a receptive, docile public of repentant sinners. A wandering mob of penitents is literally herded by a group of black-hooded monks (Dominicans according to the script) as the participants "whip themselves and each other, howling ecstatically . . . in violent, almost rhythmic outbursts" (38). The sequence begins on an audio dissolve; as their song ends, Jof and Mia are framed by the camera in a two-shot as a discordant chant begins over the music. The camera stays with the performers, zooming in to register their reactions as the chanting grows louder. The performers are transformed into the audience, as the flagellants drown them out altogether. Bergman films the procession to maximize the sense of threat, to intensify the horror. He positions a still camera in front of the line of flagellants at a low angle, in a shot that places the viewer in the midst of the procession for nearly a minute as the group moves from the back of the shot toward the front and passes by. Because the camera severely limits what we can see of the whole, we experience it as a kind of ordered chaos. We are denied any distance from the spectacle. Rhythmic chanting is punctuated by a drum, but the rhythm is disordered by the flagellants screaming, howling, crying, and praying as they whip one another into a frenzy. Smoke from censers alternately obscures the procession and reveals it, casting an eerie pall over the proceedings. The mise-en-scène is saturated by the iconography linking religious fanaticism and death: the penitents carry a cross, several wear crowns of thorns, bodies are literally dripping blood, a skull is held aloft by a monk.

Once again the shot–reverse shot technique, the suturing of performance and audience, shapes the unruly crowd into a particular kind of public. The camera begins to pan a chastened crowd; they are now kneeling, hands folded in prayer, expressions of fear and awe on their faces. The monk's speech reinforces this connection through direct address to the crowd: "You there, who stand staring like a goat, will your mouth be twisted into the last unfinished gasp before nightfall? And you, woman, who bloom with life and self-satisfaction, will you pale and become extinguished before the morning dawn?" (39). The reactions of the principal characters direct the responses of the cinematic audience. The first cutaway offers an artistically composed three-shot of Block, the mute girl, and Jöns arrayed in a diagonal. Their proximity to the camera, determined by the diagonal, suggests three very different reactions in one shot. Block, who is closest to the camera, seems to have the least distance from what he observes. His close-up takes up the left side of the screen. Jöns, furthest away, almost in long shot, seems to have the most distance, with the mute girl in the middle.

Jöns's detached irony is given the final word: "Is that food for the minds of modern people? Do they really expect us to take them seriously?" (40). Habermas's public sphere is replaced by Debord's society of the spectacle as "the material reconstruction of the religious illusion" (Debord, par. 20). The flagellants' procession does not create a public sphere for "modern people"; it is thoroughly medieval. Although Jöns asks the question, it is really Block's question. Block seeks a Habermasian public sphere where rational debate and philosophical exchange could open spaces for him to find answers to the kinds of questions that have been raised by his participation in the Crusades and that, for the audience, have been raised by the prospect of annihilation. What he finds, however, is the society of the spectacle.

Public spectacle always involves audience complicity. If the unruly crowd of the acting troupe's performance has been chastened and domesticated by the spectacle of flagellants, they seem to take from it not proper repentance but only the manipulations of a theater of cruelty. Not only might the public be more interested in a corpse than in a naked woman, it participates in the spectacle, perhaps even to the point of producing the corpses it desires. The next scene opens inside the inn, which is now "full of people eating and drinking to forget their newly aroused fears of eternity" (45). Raval finds easy distraction in torturing and humiliating Jof into reproducing a grotesque parody of his earlier performance for a much more appreciative crowd. Having failed to sell Jof the bracelet he had previously stolen from a corpse, and discovering that the smith's wife has run off with Skat, Raval demands that Jof dance like a bear.[32] Jof's comic performance now takes a darker turn. Amid talk of heaven and hell, nervousness that "the Riders of the Apocalypse stand at the bend in the village road," Raval provides the inn patrons with a brief moment in which they can feel in control, if not of their world, at least on a smaller scale, of this piece of it. Raval plays both playwright and director, intimidating his actor, Jof, with threats of violence. The audience for this production is initially shown in a quick montage of reaction shots, close-ups that convey their sense of expectancy and perhaps even pent-up cruelty. As Raval forces the actor to perform by holding a lit torch to his feet, Jof becomes simultaneously monstrous and domesticated—a dancing bear. The patrons insinuate themselves into Jof's performance, banging their cups on the table in rhythm to the dancing, both audience and accompaniment. Once again, the crosscutting between performance and audience sutures the audience to the performance, implicating them in a particular kind of publicity, of capitulation to the spectacle. There is something positively *unheimlich* in Bergman's lighting of the shots of Jof dancing; his looming shadow creates a kind of blot. Even as the audience displaces its sense of dread onto Jof's humiliation by laughing and clapping, the shadow—a constantly moving black hole within the shot—seems an ominous reminder that soon they will be dancing with Death.

The scene of ideal private life that follows, the much-discussed feast of strawberries and milk that finally brings Block's retinue together with the "holy family" of actors, besides allowing Block to continue his combat with Death, provides a moment of respite before the series of grotesque pageants that will propel the narrative to its end. The first series of pageants provide comic relief. As Block's entourage, which now includes Jof, Mia, Mikael, and Plog, moves toward his castle, they are reunited with Skat and Plog's wife, Lisa, who have just returned from their tryst. To circumvent Plog's revenge, Skat enacts an elaborate and comic suicide, gleefully appreciated by all—"He's dead," exclaims Jof, "the deadest actor I've ever seen"—except Plog, who mourns, "I didn't mean it like that. . . . I was beginning to like him." Having effected his escape from the angry blacksmith, Skat climbs a tree, believing himself safe. Death enters and cuts down the tree, in a performance that mimics one of the church frescoes around which Bergman structured his film. Both Skat's faked suicide and his "real" death are marked by comic theatricality. Just as Raval manipulates the fears and pleasures of the tavern audience, making them complicit in Jof's torture, here Bergman manipulates the cinematic audience into desiring Skat's death. It is an hour into the film and we are ready to see Death in action. Skat has mocked Death in faking his suicide and so is made a performer in his own even more absurd demise. When Skat tries to negotiate ("No, I have my performance"), Death responds, "Cancelled—owing to death." Much of the pleasure in this scene derives from Bergman's comic metanarrative on theater professionals: "Is there no exemption for actors?" Skat begs. If Skat is an actor or director, Death is a producer. When you mock Death, Death mocks back.

The comic grotesquerie of Skat's "execution" is followed by a much more horrific one, a witch-burning in which Bergman directly ponders the function of audience involvement and complicity in the society of the spectacle. Jöns suggests that the townspeople might enjoy the "diversion," but the executioners indicate that witnessing might be tantamount to complicity, that it might make the audience susceptible to the devil who has possessed the girl. The cinematic audience, however, does watch the witch burn, forcing us to consider the voyeuristic pleasures derived from public execution—largely abolished in modern society—and our willingness to participate in so "medieval" a performance in which ecclesiastical spectacle creates social control. Bergman complicates the scene by clearly identifying the girl's execution with the crucifixion.

The references to Christ's death on the cross are accepted by its audience as parodic—both the witch and her executioners believe that the devil is being crucified and that this death will forestall the plague. For the cinematic audience, however, the references may recall the image of the suffering Christ interjected throughout Block's confession and reappearing in the procession of the flagellants. For Block this anticrucifixion is an empty gesture; it depicts only a madwoman's pathetic resignation to her role as a scapegoat in the society of the spectacle. In a sequence formally parallel to the earlier confessional scene—Block is separated from the witch by the bars on the side of the cart that echo the earlier confessional grate—Block repeats his questions, demanding ocular proof of some transcendent order. Can she see the devil? She tells him to look into her eyes, but he sees there only "an empty numb fear." She maintains the devil will protect her from the fire. When he demands to know if the devil himself told her this, she insists only, "I know." Her certainty, however, cannot satisfy Block's obsessive need for empirical proof of God's existence. There are no answers to Block's questions forthcoming from the society of the spectacle: not from the confessional, not from the flagellants, and least of all from a fourteen-year-old condemned witch. All are the instruments of the spectacle designed to satisfy voyeuristic desires as a mechanism of social control.

A rational public sphere cannot exist in the absence of a functioning community. Whereas the Habermasian public sphere promotes community, the society of spectacle, that is "social relations . . . mediated by images," creates social dislocation and fragmentation—anomie. Block's frustrations with the society of spectacle reach their apotheosis with the witch burning. Told that his time is up, Block demands that Death provide him with answers:

BLOCK. And you will divulge your secrets.
DEATH. I have no secrets.
BLOCK. So you know nothing.
DEATH. I have nothing to tell.

His questions go unanswered. Death is indifferent; questions of good and evil are not in his purview. All Block can do is resign himself to Death, and the plot moves swiftly to its consummation.

But before he dies, Block believes, as Tennyson's Ulysses says, "Some work of noble note may yet be done." In his final showdown with Death, witnessed as a vision by Jof, "He pretends to be clumsy and knocks the chess pieces over with the hem of his coat" (77), covering Jof and Mia's escape. But Bergman's ending seems a bit of bad faith. While Block and his entourage are killed, are we to believe that Jof and his family are spared because they are good? Peter Cowie describes Jof and Mia as "the faultless souls who survive to start a train of hope for humanity again" (144) as the "holy family" rides off into the dawn, the morning after. Bergman's own words validate this reading of the ending: "Whenever I feel in doubt or uncertain I take refuge in the vision of a simple and pure love. I find this love in those spontaneous women who . . . are the incarnation of purity" (quoted in Cowie, 145). As in *The Virgin Spring*, the nuclear family, isolated from any other forms of community, is offered as the antidote to contemporary social anomie. But if death is indifferent to good and evil, then Bergman's ending contradicts the philosophical modernism of the rest of the film; it presents in place of the meaninglessness of modern life—its alienation, despair, and anomie—a sentimental, romanticized, and false ending, expecting the cinematic audience to take this turn as well.

Bergman offers in *The Seventh Seal* both the organic and the barbaric Middle Ages. In Jof, Mia, and the painter he finds the artless art he attributes to the period, while in the cleric Raval, the flagellant procession, and the execution of the witch he finds its theater of cruelty. The film's final spectacle—Jof's vision of the dance of death, a distant silhouette wending its way toward the "dark lands"—returns us to the medieval, to the church frescoes that provide the inspiration for the film. The dance of death is an iconic shot, briefly glimpsed, but it suffices to direct the cinematic audience away from Antonius Block's persistent, troubling, and ultimately unanswerable questions—questions that critique the pervasive anomie of contemporary society—and plunge us into the realm of nostalgia, into a longing for the easy faith provided by the society of the spectacle. Perhaps it is our acceptance of this compelling image that allows for the film's final sleight of hand, the survival of the "holy family."

Fight the Future: *The Navigator*

At the end of *The Seventh Seal* Jof recounts his vision of the "Dance of Death": "I see them Mia! I see them! They are all there. The smith and Lisa and the knight and Raval and Jöns and Skat. And Death, the severe master, invites them to dance. He tells them to hold each other's hands and then they must tread the dance in a long row. And first goes the master with his scythe and hourglass" (82). The shot that Bergman created to illustrate this vision, on a whim at the end of a day's shooting when the lighting was just right, shows Death leading the dance in silhouette, identifiable by his scythe. This iconic tableau has been much parodied, most famously in Woody Allen's *Love and Death*. About two-thirds of the way through *The Navigator: A Mediaeval Odyssey*—Vincent Ward's 1988 film about a group of fourteenth-century Cumbrian miners who set out to tunnel to the other side of the world to save their village from the oncoming plague and end up in twentieth-century Auckland—Bergman's image of Death appears. Ward cinematically alludes to a 1987 television ad, created by Australia's National Advisory Council on AIDS (NACAIDS), that picks up on and parodies Bergman's iconic representation, particularly noting the Swedish director's conceit of playing games with Death.[33] The ad emphasizes the indiscriminateness of the AIDS epidemic by featuring a whole bowling league of skeletal grim reapers, identifiable by their black robes and hoods. Scythes in one hand, the reapers clutch bowling balls in the other. At the end of the bowling lane stand the tenpins—groups of men, women, and children at whom the reapers take aim. The spare carries the message with a grim humor. A reaper, having left one pin standing—a mother clutching her infant, the hope of reprieve written on her face—picks up the ball and nails the spare, sending the baby flying. Afterward, he pumps the air with his scythe in a gesture of victory. The ominous voice-over describes AIDS as an apocalyptic threat to the entire community: "At first only gays and IV drug users were being killed by AIDS, but now we know that any one of us could be devastated by it." If left unchecked, it will kill "more Australians than World War II."

The AIDS commercial appears in the Auckland section of the film, as the miners follow a small boy, Griffin, whose visions—fragmented images he struggles to weave into coherent narratives—guide them through the wonders and horrors of a terrifying and incomprehensible modern world. The group has lost its way in its quest to erect a cross on the top of a cathedral, when Griffin wanders in front of a bank of television monitors. Mesmerized, he watches the replicated images he cannot comprehend, a metonymy for the bewildering visions he cannot quite bring into focus. On the monitors a hawk swoops down on a fleeing rabbit, a talking head discusses New Zealand's 1987 creation of a Nuclear Free Zone, and, finally, the last frames of the "Grim Reaper" AIDS commercial appear. Ward was attracted to this ad because of its "medieval death figures": "it had such a lovely feel to it. . . . It was a really well realized piece of short cinema" (Ward, "A Dialogue with Discrepancy," 14). In this brief encounter with the contemporary world—the entire sequence lasts only a minute and a half—Ward encapsulates the major themes of his film.[34] The images move from death and destruction in the natural world to the threat of nuclear annihilation to the devastation created by global pandemic. The scene subtly contrasts an almost Habermasian belief in the interconnectedness of community with the Debordian society of the spectacle created by advanced capitalism; Ward suspends us between the two. We live and die together; that is the point of the AIDS commercial and the point made by the talking head: "There is no refuge, no pocket, no escape from the real world." Yet capitalism isolates and alienates us, like the bank of identical monitors, each replicating exactly the same image closed off in its own little box, a perfect trope for the society of the spectacle. The scene calls on product placement (the bank of monitors are part of a Samsung display, and the logo is prominently featured), advertising, and mass media to disseminate its message. "The devil's in every window," insists Searle, one of the expedition's leaders, on seeing the monitors; Debord could not have said it better. Capitalism and the regime of the image strand the individual within an alienated existence, and at the same time technology extends the global reach of our communities to the point where New Zealand's attempt to distance itself from American militarism seems quixotic.

In a number of ways Ward's film enters into a dialogue with and remakes Bergman's *The Seventh Seal* thirty years later, creating a "dance of death" more suited to a postmodern, postcolonial, postnuclear, postindustrial, and post-AIDS world. In this world the sources of potential annihilation have multiplied, like the mechanized hydras Connor encounters on his journey to the bell tower, while the sources of social cohesion have further eroded; culture has become fragmented, and the individual is left stranded within the regime of the image, isolated and alienated. Ward's film globalizes Bergman's vision. If *The Seventh Seal* takes place in an indeterminate space, it is most definitely Swedish space—almost provincially European. Ward's English miners, themselves provincials, travel (at least imaginatively) to the other side of the world, to the antipodes, and emerge in contemporary postcolonial space—the very space that has been violently appropriated by their countrymen in the 540 years intervening between 1348 and 1988. With an almost Marxist faith in the ability of workers to form their own communities without either the guidance or protection of aristocrats or bosses, *The Navigator* repudiates *The Seventh Seal's* ending, especially Bergman's valorization of the idealized but isolated nuclear family, offering us instead a Habermasian vision of communal cooperation and individual sacrifice as the solution to twentieth-century social anomie.

The Navigator adopts an idiosyncratic narrative structure. While conventional Hollywood filmmaking tells a story through the juxtaposition of shots (montage), in representing the boy Griffin's visions, Ward provides a succession of maddeningly disconnected images that cannot be resolved into any narrative coherence simply through passive viewing. Ward's cinematic tactics demand that viewers perform the same kind of narrative work the visionary must undertake. We must discover the context and the set of connections that will resolve a series of disconnected shots into a coherent narrative. Like Griffin, we will not have the information necessary to complete that work until the end of the film. In the film, vision is always fragmentary, partial, and so open to misinterpretation and misreading—in Griffin's case fatal misreading. To be sure, fragmentation is a defining feature of postmodern narrative, and Ward's postmodern style contrasts with Bergman's modernist sensibilities, but it also suggests how visions must work; they arrive not as tidy, lucid narratives (like the visions Jof relates) but as frustratingly partial glimpses of alien worlds whose incoherence bewilders and frightens.

The film's opening "swirls around maddeningly," in the words of one online reviewer. Ward eschews conventional exposition,[35] plunging us immediately into Griffin's visions by alternating black-and-white close-ups of the child (at this point the viewer does not know the child's name or his relation to the plot) with a series of otherworldly images: a moon covered by clouds, a nighttime sky, water, a torch falling into the abyss, men operating an engine to break rock, water bubbling as something rises up from it, a church tower, the child blindfolded walking, hands climbing a ladder, someone falling from the tower, a tower stairwell, a glove floating through the air, a hooded figure raising a Celtic cross on a steeple, a figure in water pushing away a coffin, a metal Celtic cross submerged in water. This series of crosscut images goes on for the first five minutes of the film, for the most part with no dialogue or underscoring, only the Foley sound that magnifies ambient noises, making them seem portentous: the whoosh of the falling torch, the lapping of the water, the blowing wind. At best, the crosscutting might connect these random images to the repeated figure of the child, identifying him as the source or recipient of the images. But the montage does not allow the viewer to string those images together into a coherent vision; the work of the film will be to create a narrative that can fill in the gaps to explain these images. The viewer must undertake, with the child and his followers, the process of learning, composing, and retelling the story that will forge these disconnected images into a coherent account, a narrative that can protect the village from the approaching Black Death.

For the viewer willing to make the journey, Ward manages to fashion a compelling tale out of these images. Avoiding the usual style of filmic medievalism— "Robin Hood myths, myths of the wealthy, and legendary figures, Arthurian figures" (Ward, "A Dialogue with Discrepancy," 11)—he offers a grim black-and-white frozen wasteland of snow, mountains, water, and mines. The film's exposition begins once the boy wakes, standing in the freezing water as other children pelt him with snowballs and mock him: "Our Griff gets out of bed with angels in his head" (4).[36] We learn that Griffin is frequently visited with these waking dreams: "that's the fourth time this week" (4). The villagers are superstitious. They believe in relics like St. Augustine's fingerbowl and feathers from the Archangel Gabriel, believe that witches' spikes can protect them from ill fortune or that the pilgrimage Griffin dreams to make an offering in a distant church can save them from plague: "In my dream we were tunneling . . . through to the farthest part of the earth. . . . We reached the cathedral and placed the spike," Griffin tells the miners (17).

Ward uses this isolated mining village to examine how communities survive extreme trauma. On the one hand, Ward heavily idealizes his community of Cumbrian miners. Their society seamlessly integrates children, the old, and both the physically and mentally handicapped; one critic describes it as "collective, egalitarian, democratic" (Campbell, 16). Even the disjointed ravings of the visionary boy, Griffin, become an integral part of the communal exchange of ideas. On the other hand, news of the oncoming plague hints at the social dislocations that accompany the disease. Connor, one of the few members of the village to have seen what lies beyond it, reports on the cultural catastrophe he has witnessed in the "outside world" in terms that echo Boccaccio's descriptions:

> I've seen the pilgrims. . . . I've seen so many bodies that there was not enough
> of the living to bury the dead. I've seen monks refuse the rites to the dying and
> the mobs chase them from their abbeys. Is it these same monks that head west
> as pilgrims . . . ? There are people no more than animals. You can trust no one.
> Children begged me for food, but I didn't dare go near them. They had black
> boils under their armpits, the size of shillings and they pretended they didn't
> have the plague! The churches are empty. (14)

The epidemic has undermined all institutions of cultural exchange and cohesion. The very center of the medieval world has been subverted—church officials refuse their duties. Nobody goes to church. Communities have been shattered as their members scatter, attempting to outrun the plague—invariably taking it with them as they flee. Even the notion of pilgrimage has been turned upside down; instead of a journey toward transcendence, the word is now used to describe the inexorable forward motion of disease carriers to their horrific deaths. Before, Connor could not have imagined his isolated village of Cumbrian miners behaving in such a fashion, but his travels have given him reason to believe in the inevitability of the plague's corrosive effect: "We have a month, maybe two, to be with the ones we love" (14). He seems to fear the social chaos far more than the possibility of death.

Connor's worst fears are realized when a shipload of these "pilgrims" attempts to land at his village. These could just as well be foreign workers threatening the jobs of the miners, but plague exacerbates fears of the alien, and the result is armed hostility. The stage directions in the screenplay point to the extremity of social unraveling:

> The villagers of Gosford are staving the boat away from the shore with long poles. Others hurl missiles, and some of the boat people are responding. Someone wades out with a torch, brandishing it. A sudden leap of flames silhouettes the mast of the refugee boat. It flares briefly as the black figures on board rush to quench the fire. (15–16)

This breakdown of social institutions, of human charity, in the face of epidemic is problematized by Ward's uses of the words *refugees* and *boat people* to describe the victims. Such references hint at the flotillas of Vietnamese, Cuban, and Haitian immigrants who, during the 1970s and 1980s, sought sanctuary from brutal and repressive regimes. The immigration policy of the Cumbrian miners toward the wretched refuse threatening their shores—and the refugees constitute a very real threat, as evidenced by their plague-ravaged bodies—compounds the human tragedy that has befallen them. The apparently kind and open society becomes closed and intolerant; the peaceful camp becomes hostile and militaristic. Ward's camera lingers on stricken, drowning women and children. This is an unequal fight fostered by a society determined to protect its borders. If Ward's film evokes an idealistic nostalgia for the communitarian values of the Middle Ages, it balances that nostalgia with an appreciation of the darker side of such communities: their determination to expel by whatever means necessary threats from the outside world. The plague both poisons and intensifies community, reminding us that the tightly integrated communities we idealize are always built on the abjection of the other, the "not-us." The miners' willingness to destroy the diseased refugees results from their understanding of contagion, but it seems likely to be a futile gesture. They imagine the plague as "the evil [that] keeps striding forward with each full moon": "its full moon," says Connor, "bears contagion before it like a sack. At sunrise she lets it fall—on us."

Yet the villager's superstition provides space for Griffin's visions of redemption to serve as a focal point for the community. It enables them to believe that together in one night they can make a journey to the other side of the world and

raise a spike on a great church, an offering of "Cumbrian copper" that will forestall death. Such a journey, like Dante's great journey, can only be undertaken
imaginatively. Critics of the film have taken Ward to task for offering medieval answers to contemporary problems; the film, they complain, offers "fanciful (childish, religious, magic) solutions" to some of the most serious social and political
issues of our day: "the ignorance, fear and superstition experienced by the miners," writes Barbra Luby, "is hardly likely to be relevant to those trying to be more
responsible about the management of AIDS, when knowledge, understanding,
acceptance and informed resistance might indicate a more reasoned approach to
the phenomenon" (quoted in Campbell, 15). But Russell Campbell suggests another approach to the film's mysticism, its "obsessive repetition of images" that
seem like "necromantic fetishes" (15). The film deliberately short-circuits the
kind of commonsense thinking Luby calls for, refusing rational deliberation in
order to explore our collective cultural unconscious. Citing Herbert Marcuse,
Campbell argues that the film shares the belief of the surrealists in unlocking the
unconscious as a "revolutionary process by which the thralldom of established
modes of thinking and living could be overthrown" (15). The successful accomplishment of this ludicrous task does not constitute the talisman against the
plague; rather it is the imaginative process of undertaking Griffin's quest, of solv-
ing the problem he sets collectively.

   Ward creates a set of preternatural connections between the two distinct
chronotopes (medieval Cumbria and modern New Zealand) that give the film a
mystical quality, no doubt the very quality that has raised critics' hackles. At the
beginning of the film, the visionary child Griffin dreams of "a big fish—evil—a
queenfish" that turns out to be a submarine called the *Queenfish*. The church they
find in twentieth-century Auckland is coincidentally awaiting a cross for its
steeple, and the mold for that cross has already been cast by a smith whose name
just happens to be Smithy. *The Navigator* disrupts the process Eco describes as
"dreaming the Middle Ages"; instead, the Middle Ages dreams us (or, more accurately, we dream it dreaming us). The film stages an intervention into our routine
ways of experiencing the world. To understand what consolation or solution the
film might offer for contemporary forms of social anomie requires that we focus
not on the latent or manifest content of this strange collective dream but on the
dream-work, what Freud considered to be the "essence of dreaming" and the explanation of its peculiar nature; we must explore the processes by which the unconscious comes into being. The collective dream of Griffin, Connor, and the
other miners explores the cultural unconscious of the West's infatuation with its

image of itself, and if, as we argued in chapter 1, the medieval is the repressed of the West's self-representation, then that dream must uncover that repression.

The central conceit of the film, which Ward admits he created "for the sheer gall of it" (9), connects the fourteenth century and the twentieth by means of a tunnel through the earth, a child's myth of digging in the sand. Ward inverts the conventional formula of time travel movies in which a modern protagonist travels back to the Middle Ages to flaunt the superiority of modern technology to ignorant preindustrial peoples.[37] *The Navigator*'s conceit of the tunnel intervenes in modernist fantasies of the Middle Ages as the West's origins—the time before modernity—and that against which modernity has been fashioned. The tunnel effects a rift in the discourses of modernity that use the Middle Ages as "a kind of Jurassic Park," a place to smuggle in "an ideal of totality" that we disavow in the modern (Strohm). The myth of the Middle Ages is that it is simultaneously simple and whole, backward and barbaric. Instead, Ward creates a Middle Ages of "motile signs, 'category confusions,' representational swerves and slippages, partial and competing and . . . irreconcilable narrations" (Strohm). The nighttime journey the miners take to raise a copper cross on the cathedral steeple imaginatively occupies the liminal spaces between the full moon and sunrise, night and day, past and present, heaven and hell, medieval and modern.

The tunnel connects two chronotopes normally thought of as occupying opposite sides of a geographical, as well as temporal, split to interrogate yet another myth of the Middle Ages as the "imaginary space of the Third World," the atemporal site of postcolonial "people without history" (Biddick, "Review of *The Navigator*," 1152).[38] Ward suggests that he had something like this in mind: "[white] New Zealanders are of Celtic origin. . . . They came here from the potato famines in Ireland, the Highland Clearances in Scotland. . . . We have as much claim to the middle ages as the English do, or the French, or anybody else" (Ward, "A Dialogue with Discrepancy," 10–11). But what his account represses is the work of colonization that brought his Celtic ancestors to the other side of the world. White New Zealanders' claims to the Middle Ages may be unassailable, but their claim to the land of New Zealand is more suspect; Ward does not probe that claim—at least not consciously. Those who were colonized in England (Celtic Cumbrians) became, in New Zealand, the colonizers, who, in the film, face their ancestors. The technological advances of the Middle Ages—mining and metalworking included—are revealed as the motor of the colonial enterprise when the film brings white New Zealanders and their ancestors together. The two timespaces of the film are connected by the long reach of British imperialism, which may be recognized only by the presence of a single Maori among the foundry workers the miners encounter.

By disrupting the foundational myths of medievalism as a site of rupture between medieval and modern, the film inverts other common tropes of medievalism that attend the time-travel formula—the valuations of urban and rural, center and periphery, nature and technology. The miners' journey describes not the movement from the geographical center of the metropole to the colonial periphery, from the city to "nature," that was the trajectory of British colonialism, but a journey from one margin to another, from rural England to an urban New Zealand that seems a haven surrounded by a hostile and menacing natural landscape. In fourteenth-century Cumbria, Ward has chosen a site that was undoubtedly as marginal, as isolated, and as far-flung to the fourteenth-century European as New Zealand today seems to Europeans and Americans. Cumbria sits at the border between England and Scotland, the desolate marches that in the fourteenth century must have seemed like postcolonial wild space. Medieval maps representing Jerusalem as the center of the civilized world situate England in the far-flung north at the edges of the map. In fact, one map in a fifteenth-century manuscript of the chronicler John Hardyng locates Scotland just south of hell.[39] Ward links these two marginal geographic spaces—rural Cumbria and urban Auckland—as a means of highlighting the historical continuities between them (visually represented by the tunnel the miners dig to connect them)—in Cumbria war, disease, and economic change; in Auckland nuclear holocaust, AIDS, and economic downsizing—suggesting that the similarities are at least as significant as the discontinuities: "People felt then as they feel now, . . . that their world was under serious threat, and that they couldn't do much about it. The devastation of the Black Death combined with vast wars has not been matched until this century. . . . Everything that we take for granted in the twentieth century, you can see its beginnings in the Middle Ages" (Ward, "A Dialogue with Discrepancy," 10).

Once they reach their destination, the miners discover that the other side of the world is at once astonishing, beautiful, and terrible. This sense of discontinuity and defamiliarization is, of course, one of the conventions of the time-travel formula, and the audience shares the appreciation of wonder with the travelers, who are awed and delighted by the beauty of the modern metropolis, the city of Auckland illuminated, shimmering, in the night. Martin marvels, "It makes sense. Anything flat's got two sides, and if the evil was our side then surely God's goodness is—It'll be God's city all right." But, there is evil enough on the other side; this is, after all, as Martin suggests, the medieval myth of the world upside down. The miners' nightmarish encounters crossing a busy roadway, rowing across the water to be attacked by a nuclear submarine—a sea monster rising up out of the sea—encountering monstrous cranes and trains, convince some members of the expedition that they have landed in a very different place. Searle counters, "This doesn't look like God's work to me." The obstacle of the highway requires that the miners rethink their notions of community—they are going to have to split up—forcing them to negotiate some forms of twentieth-century isolation and alienation; it is after they separate that Griffin has his encounter with the TV monitors. The travelers' terror and their sense of helplessness in the face of technology are compounded when Griffin is struck by a hit-and-run driver, as good an image as any of the anomic condition of the twentieth century. Only a chance meeting with a group of foundry workers reinvigorates their belief in community and emboldens them to continue their journey. With the rescue of the travelers by the foundry workers, Ward reverses the clichéd conventions of the formula to stress the continuities between past and present. What creates community between medieval and modern laborers and enables the successful accomplishment of the quest is not, however, the Habermasian public sphere of reasoned discourse and public debate, but work.

The meeting of the medieval miners and the Auckland foundry workers provides one of the most striking set pieces of the film. The miners arrive at the foundry by, literally, following their noses. At first, the foundry men are unsure what to make of the strangers; are they "Hare Krishna"? "Well, it looks like they've been in the bush awhile," one of them says (34), falling back on that European mind-set that associates the colonized "primitive" with the medieval.[40] The film deliberately links the British colonization of New Zealand to the development of industrial technologies like mining and metalworking in medieval Cumbria. Such technologies also fueled medieval warfare and made miners, according to Ward, among the most privileged of medieval workers: "medieval miners had a position that other feudal peasants did not have. . . . They had effectively 'union' rights . . . and they were better paid [than other workers]. . . . Armament metal was essential, and for metal you needed miners. So they had a very privileged position in society" ("A Dialogue with Discrepancy," 10–11). Ward relied heavily on Jean Gimpel's *The Medieval Machine* for historical information on medieval miners. Gimpel stresses historical continuities, arguing that medieval Europe experienced its own industrial revolution and shared many of the same economic issues, including concerns over working conditions, that dogged the Industrial Revolution of the nineteenth century and continue to affect laborers even today.

The fourteenth-century miners are able to connect with twentieth-century foundry workers through their labor even though they do not share a common language. They are linked by their knowledge of their craft, which they know with all their senses. Griffin finds the foundry, as Connor instructs him, by smell, because, however different a foundry may look in this alien land, it will smell the same. Amidst all of the distractions of the new, the disorientation that follows from the barrage of visual stimuli, the miners are able to use their knowledge to focus by cutting off sight and relying on other sensory input (as later Griffin will have to be blindfolded and navigate to find the church by sound).

When they first arrive in Auckland, the travelers believe they will spot the cathedral easily since it should be the tallest building in the city: "nothing's higher than a church spire." However, it proves to be far more difficult than they expected; skyscrapers—urban monuments to corporate capitalism—obscure their vision. In the twentieth century, capital has replaced religion as the ordering institution of social life, giving value to labor and aspiration (this of course is Debord's complaint). The foundry workers are facing traumas of their own; capitalism has failed them as religion has failed the miners. Under capitalism labor exists only to create surplus value; it is alienated. Capitalism creates transient communities of workers that hold together only as long as they are supported by capital; this particular community of laborers is being dislocated by the economic calculation of late capitalism. The founders will be unemployed as their jobs move elsewhere, where cheaper labor will create greater surplus value.

The miners provide the foundry workers with an opportunity to consider their own economic obsolescence in the light of the church's displacement by capital in contemporary culture. The medievals understand the cross they want cast as a gift, one of many gifts designed to ward off evil that would be brought by pilgrims to a great church. Martin says, "Surely people have come, as we did, with gifts? From across the world." The foundry workers are bemused: "Gift," Smithy replies. "You'd probably be the first." When the miners ask the founders to cast the spike, the foundry workers misrecognize the cross as a mold they have already created but have never poured:

> TOM. . . . must be for the same church spire—but we were going to pour it
> two months ago. We've run out of money—(Crooks his thumb and finger
> in the shape of a coin.) The Church hasn't paid us. The full casting bed's
> been stacked here for months while the Church scratches around for
> enough money to buy the metal. (37)

This information mystifies the miners and not because the very mold they need has somehow mysteriously been there all along. Martin is shocked:

MARTIN. The Church . . . is poor?

TOM. Well, just like any other business . . . if people don't like what you're selling.

MARTIN. Selling!! (37)

What the medievals cannot understand is the shift capitalism effects from an economy of gift-giving to an economy of exchange. In the former, with which they would be familiar, wealth would have been determined by how much could be given away; in the latter it is determined by how much surplus value can be accumulated. Under the regime of capital, the church has become just another business, and a poor one at that. While the foundry workers are obsolete because they don't generate enough surplus value, the church is obsolete because, as a remnant of a gift economy, it doesn't generate any.

A night with these weird strangers who have popped up inexplicably on their doorstep offers these displaced founders a reinvigorated love of their craft and a sense of the possibilities beyond surplus value that their labor offers. In a speech included in the script but cut from the film, the aptly named Smithy muses, "I think it's something we'd almost forgotten . . . love of the trade. It'd make you cry. The night they close us down is the night—I dunno—something comes along to show you how wonderful it could have been" (38). The process of casting the spike and erecting it on the church spire offers the foundry workers a glimpse of a very different kind of community—a community bound not by the surplus value work creates but by the joy of work and creativity, the results of which can only be given as a gift. Miners and foundry workers together share a moment of delight when Smithy announces "good copper" and Searle concurs, "Cumbrian copper."

The medievals understand the process of forging metal and take to the refinements of modern industrial processes far more quickly than they do to the Foster's beer with which they toast the forging of the cross. Ward spends a great deal of screen time taking the audience through the process of metalworking in some detail—extracting the metal from the ore, refining it, pouring the mold, and cooling it—in a montage that suggests conviviality through Celtic music, laughter, and smiles amid flying sparks. The culmination of the montage, the pouring of the copper into the mold is a visual delight that evokes a kind of religious awe: Martin even recites a Latin prayer. The workers' collective knowledge and the pleasures of collaborative labor—values incomprehensible to capitalism—smooth over the initial differences between the groups and convince the foundry workers to finish the job by helping to raise the spike.

The moment the miners plant their spike, they are returned to medieval Cumbria, and the audience discovers that all—miners and viewers alike—have been party to a collective dream, which, through our labor, we have successfully worked out. But some portions of the puzzle remain unresolved—Griffin had promised that someone would die, and throughout the film we are encouraged to believe that person will be Connor. Amid the celebration in the mining town, those pieces fall into place. Griffin realizes, as we do, that a sacrifice still needs to be made; we still need to make sense of the image of the coffin being sent off on the water. It turns out that Connor has brought the plague home from his many travels after all, and, while he kept himself from all the others, including his pregnant wife, he has infected his younger brother. Griffin will be the victim, the scapegoat. The labor of collectively using the imagination to find a solution to the problems of both medieval plague and modern anomie has been insufficient to save the navigator.

But does Griffin's sacrificial death—suggested by the image of Connor pushing his coffin out to sea—really, as Griffin claims, avert the plague? Griffin insists the infection won't break loose (although we find that hard to believe after viewing the shot of Griffin waving his shirt around in triumph). What sense are we to make of Griffin's final words: "I want them to know the threat is gone . . . the village safe. You'll tell them. You'll bring them around, make them believe my story. They must. You'll tell them. . . . That's when they'll believe it" (75). As he is dying, he seems less fearful of the disease than of the threat of social disruption of the community that it brings. The job he bequeaths to Connor is to maintain the community that has been woven together through his vision. The success of the quest lies not in having erected the cross. It is not the villagers' belief in religion or in mysticism that saves them but the process of working together creatively to solve a problem. It is the journey they take and not the end result, the willingness of individuals to sacrifice their own interests for a common good.

Fashioning the Middle Ages as a jumping-off point to explore the causes and repercussions of twentieth-century anomie, Bergman and Ward create films that are visually arresting and intellectually compelling. Nevertheless, both in their style and in their substance, *The Virgin Spring, The Seventh Seal,* and *The Navigator* are also foreboding, appealing primarily to a coterie audience of cineastes. While art house patrons gather in very small groups to share anxieties about the uneasy relationships created by capitalist culture, Cineplex audiences seem more interested in celebrating fantasies about the role of the autonomous individual in a consumerist world. It is for this group—consisting primarily of male adolescents—that Hollywood expends most of its energies and nearly all of its capital. It is from this group that the greatest financial reward may be received. In our final chapter we will discuss how the Middle Ages has become, for the film industry, just another device to manipulate materialist desire in the young.

Chapter Ten

Forever Young

The Teen Middle Ages

T he spin-off music video for Brian Helgeland's 2001 film *A Knight's Tale* features Robbie Williams and Queen performing the old Queen stan- dard "We Are the Champions" (dir. Evan Bernard), an anthem imme- diately recognizable to anyone who even casually follows modern sporting events. The video sets a rock concert in medieval London. Intercutting clips from the film into the concert, this gimmick creates a series of equivalencies between the medieval jousting knight, the rock star, and the sports hero that makes the knight the object of the kind of celebrity enjoyed in our culture by both popular musi- cians and athletes. The equivalency suggests that all three—the rock star, the ath- lete, and, by analogy, the knight—are interchangeable commodities in a com- modity culture, all material boys living in a material world. In the video fans cross a bridge over the Thames, passing both ticket scalpers ("Who needeth one?") and souvenir sellers hawking the concert "tabard," the medieval version of the T-shirt. In voice-over an announcer proclaims, "Art thou ready to ruckus!" There are goth maidens screaming, "We love thee Robbie," and young men dressed in medieval attire, including a makeshift medieval beer hat. The concert itself is held in a torch-lit room. Bouncers dressed as knights remove screaming groupies from the stage area and offensive jesters from the after-party. The lead guitarist wields a six-string "axe" (literally), and backup singers are dressed as monks. Robbie Williams sports leather breeches and a chain-mail wife-beater. There is even an "interview" during which Williams, the beleaguered medieval showman, complains of having been misunderstood, his statements "taken out of context." Paraphrasing John Lennon's notorious 1966 remark comparing the Beatles with Jesus, he claims, "I never said we were better than the king. I said we were more popular." The scalpers, vendors, groupies, beer hat, bouncers, interviews, and even embarrassing off-the-cuff remarks are all necessary components of that complex web of exchanges that constitutes the performance, whether musical or sporting, for twenty-first-century audiences.

Neither teen movies nor teen culture are new phenomena; a distinct teen culture as we know it was born out of the same postwar prosperity that drove baby boomers' parents to the suburbs.[1] The Robbie Williams/Queen music video provides a starting point for exploring the key features of contemporary youth culture that structure the representation of the medieval in the two teen movies we examine in this final chapter. The most obvious feature is the video's participation in the set of practices we call rock and roll. Todd Gitlin, in his attempts to define the zeitgeist of the 1960s, writes that "nothing influenced me, or the baby-boom generation as a whole, as much as movies, music, and comics did" (31); and, of the three, it is probably the music—rock music—that has become both then and now the defining feature of youth culture. Rock music is youth culture, no less today than for Gitlin's baby boomers. "Rock announced: Being young means being able to feel rock. Whatever it is you're in, kid, you're not alone; you and your crowd are where it's at, spirited or truculent or misunderstood, and anyone who doesn't get it is, well, square" (Gitlin, 37). Rock's ascendancy was fueled by the availability in the 1950s of new consumer electronics like television and the transistor radio, both of which helped to create the teenager as a category of consumer at the same time that they offered a focal point for the collective fantasies—and rebellions—of a generation. Rock music has always, but even more so since the 1980s, been relentlessly driven by technology and consumerism; it is material culture par excellence. Its cultural landscape has been transformed by cable television and MTV, computers and video games, boom boxes, Walkmans, CDs and iPods, VCRs and DVDs, the Internet and cell phones, email, text messaging, and instant messenger.

Since the debut of MTV in 1981 music videos have become a lucrative marketing device, exploiting the synergy between the music teenagers listen to and the movies they watch. Initially, music videos were produced as advertisements for records. They have, however, become central participants in the contemporary teen economy, selling everything from music and celebrity to fashion, movies, and new electronic devices. Music videos have become a mediating technology between popular music and popular film. These days, however, it is more difficult to tell the marketing device from the product, as horizontal integration (the integration within single corporations of various media—movies, television, music, video games, radio, and Internet) increasingly shapes teen culture.[2] This corporate strategy has radically transformed the nature of rock performances. Since the 1980s, visuals have come to dominate even the music, which is increasingly relegated in performance to lip-synching, the better to achieve in live performance the perfection of the video (DeCurtis, 4). And as directors of music videos turn to making feature-length films, the styles developed for the music video insinuate themselves into those films.

Brian Helgeland self-consciously incorporates the aesthetic apparatus of the rock video, as well as the horizon of expectations of the audience he is targeting, into *A Knight's Tale*. The film even replicates the style of the Queen video in its opening credits, which are played over a rendition of the band's "We Will Rock You," the companion piece to "We Are the Champions" and a song that virtually distills the "performance" of fandom in modern sports. The tournament in which the film's protagonist, William Thatcher, will impersonate his master is represented as a stadium event, but even that designation does not suggest the extent to which it is not a single performance but a whole series of interrelated and routinized performances that, like the imaginary medieval rock concert, involve participants, audience, officials, patrons, and vendors.[3] In the opening credits the camera watches the crowd, not the jousters. The signature drumbeat of "We Will Rock You" is heard as an overlay in the sound track, even before the cut to the tournament crowd in a stadium, which we recognize as a stadium precisely because the people in it behave as people in stadiums routinely do. In *A Knight's Tale* rock music is not used primarily to set the tone, to provide a vague historical context (a technique George Lucas pioneered in his 1973 teen movie, *American Graffiti*), or to be performed diegetically as in a musical. Rather it is brought into the action and, in several scenes, such as this one, structures both action and camera movement. As in the rock video, everything in this scene is synchronized with the music, which serves to link the celebrity of the sports hero to that of the jousting knight. In the establishing shot the crowd pounds the stands and claps in time to the drumbeat. The knights join in by clapping their gauntlets and banging their breastplates. As the camera pans the crowd, the characters we associate with modern sporting events appear. A herald is "cheerleading." There are four drunken, overweight, middle-aged male fans, naked from the waist up. The aristocrats, set apart from the crowd in their "skyboxes," look bored and annoyed at the crowd's antics. There are children with painted faces waving pennants, a girl dancing to the music, a "security" guard singing along; the crowd performs the wave. Eventually even the aristocrats get caught up in the beat of the music, as the patron begins tapping his fingers and singing, and one contestant waves his fist in time to the music. This Bakhtinian carnival of performances overshadows any actual jousting. This montage is a veritable cultural study of the "signs" constituting the modern entertainment industry, easily read by anyone who has ever attended a rock concert or a football game. Without the music, however, without Queen's "We Will Rock You," the scene would make little or no sense. As in a music video, the song is the glue that holds the visual sequence together.

It is all wildly anachronistic, and its anachronism is wildly beside the point; it would be churlish even to point it out. "Whatever century you're in, you need an awesome soundtrack," exclaims the advertising for the film's CD. A feature that marks both the music video and the film—and indeed is a source of much of their humor—is the relentless mixing of cultural signs from different historical periods. Enjoyment of the macaronic language of "Art thou ready to ruckus," the silly beer hat, and the medieval spectators' participation in the 1970s Queen anthem depends on one's ability to read against the grain of the conventional historical time produced by academic histories. The film's comedy springs from a view of the past in which the medieval—far from constituting the break between the modern and what came before—can proleptically anticipate the key features of contemporary teen culture. This view of history structures the film to the tiniest detail; witness the establishing shots of Paris and London. The observant viewer may detect faint, chiaroscuro images of the Eiffel Tower and the Eye of London. The very faintness of the images (London is shot at night and the Eye is almost completely enveloped in clouds) in what are, after all, constructed models, suggests that the filmmakers went to a lot of trouble to produce these anachronisms and then to hide them; they were quite deliberately creating a joke that implies an attitude toward anachronism that might best be described as "dialogic," in Bakhtin's sense of the word, "the intense interaction and struggle between one's own and another's word, . . . in which [these words] oppose . . . or interanimate one another" (*The Dialogic Imagination*, 354). In both film and video, medieval culture and contemporary teen culture jostle one another to produce a visual polyglossia that includes numerous such jokes.

Eighteen Forever

Jokes like these highlight the presentism of teen culture, in which past and future are always subordinated to the now. The linguist Émile Benveniste has pointed out that a speaker's present is "the axis around which all of our subjective as well as linguistic sense of time is organized," but in youth culture there is, to paraphrase Gertrude Stein, no "then then." There is *only* now. In the logic of teen culture, to be young is to be in the here and now.[4] The past is completely flattened out, the future a blank. Undoubtedly, this focus on the present moment serves the ends of consumerism, creating the desire for the most up-to-date fashion, music, and merchandise, but it also reflects the liminality of adolescence, that period between childhood restriction and adult responsibility. There can be no past or future because both imply the inevitability of growing old for adolescents (not to mention for nostalgic adults who create rock videos and teen movies or who write about them) who desire to remain, in the words of the alternative rock band Brand New, "eighteen forever." Their single, "Soco Amaretto Lime," sums up the extreme presentist bias of youth culture. Songwriter Jesse Lacey sings of teen years marked by cool indifference to everything that has been done and said, where continuous revelry—the song's title refers to a potent drink made with Southern Comfort and Amaretto—replaces any obligation to history. Why listen to adult authorities, Lacey asks, when they are just jealous of your youth and vitality? In a YouTube video of the song, Brand New's Birmingham, England, audience provides word-for-word accompaniment, forming a community living for and in the moment.[5] As with Cher in Amy Heckerling's 1995 *Clueless,* the worst thing one can say about something in teen culture is that it is "so five minutes ago." This perhaps explains why the Middle Ages is barely representable in teen culture.[6]

In the "We Are the Champions" video, one of the few that actually does admit a past, although not one we would recognize as historical by any means, time collapses to allow both the Middle Ages and the 1970s ("We Are the Champions" was first released in 1977) to serve the contemporary teen marketplace. Robbie Williams becomes both a medieval knight and Freddy Mercury, the deceased lead singer of Queen, but he is always Robbie Williams, the bad boy of pop music. The gesture, characteristic of teen culture's attitude toward history, appropriates and annihilates the past. It mocks the idea of a stable identity authorized by a documentable and documented history. It offers a view of temporality and history that, in the words of Carla Freccero, "does not necessarily take seriously the pieties of the discipline that would require the solemn, even dour, marshalling of empirical evidence to prove its point" (3). Like the sensibility of the "queer" that is Freccero's subject, teen culture draws on intertextuality and anachronism that "proceed otherwise than according to a presumed logic of cause and effect, anticipation and result; and otherwise than according to a presumed logic of the 'done-ness' of the past" (5).[7] Williams channels (or channel surfs) the past, usurping all possible celebrities, even John Lennon, moving toward a place where both he and the members of Queen can profit from something akin to identity theft (the paranoia par excellence of the twenty-first century). Reproducing *A Knight's Tale*'s play on identity theft, Bernard's music video not only has Williams replacing Freddy Mercury; it also replaces the surviving members of the original band with younger performers who mimic playing the instruments. Though it is likely that the audio dubbing was done by Brian May and Roger Taylor, these original members of the band seem to be unrepresentable within the *visual* iconography of the rock video precisely because of their age.

The symbiotic relationship formed when Robbie Williams teams up with Queen to perform their signature song highlights a third key feature of youth culture: the complex web of exchanges necessary for the creation and maintenance of celebrity. Teen culture is relentlessly performative, creating what one commentator has described as an "alienating superstar juggernaut" (DeCurtis, 3). The creation and selling of an image is today an essential component of celebrity that relies heavily on horizontal integration, here of the particular celebrity—whether rock star, movie star, or athlete—who may be involved in videos, video compilations, long-form videos, movies, corporate sponsorships, product endorsements, T-shirts, book deals, interviews, television appearances, movie tie-ins, songs for sound tracks (DeCurtis, 5). The usual institutions for fashioning stardom—fan clubs, fan magazines, fan mail, appearances—have all been ratcheted up on the Internet, where fan-maintained Web sites abound and where you can talk to your favorite star in specialty chat rooms.[8] The music video cover of "We Are the Champions" becomes part of the celebrity machine. Robbie Williams was willing to record the song because he needed Queen's iconic rock status to gain a reputation with U.S. audiences. Conversely, in the visual culture of celebrity—where a young Andre Agassi once proclaimed, as part of a campaign for Canon cameras, that "image is everything"—Queen needed Williams's youth. The exchange furthered the celebrity status of both.

There is one last feature of teen culture illustrated by our exemplary music video: the performance of masculinity. While teen culture reserves pockets for girls, it remains a highly masculinized subculture, especially when formed around rock and roll and sports. The performance of rock music remains to this day a largely male preserve (despite the success of female rockers like Chrissie Hines, Deborah Harry, and Joan Jett). Like so many music videos, the Robbie Williams / Queen video walks a fine line in its attempt to appeal both to male and female audiences. But gender roles are clearly delineated. Males are performers, females adoring fans. All of the musicians are men; all other active roles—the vendors, scalpers, promoters, announcers, bouncers, and entourage belong to men (and they do seem like men, not adolescents). The only roles allowed women are the adoring fans. And they seem more like girls. They scream, "We love thee Robbie." They chase his "coach" through the streets. One groupie jumps up on the stage and wraps herself around Williams's waist so that she has to be pulled away by the bouncers. The paradigmatic shot sequence for concert videos since Elvis Presley's appearance on *The Milton Berle Show,* and one that appears at several points in "We Are the Champions," cements these gender roles by cutting away from the musician to shots of the screaming female fans, imitating "the shot/reverse shot sequence that structures the gaze in narrative cinema" (Shumway, 127). The performance of masculinity in rock, however, is never as straightforward as it appears in narrative cinema; it offers its own distinct pleasures and dangers. As David Shumway has noted, Elvis, who set the standard for rock's performance of masculinity in the 1950s, was "the first male star to display his body as an overt sexual object" (126), a position usually reserved in patriarchy for women. In this he not only offended conventional morality; he violated taboos about male sexual display. Since then, from Mick Jagger through Robbie Williams, male rock stars have presented themselves as objects of a sexualized gaze, troubling the usual erotics of looking described by Mulvey, where women offer themselves as objects to be looked at by men. Shumway even reads the transvestism of later male rockers as a means of taking on the markers of the sexualized gender (127). The only way to neutralize the threat of homoeroticism in this display is to demonstrate that those who look are clearly female, so that while both males and females may buy concert tickets in more or less equal numbers, the audience cutaways always show female fans. Throughout "We Are the Champions" Williams pouts, gyrates, thrusts his pelvis, and casts come-hither looks to his exclusively female audience.

Before turning to discussions of *A Knight's Tale* and *Black Knight* as representative films of the teen Middle Ages, we should point out that our discussion of teen culture in this chapter describes a paradox. We are referring to a large group of diverse individuals between the ages of thirteen and twenty. Even within the borders of the United States these individuals are white, black, Asian, Latino, male, female, rich, middle class, poor, urban, rural, suburban, and so on. Individually and collectively they engage in certain cultural and consumer practices—going to movies, watching television, shopping, listening to music—that have particular meanings for them and over which they exercise some agency. But it also refers to the creation of a hypostatized category, a demographic that producers hope to shape to their own ends by imagining it and marketing to it as a monolith (and, for the most part a white, middle-class, straight, and male monolith). This paradox has led Scott Long to suggest that the category of teenager is entirely imaginary: "One expects a certain clarity to come from admitting that the teenager *is* a representation: adolescence is a fake. The rhetoric of its liminality merely drowns out the clatter of its making. A marginal moment when the subject stands between two worlds, poised with innocence on the one hand and experience on the other. . . . The teen years are an invented transition between two carefully constructed norms, childhood and adulthood" (156). While Long makes a good case for the obsolescence of adolescence as a developmental stage (an "empty identity") and even as a training ground for consumerism (children are learning to be consumers from the cradle), he overlooks the economic incentives for maintaining a prolonged period of adolescence. Teenagers are more likely than children to have their own disposable incomes, while they are at the same time generally freer than adults to pursue leisure spending. We prefer to maintain in our analysis a tension between the agency of particular teenagers (the "social audience" of teen movies)[9] and the creation of a consumer category by an industry run by adults, locating our readings of the teen Middle Ages somewhere between the "rebellion against mass-production and the mass-production of rebellion" (Long, 158). The creators of teen culture—adults, after all, own the means of production even of youth culture—must manage the same juggling act. Teenagers are the product of teen culture, but they are never simply automatons, passively receiving that culture. They can and do appropriate that culture to their own ends, just as advertisers are capable of appropriating the kinds of spontaneous culture kids create.

I See by Your Outfit That You Are a Knight, Boy

If the conceit of the Robbie Williams/Queen video is that rock stars can be knights, the conceit of *A Knight's Tale* is that knights can be rock stars. The film's tagline, "He will rock you," encapsulates the system of equivalences the film sets up. It simultaneously signifies the brutality of the joust, the exuberance of rock music, the boisterousness of sports fans who have made the Queen anthem their own, and the star quality of its leading man. The film, which plots the rise of William Thatcher from "peasant squire" to knight and world jousting champion, casts teen idol Heath Ledger, who had already proven his profitability in *10 Things I Hate about You* (Gil Junger, 1999), in a role that basically illustrates how to manipulate identity to create a bankable star. The job of transforming Ledger's William Thatcher into Sir Ulrich von Lichtenstein, thereby demonstrating "the meaningless mechanics of fabricated fame" (Gamson, 46), falls to Geoffrey Chaucer, the poet who, in his allegory *House of Fame*, wrote about fame as, among other things, a fart, which "Loud or private, foul or fair" can never be anything more than "broken air" (lines 767, 770; our translation).

A Knight's Tale opens on the entourage of Sir Ector, an aging knight who dies unexpectedly in the middle of a tournament. His untimely demise creates a vacuum, the need for a replacement who can assume and refurbish Ector's tarnished reputation. His entourage—Thatcher, Wat, and Roland—are young men nervous about the sudden absence of their meal ticket and, at least initially, at a loss as to what to do. Ector is a jousting knight, a performer, and the entourage buys into a mythology that locates his celebrity in his class status. Jousting, the opening titles explain, is a "sport," not a tournament, not training for warfare, not a ritual, but a competition; however, only "noble knights" can compete. The film's opening sequences establish the tournament as an event simultaneously designed to foster social integration, uniting "noble and peasant fans alike," and to establish clear demarcations between classes, since only nobles can participate. These scenes further suggest that modern stadium events—from rock concerts to the Super Bowl—share the same ideological function as medieval spectacles like the tournament at Smithfield that Geoffrey Chaucer helped organize in 1390 (Carlson, 26; Ganim, *Chaucerian Theatricality*, 41). Within a very short space of time, however, before even the film's title and opening credits, this mythology is thoroughly dismantled, and what is offered is the joust as a performance, as theatrical event. Ector's ignoble death—as Roland puts it, "The spark of his life is smothered in shite. His spirit has left him but the stench remains"—already undermines the notion that noble knights are better than anyone else; like everyone else, they excrete and die. William's decision to impersonate his lord and finish the competition himself suggests that jousting is really a performance, and, if it is, then anyone—even a thatcher's son—might "perform" it. All he needs to assume or "steal" Sir Ector's identity is armor and the willingness to take a blow.

Thatcher is able to claim a prize in Ector's name because his helmet has been so dented from his first encounter in the lists that he cannot raise his visor and give away his true identity.[10] He then argues, over the objections of Wat and Roland—who want to cash in and go home—that greater profit can be accrued if they take this identity theft to the next level. He proposes that they counterfeit knightly identity and roam the tournament circuit picking up whatever rewards they can—a crime not without risk since it is punishable by death if discovered. Their scam lacks only the patents of nobility that would testify to their holder's aristocratic position. Traditionally, the claim to class status—to nobility—is based on the ability to document one's past. The fiction of aristocracy is that it derives from links that stretch far back into the past and therefore into the future. The aristocrat imagines that identity will survive death by being passed on to heirs, continuing a link forged in the distant past. Hence the significance in the film of patents of nobility—written documents that demonstrate at least four generations of nobility, that show a stable identity based on a historical record. These patents of nobility differentiate those who sit in the skybox from the masses in the stands and the participants from the fans. This historical conception of identity as fixed and unchangeable, as essence and depth, the film suggests, is anathema to its youth audience, which sees identity only as a series of performances in the present moment. Identity, as the film's protagonist reshapes it, can be put on like so much armor; it can be invented, forged, assumed.[11] After William and his friends meet a destitute, "trudging" Geoffrey Chaucer, the small group hatches a plan to recreate William as a bona fide knight by forging the patents of nobility that will make him Sir Ulrich von Lichtenstein of Gelderland by manufacturing (much as medieval chroniclers did) noble ancestors.

In the film's view of identity, surface and appearance are everything. You are who you appear to be. The film taps into the paradigmatic anxiety of twenty-first-century middle-class life—identity theft. While identity theft includes practices as various as mail fraud, credit card theft, and even such low-tech scams as "dumpster diving," what most people actually fear are various forms of high-tech *computer* identity theft.[12] These fears stem at least in part from the recognition that computer technology introduces yet another break between the individual and the signifiers of her or his identity. In middle-class American culture the signs of identity include things like property and credentials. We fear that we have dispersed these signs of our identities into cyberspace where, unmoored from us, they are just waiting to be stolen by someone, usually imagined as a gawky adolescent male hacker, whose computer expertise exceeds our own. We imagine the hacker to be a teenager because in middle-class America, teenagers are not likely to own property or credentials, so they have less investment in either marker of middle-class identity. They can and do play more fluidly with identity. Anyone can be anyone else if he or she has access to certain powerful technologies. In our culture it is the computer; in the Middle Ages it was literacy.

Writing constitutes identity at the same time that it detaches it from the body of the individual designated by the identity. This makes sense of the film's return to the Middle Ages. In doing so, it addresses the first break between the self and the signifiers of identity—writing. As early as *Phaedrus,* Plato turns to mythology to illustrate the dangers posed by the technology of writing, relating the story of the god Thoth, who offers the gift of writing to the Egyptian king Thamus. The king declines the offer, arguing that the dangers of writing exceed its cultural advantages. According to Christopher Norris, for Plato the pernicious effect of writing is "to break those peculiar ties—of paternal sanction on the one side and filial obligation on the other—that serve to ensure the passage of authentic truth from each generation to the next" (31),[13] exactly the notion of identity perpetuated by an aristocracy and, in the film, by a rule that says only nobles may joust. However, it is precisely the patents of nobility—designed to serve as the proof of nobility—that introduce the possibility of counterfeiting it, because they separate the title from the body of the nobleman, making it possible for those who control the technology of proof—individuals like Chaucer—to manipulate it to their own— or their patrons'—ends. Chaucer is required to "sell" Thatcher's forged proof of nobility to the tournament "officials"—"May I present my Lord Ulrich, whose mother's father was Shelhard von Rechberg, son of the Duke Guelph of Saxony, son of Ghibellines, son of Wendish the fourth earl of Brunswick, the same Wendish who inherited the fief . . ." This vaguely medieval hodgepodge, which includes references to rival Italian political factions and the Frankish name for the Slavs of north central Europe, makes hash of the genre of medieval genealogy, its humor deriving from its long-winded gibberish (the official stops him in mid-sentence). In point of fact it resembles nothing so much as the actual genealogies offered by many a medieval chronicler; both attempt to generate legitimacy by filling out the empty forms of nobility with nonsensical but plausible-sounding signs.

Rather than succumbing to paranoia about unmoored identity present in a movie like *The Net* (1995), however, *A Knight's Tale* celebrates its playful possibilities. With the death of their master, Thatcher, Wat, and Roland are without identity. They exist in much the same position of cultural flux as the teenagers who are imagined as the film's audience.[14] The willingness of the three squires to participate in identity theft springs from their desire to access aristocratic culture, although they do not really want to become part of that culture. They do not want to become responsible knights who might have to go to war (as the villain, the "real" knight, Adhemar does) or to govern (like the Black Prince). The film only marginally recognizes that knighthood is about either of these things; it shows only the desire to "play," that is to joust. In this Thatcher and his friends are like the teenagers of "Soco Amaretto Lime," who construct their time as a series of never-ending parties. The white middle-class teenagers who are the target audience for this film can be anything they want to be because they are all potential. They are less threatened by the ways in which computers destabilize identities because they have less to lose, just as William Thatcher and his friends are less anxious than, say, Adhemar, a member of the aristocracy, about the threat their impersonation poses to aristocratic identity. Thatcher's rebirth into the aristocracy is marked by his creation of a faux heraldic emblem, three phoenixes rising, symbolizing each team member's desire to spring from his own platonic conception of himself—a scene that was cut from the motion picture but included in the DVD extras.

A Knight's Tale unpacks the complex web of exchanges that constitutes twenty-first-century notions of celebrity as performance—in music, in film, in entertainment, in athletics, in poetry, even in romance—by removing them from their familiar locus in contemporary life and relocating them to the more alien Middle Ages. The jousts themselves constitute the central performance, and these, as Helgeland notes obsessively in his commentary, are framed by all of the tricks of the MTV trade: slow motion, overhead shots, montage, rhythmic cutting, and camera movements that "the MTV generation," as Helgeland calls his teen audience, enjoys. Around the "sport" of jousting circulates the performance of spectatorship, not only in the opening credits but in crowd shots scattered throughout the film that trade on the audience's knowledge of sports spectatorship: in vendors who sell "cat meat," in crowds reaching for flying helmets the way baseball fans go after a home-run ball, in Kate the blacksmith giving William free armor as an endorsement so that others will see and want it, even in the suggestion of such contemporary commercial "signs" as the Nike swoosh on that armor, an instance of product placement for which, as Helgeland nervously remarks, "no money changed hands." This suggests that, even in the absence of lucrative placement deals, allusions to contemporary fashion are a required element of the teen movie. If they can provide an in-joke, a sense that the film's spectator is "in the know," so much the better. When Kate calls the swoosh "the marks of my trade, should another knight admire my work," she provides a subtle reference to Nike's founder Phil Knight. In this scene the medieval "anticipates" the origins of a horizontal integration that links athletic performance to commercial products through endorsements.

The careers of the heralds who announce the jousters also circulate around the athletic performances. Bettany's Chaucer creates Sir Ulrich von Lichtenstein of Gelderland literally out of thin air, through his bravura performances in the role of herald, inflating the reputation of his patron like a medieval Don King. These performances locate the roots of Chaucer's poetry in the popular entertainments of the day; they provide models for Chaucer's portraits not only of the Knight, but of the Summoner and Pardoner as well, in his adventures with William and his entourage. This may suggest why Helgeland chooses to make Chaucer the poet the pretext for his movie.[15] Chaucer, as John Ganim has persuasively argued, found inspiration for his poetry in the entertainments of his day, both civic and courtly—entertainments like the tournaments that dominate the action of *A Knight's Tale* and the first of *The Canterbury Tales* (see Ganim, *Chaucerian Theatricality*). In the figure of Chaucer, *A Knight's Tale* exploits the parallel between the theatricality of contemporary teen culture—in stadium events like rock concerts and sports—and the theatricality of medieval life—its tournaments, processions, disguisings, festivals, mimes—that give Chaucer's poetry its provisional and improvisational character. Chaucer and Helgeland, as Haydock notes, evince "a shared devotion to public spectacle" (*Movie Medievalism*, 101).

Ganim argues that, in his poetry, "the figure of Chaucer himself, is theatrically represented, . . . so much so that it has become one of the tropes of modern Chaucer criticism to address his degree of fictionality, precisely that which theatricality simultaneously invites and frustrates" (*Chaucerian Theatricality*, 6–7). *A Knight's Tale* is set in 1370, a year during which Chaucer goes missing from the historical record for six months while on the continent.[16] It gives us not Chaucer the bookish, ineffectual, slightly pudgy, middle-aged poet represented both in Chaucer's poetry and in the various portraits, such as that included in the Ellesmere manuscript (Figure 19).[17] Paul Bettany's turn as a long and lean (and occasionally naked) Geoffrey Chaucer gives us the poet as a young man, raconteur, and jack-of-all-trades, literally scrambling to keep the clothes on his back: "Geoffrey Chaucer's the name, writing's the game" (Figure 20). In fact, allowing for considerable poetic license, Bettany's Chaucer is not all that far from the Chaucer who emerges in David Carlson's recent study of Chaucer's jobs, at least from his early years in domestic service. Carlson argues that in those years Chaucer was a "lackey," "a domestic servant," "servile, doing useful work" (1), "dependent on the patron's munificence even for such basic requisites as food, shelter, and clothing" (5). In the film, Thatcher pays off Chaucer's gambling debts with his tournament winnings, literally providing the poet with the clothes on his back, and at that moment Chaucer becomes dependent on Thatcher's success for his own livelihood. As in his life, in the film Chaucer's poetic endeavors make up only a small part of the services on offer, although the film clearly designates him as an exemplar of what Anne Middleton calls "textworkers" (in whose ranks she includes "scriveners as well as versifiers, ecclesiastical and legal odd-job and regular-service men of several sorts"; quoted in Carlson, 75): "for a penny, I'll scribble you anything you want: summonses, decrees, edicts, warrants, patents of nobility; I've even been known to jot down a poem or two if the Muse descends." As a wordsmith Chaucer settles scores not by fighting (as William does) but by immortalizing his enemies in writing. To the Pardoner and Summoner who hold his gambling debts he threatens to "eviscerate you in fiction, every last pimple, every last character flaw. I was naked for a day; you will be naked for eternity."

Bettany's Chaucer is not simply an observer of court entertainments; he participates in—and even creates—their theatricality. Just as Ganim stresses the poet's role as a "master of ceremonies" in works like *The Canterbury Tales*, Bettany's Chaucer, in his role as herald, serves as an intermediary between the spectators at the joust and its participants. For this reason it is worth examining in detail at least one of Bettany's performances, noting how both acting and editing create from a clever bit of writing a dialogic interanimation between contemporary and medieval popular entertainments—how they create this ersatz knight's fame literally out of "broken air," out of words. The first and longest set piece occurs during the tournament at Rouen. The scene begins in midsentence with an introduction by the herald who precedes Chaucer and announces Thatcher's op-

Figure 19. Ellesmere portrait of Chaucer, ms. 26 C9, fol. 153v. Reproduced by permission of the Huntington Library, San Marino, California.

ponent, Sir Thomas Colville (who we later discover is none other than the Black Prince himself; Thatcher is not the only knight hiding his identity). This brief routine sets the audience's expectations for the genre. It begins with a medium shot of the herald, who addresses the nobility on the dais sedately and not a little

Figure 20. Paul Bettany as Chaucer in *A Knight's Tale* (Brian Helgeland, 2001).

smugly; while he speaks, he takes up very little space and moves hardly at all, a sign of his servility. Midway through, a cut to long shot from behind him shows how excluded and uninvolved the crowd is. This exchange, ending with the herald's obsequious bow, takes place exclusively between the herald and the nobility whose wealth and status the tournament promotes.

Bettany's Chaucer plays off of and repudiates just this generic expectation of deference in a manner we might define as positively "Chaucerian." The reaction shots of his audience suggest just how audacious his performance is. He begins by quietly imitating his predecessor with a bow and deferential nod toward the nobility's social rank, "My lords, my ladies . . ." A pause, filled by a reaction shot, shows their acknowledgment of his respect. He then immediately turns on its head this perfunctory piece of courtesy designed to solidify class difference. A long shot shows him waving his hand as if pointing to the whole audience; he finishes, ". . . and everybody else here not sitting on a cushion." The shot takes in the crowd's enthusiastic response, quickly followed by a shot showing the bewilderment of Thatcher and his crew. Together these reactions tell us his tactic is effective but dangerous. Besides the obvious reference to the class distinction in Elizabethan theaters between the groundlings and those who could afford to sit, familiar to most high school students of Shakespeare, this line also contains an allusion to the Beatles' 1963 appearance at a Royal Variety Performance in London, attended by Queen Elizabeth, the Queen Mother, and Princess Margaret, in which John Lennon famously exhorted the audience by shouting, "Will the people in the cheaper seats clap your hands? The rest of you, just rattle your jewelry" (DVD commentary). Chaucer's speech takes a decidedly populist turn: "Today you find yourselves equals." Reaction shots show the approval of the crowd and the uneasiness of the nobility at such a subversive statement. The punch line—"for you are all equally blessed" by the opportunity to see his patron in action—stresses the ways in which audience participation in the tournament could serve as a form of social integration that levels class distinctions without entirely eliminating them. The speech commands the audience's assent by employing artificial rhetorical devices like alliteration—"I have the pride, the privilege, nay the pleasure"—and anaphora—"a knight sired by knights" to structure repetitions that enhance his patron's fame. In later variations on this performance, as in Paris, he will add simple rhymes, reminiscent of modern-day sports performances: ". . . the harasser of Parasser, he gave them hell at La Rochelle."

Genealogy is another strategy through which "Chaucer" constructs "Sir Ulrich's" nobility, a tactic the speech shares with medieval chronicle and romances. Sir Ulrich, Chaucer claims, can trace his ancestry back in a lineage older than Charlemagne; this is perhaps no wilder a claim than Malory's that Lancelot and his son, Galahad, could trace theirs through Joseph of Arimathea to Jesus or Geoffrey of Monmouth's that the kings of England could trace theirs back to the Trojan Brutus. Knighthood, however, rests on the contradictory claims that one is both born into it and must achieve it. Sir Ulrich requires prior feats of strength to attest to his "fame." In a link to the General Prologue portrait of the Knight, Chaucer insinuates his patron's achievements obliquely through periphrastic references to the Crusades—"I first met him atop a mountain near Jerusalem praying to God asking forgiveness for the Saracen blood spilt by his sword"—and later in Italy, "saving a fatherless beauty from the would-be ravishings of her dreadful Turkish uncle."[18] As in *The Canterbury Tales*' portrait of the Knight, Ulrich's opponents are the Saracen "others." And, as in "Sir Thopas," meaningless hyperbole fills out the rest of his portrait: "In Greece he spent a year in silence [beat] just to better understand the sound of a whisper." Despite this flurry of medieval references and rhetorical flourishes, however, Bettany admits that he prepared for these performances by watching videotapes of the World Wrestling Federation's Vince McMahon, modeling his own performance on those of the popular wrestling promoter and announcer.

Although the film's primary interest lies in the relationship of William Thatcher to his makeshift retinue of "retainers"—Wat, Roland, Kate, and Chaucer—and with the villain, Adhemar of Anjou (played by Rufus Sewell), there is a perfunctory love story. Its primary purpose, however, seems to be to create a pretext for the rivalry between William and Adhemar to be staged. Jocelyn provides both an audience and a prize for that rivalry. Shannyn Sossamon, in her first film, performs here primarily as a fashion model; like Eva Green in *Kingdom of Heaven*, she is blank but comely. Sporting a new outfit in every appearance, she looks more like Audrey Hepburn (in *Roman Holiday* or *Sabrina*) than a medieval princess. As Helgeland notes in his commentary, Caroline Harris's costumes seem vaguely medieval, but at the same time they reference contemporary and even retro fashion. In the perfunctory love story Jocelyn is little more than quarry to be pursued; indeed, much of the dialogue between the two lovers relies on metaphors that make her a hunted animal (Haydock, *Movie Medievalism*, 103).

The exchanges between the two lovers—William and Jocelyn—take place almost exclusively in public places—in churches, in the lists, at a dance—in front of an audience. Even the most private, intimate moments, however, are imaginable only as performances. When Jocelyn comes to William's tent at night to offer herself up to him, the pair is observed by Chaucer; indeed, we see the scene, at least initially, from his point of view. The traditional Hollywood techniques for representing intimacy are often missing where one would expect them. A case in point is the scene in the cathedral (presumably Notre Dame since this tournament takes place in Paris) between William and Jocelyn in which she commands him to prove his love for her by losing in the tournament. The scene is shot in long shot inside a cathedral in a single take that lasts more than three minutes. As the characters move through the church up and down its central aisle, they are framed by pillars, which create the effect of a proscenium arch. A stained-glass window is centrally located between each set of pillars providing a diegetic light source, as well as some color contrast to the drabness of the stone. Bystanders kneel, stand, walk through the shot, observing the lovers as they "woo" in a language that sounds badly rehearsed. We are encouraged to read the scene as a theatrical performance rather than an intimate moment. Undoubtedly, the scene was shot this way for financial, as much as for aesthetic, reasons. In the DVD commentary Helgeland explains that "a lot of people thought this [the three-minute tracking shot] was a bold move," but, in fact, he had simply run out of time to shoot on that set and could save $130,000 by filming it as a master shot. Whatever his reasons, the scene works because it shows William's and Jocelyn's love as essentially a performance. Their love unfolds not in private, intimate moments indicated by the usual filmic language of close-up, shot–reverse shot, and two-shot composition but in public, always in front of an audience in a theatrical space.

Through its dialogic interchange between medieval and contemporary popular entertainments, *A Knight's Tale* asks us not to imagine that medieval theatricals like the joust were exactly like modern stadium events but that they share common, if occasionally contradictory, features like improvisation and artificiality, dignified ritual and exuberance, subversion and affirmation of the status quo. Helgeland's creation shows a keen understanding of his target audience and even of the medieval texts around which he structures the screenplay. Teenagers are more than competent participants in most forms of mass entertainment, including film. This kind of theatricality is a major component of their culture, from rap music and slam poetry to rock concerts and, yes, even professional wrestling, which, after all, is no more inane than jousting as an entertainment. Not surprisingly, *A Knight's Tale*, which cost $41 million to make, was modestly successful, grossing $56 million in the United States alone, attesting to the film's ability to bridge medieval and modern for a contemporary teen audience.

Inner-City Chivalry

Adolescence, whether perceived as a category of consumption or a psychological state of liminality, thrives on performance. For this reason teen culture is playfully mimetic, appropriating everything and internalizing nothing. Though a less-skilled comedy than Helgeland's (it was universally panned by the critics and domestically grossed only $33 million of its $50 million investment),[19] Gil Junger's 2001 film *Black Knight* offers an intriguing postcolonial teen fantasy that plays the very real oppression of urban modernity in inner-city communities like South Central Los Angeles off against a commodified version of ghetto culture, transporting to the Eurocentric Middle Ages a hip-hop culture immediately identifiable to any teenager, white or black, who has listened to popular music, watched MTV, or enjoyed the latest Martin Lawrence comedy vehicle. Because teen culture shares with at least the most superficial aspects of the postcolonial a relentless hybridity, a tendency, common to those who feel marginalized by their circumstances, to appropriate and resignify cultural signs, *Black Knight* indulges adolescent fantasies of unmoored signification that cavalierly mix and match whatever identities are at hand. This crossover film, designed to appeal to teenage males who constitute Lawrence's fan base, attempts to use the experience of the Middle Ages to relieve the traumas of urban modernity by calling on Mark Twain's *Connecticut Yankee* formula.

At first glance nothing could seem a less-appropriate—and hence less-realistic—setting for a time-travel movie about the Middle Ages than the inner city ghetto. The first thing everybody notices (or perhaps does not even need to notice) about films set in the Middle Ages is that all the characters are usually white. The fantasy of the Middle Ages has always been the exclusive province of

European colonialism, representing the historical legitimation of white Christian European domination; a nonwhite character in such a landscape would surely seem "unrealistic" and need explaining.[20] The real point of interest in *Black Knight* is to see how this unlikely mélange of Martin Lawrence hip-hop comedy and medieval swashbuckling will connect the twentieth-century young urban black man with the "black knight" of chivalric fantasy and so realize the pun in the title.

To make this connection, it is necessary to explore more fully the ways in which cultural differences, as Homi Bhabha notes, destabilize the binary oppositions between "past and present, tradition and modernity, at the level of cultural representation and authoritative address" (*The Location of Culture*, 35). We need to understand more fully how, "in signifying the present," twentieth-century hip-hop culture "comes to be repeated, relocated and translated in the name of tradition, in the guise of a pastness that is not necessarily a faithful sign of historical memory but a strategy of representing authority in terms of the artifice of the archaic" (35). Perhaps the film, for all its silliness, recognizes how strongly the colonial impulse still thrives. Or perhaps it doesn't and simply reproduces the cultural imaginary of colonialism. Whichever explanation we accept, the inhabitants of *Black Knight*'s South Central LA, and most especially, its central figure, Martin Lawrence's Jamal Walker, inhabit what Anne McClintock calls the "anachronistic space" of colonization (40). Excluded from the history of modernity, they are the "prototypes of anachronistic humans: childlike, irrational, regressive and atavistic, existing in a permanently anterior time within modernity" (42).[21] For this very reason they are ideally situated to realize the colonial and postcolonial elements present in the *Connecticut Yankee* formula. The cultural differences—the differences between white and black, Europe and America, medieval and modern, teenager and adult—that are the subject of the film trouble the binary oppositions Bhabha identifies.

The link between the main character and the primitive past is established from the opening credits, which feature Walker, only marginally distanced from comic Lawrence portraying him, mugging in front of the camera as he performs simple acts of grooming—brushing, flossing, combing, cleaning. The film offers cleanliness as a marker of modernity; the Middle Ages is identified by the prevalence of filth, particularly excrement. Walker's toilette, his obsessive efforts to remove or control physiological surplus—hair, tartar, earwax, body odor—connect him to the market commodities of the twentieth and twenty-first centuries, which hold out the promise that humanity's animal nature can be repressed, perhaps even denied. His self-fashioning as modern man is established by his use of grooming aids: toothpaste, dental floss, Q-tips, and so forth. This scene, along with a later scene in which Walker offers the drunken knight Knolte money to purchase soap and Tic Tacs, establishes hygiene as that which separates the medieval from the modern. But it is, after all, more than just hygiene that separates the historical periods; it is how hygiene falls under the sway of the commodity. Walker is, if nothing else, a child of the contemporary marketplace. His toilette is determined by the commercials he watches on television, determined by his viewing of films, like *Black Knight,* which derive at least a portion of their initial investment from product placement. *Black Knight* suggests that if the Middle Ages were filthy, it is because capitalism had not yet made cleanliness a desirable commodity.

But *Black Knight* suggests that, even as we live in our bodies, we necessarily live in the Middle Ages, a Middle Ages figured as bodily surplus. While the strong beat of a rap song, "I Like the Way," performed by Beenie Man, fills the sound track, no language issues from Walker/Lawrence; only various animalistic noises punctuate his performance. There are shots, particularly one in which Lawrence inserts Q-tips into his ears and another in which he raises a leg like a urinating dog, in which it would take an act of self-will not to imagine animals. In this sequence we are encouraged to see Walker not as a mature black man (perhaps too threatening for a mainstream comedy) but as a childlike innocent, a primitive—maybe even a teenager. In this simple scene, which does nothing to further the plot and everything to overdetermine the ways in which viewers perceive the central character, we can read the denial of modernity and of its complexities to the characters. The denizens of Walker's world are "urban primitives," occupying anachronistic space, the space of the past. In short, they are everything represented by the term *medieval* because what else does the term connote except that which is not modernity? As Carolyn Dinshaw notes in her reading of *Pulp Fiction,* the medieval is "that space of abjection and otherness—the space where sodomy, sadomasochism, southernness, and blackness get dumped in the creation of a unified straight white masculinity" (205).

Black Knight's Walker is underemployed at an amusement park called Medieval World. Like the restaurant Medieval Times in Ben Stiller's *The Cable Guy,* Medieval World is a tawdry recreation of the past in which the Middle Ages becomes a commodity just like any other, so much junk. However, there is very little medieval about this battered and graffitied ersatz castle surrounded by a moat filled with the detritus of modern urban life. The illusion of a romanticized and perhaps simpler past is undercut by the broken-down rides and derelict batting cages inside. Medieval World is a failing institution, unable to provide either an idealized history for its customers or economic sustenance for a community alienated both by culture and poverty. This situation is sketched out with remarkable economy and little dialogue in an early scene, in which Walker and his boss, Mrs. Bostick (Isabell Monk), trade the tired clichés of a liberal capitalism that has mostly failed African American communities. Mrs. Bostick claims she has provided "quality jobs" for the community for twenty years. But Walker understands perfectly well that he holds down a teenager's job[22]—low-paying alienated labor in which workers are bored, interchangeable, and expendable—and he articulates his alienation through his indifference. "Cash out," Walker counters. Responding to what she sees as adolescent irresponsibility, she retorts, "Look outside yourself and buckle down." He parries, "Help yourself, forget about the community." Mrs. Bostick's bootstrap approach to combating the economic adversity of inner-city life—"I had high hopes for you"—is unintelligible to Jamal's cynical despair: "Take what money you got—and jet." He gestures toward the prodigality of those who have nothing, those who in their powerlessness are culturally marked as children.

Medieval World is threatened by the opening of a better, more "real," amusement park called Castle World. The film explicitly links economic viability and cultural verisimilitude by way of Eco's "hyperreality." The imagination and taste of the "average American" participates in the philosophy of the hyperreal, a philosophy that "demands the real thing and, to attain it, must fabricate the absolute fake; where the boundaries between game and illusion are blurred" (8). Reproduction in the mode of hyperreality attempts to improve on the real, to make it better, all in the interest of selling something. Castle World comes as a threat from outside the South Central community; it represents corporate interests that appropriate all authentic culture. Corporate interests alone can bring together and level the difference between the hip-hop culture of the inner city and that of medieval England. All cultural pasts are reduced to the same process of commodification and so become interchangeable. The film itself mimics that very process as the corporate interests represented by Regency Enterprises and Twentieth Century Fox have brought these worlds together with the help of Martin Lawrence, the film's executive producer and an "authentic" representative of hip-hop culture.

Ironically, Castle World is never shown in the film, except as an ad in a newspaper. Instead, the film consciously deconstructs the binary between real and fake, as it does between past and present, both critiquing and participating in the cultural appropriations outlined above, as Walker is magically transported back in time and space to fourteenth-century England, where he finds himself in the real thing (a castle world), which he mistakes for the reproduction (Castle World). Walker reacts to the "real" fourteenth century as if it were its twentieth-century reproduction. He can only understand his experiences through the philosophy of hyperreality, which dictates that this castle world must be a truly authentic *reproduction* of the real Middle Ages. This is the basis of all the jokes in the scene in which Walker first finds himself in fourteenth-century England. His encounter with the intoxicated, outcast knight Knolte can only be understood by Walker as the aftermath of the "opening party for Castle World." The knights who nearly run him over must be "dumb-ass actors takin' their job way too seriously." As Walker notes, "Castle World got it goin' on—horses, costumes, smells." It is an authentic medieval world right down to its gross smells, because to the hyperclean Jamal, the medieval must invariably smell. It is made of "real brick, none of that fake stuff." Walker concludes, "Miz Bostick, you in trouble."

At the same time, Walker finds the fourteenth century, as measured by the yardstick of hyperreality, somewhat disturbing. It threatens his conviction, which he undoubtedly shares with the film's target teen demographic, that contemporary appropriations of the Middle Ages (like Castle World) must necessarily be Disneyfied, must be brought within the hygienic regime of commodity culture. Mistaking the medieval castle of King Leo for a modern, theme-park hotel, for instance, he insists: "You think you gonna charge people money to stay here and wipe their asses with straw? No. Seriously." Walker longs to be an accidental tourist in the fourteenth century. He longs not for an authentic Middle Ages but a hyperreal one, where, like the Middle Ages of the Medieval Times restaurant chain, he can order a Pepsi from some "serving wench."

Black Knight spoofs the cultural industries that turn everything they touch into a reproduction of reality; at the same time, though, it participates in that very enterprise. The castle world of *Black Knight* is an authentic reproduction of a medieval castle, complete with actors and extras in authentic-looking costumes. It *is* a movie set (the film was shot in North Carolina), although unlike *Monty Python and the Holy Grail* the film never breaks its diegesis to remind us of that; and it is represented with all of the cinematic "signs" of medievalness. The "Middle Ages" appears in this scene virtually out of nowhere, as a sharp, deep focus, and well-lit scene shifts suddenly to smoky mists that part to reveal knights on horseback galloping into the frame in slow motion. The moment is meant to create some drama as it imitates the conventions of countless scenes from both medieval movies and westerns. The time shift is revealed as much by the technological apparatus of the film as by any content. These characters can easily be mistaken for movie actors "playing" at the Middle Ages because they are. Here we have the *mise en abyme* of reproduction and reality, except all is reproduction, all hyper-reality. There is no accessible real.

Black Knight's appropriation of the *Connecticut Yankee* formula frames a contrast between a superior "modern" technology and a benighted and atavistic past, linking certain elements in contemporary culture, the homeless for instance, to a primitive Middle Ages. But the film also offers an interesting and somewhat contradictory take on that ideology. After connecting Jamal (and by extension African Americans) early in the credits with the primitive, the film then transports him to a medieval past where, ultimately, as a representative of a superior, more advanced "race," he is able to solve their problems—and coincidentally his own—through the application of his wits and superior technology.

Walker's transformation into the redemptive Black Knight—literally his maturation—does not, however, come easily or, it would seem, naturally. Junger's *Black Knight* draws its inspiration less from Mark Twain's *A Connecticut Yankee in King Arthur's Court* than from the 1949 Tay Garnett film of the same title—replicating, at times, the Garnett film almost shot for shot. The Junger project, however, casts its protagonist in a very different role than either of its two intertexts. Arriving in the Middle Ages, Hank Morgan, the hero of Twain's original story, is more than a product of the Industrial Revolution, more than a representative from a technologically advanced culture. He possesses the astonishing self-assurance of a successful, free, white, nineteenth-century American *man* who enjoys the luxury of being simultaneously disgusted with, yet undeniably profiting from, both the genocide of Native Americans and the institution of slavery. He sees himself as, and has himself knighted, "Sir Boss," a nod to his smug masculinity. At least a portion of Twain's critique of American society is directed at Morgan's arrogance: "I could make anything a body wanted—anything in the world, it didn't make any difference what; and if there wasn't any quick new-fangled way to make a thing, I could invent one—and do it as easily as rolling off a log" (7). Garnett's film completely strips away Twain's critique of American exceptionalism, leaving a supremely confident protagonist, Hank Martin, to work his desires on medieval England. As Rebecca and Sam Umland note, Martin, as played by Bing Crosby, embodies certain characteristics that would have been regarded by post–World War II America as "cool": "A refusal to sentimentalize, self-deprecation, and self-effacement, wisecracks, emotional distance and restraint, and self-reflexivity" (43). These qualities, the Umlands suggest, were racially encoded for the postwar generation: "The word 'cool' emerged from 1940s American jazz culture known as 'bebop'" (41). But in Garnett's film this African American "cool" has been almost seamlessly merged with the star persona represented by Bing Crosby to display the power and authority of America's dominant, white, middle-class culture, a culture that can co-opt African American language and styles as effortlessly as it can its own medieval past. In *Black Knight* the casting of a black man in this role pushes the formula even further in the direction of what Bhabha defines as "hybridity" in which "other 'denied' knowledges enter upon the dominant discourse and estrange the basis of its authority" (*The Location of Culture*, 114).

Jamal Walker, unlike Hank Martin, proceeds among the white people of fourteenth-century England with the caution of the marginalized. He is twice an outsider in medieval England: black and from another time. Hailing from the corner of Florence and Normandie in South Central Los Angeles, where black men like Rodney King are routinely beaten by the authorities,[23] Walker is hypervigilant about his status as an African American. Mistaken for the Norman ambassador to the court of King Leo, Walker receives a warm welcome, thanks in no small part to the fortunate geographical pun realized in his South Central neighborhood.[24] But he remains anxious, distrustful of the agendas of the Eurocentric world into which he has fallen. He hears, for instance, in the constant reiteration of the descriptor "Moor," the potential for a racial epithet, which he proclaims to like "less and less." Walker's response to his cultural alienation in the Middle Ages coalesces with stereotypes taken on by African Americans to alleviate some of their suffering in contemporary society. He plays the clown, identifying himself as both an ambassador and a court jester. Bhabha locates in this behavior—"in enigmatic, inappropriate signifiers" such as stereotypes and jokes—"colonial doubling," a "strategic displacement of value" where we get a "sense of a specific space of separation," of what he means by hybridity (*The Location of Culture*, 120). This reversion to ethnic stereotype, this recollection of the black man as minstrel, suffering a series of humiliations to amuse his white audience, garners only a grudging approval from King Leo, who notes, "I have to admire his commitment. It is no longer funny, but he refuses to give up on the joke"—perhaps because it defines his cultural hybridity as well as his cultural insecurities.

Jamal Walker (the name itself suggests hybridity) does not participate in the romantic belief in American exceptionalism and its promise of limitless possibilities that motivates Hank Morgan and Hank Martin. Morgan and Martin carry with them a sense of entitlement, the privilege enjoyed by white American males.

Walker possesses no such motivation, and his self-fashioning borders on the tragic, at least initially. When Victoria, a young black woman wildly out of place in the court of King Leo, asks Walker a perfectly reasonable question, given that she lives in the fourteenth century, "You can read and write?" Walker's response highlights the sad state of education among America's urban poor: "Yeah. Who you been datin'? You got to raise the bar." When King Leo inquires, "What news from Normandy?" Walker replies, remarking on the desperation of America's inner cities, "What news? A couple of drive-bys. Other than that, same old, same old." In fact, Junger's film seems to make the case that Walker may be better suited to the time-travel adventure of returning to the Middle Ages than either Morgan or Martin. With its dehumanizing treatment of women, its ultraviolence—so extreme, in fact, that even Walker is unnerved while witnessing an execution—and its brutality toward the working poor, Junger's medieval England does not seem as alien to America's inner cities as it first appears. By learning to negotiate the problems of the past, therefore, Walker, at least in the film's fantasy, learns to address the problems of his violent and impoverished present.

To accomplish his transformation from urban primitive to American capitalist, Walker must reinvent himself as an adult, as he calls on his expertise in African American popular culture to negotiate the dangers of King Leo's court. Lawrence's Walker survives—and even thrives—in this alien environment not because he possesses some kind of authentic blackness but precisely because of his skill in forging hybrid cultural forms. This tactical use of hybridity is demonstrated by the film's advertising poster, which shows the star, Lawrence, centered in front of a castle, sporting a bewildering array of mismatched cultural signs. His backwards baseball cap, football jersey, sunglasses, baggy pants, and Nikes identify him with a teen hip-hop culture whose appeal has crossed over from inner-city "gangsta" to white suburban wannabe. At the same time he carries a sword and helmet, and his arms and legs are encased in medieval armor. Lawrence's name dominates the top of the poster, and beneath it in smaller letters there is a caption that reads "He's about to get medieval on you," a reference to the medieval in Quentin Tarentino's *Pulp Fiction* (1994).

The same cultural hybridity marks every nuance of Lawrence's performance in this film. Through the herald's introduction he refashions his character's identity: "Starting at small forward from Inglewood High, two-time, all-county, conference player of the year, the messenger from Normandy, Jamal 'Sky' Walker." The allusion immediately calls to mind George Lucas's groundbreaking 1977 movie *Star Wars*, which, telescoping time, offers a future in which Jedi knight Luke Skywalker battles enemies with a light saber and a mystical power called "the force." But the introduction has an Afrocentric referent as well. In 1974 North Carolina State University won the NCAA basketball tournament, putting an end to the dynasty of John Wooden's UCLA Bruins. NC State was led by forward David "Skywalker" Thompson, who, along with the likes of Julius Erving, would ultimately redefine the game of basketball. Thompson, Erving, and a number of other young African American players seemed to fly above their peers, bringing to the game an extraordinary athleticism and the sense of razzle-dazzle showmanship that would ultimately reach its apotheosis in the figure of Michael Jordan (who was an admirer of Thompson's and whose number 23 Jamal sports on his jersey). When Walker walks into—onto—King Leo's "court," the identity he assumes with the name "Skywalker" is that of a black man, a champion, an NBA Hall of Famer, a founding father of the kind of basketball that has become an integral part of hip-hop culture.

The scene in which Walker teaches King Leo's court how to dance parodies almost shot for shot a similar scene of cultural hybridity in Garnett's *A Connecticut Yankee in King Arthur's Court*. In that film Martin/Crosby, impatient with medieval music and dance—which, as they are depicted in the film, have very little in common historically with medieval music and dance—instructs King Arthur's musical ensemble on how to create a twentieth-century big band sound and shows the court the pleasures of couples dancing. Martin/Crosby's gesture is one of dominance, imposing a "higher"—or at least "cooler"—cultural standard on plodding primitives. The primitives, King Arthur's knights and their ladies, attempt to adopt this standard, but their efforts prove awkward, at best, demonstrating that only the most exceptional whites—individuals like Bing Crosby—can achieve true "cool." The pleasure in this scene derives from the twentieth-century audience's feeling superior to the fumbling medievals. Perhaps a portion of the pleasure also comes, as it certainly does in Twain's novel, from the fantasy of an American reversing the history of English colonialism, forcing the culture of the onetime colonized down the throats of its former oppressors. Such an appreciation of this scene would require Garnett's audience conveniently to forget America's own history of colonialism, a bit of amnesia that Twain resists.

Black Knight seems less concerned with dominance than with the display of cultural hybridity, whether in the service of racial conciliation or assimilation is less clear. The dance scene begins nervously, as King Leo comments to Walker, "I'm interested in learning more about your culture. It is my understanding the Normans are excellent dancers." Walker, reading Leo's inquiry through the eyes of a twenty-first-century African American, assumes that he has been patronized and responds: "No offence, king, but, you know, that thing about dancing, that is a very stereotypical thing you said." Walker is ultimately intimidated into a performance. Unlike Martin/Crosby, who whistles a melody for the medieval band to learn, Walker racially marks his pedagogical moment, laying down a bass line, nudging King Leo's group toward improvisation, with the caveat, "Now this is a pretty white crowd, so nothing too crazy. My life depends on it."

The song that emerges from the collaboration between Walker and the medieval musicians is Sly and the Family Stone's "Dance to the Music." For moviegoers aged eighteen to twenty-five, *Black Knight*'s primary demographic, this song from the late 1960s is just one more piece of history thrown into the cinematic blender, along with the Middle Ages and Mark Twain. All pasts are indistinguishable, able to be fused and confused. But the choice of "Dance to the Music" does not seem all that arbitrary to an audience that entered its teen years in the 1960s. As that decade drew to a close, rock audiences were becoming increasingly segmented by race. With their brand of psychedelic soul, Sly and the Family Stone bridged the divide, offering a musical mix popular among both white and African American audiences. At the 1969 Woodstock music festival, despite the scarcity of nonwhite faces both in the audience and onstage, Sly and the Family Stone were a huge hit. Walker conjures this spirit of racial harmony, simultaneously saving his own life and making the court of King Leo just a bit hipper.

The politics of Walker's dance extend beyond his musical choice. The performance was choreographed by Paula Abdul, a multiethnic performer whose credits include, but are by no means limited to, teaching dance moves to the Los Angeles Lakers cheerleaders, Janet Jackson, and ZZ Top. Abdul, both Canadian and Syrian by birth, had a short but highly successful career as a singer-dancer, merging, at times, a pop sensibility with hip-hop grooves. She has since become hugely successful sitting between the African American Randy Jackson and the white Englishman Simon Cowell as a judge on the television phenomenon *American Idol*. Whereas Martin/Crosby teaches Arthur's court a dance that emphasizes their inadequacy, that humiliates them, the dance that Abdul provides for Walker, though filled with little hip-hop moves, is one that King Leo and his followers take to quickly and easily. It is a dance that gives them pleasure. Walker emerges as a figure who can solve problems, even those as complicated as race in twenty-first-century America, or so the film suggests.

Black Knight would have us believe that the encounter with a culture more barbaric and lawless than that of twentieth-century South Central Los Angeles ultimately resituates Jamal. On the one hand, Walker's Middle Ages are savage and atavistic, a place of violence, betrayal, foul actions and foul odors, but perhaps no more so, the film suggests, than Walker's neighborhood. On the other hand, in the Middle Ages Jamal finds the organic, precapitalistic communitarianism he earlier mocked. In his efforts to restore a medieval queen—a surrogate for his own Mrs. Bostick—to her throne, he struggles to reimpose the very sort of centralized, organized, and just governance missing from his inner-city experience. Since, as Lloyd argues, the Middle Ages contains "seeds of the transition to capitalism," Walker must return there to receive the enculturation he lacks. In the Middle Ages he is not just another passive consumer of a throwaway commodity culture. Like his *Connecticut Yankee* antecedents, Walker has to apply what he knows about his own world to the problems he encounters in the medieval. As he assembles his medieval army to restore the queen, he argues, contra Rodney King, "sometimes we can't just get along; sometimes we've got to take up arms." Walker finally can put to use the lessons twentieth-century capitalism has taught him. Because he does not know how to be a medieval warrior, he is at a decided disadvantage in the climactic single combat against the movie's villain, Sir Perceval (played by Vincent Regan, looking more than just a little bit like Rufus Sewell), but he can draw on the stereotype that makes black men sports prodigies—in certain sports. While Perceval mocks Walker for his ineptitude with a sword, Walker defeats his opponent by calling on his skills first in baseball and basketball—sports that African Americans have dominated for the last half century. Finally, he uses his knowledge of golf—perhaps the most Eurocentric of all contemporary sports—to finish Perceval off. "You can thank Tiger for that," he sneers, invoking the most visible symbol of cultural hybridity for popular-sports audiences at the turn of the century—Tiger Woods.

Bending to the pressures of both the *Connecticut Yankee* formula and the expectations of its audience that *Black Knight* deliver a fantasy of the American dream's promise of limitless possibilities, the film's conclusion attempts to repress, to smooth over, Walker/Lawrence's gestures toward hybridity. The conclusion repudiates the rest of the film by asking us to believe that Walker returns from the Middle Ages rehabilitated, no longer a self-fulfilling ethnic stereotype, no longer a member of the marginalized deploying signs of hybridity, no longer an adolescent, but an American capitalist, confident, powerful, responsible, filled with middle-class values. Calling on the whole ideology of Americanness that Hank Morgan—and Hank Martin—represents in *A Connecticut Yankee in King Arthur's Court*, Junger's film asks its viewers to consider Jamal Walker no longer as an *African* American but as an American. By experiencing the European past, he has been socialized into capitalism, heteronormativity, and the family—the foundations of the American middle-class dream. The Medieval World to which Walker returns, however, is as much a fantasy as the "real" medieval world to which he was transported. In a mere six weeks, the film tells us, working with no money and a still largely recalcitrant crew, Walker and Mrs. Bostick transform a seedy and empty theme park in the middle of the ghetto into a going concern—a profitable investment in the hyperreal. Even more remarkable, after the revitalization, this inner-city enterprise seems to be patronized almost exclusively by white people; Medieval World has been gentrified, its previous African American patrons mysteriously vanished. The Middle Ages have been reclaimed for whiteness. The film promises its audience a happy ending that is, of course, impossible. Walker cannot bring the organic, precapitalist communitarianism of the nostalgic Middle Ages back to South Central. He cannot really save Mrs. Bostick's inner-city Medieval World from its inevitable decay any more than he can rehabilitate his neighborhood. He continues to live in white America, which requires hybridity, not dominance, from African American men. He may be a better man for his excellent medieval adventure, but he is still black, poor, underemployed, and living in the hood.

Plato's Cave Redux

Black Knight returns us to the metaphor of time travel with which we began this project. We opened with a discussion of a teenage medievalist's search for the "real" Middle Ages. Kivrin, the protagonist of Connie Willis's *Doomsday Book*, hopes to confront and to escape the very modern problems of the twenty-first-century dystopia in which she lives, a planet ravaged by a global pandemic that functions as a trope for the economic and social dislocation wrought by modernity, by traveling through time back to the Middle Ages. Our desire to travel across time—to return, say, to the Middle Ages—likely contains some portion of the same objectives: to recover the past, to remake it in our own image, to use it as a fantasy against the terrors of the real or of the Real. As we conclude this volume, it seems appropriate to return to the argument with which we began: that the medieval in film has frequently served as an abjected other against which modernity has defined itself, even as it simultaneously functions as the seed from which modernity emerged, as well as a fantasy frame through which the "reality" of modernity might be apprehended, deconstructed, and reconstructed. We might dismiss this fantasy as mere escapism or examine the ways in which fantasies like these function as a support to "give consistency to what we call reality" (Žižek, *The Sublime Object of Ideology*, 44).

We have concluded with discussions of *A Knight's Tale* and *Black Knight* not because these films are remarkable but because they are so very typical. They are products of cinema mass-produced for the masses, their appropriation of the Middle Ages bound up with and intended to advance the agendas of late capitalism. But they also testify to the ways in which the Middle Ages resonate, even with adolescents, a group not generally associated with antiquarian interests. *A Knight's Tale* and *Black Knight*, with their appropriation of twenty-first-century teen culture, remake the Middle Ages into a hospitable place for adolescent play, a kind of Middle Ages R Us. On the one hand, these films find in the Middle Ages "the dense, unvarying, and eminently obvious monolith against which modernity and post-modernity groovily emerge" (Dinshaw, 16). The ideologies of adolescence they offer are simply vulgar versions of the "modernizing avant-gardes" that Bruno Latour criticizes for possessing "a peculiar propensity for understanding time that passes as if it were really abolishing the past behind it" (*We Have Never Been Modern*, 68). On the other hand, these films remind us of Latour's assertion that "we have never been modern." They offer up a belief that the present can only be remediated by returning to medieval times (just as Chip Douglas, the Cable Guy, believes that he must return to the Medieval Times themed restaurant to remediate the soullessness of his contemporary existence).

Lee Patterson worries that, within the academy, medieval studies is conceived of as "a place to escape from the demands of modern intellectual life" (87). His concerns are exacerbated by the appropriation of the Middle Ages in film—especially in popular, Hollywood-driven films like *A Knight's Tale* and *Black Knight*—and by the power of cinema to organize, manipulate, and control fantasies. Toward the end of *A Singular Modernity*, Fredric Jameson recounts a story that Simone de Beauvoir narrates about the existentialist philosopher Jean Paul Sartre in *Adieux: A Farewell to Sartre*. For us the anecdote fleshes out the connections between certain fantasies of the Middle Ages—fantasies that create the kinds of anxieties Patterson relates about academic medieval studies—and the power of film to provide a fantasy that gives consistency (at least temporarily) to the chaotic flux of existence. Sartre explains that "to come out of a theatre of human and humanly produced images was to undergo the shock of existence of a real world of noisy and chaotic urban daylight." In this epiphany he seems to understand that the experience of the real, with its confusion and disorder "is thus not only dependent on a certain perception of the world, it also has as its fundamental precondition an experience of form with which that world is dramatically juxtaposed" (Jameson, *A Singular Modernity*, 207). Sartre offers up an existentialist twist on the image of Plato's cave, the icon with which we began this volume. In the *Republic* Plato's prisoners inside the cave—his trope for humanity immersed in day-to-day existence—think they are experiencing reality, but they perceive only illusions, "the shadows cast by the fire on to the cave wall directly opposite them" (*Republic* 7.515a), so much like the flickering images of a darkened movie theater. For Plato the day-to-day world of human life, the world of noise and chaos—the world projected inside the cave—is merely an illusion, signifying the excess of things unassimilable to the Platonic forms, which Plato insists are the only true reality. By contrast, Sartre, as moviegoer, imagines himself emerging from the theater, where the flickering images offer up a vision that masters contingency through representation, where the flickering images offer the organization and stability hinted at by Plato's notion of the "real." But, Sartre argues, that representation of order and coherence is the illusion, is the prison of the cave. It is only when he emerges from the cocoon of the theater that he experiences "reality," which is the shock of "the existence of a real world of noisy and chaotic urban daylight." *A Knight's Tale* and *Black Knight* imagine both the Middle Ages and movie theaters as versions of Plato's Cave, comfortable spaces that refuse the complexities, the shock, of the "real," the shock of modernity. They represent a Middle Ages of fantasy in which the terrors of modernity can be mastered for the cost of a ticket. It has been the project of this book to deconstruct such facile binaries between reality and illusion. The division of the medieval from the modern—like Sartre's separation of the movie house from the "real world"—is just another restaging, just another "theatre of human and humanly produced images." Is it, we might ask, any more possible to leave the Middle Ages behind, to constitute an absolute break with the past, than to refuse allowing the stuff of movies to seep into our everyday existence? How much of our "real world" is organized around inheritances from the Middle Ages, how much determined by fantasies we have internalized from film?

It is not surprising that popular culture embraces movies about the medieval past; as Umberto Eco has so famously noted, the contemporary West is in a constant state of "dreaming the Middle Ages." These dreams often involve kinds of nostalgia—Eco's "Ten Little Middle Ages"—but he also notes that "our return to the Middle Ages is a quest for our roots and, since we want to come back to the real roots, we are looking for 'reliable Middle Ages,' not for romance and fantasy"

(65). But Eco's differentiations between real and presumably historically verifiable "roots," on the one hand, and "romance and fantasy," on the other, as we have tried to show, continually collapse. Even in the most fanciful films about the medieval period, writers, actors, costumers, set designers, makeup artists, hairstylists, and directors—as well as, often enough, scholarly consultants—conspire to bring us a Middle Ages that is credible, if not entirely historically spot-on. Cinema provides an intersection between nostalgia and the illusion of the recovery of a transparent past. But perhaps we desire even more. We take pleasure in recognizing that the Middle Ages supply the materials for both modern and postmodern identities. Shifts that began during the Middle Ages continue to fashion how we labor and why, who we conceive of as our political friends and who we conceive of as our political enemies, the ways we construct hierarchies of governance, the ways religion plays into our lives. The Middle Ages have taught us the various languages of human relations, both intimate and far-reaching. Through cinema we continually return to the past to reimagine our present. Through cinema we continually revisit the Middle Ages to find ourselves.

Notes

CHAPTER ONE: Traversing the Fantasy

1. Hayden White argues that we cannot understand history as a reproduction, like a model airplane, that we can compare against some original: "we cannot go and look at [historical events] in order to see if the historian has adequately reproduced them in his narrative. Nor should we want to, even if we could; for after all it was the very strangeness of the original as it appeared in the documents that inspired the historian's efforts to make a model of it in the first place. . . . We would have no reason to think that anything at all had been *explained* to us" (White, "The Historical Event as Literary Artifact," 1718).

2. Umberto Eco has coined the term *hyperreal* to describe "a philosophy of immortality as duplication" in which "the past must be preserved and celebrated in full-scale copy" (6). Eco describes hyperreality as a peculiarly, although perhaps not exclusively, American phenomenon: the imagination and taste of the "average American," Eco argues, participates in the philosophy of the hyperreal, a philosophy that "demands the real thing and, to attain it, must fabricate the absolute fake" (8).

3. We have limited our study to what might loosely be termed "costume dramas," that is to films actually set in the Middle Ages. We do not examine works—like *Knightriders* (George Romero, 1981), *The Fisher King* (Terry Gilliam, 1991), or *Indiana Jones and the Last Crusade* (Steven Spielberg, 1989)—that use contemporary settings to explore medieval themes. For exemplary readings of these films see Aronstein, *Hollywood Knights*, 122–43, 160–65. See also Kevin J. Harty, "Cinematic American Camelots Lost and Found." Sue Harper distinguishes between historical films, which she defines as films that deal with historical persons or events, and costume dramas, which "use the mythic and symbolic aspects of the past as a means of providing pleasure, rather than instruction" (127). However, the opposition she posits between historical "truth" and pleasurable fiction is precisely the binary that this study intends to trouble.

4. See Burt, "Getting Schmedieval."

5. See Latour, "Why Has Critique Run Out of Steam?"

6. Gabrielle Spiegel uses the term "social logic" to describe the historical circumstances that are displayed openly in a given text, as well as those that reside in its silences, gaps, and contradictions (84). We have borrowed her concept and extended it to an examination of the ways in which the formal features of a fantasy (in historical

films, for instance) carry social meanings. Susan Aronstein's *Hollywood Knights* engages in a similar project, examining the ways in which the fantasies of Arthurian narratives work in film both to mask and engage with contemporary social issues, although she uses neither the term "social logics" nor the theoretical framework we are invoking here, which we believe enables us to articulate the political importance of fantasy.

7. See Žižek, *Looking Awry*, 3, 10, 91; Žižek, *The Metastases of Enjoyment*, 118; and Žižek, "Grimaces of the Real," 44–48, for discussions of the anamorphotic blot. See also Myers, 99–102.

8. Žižek points to the *X File*'s tagline, "The truth is out there" (*The Plague of Fantasies*, 3).

9. "Enjoyment" is Žižek's translation of Lacan's *jouissance*, a nearly intolerable level of excitation, of pleasure and pain.

10. Analysis of the commodification of the Middle Ages in popular culture has become something of a publishing industry since Eco's book; see Sklar and Hoffman, esp. Sklar, "Marketing Arthur"; Aronstein and Coiner; and Marshall.

11. For a history of British and American medievalism since the fifteenth century, see Aronstein, *Hollywood Knights*, 11–27; though by no means an exhaustive list, works by Bloch and Nichols; Cantor; Chandler; and Alan and Barbara Lupack offer an overview of the field, and rather than repeat that history, we will focus on the founding theoretical assumptions of medievalism as a scholarly field.

12. This description of the field was reproduced on the *Studies in Medievalism* Web page until recently but was replaced with the current description (quoted below) when T. A. Shippey took over as editor.

13. In *Medievalism and the Modernist Temper* Stephen G. Nichols uses the phrase "hard-edged alterity" to describe the break between "past and present, history and theory, medieval studies and medievalism" (49); see also Biddick, *The Shock of Medievalism*, 4.

14. See Biddick, *The Shock of Medievalism*; Ganim, *Medievalism and Orientalism*; Bloch and Nichols, *Medievalism and the Modernist Temper*; Finke and Shichtman, "Profiting Pedants."

15. Shippey, "Studies in Medievalism," www.medievalism.net/about.html (accessed June 23, 2008).

16. As has the term *neomedievalism*, which Bruce Holsinger uses to describe a recent school of thought in International Relations "whose emergence is closely tied to the rise of non-state global actors—NGOs, transnational corporations, organizations like al Qaeda, corporate militias, and so on—as dominant forces in the international political sphere" (Holsinger, *Neomedievalism, Neoconservatism, and the War on Terror*, v).

17. In his essay "Interpreting the Variorum" Stanley Fish has made the same point about formalist literary criticism, arguing that the "formal features [of a text] do not exist independently of the reader's experience" (147) and drawing on the concept of interpretive communities to explain how readers come to "see" the same things "in" texts, as well as how they negotiate their disagreements.

18. We refer here to the narrative related in *The Trials of Arthur: The Life and Times of a Modern-Day King*, by Arthur Pendragon and Christopher Stone (50–51, 82).

19. By "nostalgia" here we mean the longing for an imaginary past that never was.

20. In *The Premodern Condition* Bruce Holsinger documents the fascination the Middle Ages held for the founders of postmodern theory, among whom he includes Zumthor. He argues that "in its variegated assault on the legacy of the Enlightenment, the critical generation of this era turned to the Middle Ages not in a fit of nostalgic retrospection, but in a spirit of both interpretive and ideological resistance to the relentless inevitability of modernity" (5).

21. Lee Patterson has argued that a too-easy acceptance of such views has marginalized medieval studies: "If . . . the master narrative first put in place by the Renaissance is the cause of all our woe as medievalists, then surely we should struggle against it at every level. And yet medieval studies has been all too eager to accept this account, and the professional sequestration it entails" (101). However, the belief that the medieval as a period is significantly different from other periods persists, in the popular imagination, as well as among academics.

22. Kim Moreland, in *The Medievalist Impulse in American Literature*, asks whether for America the Middle Ages might represent a "mythic golden past" (26), a view that is certainly present in Emerson's medievalism (Aronstein, *Hollywood Knights*, 20).

23. For a fascinating reading of the post-9/11 war on terror that explores the fantasy of the medieval as barbarism see Holsinger, *Neomedievalism, Neoconservatism, and the War on Terror*.

24. See "In the Middle," http://jjcohen.blogspot.com/2006/08/dear-capital-one .html (accessed Jan. 27, 2009); see also Haydock, *Movie Medievalism*, 13.

25. Less than a year after we wrote these words, the collapse of global financial markets made this commercial seem almost prophetic.

CHAPTER TWO: Signs of the Medieval

1. See "Discourse in the Novel," in Bakhtin, *The Dialogic Imagination*, 259–422. As early as 1927 the great formalist Boris Eichenbaum was already arguing for applying literary and linguistic models to film studies; see Eichenbaum, "Problems of Film Stylistics."

2. Eisenstein's *October* was released in 1928, the same year in which P. N. Medvedev's *The Formal Method in Literary Scholarship* (a text attributed by some Bakhtin scholars to Bakhtin himself) appeared and a year before the appearance of *Marxism and the Philosophy of Language* (attributed to V. N. Vološinov but also thought by some to have been authored by Bakhtin) and *Problems of Dostoevsky's Poetics*. In "The Problem of the Text" Bakhtin leaves room for the analysis of nonlinguistic signs: "Any sign system (i.e., any language), regardless of how small the collective that produces its conventions may be, can always in principle be deciphered, that is, translated into other sign systems (other languages). Consequently, sign systems have a common logic, a potential single language of languages (which, of course, can never become a

single concrete language, one of the languages)" (*Speech Genres and Other Late Essays*, 106). For discussions of the authorship question in Bakhtin scholarship see Todorov, 6–13; Clark and Holquist, 146–70; and Morson and Emerson, 31–48.

3. *Remediation* is the term Bolter and Grusin use to describe "the formal logic by which new media refashion prior media forms" (273); in the case of film criticism this logic pertains to the ways in which film refashions earlier media, like the book or the manuscript.

4. Remediation, immediacy (transparency), and hypermediacy (opacity) are the three traits identified by Bolter and Grusin in their genealogy of the so-called new media. While immediacy aims to render the medium transparent, hypermediacy calls attention to the medium.

5. Nickolas Haydock discusses the technical processes through which Boorman achieved this effect (*Movie Medievalism*, 70).

6. We are grateful to our colleague Sarah Blick of the Department of Art History at Kenyon College for pointing this out to us, as well as for her insightful observations on this image. Martha Driver has also noted some ways in which modern films "remediate" medieval manuscripts; see "What's Accuracy Got to Do with It?"

7. As early as 1975 Raymond Williams was denouncing the belief that new technologies "are discovered, by an essentially internal process of research and development, which then sets the conditions for social change and progress" (13).

8. A process already begun with the introduction of the Sony Walkman in the 1980s; see du Gay et al., 113–18.

9. Close readings of the formal features of Dreyer's *La Passion de Jeanne d'Arc* by David Bordwell in 1973 and 1981 and of that same film's textual variants by Tony Pipelo in 1988 employed this technology.

10. Criterion releases come with cases sporting a somber black label with the director's signature and the legend "Director Approved Special Edition."

11. A sophistication that Sobchack, as coauthor of an introductory film textbook and author or editor of numerous film books, certainly possesses.

12. *Translinguistics* is the term coined by Julia Kristeva to describe Bakhtin's project, a translation of a Russian term he uses in "The Problem of the Text in Linguistics, Philology, and the Human Sciences" (Bakhtin, *Speech Genres and Other Late Essays*, 103–31). On the theoretical problems associated with describing film semiotics as a "language" see the essays by Buckland and by Currie in Miller and Stam, 84–104, 105–22.

13. We do not intend to engage in the debate between psychoanalytic and cognitive film theory, but given its prominence in current film studies, it does form a backdrop to our study. Both tendencies in film theory, to our mind, tend toward the formalist and ignore the sociohistorical dimensions of film. A Bakhtinian approach provides a salutary corrective. For an introduction to this debate see Bordwell and Carroll, *Post-Theory*; Žižek, *The Fright of Real Tears*; and the essay by Gregory Currie in Miller and Stam, 105–22.

14. The protagonist's name was first changed from Twain's Hank Morgan in David Butler's 1931 film version starring Will Rogers.

15. See Finke and Shichtman, "No Pain, No Gain," 121–22.

16. Throughout the film Jones and Gilliam play extensively with depth of field as a way of minimizing Arthur's significance. He is literally "cut down to size," frequently shown as a tiny figure in the extreme background of a shot.

17. For a useful discussion of the cognitive bases of the shot–reverse shot sequence see Bordwell, "Convention, Construction, and Cinematic Vision."

18. Our argument here is not all that far from David Day's analysis of the film, which claims that the "vehicle of the film" is the first and most obvious target of satire (see Day, "Monty Python and the Medieval Other," 83).

CHAPTER THREE: Celluloid History

1. Among the ranks of "new history films," Rosenstone includes *Hitler: A Film from Germany* (Hans-Jürgen Syberberg, 1977), *Hiroshima mon amour* (Alain Resnais, 1959), *Distant Voices, Still Lives* (Terençe Davies, 1988). See also Lindley, "The Ahistoricism of Medieval Film," on *The Seventh Seal* (Ingmar Bergman, 1957) and *The Navigator* (Vincent Ward, 1988).

2. Norris Lacy describes his participation as a talking head in the documentary representation of Arthurian culture in his essay "The Documentary Arthur" (see 77–86). See Haydock's reading of this scene (*Movie Medievalism,* 12). Later in this chapter we will examine more closely one Monty Python director's excursion into documentary filmmaking.

3. The film's credits identify the historian as "not A. J. P. Taylor," the controversial left-wing British historian famous for his frequent appearances on television news shows and BBC documentaries. Taylor, who also makes a cameo appearance in Terry Gilliam's 1981 *Time Bandits*, becomes, for Python, the emblem of the historian authorized as "talking head." However, this identification can finally exist only as an in-joke among academic historians. For the majority of the film's viewers the documentary's historian will always be anonymous (*not* A. J. P. Taylor). On Eric Idle's revisions of this character for his 2005 Broadway musical *Spamalot* see Finke and Aronstein, 4–5.

4. Haydock identifies the knight as Lancelot; however, the knight in this scene is not wearing on his tunic the insignia that has identified Lancelot throughout the rest of the film.

5. The reference here is to John Grierson, the Scottish filmmaker who inaugurated the British documentary film movement in the 1930s.

6. In *The Formal Method in Literary Scholarship* Medvedev defines tact as "the ensemble of codes governing discursive interaction," which are determined by "the aggregate of all the social relationships of the speakers, their ideological horizons, and, finally, the concrete situation of the conversation" (Stam, 45). Stam argues that tact is a useful concept for film theory, "applying literally to the verbal exchanges within the diegesis, and figuratively to the tact involved in the metaphorical dialogue of gen-

res and discourses within the text, as well as to the 'dialogue' between film and spectator" (45).

7. On history's claims to represent the real see Finke and Shichtman, *King Arthur and the Myth of History*, 10–21. The situation for documentary film is not nearly as simple or straightforward as Carroll would have us believe. Todd Phillips and Andrew Gurland's 1998 award-winning documentary *Frat House* is a salutary case in point. Commissioned by HBO and highly praised by critics, this study of college fraternity hazing practices never aired because of allegations that the hazing footage was not authentic but had been recreated by Phillips and Gurland using fraternity members from Muhlenberg College in Pennsylvania as actors. On the other hand, in Michael Block's 1973 *No Lies*, a documentary that is entirely staged, the interviewer we see onscreen with a handheld camera interviewing a woman about a recent rape is, in fact, an actor, as is the woman. The film offers a metacommentary on the abuses of journalism that "risk . . . turning people into victims so that we can learn about their suffering and misery" (see Nichols, *Introduction to Documentary*, 12–13).

8. For a more detailed discussion of Crusades history and filmmaking see chapter 7.

9. Hayden White would argue that what is at stake is how the Crusades are narrativized; see "The Historical Event as Literary Artifact," 1720. In *Neomedievalism, Neoconservatism, and the War on Terror* Bruce Holsinger offers a more nuanced analysis of the ways in which the Crusades resonate in current international relations, especially around the Middle East and the so-called war on terror.

CHAPTER FOUR: Mirror of Princes

1. John of Salisbury, 67. Christine de Pisan, whose *Book of the Body of Policy* (1406) was written about a century earlier than *The Prince* and translated into English in 1470 by Anthony Woodville, Edward IV's brother-in-law, offers another example of this genre. For a comparison of the corporeal metaphor of the body politic in these two medieval writers, see Forhan, "Polycracy," and Finke, "The Politics of the Canon."

2. On women's exclusion from the original liberal social contract see Pateman, 33–57, and Wendy Brown, 162–64.

3. On American Arthurian films see Aronstein, *Hollywood Knights*; for a comprehensive filmography of Arthurian films see Harty, *Cinema Arthuriana*, 253–301.

4. Our discussion of this scene is indebted to Aronstein, *Hollywood Knights*, 112–13; Day, "*Monty Python and the Holy Grail*," 131; and Burns, "Nostalgia Isn't What It Used to Be," 92.

5. Aronstein describes this scene using Althusser's notion of interpellation. Arthur's attempts to "hail" the peasants as his subjects are consistently refused (*Hollywood Knights*, 113–14).

6. This same shot, ironically, turns up in the Grail sequence of *Excalibur*, serving a very different purpose. In that film, as Arthur's knights ride throughout the wasteland in search of the Grail, one of them comes on a group of peasants digging in the

mud. Here, however, the scene works in the service of the view that sees the Middle Ages as an integrated society. In *Excalibur*'s mythic world, because "the land and the king are one," the land cannot prosper without the authority and power of the king. In his absence it becomes wasteland—mud.

7. This image is accessible at Wikimedia Commons: http://commons.wikimedia .org/wiki/Image:Edmund_blair_leighton_accolade.jpg (accessed March 1, 2009).

8. Aronstein describes the American context into which the film was released; see *Hollywood Knights*, 109–10.

9. The film's financial records are appended to the script; see Monty Python, 91–92.

10. See Friedman for a discussion of British film during the Thatcher years.

11. The theme is repeated nine times in the film, but these first three segments contain more than half of the occurrences. As early as 1911, the Wagnerian technique of assigning musical motifs to particular characters, objects, or actions was a well-established filmic technique: "To each important character, to each important action, motif, or idea, and to each important object (Siegmund's sword, for example), was attached a suggestive musical theme. Whenever the action brought into prominence any of the characters, motifs, or objects, its theme or motif was sung or played" (Clarence Sinn, quoted in Paulin, 70).

12. Sontag argues that this aesthetic is neither tied to a specific historical period nor confined to the politics of the radical right. It can be found, for instance, in Walt Disney's *Fantasia*, Busby Berkeley's *The Gang's All Here*, and Stanley Kubrick's *2001* (91), as well as in movements as diverse as "youth/rock culture, primal therapy, antipsychiatry, Third World camp-following, and the belief in the occult" (96). For a fuller discussion of the fascist sensibility and its attraction to things medieval see Finke and Shichtman, *King Arthur and the Myth of History*, 186–214.

13. The transformation of Arthur's kingdom into the wasteland is illustrated by the change in seasons from the lush greens of Lancelot and Guenevere's love scene to the barren landscape through which the knights ride.

14. *Excalibur* was virtually the first American film to use this musical piece in its score. Orff's cantata was popular in Nazi Germany.

15. In this regard it is worth remembering that the French government did not disestablish the church until 1905, only about fifty years before Anouilh's play; up until that point the Catholic Church had been the state religion of France.

16. Although "homosociality" can describe same-sex affective bonds between either males or females, it most often describes the institutionalized, erotically charged bonds between men that empower them socially. We use this term to emphasize the structure of men's relationships under patriarchy, the relation of male bonding to institutionalized heterosexuality.

17. The phrase is Gayle Rubin's; see also Sedgwick, *Between Men*.

18. There is, however, evidence that, as archbishop, Becket did surround himself with Saxon clergy, including his good friend John of Salisbury, who was born in Old Sarum (Winston, 100).

19. "Becket or the Honor of God," unsigned review, http://brothersjudd.com/index .cfm/fuseaction/reviews.detail/book_id/995/Becket%20or%20Th.htm (accessed Feb. 4, 2009).

20. In the play Anouilh includes in a later scene the following remark from the king: "Saxons are always called 'dog.' I can't think why, really. One could just as well have called them 'Saxons' " (14).

21. Later in the same scene, as Becket and Henry discuss gold plate and forks, Becket is revealed as wealthier and more civilized than his Norman conquerors and even than the king himself (a belief no doubt shared by the twentieth-century French about their German occupiers). The dinner scene that follows is designed to highlight this disparity, showcasing Becket's wealth and taste.

22. In the play Becket displaces his own collaboration onto his father: "He managed, by collaborating, to amass a considerable fortune. As he was a man of rigid principles, I imagined he contrived to do it in accordance with his conscience. That's a little piece of sleight of hand that men of principle are very adept at in troubled times" (Anouilh, 4).

23. In fact, England required, from the fifth century on, a class of professional interpreters, called *latimarii*, who acted as "intermediaries and translators between one race and another" (Salter, 9; see our discussion in *King Arthur and the Myth of History*, 125, 129). After the Conquest this group became even more important in managing the cultural Babel created by frequent intermarriages among speakers of French, Breton, English, Welsh, Scandinavian, Cornish, and Irish (not to mention the ubiquitous presence of Latin-speaking clerics) in the Anglo-Norman courts and their anxious coexistence within hierarchically integrated households bound tightly together by patronage ties. Anouilh's focus on collaboration is encouraged by Thierry's nineteenth-century romantic nationalism and born of a post-Holocaust world in which the question, "Can one collaborate with honor?" would be pressing.

24. The triumphant entry into the French city and Becket's investiture as archbishop of Canterbury are examples of other such scenes. In some ways, so is his death scene. Glenville generally marks his scenes of "fascist dramaturgy" with the camera moving downward. This calls to mind Riefenstahl's technique in *Triumph of the Will* in which scenes generally tend to move from high to low, from the sky to the earth.

25. Goldman's play premiered at the Ambassador Theater in New York City on March 3, 1966. Robert Preston played Henry, Rosemary Harris a very young Eleanor (thirty-nine, compared to Hepburn, who was sixty-one in 1968), and Christopher Walken played Philip of France (Goldman, ix). It ran for ninety-two performances, closing in May of 1966 and won Tony Awards for Best Actress and Best Direction.

26. This film jump-started the film careers of many of its principals. This was both Nigel Terry's and Timothy Dalton's first film (*Excalibur* was Terry's second) and only Anthony Hopkins's third. After Hepburn and O'Toole, Jane Merrow was perhaps the most accomplished actor, having already appeared in at least thirteen films, and she gets billing over all three male newcomers whose careers have since eclipsed hers.

27. This reference to *King Lear* is in Goldman's original play, but it occurs later, after the first audience with Phillip, and Henry relates it to Eleanor, not Alais. During Henry II's lifetime, knowledge of the story of Lear would have been available through Geoffrey of Monmouth's account in *Historia Regum Brittanniae,* but Goldman is almost certainly referencing Shakespeare. John did indeed become king of England after his brother Richard's death and promptly managed to lose Henry's land to France, earning him the appellation John Lackland and making Henry's words seem bitterly ironic in retrospect.

28. That the psychological language of family dysfunction has found its way into popular discussions of public figures is suggested by an article on royal scandals that appeared in *Psychology Today* in 1992; see Montefiori, who asserts of the United Kingdom's house of Windsor that "the press's feverish pursuit of even the slightest detail of royal life is to blame for their dysfunctional family unit" (33).

29. Pateman goes on to argue that the repression of the private sphere of the home from political theorists' accounts of the public sphere makes room for the emergence of yet another public-private dichotomy, that between public or common weal and private enterprise (122).

30. We are not reading *The Lion in Winter* through psychoanalysis, nor are we drawing on any particular brand of psychoanalysis; instead, we argue that psychoanalysis has provided a cultural narrative about the domestic sphere that was readily available to both writer and director and that they have used it to shape their account of late-twelfth-century British and French politics.

31. While he has only a small role in the film, William Marshal did indeed serve as marshal of England under Henry II and was his closest adviser. Henry died in 1189, Marshal in 1219. For accounts of Marshal's life, based on the vita his son had written after his death, see Duby, *William Marshal: The Flower of Chivalry,* and Crouch, *William Marshal: Knighthood, War, and Chivalry, 1147–1219.*

32. Since all of the action of Goldman's play takes place in Chinon castle, these scenes were added for the film, primarily to introduce each of the principals, whom we might compare with Goldman's stage directions: John is a "charming-looking boy," despite his pimples; Richard, "a famous soldier since his middle teens, and justly so; war is his profession and he is good at it"; and Geoffrey, "charming and owner of the best brain of a brainy family" (9).

33. In his DVD commentary Anthony Harvey suggests that Barry's music in this scene was inspired by Benjamin Britten's *Peter Grimes,* which the director had used as a temp track in an early cut of the film.

34. "He wears, as always, plain and unimpressive clothes" (Goldman 3).

35. *Becket* also creates a distinction in styles between the French and English monarchies. Scenes set in the French court are much more brightly lit than those in the English castle and its king and courtiers much more fashionably and colorfully dressed.

36. Henry refers to Eleanor as "a woman out of legend." Tolhurst describes her as "an Everywoman whom each male historian or poet uses to praise or critique the

women in his own culture and time" (9), although Eleanor is perhaps too larger-than-life, too legendary, to be Everywoman. Richard shows up frequently in medieval films, in both Robin Hood and Crusades films (see chapter 7). The Third Crusade, as Aberth argues, has proven irresistible as a film subject because of its romantic pairing of two legendary figures, Richard and Saladin (70). Even an Arab film like Youssef Chahine's 1963 *Saladin* portrays Richard as a figure of romance. For another filmic revision of Richard's legend see Richard Lester's 1976 *Robin and Marian*, where an aging Richard, played by Richard Harris, is a grotesque and bloodthirsty figure.

37. *The Lion in Winter* challenges any auteur theory of filmmaking. In fact, in his DVD commentary Harvey relates how it was O'Toole who asked him to direct the film, suggesting that the actors, because of their star status, had more creative input than is usual. He also highlights the contributions of several other artists to the film, including his composer, editor, and cinematographer. While Harvey undoubtedly had an aesthetic vision for this film, he is also conscious of the collaborative nature of the art.

38. The film subscribes to a pathology model of homosexuality largely derived from a popular Freudianism that saw it as the result of family dysfunction: an absent father and overinvolved mother. This view, which replaced an earlier sin model, was prominent in the pre-Stonewall 1960s as American movies were beginning to break the Production Code's taboo on naming homosexuality.

CHAPTER FIVE: The Politics of Hagiography

1. Robin Blaetz has examined uses of Joan of Arc in American film and culture in *Visions of the Maid*. For a detailed history of the saint see Pernoud and Clin; for a brief summary of her life and achievements see Aberth, 257–77. Throughout this chapter we use the English version of the saint's name (Joan of Arc) except when we are describing a French film, such as Dreyer's, which uses the French "Jeanne d'Arc."

2. The Miracle of St. Joseph, www.themiracleofstjoseph.org/speaker1678.html (accessed Sept. 6, 2008). Here is a sample from a revelation given to Klug on March 13, 1985. Joan speaks:

My death was a terrible death, not because I was so young, but I was forced into a position where I could not run. I was tied and I was abandoned by many of those whom I loved. But the words at the end, when I knew I could no longer fight for what I knew was right, have never been given to the world correctly. I am Saint Joan of Arc. My words were these: If I have failed You, my God, forgive me. If I have done one impure thing that was my own fault, forgive me. And now that man has judged me and I go to Your Judgment, have mercy on me, for in my littleness, if I have failed You, I ask Your Forgiveness. Do not let the evil one touch me. I could not bear the stench of his place. Please God, take me to Where You are, for my Soul's sake. So be it.

3. She is included, for instance, in Ruth Ashby's and Deborah Gore Orhn's *Herstory: Women Who Changed the World* (38), a collection, aimed at an audience of "young

women," of some 120 biographical sketches of famous women, from Sappho to Evita Peron, from Sultana Razia in thirteenth-century India to the 1991 Nobel Peace Prize winner, Aung San Suu Kyi.

4. It is easy in retrospect to see Joan's canonization as inevitable and therefore important to remember that it was vigorously debated. Many believed that, while Joan was certainly a heroic figure in French history, her life did not provide evidence of any special sanctity. On the arguments against Joan's canonization see Henry Ansgar Kelly's essay on the Devil's Advocate (the Promoter of the Faith), the cleric charged with assembling the case against canonization.

5. Formal proceedings for her canonization began only in 1869 with a petition to Rome from Felix Dupanloup, bishop of Orléans (Henry Kelly, 206). On Joan's connection with nineteenth-century nationalist movements see Winock, 103–10; Weber, *The Nationalist Revival in France*, 69–71; and Warner, 255–65.

6. In 1895 a Jewish military officer, Alfred Dreyfus, was convicted of treason. Based on new evidence, he was retried in 1899 and once again found guilty. He was finally exonerated in 1904 after the leftists took power. The fallout from these trials consumed French politics for decades after the trials were over, polarizing public opinion for and against Dreyfus and by extension French Jews. For details see Winock, 114–16.

7. For a discussion on the significance of Joan's virginity see McInerney, 195–211.

8. Both Dreyer's original print and a second print he made from outtakes were destroyed by fire. In 1981 a nitrate print of the film was discovered in a mental hospital outside of Oslo. Medievalists, more than anyone, can appreciate the textual problems presented by Dreyer's film. As with medieval manuscripts, the "text" of the film exists in several different versions, none of which is the "original." Like the modern editions of medieval texts that we use in our classrooms, *La Passion de Jeanne d'Arc* may be viewed only as a reconstruction governed by the principles of "mouvaunce" (see Pipelo, 301–2; on the "mouvaunce" of the medieval text see Zumthor).

9. In *Filmguide to "La Passion de Jeanne d'Arc,"* Bordwell explicitly links the film with the avant-garde artistic experimentation of 1920s Paris (see 13–14).

10. As Paula Marantz Cohen has suggested, the term *popular audience* can be a marker of both class and nationality. Formalism and experimentation are seen as upper class and European; the popular cinema is understood as middle- to lowbrow and American; the innovation in special effects and editing by the Hollywood film industry is rarely viewed as experimental or avant-garde (10–11).

11. Dreyer's notion of abstraction is remarkably reified in Picasso's series of lithographs of a bull that successively strip away (or abstract) features until there is nothing left but nine lines to convey the form of the bull. Similarly, Dreyer began with realistic sets, costumes, and props and then through his camera work stripped them away.

12. This is a point that escaped at least one of the film's reviewers. The 1929 *Variety* reviewer clearly thought the film's title was promising something much more than it delivered: "This 'Passion of Joan of Arc' isn't worth a dollar to any commercial reg-

ular picture theatre in the U.S. Unless the theatre is willing to rely upon the deceptive 'Passion' of the title which is meaningless on the screen" (April 10, 1929).

13. It is possible, with a lot of help, to figure out the names of Jeanne's judges in the film, although none are named anywhere in the intertitles. Caspar Tybjerg's commentary on the Criterion Collection DVD of the film is extremely helpful in this regard. However, initially the film was screened without credits, and the casual viewer would be hard put to associate any names with the various judges without a great deal of research; viewers are much more likely to think of them as the tall thin one, the fat one with hair like horns, etc. The cast, in fact, included a very young Antonin Artaud, promoter of the "theater of cruelty," as the priest Massieu.

14. Seldom has a work in feminist theory been as foundational as Mulvey's essay. Virtually all work in feminist film studies since 1975 has been a response to "Visual Pleasure and Narrative Cinema," including Mulvey's own "Afterthoughts on 'Visual Pleasure and Narrative Cinema' inspired by King Vidor's *Duel in the Sun* (1946)." In his 1982 book, *The Imaginary Signifier*, Christian Metz followed Mulvey in arguing that the voyeuristic qualities of the film screen aligns the spectator with sadism—with mastery, possession, and control of the screen object. E. Ann Kaplan's 2000 volume *Feminism and Film* collects important feminist essays from the 1980s that "debated, argued against, or built out from" Mulvey's essay. These include Mary Ann Doane's "Film and the Masquerade: Theorising the Female Spectator" (1982); Kaplan's "Is the Gaze Male?" (1983); Steve Neale's "Masculinity as Spectacle: Reflections on Men and Mainstream Cinema" (1983); and Gaylyn Studlar's "Masochism and the Perverse Pleasures of the Cinema" (1984).

15. On the glamour shot see Turner, 54; on the star system see Dyer. Leni Riefenstahl in *The Wonderful, Horrible Life of Leni Riefenstahl* (Ray Müller, 1993) describes how she lit men and women differently. In her fiction films *Blue Light* and *Tiefland* the men were lit from the side so that their features stood out. Women, she states, should be lit to look "young and lovely"; she usually accomplished this by means of a very soft light from the front.

16. In "Remembering Women: Psychical and Historical Constructions in Film Theory," Mary Ann Doane criticizes gaze theory for its lack of flexibility. Because the masculine gaze is always posited as the site of mastery and control, while the feminine is marked by submission to the gaze, the "totalizing nature of its analysis of patriarchy leaves little room for resistance" or alternative practices (47). Sue Ellen Case argues that the paradigm locks the activity of looking into an Oedipal heterosexuality: "The hegemonic spread of the psychoanalytic [visual apparatus] does not allow for an imaginary of the queer," she writes (11). Norman Bryson points out that theories drawing on a visual apparatus based on a gendered split between female object and male voyeur remain "relatively undeveloped in dealing with what is at stake in the male gaze upon another male" (230).

17. Quoted in Bordwell, *Filmguide to "La Passion de Jeanne d'Arc,"* 19. Dreyer shot this film entirely in sequence (unusual for narrative filmmaking) so that his actors would experience Jeanne's story as it unfolded.

18. This perhaps explains why the acting in the film seems more naturalistic to modern audiences than conventional silent film acting usually does.

19. Gish, ironically, was one of the actresses Dreyer considered for his Jeanne before choosing Falconetti.

20. To be sure, contemporary feminist film theory does offer alternative conceptions of the gaze that do not rely on sadism, objectification, distance, and possession. These alternatives tend to be aligned most closely with the maternal and the pre-Oedipal period of object relations. Gaylyn Studlar, in "Masochism and the Perverse Pleasures of the Cinema," turns to the psychoanalytic theories of masochism advanced by Gilles Deleuze to describe the cinematic gaze. E. Ann Kaplan, in "Is the Gaze Male?" and "The Case of the Missing Mother," and Linda Williams, in " 'Something Else besides a Mother,' " focus on the genre of maternal melodrama and its connection to the pre-Oedipal in an attempt to define a kind of female spectatorship.

21. Holy cards are small cards around 2½" by 4½" often given to Catholic children in school as rewards or gifts or distributed at funerals as memorials. The cards usually have a religious image of some kind on one side and text—either a prayer or information about the deceased or the image—on the reverse side; see Petruzzelli. While such cards date back as far as the fifteenth century, they became especially popular during the nineteenth century and continue in use even today.

22. Initially Dreyer had wished to make a sound picture (*La Passion de Jeanne d'Arc* was released in the same year as the first "talkie"), but he discovered that European studios were not yet equipped for sound (Bordwell, *Filmguide to "La Passion de Jeanne d'Arc,"* 14).

23. This is the version of the final intertitle used in the Criterion DVD. At least two other variations exist. Dreyer's screenplay reads, "As the sun went down Joan's heart was sunk in the river, the heart which from that time became the heart of France, just as she herself was the incarnation of the eternal Flame" (Dreyer, *Four Screenplays,* 76). The version on the video recording reads: "and amid the flames the white soul of Jeanne rose heavenwards, that soul which has become the soul of France, as Jeanne herself has become the incarnation of imperishable France."

24. Bernstein, *Walter Wanger,* xiv, 239–45; the film needed to recoup $4,600,000 in negative costs, according to a *Variety* reviewer (Oct. 20, 1948).

25. Bosley Crowther of the *New York Times* wrote that the film, "while honestly intended, fails to come finally to life or to give a profound comprehension of the torment and triumph of Joan" (Nov. 12, 1948).

26. See Legion of Decency, *Motion Pictures Classified by National Legion of Decency.* By way of comparison, Shaw's *Major Barbara* was given a B rating for "irreverence and cynicism toward religious matters and marriage" (F. Walsh, 141). The vast majority of B and C films between 1936 and 1959, however, were foreign made. Rossellini's modern religious parable *The Miracle* (1948) was condemned (C rating) as "a sacrilegious and blasphemous mockery of Christian and religious truth" (Black, 94).

27. The New York office operated on a shoestring budget, its staff consisting of a director, Father John J. McClafferty; a secretary; and a coordinator of the volunteer

reviewers, Mary Looram, who was the head of the IFCA (International Federation of Catholic Alumnae) Motion Picture Bureau.

28. Richard Maltby has explored the failure of Protestant religious groups to exercise the kind of influence over film censorship that Catholic organizations did; see *"The King of Kings* and the Czar of all the Rushes."

29. *The Robe's* rating comes with the following caveat: "While this film deals with incidents of Sacred history in a reverent and inspirational manner, it is to be noted that it is a fictional narrative and contains variance from and omissions of Scriptural and historical accuracy" (F. Walsh, 197).

30. For films released after 1960 we have relied on the ratings of the Legion of Decency's successor organization, the United States Conference of Catholic Bishops' Office for Film and Broadcasting, which currently maintains its own movie ratings (www.usccb.org/movies [accessed Sept. 7, 2008]).

31. Shaw's *St. Joan* was finally made into a film in 1957 by Otto Preminger. This film is perhaps most noteworthy for Preminger's nationwide search to find a teenage Joan, a search that culminated in Jean Seberg, and then for almost incinerating his star in the execution scene when the gas jets exploded.

32. The version of the film that premiered in 1948 ran 146 minutes. When it failed to produce the kind of profits needed to recoup costs, the film was almost immediately cut to 100 minutes to make it more saleable. At this point the narration and maps were added to assist the audience, although, in fact, the narration provides more commentary than exposition. In May 2004 Image-Entertainment released on DVD the University of California Film and Television Archive's restoration of the 146-minute version, which had not been seen for more than half a century. Although it is tempting to view this newly restored print as the best realization of the filmmakers' original intention and to relegate the shorter version to the status of "butchered" masterpiece, we reject this view as naive and ahistorical auteurism. We prefer instead to try to articulate the historical meanings produced by different prints of the same films (see note 8 above), in much the same way that we have argued elsewhere for the need to articulate the historical meanings produced by the variability of medieval manuscripts (see Finke and Shichtman, "Profiting Pedants"). We view each version as a unique event, representing not only the labor of artists but also the activities of viewers, reviewers, censors, financiers, museum curators, and preservationists. For this reason our analysis of the film and its relationship to American ideologies in the postwar period will draw on both versions.

33. Naish emphasizes Luxembourg's villainy through facial deformations. He sports a scar and a deformed eye. His performance illustrates how casting can shape a film's meanings (Turner, 105–6). Naish had already appeared in several horror films, including *Dr. Renault's Secret* (1942), *Calling Dr. Death* (1943, with Lon Chaney Jr.), *The Monster Maker* (1944), and *House of Frankenstein* (1944), which made it easy for audiences at the time to identify him as a villain.

34. On changes in women's roles during the war and the propaganda campaigns

that encouraged women's entry into the workforce see Blaetz, 118–19; Dabakis; Rupp; and Honey. On women's lives during the 1950s see Harvey and see Coontz.

35. Early in the film Joan mentions that she would rather be with her mother sewing than saving France, and after her capture she is shown sewing with the countess of Luxembourg, who comments on the excellence of her spinning and sewing.

36. Blaetz argues that this change borrows structurally from film noir, moving backward from a "fixed, morbid end" (135).

37. The shortened version also eliminates references to Joan's refusal to give up wearing men's clothing, another central issue in her trial that the longer version restores.

38. This threat is also represented by repeated characterizations of Joan as a "green country girl" by both friends and enemies.

39. One exception is Jean-Pierre Dufreigne, reviewing the film for the French weekly *L'Express*, who thought the sequences worked precisely because, since Besson couldn't hope to measure up to Robert Bresson's presentation of the trial sequences (in his 1962 *Procès de Jeanne d'Arc*), the scenes with The Conscience offer at least a novel approach to this part of Jeanne's story (Oct. 28, 1999). Nickolas Haydock's perceptive essay on this film discusses Dustin Hoffman's role as a figure for "postmodern doubt," in a reading that intersects with ours at several points. Haydock notes that in the screenplay Hoffman's character was called simply "Man," a designation with quite a different valence from "The Conscience," which is how he is finally billed in the credits (see Haydock, "Shooting the Messenger," 257–63).

40. Haydock treats this scene primarily from Birkin's screenplay, which he believes creates "a more uncanny figure, morally indeterminate rather than just stern and uncompromising" (260), than the film presents. Our analysis derives primarily from the film text.

41. The "paratext," as the term is used by Richard Burt, comprises a film's "title sequences, trailers, movie posters, interviews with filmmakers, historian consultants, and their extension and dispersal through new digital and electronic media: DVD audio commentaries by directors and historians, deleted scenes, animated menus, official film websites, fan websites; trailer websites; and so on" (Burt, 218).

42. The presence of Gilles de Rais, who was a notorious sexual predator and serial killer, in Joan of Arc films (he is also a character in Fleming's *Joan of Arc*) raises some interesting questions about Joan's story, although we do not have the space to pursue them here.

43. See Haydock's perceptive analysis of the scene ("Shooting the Messenger," 248–49).

44. Cynical in Žižek's terms because Besson and his viewers know perfectly well that Joan is mad, but they act as if she were a saint. (Or alternatively, they know perfectly well that she is a saint, but they act as though she is mad.) On cynicism see Žižek, *The Sublime Object of Ideology*, 28–30. In this respect *The Messenger* seems an odd film because both Besson and his leading lady, when they talk about the film, act as if they believe Joan was a saint and hero yet present her as if she were mad.

45. In Haydock's reading of this scene Joan is compared to the vampire child played by Kirsten Dunst in Neil Jordan's *Interview with the Vampire* (1994) (see "Shooting the Messenger," 250).

46. On medieval mystics see Finke, *Feminist Theory, Women's Writing*, 84–98, and Finke, *Women's Writing in English*, 126–45. Haydock also points to small details that "seem to derive from the golden legend" of Opus Dei's founder, Josemaria Escrivá, without considering that such details are conventional for the genre of hagiography (see "Shooting the Messenger," 266).

47. Although there is much debate about the validity of lumping all sectarian religious movements under the banner of "fundamentalism," one belief that the religious movements that get so labeled share is a suspicion of modernization and secularization (although these suspicions are often highly selective; see Aho). For a survey of the sociological literature on religious fundamentalism see Emerson and Hartman; on Conservative Protestants in the United States see Woodberry and Smith.

48. See Cuneo, 84. Modernism is the heresy condemned by Pius X at the turn of the century; it might be described most simply as the desire to adapt Catholic dogma to the intellectual, moral, and social needs of the contemporary or modern world. Traditionalists frequently cite Pius IX's *Syllabus of Errors* (1864), which denounces the view that the pope "can or should reconcile himself to, or agree with, progress, liberalism, and modern civilization" (Cuneo, 195). Kevin Smith parodies the reformism of Vatican II in *Dogma* through the character of Cardinal Glick and his "Buddy Christ" icon. *Dogma* was released at almost the same time—late 1999—as *The Messenger* and was frequently paired with it in reviews.

49. Opus Dei has tended to generate a great deal of polemical writing. For defenses see Le Tourneur and see O'Connor. For an exposé see M. Walsh. The most balanced sociological treatment of Opus Dei is the Spanish sociologist Joan Estruch's *Saints and Schemers*. The organization has perhaps been most notorious for its appearance in Dan Brown's popular novel *The Da Vinci Code*.

50. For more on this conflict see www.sspx.org (accessed Sept. 7, 2008).

51. For a full description of these groups see Cuneo. While these groups' numbers represent only a small percentage of the world's Catholics, the release in 2004 of *The Passion of the Christ* propelled them into the limelight as newspapers began to run stories about Mel Gibson's traditionalist beliefs and the chapel he founded in Malibu. Gibson's film, which draws heavily on the visionary writing of the eighteenth-century German mystic Anna-Katarina Emmerick, reveals its ultraorthodox Catholicism at every turn; it seems more medieval passion play than biblical history. If Catholic dissidents turn to the Middle Ages for their religious doctrine, however, their embrace of the Internet as a way of getting out their message marks them as thoroughly modern. Each of the schismatic and millenarian groups has its own extensive Web site, from SSPX (www.sspx.org) and SSPV (www.sspv.net) to the Fatima Crusade (www.fatima.org; see Cuneo, 134–52) and the Bayside Movement of Veronica Lueken (www.tidm.org; Cuneo, 152–77).

52. "Jean Marie Le Pen in Athens," Hellenic Lines, www.e-grammes.gr/2005/01/lepen_en.htm (accessed Feb. 9, 2009).

53. For a fuller discussion of the interplay of violence and the gaze in Besson's early films see Hayward, 77–125.

54. A Web site titled Catholics in the Military publishes a list of "military saints" (www.catholicmil.org [accessed March 18, 2009]); however, with the exception of Joan of Arc, they are more notable for their martyrdom than for any military exploits, more likely to be the objects than perpetrators of violence. Kelly DeVries attempts to sort out Joan's military career in *Joan of Arc: A Military Leader,* noting that the siege of Orléans is remembered as one of the bloodiest engagements of the Hundred Years' War (87).

55. See Haydock's description of the phallic implications of such military technology ("Shooting the Messenger," 251–53).

56. Even Mulvey's paradigmatic example of the power of voyeurism, Hitchcock's *Vertigo,* is more ambiguous than she suggests. Although its protagonist, Scottie, does have the power to reshape Judy/Madeleine to fulfill his erotic fantasies, Hitchcock also feminizes the character, who appears weak, neurotic, and fairly pathetic (early in the film he makes reference to the "girdle" he is wearing). His paralysis, his neurotic inability to act, precipitates the tragedies of the film.

57. On virginity as it was understood in the Middle Ages see Bloch, *Medieval Misogyny and the Invention of Western Romantic Love,* 93–109; Kathleen Coyne Kelly, 17–39; and McInerney.

58. Kathleen Coyne Kelly has documented the legal practice that called on "juries of matrons," women of good reputation or probity, to examine and testify to the virginity of a woman. While physiological signs of virginity might have included an intact hymen, it is not clear that this was the only or even best way to make that determination. Other signs that would have been examined in the Middle Ages included urine, blood, and the tightness and shape of the uterus, cervix, or vagina.

CHAPTER SIX: The Hagiography of Politics

1. Alan Jay Lerner enumerates the musical's difficulties: the costume designer, Adrian, died of a heart attack when the costumes were only half finished; Lerner got sick and was hospitalized the day after the play opened; the director, Moss Hart, suffered a heart attack and would not return until four months after its opening; finally the running time in Toronto was more than four hours, necessitating drastic cuts (*The Musical Theatre,* 205–6).

2. Figures are from the Internet Broadway Database (ibdb.com).

3. See discussions in Aronstein, *Hollywood Knights,* 89–98; Morgan, 187–88; Aberth, 17–20; Grellner, 74–81; and Davidson, 63–68. For a discussion of the Kennedy presidency by an iconic 1960s figure see Gitlin, 81–97, whose section on the early Kennedy years is entitled "Uneasy in an Anteroom in Camelot."

4. All three quotations are cited in Redfield (59). Roberta Davidson argues that

the claims of Arthurian films that their Arthur is the "true" and real Arthur functions as a mechanism of political idealization.

5. In Knapp see also chapter 5, "Whose (Who's) America" (103–18). Many other scholars of the musical have explored the nationalist ideologies of Broadway musical comedy; see, e.g., Altman, *The American Film Musical*; Mast, *Can't Help Singin'*; Walsh and Platt, *Musical Theater and American Culture*; and Most, *Making Americans*.

6. For a discussion of Hollywood filmmakers' responses to 1960s radical movements see Ryan and Kellner, esp. 17–48: "The psychosocial effects of economic instability, the loss of the Vietnam War and of national prestige, social divisiveness, threats to the traditional patriarchal family and to conservative sexual mores, revelations of corruption in government and business, fears of environmental poisoning and of nuclear war are on ample display in film" during this period (7). On the 1960s see also Hoberman and see Gitlin. For a discussion of the "cinema of dissent" of the late 1960s, see Aronstein, *Hollywood Knights*, 89–98.

7. By this time even Broadway was attempting to attract youth audiences. A year after *Camelot*'s release *Hair*, the first musical to integrate rock music into the genre of the musical, opened (April 29, 1968).

8. Altman makes much the same point in *The American Film Musical*: "the musical's dual focus on a pair of characters permits the introduction of diametrically opposed values or value systems which are 'carried' by the would-be lovers. The resolution of the love plot thus assures not only the coupling and marriage of the lovers but the merging of cultural values once defined as mutually exclusive" (145; see also 45–50).

9. Lerner and Loewe were prevented from using this material from T. H. White because Disney Studios already owned and exercised the rights in their 1963 cartoon feature film *The Sword in the Stone* (Lees, 174).

10. Logan claims that he chose Redgrave to play Guenevere on the advice of his sixteen-year-old son, who, after seeing her in *Morgan* (1966; dir. Karel Reisz), found her to be "acres of beautiful" (196).

11. What made the analogy between Camelot and the Kennedy White House so compelling was the close resemblance between Guenevere and Jacqueline Kennedy, who, in contrast to her Irish upstart husband, was descended from American aristocracy, wealth, and privilege. And like Guenevere, Jackie Kennedy knew how to use her aristocratic bearing to further her own and her husband's agenda. We thank Mary Ramsey for this suggestion.

12. The film glosses over, for instance, the Arthur who, in the first book of the *Morte Darthur*, out-Herod's Herod by ordering that all children born on May Day (the day of Mordred's birth) be slain.

13. As Altman notes, montage scenes like this one create "musically unified sequences" by breaking the spatiotemporal unity of the theatrical "scene" (*The American Film Musical*, 152). This was technologically possible once playback and dubbing were available to directors (as early as 1930) and action could be freed from sound.

14. That major third might well be an apt symbol for Lancelot, who considers

himself perfect and who will become the third in the relationship between Arthur and Guenevere; our thanks to Mary Ramsey for this observation.

15. Franco Nero, who played Lancelot, did not actually sing in the movie; his voice was dubbed by Gene Merlino.

16. Altman describes the contrast between the outlaw, who represents danger, passion, and excitement, and his law-abiding, morally restrained, and dull alter ego as a central feature of the subgenre he calls the fairy tale musical.

17. See Spisak and Matthews, 1:555. For a discussion of the Arthurian theme celebrating the pleasures afforded by peacetime in the Anglo-Norman poet Wace see Finke and Shichtman, *King Arthur and the Myth of History*, 79–94.

18. For a discussion of this split and its political ramifications, especially for women's citizenship, see Eisenstein, 14–30, and Pateman, 118–40.

19. In both Malory's *Morte Darthur* and White's *The Once and Future King*, the blood feuds perpetuated by Gawain and his brothers over wrongs to their family (Pellinore's killing King Lot, their father; Lancelot killing Gareth) are identified as the immediate cause of the Round Table's destruction.

20. In section 3 of *The Once and Future King*, "The Ill-Made Knight," White writes of Lancelot, for instance, "It was hard for him at eighteen to have given his life to a king, only to have been forgotten . . . hardest of all to have broken his body for the older man's ideal, only to find this mincing wife stepping in at the end to snatch away his love at no cost at all. Lancelot was jealous of Guenever, and he was ashamed of himself for being so" (328).

21. The lyrics are not included in the 1962 vocal score; see Loewe and Lerner.

22. See the reading of courtly love by Laurie Finke in *Feminist Theory, Women's Writing*, 33–48.

23. The plot of Mark Sandrich's 1934 musical *The Gay Divorcée* provides an example of a fictional attempt to "stage" a scene of adultery for the purposes of obtaining a divorce. In the film Fred Astaire is mistaken for what Altman euphemistically calls a "professional correspondent" in Ginger Rogers's divorce. The first no-fault divorce law was signed into law in 1969 by Ronald Reagan as governor of California.

24. The phrase references Jean Renoir's 1939 *La Règle du jeu* (*The Rules of the Game*), in which the director, noting the willful apathy of the French bourgeoisie on the eve of World War II, accused them of "dancing on the edge of a volcano."

25. The film failed to recuperate its $17 million in negative costs.

26. *The Passion of the Christ* enjoyed considerable success among conservative Protestants despite significant doctrinal differences between Gibson's Catholic traditionalism and conservative and evangelical Protestant sects. On Catholic traditionalism see Cuneo; Lawler; and Stoekl. On the religious right and the differences among the various Protestant sects labeled as evangelical and fundamentalist see Woodberry and Smith, 27–33.

27. An exception may be Thomas Byers, who is not a medievalist. His work on *Braveheart* describes what we might call the "Christian nationalism" of the film. He notes, for instance, the ways in which Gibson creates his story about the origins of the

Scottish nation by weaving together the strands of certain foundational narratives of American nationalism, including both the American Revolution and "*The Birth of a Nation* without blacks" (4); we thank Professor Byers for generously sharing his paper with us. Our reading of *Braveheart* is in dialogue with perceptive readings of the film by Byers, Colin McArthur, William Luhr, and Sid Ray.

28. These German phrases are never translated in the show; its largely non-German-speaking audience would surely miss the subtlety of the joke, becoming, like the South Park mob, unwitting participants in Cartman's pogrom. Only Cartman's "uniform" supplies a semiotic code for the joke.

29. See Jeffords, *Hard Bodies*, 24–63, and Jeffords, *The Remasculinization of America*. Michael Ryan and Douglas Kellner make much the same argument in *Camera Politica* (see esp. 194–243). The growing obsession with and anxieties surrounding masculinity in political discourse during the 2004 election have been documented by Stephen Ducat in *The Wimp Factor*.

30. On the rise of the religious right see Woodberry and Smith, 44–48. They locate the beginnings of the religious right's involvement in politics in the 1976 campaign of Jimmy Carter and link its political ascendancy (which they see as limited) to Ralph Reed's 1989 founding of the Christian Coalition, which attempted to unite not only conservative white Protestants but their African American counterparts, Catholics, Mormons, and conservative Jews around issues such as abortion, homosexuality, the loss of family values, and the separation of church and state, all of which they saw as contributing to America's moral decline.

31. Byers's reading does not so much contradict as complement Colin McArthur's perceptive discussion of the film in the context of Scottish nationalism.

32. We have been aided in our thinking about medieval ideas of freedom by Peter Larson, who generously shared with us his unpublished paper "Freedom and Unfreedom in Late Medieval Durham"; on medieval serfdom and ideas of freedom see the classic essay by Rodney H. Hilton.

33. On January 30, 2004, the PBS show *Religion and Ethics Newsweekly* reported that Gibson marketed *The Passion of the Christ* heavily to religious groups, both Protestant and Catholic, even releasing a four-minute trailer specifically designed for churches that contained an endorsement from the evangelical author of *The Case for Christ*, Lee Strobel. This DVD was sent free of charge to thousands of pastors across the country but not released to the media (www.pbs.org/wnet/religionandethics/week722/news.html [accessed July 29, 2008]).

34. For a popular nonfiction history of Edward and Isabella see Paul Doherty.

35. Sid Ray offers the most complete analysis of Gibson's characterization of the first prince of Wales.

36. Of course, neither of Edward's "favorites" was named Phillip. Both of his favorites, Piers Gaveston and Hugh de Spenser, were executed (as was Edward) but not by defenestration. The grotesque execution of Hugh de Spenser, which in many ways parallels Gibson's depiction of Wallace's, is described in Froissart's *Chronicles* 44. For

a very different film representation of Edward II's homosexuality see Derek Jarman's 1991 *Edward II*, based on the Christopher Marlowe play.

37. On the intersections of hyperviolence and comedy see Charney, 58–61, and Tetzlaff, 269–85.

38. In fact, the scene is reminiscent of nothing so much as the wedding scene in the Lerner and Loewe musical *Brigadoon*.

39. On the male body in pain in Gibson's *The Passion of the Christ* see Stanbury, "Pathos and Politics."

40. See Luhr for a somewhat different reading of Gibson's "sudden graphic reticence" (242) in displaying Wallace's castration: "When considered in relation to *Braveheart*, one might say that for Christ to become a man, he had to acquire genitals, and for Wallace to become sacred, he had to lose his" (244).

41. It was, however, a largely pyrrhic victory and quickly lost.

CHAPTER SEVEN: The Crusades

1. Bin Laden wrote, "The Arabian Peninsula has never—since Allah made it flat, created its desert, and encircled it with seas—been stormed by any forces like the crusader armies spreading in it like locusts, eating its riches and wiping out its plantations" (quoted in Holsinger, *Neomedievalism, Neoconservatism, and the War on Terror*, 20). The complete text of bin Laden's "Fatwah Urging Jihad against Americans" can be found at www.mideastweb.org/osamabinladen1.htm (accessed Feb. 11, 2009).

2. See Aberth, 63; Haydock, *Movie Medievalism*, 218n15. "The West won the world not by the superiority of its ideas or values or religion . . . but rather by its superiority in applying organized violence. Westerners often forget this fact, non-Westerners never do" (Huntington, 51).

3. Holsinger, *Neomedievalism*, provides a fascinating account of the dominant journalistic and political paradigm that understands America's perceived enemies as "medieval," but he also documents an emerging paradigm in International Relations that understands the prominence of nonstate global actors—NGOs, transnational corporations, drug cartels, and terrorists—as a new form of medievalism.

4. Of Huntington's thesis Edward Said wrote in *The Nation:* "the personification of enormous entities called 'the West' and 'Islam' is recklessly affirmed, as if hugely complicated matters like identity and culture existed in a cartoonlike world where Popeye and Bluto bash each other mercilessly, with one always more virtuous pugilist getting the upper hand over his adversary" ("The Clash of Ignorance," 12).

5. See Runciman and see Riley-Smith, *The Crusades*. The History Channel documentary on the Crusades included in the DVD release of *Kingdom of Heaven* is rife with scholars proclaiming the piety of the first crusaders, while denying that it represented a land grab on the dubious evidence that outfitting a crusader was an expensive proposition. The films, however, are actually consistent with at least one long-lived strain of Crusades historiography that reflects Enlightenment attitudes toward religion and the anti-Catholic sentiment often present in Great Britain in the eighteenth

and nineteenth centuries. In his 1761 *History of England* the Scottish philosopher David Hume describes the "tumult of the crusades" as "the most signal and durable monument of human folly that has yet appeared in any age or nation," while early in the nineteenth century, in *History of the Crusades,* Charles Mills concludes that the movement "retarded the march of civilization, thickened the clouds of ignorance and superstition; and encouraged intolerance, cruelty, and fierceness" (Hume and Mills quoted in Siberry, 2, 12). On Crusades historiography see Siberry, 1–38.

6. Notwithstanding Pat Robertson's remark, reported by CNN on January 6, 2006, that Israeli Prime Minister Ariel Sharon suffered a stroke because "he was dividing God's land, and I would say, 'Woe unto any prime minister of Israel who takes a similar course to appease the [European Union], the United Nations or the United States of America.'"

7. *Rambo III* sits on the cusp of this cultural shift in American popular cultural views of world conflict as a clash of civilizations. In this 1988 film, the third in a series about this cold war hero, Rambo comes to the aid of Afghani freedom fighters rebelling against Soviet occupation. In 1994 Susan Jeffords could write about this film as an expression of American conflicts with "the evil Soviet empire" that followed logically from the first two installments in the series (41). In the wake of the fall of the Soviet Union, however, and the emergence of the war on terror, the film reads very differently. The site of the film's conflict—Afghanistan—becomes one of the sites of a latter-day American "Crusade" to oust the very group—the Taliban—that Rambo empowers in the film.

8. The literature on postcolonialism is vast and contentious. For historical introductions to postcolonialism see Young, 2001 and 2003. Edward Said's foundational work, *Orientalism,* must figure in any account of postcolonialism, as must Gayatri Spivak's essay "Can the Subaltern Speak?" and the work of Homi Bhabha and the Subaltern Studies Group.

9. See McClintock, 40, 42. The colonists "made us leave history, our history, to follow them, right at the back, to follow the progress of their history" (Amilcar Cabral, quoted in Young, *Postcolonialism: A Very Short Introduction,* 18). In *The Politics of Dispossession* Edward Said writes that, for the U.S., "Islam had existed in a kind of timeless childhood, shielded from true development by an archaic set of superstitions, prevented by its strange priests and scribes from moving out from the Middle Ages and into the modern world" (59).

10. Gayatri Spivak's 1983 essay "Can the Subaltern Speak?" offers a now classic formulation of the problem of subaltern knowledges. Spivak argues that simply being postcolonial or a member of an ethnic minority does not make one "subaltern"; rather the term indicates "the sheer heterogeneity of decolonized space" (*A Critique of Postcolonial Reason,* 310). Nabil I. Matar examines the Arab-Islamic counterpart of Said's discourse on Orientalism, which he calls "Occidentalism" (154).

11. See, e.g., Deleuze and Guattari, 25–27.

12. Focusing on the work of the Subaltern Studies Group, Bruce Holsinger has explored the ways in which particular views of the Middle Ages ground current post-

colonial theory. See Holsinger, "Medieval Studies, Postcolonial Studies, and the Genealogies of Critique." For postcolonial work in medieval studies see the collections by Jeffrey Jerome Cohen; Ingham and Warren; and Kabir and Williams.

13. See Said, *Orientalism*, 171, 206, and Ganim, *Medievalism and Orientalism*, 107. Ganim explores the "crosspollination" of space and time in the presentation of an orientalized Middle Ages and a medieval orient: "this dual understanding of the medieval as embodying the imaginative and creative abilities of an East imbued with the gift of fantasy as well as the primal record of historical origins" (7). Other studies of the relationships between medievalism and Orientalism include Kathleen Biddick's "Coming Out of Exile," an analysis of the underlying medievalism of Said's groundbreaking study.

14. Said demonstrates this prominent stereotype through a 1975 course guide written by Columbia University undergraduates that describes the Arab language as a reflection of the "Arab mind," both "violent" and "bombastic" (see *Orientalism*, 287).

15. The expression by King Richard and his knights of anti-Scottish sentiments suggests a link between the "Scottish barbarians," England's colonized neighbor to the north, represented by Sir Kenneth, and the Muslim enemy represented by Saladin. Indeed, by the film's climax, Richard has challenged both men to single combat.

16. Perhaps the ideals of courtly love made bearable the political realities of the relations between the sexes among the European aristocracy of the time. Elsewhere, Laurie Finke has argued that courtly love may have provided a conduit for patronage exchanges between men (*Feminist Theory, Women's Writing*, 33–48). Aristocratic marriage, at this time, had more to do with property than with love. For instance, there is no evidence that the childless marriage between the historical King Richard and his wife, Berengaria, was ever even consummated. Richard's union with this heiress of Navarre did more to secure the southern border of Aquitaine than to promote idealizations of love and women.

17. Régine Pernoud (85–99) and, more recently, Tyerman (75–76) document the historical presence of women in crusader armies. Because he married her en route, Richard did take Berengaria with him on crusade, though they returned from the Holy Land separately. Other women crusaders included Eleanor of Aquitaine, Margaret of Provençe (a queen of France), and Eleanor of Castile (another queen of England); see Tyerman, 75.

18. On the ambiguous meanings given to the veil in Muslim cultures, as well as its orientalizing meanings for Western culture, see Young, *Postcolonialism: A Very Short Introduction*, 80–92, and Davis; for a history of veiling in Muslim cultures see Mernissi.

19. In his 1981 book *Covering Islam* Said writes that images "regularly rendered by television pictures of chanting 'Islamic' mobs accompanied by commentary about 'anti-Americanism' " limit our understanding of Islam to these characteristics. Since "Islam is 'against' us and 'out there,' the necessity of adopting a confrontational response of our own towards it will not be doubted" (44).

20. See Fawal, 158; Kiernan, 135; Malkmus and Armes, 152; Ganim; Shafik, 67; and Aberth, 103–6. Shafik describes *Saladin* as "still one of the most remarkable his-

torical movies of Egyptian film history, due in part to Chahine's skill in handling fierce battle scenes but also to the careful set and costume designs of Wali al-Din Samih and Chadi Abedessalam" (67).

21. A Western director would almost certainly have located Saladin in a tent, an Orientalist trope familiar to Western audiences from films like *King Richard and the Crusaders* and, more recently, *Kingdom of Heaven*.

22. Arab audiences contemporary with the film would most likely have identified this character as Saladin more quickly than, say, an American audience. Ahmed Mazhar, the actor playing Saladin, was an Egyptian matinee idol at the time whose familiarity to Egyptian audiences would have aided in recognition.

23. As Ganim notes, the film's score was written by Italian composer Angelo Lavignino: "Lavagnino's score has the same flexible quality one hears in *cinecetta* films of the 1950s, with their loose relationship to the action on screen, useful and adaptable to relatively rough editing and uncertain post-production conditions" ("Reversing the Crusades," 50).

24. We maintain the illusion that we are looking at a face longer if we run the tape backward; as we noted with the opening teaser, beginning from the whole and moving to the part renders an object more coherent than the reverse. This, of course, is the whole basis of impressionistic art. Chahine's play with this perceptual puzzle suggests that cognitive approaches to film are not nearly as incompatible with semiotic theory as the often vitriolic antitheoretical essays contained in the anthology *Post-Theory* suggest; see Bordwell, "Convention, Construction, and Cinematic Vision," 94, and Peterson, 111–12.

25. Adeed Dawisha argues that the disinterest on the part of the architects of Arab nationalism in creating democratic institutions that could transcend the personality of a particular leader led to the failure of pan-Arabism. He cites R. Stephen Humphreys: "Arab nationalist thinkers . . . had looked at the crucial problems confronting them and their people as one of identity rather than as one of institutions. The question was, who is an Arab, not how can the Arabs build a common political life and effective institutions of government? . . . Very few writers asked seriously how [the projected Arab] state would be constituted, how the relationships among its many disparate regions were to be defined, and how different social groups would be represented within the political system" (Dawisha, 297). See also Abu-Rabi, 133; Moaddel, 121–46.

26. In his documentary on the Crusades Terry Jones includes a clip from *Saladin* in his discussion of the Battle of Hattin (Part 3: *Jihad*).

27. For a brief history of the Third Crusade see Aberth, 70–76; more complete histories include Prawer; Riley-Smith, *The Crusades*; Hillenbrand; and Tyerman. These works demonstrate that Saladin was not nearly as heroic as his hagiographic portraits would suggest. However, this debunking of political "saints" frequently obscures the reasons that such figures become national heroes and the functions such political hagiographies serve (see chapter 6).

28. Louise's name obliquely references one of the most powerful members of the

Frankish aristocracy in the East during the final years of the Crusader Kingdom—Guy de Lusignan, the husband of Sibylla, the last queen of Jerusalem (see below).

29. On the issue of miscegenation between Arab and Christian in the Middle Ages see Kinoshita.

30. While Greek fire *(naft)* was an ancient form of military technology, it was improved in the seventh century by a Syrian named Kallinikos and exploited by the Byzantines in their conflicts with the Arabs. According to Hillenbrand (528–29), it was the Arabs' preferred response to the Frankish siege engines.

31. We would argue, on the contrary, that Chahine's filmmaking taken as a whole evinces an interest in the status of women in the Arab world, often presenting quite complex representations. His 1958 film, *Jamilla the Algerian,* presents another kind of woman warrior who forgoes marriage and children to join the Algerian struggle for independence. Fawal has compared Chahine's portrait of her imprisonment, torture, and death to Dreyer's cinematic vision of Joan of Arc (81–88). Chahine's most recent film, *Destiny* (1997), despite its focus on religious fundamentalism, avoids entirely any predicable images of veiled women. The women in the film move quite freely in public; they are singers and dancers, scribes and students, as well as wives and mothers (see Fawal, 178–86; and Hoffman, "Chahine's *Destiny*").

32. From the film's map, Aurocastro appears to be located somewhere between modern-day Bari and Brindisi on Italy's east coast.

33. Lindley, in "Once, Present, and Future Kings," notes the indebtedness of Crusades movies to the generic conventions of the western (see 17–20).

34. See above (p. 195). In fact, Taranto was last invaded by Arabs in the ninth century, two centuries before the time in which the film is set. It was, however, conquered by the Normans in 1063, some thirty-three years before the crusading armies set out from Europe for Jerusalem. If any fighting was going on in Aurocastro around the time of Peter's birth, it would have been against invading Normans, not invading Saracens, as the film's opening scene suggests.

35. *The Deer Hunter* (1978), *Coming Home* (1978), and *Apocalypse Now* (1979) launched the Vietnam War genre; these were quickly followed by the three *Rambo* films (in 1982, 1985, and 1986), *Platoon* (1986), *Good Morning, Vietnam* (1987), *Gardens of Stone* (1987), and Stanley Kubrick's *Full Metal Jacket* (1987). Randall Wallace's *We Were Soldiers* (2002) represents an attempt to redeem the genre.

36. For an account of these films' project of masculinity see Jeffords, *Hard Bodies,* and Jeffords, *The Remasculinization of America.*

37. Thus he becomes a victim of "friendly fire." During the Gulf War a high percentage of coalition casualties were the result of friendly fire.

38. On the Tomb of the Unknown Soldier as a focus for imagining the nation see Anderson, *Imagined Communities,* 9–11; Anderson, *The Spectre of Comparison,* 51–57; and Redfield, 11–12; the quotation is from *Imagined Communities,* 9.

39. Its final scene shows Richard, traveling through France on his way to recapture Jerusalem, asking directions to the Holy Land from the recently returned Balian.

On the historical inaccuracies of the film see Lindley, "Once, Present, and Future Kings," 17–20.

40. The Leper King of Jerusalem was Baldwin IV, who came to the throne at thirteen and died at twenty-four (1161–85); see Hamilton, *The Leper King and His Heirs*, esp. 245–58, on the progress of his disease; see also Lindley, "Once, Present, and Future Kings," 17, 19.

41. This is the term used by the French film theorist Michel Chion to describe sound not anchored to the diegesis of the film. Here Baldwin's voice, through the mediation of the mask, becomes detached from his body. We will explore the theoretical implications of acousmatics more fully in the next chapter.

42. That Ridley Scott and most of the cast (including Orlando Bloom, who plays Balian) are British and European by birth seems beside the point; the film is a Hollywood film saturated with core American ideologies.

43. According to the description of Hrabanus Maurus, *umbilicus regionis et totius terre* (see Finke and Shichtman, *King Arthur and the Myth of History*, 142; Akbari, 21; and, in connection with *Kingdom of Heaven*, Lindley, "Once, Present, and Future Kings," 16).

44. Historically, in fact, it was Balian of Ibelin who organized the final defense of Jerusalem. This was undoubtedly the inspiration for Monahan's screenplay, although see Haydock's description of the film's legal battles with James Reston, who claimed that his book *Warriors of God* was the source of Monahan's screenplay (*Movie Medievalism*, 143).

45. See Hamilton, "Women in the Crusader States," 169–72; women served several functions in the Crusader Kingdom. Not only were many tasks delegated to women while their husbands were at war, but the survival rate in the Frankish kingdom among girls was higher than that of boys. They provided continuity for the land and spouses for fresh recruits from the West (143).

46. The Crusades historian Jonathan Smith-Riley, for example, was frequently quoted by news sources as claiming, somewhat hyperbolically, that *Kingdom of Heaven* was "Osama bin Laden's version of history. It will fuel the Islamic fundamentalists," while UCLA Islamic law professor Khaled Abou El Fadl maintained, "I believe this movie teaches people to hate Muslims" (*Washington Post*, May 1, 2005).

47. Ironically, women were prominent in the Egyptian film industry from its inception, both as producers and directors. *Saladin* was produced by the Lebanese actress Assia Daghir. On women in the Egyptian film industry see Shafik, 25.

48. If the film inaccurately portrays Guy as king, what it gets right is the inevitable factionalization created in the Crusader Kingdom between a nobility that had ruled Jerusalem for nearly two centuries—represented by Baldwin and Sibylla, as well as Tiberius (Jeremy Irons)—those whose ancestors participated in the First Crusade—and the newcomers from the West—opportunists like Guy de Lusignan and Reynald of Chatillon. The historical Balian of Ibelin was in fact a member of one of the old crusading families, not, as in the film, a newcomer to the Holy Land. The real Balian married the second wife of Sibylla's father, Amalric, the Byzantine princess Maria Comnena. His brother, Baldwin, however, schemed unsuccessfully to marry

Sibylla and eventually make himself king of Jerusalem (Hamilton, "Women in the Crusader States," 166). Bernard Hamilton quotes one hostile English source that describes the partnership between Balian and Maria in less than complimentary terms: "where he was savage, she was godless; where he was shallow-minded, she was fickle; where he was treacherous, she was scheming" (165). Eventually, as Sibylla notes in the film, her mother married her off to Guy de Lusignan, temporarily resolving what amounted to a struggle between court factions literally over Sibylla's body. Scott and Monahan alter both Balian's origin and his character because, as hero, he must be kept above the political fray that divides—and ultimately leads to the destruction of— the Crusader Kingdom.

49. See Young, *Postcolonialism: A Very Short Introduction*, 80–92, and Mernissi. On veiling and its association with the harem see Richon, 9–10.

CHAPTER EIGHT: Looking Awry at the Grail

1. With the aid of supplementary technology such as screen capturing one might freeze the image for closer examination and perhaps decide that the object is the head of a spear, perhaps a reference to the spear that pierced Christ's side that is associated with Grail legends. However, a viewer could not hope to make out the image in the short amount of screen time Bresson gives it.

2. The connection of the Grail to the Eucharist is briefly explored by Miri Rubin, 139–42. *The New Advent Catholic Encyclopedia* describes the attitude of the church toward Grail legends:

> It would seem that a legend so distinctively Christian would find favour with the Church. Yet this was not the case. Excepting Helinandus [a thirteenth-century Cistercian chronicler who wrote about the Grail], clerical writers do not mention the Grail, and the Church ignored the legend completely. After all, the legend contained the elements of which the Church could not approve. Its sources are in apocryphal, not in canonical, scripture, and the claims of sanctity made for the Grail were refuted by their very extravagance. Moreover, the legend claimed for the Church in Britain an origin well nigh as illustrious as that of the Church of Rome, and independent of Rome. It was thus calculated to encourage and to foster any separatist tendencies that might exist in Britain. As we have seen, the whole tradition concerning the Grail is of late origin and on many points at variance with historical truth. (www.newadvent.org/cathen/ 06719a.htm [accessed Aug. 9, 2008])

3. It is beyond the scope of this chapter to speculate about whether the Grail was a stranded object for its medieval audiences, although we suspect it was, even at the same time that it may have served to legitimize the power of the military orders of knighthood.

4. From the French press book for the film (www.mastersofcinema.org/bresson/ Words/LancelotDuLac_pressbook.html [accessed Aug. 9, 2008]).

5. This film at times suffers as a result of film parodies released at about the same time. It is virtually impossible not to see in the film's opening decapitation Monty Python's parody of film violence in the Black Knight sequence of *Monty Python and the Holy Grail*, which appeared a year later (see Haydock, *Movie Medievalism*, 12). Similarly, the acousmatic neighing of horses throughout the film repeatedly brings to mind Mel Brooks's *Young Frankenstein*, which was released in the same year.

6. We have already examined the relationship of the long shot to the close-up in our analysis of Dreyer's refusal of this system in *La Passion de Jeanne d'Arc*. For a summary of other theoretical approaches to the system of suture that traces its evolution from Lacanian psychoanalysis to film theory, see Žižek, *The Fright of Real Tears*, 31–54; Dayan; Rothman; and Silverman.

7. On the theory of montage see the essays by Pudovkin and Eisenstein in Braudy and Cohen, 9–14 and 15–42.

8. The dialogue in this scene is between Arthur and Gauvain. Lancelot, the title character, remains curiously detached from their anguish throughout the scene.

9. The opening gag in *Monty Python and the Holy Grail* plays on this suturing technique by substituting the sound effect (the coconuts) for actual horses, the object the sound represents.

10. Kevin Harty suggests in a personal communication that the sound is a Breton bagpipe, but we would stress that it is motivated by nothing in the film's diegesis and, at best, would be identifiable by no one but an expert.

11. We understand that our invocation of this Lacanian slogan is risky and assume the risk because it helps make sense of Bresson's technique. Feminists have long debated the question of whether Lacanian formulations about women are misogynist or useful to feminist analytics (see, e.g., Grosz). Žižek's writing presents similar challenges. The political astuteness that characterizes much of his other writing seems missing when he turns to women, his Lacanianism a regrettable blind spot. However, for a discussion of Žižek's formulations on women see Myers, 79–92. Myers understands these texts as more feminist than they may at first appear (or at least less misogynous). We would argue that, whether they are finally feminist or misogynist, Žižek's rereading of Lacan's aphorism that woman is man's symptom accurately describes Bresson's treatment of Guinevere in this film and so provides a useful starting point for a reading of that character.

12. A still of this shot has been reproduced in several articles on the film—with one interesting difference. In the still, Condominas is clothed, not nude as she is in the film; a strap is clearly visible on her shoulder. This still appears in Rider et al.'s essay in Harty, *Cinema Arthuriana*, 154, and in Michael Dempsey's essay in Quandt, 373. On the distinction between naked and nude see Berger, 45–64.

13. Bruce Beatie is one of the few critics who dissents in this critical consensus about the Passion play's significance, describing the Passion play as the only place where "Rohmer makes a purely filmic decision, freed from the tyranny of his textual model" (257).

14. Beatie also dissents from other critics in privileging the film's final shot,

which depicts Perceval returning once again to the "cyclic movement through the endless forest," arguing that the "broken quest"—and not the Passion play—becomes a "metaphor of transcendence" in the film (262).

15. "Eric Rohmer and the Holy Grail," 584; Williams offers perhaps the best description of Rohmer's techniques in this film (see 584–89; see also Crisp, 82–85).

16. Beatie is the one critic who at least mentions the authenticity of Jacques Schmidt's costumes (254). Bresson uses much the same technique in *Lancelot du lac* to bring some color to his monochromatic cinematography. The main sources of color in that film are the knights' breeches and the blankets they put on their horses, for which he uses bright, vivid colors.

17. See Žižek, *The Metastases of Enjoyment*, 89–112; Lacan, *The Ethics of Psychoanalysis;* and Kristeva, *Tales of Love,* 280–96.

18. David Lynch's *Blue Velvet* (1986) shows a perverse version of this narrative at work in contemporary drama in the role playing among Kyle MacLachlan's Jeffrey, Isabelle Rossellini's Dorothy Valens, and Laura Dern's Sandy (the opposition between the two women perhaps corresponding to the difference between large and small sleeves, that is, the sexually available and unavailable woman).

19. "The action of clothing or robing" (OED, 2nd edn. s.v. "investiture").

20. For more on Nazi medievalism see Finke and Shichtman, *King Arthur and the Myth of History,* 186–214.

21. On Syberberg's project of mourning see Santner, "The Trouble with Hitler," 716; Santner, *Stranded Objects,* 103–49; and Jameson, "In the Destructive Element Immerse," 100.

22. Santner calls Syberberg's political statements "obscene." He argues that for Syberberg the "super-egoic figures of postwar culture all have Jewish names" ("The Trouble with Hitler," 723). One example from his writing should suffice to demonstrate Syberberg's opinion that the Jews have tainted post-1945 intellectual and cultural life. Syberberg writes:

> The aesthetics of Adorno and Bloch to Benjamin, Marcuse and Kracauer determined . . . the cultural life of Germany after 1945. Untainted by Hitler, they became the spiritual patrons of Germany's postwar history. . . . What hounded . . . art in Germany after the last war was the curse of guilt which offered itself as a tool of intimidation by the left, in that leftists saw themselves as innocent and because Hitler persecuted the Jews—now in an unholy alliance of Jewish leftist aesthetics directed against the guilty, creating boredom and numbing all cultural life with lies, so that guilt could become a business, deadly for all fantasy life. . . . Whoever went with the Jews and the left had it made." (quoted in Santner, "The Trouble with Hitler," 719)

23. Exegesis is the approach taken by Solveig Olsen in her book, *Hans Jürgen Syberberg and His Film of Wagner's "Parsifal,"* which attempts to read Syberberg's film through the lens of Jungian analysis.

24. Arguably we avoid the most important "blot" in the film, Wagner's music,

which we barely mention in our analysis, to some extent because we do not have the necessary musicological training but also because our focus is on the "surplus" represented by Syberberg's film, what Syberberg, as a director, has added to Wagner's musical drama.

25. "The action unfolds in, on, and around the huge concrete model of Richard Wagner's death mask. This stony landscape has been divided into fourteen sections. . . . Their arrangement can change the environment as needed into passages, chambers, or a large hall. Besides combining flexibility with unity of location, this environment is also an unsurpassed solution to the problem of finding a setting for a utopian story. . . . The Grail Kingdom remains inaccessible to so many because it is not so much a geographic site as a state of mind, a phase in an individual's spiritual development" (Olsen, 145).

26. See Shichtman, "Whom Does the Grail Serve?"; Friedlander, 171–73; and Abbate, 114–15.

27. As, for instance, his repeated command that his son "Uncover the Grail!"

28. Syberberg's criticism of his contemporary Rainier Werner Fassbinder provides an example: "The man who once, in his early work, had rejected the customary shot/countershots, tracks, and zooms became in the end a master of a style he had himself discredited, the practitioner of a banal craft" (Sharrett, 462).

29. Is this not what Žižek posits as the dilemma with which Wagner presents us: "Is it still possible, after we fully accept the anti-Semitic, protofascist side of Wagner, to enjoy his music?" What if, he asks, "the very sublime effect of Wagner's music, what all of us cannot resist enjoying, is only possible against the background of, on the basis of, his darker side" ("There Is No Sexual Relationship: Wagner as a Lacanian," 34).

30. To medievalists it suggests a hell-mouth.

31. In *Parsifal* only Robert Lloyd, who plays Gurnemanz, and Aage Haugland, who plays Klingsor, act *and* sing their parts, though not at the same time. Even they are dubbed.

32. To be sure, there are practical reasons for casting actors rather than opera singers in the film; it allows the director to get the look he wants, for instance a very young androgynous Parsifal, without sacrificing voice, which is the point of opera. In this instance, however, Syberberg calls attention to the device rather than allowing it to work seamlessly.

33. See Žižek, " 'The Wound Is Healed Only by the Spear That Smote You,' " 204. It would be difficult to characterize as feminist this "eschatological ritual," which, in Santner's paraphrases of Syberberg, resolves "all separations, injuries, restlessness—embodied by the Wandering Jew and the 'evil' of woman"—in the final Sabbath "celebrated by the death cult of the grail" (*Stranded Objects,* 192). Olsen offers a detailed Jungian reading of this split (see 250–52). Žižek warns against reading Wagnerian femininity as a protest against "the male universe of contracts and brutal exercise of power": "the reference to the eternal feminine toward which the male subject [Parsifal] adopts a passive attitude is the ultimate metaphysical support of the worldly aggressive attitude" ("There Is No Sexual Relationship," 220).

34. The projection resembles the kinds of classical nude paintings John Berger explores in his chapter on nudes in *Ways of Seeing* (45–64).

35. Linda and Michael Hutcheon argue persuasively that the disease from which Amfortas suffers must be syphilis, a sexual disease that becomes a figure for social disorder.

36. Žižek uses the phrase "static diatonics" to suggest how the music represents the mythical timelessness of the Grail community through its manipulation of diatonic intervals.

37. Lest we miss that Klingsor is the villain of the piece, in the transition to the Flower Maiden scene Syberberg punctuates Wagner's melodrama by having Klingsor draw his cloak (coat) over his face Snidely Whiplash–style and projecting the flower garden onto it.

38. Santner examines this connection between anti-Semitism and the disintegrative effects of modernity in Syberberg in "The Trouble with Hitler" (see esp. 720–23).

39. We have examined these narratives about Hitler's possession of Grail objects in *King Arthur and the Myth of History* (186–214). Syberberg indicates his familiarity with pseudohistory that links the two objects when, in *Hitler: A Film from Germany,* he draws from material in both Angebert's *The Occult and the Third Reich* and Ravenscroft's *Spear of Destiny* in the wild Magician's rant:

> Here it is: Adolf's sperm; from a stand-in, of course. . . . The real capsule lies well preserved in an Alpine glacier, where someday, when the time is ripe, the capsule, closely guarded every summer by trained men, will be resurrected from the lead canisters as a rebirth when the moment is ripe, in an action prepared for since 1945. . . . The Holy Grail, the Black Stone. The treasure of all European legends and kings, found by Himmler at Montségur, France, during the war and planned as the central point of the new Reich at Bayreuth. Then as the shrine of the aforementioned relic, now well guarded until the new liberation, demanding annually live sacrifices in secret combats amidst the Alpine lakes and mountains. . . . Plus that Holy Lance . . . from the Vienna Treasury, possession of which allowed the Hapsburgs to achieve world domination after the Roman Empire. That was the lance that was thrust into the Saviour's side by that Roman legionnaire, Longinus, later celebrated in *Parsifal*. It passed into the possession of Thomas the apostle, St. Maurice, Constantine the Great, Charlemagne, Otto and Henry and Barbarossa and the Hapsburgs and Hitler. Who will be next to rule over the earth?" (*Hitler: A Film from Germany,* 105–6)

CHAPTER NINE: Apocalyptic Medievalism

1. Orru, *Anomie,* 2; Passas and Agnew, 3. Orru argues, and his book demonstrates, that the term has a long history in Western social theory, dating back to ancient Greece. Furthermore, he argues that American sociologists have revised Durkheim's conceptualization of anomie, divorcing it from its critique of modernity: "for Durkheim anomie refers to the ill-conceived cultural goals of industrial societies, whereas

for American sociologists anomie refers to the inadequacy of means for the fulfillment of society's culturally sanctioned goals" (119).

2. On anomie theory's focus on the individual within the public sphere see Orru,
"The Ethics of Anomie," and Passas and Agnew. On the division between public and
private spheres in liberal individualism see Eisenstein; Pateman; Coontz; and chap-
ters 3 and 5 above.

3. In the booklet accompanying the Criterion DVD, however, Cowie calls it "one of
the highest peaks in the Bergman range." *The Virgin Spring* is also noteworthy as the beginning of Bergman's collaboration with the cinematographer Sven Nyqvist; see Ford.
Cowie (182–90) offers the most extensive discussion of *The Virgin Spring* to date.

4. The grammatical ambiguity of this last sentence is apt. The boy's and Ingeri's
paralysis become ours, as our gaze merges with theirs.

5. Melvyn Bragg also describes what he calls Bergman's "swooning toward Hitler
and Nazism" in the 1930s (44).

6. Töre's face is more likely to be obscured than is his wife's or daughter's. One
shot, in particular, in this scene, as he turns to pick up his sword, with his face half
obscured by shadows, links him to Ingeri's darkness in the previous scene and perhaps foreshadows something ominous in his character.

7. For the Peale quotation see Online Focus, "Remembering Dr. Spock," March
16, 1998, www.pbs.org/newshour/bb/health/jan-june98/spock_3–16.html (accessed
Aug. 13, 2008); for the Agnew quotation see *The Cambridge Encyclopedia*, vol. 9,
http://encyclopedia.stateuniversity.com/pages/2582/Benjamin-McLane-Spock.html
(accessed Aug. 13, 2008).

8. In the authoritarian patriarchal family of the Victorian age "parents were ad-
vised to 'break the will of their child,' by imposing strict controls. If they did not their
child would surely go to hell. Obedience to authority, in particular the authority of
the father, was an important feature of family life during the nineteenth century. For
a child to disobey was regarded not only as a rebellion against her parents, but also
against God" (Richardson, 29).

9. *The Virgin Spring* rewrites H. G. Wells's *The Time Machine*. In Wells's dystopian
vision of a European civilization overrun by the monstrous "other," the postapocalyp-
tic, dark, cave-dwelling Morlocks provide the labor that supports the beautiful, white,
and innocent Eloi, whom they ultimately eat. Wells's tale expresses turn-of-the-
century fears that the exploited underclasses, both at home and in the colonies, might
someday rise up and exterminate their oppressors. In the wake of European colonialism, however, the Morlocks don't eat the Eloi; they just work for them. In *The Virgin
Spring* the Morlocks (the dispossessed underclass) try to destroy the Eloi (the superior white upper classes) and get violently punished for it.

10. Aberth establishes a causal link between the Crusades and the outbreak of
plague in Europe by relating an apocryphal anecdote suggesting that the plague
reached Europe through a kind of "germ warfare" when invading Mongol armies at
Caffa on the north coast of the Black Sea flung infected corpses at the "infidel Christians" holding the city (197).

11. This is not entirely surprising since Bergman provides very little social context. The geographical location in which events unfold is never mentioned; Arthur Lindley describes it aptly as "nominally if namelessly Swedish" ("The Ahistoricism of Medieval Film," par. 3); Haydock describes it as "anyplace-whatever," arguing that Bergman's use of depth of field establishes not a location but a mental state (*Movie Medievalism*, 44). On Bergman and existentialism see Aberth, 226–27, and Ketcham. For a reading of *The Seventh Seal* through Deleuze's notion of the time-image see Haydock, *Movie Medievalism*, 40–46.

12. For both readings see Steene (88 and 94, respectively).

13. See Aberth, 219–21; the comparison between the film and the medieval morality play, however, is not entirely unjustified. Melvyn Bragg relates that, before beginning *The Seventh Seal*, Bergman had directed Hugo von Hofmannsthal's *Play of Everyman* for the radio (49); see also Schildt in Steene (47).

14. Lindley, "The Ahistoricism of Medieval Film"; but see Paden, who argues that "Bergman had reconstituted the past more faithfully than available traces gave him any apparent means to do" (288).

15. The confusion is exacerbated by the existence of at least three distinct strands of anomie theory within classical sociological theory: the nineteenth-century French philosopher Jean-Marie Guyau described anomie as the motor of innovation in society, while for the French sociologist Émile Durkheim, "normlessness" is the cause of much contemporary alienation and despair. Finally, the American sociologist Robert Merton described it as "a symptom of dissociation between culturally defined aspirations and socially structured means" (674); on these different strands see Orru, "The Ethics of Anomie," and Passas and Agnew, 2–4, 9–12. There has also been debate on whether anomie is best understood as a phenomenon on the macro or micro level. *The Seventh Seal* demonstrates the way in which this concept can move fluidly between the two scales, between public and private, social and individual, macro and micro.

16. According to Giddens, all social rules are, in the final analysis, constitutive of the social order. For Giddens's analysis of rules see *The Constitution of Society*, 16–21, esp. 21. Quotations from *The Seventh Seal* are from the Malmström and Kushner script unless otherwise indicated. While in most instances the DVD's subtitles convey substantially the same sense as the script, there are occasionally some significant differences in the two translations, which we will note where appropriate. The script represents a shooting script rather than a transcription of the final cut of the film.

17. This version, from the DVD subtitles, expresses clearly the social hierarchy that governs the relationship between Block and Jöns. Malmström and Kushner give a very different sense of these lines: "Between a strumpet's legs to lie / Is the life for which I sigh" (Ingmar Bergman, 15).

18. On the contrast between the classical and grotesque bodies in Western culture see Stallybrass and White's reading of Bakhtin's *Rabelais and His World* (*The Politics and Poetics of Transgression*, 9–26). Later in the film, to indicate his puzzlement at the flagellant procession he has witnessed, Jöns, reversing the metaphoric terms of the "body of the state" (see chapter 4 above), explicitly articulates his philosophy of the body:

"My little stomach is my world, my head is my eternity, and my hands, two wonderful suns. My legs are time's damned pendulums, and my dirty feet are two splendid starting points for my philosophy. Everything is worth precisely as much as a belch, the only difference being that a belch is more satisfying" (Ingmar Bergman, 40).

19. In an interview by Jean Béranger in 1958, Bergman spoke of his own religious belief: "I believe in God but not in the Church, Protestant or any other. I believe in a superior idea that we call God. I want to and have to. I believe it is absolutely necessary." In the same volume Jurgen Schildt describes him as a "believing skeptic" (Steene, 13, 46).

20. Aberth (219) notes that it is unlikely that a fourteenth-century Swedish knight would have been crusading in the Holy Land. He suggests that Russia would be a more historically accurate location for a Swedish crusader; a Russian crusade, however, would not suggest for late-twentieth-century viewers the sense of holy mission that crusading in the Holy Land evokes.

21. The first reviews of *The Seventh Seal* frequently refer to it as a medieval morality play; Jurgen Schildt wrote that Bergman's "world is, like that of the medieval morality plays, a world of black and white, a battlefield between good and evil, Satan and—no—not God but Something Else" (Steene, 46); and Peter John Dyer notes that Bergman's "main images are familiar from any number of medieval morality plays and Chaucerian comedies" (Steene, 58).

22. The DVD subtitles read, "How are we to believe the believers when we don't believe ourselves?" The loss of the preposition completely changes the meaning of the line.

23. In the program notes Bergman could be describing this church when he describes his childhood memories of "the church's mysterious world of low arches, thick walls, the smell of eternity, the colored sunlight quivering above the strangest vegetation of medieval paintings and carved figures on ceiling and walls" (quoted in Aberth, 221).

24. On the performative dimensions of medieval visionary literature see the collection of essays edited by Suydam and Zeigler.

25. These alternatives correspond to reactions to the plague described by medieval commentators. Henry of Herford, for instance, describes the spectacle of public flagellations in Germany: "the scourged skin swelled up black and blue and blood flowed down to their lower members and even spattered the walls nearby. I have seen, when they whipped themselves, how the iron points . . . became so embedded in the flesh that sometimes one pull, sometimes two, was not enough to extract them." As for their effects on their audiences, "One would need a heart of stone to be able to watch this without tears" (quoted in Aberth, 210). In his introduction to *The Decameron* Boccaccio describes those who "believed that drinking too much, enjoying life, going about singing and celebrating, satisfying in every way the appetites as best one could, laughing, and making light of everything that happened was the best medicine for such a disease" (5). The painter is usually identified as the Swedish painter Albertus Pictor (1445–1509), who actually did paint a fresco of Death playing

chess. His historical dates place him, however, about a century later than the purported time of the film.

26. On film as an institution of the public sphere see Donald and Donald.

27. The film's various performances, especially of the acting troupe and the flagellants, might usefully be thought of as examples of Habermas's precursor or literary public sphere; see Habermas, *The Structural Transformation of the Public Sphere*, 29.

28. Habermas's critics frequently argue that even the public sphere Habermas idealizes, the institutions of eighteenth- and nineteenth-century political debate, was hardly open and free to all, nor was it nearly as rational as Habermas suggests. In fact, the ideal public sphere remains in Habermas more possibility and model than historical reality. Habermas himself noted that the eighteenth- and nineteenth-century public sphere was made possible by exclusion, by the homogeneity of its members. As "the public body expanded beyond the bounds of the bourgeoisie," as it lost its social exclusivity, it lost its coherence ("The Public Sphere," 54).

29. For a reading of *The Seventh Seal*'s gender politics see Blackwell (71–97).

30. The link between watching a film and voyeurism has been a staple of film criticism since Mulvey's 1975 essay.

31. Peter Cowie argues in his DVD commentary that this scene anticipates Tony Richardson's notorious eating scene in *Tom Jones* (1963).

32. Bergman seems to be having a small joke on actors in this scene.

33. As of this writing, the commercial may be viewed online at www.youtube .com/watch?v=U219eUIZ7Qo (accessed Feb. 17, 2009).

34. "I tried to keep it in the background of the shot, rather than alone and direct, so it would become a background statement rather than the main statement. It was meant to be subtextual" (Ward, "A Dialogue with Discrepancy," 14).

35. The only expository information he gives is the time—1348—the place—Cumbria—and an intertitle explaining the arrival of the Black Death in England.

36. Quotations are from the published script; see Ward, *The Navigator*.

37. See our analysis of the time-travel formula in *A Connecticut Yankee in King Arthur's Court* (chapter 2) and of *Black Knight* (chapter 10).

38. The title of a 1982 book by Eric R. Wolf.

39. See Finke and Shichtman, *King Arthur and the Myth of History*, 141–45, for a discussion of the Hardyng invasion map.

40. In a moment of postcolonial bravura, the script originally made this point much more clearly by having the foundry workers mistake the miners for Maori (the indigenous peoples of New Zealand who were displaced by the British settlers), even though one of their own number is clearly recognizable as an urban Maori.

CHAPTER TEN: Forever Young

1. The creation of the baby boomers' youth culture is eloquently described by Todd Gitlin; see esp. 11–44. On the postwar creation of the suburbs see Coontz.

2. According to Thomas Schatz, "the New Hollywood has been driven (and shaped)

by multipurpose entertainment machines which breed movie sequels and TV series, music videos and sound track albums, video games and theme park rides, graphic novels and comic books, and an endless array of licensed tie-ins and brand-name consumer products" (quoted in Wee, 90).

3. See Shumway for a discussion of rock and roll as a set of performative cultural practices that have, since the 1970s, become "routinized." Kathleen Forni notes that Helgeland's film uses its performances to "revivify the staid historical romance by capturing the exuberant pageantry, gritty spectacle, and youthful rebellion that presumably characterized the tournament 'circuit.' The soundtrack and costumes associate chivalry with the exhibitionist, homosocial, glam-rock genre of the 1970s—defiant men on parade whose primary audience was adolescent men—and provide a hint of what Paul Strohm has called the 'homoerotics of chivalry,' in which the lady 'serves as a chivalric pretext, enabling a relation of greater intensity between men.'" Helgeland's use of the Queen stadium anthems, she argues, reinforces his vision, "in which the medieval joust becomes an early version of an Xtreme full-contact sport" (256).

4. Benveniste, 76. The title of DeCurtis's 1992 collection of essays on rock and roll says it all: *Present Tense.*

5. The performance may be found online at www.youtube.com/watch?v=ntASb 63rN2k (accessed Sept. 11, 2008).

6. We were able to find very few instances of the medieval in teen culture. Crosby, Stills, Nash, and Young recorded a song in 1970 called "Guinnevere," Leonard Cohen wrote a "Joan of Arc" ballad (1970), Neil Young's "After the Gold Rush" begins with the lyrics, "Well I dreamed I saw the knights in armor coming, / Saying something about a queen." There is a short medieval scene in *Bill and Ted's Excellent Adventure* (see chapter 2). We do not count in this tally medieval juvenilia. The title of Elizabeth Sklar's essay "Twain for Teens," while catchy, does not accurately describe the audience for films like *A Kid in King Arthur's Court,* which appeal more to prepubescents. Costume dramas are indeed a rarity in teen films. The sole exception might be nostalgia films like *American Graffiti,* which began to appear in the 1970s—about the time when baby boomers were advancing into middle age. These films tend to recall the adolescence of their creators. *American Graffiti, Animal House* (1978), and *Grease* (1978), all set in the 1950s, idealize the adolescence of the newly middle-aged. For a brief history of the teen movie from the 1950s up through the 1990s see Giroux, 28–32.

7. Although we have found Freccero's comments about different temporalities productive in thinking about *Knight's Tale's* deliberate anachronisms as a lens through which to view popular teen culture, we are not arguing for the "queerness" of this relatively "straight" film marked by the compulsory heterosexuality of most mainstream teen culture; we are not even arguing that the film is particularly subversive. Rather, because Freccero offers up a conception of time that accords well with the presentist bias of the contemporary teen culture represented in the film, we highlight the film's marshalling of prolepses that put the Middle Ages and the middle age between childhood and adulthood into dialogue.

8. There was, for instance, an entire fan Web site—Herald: The Chaucer Fan-listing—devoted to Paul Bettany's role as Chaucer in *A Knight's Tale* (http://fan .a-beautiful-life.net/herald/ [accessed July 12, 2006]). Typical of the short lifespan of many Web sites, however, this one had disappeared by September of 2007.

9. Annette Kuhn coined the term *social audience* to distinguish the actual group of people sitting in the audience, looking *at* a film, from the *spectator*, "the subject constituted in signification, interpellated by the film" (442).

10. Helgeland relates in his DVD commentary that he took this detail from a story about William Marshal, whose *vita* formed part of his research for the film. Marshal, who died in 1219, more than a century before the fictional setting of *A Knight's Tale*, is not a bad model for William Thatcher. A younger son of a minor nobleman, Marshal's lineage offered him few prospects for advancement; however, he rose to some prominence, becoming marshal to Henry II, guardian of his son and heir, and, through marriage, one of the wealthiest men in England. Much of Marshal's reputation was based on his performance in tournaments, where between 1170 and 1183, he was undefeated; see Duby, *William Marshal*, and Crouch.

11. Steven Spielberg's *Catch Me If You Can* (2002) explores this motif of fluid identity in a contemporary setting. It tells the story of Frank Abagnale Jr., a teenage con artist who impersonated, among other things, a pilot, a doctor, and a prosecutor.

12. Truhon and Walker point to *The Return of Martin Guerre* (Daniel Vigne, 1982), a film based on events documented by the historian Natalie Zemon Davis, to suggest that identity theft has a long history that has not required particularly advanced technologies to succeed (173). Most of the literature on computer identity theft is concerned to define it, to offer mechanisms for prevention, or to describe legal means of redressing it. There is some limited psychological research (Truhon and Walker, 177). All of these approaches remain within what Mark Poster calls an "instrumental framework" (3), which asks how technologies like the Internet might benefit or harm existing social goals. He contrasts this instrumental framework with a cultural studies approach. Although there has been little cultural analysis of how identity theft might destabilize the concept of identity, Poster writes, "The question of culture in relation to the Internet involves a risk, a step into the unfamiliar precisely with respect to the figure of the self. If this question is foreclosed, one cannot examine critically the political culture of the new media" (3, see also 6–11).

13. See, however, Poster, who argues that "the material character of print as disembodied signs, stable on the page, open to visual reception, and generally received in isolated circumstances all nurtured the growth of critical, cognitive functions and a cultural identity priding itself on these traits. The question is not whether this Cartesian subject is possible without print, is 'real' in a transcendental sense. The historical fact is that with print that figure was born, grew, and came to dominate modernity" (14).

14. The film's cast was, in fact, extremely young. Whereas Helgeland was forty at the time he directed the film, Heath Ledger and Shannyn Sossamon were only twenty-two, barely themselves out of their teens; Paul Bettany and Alan Tudyk were

thirty; Rufus Sewell was thirty-four; and Mark Addy was the old-timer of the cast at thirty-seven.

15. Although Chaucer is the preeminent poet of the Middle Ages and his *Canterbury Tales* among the most frequently read medieval texts, few films have been made from his works. On Chaucer filmmaking see Harty, "Chaucer in Performance." The most recent attempt to remake *The Canterbury Tales* was a 2003 BBC miniseries that set each of six *Canterbury Tales* in contemporary settings.

16. In the introduction to *The Riverside Chaucer* Martin Crow and Virginia Leland note that there are no records to indicate the nature of "the king's business that took Chaucer to 'parts beyond the seas' in 1370" (Chaucer, xix), providing Helgeland an opportunity to play around with Chaucer's character, imagining a life that would lead up to the composition of *The Canterbury Tales*, Chaucer's most famous work. On Brian Helgeland's identification with Geoffrey Chaucer, and on the director's use of "anachronistic" notions of authorship to create William Thatcher as a figure of "transcendent masculinity," see Crocker.

17. See Haydock's discussion of Chaucer's portraiture in *Movie Medievalism*, 105–10, which makes several of the same points about the film's adolescent audience that we do.

18. Compare to Chaucer's portrait of the Knight in the General Prologue, which lists the battles in which he has fought, all of which are associated with various crusades in the Near East, Spain and North Africa, and Russia and Lithuania; see Jones, *Chaucer's Knight*.

19. While Caroline Jewers sees this film as mostly without redeeming value—"a bland plot that increases in banality as it limps along" (205), Aronstein finds it "surprisingly political" (*Hollywood Knights*, 183).

20. This is not the first film to introduce a black character into a medieval setting. Richard Fleischer's 1958 *The Vikings* presented black actor Edric Connor as a Viking slave. The 1950s British television series *Robin of Sherwood* included a Moor named Nazir. In 1991 Kevin Costner's *Robin Hood: Prince of Thieves*, gave us Morgan Freeman as Azeem, Robin Hood's "Moorish" companion, an effort that met with considerable derision in Mel Brooks's 1993 parody, *Robin Hood: Men in Tights*, which cast Dave Chappelle and Isaac Hayes as the Moors Ahchoo and Asneeze; see Aberth, 44, and Sklar, "Twain for Teens," 97–108.

21. Despite the radical presentism of teen culture—or perhaps because of it—the teenager also occupies this anachronistic space of the primitive. Teen culture offers up the fantasy that teenagers can seamlessly and simultaneously occupy more than one temporal space. This cultural *bricolage* can imagine a caveman as an American high school student *(Encino Man)* or the medieval woman warrior Joan of Arc as an aerobics instructor *(Bill and Ted's Excellent Adventure)*.

22. Lawrence was thirty-six years old when he made this film, well into middle age.

23. We are indebted to Lauryn S. Mayer for this insight, and we thank her for sharing her unpublished essay on *Black Knight* with us.

24. Like Helgeland, the writers capitalize on the anachronisms they believe will appeal to their teen demographic, feeding the adolescent fantasy that all time is simultaneous; there was a Florence and Normandy then, and there's a Florence and Normandie now.

𝕭𝖎𝖇𝖑𝖎𝖔𝖌𝖗𝖆𝖕𝖍𝖞

Abbate, Carolyn. *In Search of Opera.* Princeton, NJ: Princeton University Press, 2001.

Aberth, John. *A Knight at the Movies: Medieval History on Film.* New York: Routledge, 2003.

Abu-Rabi, Ibrahim M. *Contemporary Arab Thought: Studies in Post-1967 Arab Intellectual History.* London: Pluto, 2004.

Adorno, Theodor W. "Freudian Theory and the Pattern of Fascist Propaganda." In *The Culture Industry: Selected Essays on Mass Culture,* ed. J. M. Bernstein, 132–57. London: Routledge, 1991.

Aho, James A. "The Apocalypse of Modernity." In *Millennium, Messiahs, and Mayhem: Contemporary Apocalyptic Movements,* ed. Thomas Robbins and Susan J. Palmer, 61–72. New York: Routledge, 1997.

Akbari, Suzanne Conklin. "From Due East to True North: Orientalism and Orientation." In Cohen, *The Postcolonial Middle Ages,* 19–34.

Althusser, Louis. *Lenin and Philosophy and Other Essays.* Trans. Ben Brewster. New York: Monthly Review Press, 1971.

Altman, Rick. *The American Film Musical.* Bloomington: Indiana University Press, 1987.

———, ed. *Genre: The Musical.* London: Routledge and Kegan Paul, 1981.

Anderson, Benedict. *Imagined Communities: Reflections on the Origins and Spread of Nationalism.* London: Verso, 1983.

———. *The Spectre of Comparisons: Nationalisms, Southeast Asia, and the World.* London: Verso, 1998.

Andrew, Dudley. "The Post-War Struggle for Colour." In de Lauretis and Heath, *The Cinematic Apparatus,* 61–75.

Angebert, Jean-Michel. *The Occult and the Third Reich: The Mystical Origins of Nazism and the Search for the Holy Grail.* Trans. Lewis A. M. Sumberg. New York: Macmillan, 1974.

Anouilh, Jean. *Becket, or the Honor of God.* Trans. Lucienne Hill. New York: Samuel French, 1960.

Apter, Emily. *Continental Drift: From National Characters to Virtual Subjects.* Chicago: University of Chicago Press, 1999.

Armstrong, Dorsey. *Gender and the Chivalric Community in Malory's "Morte d'Arthur."* Gainesville: University Press of Florida, 2003.

Aronstein, Susan. *Hollywood Knights: Arthurian Cinema and the Politics of Nostalgia.* New York: Palgrave, 2005.

———. " 'The Violence Inherent in the System': Anti-Medievalism in *Monty Python and the Holy Grail.*" Paper presented at the Congress on Medieval Studies, Kalamazoo, Michigan, May 2003.

Aronstein, Susan, and Nancy Coiner. "Twice Knightly: Democratizing the Middle Ages for Middle-Class America." In Verduin, *Medievalism in North America,* 212–31.

Ashby, Ruth, and Deborah Gore Orhn. *Herstory: Women Who Changed the World.* New York: Viking, 1995.

Ashcroft, Bill, Gareth Griffiths, and Helen Tiffin. *Post-Colonial Studies: The Key Concepts.* London: Routledge, 2003.

Bacon, Francis. *The Advancement of Learning.* Ed. William Aldis Wright. Oxford: Clarendon Press, 1926.

Baigent, Michael, Richard Leigh, and Henry Lincoln. *Holy Blood, Holy Grail.* New York: Dell, 1982.

Bakhtin, M. M. *The Dialogic Imagination.* Trans. Caryl Emerson and Michael Holquist. Austin: University of Texas Press, 1981.

———. *Rabelais and His World.* Trans. Hélène Iswolsky. Bloomington: Indiana University Press, 1984.

———. *Speech Genres and Other Late Essays.* Trans. Vern W. McGee. Ed. Caryl Emerson and Michael Holquist. Austin: University of Texas Press, 1986.

Balázs, Béla. *Theory of the Film.* New York: Roy Publishers, 1953.

Balibar, Etienne. "The Nation Form: History and Ideology." In Etienne Balibar and Immanuel Wallerstein, *Race, Nation, Class: Ambiguous Identities,* 86–106. Trans. Chris Turner. London: Verso, 1991.

Barber, Richard, ed. *King Arthur in Music.* Woodbridge, Suffolk: D. S. Brewer, 2002.

Barker, Francis, Peter Hulme, Margaret Iversen, and Diana Loxley, eds. *Europe and Its Others.* Vol. 1. Colchester: University of Essex, 1985.

Barlow, Aaron. *The DVD Revolution: Movies, Culture, and Technology.* Westport, CT: Praeger, 2005.

Barrett, W. P., ed. and trans. *The Trial of Jeanne d'Arc.* New York: Gotham House, 1932.

Barta, Tony, ed. *Screening the Past: Film and the Representation of History.* Westport, CT: Praeger, 1998.

Barthes, Roland. *The Fashion System.* Trans. Matthew Ward and Richard Howard. New York: Hill and Wang, 1983.

———. "The Romans in Film." In *Mythologies.* Trans. Annette Lavers, 26–28. New York: Hill and Wang, 1972.

Baudry, Jean-Louis. "The Apparatus: Metapsychological Approaches to the Impression of Reality in Cinema." In Rosen, *Narrative, Apparatus, Ideology,* 299–318.

———. "Ideological Effects of the Basic Cinematographic Apparatus." In Rosen, *Narrative, Apparatus, Ideology,* 286–98.

Bauman, Zygmunt. "Britain's Exit from Politics." *New Statesman and Society* 29 (1988): 34–38.

Beatie, Bruce A. "The Broken Quest: The 'Perceval' Romances of Chrétien de Troyes and Eric Rohmer." In Mancoff, *The Arthurian Revival*, 248–65.

Belton, John. "Technology and Aesthetics of Film Sound." In Braudy and Cohen, *Film Theory and Criticism*, 376–84.

Benjamin, Walter. "The Work of Art in the Age of Mechanical Reproduction." In *Illuminations: Essays and Reflections*. Trans. Harry Zohn, 217–51. New York: Schocken, 1968.

Benveniste, Émile. *Problems in General Linguistics*. Trans. Mary Elizabeth Meek. Coral Gables, FL: University of Miami Press, 1971.

Berger, John. *Ways of Seeing*. London: Penguin, 1973.

Bergman, Ingmar. *The Seventh Seal*. Trans. Lars Malmström and David Kushner. New York: Lorrimer, 1960.

Bergman, Ingrid, and Alan Burgess. *Ingrid Bergman: My Story*. New York: Delacorte, 1972.

Bergom-Larsson, Maria. *Film in Sweden: Ingmar Bergman and Society*. Trans. Barrie Selman. London: Tantivy Press, 1978.

Berlant, Laura, ed. *Intimacy*. Chicago: University of Chicago Press, 2000.

Berlant, Laura, and Michael Warner. "Sex in Public." In Berlant, *Intimacy*, 311–30.

Bernstein, Matthew, ed. *Controlling Hollywood: Censorship and Regulation in the Studio Era*. New Brunswick, NJ: Rutgers University Press, 1999.

———. "Hollywood Martyrdoms: *Joan of Arc* and Independent Production in the Late 1940s." In *Current Research in Film: Audiences, Economics, and Law*, ed. Bruce A. Austin, 4:89–113. New York: Ablex, 1988.

———. *Walter Wanger: Hollywood Independent*. Berkeley: University of California Press, 1994.

Besson, Luc, and Jack English. *L'Histoire de "Jeanne d'Arc": Aventure et découverte d'un film*. Paris: Intervista, 1999.

Bhabha, Homi. *The Location of Culture*. London: Routledge, 1994.

———. "Postcolonial Criticism." In Greenblatt and Gunn, *Redrawing the Boundaries*, 437–65.

"Biblical Boom." *Newsweek*, July 5, 1955, 79.

Biddick, Kathleen. "Coming Out of Exile: Dante and the Orient(alism) Express." *American Historical Review* 105 (2000): 20–35.

———. "Review of *The Navigator: A Medieval Odyssey*." *American Historical Review* 97 (1992): 1152–53.

———. *The Shock of Medievalism*. Durham, NC: Duke University Press, 1998.

Black, Gregory D. *The Catholic Crusade against the Movies, 1940–1975*. Cambridge, UK: Cambridge University Press, 1997.

Blackwell, Marilyn Johns. *Gender and Representation in the Films of Ingmar Bergman*. Columbia, NC: Camden House, 1997.

Blaetz, Robin. *Visions of the Maid: Joan of Arc in American Film and Culture*. Charlottesville: University of Virginia Press, 2001.

Bloch, R. Howard. *Medieval Misogyny and the Invention of Western Romantic Love*. Chicago: University of Chicago Press, 1991.

Bloch, R. Howard, and Stephen G. Nichols, eds. *Medievalism and the Modernist Temper*. Baltimore: Johns Hopkins University Press, 1996.

Boccaccio, Giovanni. *The Decameron*. Trans. and ed. Marc Musa and Peter E. Bondanella. New York: Norton, 1977.

Bolter, Jay David, and Richard Grusin. *Remediation: Understanding New Media*. Cambridge, MA: MIT Press, 1999.

Bordwell, David. "Convention, Construction, and Cinematic Vision." In Bordwell and Carroll, *Post-Theory*, 87–107.

———. *Filmguide to "La Passion de Jeanne d'Arc."* Bloomington: Indiana University Press, 1973.

———. *The Films of Carl-Theodor Dreyer*. Berkeley: University of California Press, 1981.

Bordwell, David, and Kristin Thompson. *Film Art: An Introduction*. 2nd edn. New York: Alfred Knopf, 1986.

Bordwell, David, and Noël Carroll. *Post-Theory: Reconstructing Film Studies*. Madison: University of Wisconsin Press, 1996.

Bragg, Melvyn. *The Seventh Seal*. London: BFI, 1993.

Braudy, Leo, and Marshall Cohen, eds. *Film Theory and Criticism: Introductory Readings*. 5th edn. Oxford: Oxford University Press, 1999.

Bresson, Robert. *Notes on Cinematography*. Trans. Jonathan Griffin. New York: Urizen, 1975.

Brown, Eryn. "Beyond the Trappings." *Los Angeles Times*, Feb. 15, 2004.

Brown, Wendy. *States of Injury: Power and Freedom in Late Modernity*. Princeton, NJ: Princeton University Press, 1995.

Brownlee, Marina S., Kevin Brownlee, and Stephen G. Nichols, eds. *The New Medievalism*. Baltimore: Johns Hopkins University Press, 1991.

Bryson, Norman. "Géricault and 'Masculinity.'" In *Visual Culture: Images and Interpretations*, ed. Norman Bryson, Michael Ann Holly, and Keith Moxey, 228–59. Hanover, NH: Wesleyan University Press, 1994.

Buckland, Warren. "Film Semiotics." In Miller and Stam, *A Companion to Film Theory*, 84–104.

Buhler, James, Caryl Flinn, and David Neumeyer, eds. *Music and Cinema*. Hanover, NH: Wesleyan University Press, 2000.

Burde, Mark. "Monty Python's Medieval Masterpiece." In *Arthurian Yearbook 3*, ed. Keith Busby, 3–20. New York: Garland, 1993.

Burns, E. Jane. *Courtly Love Undressed: Reading through Clothes in Medieval French Culture*. Philadelphia: University of Pennsylvania Press, 2002.

———. "Nostalgia Isn't What It Used to Be: The Middle Ages in Literature and Film." In Slusser and Rabkin, *Shadows of the Magic Lamp*, 86–97.

Burt, Richard. "Getting Schmedieval: Of Manuscript and Film Prologues, Paratexts, and Parodies." *Exemplaria* 19 (2007): 217–42.

Byers, Thomas B. "Nationalism, Patriarchy, War: *Braveheart* and US Gender Politics." Unpublished paper.

Cable, James, trans. *The Death of King Arthur*. Baltimore: Penguin, 1971.

Callahan, Leslie Abend. "*Perceval le Gallois*: Eric Rohmer's Vision of the Middle Ages." *Film and History* 29 (1999): 46–53.

Campbell, Russell. "The Blindfold Seer." *Illusions* 10 (1989): 15–16.

Cannadine, David. "The Context, Performance and Meaning of Ritual: The British Monarchy and the Invention of Tradition." In *Politics and Ideology*, ed. James Donald and Stuart Hall, 121–37. Philadelphia: Open University Press, 1986.

Cantor, Norman. *Inventing the Middle Ages: The Lives, Works, and Ideas of the Great Medievalists of the Twentieth Century*. New York: William and Morrow, 1991.

Card, James. *Seductive Cinema: The Art of Silent Film*. Minneapolis: University of Minnesota Press, 1994.

Carlson, David R. *Chaucer's Jobs*. New York: Palgrave, 2006.

Carroll, James. *Crusade: Chronicles of an Unjust War*. New York: Metropolitan Books, 2004.

Carroll, Noël. "Nonfiction Film and Postmodern Skepticism." In Bordwell and Carroll, *Post-Theory*, 283–306.

Case, Sue-Ellen. "Tracking the Vampire." *Differences* 3 (1991): 1–20.

Cerquiglini, Bernard. *In Praise of the Variant*. Trans. Betsy Wing. Baltimore: Johns Hopkins University Press, 1999.

Chahine, Youssef, and Joseph Massad. "Art and Politics in the Cinema of Youssef Chahine." *Journal of Palestine Studies* 28 (1999): 77–93.

Chandler, Alice. *A Dream of Order: The Medieval Ideal in Nineteenth-Century English Literature*. Lincoln: University of Nebraska Press, 1970.

Charney, Leo. "The Violence of a Perfect Moment." In Slocum, *Violence and American Cinema*, 47–62.

Chaucer, Geoffrey. *The Riverside Chaucer*. 3rd edn. Ed. Larry D. Benson. Boston: Houghton Mifflin, 1987.

Chion, Michel. *The Voice in Cinema*. Trans. Claudia Gorbman. New York: Columbia University Press, 1999.

Chrétien de Troyes. *Arthurian Romances*. Trans. D. D. R. Owen. London: Everyman, 1991.

Churchill, Winston S. *The Birth of Britain*. Vol. 1 of *A History of the English Speaking Peoples*. New York: Dodd, Mead, 1956.

Ciment, Michel. *John Boorman*. Trans. Gilbert Adair. London: Faber and Faber, 1985.

Clark, Alice. *Working Life of Women in the Seventeenth Century*. London: Cass, 1968.

Clark, Danae. *Negotiating Hollywood: The Cultural Politics of Actors' Labor*. Minneapolis: University of Minnesota Press, 1995.

Clark, Katerina, and Michael Holquist. *Mikhail Bakhtin*. Cambridge, MA: Belknap Press of Harvard University, 1984.

Clegg, Cyndia. "The Problem of Realizing Medieval Romance in Film: John Boorman's *Excalibur*." In Slusser and Rabkin, *Shadows of the Magic Lamp*, 98–111.

Codel, Julie F. "Decapitation and Deconstruction: The Body of the Hero in Robert Bresson's *Lancelot du Lac*." In Mancoff, *The Arthurian Revival*, 266–82.

Cohen, Jeffrey Jerome, ed. *The Postcolonial Middle Ages.* New York: St. Martin's, 2000.

Cohen, Paula Marantz. *Silent Film and the Triumph of the American Myth.* Oxford: Oxford University Press, 2001.

Coontz, Stephanie. *The Way We Never Were: American Families and the Nostalgia Trap.* New York: Basic Books, 1952.

Corman, Roger, with Jim Jerome. *How I Made a Hundred Movies in Hollywood and Never Lost a Dime.* New York: Random House, 1990.

Cotter, Jerry. "Hollywood Goes Reckless." *Sign* 39 (April 1960): 40–42.

———. "Review of *Joan of Arc.*" *Sign* 28 (Nov. 1948): 53–54.

Cowie, Peter. *Ingmar Bergman: A Critical Biography.* New York: Scribner, 1982.

Crawford, Paul. "Crusades: A Commentary on the BBC Series." The Orb: On-line Reference Book for Medieval Studies. http://the-orb.net/non_spec/bbcx.html (accessed March 2, 2009).

Crisp, C. G. *Eric Rohmer: Realist and Moralist.* Bloomington: Indiana University Press, 1988.

Crocker, Holly A. "Chaucer's Man Show: Anachronistic Authority in Brian Helgeland's *A Knight's Tale.*" In Ramey and Pugh, *Race, Class, and Gender in "Medieval" Cinema,* 183–97.

Crouch, David. *William Marshal: Knighthood, War, and Chivalry, 1147–1219.* New York: Longman, 2002.

Cuneo, Michael W. *The Smoke of Satan: Conservative and Traditionalist Dissent in Contemporary American Catholicism.* Oxford: Oxford University Press, 1997.

Cunneen, Joseph. *Robert Bresson: A Spiritual Style in Film.* New York: Continuum, 2003.

Currie, Gregory. "Cognitivism." In Miller and Stam, *A Companion to Film Theory,* 105–122.

Dabakis, Melissa. "Gendered Labor: Norman Rockwell's *Rosie the Riveter* and the Discourses of Wartime Womanhood." In *Gender and American History Since 1890,* ed. Barbara Melosh, 155–81. London: Routledge, 1993.

Dahlhaus, Carl. "Parsifal." In Groos and Lacy, *Perceval/Parzival,* 287–99.

Damico, James. "Ingrid from Lorraine to Stromboli: Analyzing the Public's Perception of a Film Star." In *Star Texts: Image and Performance in Film and Television,* ed. Jeremy G. Butler, 240–53. Detroit: Wayne State University Press, 1991.

Davidson, Roberta. "The *Reel* Arthur: Politics and Truth Claims in *Camelot, Excalibur,* and *King Arthur.*" *Arthuriana* 17 (2007): 62–84.

Davis, Kathleen. "Time behind the Veil: The Media, the Middle Ages, and Orientalism Now." In Cohen, *The Postcolonial Middle Ages,* 105–17.

Dawisha, Adeed. *Arab Nationalism in the Twentieth Century: From Triumph to Despair.* Princeton, NJ: Princeton University Press, 2003.

Day, David D. "*Monty Python and the Holy Grail:* Madness with a Definite Method." In Harty, *Cinema Arthuriana,* rev. edn., 127–35.

———. "Monty Python and the Medieval Other." In Harty, *Cinema Arthuriana,* 83–92.

Dayan, Daniel. "The Tudor-Code of Classical Cinema." In Braudy and Cohen, *Film Theory and Criticism*, 118–29.

Dean, Jodi. *Žižek's Politics*. New York: Routledge, 2006.

Debord, Guy. *The Society of the Spectacle*. New York: Zone, 1994.

DeCurtis, Anthony, ed. *Present Tense: Rock and Roll and Culture*. Durham, NC: Duke University Press, 1992.

De Lauretis, Teresa, and Stephen Heath, eds. *The Cinematic Apparatus*. New York: St. Martin's, 1980.

Deleuze, Gilles. *Coldness and Cruelty in Masochism*. New York: Zone, 1991.

Deleuze, Gilles, and Félix Guattari. *A Thousand Plateaus: Capitalism and Schizophrenia*. Trans. Brian Massumi. Minneapolis: University of Minnesota Press, 1987.

Dempsey, Michael. "Despair Abounding: The Recent Films of Robert Bresson." In Quandt, *Robert Bresson*, 373–92.

Desmond, Marilynn, and Pamela Sheingorn. *Myth, Montage, and Visuality in Late Medieval Manuscript Culture: Christine de Pizan's "Epistre Othea."* Ann Arbor: University of Michigan Press, 2003.

DeVries, Kelly. *Joan of Arc: A Military Leader*. Stroud, Gloucestershire: Sutton, 2002.

Dickinson, Kay, ed. *Movie Music: The Film Reader*. London: Routledge, 2003.

———. "Pop, Speed, Teenagers and the 'MTV Aesthetic.'" In Dickinson, *Movie Music*, 143–51.

Dinshaw, Carolyn. *Getting Medieval: Sexualities and Communities, Pre- and Post-Modern*. Durham, NC: Duke University Press, 1999.

Doane, Mary Ann. "Film and the Masquerade: Theorising the Female Spectator." In Kaplan, *Feminism and Film*, 418–36.

———. "Remembering Women: Psychical and Historical Constructions in Film Theory." In *Psychoanalysis and Film*, ed. E. Ann Kaplan, 46–63. New York: Routledge, 1990.

Doherty, Paul. *Isabella and the Strange Death of Edward II*. New York: Carroll and Graf, 2003.

Donald, James, and Stephanie Hemelryk Donald. "The Publicness of Cinema." In *Reinventing Film Studies*, ed. Christine Gledhill and Linda Williams, 114–29. London: Arnold, 2000.

Doncoeur, Paul, S.J. "Ingrid Bergman and Joan of Arc." *America* 80 (Nov. 13, 1948): 158–59.

———. "Joan of Arc." *Sign* 28 (Nov. 1948): 26–28.

Dreyer, Carl Theodor. *Four Screenplays*. Bloomington: Indiana University Press, 1964.

———. "Thoughts on My Craft." In *Film: A Montage of Theories*, ed. Richard Dyer MacCann, 312–17. New York: Dutton, 1966.

Driver, Martha W. "What's Accuracy Got to Do with It?" In Driver and Ray, *The Medieval Hero on Screen*, 19–22.

———. "Writing about Medieval Movies: Authenticity and History." *Film and History* 29 (1999): 5–7.

Driver, Martha W., and Sid Ray, eds. *The Medieval Hero on Screen: Representations from Beowulf to Buffy.* Jefferson, NC: McFarland, 2004.

Duby, Georges. *Three Orders: Feudal Society Imagined.* Trans. Arthur Goldhammer. Chicago: University of Chicago Press, 1980.

————. *William Marshal: The Flower of Chivalry.* Trans. Richard Howard. New York: Pantheon, 1985.

Ducat, Stephen. *The Wimp Factor: Gender Gaps, Holy Wars, and the Politics of Anxious Masculinity.* Boston: Beacon, 2004.

du Gay, Paul, Stuart Hall, Linda Janes, Hugh Mackay, and Keith Negus. *Doing Cultural Studies: The Story of the Sony Walkman.* London: Sage, 1977.

Dyer, Richard. *Heavenly Bodies: Film Stars and Society.* New York: Macmillan, 1987.

————. *Stars.* London: BFI, 1979.

Eagleton, Terry. "Brecht and Rhetoric." In *Against the Grain: Essays 1975–1985,* 167–72. London: Verso, 1986.

Eco, Umberto. *Travels in Hyperreality.* Trans. William Weaver. New York: Harcourt Brace Jovanovich, 1986.

Eichenbaum, Boris. "Problems of Film Stylistics." Trans. Thomas Aman. *Screen* 15 (1974): 7–32.

Eisenstein, Zillah R. *The Radical Future of Liberal Feminism.* New York: Longman, 1981.

Emerson, Michael O., and David Hartman. "The Rise of Religious Fundamentalism." *Annual Review of Sociology* 32 (2006): 127–44.

Eng, David L., and David Kazanjian, eds. *Loss: The Politics of Mourning.* Berkeley: University of California Press, 2003.

Estruch, Joan. *Saints and Schemers: Opus Dei and Its Paradoxes.* Trans. Elizabeth Ladd Glick. Oxford: Oxford University Press, 1995.

Everett, William A. "King Arthur in Popular Musical Theatre and Musical Film." In Barber, *King Arthur in Music,* 145–60.

Fawal, Ibrahim. *Youssef Chahine.* London: BFI, 2001.

Feinberg, Leslie. *Transgender Warriors: Making History from Joan of Arc to RuPaul.* Boston: Beacon, 1996.

Finke, Laurie A. *Feminist Theory, Women's Writing.* Ithaca, NY: Cornell University Press, 1992.

————. "The Politics of the Canon: Christine de Pisan and the Fifteenth-Century Chaucerians." *Exemplaria* 19 (2007): 16–38.

————. "Sexuality in Medieval French Literature: Séparés, on est ensemble." In *Handbook of Medieval Sexuality,* ed. Vern L. Bullough and James A. Brundage, 345–68. New York: Garland, 1996.

————. *Women's Writing in English: The Middle Ages.* London: Longman, 1999.

Finke, Laurie A., and Martin B. Shichtman. *King Arthur and the Myth of History.* Gainesville: University Press of Florida, 2004.

————. "Magical Mistress Tour: Patronage, Intellectual Property, and the Dissemination of Wealth in the *Lais* of Marie de France." *Signs* 25 (2000): 479–503.

———, eds. *Medieval Texts and Contemporary Readers*. Ithaca, NY: Cornell University Press, 1987.

———. "No Pain, No Gain: Violence as Symbolic Capital in Malory's *Morte Darthur*." *Arthuriana* 8 (1998): 115–33.

———. "Profiting Pedants: Symbolic Capital, Text Editing, and Cultural Reproduction." In *Disciplining English: Alternative Histories, Critical Perspectives*, ed. David R. Shumway and Craig Dionne, 159–78. Albany: State University of New York Press, 2002.

Finke, Laurie A., and Susan Aronstein. "Got Grail? Monty Python and the Broadway Stage." *Theatre Survey* 48 (2007): 289–311.

Fish, Stanley. "Interpreting the Variorum." In *Is There a Text in This Class? The Authority of Interpretive Communities*, 167–80. Cambridge, MA: Harvard University Press, 1980.

Ford, Hamish. "The Radical Intimacy of Bergman." *Senses of Cinema* (Nov. 2002): www.sensesofcinema.com/contents/directors/02/bergman.html (accessed Sept. 9, 2008).

Forhan, Kate Langdon. "Polycracy, Obligation, and Revolt: The Body Politic in John of Salisbury and Christine de Pizan." In *Politics, Gender, and Genre: The Political Thought of Christine de Pizan*, ed. Margaret Brabant, 33–52. Boulder, CO: Westview Press, 1992.

Forni, Kathleen. "Reinventing Chaucer: Helgeland's *A Knight's Tale*." *Chaucer Review* 37 (2003): 253–64.

Foucault, Michel. "Sexuality and Solitude." In *On Signs*, ed. Marshall Blonsky, 365–72. Baltimore: Johns Hopkins University Press, 1985.

Fradenburg, Louise O. " 'Fulfild of fairye': The Social Meaning of Fantasy in the Wife of Bath's Prologue and Tale." In *The Wife of Bath*, ed. Peter G. Beidler, 205–20. Boston: Bedford, 1996.

Freccero, Carla. *Queer/Early/Modern*. Durham, NC: Duke University Press, 2006.

Friedlander, Saul. "Hitler und Wagner." In *Richard Wagner im dritten Reich*, ed. Saul Friedlander and Jörn Rüsen, 167–78. Munich: C. H. Beck, 2000.

Friedman, Lester. *Fires Were Started: British Cinema and Thatcherism*. Minneapolis: University of Minnesota Press, 1993.

Frith, Simon, Will Straw, and John Street. *The Cambridge Companion to Pop and Rock*. Cambridge, UK: Cambridge University Press, 2001.

Froissart, Jean. *Chronicles*. Ed. Geoffrey Brereton. Baltimore: Penguin, 1968.

Gamson, Joshua. *Claims to Fame: Celebrity in Contemporary America*. Berkeley: University of California Press, 1994.

Ganim, John M. *Chaucerian Theatricality*. Princeton, NJ: Princeton University Press, 1990.

———. *Medievalism and Orientalism: Three Essays on Literature, Architecture, and Cultural Identity*. New York: Palgrave, 2005.

———. "The Myth of Medieval Romance." In Bloch and Nichols, *Medievalism and the Modernist Temper*, 148–66.

——. "Reversing the Crusades: Hegemony, Orientalism, and Film Language in Youssef Chahine's *Saladin.*" In Ramey and Pugh, *Race, Class, and Gender in "Medieval" Cinema,* 45–58.

Garet, Ronald R. "Arthur and President Kennedy: The Myth of Kingship." *RAIN* 57 (1983): 5–8.

Giannetti, Louis. *Understanding Movies.* 9th edn. Upper Saddle River, NJ: Prentice Hall, 2002.

Giddens, Anthony. *The Constitution of Society: Outline of the Theory of Structuration.* Berkeley: University of California Press, 1984.

Gilchrist, Roberta. *Gender and Material Culture: The Archaeology of Religious Women.* London: Routledge, 1994.

Ginsberg, Terri, and Kirsten Moana Thompson, eds. *Perspectives on German Cinema.* New York: G. K. Hall, 1996.

Giroux, Henry A. "Teenage Sexuality, Body Politics, and the Pedagogy of Display." In *Youth Culture: Identity in a Postmodern World,* ed. Jonathan S. Epstein, 24–55. Oxford: Blackwell, 1998.

Gitlin, Todd. *The Sixties: Years of Hope, Days of Rage.* New York: Bantam, 1987.

Goldman, James. *The Lion in Winter.* New York: Random House, 1966.

Gourevitch, Phillip. "The Unthinkable." *New Yorker,* April 27, 1997, 110–19, 139–43, 147.

Grant, Barry Keith, and Jeannette Sloniowski, eds. *Documenting the Documentary.* Detroit: Wayne State University Press, 1998.

Greenblatt, Stephen, and Giles Gunn, eds. *Redrawing the Boundaries: The Transformation of English and American Literary Studies.* New York: Modern Language Association, 1992.

Grellner, Alice. "Two Films That Sparkle: *The Sword in the Stone* and *Camelot.*" In Harty, *Cinema Arthuriana,* 71–81.

Grimbert, Joan Tasker. "Distancing Techniques in Chrétien de Troyes *Li Contes del Graal* and Eric Rohmer's *Perceval le Gallois.*" *Arthuriana* 10 (2000): 33–44.

Groos, Arthur, and Norris Lacy, eds. *Perceval/Parzival: A Casebook.* New York: Routledge, 2002.

Grossberg, Lawrence. "Cinema, Postmodernity and Authenticity." In Dickinson, *Movie Music,* 83–98.

Grosz, Elizabeth. *Jacques Lacan: A Feminist Introduction.* London: Routledge, 1989.

Gunning, Tom. "The Cinema of Attractions: Early Film, Its Spectator and the Avant-Garde." In *Early Cinema: Space, Frame, Narrative,* ed. Thomas Elsaesser and Adam Barker, 95–103. London: BFI, 1990.

Habermas, Jürgen. "The Public Sphere: An Encyclopedia Article (1964)." Trans. Sara Lennox and Frank Lennox. *New German Critique* 3 (1974): 49–55.

——. *The Structural Transformation of the Public Sphere: An Inquiry into a Category of Bourgeois Society.* Trans. Thomas Burger. Cambridge, MA: MIT Press, 1989.

Halim, Hala. "The Signs of *Saladin*: A Modern Cinematic Rendition of Medieval Heroism." *Alif: Journal of Comparative Poetics* 12 (1992): 78–94.

Hall, Stuart. "The Toad in the Garden: Thatcherism among the Theorists." In *Marxism and the Interpretation of Culture*, ed. Cary Nelson and Lawrence Grossberg, 35–73. Urbana: University of Illinois Press, 1988.

Hamilton, Bernard. *The Leper King and His Heirs: Baldwin IV and the Crusader Kingdom of Jerusalem.* Cambridge, UK: Cambridge University Press, 2000.

———. "Women in the Crusader States: The Queens of Jerusalem, 1100–90." In *Medieval Women*, ed. Derek Baker, 143–74. Oxford: Blackwell, 1978.

Hanlon, Lindley. *Fragments: Bresson's Film Style.* Rutherford, NJ: Fairleigh Dickinson University Press, 1986.

Hanning, Robert W. "'I Shal Finde It in a Maner Glose': Versions of Textual Harassment in Medieval Literature." In Finke and Shichtman, *Medieval Texts and Contemporary Readers*, 27–50.

Harper, Sue. "Bonnie Prince Charlie Revisited: British Costume Film in the 1950s." In *The British Cinema Book*, 2nd edn., ed. Robert Murphy, 127–34. London: BFI, 2001.

Harty, Kevin J. "Chaucer in Performance." In *Chaucer: An Oxford Guide*, ed. Steve Ellis, 560–72. Oxford: Oxford University Press, 2005.

———, ed. *Cinema Arthuriana: Essays on Arthurian Film.* New York: Garland, 1991; rev. edn. 2002.

———. "Cinematic American Camelots Lost and Found: The Film Versions of Mark Twain's *A Connecticut Yankee in King Arthur's Court*." In Harty, *Cinema Arthuriana*, rev. edn., 96–109.

———. "Jeanne au cinema." In Wheeler and Wood, *Fresh Verdicts on Joan of Arc*, 237–64.

———. *King Arthur on Film: New Essays on Arthurian Cinema.* Jefferson, NC: McFarland, 1999.

———. "Parsifal and Perceval on Film: The Reel Life of a Grail Knight." In Groos and Lacy, *Perceval/Parzival*, 300–312.

———. *The Reel Middle Ages: Films about Medieval Europe.* Jefferson, NC: McFarland, 1999.

Harvey, Brett. *The Fifties: A Woman's Oral History.* San Jose, CA: ASJA Press, 1993.

Haydock, Nickolas. *Movie Medievalism: The Imaginary Middle Ages.* Jefferson, NC: McFarland, 2007.

———. "Shooting the Messenger: Luc Besson at War with Joan of Arc." *Exemplaria* 19 (2007): 243–69.

Hayward, Susan. *Luc Besson.* Manchester: Manchester University Press, 1998.

Heath, Stephen. "Narrative Space." In Rosen, *Narrative, Apparatus, Ideology*, 379–420.

Hillenbrand, Carole. *The Crusades: Islamic Perspectives.* Chicago: Fitzroy Dearborn, 1999.

Hillier, Jim, ed. *Cahiers du Cinéma. The 1950s: Neo-Realism, Hollywood, New Wave.* Cambridge, MA: Harvard University Press, 1985.

Hilton, Rodney H. "Freedom and Villeinage in England." *Past and Present*, 31 (1965): 3–19.

Hoberman, J. *The Dream Life: Movies, Media, and the Mythology of the Sixties.* New York: New Press, 2003.

Hoffman, Donald L. "Chahine's *Destiny:* Prophetic Nostalgia and the Other Middle Ages." In Ramey and Pugh, *Race, Class, and Gender in "Medieval" Cinema,* 31–44.

———. "Not Dead Yet: *Monty Python and the Holy Grail* in the Twenty-first Century." In Harty, *Cinema Arthuriana,* rev. edn. 136–48.

———. "Re-Framing Perceval." *Arthuriana* 10 (2000): 45–56.

Holsinger, Bruce W. "Medieval Studies, Postcolonial Studies, and the Genealogies of Critique." *Speculum* 77 (2005): 1195–1227.

———. *Neomedievalism, Neoconservatism, and the War on Terror.* Chicago: Prickly Paradigm Press, 2007.

———. *The Premodern Condition: Medievalism and the Making of Theory.* Chicago: University of Chicago Press, 2005.

Honey, Maureen. *Creating Rosie the Riveter: Class, Gender, and Propaganda during World War II.* Amherst: University of Massachusetts Press, 1984.

Howe, Nicholas. "The Center on the Margin, or, Self-Fulfilling Prophecies for Medievalists." Medieval Academy of America, *Medieval Academy News.* www.medieval academy.org/medacnews/news_howe.htm (accessed Feb. 19, 2009).

Huntington, Samuel P. *The Clash of Civilizations and the Remaking of World Order.* New York: Simon and Schuster, 1996.

Hutcheon, Linda, and Michael Hutcheon. "Syphilis, Sin, and the Social Order: Richard Wagner's *Parsifal.*" *Cambridge Opera Journal* 7 (1995): 261–75.

Ingham, Patricia Clare. "Contrapuntal Histories." In Ingham and Warren, *Postcolonial Moves,* 47–70.

Ingham, Patricia Clare, and Michelle R. Warren, eds. *Postcolonial Moves: Medieval through Modern.* New York: Palgrave, 2003.

Jacobs, Lea. "Industry Self-Regulation and the Problem of Textual Determination." In Bernstein, *Controlling Hollywood,* 87–101.

Jameson, Fredric. "In the Destructive Element Immerse: Hans-Jürgen Syberberg and Cultural Revolution." *October* 17 (1981): 99–118.

———. "Postmodernism and Consumer Society." In Leitch et al., *The Norton Anthology of Theory and Criticism,* 1960–74.

———. *Postmodernism, or, The Cultural Logic of Late Capitalism.* Durham, NC: Duke University Press, 1991.

———. *A Singular Modernity: Essay on the Ontology of the Present.* London: Verso, 2002.

Jeffords, Susan. *Hard Bodies: Hollywood Masculinity in the Reagan Era.* New Brunswick, NJ: Rutgers University Press, 1994.

———. *The Remasculinization of America: Gender and the Vietnam War.* Bloomington: University of Indiana Press, 1989.

Jewers, Caroline. "Hard Day's Knights: *First Knight, A Knight's Tale,* and *Black Knight.*" In Driver and Ray, *The Medieval Hero on Screen,* 192–210.

John of Salisbury. *Policraticus.* Ed. and trans. Cary J. Nederman. Cambridge, UK: Cambridge University Press, 1990.

Jones, Terry. *Chaucer's Knight: The Portrait of a Medieval Mercenary.* New York: Methuen, 1980.

Kabir, Ananya, and Deanne Williams, eds. *Postcolonial Approaches to the European Middle Ages: Translating Cultures.* Cambridge, UK: Cambridge University Press, 2005.

Kaminsky, Stuart. "The Torment of Insight: Youth and Innocence in the Films of Ingmar Bergman." *Cinema Journal* 13 (1974): 11–22.

Kaplan, E. Ann. "The Case of the Missing Mother: Maternal Issues in Vidor's *Stella Dallas.*" In Kaplan, *Feminism and Film,* 466–78.

———, ed. *Feminism and Film.* Oxford: Oxford University Press, 2000.

———. "Is the Gaze Male?" In Kaplan, *Feminism and Film,* 119–38.

Kashner, Sam, and Jennifer MacNair. *The Bad and the Beautiful: Hollywood in the Fifties.* New York: Norton, 2002.

Kay, Sarah. *Žižek: A Critical Introduction.* Cambridge, UK: Polity Press, 2003.

Kelly, Henry Ansgar. "Joan of Arc's Last Trial: The Attack of the Devil's Advocate." In Wheeler and Wood, *Fresh Verdicts on Joan of Arc,* 205–35.

Kelly, Kathleen Coyne. *Performing Virginity and Testing Chastity in the Middle Ages.* London: Routledge, 2000.

Ketcham, Charles B. *The Influence of Existentialism on Ingmar Bergman: An Analysis of the Theological Ideas Shaping a Filmmaker's Art.* Lewiston, NY: E. Mellen Press, 1986.

Kiernan, Maureen. "Cultural Hegemony and National Film Language: Youssef Chahine." *Alif: Journal of Comparative Poetics* 15 (1995): 130–52.

Kinoshita, Sharon. "The Romance of MiscegeNation: Negotiating Identities in *La Fille du comte de Pontieu.*" In Ingham and Warren, *Postcolonial Moves,* 111–31.

Kipnis, Laura. "Adultery." In Berlant, *Intimacy,* 9–47.

———. "Response." In Berlant, *Intimacy,* 434.

Kleis, John Christopher. "The Arthurian Dilemma: Faith and Works in Syberberg's *Parsifal.*" In Harty, *King Arthur on Film,* 109–22.

Knapp, Raymond. *The American Musical and the Formation of National Identity.* Princeton, NJ: Princeton University Press, 2005.

Kristeva, Julia. "On the Melancholic Imaginary." Trans. Louise Burchill. In *Discourse in Psychoanalysis and Literature,* ed. Shlomith Rimmon-Kenan, 104–23. London: Methuen, 1987.

———. *Tales of Love.* Trans. Leon S. Roudiez. New York: Columbia University Press, 1981.

Kuhn, Annette. "Women's Genres." In Kaplan, *Feminism and Film,* 437–49.

Lacan, Jacques. *The Ethics of Psychoanalysis.* New York: Norton, 1992.

Lack, Russell. *Twenty-Four Frames Under: A Brief History of Film Music.* London: Quartet Books, 1997.

Lacy, Norris J. "The Documentary Arthur: Reflections of a Talking Head." In Sklar and Hoffman, *King Arthur in Popular Culture,* 77–86.

Landy, Marcia, ed. *The Historical Film.* New Brunswick, NJ: Rutgers University Press, 2001.

Latour, Bruno. *We Have Never Been Modern.* Trans. Catherine Porter. Cambridge, MA: Harvard University Press, 1993.

———. "Why Has Critique Run Out of Steam? From Matters of Fact to Matters of Concern." *Critical Inquiry* 50 (2004): 225–48.

Lawler, Michael G. "Sectarian Catholicism and Mel Gibson." *Journal of Religion and Film* 8 (2004): www.unomaha.edu/jrf/2004Symposium/Lawler.htm (accessed March 21, 2009).

Lees, Gene. *Inventing Champagne: The Worlds of Lerner and Loewe.* New York: St. Martin's, 1990.

Legion of Decency. *Motion Pictures Classified by National Legion of Decency.* New York: National Legion of Decency, 1959.

Le Goff, Jacques. *Time, Work, and Culture in the Middle Ages.* Trans. Arthur Goldhammer. Chicago: University of Chicago Press, 1980.

Leitch, Vincent B., William E. Cain, Laurie Finke, Barbara Johnson, John McGowan, and Jeffrey J. Williams. *The Norton Anthology of Theory and Criticism.* New York: Norton, 2001.

Lerner, Alan Jay. *The Musical Theatre: A Celebration.* London: Collins, 1986.

Lerner, Gerda. "Joan of Arc: Three Films." In *Past Imperfect: History According to the Movies,* ed. Ted Mico, John Miller-Monzon, and David Rubel, 54–59. New York: Henry Holt, 1995.

Le Tourneau, Dominique. *What Is Opus Dei?* Dublin: Mercier Press, 1991.

Levin, Thomas Y. "Iconology at the Movies: Panofsky's Film Theory." *Yale Journal of Criticism* 9 (1996): 27–55.

Lewis, Lisa. *Gender Politics and MTV.* Philadelphia: Temple University Press, 1990.

Linderman, Deborah. "Uncoded Images in the Heterogeneous Text." In Rosen, *Narrative, Apparatus, Ideology,* 143–52.

Lindley, Arthur. "The Ahistoricism of Medieval Film." *Screening the Past* 3 (1998): www.latrobe.edu.au/screeningthepast/firstrelease/fir598/ALfr3a.htm (accessed Feb. 17, 2009).

———. "Once, Present, and Future Kings: *Kingdom of Heaven* and the Multitemporality of Medieval Film." In Ramey and Pugh, *Race, Class, and Gender in "Medieval" Cinema,* 15–30.

Lloyd, Ann, ed. *Movies of the Silent Years.* London: Orbis, 1984.

Lloyd, David. "The Medieval Sill: Joyce, 'Medieval Ireland' and Postcolonialism." Unpublished paper presented at "Medieval Temporalities and Colonial Histories," Princeton University, May 16, 2003.

Locke, John. *The Second Treatise of Civil Government* (1690). The Constitution Society. www.constitution.org/jl/2ndtreat.htm (accessed Sept. 1, 2008).

Loewe, Frederick, and Alan Jay Lerner. *Camelot.* Edited by Franz Allers. Piano Reduction by Trude Rittman. New York: Chappell Music, 1962.

Logan, Joshua. *Josh: My Up and Down, In and Out Life.* New York: Delacorte, 1976.

Long, Scott. "Nightmare in the Mirror: Adolescence and the Death of Difference." *Social Text* 24 (1990): 156–66.

Luhr, William. "Mutilating Mel: Martyrdom and Masculinity in *Braveheart*." In *Mythologies of Violence in Postmodern Media*, ed. Christopher Sharrett, 227–46. Detroit: Wayne State University Press, 1999.

Lupack, Alan, and Barbara Tepa Lupack. *King Arthur in America*. Cambridge, UK: D. S. Brewer, 1999.

Madden, Thomas F. "Crusade Propaganda: The Abuse of Christianity's Holy Wars." *National Review*, Nov. 2, 2001. www.nationalreview.com/comment/comment-madden110201.shtml (accessed March 20, 2009).

Malkmus, Lizbeth, and Roy Armes. *Arab and African Filmmaking*. London: Zed, 1991.

Maltby, Richard. "*The King of Kings* and the Czar of all the Rushes: The Propriety of the Christ Story." In Bernstein, *Controlling Hollywood*, 60–86.

Mancoff, Debra N., ed. *The Arthurian Revival: Essays on Form, Tradition, and Transformation*. New York: Garland, 1992.

Mann, Thomas. "The Suffering and Greatness of Richard Wagner." In *Essays of Three Decades*. Trans. H. T. Lowe-Porter. New York: Knopf, 1947.

Marcuse, Herbert. *One-Dimensional Man*. Boston: Beacon, 1964.

Margolis, Nadia. "The 'Joan Phenomenon' and the French Right." In Wheeler and Wood, *Fresh Verdicts on Joan of Arc*, 265–88.

Marie, Michel. *The French New Wave: An Artistic School*. Trans. Richard Neupert. Oxford: Blackwell, 2003.

Markley, Robert. *The Far East and the English Imagination, 1600–1730*. Cambridge, UK: Cambridge University Press, 2006.

Marshall, David W., ed. *Mass Market Medieval: Essays on the Middle Ages in Popular Culture*. Jefferson, NC: McFarland, 2007.

Mast, Gerald. *Can't Help Singin': The American Musical on Stage and Screen*. New York: Overlook Press, 1987.

Matar, Nabil I. "The Question of Occidentalism in Early Modern Morocco." In Ingham and Warren, *Postcolonial Moves*, 153–70.

Matthews, Peter. "The Hard Stuff." *Sight and Sound* 12 (2002): 24–26.

Maxwell, Ronald F. "The Messenger: Dumbed Down Dame." www.ronmaxwell.com/messenger.html (accessed March 24, 2009).

McArthur, Colin. "*Braveheart* and the Scottish Aesthetic Dementia." In Barta, *Screening the Past*, 167–88.

McClintock, Anne. *Imperial Leather: Race, Gender, and Sexuality in the Colonial Contest*. New York: Routledge, 1995.

McDowell, Linda. *Gender, Identity, and Place: Understanding Feminist Geographies*. Minneapolis: University of Minnesota Press, 1999.

McInerney, Maud Burnett. *Eloquent Virgins from Thecla to Joan of Arc*. New York: Palgrave, 2003.

Medvedev, P. N., and M. M. Bakhtin. *The Formal Method in Literary Scholarship: A Crit-*

ical Introduction to Sociological Poetics. Trans Albert J. Wehrle. Baltimore: Johns Hopkins University Press, 1978.

Merchant, Carolyn. The Death of Nature: Women, Ecology, and the Scientific Revolution. San Francisco: Harper and Row, 1980.

Mernissi, Fatima. The Veil and the Male Elite: A Feminist Interpretation of Women's Rights in Islam. Trans. Mary Jo Lakeland. Reading, MA: Addison-Wesley, 1987.

Merton, Robert K. "Social Structure and Anomie." American Sociological Review 3 (1938): 672–82.

Metz, Christian. The Imaginary Signifier. Trans. Celia Britton, Annwyl Williams, Ben Brewster, and Alfred Guzzetti. Bloomington: Indiana University Press, 1982.

———. "Problems of Denotation in the Fiction Film." In Braudy and Cohen, Film Theory and Criticism, 75–89.

Meuwese, Martine, ed. King Arthur in the Netherlands. Amsterdam: In De Pelikaan, 2005.

Middleton, Anne. "Medieval Studies." In Greenblatt and Gunn, Redrawing the Boundaries, 12–40.

Middleton, W. L. "New French Films." New York Times, Aug. 12, 1928.

Miller, Scott. Deconstructing Harold Hill: An Insider's Guide to Musical Theatre. Portsmouth, NH: Heinemann, 2000.

Miller, Toby, and Robert Stam. A Companion to Film Theory. Oxford: Blackwell, 1999.

Mitchell, Elvis. "Everyone's a Film Geek Now." New York Times, Aug. 17, 2003.

Moaddel, Mansoor. Islamic Modernism, Nationalism, and Fundamentalism. Chicago: University of Chicago Press, 2005.

Montefiori, Simon Sebaq. "Royal Scandal—Private Lives of Public People." Psychology Today (1992): 32–37.

Montrose, Louis. "Professing the Renaissance: The Poetics and Politics of Culture." In The New Historicism, ed. Aram Veeser, 15–36. New York: Routledge, 1989.

Monty Python. Monty Python and the Holy Grail (Book). London: Methuen, 1977.

Mordden, Ethan. Open a New Window: The Broadway Musical in the 1960s. New York: Palgrave, 2001.

Moreland, Kim. The Medievalist Impulse in American Literature: Twain, Adams, Fitzgerald, Hemingway. Charlottesville: University of Virginia Press, 1996.

Morgan, Pamela S. "One Brief Shining Moment: Camelot in Washington, D.C." In Verduin, Medievalism in North America, 185–211.

Morson, Gary Saul, and Caryl Emerson. Mikhail Bakhtin: Creation of a Prosaics. Stanford, CA: Stanford University Press, 1990.

Most, Andrea. Making Americans: Jews and the Broadway Musical. Cambridge, MA: Harvard University Press, 2004.

Müller, Ulrich. "Blank, Syberberg, and the German Arthurian Tradition." Trans. Julie Giffin. In Harty, Cinema Arthuriana, rev. edn., 177–84.

Mulvey, Laura. "Visual Pleasure and Narrative Cinema." In Kaplan, Feminism and Film, 34–47.

Myers, Tony. Slavoj Žižek. London: Routledge, 2003.

Neale, Steve. "Masculinity as Spectacle: Reflections on Men and Mainstream Cinema." In Kaplan, *Feminism and Film*, 253–64.

Nederman, Cary J., and Kate Langdon Forhan, eds. *Medieval Political Theory—A Reader: The Quest for the Body Politic, 1100–1400*. London: Routledge, 1993.

Nichols, Bill. *Introduction to Documentary*. Bloomington: Indiana University Press, 2001.

———. *Representing Reality: Issues and Concepts in Documentary*. Bloomington: Indiana University Press, 1991.

Norris, Christopher. *Derrida*. Cambridge, MA: Harvard University Press, 1987.

O'Connor, William. *Opus Dei: An Open Book. A Reply to "The Secret World of Opus Dei" by Michael Walsh*. Dublin: Mercier, 1991.

Olsen, Solveig. *Hans Jürgen Syberberg and His Film of Wagner's "Parsifal."* Lanham, MD: University Press of America, 2006.

Orru, Marco. *Anomie: History and Meanings*. Boston: Allen and Unwin, 1987.

———. "The Ethics of Anomie: Jean Marie Guyau and Émile Durkheim." *British Journal of Sociology* 34 (1983): 499–518.

Osberg, Richard H., and Michael E. Crow. "Language Then and Now in Arthurian Film." In Harty, *King Arthur on Film*, 39–66.

Paden, William D. "Reconstructing the Middle Ages: The Monk's Sermon in *The Seventh Seal*." In *Medievalism in the Modern World: Essays in Honour of Leslie J. Workman*, ed. Richard Utz and Tom Shippey, 287–306. Turnhout, Belgium: Brepols, 1998.

Panofsky, Erwin. "Style and Medium in the Motion Pictures." In Braudy and Cohen, *Film Theory and Criticism*, 273–92.

Paquette, Jean-Marcel. "Lancelot's Last Metamorphosis." In *Lancelot and Guinevere: A Casebook*, ed. Lori Walters, 193–202. New York: Garland, 1996.

Passas, Nikos, and Robert Agnew, eds. *The Future of Anomie Theory*. Boston: Northeastern University Press, 1997.

Pateman, Carole. *The Disorder of Women: Democracy, Feminism, and Political Theory*. Stanford, CA: Stanford University Press, 1989.

Patterson, Lee. "On the Margin: Postmodernism, Ironic History, and Medieval Studies." *Speculum* (1990): 87–108.

Paulin, Scott D. "Richard Wagner and the Fantasy of Cinematic Unity." In Buhler, Flinn, and Neumeyer, *Music and Cinema*, 58–84.

Pendragon, Arthur, and Christopher James Stone. *The Trials of Arthur: The Life and Times of a Modern-Day King*. London: Element, 2003.

Pernoud, Régine. *The Crusaders*. Trans. Enid Grant. Edinburgh: Oliver and Boyd, 1963.

Pernoud, Régine, and Marie Veroniqué Clin. *Joan of Arc: Her Story*. Trans. Jeremy Duqesnay Adams. New York: St. Martin's, 1998.

Peterson, James. "Is a Cognitive Approach to the Avant-Garde Perverse?" In Bordwell and Carroll, *Post-Theory*, 108–29.

Petruzzelli, James F. "Catholic Holy Cards: Visual, Verbal, and Tactile Codes for the (In)visible." In *The Other Print Tradition: Essays on Chapbooks, Broadsides, and Re-*

lated Ephemera, ed. Cathy Lynn Preston and Michael J. Preston, 266–83. New York: Garland, 1995.

Pipelo, Tony. "The Spectre of Joan of Arc: Textual Variations in the Key Prints of Carl Dreyer's Film." Film History 2 (1988): 301–24.

Pisan, Christine de. Ditié de Jehanne d'Arc. Ed. Angus J. Kennedy and Kenneth Varty. Oxford: Society for the Study of Mediaeval Languages and Literature, 1977.

Plato. Republic. Trans. Robin Waterfield. Oxford: Oxford University Press, 1993.

Poster, Mark. What's the Matter with the Internet? Minneapolis: University of Minnesota Press, 2001.

Prawer, Joshua. The Crusaders' Kingdom: European Colonialism in the Middle Ages. New York: Praeger, 1972.

Quandt, James, ed. Robert Bresson. Toronto: Toronto International Film Festival Group, 1998.

Quart, Leonard. "The Religion of the Market: Thatcherite Politics and the British Film of the 1980s." In Friedman, Fires Were Started, 15–34.

Ramey, Lynn T., and Tison Pugh, eds. Race, Class, and Gender in "Medieval" Cinema. New York: Palgrave, 2007.

Rauschning, Hermann. Hitler Speaks: A Series of Political Conversations with Adolf Hitler on His Real Aims. London: T. Butterworth, 1940.

Ravenscroft, Trevor. Spear of Destiny: The Occult Power behind the Spear Which Pierced the Side of Christ. New York: Putnam, 1973.

Ray, Sid. "Hunks, History, and Homophobia: Masculinity Politics in Braveheart and Edward II." Film and History 29 (1999): 22–31.

Reader, Keith. Robert Bresson. Manchester: Manchester University Press, 2000.

Redfield, Marc. "Imagi-nation: The Imagined Community and the Aesthetics of Mourning." Diacritics 29 (1999): 58–83.

"Review of Joan of Arc." America 80 (Nov. 20, 1948): 189–90.

"Review of Joan of Arc." Commonweal (Nov. 19, 1948): 143.

Richards, Jeffrey. Swordsmen of the Screen: From Douglas Fairbanks to Michael York. London: Routledge and Kegan Paul, 1977.

Richardson, Diane. Women, Motherhood and Childrearing. New York: St. Martin's, 1993.

Richon, Olivier. "Representation, the Despot and the Harem: Some Questions around an Academic Orientalist Painting by Lecomte-du-Noüy (1885)." In Barker et al., Europe and Its Others, 1–13.

Rider, Jeff, Richard Hull, Christopher Smith, Michael Carnes, Sasha Foppiano, and Annie Hesslein. "The Arthurian Legend in French Cinema: Robert Bresson's Lancelot du Lac and Eric Rohmer's Perceval le Gallois." In Harty, Cinema Arthuriana, rev. edn., 149–62.

Riley-Smith, Jonathan. The Crusades: A Short History. New Haven, CT: Yale University Press, 1987.

———. The First Crusaders, 1095–1131. Cambridge, UK: Cambridge University Press, 1997.

———. "Jihad Crusaders: What an Osama bin Laden Means by 'Crusade.' " *National Review*, Jan. 5, 2004. www.nationalreview.com/comment/riley-smith200401050839.asp (accessed March 20, 2009).

Rosen, Philip. *Change Mummified: Cinema, Historicity, Theory.* Minneapolis: University of Minnesota Press, 2001.

———, ed. *Narrative, Apparatus, Ideology: A Film Theory Reader.* New York: Columbia University Press, 1986.

Rosenbaum, Jonathan. *Movies as Politics.* Berkeley: University of California Press, 1997.

Rosenstone, Robert A. "The Future of the Past: Film and the Beginnings of Postmodern History." In *The Persistence of History: Cinema, Television, and the Modern Event,* ed. Vivian Sobchack, 201–18. New York: Routledge, 1996.

———. "The Historical Film: Looking at the Past in a Postliterate Age." In *Learning History in America: Schools, Cultures, and Politics,* ed. Lloyd Kramer, Donald Reid, and William L. Barney, 141–60. Minneapolis: University of Minnesota Press, 1994.

———. "History in Images / History in Words: Reflections on the Possibility of Really Putting History onto Film." *American Historical Review* 93 (1988): 1173–85.

———, ed. *Revisioning History: Film and the Construction of a New Past.* Princeton, NJ: Princeton University Press, 1995.

———. *Visions of the Past: The Challenge of Film to Our Idea of History.* Cambridge, MA: Harvard University Press, 1995.

Rothman, William. "Against 'The System of Suture.' " In Braudy and Cohen, *Film Theory and Criticism,* 130–36.

Rubin, Gayle. "The Traffic in Women: Notes on the Political Economy of Sex." In *Toward an Anthropology of Women,* ed. Rayna R. Reiter, 157–210. New York: Monthly Review Press, 1975.

Rubin, Miri. *Corpus Christi: The Eucharist in Late Medieval Culture.* Cambridge, UK: Cambridge University Press, 1991.

Rubino, Carl. "The Invisible Worm: Ancients and Moderns in *The Name of the Rose.*" *SubStance* 47 (1988): 54–63.

Runciman, Steven. *A History of the Crusades.* 3 vols. Cambridge: Cambridge University Press, 1951–54.

Rupp, Leila J. *Mobilizing Women for War: German and American Propaganda, 1939–1945.* Princeton, NJ: Princeton University Press, 1978.

Ryan, Michael, and Douglas Kellner. *Camera Politica: The Politics and Ideology of Contemporary Hollywood Film.* Bloomington: Indiana University Press, 1988.

Said, Edward W. "The Clash of Ignorance." *The Nation,* Oct. 4, 2001, 11–13.

———. *Covering Islam: How the Media and the Experts Determine How We See the Rest of the World.* New York: Pantheon, 1981.

———. *Orientalism.* New York: Vintage, 1978.

———. "Orientalism Reconsidered." In Barker et al., *Europe and Its Others,* 14–17.

———. *The Politics of Dispossession.* New York: Vintage, 1995.

Salter, Elizabeth. *English and International: Studies in the Literature, Art and Patronage of Medieval England.* Ed. Derek Pearsall and Nicolette Zeeman. Cambridge, UK: Cambridge University Press, 1988.

Santner, Eric L. *Stranded Objects: Mourning, Memory, and Film in Postwar Germany.* Ithaca, NY: Cornell University Press, 1990.

———. "The Trouble with Hitler: Postwar German Aesthetics and the Legacy of Fascism." In Ginsberg and Thompson, *Perspectives on German Cinema,* 714–30.

Schrader, Paul. *Transcendental Style in Film: Ozu, Bresson, Dreyer.* New York: Da Capo, 1972.

Schubart, Rikke. "Passion and Acceleration: Generic Change in the Action Film." In Slocum, *Violence and American Cinema,* 192–207.

Sedgwick, Eve Kosofsky. *Between Men: English Literature and Male Homosocial Desire.* New York: Columbia University Press, 1985.

Shafik, Viola. "Egyptian Cinema." In *Companion Encyclopedia of Middle Eastern and North African Film,* ed. Oliver Leaman, 23–129. London: Routledge, 2001.

Sharrett, Christopher. "The Last Stranger: *Querelle* and Cultural Stimulation." In Ginsberg and Thompson, *Perspectives on German Cinema,* 462–73.

Shaw, George Bernard. "George Bernard Shaw on Film Censorship." *New York Times,* Sept. 14, 1936.

———. *Saint Joan: A Chronicle Play in Six Scenes and an Epilogue.* New York: Brentano's, 1924.

"Shaw 'Muddled,' Catholics Hold." *New York Times,* Sept. 15, 1936.

Shichtman, Martin B. "Hollywood's New Weston: The Grail Myth in Francis Ford Coppola's *Apocalypse Now* and John Boorman's *Excalibur.*" *Post Script* 4 (1984): 35–48.

———. "Politicizing the Ineffable: The *Queste del Saint Graal* and Malory's 'Tale of the Sankgreal.'" In *Culture and the King: The Social Implications of the Arthurian Legend,* ed. Martin B. Shichtman and James P. Carley, 163–79. Albany: State University of New York Press, 1994.

———. "Whom Does the Grail Serve? Wagner, Spielberg, and the Issue of Jewish Appropriation." In Mancoff, *The Arthurian Revival,* 283–97.

Shippey, T. A. "Studies in Medievalism." www.medievalism.net/about.html.

Shumway, David R. "Rock and Roll as a Cultural Practice." In DeCurtis, *Present Tense,* 117–33.

Siberry, Elizabeth. *The New Crusaders: Images of the Crusades in the Nineteenth and Early Twentieth Centuries.* Aldershot, UK: Ashgate, 2000.

Silverman, Kaja. "On Suture." In Braudy and Cohen, *Film Theory and Criticism,* 137–47.

Sklar, Elizabeth S. "Marketing Arthur: The Commodification of Arthurian Legend." In Sklar and Hoffman, *King Arthur in Popular Culture,* 9–23.

———. "Twain for Teens: Young Yankees in Camelot." In Harty, *King Arthur on Film,* 97–108.

Sklar, Elizabeth S., and Donald L. Hoffman, eds. *King Arthur in Popular Culture.* Jefferson, NC: McFarland, 2002.

Slocum, J. David, ed. *Violence and American Cinema.* New York: Routledge, 2001.

Slusser, George, and Eric S. Rabkin, eds. *Shadows of the Magic Lamp: Fantasy and Science Fiction in Film.* Carbondale: Southern Illinois University Press, 1985.

Smith, Anthony D. *Theories of Nationalism.* New York: Holmes and Meier, 1983.

Smith, Neil. "Contours of a Spatialized Politics: Homeless Vehicles and the Production of Geographical Scale." *Social Text* 33 (1992): 54–81.

Snyder, Susan. "The Left Hand of God: Despair in Medieval and Renaissance Tradition." *Studies in the Renaissance* 12 (1965): 18–59.

Sobchack, Thomas, and Vivian C. Sobchack. *An Introduction to Film.* 2nd edn. Glenview, IL: Scott, Foresman, 1987.

Sobchack, Vivian. "The Insistent Fringe: Moving Images and Historical Consciousness." *History and Theory* 36 (1997): 4–20.

Sontag, Susan. "Fascinating Fascism." In *Under the Sign of Saturn,* 73–108. New York: Farrar, Straus, Giroux, 1980.

Sorlin, Pierre. *The Film in History: Restaging the Past.* Oxford: Basil Blackwell, 1980.

Spiegel, Gabrielle. *Romancing the Past: The Rise of Vernacular Prose Historiography in Thirteenth-Century France.* Berkeley: University of California Press, 1993.

Spisak, James W., and William Matthews, eds. *Caxton's Malory: A New Edition of Sir Thomas Malory's "Le Morte Darthur" Based on the Pierpont Morgan Copy of William Caxton's Edition of 1485.* 2 vols. Berkeley: University of California Press, 1983.

Spivak, Gayatri Chakravorty. "Can the Subaltern Speak?" In *Marxism and the Interpretation of Culture,* ed. Cary Nelson and Lawrence Grossberg, 271–313. Urbana: University of Illinois Press, 1988.

———. *A Critique of Postcolonial Reason: Toward a History of the Vanishing Present.* Cambridge, MA: Harvard University Press, 1999.

Stallybrass, Peter, and Allon White. *The Politics and Poetics of Transgression.* Ithaca, NY: Cornell University Press, 1986.

Stam, Robert. *Subversive Pleasures: Bakhtin, Cultural Criticism, and Film.* Baltimore: Johns Hopkins University Press, 1989.

Stanbury, Sarah. "Pathos and Politics: Nicholas Love's *Mirror* and Mel Gibson's *The Passion of the Christ.*" In *The Four Modes of Seeing: Approaches to Medieval Imagery in Honor of Madeline Harrison Caviness,* ed. Evelyn Staudinger Lane, Elizabeth Carson Pastan, and Ellen M. Shortell, 624–50. Aldershot, UK: Ashgate, 2009.

———. "Regimes of the Visual in Premodern England: Gaze, Body, and Chaucer's Clerk's Tale." *New Literary History* 28 (1997): 261–89.

Stearns, Peter N. *Growing Up: The History of Childhood in a Global Context.* Waco, TX: Baylor University Press, 2005.

Steene, Birgitta A., ed. *Focus on "The Seventh Seal."* Englewood Cliffs, NJ: Prentice-Hall, 1972.

Stewart, Suzanne R. "The Theft of the Operatic Voice: Masochistic Seduction in Wagner's *Parsifal.*" *Musical Quarterly* 80 (1996): 597–628.

Stoekl, Allan. "French Catholic Traditionalism and the Specter of Reactionary Politics." *South Central Review* 23 (2006): 89–106.

Strohm, Paul. "Conference Commentary." *Cultural Frictions*, Conference Proceedings, Georgetown University, Oct. 27–28, 1995. www8.georgetown.edu/departments/medieval/labyrinth/conf/cs95/papers/strohm.html (accessed Sept. 9, 2007).

Studlar, Gaylyn. "Masochism and the Perverse Pleasures of the Cinema." In Kaplan, *Feminism and Film*, 203–25.

Sutherland, John. *Is Heathcliff a Murderer? Great Puzzles in Nineteenth-Century Literature.* Oxford: Oxford University Press, 1996.

———. *Who Betrays Elizabeth Bennett? Further Puzzles in Classic Fiction.* Oxford: Oxford University Press, 1999.

Suydam, Mary, and Joanna E. Zeigler, eds. *Performance and Transformation: New Approaches to Late Medieval Spirituality.* New York: St. Martin's, 1999.

Syberberg, Hans-Jürgen. *Hitler: A Film from Germany.* Trans. Joachim Neugroschel. New York: Farrar, Straus, Giroux, 1982.

———. *Syberbergs Filmbuch.* Frankfurt: Fischer, 1978.

Tetzlaff, David. " 'Too Much Red Meat!' " In *New Hollywood Violence,* ed. Steven Jay Schneider, 269–85. Manchester: Manchester University Press, 2004.

Theweleit, Klaus. *Male Fantasies.* Trans. Stephen Conway. 2 vols. Minneapolis: University of Minnesota Press, 1987.

Thompson, Kristin. *Breaking the Glass Armor: Neoformalist Film Criticism.* Princeton, NJ: Princeton University Press, 1988.

Todorov, Tzvetan. *Mikhail Bakhtin: The Dialogic Principle.* Trans. Wlad Godzich. Minneapolis: University of Minnesota Press, 1984.

Tolhurst, Fiona. "The Outlandish Lioness: Eleanor of Aquitaine in Literature." *Medieval Feminist Forum* 37 (spring 2004): 9–13; typescript available online at http://las.alfred.edu/english/docs/The-Outlandish-Lioness.pdf (accessed Feb. 20, 2009).

Tripp, Anna, ed. *Gender.* New York: Palgrave, 2000.

Truhon, Stephen, and W. Richard Walker. "Digital Dangers: Identity Theft and Cyberterrorism." In *Cognitive Technology,* ed. W. Richard Walker and Douglas J. Herrmann, 172–84. Jefferson, NC: McFarland, 2005.

Turner, Graeme. *Film as Social Practice.* 3rd edn. London: Routledge, 1999.

Twain, Mark. *A Connecticut Yankee in King Arthur's Court.* New York: Modern Library, 2001.

Tyerman, Christopher. *The Invention of the Crusades.* Toronto: University of Toronto Press, 1998.

Umland, Rebecca A., and Samuel J. Umland. *The Use of Arthurian Legend in Hollywood Film: From Connecticut Yankees to Fisher Kings.* Westport, CT: Greenwood Press, 1996.

Utz, Richard. " 'Mes souvenirs sont peut-être reconstruits': Medieval Studies, Medievalism, and the Scholarly and Popular Memories of the 'Right of the Lord's First Night.' " *PhiN* 31 (2005): 49–59.

Valassopoulos, Anastasia. "*The Silences of the Palace* and the Anxiety of Musical Creation." In Dickinson, *Movie Music*, 99–108.

Vasey, Ruth. "Beyond Sex and Violence: 'Industry Policy' and the Regulation of Hollywood Movies, 1922–1939." In Bernstein, *Controlling Hollywood*, 102–29.

Verduin, Kathleen, ed. *Medievalism in North America*. Cambridge, UK: D. S. Brewer, 1994.

Vološinov, V. N. *Marxism and the Philosophy of Language*. Trans. Ladislaw Matejka and I. R. Titunik. Cambridge, MA: Harvard University Press, 1986.

Wagg, Stephen. "'You've Never Had It So Silly': The Politics of British Satirical Comedy from Beyond the Fringe to Spitting Image." In *Come On Down? Popular Media Culture in Post-war Britain*, ed. Dominic Strinati and Stephen Wagg, 254–84. London: Routledge, 1992.

Wagner, Richard. *Religion and Art*. Trans. William Ashton Ellis. Lincoln: University of Nebraska Press, 1994.

Wakeman, Ray. "*Excalibur*: Film Reception and Political Distance." In *Politics in German Literature*, ed. Beth Bjorklund and Mark E. Cory, 166–76. Columbia, SC: Camden House, 1998.

Walsh, David, and Len Platt. *Musical Theater and American Culture*. Westport, CT: Praeger, 2003.

Walsh, Frank. *Sin and Censorship: The Catholic Church and the Motion Picture Industry*. New Haven, CT: Yale University Press, 1996.

Walsh, Michael. *The Secret World of Opus Dei*. London: Grafton Books, 1989.

Ward, Vincent. "A Dialogue with Discrepancy: Vincent Ward Discusses *The Navigator*." *Illusions* 10 (1989): 9–14.

———. *The Navigator: A Medieval Odyssey*. London: Faber and Faber, 1989.

Warner, Marina. *Joan of Arc: The Image of Female Heroism*. New York: Alfred Knopf, 1982.

Watson, Derek. "Wagner: *Tristan und Isolde* and *Parsifal*." In Barber, *King Arthur in Music*, 23–34.

Weber, Eugen. *The Nationalist Revival in France, 1905–1914*. Berkeley: University of California Press, 1968.

Wee, Valerie. "Selling Teen Culture: How American Multimedia Conglomeration Reshaped Teen Television in the 1990s." In *Teen TV: Genre, Consumption, Identity*, ed. Glyn Davis and Kay Dickinson, 87–98. London: BFI, 2004.

Weisl, Angela Jane. *The Persistence of Medievalism: Narrative Adventures in Contemporary Culture*. New York: Palgrave, 2003.

Wheeler, Bonnie, and Charles T. Wood. *Fresh Verdicts on Joan of Arc*. New York: Garland, 1996.

Whitaker, Muriel. "Fire, Water, Rock: Elements of Setting in *Excalibur*." In Harty, *Cinema Arthuriana*, 135–43.

White, Hayden. "The Historical Event as Literary Artifact." In Leitch et al., *The Norton Anthology of Theory and Criticism*, 1712–29.

———. "Historiography and Historiophoty." *American Historical Review* 93 (1988): 1193–99.

White, T. H. *The Once and Future King*. New York: Ace Books, 1987.

White, Theodore H. *The Making of the President, 1960*. New York: Atheneum, 1961.

Williams, David John. "Looking at the Middle Ages in the Cinema: An Overview." *Film and History* 29 (1999): 9–19.

Williams, Linda. "Eric Rohmer and the Holy Grail." In *The Grail: A Casebook*, ed. Dhira B. Mahoney, 575–90. New York: Garland, 2000.
———. " 'Something Else besides a Mother': *Stella Dallas* and the Maternal Melodrama." In Kaplan, *Feminism and Film*, 479–504.
Williams, Raymond. *Television: Technology and Cultural Form*. New York: Schocken, 1975.
Willis, Connie. *Doomsday Book*. New York: Bantam, 1992.
Winock, Michel. *Nationalism, Anti-Semitism, and Fascism in France*. Trans. Jane Marie Todd. Stanford, CA: Stanford University Press, 1998.
Winston, Richard. *Thomas Becket*. London: Constable, 1967.
Wise, Naomi. "Review of *Perceval*." *Film Quarterly* 33 (1979–80): 48–53.
Witt, Mary Ann Frese. *The Search for Modern Tragedy: Aesthetic Fascism in Italy and France*. Ithaca, NY: Cornell University Press, 2001.
Wolf, Werner. *The Musicalization of Fiction: A Study in the Theory and History of Intermediality*. Amsterdam: Rodopi, 1999.
Wood, Robin. *Ingmar Bergman*. New York: Praeger, 1969.
Woodberry, Robert D., and Christian S. Smith. "Fundamentalism et al: Conservative Protestants in America." *Annual Review of Sociology* 24 (1998): 25–56.
Wright, Elizabeth, and Edmond Wright. *The Žižek Reader*. Oxford: Blackwell, 1999.
Young, Robert J. C. *Postcolonialism: An Historical Introduction*. Oxford: Blackwell, 2001.
———. *Postcolonialism: A Very Short Introduction*. Oxford: Oxford University Press, 2003.
Žižek, Slavoj. *The Fright of Real Tears: Krzysztof Kieslowski between Theory and Post-Theory*. London: BFI, 2001.
———. "Grimaces of the Real, or When the Phallus Appears." *October* 58 (1991): 44–68.
———. *Looking Awry: An Introduction to Jacques Lacan through Popular Culture*. Cambridge, MA: MIT Press, 1992.
———. *The Metastases of Enjoyment: Six Essays on Women and Causality*. London: Verso, 1994.
———. *The Plague of Fantasies*. London: Verso, 1997.
———. *The Sublime Object of Ideology*. London: Verso, 1989.
———. "There Is No Sexual Relationship." In *Gaze and Voice as Love Objects*, ed. Renata Salecl and Slavoj Žižek, 208–49. Durham, NC: Duke University Press, 1996.
———. "There Is No Sexual Relationship: Wagner as a Lacanian." *New German Critique* 69 (1996): 7–35.
———. " 'The Wound Is Healed Only by the Spear That Smote You': The Operatic Subject and Its Vicissitudes." In *Opera through Other Eyes*, ed. David J. Levin, 177–214. Stanford, CA: Stanford University Press, 1994.
Zumthor, Paul. *Speaking of the Middle Ages*. Trans. Sarah White. Lincoln: University of Nebraska Press, 1986.

Index

Page numbers in *italics* indicate illustrations.